Screened Encounters

Film and the Global Cold War

Published by Berghahn Books and the DEFA Film Library at the University of Massachusetts Amherst

Series Editor
Skyler J. Arndt-Briggs, Executive Director, DEFA Film Library, University of Massachusetts Amherst

Editorial Board
Seán Allan, University of St Andrews
Barton Byg, University of Massachusetts Amherst
Anne Ciecko, University of Massachusetts Amherst
Thomas Lindenberger, Hannah Arendt Institute for the Study of Totalitarianism at Technische Universität Dresden
Ralf Schenk, DEFA Foundation

This interdisciplinary publication series explores the multiple and particular ways in which films, filmmaking, and film industries participated in and were shaped by the Cold War. It proceeds from the premise that the Cold War organized global interrelationships for nearly half of the twentieth century, just as colonialism had in preceding centuries. Films in this period were intimately involved in both state aspirations and national cultures, while at the same time their creation, distribution, and consumption were part of broader transnational trends. Because film connects a range of domains—including art, advertising, propaganda, information, and individual creative labor—it also offers privileged insights into a wide variety of sociocultural contexts, all of them shaped by the era's aesthetic, ideological, political, and economic forces.

Volume 1
Screened Encounters: The Leipzig Documentary Film Festival, 1955–1990
Caroline Moine

SCREENED ENCOUNTERS
The Leipzig Documentary Film Festival, 1955–1990

Caroline Moine

Translated from the French by John Barrett

Edited by Skyler J. Arndt-Briggs

berghahn
NEW YORK · OXFORD
www.berghahnbooks.com

First published in 2018 by
Berghahn Books
www.berghahnbooks.com

English-language edition
© 2018, 2025 Berghahn Books
First paperback edition published in 2025

French-language edition
© 2014 Publications de la Sorbonne – Paris, France

Originally published by Publications de la Sorbonne as
Cinéma et guerre froide: histoire du festival de films documentaires de Leipzig (1955–1990)

Translation supported by the Department of Human and Social Sciences at the Université Paris-Saclay and the DEFA Film Library at the University of Massachusetts Amherst

All rights reserved. Except for the quotation of short passages for the purposes of criticism and review, no part of this book may be reproduced in any form or by any means, electronic or mechanical, including photocopying, recording, or any information storage and retrieval system now known or to be invented, without written permission of the publisher.

Library of Congress Cataloging-in-Publication Data

A C.I.P. cataloging record is available from the Library of Congress

British Library Cataloguing in Publication Data

A catalogue record for this book is available from the British Library

ISBN 978-1-78533-909-7 hardback
ISBN 978-1-83695-047-9 paperback
ISBN 978-1-83695-164-3 epub
ISBN 978-1-78533-910-3 web pdf

https://doi.org/10.3167/9781785339097

Contents

List of Illustrations and Figures	vii
Preface. The Cold War's Documentary Crossroads: Leipzig in the Galaxy of Festivals *Dina Iordanova*	ix
Acknowledgments	xix
Introduction. A Festival at the Heart of the Cold War	1

Part I. A Cold War Festival (1949–1964)

Chapter 1. The Genesis of the Leipzig Film Festival	17
Chapter 2. Opening to the World	43
Chapter 3. Between Propaganda and *Cinéma Vérité*	71

Part II. Between Provincialism and International Dialogue (1964–1973)

Chapter 4. When the Tide Turns . . .	101
Chapter 5. Toward Documentaries with a Human Face	130
Chapter 6. Documentaries in the Service of International Solidarity	157

Part III. A Trompe L'Oeil Mise-en-Scène? (1973–1983)

Chapter 7. Wide Angle on Socialist Society	189
Chapter 8. Don't Wait for Better Times	219

Part IV. Toward New Horizons (1984–1990)

Chapter 9. An Opening in the East? 247

Chapter 10. Revolution on the Screen, on the Street 279

Conclusion. Beyond the Cold War: A Memory in the Making 307

Appendices 318

Glossary 327

Bibliography 330

Index 358

Film Index 368

Illustrations and Figures

1.1.	Poster by John Heartfield for A. Thorndike's *You and Some Comrade* (1956)	23
1.2.	Poster for J. Ivens's *Song of the Rivers* (1954)	29
2.1.	Poster for the 1955 Leipzig Festival	45
2.2.	Poster for the 1960 Leipzig Festival	55
2.3.	Poster for the 1962 Leipzig Festival	63
3.1.	1964 gathering of important documentarists at the Leipzig Festival	73
3.2.	Award ceremony on stage at the Capitol Theater, the Leipzig Festival's main venue, in 1963	78
3.3.	Jürgen Böttcher and crew shooting *Furnace Makers* (1962)	85
4.1.	The Golden Dove grand prize medal, with the festival motto and Picasso's dove (1963)	112
4.2.	Wolfgang Klaue at the festival in 1970	114
4.3.	GDR poster for M. Romm's *Ordinary Fascism* (1965)	116
5.1.	1968: Streamers, posters, and the flags of all countries represented at the festival decorated the center of Leipzig	141
5.2.	Joris Ivens with festival director Wolfgang Harkenthal at the 1968 Leipzig Festival	143
5.3.	1967: Rooms with televisions now supplemented the main screening venue and projection booths	152
6.1.	Collecting for International Solidarity at the Leipzig Festival soon after the coup d'état in Chile in 1973	160

6.2.	Cuban documentarist Santiago Álvarez at the festival's opening gala in 1983	165
6.3	Jane Fonda visits the 1974 Leipzig Festival	168
6.4.	The Free German Youth (FDJ) call for international solidarity at the 1975 festival, with posters and music against the Chilean coup and apartheid	173
6.5.	Dean Reed's debut at the Leipzig Festival in 1971	174
7.1.	French documentarist René Vautier at a festival discussion in 1976	191
7.2.	Winfried Junge and cinematographer Hans-Eberhard Leupold shooting the first film in the Golzow Series, as the children start school in 1961	200
7.3.	Shooting *Eleven Years Old* in Golzow in 1966	201
7.4.	Volker Koepp shooting in Wittstock in 1975; here the crew films Edith walking with friends	208
7.5.	Elsbeth—nicknamed Stupsi—at work in Wittstock in 1984	210
7.6.	Poster for the 1975 Leipzig Festival	212
8.1.	Still from J. Böttcher's *Shunters* (1984)	227
9.1.	Poster for the 1987 Leipzig Festival	249
9.2.	GDR rock icon Tamara Danz and director Dieter Schumann shooting *whisper & SHOUT* (1988)	267
9.3.	Still from D. Schumann's *whisper & SHOUT* (1988)	268
9.4.	Helke Misselwitz awarded the Silver Dove in 1988; behind her stands Annelie Thorndike	272
10.1.	1989: Street scene before the Capitol Theater	280
10.2.	Still from A. Voigt and G. Kroske's *Leipzig in the Fall* (1989)	290
10.3.	Poster for R. Steiner's *Our Children* (1989)	296
10.4.	Jürgen Böttcher, Thomas Plenert, and Gerd Kroske shooting *The Wall* (1989–1990)	302
A.1.	Number of awarded films by country, 1955–86	325
A.2.	Invited GDR and foreign guests	326
A.3.	Audience numbers	326

||||||||||||||||||||

Preface
The Cold War's Documentary Crossroads
Leipzig in the Galaxy of Festivals

Dina Iordanova

Some years back, I attended an event featuring the celebrated Uruguayan political documentarist Mario Handler. His life's work has been dedicated to matters such as leftist student movements, workers' struggles, flawed elections, military dictatorships, political exile, poverty, and the adverse effects of globalization. His career evolved transnationally across Latin America, in places like Argentina, Venezuela, Chile, Cuba, Bolivia, and Mexico. Through the decades, Handler worked closely with people like Raúl Ruiz, Santiago Álvarez, Octavio Getino, and Fernando Solanas. Born in 1935 (and now living in Berlin), Handler graduated from the FAMU film school in Prague, Czechoslovakia. When asked about his career in the 1960s, Handler said that the most important professional encounters of the period had taken place at the Leipzig Documentary Film Festival. This event, based in a secondary city of seemingly isolated East Germany, had in fact provided a career-defining moment for him, bringing together aspiring filmmakers from Latin America with like-minded documentarists from elsewhere.

Around the same time, I also had the opportunity to attend a discussion with the famous Serbian documentary filmmaker Želimir Žilnik. Born in 1942, his oeuvre has focused on matters such as student protests, the contradictions of state socialism, political violence, corruption, immigrant exploitation, ethnic cleansing, extreme nationalism, and labor inequalities and mistreatment. His career, too, evolved transnationally—starting in unified Yugoslavia, then moving on to Italy and Germany, then winding up in a newly minted, nationalist Serbia, now surrounded by independent and similarly nationalistic Croatia, Slovenia, Bosnia, Macedonia, Kosovo, and Montenegro. Over the decades,

Žilnik worked closely with directors including Dušan Makavejev, Karpo Godina, and Reiner Werner Fassbinder. Although he had been more connected with the West German film festivals in Oberhausen and Berlin (where his film *Rani Radovi* [1969, *Early Works*] won the Golden Bear), Žilnik also said that in his opinion the Leipzig Festival was the seminal place for exchanges around documentary film.

Coming from opposite ends of the planet, it was striking that both of these documentarists considered the Leipzig Documentary Film Festival to have been a cultural event of defining importance for their careers. Many other world-famous documentarists would probably provide a similar testimony—because, as one learns in this history of the festival by French historian Caroline Moine, Leipzig was a true documentary crossroads of the Cold War. And the transnational interactions enabled by the Leipzig Festival were one of its most important contributions. It stands out as a node for networking and industry—a place where films were exhibited, but also where production teams were put together and distribution deals closed.

In *Screened Encounters,* Caroline Moine offers us a transnational cultural history of the Cold War through the prism of a singular cultural institution. It presents the Leipzig Festival, from its founding in 1955 to German unification in 1990, as well as the people who ran it, the people who attended it, and (some of) the films that played there. It describes successive dynamic configurations of festival stakeholders—including the festival leadership, foreign guests, local government, ideological overseers, security services, and filmmakers—who navigated the festival's field through congregations and confrontations. The study also highlights the specific dynamics of the circuit of festivals in East Central Europe and the East Bloc as well as the dynamics of festivals in Germany. It sets the scene for scholars interested in the defining force of cultural exchange in the transitional postcommunist period, the basic premises of which were already laid out in the 1980s perestroika period. And, finally, it offers readers the opportunity to observe the film festival as a crossroads of cultures—in this instance, as a meeting place for filmmakers of what used to be called "the progressive world."

* * *

During the Cold War, East Germany (the German Democratic Republic, or GDR) became a showcase for the state socialism that unfolded across the countries in what was designated the Soviet sphere of influence. The country was home to a variety of international democratic organizations; it often hosted large events of cultural diplomacy. The GDR's cultural policies were thus not only of importance in the complex dialogue within divided Germany but also of metaphorical value in creating a display window for the achievements of socialism at large.

Known today as DOK Leipzig, the International Leipzig Festival for Documentary and Animated Films, the festival is one of the rare East German cultural institutions to have survived the collapse of the regime and continued to evolve successfully after 1990. Launched in 1955 as the Leipzig Culture and Documentary Week, its earlier decades were closely associated with all the twists and turns of culture in the East Block. With a wealth of screenings of new films, retrospective programs, and moderated debates, the festival provided a meeting place for politically engaged filmmakers and film enthusiasts from diverse backgrounds, hosted a forum for international professionals from across Europe and beyond, and made generations of GDR documentarists known abroad. In Moine's hands, the history of the Leipzig Festival thus offers an opportunity to examine not only the evolution of East German cultural policies and cultural diplomacy but also the power relations that mobilized nonstate actors across state socialist countries as well as their specific understandings of internationalism.

A reputable film festival brings great benefits to a domestic film industry, and this text presents plenty of examples showing how the East German film industry and others profited from Leipzig's success. It was the presence of the festival that, to a large extent and despite political intricacies, allowed the GDR's DEFA Studios to stay clear of pressures that would have engaged it in blunt propaganda. It was the existence of the festival that ensured a delicate balance between the two fundamental themes that dominated documentary film production in the GDR—the question of divided Germany and international political issues. And it was the festival that gave an outlet to East German films, including those of the internationally known outlier Studio H&S—the documentary duo Walter Heynowski and Gerhard Scheumann—which undertook controversial investigative projects independent of DEFA.

Perhaps most importantly, the persistence of the festival allowed the growth of a specific kind of documentary that was fostered in the East Bloc—a sociological-humanist documentary cinema that was committed to tackling important social issues and trends and was produced at a number of documentary studios in socialist countries. In the West, this type of filmmaking is often associated with the names of René Vautier and Chris Marker. By presenting concrete examples, however, Moine shows that there was in fact an amazing array of documentary auteurs working in this vein, including Judit Elek and Márta Mészáros in Hungary; Krzysztof Kieslowski, Tomasz Zygadło, Marek Piwowski, and Marcel Łoziński in Poland; the Slovak director Dušan Hanák; and the Latvian Herz Frank.

I would add the names of the Bulgarian directors Nevena Tosheva, Romanian Paula, and Doru Segall as well as the Yugoslavian director Lordan Zafranović. By consistently featuring this work, Moine remarks, "The Leipzig Festival effectively allowed the government to showcase the sheer normalcy and universality of life in East Germany" (p. 215) as well as optimistically showing how these played out in the "evolution of socialist society" (p. 213), even in instances where the tone of the films was critical. In all these ways, Leipzig was indeed a festival positioned at the heart of the Cold War.

Moine's discussion of censorship, a recurring theme in the book, is particularly fascinating. She describes how socialist ideological oversight and censorship operated over the thirty-five years of the festival's life in the GDR—mostly not through outright banning but often by producing just a few prints of a film and then granting it a very limited release. Situations where such censorship came to the surface in 1968, for example, are contextualized in relation to both Western protest movements and the Prague Spring, which presented a rare opportunity to voice criticism and openly express challenges to the regime. Similarly, reports on events related to Wolf Biermann in the 1970s and incidents that took place in the 1980s reveal the double dynamic that characterized the way censorship operated—on one hand, trying to control the image and perceptions of socialism in the West while, on the other hand, determined by a changing ideological climate and the rise of outspoken dissident groups within the East Bloc itself.

The Leipzig Festival team often had to navigate treacherous and unpredictable waters. Moine draws attention to some of the personalities involved in the festival leadership, persuasively showing how individual leaders shaped the character of the organization. Such was the case with Wolfgang Kernicke—festival director until 1963, who spoke French and involved many French intellectuals—and the remarkable Annelie Thorndike, president of the honorary presidium from 1963 to 1966 and then its de facto permanent president until 2004, when Claas Danielsen became the first West German–born director in the festival's history.

Leipzig's interactions with other festivals in Germany—all West German—reveal, first and foremost, that film festivals were seen as the definitive platform for showcasing the cultural scene in a state socialist country. The festival in Mannheim opened in 1952, the one in Oberhausen in 1954; the Berlin International Film Festival—known as the Berlinale—also entered the field in 1954 to complicate (and enrich) the picture; and the *documenta* art exhibition, in Kassel—a seemingly unrelated and yet impactful presence—was launched in 1955 near the internal border between the two German states. It was in this context that the East German Leipzig Festival, also launched in 1955, was compelled to forge its own specific identity. The choice of location was not accidental and had a certain political significance. Individuals from the language, literature, and journalism departments of Leipzig University were involved with the festival—often working there over the years—as were local businesses. The festival survived the construction of the Berlin Wall in 1961, and the number of films it showed grew rapidly. Even though finances are not a focus of this study, there is sufficient detail to infer the state's generous approach to financing culture (and propaganda) under socialism.

Although the role of the Leipzig Festival, as far as the state was concerned, was to uphold and project socialist values, it is interesting to note that cooperation with the other German festivals never ceased. Programmers from Oberhausen, for example, came to Leipzig from the outset; already in the first year, they took a selection of films by the Czech puppet animation master Jiří Trnka—which had played at the inaugural Leipzig event—to show in West Germany. Such exchanges did not only occur with German festivals, however. Leipzig also had multiple interactions with other contemporary film festivals across the East Bloc. The oldest one in this part of the world was established in the Czech spa town of Mariánské Lázně in 1946 but soon moved to nearby Karlovy Vary, where it became one of the two most important official showcases for fiction films in the Soviet sphere, alternating with the festival in Moscow over a number of years.

The documentary festival circuit is perhaps best understood when explored through the prism of a specific festival, as it is in this case, where one festival can in some sorts be seen as representing all documentary forums. Comprising festivals dedicated to nonfiction cinema, the documentary circuit has its own political agenda, with such festivals being particularly important in the context of high-control societies. Leipzig was always one of the biggest and most significant of the documentary festivals, showing over a hundred films as early as the 1960s and displaying both dedication to a progressive leftist cinema and intolerance of the "apolitical."

At that time, the Leipzig Festival also interacted with festivals in Krakow (Poland), Venice (Italy), and Tours (France) as well as with the festivals in Carthage (Tunisia) and Tashkent (Soviet Uzbekistan), both of which cultivated a focus on documentary filmmaking in the aligned and nonaligned countries of the Third World. Other, later festivals have played a similar transnational function as Leipzig, including the festival in Hong Kong—which provided the first opportunities for filmmakers in the diverse and politically divided regions of the Chinese-speaking world to meet in the early 1980s—and the Yamagata International Documentary Festival in Japan—which has served as the main location for documentarists from across Asia to meet since 1989. New documentary forums that have grown to become important players nowadays—such as the Jihlava International Documentary Film Festival in the Czech Republic or the leading IDFA in Amsterdam—are in many cases indebted to organizational models first set up at Leipzig.

Cultural integration within the socialist camp was intense, much more so than the cultural integration present across the European Union in recent years. It led to the development of a well-established distribution network for films made across the region, thus permitting the best cinematic productions to travel among East Bloc countries. Film schools were another area of integration; whole generations of filmmakers from different countries were educated together at places like FAMU in Prague (including the GDR's Frank Beyer and Karl Gass), VGIK in Moscow, and the Łódź Film School in Poland. Certain West Germans had been attending the Leipzig Festival since early on, and as of the 1970s there was a constant group of people crossing into the GDR specifically for the festival. Meantime, filmmakers, intellectuals, and dissidents from the East Bloc kept returning and revisiting the festival as well, as it supplied them with the hugely important exchanges they were deprived of under the isolated conditions of the Cold War.

The Leipzig Festival made its politics clear with its choice of retrospectives, many of which were dedicated to documentarists associated with leftist aesthetics, such as Dziga Vertov, Alberto Cavalcanti, Joris Ivens, Chris Marker, John Grierson, Roman Karmen, Jerzy Bossak, the Maysles brothers, Robert Flaherty, and many more. Leftist intellectuals, such as Jerzy Toeplitz, Georges Sadoul, and Pablo Picasso, also visited the festival. Documentary film directors from other state socialist countries — such as the Hungarian András Kovács, the Cuban Octavio Cortázar, and the Chilean Patricio Guzmán, at the time in political exile in Cuba — as well as programs on controversial political issues — such as the Vietnam War on screen or films made in and about Chile before and after the coup — defined the specific profile of Leipzig within the global festival circuit.

* * *

Moine's history expands our understanding of how regional and global festival circuits operated in the Cold War. Her observations on the growing number of foreign journalists in attendance, for example, give a very different perspective from the standard view of dynamics between East and West in the 1960s and 1970s — a period that many people believe was marked by total separation. While the Leipzig Festival did not interact with the Berlinale very much, its close dealings with West German documentary counterparts at Oberhausen and Mannheim — even though these were never officially formalized — are explored in depth. The number of West Germans routinely crossing the border to attend the festival recurs often, showing exactly how the movement of these individuals, who made new contacts and then brought programs over to events they staged back home, kept reproducing the interconnectedness of the festival circuit.

Importantly, Moine's close zoom in on the history of the Leipzig Festival allows us to study the dynamically shifting configurations of festival stakeholders. Elsewhere, I have argued (Iordanova 2017) that in order to understand a film festival one must look, first and foremost, at the specific constellation of a festival's stakeholders — as it is the interactions between stakeholders that ultimately determine the ambiance, feel, style, film selection, nature of the event, and everything else related to a specific festival. In the case of the Leipzig Festival, Moine shows quite clearly how the changing configuration of stakeholders repeatedly led to specific changes. Most elegantly this is executed in her analysis of the perestroika years, as she traces the movements of stakeholders from either side of the Iron Curtain—from the Stasi to Western guests—and the specific expectations and behaviors they displayed.

Leipzig is where actions clashed in reaction to longitudinally established, yet shifting stakes. The complex international repercussions of Soviet perestroika and glasnost, showcased at Leipzig, closely reflected the intricacies of the "mature socialist" period of Eastern Europe in the late 1980s. Moine reveals quite well how the GDR's relative isolation played out in this context. The festival decisively embraced the new developments and stood up to various attempts, coming from both state organizations and individuals, to suppress and control them. The documentary output of socialist countries during this period provides a great prism through which to understand how far things had gone over a short, but extremely intense stretch of time. All of a sudden, the moment of truth had arrived, and it was too late for censorship and ideological intervention; the genie was out of the bottle ... and various previously suppressed political movements joined forces.

The festival also became a place where outside observers could test the political temperature of the GDR. Having started some years earlier, by showcasing movies such as the Polish Solidarity film *Robotnicy '80* (1980, *Workers '80*)—by Andrzej Chodakowski and Andrzej Zajaczkowski—and the ideas of dissident intellectuals with Prague's Charter 77 and other Central European opposition movements, the festival seamlessly came to engage with the radicalism of the films of directors Yuris Podnieks, from Latvia, and Tengiz Abuladze, from Georgia. Indeed, as Moine has it, this was possible because Leipzig offered a "multilateral framework" as well as "an ideal perspective from which to grasp, in all its complexity and specificity, how East German society experienced perestroika before the GDR collapsed in the 1989 revolution" (p. 247). What followed is well-known, not least from Jürgen Böttcher's *Die Mauer* (1990, *The Wall*), yet another film that started its triumphant global journey at Leipzig.

* * *

The importance of the case study is now universally acknowledged in the field of film festival studies. Detailed discussions of the complex histories and multipronged relational activities of specific festivals have proved to best reveal the diversity of affects and effects that festivals bring together and intervene in. A festival like Leipzig—geographically positioned in Central and Eastern Europe and temporally traversing several turbulent decades—may provide a singular example, and yet it opens up a panoramic window on to a wealth of insights that permit an informed reconstruction of the diverse dimensions and dynamics of the Cold War's cultural history.

The text is straightforwardly chronological, yet this is a book of flowing rhythm. While the original edition was published in French in 2014, its English version follows in the footsteps of a collection that Moine edited with Andreas Kötzing, titled *Cultural Transfer and Political Conflicts: Film Festivals in the Cold War* (Kötzing and Moine 2017). Moine has worked on the Leipzig Festival project for nearly two decades, with interviews dating back as early as 1999. Some of these individuals who lived at the height at the Cold War—like the prolific East German documentarist Karl Gass (1917–2009) of *Das Jahr 1945* (1984, *The Year 1945*) fame—are no longer with us. Other interviewees are still active—like Eva Zaoralová (b. 1932), the artistic director of the Karlovy Vary Film Festival, who recently published a memoir on this important cultural event. This history also recalls Ulrich and Erika Gregor, born in 1932 and 1935, respectively, key figures of the German and global film festival scene who incessantly traversed the cultural territory of the Cold War. When all these people pass on, they will take the memory of these events with them. This is why the efforts of younger historians like Moine are so important, as they ensure that living memory will transform into historical record.

To me, this is what solid historical research is supposed to be—no spin, no partial reporting. Even though it is nominally classified as being about German cultural history, Moine's book offers the transnational history of a whole cultural and ideological sphere. It persuasively shows that the clusters of issues and constellations of intellectuals that existed during the Cold War are not simply German history but part of a much wider transnational cultural history. It reaches out to cover the festival's outreach to the Third World, for example—showing how the festival selected and featured films from Vietnam, China, and Algeria—and points out that it did this earlier than other festivals and at a time when other progressive festival directors were publicly decrying the lack of selected Asian and African films. Moine is conscious of the fact that the exploration of soft power and "new institutional approaches to considering culture as a fully integrated aspect of international relations" (p. 3) has repercussions for scholarly understanding far beyond the borders of Germany. In this, her work ranks alongside some of the most influential general scholarship in cultural and sociohistorical studies of importance for the whole region, even if focused on a singular country or area, for example, the work of Aleksei Yurchak (2006), Svetlana Boym (1994), and Maria Todorova (2009, also see Dimou et al. 2014).

But even with this translation, the scholarship on cultural diplomacy and Cold War film festivals remains small. Luckily, Moine is among a group of younger historians who have realized the fantastic riches of the topic and materials that a close study of the history of cultural institutions may provide. Similarly positioned studies include Stefano Pisu's *Stalin a Venezia* (2013), which discusses how Soviet cinema was represented at the world's oldest film festival during the difficult period from 1932 to 1953. There are books on the Festival of Yugoslav Film (now the Pula Film Festival, in Croatia) and on the histories of the Moscow and Karlovy Vary International Film Festivals, each published in its respective territorial language. A team of young historians at Concordia University in Canada is engaged in studying the festival in Tashkent (now Uzbekistan), which focused on Third World filmmakers during the period of anticolonial revolutions (e.g., Djagalov and Salazkina 2016). This transnational, collaborative research group represents a trend in the cultural history of the region and is producing scholarship in a variety of languages, mainly in Europe. Only a fraction of this writing is available in English, including a 1990 volume by Wolfgang Jacobsen on the history of Germany's Berlinale festival.

It is certain that we are seeing a generational change, in which younger historians are taking over from the group of historians who dominated the field in the 1990s. Those were mainly émigrés who had been at odds with the communist regimes and who, once in the West, engaged in exposing the hypocrisy of "progressive" state socialism and, in the process, uncritically adopting Cold War propaganda of the West. The new historians do not have such an agenda and can afford to look at things in their complexity. They know that the reality of state socialist culture was more diverse and multidimensional than what is suggested by the limited anecdotal evidence that has trickled down to mass audiences in the context of stripped-down narratives indicating that there was not much more to life in East Germany than the Stasi and Berlin Wall.

Caroline Moine's book thus makes a key contribution to case studies of film festivals and will soon be a recognized classic of the genre. Written by a French cultural historian specializing in East Germany, it provides a kaleidoscopic view of the Cold War period. While it focuses on one institution, the close-up it offers enables us to understand the specific modus operandi of cultural policy under state socialism. Moine's scrutiny of the Leipzig Festival over several decades provides an apposite vantage point from which to both examine sociohistorical and cultural issues that were of pan-European importance—from the separation of Germany and the construction of the Berlin Wall to perestroika and glasnost—and demonstrate the relevance of East Germany in the transformative changes that marked the evolution of the East Bloc. Thus, this history of the Leipzig Festival in some ways surpasses its original scope and ambitions. Conceived and published within the context of a growing and dynamic body of GDR cultural histories, Moine's work makes a contribution that reaches out much further and opens up pathways into two other, much larger areas: the cultural dynamics of Cold War relations and the dynamics of film festivals as key nodes for transnational cultural exchanges. Going far beyond a German angle of investigation, this project gives deep insights into the transnational nature of Cold War culture as it looked from the East Bloc.

Dina Iordanova is Professor of Global Cinema and Creative Cultures at the University of St. Andrews in Scotland. Her work on Balkan and East Central European cinema and film cultures is well known to cultural historians of the Cold War in these areas. Her more recent publications tackle contemporary issues, such as cinema and trafficking in the new Europe.

Acknowledgments

This book grew out of research for which I benefited from many valuable forms of support over the last years. Although I cannot list all the people who contributed, each in their way, to the development and completion of this project, I would like to start by thanking professors Robert Frank, Etienne François, Sandrine Kott, Thomas Lindenberger, and Christian Delage for reading and commenting upon the initial text. Among the multiple exchanges I had with the many colleagues who accompanied my research, be it in archives or in seminars and colloquia, my discussions and collaborations with Andreas Kötzing and Stefano Pisu—between Paris, Leipzig, and Padua—were some of the most fruitful. Günter Jordan's review of the text was another phase in a dialogue that has now been going on for many years and has enriched this work considerably.

I was able to write this book in France, as part of the team at the Center for Cultural History of Contemporary Societies (CHCSC) at the Université Versailles Saint-Quentin-en-Yvelines / Université Paris-Saclay, thanks to the support of the center's two successive directors, Christian Delporte and Jean-Claude Yon. Research stays in Germany were made possible thanks to financial support from DAAD (German Academic Exchange Service), CIERA (Interdisciplinary Center for Studies and Research on Germany), the DEFA Foundation and Centre Marc Bloch in Berlin, and the Centre for Contemporary Historical Research in Potsdam (ZZF). The welcome extended by the last two institutions, and my participation in different seminars and work groups there, allowed me to develop my research within an international framework and fostered particularly rich exchanges in very stimulating work environments. I deeply appreciate all those who agreed to speak with me about their experiences and memories; they shared moments of their lives with me that were sometimes painful and difficult but always fascinating. Other collaborators facilitated the long and laborious work of archival research a great deal; in particular, I would like to thank Ms. Kiel and Ms. Klawitter at the Bundesarchiv-Filmarchiv in Berlin, Ms. Schmutzer and Ms. Schmal at the Filmmuseum Potsdam, Leena Pasanen at DOK Lepzig, and Ms. Söhner at the DEFA Foundation.

The present volume is a significantly reworked version of *Cinéma et guerre froide*, which was published in French by the Publications de la Sorbonne in 2014. Its translation would not have been possible without the generous financial support of the Department of Human and Social Sciences at the Université Paris-Saclay and of the DEFA Film Library at the University of Massachusetts Amherst. This book would not have seen the light of day without the decisive support and engagement of Skyler Arndt-Briggs. Her insightful and demanding approach to this project enabled a deeply stimulating collaboration to emerge during the long process of rewriting, translating, and editing. She has my warmest gratitude. Thanks to his attentive, enriching readings and skilled translation, John Barrett revived my excitement about this text, as if it were my first voyage into the topic. Johanna Frances Yunker worked tirelessly to keep references and bibliography in order and meet our deadlines. I thank all three for their great patience.

I would like to thank Chris Chappell of Berghahn Books and the editors of the Film and the Global Cold War series for allowing this to be its opening volume. My gratitude goes to Dina Iordanova for agreeing to write the preface to a work that aspires to contribute to the field of film festival studies, for which she has done so much. Finally, all my thoughts go to my husband Jakob, our son Hugo, his sisters Veronika and Pauline, and our growing "Europa Dreieck" family—living proof that Europe can be a magnificent site of meetings and exchanges, not only screened encounters.

|||||||||||||||||||

Introduction
A Festival at the Heart of the Cold War

November 1967, German Democratic Republic:
French filmmaker Chris Marker is invited to the international documentary film festival that transforms the East German city of Leipzig for a week every year (Marker 1971, 1997). To his astonishment, he discovers that Soviet film director Alexander Medvedkin (1900–1989), whom he admires so much, is still alive![1] Marker has been profoundly influenced by Medvedkin's experiment with the *Kinopoezd*—the "ciné-train" from which he shot footage and screened it for local people across the length and breadth of the Soviet Union during the 1930s—as well as by his film *Schaste* (1935, *Happiness*).[2] Other festival guests gathered around the table where the two filmmakers drink one vodka after the other, toasting to their chance meeting. German singer-songwriter Wolf Biermann, whose critical and ironic attitude will lead to his being stripped of his East German citizenship in November 1976, can still be heard loud and clear. Beside him, equally outspoken Cuban guests contribute to vehemently animated discussions. Among them is Santiago Álvarez, a member of the festival jury, whose accusatory films against all forms of imperialism are excellent at provoking the East German government and party functionaries who are vigilant in the wings of the festival.

Everyone is talking about a young East German documentary filmmaker, Jürgen Böttcher, whose film *Der Sekretär* (1967, *The Party Secretary*) was banned from the festival but has nonetheless been screened before a packed house at Leipzig's ciné-club. Marker was there. Did this heartwarming portrait of a secretary of the Socialist Unity Party of Germany (SED) who is close to his workers really deserve to be removed from the official program? A few dance steps against the backdrop of Latin American music brings everyone together for the duration of an evening; in the midst of the Cold War, guests from East and West, North and South find themselves united by the rhythm of a Cuban rumba.

November 2004, Federal Republic of Germany:
Claas Danielsen becomes the third director of the Leipzig Festival since 1989, and the first not to come from the former German Democratic Republic (GDR). Born in 1966 in Hamburg, Danielsen studied at the University of Television and Film in Munich. Given his age and life trajectory, he represents a clean break in the festival's history, which seems to turn the page on its East German past. Danielsen (2004), however, lays claim to a legacy and expresses his determination to continue the tradition of a festival of politically engaged documentaries and to underscore its international openness to the East as well as the South. Picasso's dove of peace, which has adorned medals and other prizes conferred at Leipzig since 1962, admittedly vanishes in 2005; but it is replaced by yet another dove. Is this rupture within continuity? Continuity within rupture?

The Leipzig Film Festival is one of the rare East German cultural institutions to have survived the collapse of the regime in 1990 and has continued until today in the Federal Republic of Germany (FRG).[3] Launched in 1955 as the Leipzig Culture and Documentary Film Week (Leipziger Kultur- und Dokumentarfilmwoche),[4] for over thirty years the festival was closely associated with the policies of the East Berlin government, which sought to make it the cultural showcase for the GDR's international openness. Up until the country's final hours, the festival's motto remained: Films of the World—for Peace in the World. Collections of firsthand accounts of the festival that have been published since 1990, however, tellingly speak of a "white dove on a dark background," of "dialogue with a myth" (Gehler and Steinmetz 1998; Mauersberger 1997). Such assessments reflect ambiguities in the festival's history and in its much-vaunted openness to the world.

The continued existence of this Cold War film festival in a united Germany raises questions as to its identity, as well as its relations with the regime during the East German era. The festival also offers us an opportunity to examine East German society and power relationships through the lens of a history that mobilized non–state actors, institutional or otherwise, and constantly wavered between provincialism and international dialogue. From a transnational perspective, the festival offers an ideal opportunity to break with the idea of monolithic blocs during the Cold War. It allows us not only to grasp the cultural politics and international flow of people, ideas, and films taking place—between East and West as well as between North and South—but also to see the ways in which these evolved from the 1950s until the 1990s. The history of the festival reveals the complex domestic and international challenges that East German cultural policies attempted to address over four decades. This is because, for the duration of the festival, Leipzig represented a frontier zone where official discourse was constantly put to the test and confrontations took place—not only with the West but also and especially with other East Bloc countries as well as those from the Global South.

Cultural History of the Cold War

In recent years, the history of the Cold War in Europe is no longer solely explored in terms of diplomatic relations reduced to their political dimension and has increasingly opened up to cultural-historical approaches (Frank 2012; Jarausch et al. 2017). In this respect, it has undergone a development also seen in the history of international relations, echoing the cultural turn of the early 1980s (Frank 2003b; Ory 2010). Aside from studies focusing on cultural diplomacy,[5] researchers have explored new, less institutional approaches to considering culture as a fully integrated aspect of international relations.[6] An example is the development of the concept of American "soft power," which encompasses cultural and ideological dimensions (Dagnaud 2011; Nye 2004). The historiography of the Cold War has also adopted questions posed by a social history that regards representations and their significance in terms of both the balance of power and the definition of international influences.[7]

If we consider the Cold War as a series of confrontations and competitions in the domain of cultural practices and norms—as well as in terms of the sensitivities and values of shared imaginaries—the clash was in fact based on structures and rationales going far beyond the framework of interstate or bilateral relations and the establishment of two power blocks.[8] To operate within a truly multilateral dimension—in some sense, the only pertinent one—we must, without neglecting them, go beyond the issues that faced East and West Germany and the East and West Blocs and examine the cohesion of the two blocs as well as the role played by the Global South.

An examination of the role of mass media during the Cold War reveals both the different analytic scales and the play between them (*jeu d'échelles*, or scale shifts) that are needed to grasp the mechanisms behind a confrontation that was largely determined by transnational forces.[9] As mediators of expectations—as well as of fears and collective memories—mass media, and cinema in particular, played an essential role in ideological warfare, circumventing the borders between nations and blocs (Chapman 1998; Karl 2007; Shaw 2000; Sorlin 1998). This cultural history of East Germany, which focuses on cinematographic production and distribution as a core issue in international cultural relations of the Cold War period, affords us ample evidence of this.

Approaches to East German History

Since the 1990s, cultural history has also imposed itself on the historiography of East Germany.[10] Most research—before and since German unification in 1990—focused primarily on political and institutional history, analyzing the hierarchical political control at the heart of the East German system. These studies were based upon the theory of totalitarianism, borne of Cold War debates. This body of research considers East Germany to have been a society dominated through and through by an all-encompassing regime (*durchherrschte Gesellschaft*). For the German sociologist Sigrid Meuschel (1992), who adheres to a school of thought different from those early proponents of totalitarianism theory, the East German state was "distorted," rendered "undifferentiated," and subsequently "reduced to nothingness" by the state and party.

Other studies sought, in contrast, to no longer reduce the history of the GDR to that of its regime. East German society and its differentiated relationship to political power thus became the object of a series of studies that applied traditional social-historical approaches to the GDR yet retained the interpretation of a thoroughly subjugated society (Glaessner 1988; Kaelble 1994). Yet other studies strove to go further, postulating the existence and evolution of an autonomous society, independent of the power of the party and state. According to these scholars, opportunities for self-expression and communication existed for East German citizens, despite the undisputedly repressive nature of the regime. Here, the goal has been to gauge the limits of state power, the boundaries of dictatorship (*Grenzen der Diktatur*)—or, in other words, the accommodations, compromises, and acts of resistance that emerged during the forty-one years of GDR history (Bessel and Jessen 1996; Lindenberger 1999a). In this scenario, East German citizens are considered stakeholders in their society, having actively participated in its creation and subsequent downfall.

Building on this perspective, social history "seen from below" assumed a growing importance in the historiography of the GDR (Droit and Kott 2006). Partially disengaged from political determinisms, this approach situates social groups and citizens at the core of its argument, in the West German tradition of oral and everyday history (*Alltagsgeschichte*).[11] Thomas Lindenberger, for example, became interested in defining the formation of an *Eigen-Sinn*—in opposition to authority (*Herrschaft*)—within East German society (Lindenberger 1999b). The term *Eigen-Sinn*, which is difficult to translate, concurrently signifies a separate sphere, a sense of self, and aloof dignity or autonomy on the part of individuals or groups. The existence of social niches is posited to have allowed for the emergence of a certain margin of maneuver and empowerment (Camarade and Goepper 2016).

From this emerges a supplementary notion, namely that of diversity. The ability to distinguish different strategies at the heart of both power structures and the population makes it possible to grasp the ways in which East German society did not remain a static, monolithic entity from 1949 to 1990. On the contrary, depending on the particular period, it followed diverse social, political, and cultural trends and rationales—offering a multitude of "experiences of dictatorship"—and it evolved in response and reaction to these developments (Jarausch 1999). More radically, this approach posited that an attitude of contestation was much more significant and present in daily life than had hitherto been indicated in histories of the GDR and that it had expressed itself in a wide variety of spheres, for example in practices of consumption and music (Hübner 1995; Merkel 1996; Rauhut 1993). Such findings demonstrate the importance and relevance of cultural history.

GDR Culture and Cinema

East German authorities regarded culture as a sphere of the utmost importance (Jäger 1994). Repeating the process of national unification in the nineteenth century, they utilized the entire spectrum of arts and culture to create foundations for a collective identity (*Selbstbewusstsein*) based upon a set of values that shaped a specific vision of the world (*Weltanschauung*) and of belonging to a specific society (*Gesellschaft*). People's reactions to this attempt, which ranged from re/appropriation to refusal of the identities proposed by the regime, constitute the stakes at the core of East German history.[12]

Until the early 2000s, scholarship on literature and theater dominated cultural studies of the GDR.[13] Some works on painting, notably those on contemporary exhibitions, offered glimpses of considerable artistic output (Blume and März 2003; Damus 1991; Flacke 1995; Kuehn 1997). In these studies, the approach to culture is frequently confined to problems of representation, however. In a few rare cases, it is evoked from the standpoint of a particular social group or individual within the framework of the company or other social venue (Bazin 2015; Kott 1999). The study of cinema allows us to adopt another perspective, however.

The history of cinema in the GDR overlaps to a large extent with that of the Deutsche Film Aktiengesellschaft (DEFA), the state-owned company that exercised a monopoly over East German film production from its establishment in 1946 to the demise of the GDR in 1990.[14] Subordinate to both the central government and the SED, the official state party,[15] DEFA was part of the planned industrial economy, and everyone from film directors to technicians was a salaried employee. From the perspective of documentary film—the focus of the Leipzig Festival—examining East German cinema thus becomes a matter of probing the complex and changing relationships linking aesthetics and ideology, the artistic aspirations of individual filmmakers and the dogma of Socialist Realism (whose definition has always been problematic). To this end, we must pursue two levels of analysis, cross-referencing the institutional level—the evolution of the studios as a whole—and the individual level—which focuses on the biographical trajectories of DEFA personnel.

Several works have already been devoted to the DEFA Studios since 1989. These have been published in part by former stakeholders and observers of DEFA, who have provided a lion's share of basic documentation (Jordan 2009; Mückenberger and Jordan 1994; Schenk 1994, 2006), and predominantly by German researchers from both the East and West (Geiss 2001; Heimann 1994; Moldenhauer and Steinkopff 2001). Anglo-Saxon scholars have also been very active in this field, as well as in GDR history in general, in particular around the DEFA Film Library at the University of Massachusetts Amherst in the United States.[16] In French academic circles, where research on the topic has been scarce, East German cinema is treated within German cinema more globally.[17] The publication of historian Cyril Buffet's work in 2008 finally offered an overview of the history of the DEFA Studios in French (Buffet 2008).

Two principal characteristics emerge from these publications. First, research themes have evolved over time: a predominantly political approach, focused on the relationship between feature filmmakers and the regime, has given way to research on social and cultural history (Heimann 1991, 1994), seeking to more accurately reflect the role of fictional cinema in the evolution of East German society (Feinstein 2002). In this context, documentary film has not been entirely neglected.[18] The vast panorama devoted to this genre in 1996 by Günter Jordan and Ralf Schenk has opened up multiple avenues of research, as have the works published by the Haus des Dokumentar Films in Stuttgart (Jordan and Schenk 1996; Zimmermann 1995). Second, there are monographs in which the sole comparison envisaged is that between the two Germanys, reflecting to some degree the dominance of German scholars in this field of study and associated with work on specific memories (Kötzing 2013; Steinle 2003; Zimmermann and Moldenhauer 2000).

More recent publications, however, attest to a growing interest in the history of the global circulation of East German films (Byg 1999; Lindenberger 2009; Val 2012; Wedel and Elsaesser 2011; Wedel et al. 2013). Taking a cultural-historical approach to cinema, this study participates in this same commitment to openness. It seeks to move beyond questions of representation alone and to focus on the technical, economic, and political conditions of cinematic production in the GDR, in comparison to conditions elsewhere and incorporating, insofar as is possible, research on its reception (Ory 2004).

The choice to focus on documentary film—a valuable and intricate source for historians—also presents challenges (Moine 2010a). It is important to understand East German film, both fictional and documentary, in all its complexity—as a set of practices and productions that are anchored not only in domestic issues facing East German society and government but also in competitive Cold War cultural relationships on an international scale. Considering only the GDR would, in fact, run the risk of confining our analysis to the stakes involved in relations between dominant and dominated, between artists and authorities,[19] without unshackling it from a reductive interpretation of allegiance, propaganda, and loyalty toward the regime. The history of the Leipzig Festival thus offers the perfect opportunity to delve deeper into a cultural history of documentary cinema within an international context.

Toward a History of Festivals

While sociologists, geographers, and media studies scholars have already identified festivals as an important research topic, the subject has thus far not received much attention from historians.[20] Indicative of a new consideration of these cultural manifestations, however, is a proliferation of research projects. These include work on the history of music festivals in Salzburg and Prague and the influential theater festival in Avignon, founded in 1947 (Baecque and Loyer 2007; Charnay 2003; Fink 2009; Moine 2013; Petersen and Mazza 2011). With regard to film festivals, in particular, it is notably Anglo-Saxon researchers in the fields of media studies or information and communication sciences who have paved the way, primarily focusing on the dramatic increase in the number of festivals over recent decades (Elsaesser 2005; De Valck 2007; De Valck and Loist 2009).[21] Over the course of the 2000s, various groups of non-historians and research networks—in fields such as communications and media and film studies—were formed to gather the few studies that had surfaced in different institutions.[22]

In recent years, a historical approach to the subject that links political and cultural history has clearly evolved. In France, Loredana Latil's book (2005) on the Cannes Film Festival long remained a solitary example of work on the subject. Two recent publications—Stefano Pisu's work (2016), covering the period from the 1930s to the 1970s, and the coedited volume by Andreas Kötzing and Caroline Moine (2017), spanning the Cold War period—testify to the fruitfulness of such an approach to film festival history.

We can identify three principal challenges raised by cultural histories of film festivals.[23] The first is the need to study culture in its broadest sense. Historian Akira Iriye proposes a definition of culture that balances representations, ideologies, and mindsets, with the reproduction and dissemination of symbolic objects that constitute the "creation and communication of memory, ideology, emotions, lifestyles, scholarly and artistic works, and other symbols" (Iriye 1991: 215). One question raised by the study of an international festival is, in fact, to what extent the exchange of symbolic products can induce a change in representational system—on one or both sides of national borders—or whether the opening of the representational system abroad generates the desire to exchange symbolic products.

The history of an international festival also underlines the incontrovertible analytic significance of different spatial and temporal scales. It demonstrates the extent to which cultural policies are intertwined at the national and international level. In the case of Leipzig, considerations of scale allow us to better understand the forms assumed by the search for an East German identity — an identity that was bound not only to the question of the regime's legitimacy vis-à-vis its citizens but also to the issue of international recognition. The festival format — with its mostly annual rhythm — also allows us to integrate the temporal scale. To borrow a geological image, studying the Leipzig Festival consists in taking samples from the soil of East German society, observing its evolution at regular intervals, and analyzing different strata — cultural, social, and political — in a dynamic and progressive manner; these geological cores ensure that we avoid the pitfalls of the univocal or teleological vision that can dominate when the collapse of the GDR is regarded as the observational starting point.

Finally, film festivals raise the question of how political entities instrumentalized images during the Cold War and offer an opportunity to analyze various actors operating within these highly complex relations of power. Several successive circles are apparent here.[24] The first — and most frequently studied — are actors in the field of cultural diplomacy; these were clearly represented at the Leipzig Festival, which was a cultural event financed and organized by the state. The second — which integrates both diplomatic and nondiplomatic, official and unofficial actors — makes it possible to grasp cultural exchanges more comprehensively. Transnational cultural movements, in which cultural transfers and exchanges are developed, form a third and final circle.[25] The Leipzig Festival is located right at the heart of these different dynamics.

Writing the History of the Leipzig Film Festival

The Leipzig Festival's history, from its inception in 1955 to German unification in 1990, offers a number of research perspectives that suggest fresh ways of looking at international cultural and diplomatic geography, as well as at the role of the GDR on the European and international stage.[26] A border and contact zone, a place for screenings as well as exchanges and meetings between guests from all round the globe, Leipzig also had its own dynamics. The festival thus represents an observational vantage point of exceptional value for the historian, thanks to its programming, its staging, and the responses and memories it generated.

Analyzing the films selected in different categories, the prizes awarded, and the official and unofficial debates that took place enables us to follow the major international trends in documentary filmmaking during this period —

defense or denunciation of engaged documentary (*cinéma militant*); shift toward Direct Cinema; evolution of sociological documentary; increased competition with television—and the extent to which GDR productions remained isolated from these trends or not, as the case may be (Aitken 2005; Barnouw 1993; Gauthier 1995). In addition to grasping the numerous interactions involved in the process of making documentary films in the GDR, this study gives us a new way to approach the central issue represented by the Soviet model, which was pervasive across the East Bloc during the Cold War (Jarausch and Siegrist 1997). Throughout the festival's history, the evolution of documentary film in the USSR can effectively be traced right up until the highly fruitful glasnost period, in the latter half of the 1980s. Leipzig's history also reveals the importance of alternative points of reference for documentarists from the GDR and the East, for example, post-1958 Cuban cinema.

The research for this investigation relied on three major types of sources—written, film, and oral archives—available mainly in Berlin and the Brandenburg region of Germany. The almost complete opening of the East German archives following German unification is a well-known fact. Such an "archival revolution," however, did not come about without some technical hitches and methodological misgivings (François 1995; Weber 1992; Wolle 1992). Working in the written archives of the GDR entails being confronted with not just a pile of documents but also a monotonous uniformity in the tone of the sources, because of the political doublespeak of the East German administration.[27] The government and party archives, as well as those of the Leipzig Festival—all conserved in Berlin—nevertheless enabled me to trace the history of the festival, from the preparatory stages all the way to its critical reception, including all that unfolded in between.

The films screened at Leipzig naturally constitute the second set of sources used for this study. Putting together a corpus of nearly 150 films—which are, in part, kept in Berlin film archives or sometimes available through the filmmakers—was no easy feat.[28] The first task was to give an account of the diverse aspects of East German documentaries from 1949 to 1990—from films serving the regime's strategic discourse to censored films and films caught in between: uncensored works that received only very limited distribution.[29] The second task was to develop a list of non-German documentaries screened at the Leipzig Festival that evoked particular attention among foreign guests; these films make it possible to decisively inscribe the East German example into an international context.

Obviously, not all films are of equal importance for the present study. As a result, the method of analysis differs according to the role played by a given documentary in the general argument. Above all, I was concerned with highlighting the complexity of the term "propaganda." We would be mistaken to regard East German documentaries as exclusively a series of commissioned works, of indiscriminate propaganda in which filmmakers were simply anonymous pawns of an institutional system, mere executors devoid of any personal vision. We must go beyond this simplistic designation for DEFA documentaries, if only because propaganda was sometimes claimed by filmmakers from both blocs, even assuming positive connotations, precisely in the field of documentary filmmaking (Hahn 1997).[30] It is thus necessary to resituate these films in their sociopolitical context of production and distribution in order to establish a "more nuanced view of how [these images] were conceived and perceived" (Véray 2003). It is in this spirit that certain documentaries in the corpus, for which I had access to archives and sources, were analyzed with particular attention.[31]

I collected oral testimonies, the third set of sources, during my research stays, mainly in Berlin and in its environs. I conducted a series of interviews with twenty-one people: former DEFA film directors, technicians, dramaturgs, and erstwhile festival directors as well as French and East and West German journalists. Two groups can be distinguished: those who have overcome the turning point of 1989–1990, who have worked out their past and speak of it with a certain detachment, and those who employ the same language and apply the same interpretative grids as in the past.

Of course, we must remain conscious of the specificity of oral sources. The cognitive value of oral memoirs should not be confused with the immediate transmission of a lived past; rather the value is in the opportunity that the interview affords to scrutinize how the past is constructed, how meanings are attributed a posteriori, and how lived experiences are assimilated (*Verarbeitung*)—in a word: subjectivity (Perks and Thomson 1998; Wierling 2002). Using oral sources is particularly important in the case of the GDR, however; a series of processes essential to comprehending the lived history of the GDR were so clandestine that they were invisible to the surveillance apparatus, as highly developed and inquisitive as it was.[32]

The challenge is to understand when and how the internal disaffection felt by many in the GDR operated, the shift from total or partial adherence to resigned submission and then the mere semblance of loyalty (François 1995). Moreover, in an authoritarian state in which taboos and prohibitions prevented the expression of opinions contrary to official discourse, the written sources that survive especially privilege the voice of the regime and are therefore also skewed. Oral testimonies thus constitute a reservoir of perspectives that give rise to an alternative and multilayered image that overlaps the one furnished by written sources. And, at the end, a festival thrives on encounters, individual and collective experiences, and memories; whether a festival lives or dies is mostly determined by the impressions it leaves behind.

Historical Overview

This volume seeks to weave questions of temporal and spatial scale throughout an in-depth exploration of the Leipzig Film Festival. It follows a generally chronological schema whereby it should be noted that "chronological inflexions, or even breaks" in the festival's history do not entirely coincide with those of GDR politics (Kott 2000: 322–23); for example, the landmark dates in the festival's institutional history were 1964 and 1973, corresponding with the arrival of new festival directors who were charged with the task of modifying future festival policy. This chronological approach is overlaid by thematic focal points that allow us to trace broader developments in documentary cinema and international relations, as well as in the GDR.

The Leipzig Documentary Film Festival gradually took shape from 1949 to 1964 and was affected by the overlapping influences of inter-German relations, East and West Bloc policies, and East German intellectuals who were anxious to resist cultural isolation in the evolving political climate of the Cold War. In 1964, the entry of GDR television as the official organizer led to the professionalization of the Leipzig Festival, which was increasingly called upon to actively contribute to the GDR's cultural and diplomatic offensive in the international arena. Partly in response to the aftermath of de-Stalinization, the prevailing international ambience reflected the political effervescence and globalized culture of the 1960s, which were also apparent in various forms of cinematic new waves.

After the GDR finally achieved widespread diplomatic recognition in 1973, it became necessary to deliberate on fresh challenges confronting the Leipzig Festival; dividing lines between East German society and cinema, on the one hand, and ongoing political and cultural developments, on the other, were becoming increasingly permeable in the East, as in the West. Over the course of the 1980s, the documentary films being produced at DEFA underwent profound changes, in line with the international momentum initiated by the institution of reforms in the USSR as of 1985. Finally, in 1989 East Germany's peaceful revolution played out not only on the streets of Leipzig but across the screens of its festival as well.

Notes

1. As of March 1967, Marker had participated in shooting a film on the workers' occupation of a factory in Besançon, in the French provinces; he worked side by side with worker-filmmakers, who then formed the Medvedkin Group in December 1967.

2. Much later, Marker paid Medvedkin a marvelous cinematic tribute in his 1992 film *Le tombeau d'Alexandre* (*The Last Bolshevik*).
3. See the official film festival website: http://www.dok-leipzig.de/.
4. Over time, the festival has had different names: Leipziger Kultur- und Dokumentarfilmwoche (1955–1956); Internationale Leipziger Dokumentar- und Kurzfilmwoche (International Leipzig Documentary and Short Film Week; 1960–1967); Internationale Leipziger Dokumentar- und Kurzfilmwoche für Kino und Fernsehen (International Leipzig Documentary and Short Film Week for Cinema and Television; 1968–1989); Internationale Leipziger Filmwoche für Dokumentar- und Animationsfilm (International Leipzig Film Week for Documentary and Animated Film; 1990); Internationales Leipziger Festival für Dokumentar- und Animationsfilm (International Leipzig Festival for Documentary and Animated Film; 1991–present). Informally, the festival was often simply referred to as the Dokfilmwoche; it is now referred to as DOK Leipzig.
5. See Dubosclard et al. 2002; Paulmann 2005.
6. See Berghahn 2004; Caute 2003; Gienow-Hecht 2009b; Rolland 2004; Saunders 1999.
7. See Gienow-Hecht 2009a; Major and Mitter 2006; Sirinelli and Soutou 2008; Vowinckel et al. 2012.
8. See Iriye 1991.
9. On this vast topic see "The Cold War and the Movies" 1998; Buffet and Maguire 2014; Niemeyer and Pfeil 2014; Shaw and Youngblood 2010; Lindenberger 2006; Mattelart 1995.
10. See Bispinck et al. 2005; Eppelmann et al. 2003; Lindenberger 2014; Port 2013. For an overview of historiographic issues, see Kott 2002.
11. See Kott 2000, 2011; Lüdtke 1998.
12. See Carter 2001.
13. In France, see Hähnel-Mesnard 2007; Poumet 1990.
14. There were also army studios and a studio that specialized in the production of publicity films, but these remained marginal. One must also note the films that were made clandestinely—amateur films and other forms of an underground cinema—which developed especially as of the 1970s with the emergence of new technologies, such as Super-8 and video (Fritzsche and Löser 1996; Löser 2011; interview by the author with Thomas Heise, Nyon, Switzerland [25 April 2002]).
15. SED stands for Sozialistische Einheitspartei Deutschlands, the Socialist Unity Part of Germany, a pillar of the governing regime created in 1946 by the forced fusion of the Socialist Democrat Party (SPD) and the Communist Party (KPD) of Germany in the Soviet Occupation Zone.
16. See Allan and Sandford 1999; Byg and Moore 2002; Hake 2002.
17. Béatrice Fleury-Villatte (1995) compares East and West German feature films; Bernard Eisenschitz (1999) integrates DEFA into his history of German cinema; Matthias Steinle (2008) devotes a chapter to the GDR.
18. In the West before 1989, Ernst Opgenoorth (1984) published *Volksdemokratie im Kino. Propagandistische Selbstdarstellung der SED im DEFA-Dokumentarfilm, 1946–1957*; we must also note post-1990 publications that started before 1989, such as *Erprobung eines Genres: DEFA-Dokumentarfilme für Kinder, 1975–1990* (Jordan 1991).
19. On the issues surrounding commissioned art, see Flacke 1995.
20. In France, see Ethis 2001 and Wallon 2010.

21. For a panorama of recent studies on film festivals, see Blahova 2014; Iordanova 2013; Vallejo 2014; De Valck et al. 2016.
22. See the resource provided by the Film Festival Research Network (FFRN), created by Skadi Loist and Marijke De Valck, which features a large and regularly updated online bibliography. (http://www.filmfestivalresearch.org/).
23. For an analysis of the stakes involved in the history of art festivals, in general, see the proceedings of an international colloquium held in France in 2011 (Fléchet et al. 2013).
24. See Ory 2003.
25. See the pioneering works of Espagne and Werner 1988; Werner and Zimmermann 2004.
26. This book evolved out of a series of research projects on the Leipzig Festival and other film festivals during the Cold War that the author undertook starting in 2000. They formed the basis for a 2005 thesis at the Université Paris 1 (Moine 2005a), as well as the original French version of this volume (Moine 2014a). Preceding such work, however, it is important to note the work of Christiane Mückenberger, who directed the festival from 1990 to 1993 (Mückenberger 1996). Since 2005, the festival has also been the topic of two other works. The first was conducted in information and communications sciences by Martini (2007); this monograph is problematic in several ways, especially its rather uncritical view of the complex relations between the festival and the dominant regime and the absence of any analysis of the films themselves. The work of historian Andreas Kötzing is of entirely different quality; his 2004 Master's thesis centers on the Leipzig Festival in the 1970s, while his 2013 dissertation compares the Leipzig and Oberhausen festivals from 1954 to 1972.
27. Furthermore, not all document collections are accessible yet. In addition to routine regulations limiting access to archives less than thirty years old, certain judiciary archives have not yet been made entirely accessible. See Mouralis 2008.
28. For a detailed filmography of DEFA documentary films, see Gerull and Grusser 1996. The best work to trace the principal historical stages of East German documentary filmmaking is the reference work edited by Jordan and Schenk 1996.
29. Issues with access to films make the question of an exhaustive overview moot. Please see Appendix I on Archival Sources. Directors gave me copies of some films, allowing me to fill in certain blank spots; in this regard, I would particularly like to thank Gitta Nickel, who enabled me to watch the totality of her films on VHS videocassettes, as well as Günter Jordan.
30. Also see the positions of filmmakers like John Grierson from Britain.
31. See, for example, Lindeperg 2014. This historian was able to find sources and archives that allowed her to retrace all aspects of the process of creating a film, from its early history as a project to its screening and reception. Clearly, this is not always possible.
32. On the complexity of using oral sources that face historians of the GDR, see Niethammer 1985.

PART I

A Cold War Festival (1949–1964)

CHAPTER 1

The Genesis of the Leipzig Film Festival

Ten years after the end of World War II, in a Europe increasingly polarized by Cold War politics, the Leipzig Documentary Film Festival represented a hopeful opportunity for filmmakers from East and West Germany to meet, share their work, and partake in international cinematographic developments. The festival's creation was invested with multiple expectations on both sides of the Iron Curtain, and those launching it faced serious challenges in an environment shaped by institutions, individuals, and national and international politics.

The domestic context in which the Leipzig Documentary Film Festival was established was structured by East German cultural policy during the country's formative years. Filmmaking was located at the intersection of several different institutions that often had different, and sometimes competing, interests. An examination of the trajectories and careers of individuals involved in these institutions further deepens our understanding of issues surrounding the festival's genesis. The collective portrayal of functionaries and administrators, directors and dramaturgs who shaped cultural and cinematographic policy—from the highest echelons of government and the ruling party to the DEFA Documentary Film Studio—renders the entire human dimension of a world relatively closed in upon itself and riddled by strained relations.

Administering Filmmaking in the GDR

As early as 28 April 1945, while fighting continued to rage in the heart of Berlin, the city's Soviet commander ordered the reopening of theaters, cinemas, and sports facilities (Mückenberger and Jordan 1994). Two days later, the first group of German exiles from Moscow landed in Berlin to help in reconstructing the country. On 17 May 1946 the Soviet occupation authorities formally granted a license to the Deutsche Film Aktiengesellschaft (DEFA, literally German Film Company). On 6 June 1945, the Soviet Military Administration in Germany was formally established; and in August 1945, the four military occupation zones of German territory were definitively marked out.

The majority of German film production studios were now located in the Soviet Occupation Zone,[1] and the Soviets rapidly launched an active cultural policy in which cinema became a key element (Pike 1992). Subsequently, from 1949 to 1954, the new structures of the East German state took shape, largely based on the Soviet model. Once this transition was complete, three institutions were concerned with film and film policy in the GDR: the DEFA Studios; the Central Administration for Film (HVFilm) within the Ministry of Culture; and the Central Committee (ZK) of East Germany's ruling German Socialist Unity Party (SED). Over the forty years of East Germany's existence, this framework, within which officials responsible for cinema as well as directors and other studio employees worked, would only change marginally.

The DEFA Studios

After the establishment of the GDR on 7 October 1949, the many corporations established in the Soviet Occupation Zone (SBZ) gradually came under the control of the newly founded state. This was also the case for DEFA, which was integrated into the state's political and cultural apparatus as the sole filmmaking concern in the country in 1953. Made up of several studios specializing in different types of films, DEFA—now the DEFA Studios—was administered by a managing director. In all, seven men held this position between 1949 and 1989.[2] All card-carrying members of the SED, the first few were among those German Communists who had spent the Nazi years as refugees in Moscow—a fact that a priori guaranteed their political integrity in the new state. These men were most often chosen for their experience in cultural, theatrical, or journalistic spheres.

Each of the individual DEFA studios also held the status of a "publicly owned company" (VEB) and had its own director. These were accountable to the managing director of the DEFA Studios, who himself was subject to government control. Where documentary films fit into the structure of DEFA evolved over time. Newsreels had been the first films produced at DEFA (and in Germany) after World War II, followed shortly by feature and documentary films. A separate DEFA Studio for Newsreels and Documentary Films was established in 1952. As of 1969, the DEFA Studio for Short Films combined documentary with educational and scientific shorts. Then, in 1975, all documentary production was united in the DEFA Studio for Documentary Film until the collapse of the GDR in 1990.

Among the men who directed DEFA documentary production, three stand out as having played a particularly important role in the Leipzig Festival: Günter Klein (1953–1960), Rolf Schnabel (1966–1968), and Wolfgang Kernicke (1969–1976). These men's biographies give a good preliminary sense of some of the forces at play. Born in 1922 and a prisoner of war at Stalingrad, in 1944 Klein actively participated in the communist exile group the National Committee for a Free Germany (Nationalkomitee Freies Deutschland). He arrived in Berlin in 1945. A year later, having joined the SED, he worked as a journalist in the Soviet Press Office. In 1949, he was appointed head of newsreel production in order to impose a more orthodox ideological line than hitherto taken (Jordan 2000). In 1953, he became director of the newly established DEFA Studio for Newsreels and Documentary Films. This position allowed him to play an influential role in the establishment of the Leipzig Festival in 1955. In 1960, he was appointed as a member of the state committee for East German Television (DFF), a sector tightly controlled by the SED. An apparatchik, Klein was often criticized for not ensuring the studio's proper functioning and being difficult to reach;[3] thanks to his allegiance to the SED, however, such criticisms did not hamper his career.

Rolf Schnabel, born in 1925 and enlisted in the Wehrmacht in 1943, was a member of the Free German Youth (FDJ), the SED's official youth movement, from 1946 to 1954. He subsequently joined DEFA, where he worked on newsreels. From 1963 to 1966, he continued his formation at the SED's Party School (*Parteischule*), before becoming director of the DEFA Studio for Newsreels and Documentary Films, and, as of 1968, he devoted himself entirely to directing films. Moving in the opposite direction, Wolfgang Kernicke had an active role in filmmaking before becoming the studio's director. As of 1953, he was one of the core organizers of a professional association called the GDR Filmmakers' Club (Club der Filmschaffenden der DDR). He subsequently became the first director of the Leipzig Festival before becoming the studio director in 1969.

The Central Administration for Film

The establishment of the Ministry of Culture was a crucial turning point in the evolution of cultural policy in East Germany.[4] Several months earlier, the crisis of June 1953 had marked a clear rupture in the history of the GDR; a series of uprisings in the fledgling state had exposed deep hostility toward the regime's economic, social, and political decisions.[5] In this context, artists and intellectuals were hopeful that the appointment of the poet Johannes R. Becher as minister of culture would usher in a certain liberalization. For the party, however, it was predominantly an issue of further consolidating another sector of a centralized state apparatus facing the risk of centrifugal forces.

Within the new ministry, a Central Administration for Film (HVFilm) replaced the State Committee for Cinema, which had been established on the Soviet model in 1952, and took over its main prerogatives (Heimann 2000): film production and distribution, management of movie theaters, training filmmakers, and relations with foreign countries. It was divided into three departments: artistic production; cultural policy, where authorizations for general release were decided; and planning and finance, where state subsidies were allocated. HVFilm subsequently became the government trustee of the Leipzig Festival. Anton Ackermann, a communist activist from the outset and former Moscow exile, served as the first director of HVFilm from 1954 to 1958. From 1964 to 1966, Günter Witt held the reins until being ousted from his position in the wake of the Eleventh Plenum of the SED's Central Committee.[6] Over the following decade Wilfried Maaß, Siegfried Wagner, Gert Springfeld, Günter Klein, and Johannes Starke were successively in charge. Horst Pehnert held the position continuously from 1976 to 1990 (Beutelschmidt 1995). By 1954, a highly hierarchical system for culture and film production was firmly in place, under the control of the Party.

Culture and Propaganda

From 1949 to 1989, East German film policy was ultimately decided within the Culture and the Agitation Departments of the SED's Central Committee (ZK), the party's "supreme body" between its congresses. As of 1954, as film production came under the control of HVFilm at the new Ministry of Culture, the ZK's Department of Literature and Art dealt with fictional feature films, while documentaries and newsreels remained the remit of the Agitation Department, as had been the case since 1946. Later, documentaries were set apart from newsreels and also placed under the responsibility of the Culture Department. The new distribution system led to manifold tensions among the ZK's various departments, which film directors could sometimes exploit to their own advantage, particularly during heated discussions about a given film. In 1958, Kurt Hager became the all-powerful ZK secretary—responsible for the departments of culture, popular education, and science—and remained in the post until 1989. As the regime's chief ideologist, he was responsible for implementing its policies, upon which even the minister of culture was dependent.

From 1976 to 1989, in particular, a very strong continuity was apparent within the three central groupings upon which GDR cinema depended—be it with Hans-Dieter Mäde directing the DEFA Studios; with Hans-Joachim Hoffmann at the Ministry of Culture (from 1973 to 1989) and Horst Pehnert at HVFilm (the sole nonmember of the ZK); or with Kurt Hager within the SED's ZK. This continuity bolstered the political clout of these officials within the system. It also exemplifies the inability of the East German state apparatus to renew itself and incorporate new blood into its structures during all those years. How, then, was it for directors, writers, and studio technicians working in this system?

DEFA Documentarists: Such a Small World

In 1954, the DEFA Studio for Newsreels and Documentary Films, at the time the largest in Europe (Herbst et al. 1994), had 420 employees.[7] These deserve attention, as they played a vital role in the history of the Leipzig Festival. In order to measure what influence they had within the regime's policies and to better understand DEFA's documentary production, we must try to understand their political and social identities.

Until the construction of the Wall in 1961, DEFA hired people living in all four occupied sectors (Heimann 2000), resulting in only weak ideological homogeneity in the studios. In December 1954, the newly established HVFilm took stock of the political and social situation in the Newsreel and Documentary Studio.[8] Their findings were largely negative. While 388 of the 420 studio employees were affiliated with the Free German Trade Union Federation (FDGB), only ninety-seven were card-carrying SED members.[9] The report revealed a strong sense of not only professional but also political and social continuity with the period prior to 1945; it underscored limited engagement with organizations linked to the new system and its project for a new society.

The career of documentary director Andrew Thorndike illustrates this transition period. Born in 1909, Thorndike, the son of a director at the UFA Studios (DEFA's predecessor), worked in the publicity film department there from 1931 to 1939 (Jordan 1994). Drafted into the Wehrmacht, he was taken prisoner by the Soviets in 1945 and underwent antifascist schooling until 1948, at which point he returned to Dresden (Herlinghaus 1982). Joining DEFA in 1949, he played a highly prominent role until his death in 1979. He influenced an entire generation of filmmakers and studio technicians through his lectures at the Babelsberg Film Academy (starting in 1954); through his artistic production group (KAG) at the studio (from 1967 to 1979); through his commitment to the Leipzig Festival, of which he was president of the jury from 1964 to 1966 and a member of the presidium from 1962 to 1966; and, finally, as the first president of the East German Association of Film and Television Workers (VFF; from 1967 to 1979).

Across about ten films, Thorndike represented the regime's core propaganda themes. He directed hagiographic portraits of two leading communist figures: Wilhelm Pieck (1952), the GDR's first president, and Lenin (1970). Two historical compilations reflected communist interpretations of history: one was about Germany's responsibility for both world wars—*Du und mancher Kamerad* (1956, *You and Some Comrade*)—and the other was a cinematic panorama spanning the period from tsarism to the Soviet Union (1963). His films were also critical of West Germany, including a portrayal of West German workers acclaiming the East German system—*Sieben vom Rhein* (1954, *Seven from the Rhine*)—and two films denouncing the presence of former Nazis in the FRG government in Bonn—*Urlaub auf Sylt* (1957, *Holiday on Sylt*) and *Unternehmen Teutonenschwert* (1958, *Operation Teutonic Sword*). With such films, which he effectively put at the service of the regime "with the zeal of the convert," in the words of historian Günter Jordan, Thorndike knew how to win the trust and support of GDR leaders.

Nevertheless, he was the object of much enmity, because to many he remained an erstwhile bourgeois who had to prove that he was one of them, an artist and comrade.[10] The establishment in 1967 of Thorndike's own production group within the studio merely intensified internal rivalries—notably with Karl Gass, a documentary director born in 1917 who in 1948 had opted for the Soviet zone of occupation in order to continue journalistic activities he had started after the war in Cologne. Gass entered the DEFA Studio for Newsreels and Documentary Films[11] as a screenwriter, author, and director in 1951; from 1954 to 1958, he was named artistic director and among the founders of the Leipzig Festival. The incessant rivalry between Gass and Thorndike[12] was to have ramifications, as we will see, that affected the Leipzig Festival's organization and evolution.[13]

From the point of view of HVFilm, the trick was to give voice to various actors in cultural life while retaining control over their artistic output. In part to address and bring to an end what their report indicated was too great a degree of political and social heterogeneity within DEFA, it established two separate institutions to extend control and offer training: the GDR Filmmakers' Club and the German Academy of Film (HFF) in Potsdam-Babelsberg.[14]

The Filmmakers' Club

The establishment of the East German Academy of Arts (Akademie der Künste, or AdK) in March 1950 offered grounds to hope for the relative autonomy of artists, notably thanks to such strong personalities in its ranks as the authors Bertolt Brecht and Anna Seghers. Hope, however, swiftly waned in the face of the SED's increasingly interventionist policies (Uhlmann 1993). The birth of the GDR in 1949 had ushered East Germany into a phase of "popular democracy," thereby jettisoning the preceding "democratic and antifascist"

Figure 1.1. Poster by John Heartfield for A. Thorndike's *You and Some Comrade* (1956). © DEFA Stiftung, John Heartfield.

phase. As of September 1948, there was no longer talk of a "specific German path towards socialism," as Anton Ackermann had formulated the aspiration in 1946 to a democratic model that would be distinct from Nazism but also independent of the USSR (Schröder 1998: 64).

As in the other socialist countries in Eastern Europe that depended on Moscow, the Soviet model finally prevailed over every other option, however. The creation of several associations—the Academy of Architecture in December 1951, the Association of Sculptors in April 1952, and a month later the Professional Association of Authors in the GDR (later the German Authors' League, DSV)—was decreed by the SED's ZK, hence clarifying the party's leadership in cultural matters.

The GDR Filmmakers' Club was the last to be established, in December 1953, following the creation of the GDR Cinema Committee in 1952 and the overhaul of the studios in 1953.[15] Filmmakers were merely accorded the status of a club, whose structures were looser and less autonomous than those of an association.[16] The Filmmakers' Club was not meant to function as a union or professional association—as a conduit between members and those in power—but rather as a simple forum for cultural expression and exchange. Debates and screenings were thus organized and, in the initial phase, primarily intended for a West German public (Heimann 2000). The Club became chief organizer of the Leipzig Festival in 1955.

The Film Academy in Babelsberg

The establishment in 1954 of the German Academy for Film (Deutsche Hochschule für Filmkunst) in Potsdam-Babelsberg represented an important watershed. The GDR lagged behind Poland, its neighbor to the East, which had founded the Łódź Film School in 1948 (Michalek and Turaj 1992). Yet it outpaced, and by some considerable distance, West Germany, where the German Film and Television Academy opened in West Berlin only in September 1966, followed in November 1967 by the University of Television and Film in Munich (Pflaum and Prinzler 1993). In 1969, in response to the increasing influence of television in the GDR, the academy in Babelsberg was renamed the Academy for Film and Television (HFF).

The HFF, located near the main site of the DEFA Studios in Berlin's southwestern suburbs, took as its model the State Institute of Cinematography in Moscow (VKIG), which was founded in 1919. Over a four-year degree program, an intensely orthodox political education (courses in Marxism-Leninism, economics, philosophy) paralleled technical and artistic training (acting, dramaturgy, production, editing, sound recording, cinematography, directing, film and television science; Löser 1996). After completing their training, students found work at DEFA as directors, screenwriters, and technicians. There they were mostly engaged as full-time employees, so they received a regular salary even when not working on a film[17]; this was supplemented by bonuses based on the success of a particular film or when it was awarded a prize, especially at film festivals. In this respect, their situation differed considerably from that of West German documentary filmmakers.

Another salient feature of the Babelsberg academy from the start was the presence of many foreign students. Coming from Africa, Asia, Europe, and the Middle East, they were sent by countries that were affiliated with the GDR. Erika Richter, who studied dramaturgy there starting in 1956, recalls Iraqis, Vietnamese, Greeks, Spaniards, and Africans who often came from affluent backgrounds.[18] Their admittance to the academy did not correspond to very clear artistic criteria but was instead based on political considerations (Löser 1996). As soon as they entered the academy, budding directors and technicians were thus confronted with the notion of international solidarity, a concept at the very core of the East German experiment. By way of the history of the Leipzig Festival, we will observe to what extent this solidarity was actually advocated and put into practice.

Thanks to free exchanges between film schools, the HFF also arranged special screening sessions, which featured foreign films not released in movie theaters in East Germany. This made it possible for Babelsberg students to discover newly released foreign films and motion picture classics. Beyond the confines of the academy, the Club organized screenings, but these too were reserved for professionals. Foreign cultural centers in East Berlin also screened films for those in the know. Opportunities were nevertheless limited and contacts with the outside world were still monitored. It was not possible to attend festivals abroad in a private capacity. Either one's film was officially selected or one had to be part of the delegation of Filmmakers' Club and Association members. And while there were always DEFA delegations to festivals in the East, their presence at events in the West was contingent upon existing diplomatic relations. In this context, the programming of student films at Leipzig as of 1962 presented students at Babelsberg with a valuable opportunity.[19]

The Issue of International Recognition

Establishing a film festival in the GDR thus represented a great hope for DEFA documentary filmmakers: it would enable them not only to discover what was being produced abroad but also to present their own films to a wider audience. So soon after the end of World War II, however, two questions were central: To what extent had DEFA succeeded, if at all, in making a clean break with the *Kulturfilm*[20] of the Nazi era? And what place would East German documentaries be able to forge for themselves in the international arena?

In 1946, film director Kurt Maetzig, who had shot the first German newsreels in the Soviet Occupation Zone and was one of the founders of DEFA, published an article exposing the dilemma posed by Nazi filmmaking that, with its calculated use of real images, had nonetheless fabricated a falsified representation of reality.[21] As a result, German documentary filmmaking had fallen into disrepute. One of the challenges facing DEFA was hence to revive a thoroughly discredited cinema—which had been assimilated into a regime now ostracized by the international community and, to a large extent, severed from its political and aesthetic roots—and once again give it a national, as well as worldwide role and recognition.

A Difficult Transition to Socialist Realism

In the first half of the 1950s, the Soviet model—from the mode of production to the very conception of what constituted a documentary film—was open to multiple readings, putting East German filmmakers and officials in a delicate transitional phase. A documentary film's trajectory, from the initial idea to the end of production, included no fewer than twenty-three distinct stages, according to a 1954 schema constructed within a framework determined in part by Soviet-style planning.[22] Above and beyond these constraints, artistic, and cinematographic creation was shackled to vaguely defined aesthetic and political considerations.

Between July 1950 and March 1951, the SED initiated the "struggle against formalism in art and literature, for a progressive German culture." As of this juncture, cultural debates openly became part of the stakes in play in the Cold War. A virulent East German nationalism emerged in a campaign that indiscriminately denounced formalism, objectivism, and cosmopolitanism coming from the West, which were accused of making art inaccessible to the population (Lemke 2000; Lindenberger 2005). Realism—which, according to party ideologues, provided the sole way for art to reach the masses and thus establish a truly democratic art—was replaced at the SED convention in July 1952 by the term "Socialist Realism," whose meaning was equally vague. Most importantly, the regime attributed a new social function to artists: political engagement and proximity to the people were its two principal pillars.

A conference titled To Revive Progressive German Cinema was organized in September 1952, underscoring the critical role filmmaking played in the regime's policy. Any compromise with filmmakers not toeing the official political and cultural line was ruled out ("Für den Aufschwung" 1952). Those DEFA directors living in the West ceased working with the studios.[23] Even so, East German documentary film production remained suspended between two models, the old and the new. The teachings of Kurt Maetzig and Andrew Thorndike were dominant at the Babelsberg academy, forging a "curious mixture between the *Kulturfilm,* imbued with National Socialism, and Marxist-Leninist doctrine" (Löser 1996: 344–45). Oversimplification virtually always won out: class struggle slogans, enforced educational content, demonstrative scores. . . . Amid the production of some twenty films per year, however, several works stood out, which sketched out innovative directions for documentary filmmaking, enabling DEFA to achieve recognition, even on an international level.

The German Question Onscreen

Two fundamental themes dominated film production: the German question and international political issues. With the introduction of the new course set in 1953, the theme of national unity won out over an overly aggressive vision of the West German neighbor (Steinle 2003). Their shared German classical heritage was particularly valorized and even ensured some successes for DEFA. Two documentaries by Max Jaap, *Ludwig van Beethoven* (1954) and *Friedrich Schiller* (1956), perfectly illustrate this trend. Inspired by a scenario by author Stephan Hermlin and with the help of musicologists, the Beethoven documentary was warmly received at the Karlovy Vary, Locarno, and Edinburgh festivals in 1954–1955. Unusually, its distribution rights were even bought in Switzerland and Japan, and it was broadcast by the BBC in 1956 (Heimann 1991; Knopfe 1996). Only its closing segment evoked the tenor of East German newsreels, illustrating Beethoven's Ninth Symphony with images of the "liberated and happy life of our present." With Schiller, the director created a portrait that allowed him to slip in an excerpt of Wilhelm Tell's monologue: "We want to be a single people of brothers" (Knopfe 1996: 308).

Nevertheless, East German cultural life was given pride of place in documentary film productions. Hence, Joachim Kunert's *Die Dresdner Philharmoniker* (1955, *The Dresden Philharmonic*) documented the 1955 foreign tour of the Dresden orchestra, its first since the end of the war. Grenoble, the French Riviera, Prague, Budapest, and Bucharest were the stages on a journey filmed by the director, without recourse to folkloric touches or demonstrative political commentary (Heimann 2000).

Andrew Thorndike's *Seven from the Rhine* merged the two tendencies, balancing between conciliatory and aggressive discourse on the national question. The film documents the visit by a delegation of West German workers to a factory near Dresden, which had the advantage (for the authorities) that it had remained relatively calm during the June 1953 uprising. For the project, the director selected a group of workers that he had met at the Leipzig Fair in the fall of 1953, who came from the left-wing Ruhr region. The film's message was clear: after initially expressing some doubts about the GDR, the workers recognized its superiority once they had visited the factory. Conversely, with its high unemployment, inadequate social policies, and individualism, the portrayal of the FRG was bleak. Visual takes embracing everything from the banks of the Elbe, the Dresden Opera House, and Goethe's house in Weimar strove to demonstrate to what extent the GDR was the guardian of an invaluable common heritage. The pedestrian staging of several sequences turned East German audiences off the film (Steinle 2003). That, however, did not dissuade the regime from selecting the documentary for festivals abroad, including those in West Germany.[24]

In the early 1950s, East Germany took other steps toward opening up to global cinema, programming Italian Neorealism and French, British, and Japanese films in movie theaters[25] while also developing coproduction projects with foreign countries.[26]

Joris Ivens: International Trump Card

In addition to treating international issues, such as pacifism and internationalism, the increasing presence of DEFA documentary films on the international circuit was also due to the commitment of foreign directors. One of the most renowned intermediaries between the GDR and the West was the Dutch documentary filmmaker Joris Ivens (1898–1989), a leading light of politically engaged cinema (Jordan 2018). In the early 1950s, Ivens, who had lived and worked in Germany during the interwar years, proved particularly prolific at the East German film studios. Before filming *Die Abenteuer des Till Ulenspiegel* (1956, *The Adventures of Till Eulenspiegel*) with Gérard Philipe, Ivens had directed several documentaries that actively contributed to forging DEFA's reputation abroad.

Lied der Ströme (1954, *Song of the Rivers*) was the third film Ivens directed at DEFA, assisted by his compatriot Joop Huisken, a permanent associate at the East German studios, and the Frenchman Robert Menegoz. Filmed on the occasion of the Third International Conference of the World Federation of Trade Unions, held in Vienna in 1953, the film advocated the unity of workers and laborers the world over. An epic lyrical song, politically engaged and militant, the film distinguishes itself not least because of Ivens's editing technique and its diversity of footage. From time to time, however, it indulges in excessive lyricism and descends into official postwar rhetoric celebrating China and the USSR. Images of crowds of people coming together in a common struggle intertwine with images of the world's great waterways, on whose banks human misery had yet to be confronted. The Mississippi, the Ganges, the Volga, the Nile, the Yangtze, and the Amazon offered a diversity of landscapes as well as contrasting political and social situations, as spelled out by Vladimir Pozner's commentary. Bertolt Brecht penned a poem for the film, and Dmitri Shostakovich composed the musical score. Pablo Picasso designed the cover

Figure 1.2. Poster for J. Ivens's *Song of the Rivers* (1954). © DEFA Stiftung, Horst Donth & Gerhard Münch.

for the booklet, whose publication coincided with the documentary's release. Joris Ivens had thus drawn upon his global network of artists and friends and thereby directly benefited DEFA: the film was distributed far beyond the borders of the GDR and the East Bloc.

A year later, Ivens assumed the role of artistic director for a new project undertaken with the support of the Women's International Democratic Federation. Following his departure to China to shoot yet another film project, the documentary was completed by the East German director Alfons Machalz in collaboration with Vladimir Pozner, who had written the screenplay and commentary. *Mein Kind* (1955, *My Child*) was a tribute to the mothers of the world, often forced to raise their children in harsh conditions and despite the menace of deadly conflict. Opening with a childbirth scene, the twenty-minute-long documentary culminates with a call for peace at an international congress of mothers in Lausanne.

The commentary was narrated by the actress Helene Weigel, who had settled in the GDR. With indisputable emotional and aesthetic effectiveness, the film furnished East German documentary film production with an international success in the first half of the 1950s. According to official data, the film drew nearly a million and a half spectators in the GDR over a three-week period (Heimann 2000). It received an award in 1956 at the West German Mannheim festival and was received with equal enthusiasm at Karlovy Vary in Czechoslovakia and at Montevideo in Uruguay. Through these successes and collaborations with renowned international filmmakers, the reputation of East German documentary filmmaking for pure propaganda was now tempered by an image of increasingly dynamic output and energy.

Finally, DEFA also knew how to take advantage of comparisons with West German documentary filmmaking. In the West, industrial and cultural films of mediocre quality predominated, making them difficult to market.[27] According to film historian Peter Zimmermann, West German documentaries of the period followed conventional schemas largely borrowed from the UFA Studios; the best and most popular films were about travel and animals (Zimmermann 1998). It is also worth noting that, as early as the 1950s, documentary films in the FRG were primarily produced both for and by television stations. No equivalent of the DEFA Studios existed in West Germany, a factor that hastened the incorporation of documentaries into televised news and reports on current events and influenced their style. In the GDR, the advent of television was more gradual.[28]

There was thus little doubt that, as of the mid-1950s, a certain dynamism was discernable in the DEFA documentary output, which was just emerging from the aesthetic poverty of the preceding years. An overall increase in moviegoers also bespoke a renewed interest in cinema. In 1953, some 4.8 million spectators had attended over 51,000 screenings; in 1954, more than 9 million attended nearly 89,000 screenings (Heimann 2000).[29] East German feature and documentary film, therefore, had no reason to be ashamed before its West German neighbor; the balance of power, in fact, was rather favorable for DEFA. This did not make relations between the two national productions any smoother, however, as was evidenced by the difficult birth of an inter-German festival.

Culture and Diplomacy

The founding of two German states in the fall of 1949 immediately raised the question of the German nation and its unity, particularly given the increasing integration of the two states into the opposing camps of the Cold War. From 1949 to 1955, inter-German politics vacillated between confrontation and attempts at neighborly reconciliation (Klessmann 1997). Leaders of the FRG and the GDR effected these approaches through trade and diplomatic relations, as well as more informal networks. The space created by this ambivalence and an increasing number of festivals in Europe formed the precondition for the emergence of the Leipzig Documentary Film Week.

The cultural sphere offered a precious avenue for contact and exchange between the societies of the two German states. The extremely tense and unpredictable diplomatic atmosphere meant that the endeavors of proponents of a united Germany faced stiff opposition. The East German regime championed a unitary vision of the German nation in its very constitution (Judt 1997). It attested to this in 1946 and again in 1949 at the Deutsche Kunstausstellung[30] in Dresden, which brought together artists from East and West Germany in a wide panorama of contemporary trends (Damus 1991). Likewise, DEFA presented itself as a cultural institution with pan-German, not East German ambitions. In 1951, Anton Ackermann, head of HVFilm, wrote, "Art, like all culture, is national in form, and militant, humanist, and progressive in content. It seems to me that DEFA's prime mission is to discover the national form capable of encompassing the rich content of the global struggle of a peaceful and progressive humanity" (Ackermann 1951: 8).

The situation took another turn in 1952, however, as the FRG's Konrad Adenauer refused the so-called Stalin Note of 10 March 1952, which evoked a unified, neutral Germany with its 1945 borders and own army and without Allied occupation forces. In May of that year, the FRG ratified a treaty with the Western Allies (excluding the USSR), which opened the way for West Germany to attain greater sovereignty.[31] In July, the GDR then proclaimed the "construction of socialism," thereby relegating the question of German unity to secondary importance. In the cultural domain, this resulted in the initiation of the dogma of Socialist Realism. In 1953, the third Deutsche Kunstausstellung in Dresden thus showcased a much more homogeneous image of contemporary artistic output in the two Germanys (Damus 1991).

In the wake of Stalin's death in March 1953, Moscow's policy toward the GDR took yet another change of course. As Soviet authorities began withdrawing from the East German administration, the official discourse from East Berlin with regard to West Germany became less aggressive (Loth 1994). In early June 1953, Günter Klein, managing director of the DEFA Studio for Newsreels and Documentary Films, asked his associates to avoid all caricature of living conditions in West Germany.[32] Instead, the studio was to focus on subjects that glorified a united Germany, "our beautiful homeland (*Heimat*)." Fresh tensions soon erupted between Bonn and East Berlin, however, as violent economic and political protests broke out throughout the GDR from 16 to 18 June 1953. East Berlin accused the FRG of provoking the demonstrations in concert with the CIA. In October 1954, the Paris Accords, which heralded the stabilization of relations between the FRG and the Western Allies, ended the occupation and sought the integration of a sovereign West Germany into the Western camp, further diminishing any hope of dialogue.[33]

So that East Berlin might appear to be the sole defender of German unity, on 25 November 1953, the first secretary of the SED's ZK, Walter Ulbricht, proposed convening a pan-German meeting of "renowned writers, publishers, artists, and humanist scientists, who would be granted the right to make decisions on artistic and cultural issues" (Mückenberger 1996: 366). In support of this goal, on 8 February 1954 the Documentary Studio hosted a historic meeting of key US, French, and West German directors of photography and news editors, who had come to Berlin for an inter-Allied conference. In November of the same year, scientists and artists again met in Berlin, thereby proving that "Germans of differing religious, ideological, and political persuasions could get along together if they are united in their love of country and of peace."[34]

Among the many initiatives introduced as part of this offensive, the GDR Filmmakers' Club organized discussions open to colleagues from the West. It was there that the West German journalist Ludwig Thomé, a witness to the ongoing shifts, suggested that an inter-German documentary film festival be established in East Germany. In revisiting the origins of the Leipzig Festival in 1997, however, the East German documentary filmmaker Karl Gass laid claim to the idea:

> At the festival's origin was "the struggle for the unity of Germany." Cinema, itself was meant to have political aspirations. That's why I proposed the festival. It did not come from above, but I later sought partners. My most active comrade-in-arms was Günter Klein, then managing director of the Documentary Studio. We relied

on Hans Rodenberg, [managing director of the Studio for Feature Films], who also supported the idea. (Gass et al. 1997: 26)

In effect, the name of Ludwig Thomé and his draft proposal dating from late 1954 rapidly disappeared from the official East German records of that period. Naturally, it was better to attribute the festival's origins to DEFA documentarists than to a West German journalist.

Preparations for the future festival had to adapt to a hectic political and diplomatic calendar. In January 1955, the East Bloc launched a lively campaign against the Paris Accords, which were ratified on 27 February and would lead to West Germany's membership in NATO. A first meeting between the Filmmakers' Club and Anton Ackermann, the deputy minister responsible for cinema, was then adjourned sine die.

On 5 May 1955, West Germany became a fully sovereign state, while its entry into NATO and then the Western European Union in June paved the way for its remilitarization. On 13 May, Anton Ackermann finally met with representatives of the Filmmakers' Club, and the decision was made to organize the festival in the fall. The next day, in response to the FRG's admittance into NATO, the USSR and the European people's democracies signed the Warsaw Pact, which ensured the military and political integration of its members. By June, the festival project had assumed its definitive form, closely linked to current events:

> A German Documentary Film and Cultural Film Week has been organized after the Leipzig Trade Fair in the fall in order to: safeguard the unity of German culture in the field of cinema; support the humanistic efforts of progressive West German filmmakers and strengthen the bonds that unite us to them; and introduce them to DEFA documentary films.[35]

Over the following months, the German partition only received further confirmation. The June 1955 Messina Conference announced plans to create the European Economic Community. In July, Nikita Khrushchev visited East Berlin, where he laid out his "two-state theory," according to which German reunification could only happen if "socialist gains" were retained; a rapid solution to the German national question no longer seemed to be the order of the day (Klessmann 1997). On 20 September, the Soviet Union recognized the GDR's full sovereignty. Concurrently, Bonn adopted the Hallstein Doctrine, which stipulated that diplomatic recognition of the GDR by a state other than the USSR would entail the rupture of diplomatic relations between the FRG and this state (Kilian 2001).

The festival project thus emerged in the particular diplomatic and political context of the Cold War, in a Europe unquestionably divided but also animated by a multitude of initiatives aimed at maintaining a European cultural life on either side of the Iron Curtain.

Film Festivals Emerging in Europe

From the end of World War II until the beginning of the 1960s, a series of events focusing on various artistic fields (theater, music, dance) emerged in both Western and Eastern Europe (Autissier 2008; Moine 2013). The European Association of Music Festivals, founded in December 1951, was one of the earliest initiatives launched in the name of European cultural unity. Film festivals also experienced major growth at the turn of the 1950s in both East and West, although with varying degrees of artistic and political reach (Moine 2012). This dynamic, of which the establishment of the Leipzig Festival was part, can only be understood by tracing exchanges between festivals throughout their histories.

Festivals to the East

The first European film festival established after 1945 was the international festival at Mariánské Lázně, which took place at Karlovy Vary, Czechoslovakia starting in 1950. Both these spa cities, which had welcomed tourists since the eighteenth century and were hence tapping into a well-established tradition, had the merit of being able to offer accommodations for guests and festival participants, thanks to hotel infrastructure that had in part remained untouched by the war.[36] Inaugurated in the summer of 1946, the Karlovy Vary Festival set out to introduce Czechoslovakia's recently nationalized feature and documentary film production abroad.[37] In 1948, a few months after the Communist Party seized power in Prague, the event took on a completely new dimension. Its motto, in keeping with the new official discourse, proclaimed, "For a new individual, for a more perfect world" and "For more sincere relations between peoples, and a lasting friendship between nations."

In 1951, as evidence of the festival's success, the jury became international, with representatives from the East and West but always under the presidency of a Czechoslovakian. The Karlovy Vary Festival was among the important dates on DEFA's festival calendar; as of 1949, they sent a delegation there on an annual basis.[38] In 1954, the GDR's Ministry of Culture, in agreement with the DEFA Studios, dispatched feature, animation, educational, and documentary films—including *Seven from the Rhine, Song of the Rivers,* and *Turbine 1* (1953)—as well as a series of newsreels.[39] Both the quality and quantity of films included in the selection reflected the significance accorded to the festival.

In 1954 the city of Pula in northwestern Croatia, then part of Yugoslavia, hosted the first ever Festival of Yugoslav Film, which was devoted to the national cinema and had both feature and documentary films (Munitić 1992). The often overly conventional nature of the films that won awards, however, met with increasing incomprehension on the part of the younger generation of Yugoslav filmmakers. In 1960, certain directors launched their own festival, which was dedicated to documentaries and short films[40] from both socialist and capitalist countries, in Belgrade.[41]

As the Moscow International Film Festival was established only in 1959, in the wake of the domestic political and cultural thaw overseen by Khrushchev (Karl 2007),[42] the Czechoslovakian and Yugoslav festivals represented the only ones in the East Bloc at the time. They were therefore an invaluable open window on to the world at large for East German filmmakers and journalists, giving them the opportunity to discover films from other socialist countries, as well as from other regions of the world, while allowing them to screen their own films for a foreign audience. They were also important sites of dialogue and exchange with colleagues from the West, as it remained extremely difficult to travel to any festivals held on the other side of the Iron Curtain.

Festivals to the West

In Western Europe, numerous international festivals were already in existence in the early 1950s. Among the most recognized were the Venice Film Festival, established in 1932 under the fascist regime and subsequently reinstated in 1946 (Gili 1981; Taillibert 1999; Vingt ans de cinéma à Venise 1952), and the Locarno (Volonterio 1977) and Cannes (Latil 2005) Film Festivals, both founded immediately after the war. All three of these were primarily devoted to feature films. In 1946, the prizes for short films at Cannes were awarded to Polish, Czechoslovakian, and Soviet entries, and the International Peace Prize went to *Molodost nashey strany* (1946, *Youth of Our Country*), a short documentary produced in the USSR. The presence of Eastern European countries did not subsequently wane, notwithstanding the beginnings of the Cold War the following year, whose ramifications affected the festivals in Venice, Locarno, and Cannes equally.[43]

In addition to these leading festivals, which were difficult for East German delegates to attend due to strong West German diplomatic pressure, there were less prestigious, but often equally important, festivals for DEFA. These included the London Film Festival, launched in 1965 and organized by the British Film Institute; the Edinburgh International Film Festival, inaugurated in 1947 (which the FRG incidentally forsook, because the East German national anthem was played there; Bartie 2013); and the Tours Festival from 1955 to 1968.[44]

The first Berlin International Film Festival opened in West Berlin in June 1951, in an increasingly tense diplomatic context. The festival's awards were inspired by the Berlin Bear—symbolizing West Berlin, an isolated enclave within the GDR that itself symbolized divided Germany and the Cold War.

They were thereby meant to remind the world of the city's existence and to eschew the slightest trace of provincialism. The municipal authorities had to admit the extent to which Berlin had lost its standing as a global film capital, which it had enjoyed in the interwar period, and the crisis in which the West German film economy found itself. Oscar Martay, the officer responsible for cinema within the administration of the U.S. occupation, succeeded in raising the necessary funds to launch the festival with the support of American producers who were aware of the political and commercial significance that West Germany represented.

The "Berlinale," in fact, became a showcase for Western film productions, and no East Bloc country could have a film programmed in the official selection.[45] Meanwhile, the Berlin festival posed a real challenge for its organizers. The International Federation of Film Producer Associations (FIAPF), which was playing a key role in organizing international festivals, initially preferred to assist Venice, Cannes, and Locarno (Moine 2011a). The growing interest throughout Europe for such events also raised the specter of a deluge of new festivals, whose growing number could ultimately only devalue those already in place. Competition was also turning out to be difficult; the month of June was chosen for the Berlinale so that it would be held before other West German events, scheduled in Cologne and Munich, and would not to be too close in time to the Venice Film Festival, which took place from late August to early September. Finally, the Leipzig Festival was also intended to act as a counterweight to the World Youth Festival, slated to take place in East Berlin in summer 1951 (Jacobsen 2000).

Nevertheless, the issue arose about whether and how to establish ties with the GDR. In 1952, after having noted that many journalists and guests from the West actually went to East Berlin to view DEFA films, festival organizers for a time envisaged coordinated film screenings. Ultimately, only one film was screened, however, *Film hinter dem eisernen Vorhang* (1952, *A Look behind the Iron Curtain*), a montage of excerpts of Soviet and East German feature films and newsreels intended to demonstrate Soviet propaganda methods. A year later, relations between the two sides of the city sharply deteriorated and dampened the festival's atmosphere: the Berlinale opened the day after the demonstrations of 17 June 1953, and the East German spectators (20 percent of all expected spectators) found their way blocked by the temporary closure of the border from East Berlin (Jacobsen 2000).

German Documentary Film Festivals

In 1954, the Berlin Film Festival's international recognition was confirmed, as it hosted numerous stars and enjoyed highly positive press coverage, with the exception, as always, of the socialist countries. The GDR could not hope to compete directly with the Berlinale, whose international dimensions kept expanding. It therefore had to forge a distinct profile for its future festival. The Leipzig Festival, focusing on documentaries, was in fact created strictly in the context of German-German relations, notably in response to two very recent West German developments.

Mannheim and Oberhausen in the West

The first Mannheim Week of Documentary und Cultural Film (Mannheimer Kultur und Dokumentarfilmwoche) took place in May 1952 in the river port city at the confluence of the Rhine and the Neckar Rivers. In the artistic sphere, Mannheim had hitherto been known in particular for the historic National Theatre Mannheim, where Friedrich Schiller's first play had premiered in 1780. While the new festival was partially funded by the city and the federal government, the principal organizers were the municipality and the Association of German Film Clubs (Kötz and Minas 2001). The journalist and screenwriter Kurt Joachim Fischer (1911–1979) became its director. The goal of the organizers was to champion the wealth of a new documentary cinema, liberated from conventional themes (nature, the animal world, classical fine arts), from emphatic commentary and the artificial lighting much beloved by UFA (Kötz and Minas 2001). Screenings drew 20,000 spectators over a six-day period.

DEFA's participation in the Mannheim Festival was modest. In 1954, a single DEFA film, about the reconstruction of Dresden, was screened.[46] This was followed in May 1955 by eight films, including *Vom Alex zum Eismeer* (1954, *From Alexanderplatz to the Arctic*).[47] For this documentary, Karl Gass's second, the crew embarked with fishermen from Rostock, an East German port on the Baltic coast, upon a fishing expedition that took them to the Barents Sea. The film astounded spectators with its images of storms shot from the fishing boat, vigorously testifying to the hardships endured by these fishermen, echoing John Grierson's 1929 film *Drifters*.

West Germany's second film festival was inaugurated in February 1954 in Oberhausen. Located in the industrial Ruhr region, one of the pillars of the West German economic miracle and traditionally leftist, the West German Short Film Festival (Westdeutsche Kurzfilmtage) referenced a different political and social context from Mannheim. The Oberhausen Festival was not funded by the federal government in Bonn but exclusively by the city and private supporters. Responsible for film festival programming was Hilmar Hoffmann, the director of Oberhausen's *Volkshochschule* (adult education center); Hoffmann swiftly cut loose from traditional educational films in favor of a program of short films and documentaries with greater political and aesthetic aspirations. The journalist Will Wehling—the first West German critic to visit Czechoslovakia after the war—was very active in selecting the Oberhausen program; as a result, puppet animation films by the Czechoslovakian Jiří Trnka were enthusiastically greeted by the public as of 1955.[48]

Leipzig: the Response in the East

In 1955, Oberhausen and Mannheim were still in their infancy and finding their way; the launching of a documentary festival in the GDR would be far from an insignificant occurrence for them.[49] During this particularly sensitive period of the Cold War on German soil, the sites for international cultural and political events were chosen with great care on either side of the Iron Curtain. Hence, in September 1955, the first *documenta*—a major West German exhibition of contemporary art—was held in Kassel, thirty kilometers from the German-German border, a location whose symbolic dimension was patently clear and vaunted by the organizer himself. No East German artworks were included in the exhibit (Schieder 2009). As a site for the East German film festival, the Saxon city of Leipzig swiftly asserted itself.

In fact, it offered all the necessary qualifications, with significant material advantages in addition to an undeniable symbolic dimension. Since the thirteenth century, Leipzig had been a city of fairs, which over time evolved into the world-famous Leipzig Trade Fair; in addition to being a traditional venue for international and business gatherings, the city hosted cultural events thanks to its publishers. In September 1954, Leipzig's Trade Fair also featured a series of screenings of DEFA documentaries, newsreels, and satirical films.[50] Thanks to its hotels and relatively intact infrastructure, including its well-known railway station, Leipzig could also comfortably accommodate participants.

Furthermore, Leipzig made it possible to inscribe the creation of the festival within a national cultural continuum. Since 1945, the city had been the backdrop of a very active commemorative policy. The East German regime immediately exploited Leipzig's history, focusing on key figures. In 1949, the city celebrated Goethe's 200th anniversary with great pomp (Borchmeyer 2009). In 1950, an official commemoration in Leipzig paid homage to Johann Sebastian Bach, "founder of German classical music" and "originator of the Enlightenment." In parallel, the choir of St. Thomas Church, where Bach had been the cantor, became a veritable ambassador for the East German regime's cultural policy during multiple tours organized abroad, as did Leipzig's Gewandhaus Orchestra. Lastly, Leipzig was home to the Bach Archives, which depended on the Johann Sebastian Bach Institute in Göttingen, West Germany (Veit 2009).

Leipzig also remains closely linked to the Monument to the Battle of the Nations, the Völkerschlachtdenkmal, unveiled in 1913 in honor of the 1813 victory of the coalition of nations against Napoleon's troops, which in due course had become a national myth (Schäfer 2009). The East German regime swiftly exploited this historic battle and its memory in order to lay claim to the "spirit of 1813." It argued that the policies of Bonn and the Allies were fundamentally opposed to this spirit of unity and that only the GDR wanted to end the postwar partition of the German nation. As of 1950, annual commemorations, in which the National People's Army took part, were held before the monument.

Finally, as early as 1949 Leipzig had attracted the attention of the authorities, who judged the location perfectly suited to form the vanguard of socialism (Hofmann and Rink 1990). The presence of heavy industry, in place since the Industrial Revolution, provided a favorable environment. Was it not in Leipzig that the German workers' movement had taken off? Had it not taken advantage of the strong presence of skilled workers and its long-standing tradition of trade fairs to welcome international workers' congresses much earlier than Berlin? Hence, it was in this Saxon city that the GDR's first Workers and Farmers Faculty (Arbeiter und Bauernfakultät) was founded in 1949. From 1950 to 1954, other key institutions in the regime's education policy emerged here, notably the Leipzig Music School, the Pedagogical Institute, and the School for Construction Industries. Leipzig was clearly called upon to become a model city.

On 8 May 1955, Leipzig's city council was informed that the film festival would take place in the fall, from 11 to 17 September (Mückenberger 2000).[51] This set in motion a long history, which continues to this day. Born of international Cold War tensions—between the two Germanys, but more broadly throughout Europe—as of its genesis, the festival reflected the non-linear nature of East German cultural policy and the multiplicity of actors involved in its conception.

Notes

1. The vast studios of interwar production companies (including UFA, Tobis, and the Kodak factories) on the outskirts of Berlin were now in the Soviet Occupation Zone, as were other related companies, including the Agfa plants in Wolfen, Carl-Zeiss in Jena, and Zeiss-Ikon in Dresden.
2. DEFA's managing directors were Hans Rodenberg (1952–1957), Albert Wilkening (1957–1961), Jochen Mückenberger (1961–1966), Franz Bruk (1966–1973), Albert Wilkening (again, 1973–1976), and Hans-Dieter Mäde (1976–1989).
3. Bericht über den Einsatz einer Instrukteurbrigade beim VEB DEFA-Studio für Wochenschau und Dokumentarfilme im Dezember 1954, SAPMO-BArch, DR 1/4200; Wolfgang Kernicke and Hans Wegner, Bericht über die Arbeit des Organisationsbüros der III. Leipziger Kurz- und Dokumentarfilmwoche (13–19 November 1960) Berlin,

29 November 1960, SAPMO-BArch, DY 30 IV 2/9.06/228. See Appendix I, Archival Sources, for abbreviations.
4. It is important to underline that the Federal Republic of Germany never had a federal ministry of culture; France created one only in 1959 under the direction of André Malraux.
5. In June 1953, demonstrators raised a number of issues, including the increasingly problematic economic situation and the government's May decision to increase production standards without accompanying wage increases.
6. For more, see chapter 5.
7. Bericht über den Einsatz einer Instrukteurbrigade beim VEB DEFA-Studio für Wochenschau und Dokumentarfilme im Dezember 1954, SAPMO-BArch DR 1/4200.
8. Bericht über den Einsatz einer Instrukteurbrigade beim VEB DEFA-Studio für Wochenschau und Dokumentarfilme im Dezember 1954, SAPMO-BArch DR 1/4200, p. 2–5.
9. None of the eight employees in the commerce department were members of a political party, and the youngest ones had been excluded from the Free German Youth (FDJ) as of 1953, presumably as a result of the June demonstrations (see note 5). In accounting, only five of seventeen employees were in the dominant Socialist Unity Party (SED) or the FDJ, its youth organization. Before joining the SED, the main person in charge of the plan had been a member of the Social Democratic Party of Germany (SPD) until 1933 and then the National Socialist German Workers' (or Nazi) Party from 1933 to 1945. Eighteen of the forty-six technicians had been employed at a production company before 1945; the director of photography had been with the German news. Of thirty editors, only twelve were in the SED or FDJ. Bericht über den Einsatz einer Instrukteurbrigade beim VEB DEFA-Studio für Wochenschau und Dokumentarfilme im Dezember 1954, SAPMO-BArch DR 1/4200.
10. According to Annelie Thorndike (Jordan 2000).
11. From 1946 until it was closed in 1991, the DEFA Studio system included an evolving group of complementary studios. Those that concerned documentary filmmaking were DEFA Studio for Newsreels and Documentary Films (1946–1969), DEFA Studio for Short Films (1969–1975), and DEFA Studio for Documentary Films (1975–closure). To simplify, this text simply refers to the DEFA Documentary Studio throughout.
12. Author's interview with Karl Gass, Kleinmachnow, Germany (August 2000).
13. For more, see chapter 5.
14. The Babelsberg film school—the oldest and largest in Germany—had different names at different points in its history: founded on 1 November 1954 at Schloss Babelsberg in Potsdam-Babelsberg, it was first known as the Deutsche Hochschule für Filmkunst (German Academy of Cinema Arts); in 1969, it was renamed Hochschule für Film und Fernsehen (HFF) der DDR (Film and Television Academy of the GDR); in 1985, the name of feature film director Konrad Wolf was added; in 1990, it was then formally renamed Hochschule für Film und Fernsehen (HFF; Film and Television Academy); in 2014 it was accredited as a university and renamed Filmuniversität Babelsberg Konrad Wolf (the Konrad Wolf Film University Babelsberg). To simplify, the acronym HFF is used throughout this text.
15. The Soviet Filmmakers Union was created only after Stalin's death in 1957 (Laurent 2000).
16. The club was accorded the status of association (Verband) only in 1967, as part of an attempt to bridge the deep chasm that had arisen between filmmakers and the

regime in the wake of censorship tied to the Eleventh Plenum of the ZK in December 1965. For more, see chapter 4.
17. Salaries continued even when inactivity was imposed for reasons of censorship. Author's interview with Jürgen Böttcher, Karlshorst, Germany (31 October 2000).
18. Author's interview with Erika Richter, Berlin, Germany (1 November 2000).
19. For more, see chapter 3. See also Ebbrecht-Hartmann 2017.
20. The term *Kulturfilm* first appeared in the press in 1907, but its true "birth" is considered to be the creation of the UFA's *Kulturfilm* department in 1918. They were primarily popular science documentaries that were shown before the feature film at movie theaters. Under the Nazis, they started including newsreels and became vehicles for Nazi biological determinism and sometimes other propaganda.
21. Maetzig's article "Vom Wesen des Dokumentarfilms" is reprinted in Mückenberger and Jordan (1994).
22. Bericht über den Einsatz einer Instrukteurbrigade beim VEB DEFA-Studio für Wochenschau und Dokumentarfilme im Dezember 1954, SAPMO-BArch DR 1/4200.
23. Including Wolfgang Staudte, who in 1946 had made the first postwar German feature film at DEFA, *Die Mörder sind unter uns* (*The Murderers Are among Us*; Becker and Petzold 2001).
24. For more, see chapter 2.
25. These films had the advantage of taking a critical look at the capitalist world. The French feature film selections were mainly adaptations of classics with Gérard Philipe, whose involvement with the French Communist Party (PCF) was well-known (Becker and Petzold 2001).
26. Notably with France, in collaboration with Unifrance or Pathé (Lindenberger 2005; Wedel et al. 2013).
27. In 1954, 37 percent of West German documentaries had not found a distributor.
28. For more, see chapter 4.
29. See also SAPMO-BArch DR1/4663.
30. The first of these, in 1946, was called the Erste Allgemeine Deutsche Kunstausstellung; it was the first and last German-German art exhibition until 1990. Five editions of the Deutsche Kunstausstellung were held between 1949 and 1968; from 1972 to the end of the GDR, the exhibition went by Kunstausstellung der DDR.
31. The treaty lightened the allied presence in the FRG (Seebacher-Brandt 1992).
32. Günter Klein to Sepp Schwab, 8 June 1953, SAPMO-BArch DR1/4174.
33. In March 1954, Moscow granted greater sovereignty to East Berlin, establishing bilateral interstate relations between the USSR and the GDR.
34. Gedanken zur Deutschen Begegnung 1955, archives of the Ministry of Culture, SAPMO-BArch DR1/7889.
35. Vorlage zur Sitzung am Montag, 27 June 1955, Anton Ackermann, Ministry of Culture, SAPMO-BArch DR1/4194.
36. Author's interview with Eva Zaoralová, Prague, Czech Republic (21 August 2007). See also Zaoralová and Passek (1996) and the festival website: http://2002.MFFKV.cz.
37. It was still very modest: a single film from Britain, the United States, or France shown three times a day.
38. President of the Filmmakers' Club, Andrew Thorndike, to HVFilm, Filmfestival Kalender. Januar 1964 (23 July 1965) SAPMO-BArch DR1/4306.
39. Brief des Ministeriums für Kultur, J.R. Becher an den Sekretär des ZK der SED, Genossen Paul Wandel, Berlin (19 May 1954) SAPMO-BArch DR1/4194.

40. Author's interview with Heinz Klunker, Berlin, Germany (15 September 2004). See also Jelenkovic 2013.
41. Besuch beim IX. Jugoslawischen Dokumentarfilm- und Kurzfilmfestival (April 1962) SAPMO-BArch DY 30/IV 2/906/248, p. 63; Batančev 2017; Jelenkovic 2017b.
42. The festival was held once before 1959, in 1935.
43. For more on the ties of these festivals to Moscow, see Gallinari 2007 and Pisu 2013.
44. President of the Filmmakers' Club, Andrew Thorndike, to HVFilm, Filmfestival Kalender. Januar 1964 (23 July 1965) SAPMO-BArch DR1/4306. For more on Tours, see Mazany 2015.
45. The USSR participated in the Berlinale only in 1974, the GDR in 1975.
46. Parts of a public that did not appreciate how the workers were presented as heroes hissed the film (Kötz and Minas 2001).
47. Letter from Anton Ackermann, Ministry of Culture, to the Central Committee of the SED, cinema sector (25 April 1955) SAPMO-BArch DR1/4194.
48. The GDR took part in the festival for the first time in 1956 (Holloway and Holloway 1979).
49. For more on the relations between Oberhausen and Leipzig, see Kötzing (2013).
50. In the GDR, satirical films were produced as part of the *Stacheltier* (Hedgehog) series starting in 1953. Plan zur Mobilisierung der Belegschaft des DEFA Studios für Wochenschau und Dokumentarfilm zur Vorbereitung der Volkswählen, from Günter Klein, director of the studio, to Anton Ackermann, director of HVFilm (27 August 1954) SAPMO-BArch DR1/4200.
51. See also Leipzig City Council, Culture Department (18 May 1955) BArch-Filmarchiv, Filmmakers Club Fund, 1955.

CHAPTER 2
||||||||||||||||||||

Opening to the World

The beginnings of the Leipzig Festival reveal the significance of the inter-German and international contexts in the GDR's cultural and film policy. During its slow maturation and formative years until 1961, the festival reflects the trial-and-error approach of a political and diplomatic system in search of recognition beyond the confines of the Communist Bloc. This chapter will revisit and assess the chaotic launching of this event in all the complexity of its organizational and political challenges.

First Steps: 1955–1959

The East German government immediately set itself the objective of participating in major international festivals, such as those at Venice, Locarno, and Cannes. In 1955, this task was achieved: the GDR was represented at Swiss and French festivals, not by means of selected films but by sending observers. In June, the Ministry of Culture renewed its efforts to obtain an invitation to the Venice Film Festival and underlined the need to "take part in festivals in Edinburgh, Bombay, and Argentina, should the opportunity arise."[1] They developed an intense festival-related diplomacy; by the fall of 1955, the GDR had established contacts with sufficient festivals abroad—in both the East and West—to assert itself, in turn, as an organizer of a similar event.

In early 1955, the West German Producers' Union and DEFA agreed to the principle of working together "for the unity of Germany," and a program of East German films was screened at the Mannheim Film Festival in May. In late June and early July, the East German Filmmakers' Club took advantage of the Berlinale being held in West Berlin to invite twenty-five participants, including the Italian actor and director Vittorio de Sica, to the Babelsberg studios and to various events (Mückenberger 1996). In the fall, the Leipzig Festival was to become part of continuing these initial inter-German exchanges.

Between 11 and 17 September 1955,[2] 123 spectators attended the Cultural and Documentary Film Week organized by the City of Leipzig and the Filmmakers' Club, whose vice-president, Wolfgang Kernicke, was appointed director of the festival.[3] The opening ceremony took place before a packed house at the Capitol, the city's largest movie theater. Of the fifty-three films selected, twenty-five came from the GDR, twenty-eight from the FRG.[4] The jury comprised three West Germans and three East Germans. The film critic Ludwig Thomé from Heidelberg and the producer Walter Knoop and the movie distributor Hans Appeldorn, both from Hamburg, represented the FRG. On the East German side, DEFA was represented by Herbert Theuerkauf, the director of the satirical *Stacheltier* (*Porcupine*) film series; Reinhard Stier, the director of scientific educational films at the DEFA Documentary Studio; and film director Karl Gass, the studio's artistic director and one of the founders of the festival.

The program's central theme was "Germany, our beautiful homeland," in keeping with one of the overriding expectations of then minister of culture, Johannes R. Becher. Hadn't the author, as lyricist of the GDR's national anthem "Risen from Ruins," duly reminded documentarists at DEFA of the importance of "forging patriotism, for the love of country (*Heimatliebe*)"?[5] All the ambiguity of East German official discourse was evident: it highlighted divisions between two political systems, while upholding the sentiment of a unified nation, which the concept of *Heimat* was to represent. The remainder of the program illustrated the two countries' documentary film output, in which works dealing with industrial and cultural topics dominated. Very similar to newsreels or commissioned films, they were of no real aesthetic interest. As a result, the out-of-competition, world premiere screening of *My Child* — a joint project of Joris Ivens and Vladimir Pozner directed by Alfons Machals — became all the more the centerpiece and opened the way for internationalizing the festival.[6]

The awards were presented by the two organizers, the mayor of Leipzig and the Filmmakers' Club. The two major prizes rewarded documentaries highlighting the historical and geographical continuity between the two Germanys, suggesting a soon to be restored unity. The West German film *Um die Europameisterschaft* (1951, *The European Cup*) by Walter Knoop — which focuses on an athletics competition and which ended on the national anthem "Deutschland, Deutschland über alles"[7] — won first prize. The GDR received second prize for an animated film recounting an episode from *The Adventures of Till Eulenspiegel* (Mauersberger 1997), a time-honored theme in German popular culture.[8] Another East German documentary, Joachim Kunert's *Ein*

Figure 2.1. Poster for 1955 Leipzig Festival. © Bundsarchiv-Filmarchiv, Archiv der Leipziger Dok-Filmwochen GmbH.

Strom fließt durch Deutschland (1954, *A River Flows through Germany*), received a special mention; it traces the course of the Elbe River—which constituted the natural border between the two republics—from the East German city of Dresden to the West German Hanseatic port of Hamburg.

Ultimately, the ambiguity of the positions taken on either side vis-à-vis the German question was advantageous for the Leipzig Festival. The Hallstein Doctrine, initiated around the same time by the Bonn government, did not prove to be a handicap in preparing the event. In fact, not everyone in the West German government liked the doctrine or considered attending the Leipzig Festival reprehensible. While the FRG's Foreign Ministry scrupulously defended the spirit of the doctrine, the Federal Ministry for Inter-German Affairs swiftly encouraged individual initiatives that maintained communications channels open between the two states, particularly in the cultural sphere. The goal involved doubling diplomatic relations by means of a network of individual exchanges and nonstate institutions.

Nonetheless, merely 37 of the festival's 123 official guests came from West Germany.[9] The decision of whether to participate in the festival was not without ramifications. For example, Will Wehling, a correspondent with the important West German daily *Die Welt*, who was also the program director of the Oberhausen Festival, thanked the Leipzig organizers for their invitation but requested that in the future they send it to his private address.[10] The director of the Mannheim Festival, Kurt Joachim Fischer, who initially accepted the offer to be part of the festival jury, changed his mind at the last minute for health reasons. The press, meanwhile, reacted positively and supportively, while also clearly emphasizing political differences and "fundamentally distinct social realities," according to an East German newspaper (Schehufer 1995).

1956, A Decisive Year

"It was a politically turbulent period. We were excited about what was going to happen. At the school I was attending, we were all politicized," recalls Erika Richter, then a first-year student of dramaturgy at the Babelsberg film school.[11] Indeed, 1956 was a year that saw lively discussion and profound questioning of the political and ideological model in the East Bloc. The festival would thus take place in a much more passionate and less unanimous atmosphere than the previous year, mirroring events that were perturbing international relations.

The Leipzig Week for Cultural and Documentary Film ran from 4 to 10 November 1956 as a "friendly collaboration between filmmakers for an artistic cinema that helps human beings live in peace and well-being."[12] It was meant to be an "exhibition of cultural films open to the world at large," according to Günter Klein, director of the DEFA Documentary Studio.[13] This openness took place parallel to the competition, with the so-called Information Program featuring around twenty-four non-German documentaries. This was a first for the festival and deeply altered its spirit, as evidenced by the list of 155 guests, 102 of whom were from East Germany and 53 from other countries.

The Communist Bloc was represented by the Soviet Union, Bulgaria, Czechoslovakia, and Poland, as well as by China, which at that juncture had not yet been excommunicated. Among Western countries, Switzerland, France, Belgium, the United Kingdom, and the Netherlands sent delegates.[14] Another remarkable development was that it was in 1956 that delegates and films from the "Third World" first appeared at the Leipzig Festival, thereafter never to leave. Korea, Vietnam, and Egypt featured significantly among the first countries to be represented.[15] If the Vietnamese film *Der Bambus Tanz* (*The Bamboo Dance*) was not a major topic, the Egyptian entry garnered considerably more attention (*Mitteldeutsche Neueste Nachrichten* 1956).

The first Asian-African Conference had taken place in Bandung, Indonesia, in April 1955. Known as the Bandung Conference, its stated objectives were to oppose colonialism and promote peaceful coexistence and nonalignment. It offered Egyptian leader Gamal Abdel Nasser the opportunity to assert himself on the international stage, as did the tripartite meeting in Yugoslavia with Jozip Broz Tito and Jewaharlal Nehru in July 1956, where the principles of nonalignment were reiterated during a Non-Aligned Movement summit. It was, however, the Suez Crisis of 29 October to 6 November 1956 that allowed the Egyptian president to pursue an offensive policy vis-à-vis the Western powers and to rally for a time with the Soviet Bloc. The Leipzig Film Festival, which opened before the Suez crisis had come to an end, immediately exploited these geopolitical developments.

Two documentary films "offered by the Republic of Egypt to the GDR" and devoted to the Suez Canal were screened as part of the Information Program.[16] An East German newspaper hailed the "handshake between an English film director and two Egyptian filmmakers to thunderous audience applause" (*Mitteldeutsche Neueste Nachrichten* 1956). Viewers were attending the very first demonstration and staging of "international solidarity," which were to become staples of the festival thereafter. Also in 1956, Latin America made a very discreet entrance to the festival with *Uruguay. Fernes Land nah gesehen* (1956, *Uruguay, Distant Country, Observed from Nearby*) by director and cinematographer Joop Huisken.[17]

Other developments in the fall of 1956 played an equally important role in how the festival evolved and outgrew the limited scope of a German-German framework. In Poland, on the heels of the workers' uprising in Poznan on 28 June 1956, worker and student demonstrations from 19 to 21 October occasioned the reelection of the first secretary of the Communist Party Władysław Gomułka, a moderate who had just been released from prison after being removed from power in 1948. In Budapest, Hungary, demonstrations in support of Gomułka transformed into the 24 October uprising, in the face of the refusal of reforms by Stalinists in the Hungarian Communist Party. In response, these called for Red Army reinforcements, against the desire expressed by Imre Nagy for an independent Hungary.

The ensuing bloody repression began on 3 November and was still taking place as the Leipzig Festival opened. The reforms undertaken in Poland and the attempts to follow a Polish path to socialism alarmed the East Berlin regime, which was not receptive to such experiments (Klessmann 1997). Nikita Khrushchev's revelations about Stalin at the Twentieth Congress of the Communist Party of the Soviet Union in February 1956 had also run counter to the guiding principles of those in power in the GDR. Hostile to de-Stalinization, Walter Ulbricht did his utmost to prevent Khrushchev's thaw from spreading to the GDR.

The liberalizing cultural policy in Poland had primarily affected filmmaking. As early as 1954, Socialist Realism was in decline in Poland, earlier than in Hungary or Czechoslovakia, and a "Polish School" emerged that attested to a unique spiritual and aesthetic identity (Michalek and Turaj 1992). Critical Socialism sought to present life in Polish society as it really was, and Polish filmmakers became interested in recent history. This was the source of the so-called Black Series, nurtured by critical realism inspired by Jerzy Bossak.[18] Several young graduates of the Łódź Film School had gathered around him, seeking to transform documentary film into an instrument of social analysis. The year 1955 had been decisive for Polish cinema, notably with the release of Jerzy Hoffman's short film *Uwaga, chuligani!* (1955, *Look Out, Hooligans!*). While by today's standards it may seem trivial, the film dared to articulate that all was not well for young people living in big Polish cities at the time.

In 1956, Kasimierz Karabasz and Władysław Ślesicki shot the documentary short about street children, *Gdzie diabeł mówi dobranoc* (*Where the Devil Says Good Night*), in which they particularly criticized the failings of the bureaucracy (Michalek and Turaj 1992). Karabasz was one of the leading Polish directors regularly invited to and even awarded at the Leipzig Festival, although not for one of his Critical Socialist films. In 1997, he considered the films in the Black Series to be too verbose, too close to journalism. "But," he added, "we didn't know how to do any better. We were in search of a new image to represent reality. Social conditions were catastrophic" (Karabasz 1997: 43). Between 1955 and approximately 1959, some twenty documentaries in the Black Series were produced (Hülbusch 1997; Michalek and Turaj 1992). They were never selected for the Leipzig Festival but made their mark—particularly in the West, for example at Mannheim and Oberhausen in the FRG (Holloway and Holloway 1979). German festivals therefore followed distinct paths, reflecting the state of relations between the FRG and the GDR.

"Of course, events in Budapest and Cairo cast a shadow over at least the early days [of the festival]. Many producers from the FRG cancelled at the last minute. . . . The programming was therefore anything but inter-German," noted the correspondent from the West German newspaper *Die Welt* (Wehling 1956). Indeed, the balance that had been established in the festival's opening year had vanished: DEFA presented thirty-seven films from the GDR, as opposed to just twelve from the FRG.[19] The chasm between the two systems was accentuated in 1956. On 18 January, the People's Chamber (*Volkskammer*) of the GDR voted in favor of establishing the National People's Army and a Ministry of National Defense. Meanwhile, while not yet applied in practice, the Hallstein Doctrine was in force in Bonn.

Parity was respected, however, in the composition of the eight-member festival jury. The director of the Oberhausen Festival, Hilmar Hoffmann, notably represented the FRG.[20] As for the GDR, Karl Gass and Herbert Theuerkauf sat on the jury, as in 1955. The DEFA film director Annelie Thorndike, a new jury member, commenced what were to be many long years of involvement with the festival. Finally, the Babelsberg film academy was represented in the person of its dean, Hans Rodenberg, who was also the general director of DEFA.[21] The documentarist Andrew Thorndike tried to be optimistic: "Potential co-productions were mentioned. . . . It seems that we artists in the two countries are thus in a position to contribute significantly to the struggle against the partition and division [of the German nation]" (Thorndike 1956). Its 1956 edition, however, confirmed the failure of an inter-German festival.

The quality of the output of the two Germanys proved to be mediocre. The worst entries were even awarded garden gnomes (Gass 1995; Theuerkauf 1956). And even if political tensions could have been overcome by the enthusiasm of those participating, as 30,000 spectators attended the festival, the questionable quality of the documentaries posed the risk of turning off spectators and professionals alike. Another divisive factor was that it became more and more difficult to ignore the increasingly large role devoted to the festival's political dimension. Initially conceived as a forum for exchanging views and encouraging debate between representatives of the two Germanys, the Leipzig Festival now became an official tribune for the East Berlin regime. A presidium was thus instituted for the 1956 festival, whose membership included those trusted by the regime.[22] The presidium was meant not just to appoint members of the Selection Committee, all from the GDR, but also to control their selection. The consequences were felt in the entire program.

A festival highlight, the retrospective, was dedicated to the documentarist Joris Ivens. It seemed that such a choice would muster all the votes cast, thanks to the strong personality of the Dutch director, who had been recognized in both the East and the West since the 1930s. There was an incident, however, during a screening. One of the works selected, *The Spanish Earth*, which Ivens had shot in 1937 during the Spanish Civil War, had been produced with the help of American intellectuals. The original version was thus American, with the commentary by Ernest Hemingway (Gauthier 1995). In Leipzig, the original version was shown but with a simultaneous translation read aloud during the screening. This provoked strong reactions:

> The audience muttered. Hissed. Not just because they wanted to hear Hemingway in the original version, but also to protest the "translation." . . . As the projectionist had not sufficiently reduced the volume, one could still hear, faintly but distinctly, Hemingway's text. The so-called German translation was actually "popular democratic." Whenever Hemingway spoke of "liberals, Catholics, and socialist" members of the International Brigades, they simply became the "communists." (Wehling 1956)

This anecdote not only demonstrates the attempts of the organizers to filter the films through the GDR's official discourse but also reveals how a guarded public reacted to such manipulations. Although the audience included foreign guests, most spectators came from Leipzig itself; as we will see, throughout the festival's long history there are numerous accounts that evoke the often turbulent atmosphere in movie theaters when audiences were confronted with films too blatantly propagandistic or, in contrast, with those in which ambiguity was skillfully retained. Given such an agitated political situation, the East Berlin regime had to choose which route to follow: to open up or block off dialogue or censorship. Unable to show quality German films that would have warranted overcoming political differences between the two Germanys, the Leipzig Festival was forced to find new perspectives and a new identity.

Ensuing Uncertainty

The Hungarian Uprising prompted Walter Ulbricht to put an end to the thaw that had timidly appeared in the GDR in the wake of the Twentieth Congress of the USSR's Communist Party. The SED general secretary violently condemned supporters of a possible "third way" between capitalism and Stalinist socialism. In 1957 and 1958, a series of arrests and trials took place in the context of an "intensifying international class struggle between socialism and imperialism," which in the first instance affected any opponent to Ulbricht's line.[23] In July 1958, during its Fifth Congress, the SED, emboldened by optimistic economic forecasts, declared that an additional step had to be taken to achieve socialism. The Leipzig Festival, which had proved powerless to overcome dissension in German-German relations, was no longer of interest to a regime that until 1960 remained convinced that it could overcome its diplomatic isolation on the strength and progress of its economy.

The political hardening also led to an ideological offensive in all spheres of East German society. The authorities' overriding objective was to curb the mass exodus of East Germans, who were leaving the GDR at a rate of about 250,000 people per year (Schröder 1998). The "struggle for the victory of socialism" initiated at the SED's Fifth Congress in 1958 was about not only the state and the economy but also the "socialist revolution (*sozialistische Umwälzung*) in the ideological and cultural sphere" (Weber 1987: 26). DEFA's documentary films did not measure up to the ambitions articulated by the regime. In March 1957, the SED's Central Committee denounced the ever-widening gap between the best films and DEFA's average production. They should emphasize and highlight their few high quality documentaries—such as *Song of the Rivers, You and Some Comrade, Ludwig van Beethoven,* and *My Child*—"which [had] won widespread recognition at international competitions, not only in East Germany but also abroad, and thus helped to enhance the GDR's reputation."[24]

The government was aware of the delicate situation in which the festival found itself: on one hand, it had to avoid the weakness of the 1956 East German selections, while, on the other, it had to deal with the risks encountered should the new Polish aesthetic begin to spread. Faced with this dilemma, the proposed solution was clear: in August 1957, a letter from the director of the Documentary Studio announced to the Filmmakers' Club the cancellation of the upcoming festival, without further explanation.[25] Was this the death knell for an inter-German festival?

The initial idea was not completely abandoned in high places. In an internal document in 1958, HVFilm concluded an appraisal of the collaboration between DEFA and "progressive" West German production companies:

> Film festivals offer the possibility of direct contact with West German filmmakers. This year festivals are being held at Cannes, Locarno, Karlovy Vary, and Leningrad. In the GDR, it has yet to be decided whether the Leipzig Week for Cultural and Documentary Film can still be organized. This would provide a further opportunity to establish contact with West German filmmakers.[26]

In July 1958, however, the Filmmakers' Club learned that "the Leipzig Festival [would] no longer take place in the same form" and would be replaced by an "international action of filmmakers against the atomic bomb, . . . against NATO's plans in Europe, and against the atomic rearmament of the West German army."[27] The Second Berlin Crisis, which began in November 1958, duly succeeded in rendering illusory all attempts at bilateral dialogue between the two German states, in any form whatsoever.

Aside from diplomatic issues, we should not underestimate the role of individuals in key positions, for significant changes took place in 1958 in the movement to regain control and pursue changes sought by Ulbricht. The Central Administration for Film (HVFilm) gave way to the Association of State Owned Film Enterprises (VVB-Film), directed by Ernst Hoffmann. At the Ministry of Culture, Alexander Abusch replaced Johannes R. Becher, who had been a staunch supporter of rapprochement between the GDR and the FRG and had served as minister for culture from 1954 until his death in October 1958. This resulted in a net cooling off of cultural exchanges between the two Germanys in an already unfavorable broader context.[28]

In 1959, on the tenth anniversary of the GDR's founding, the East German black, red, and yellow flag, hitherto identical to that of the FRG, sported a new coat of arms: a hammer and compass encircled by a crown of grain, symbol of the "workers' and peasants' state" (Lorrain 1994). The regime thus demonstrated more than a symbolic yearning to set itself even further apart from Bonn. On the West German side, momentum for integration into the West Bloc—which in no way led in the direction of an immediate settlement of the German national question—was increasingly gaining traction. In November 1959, the West German SPD announced its Godesberg Program, with which it abandoned all references to Marxism and declared itself a party not just for the working class but for all social strata. It also abandoned the idea of a confederation of the two German states, thus supporting policies pursued by Bonn and putting an end to discussions with the SED that had taken place over the course of the year (Klessmann 1997).

On the East German side, ramifications for the cultural sphere of the SPD's evolution were clearly discerned. Hence, in April 1959, the secretary of the Filmmakers' Club and the director of the DEFA Documentary Studio traveled to Mannheim to organize the participation of the DEFA delegation at the festival. There they had the opportunity to talk at length with the festival's founding director, Kurt Joachim Fischer, who was "close to, or possibly even a member of the SPD."[29] While Fischer did stress that the SPD's Germany policy was not clear, he felt that a confederation of both states was the best conceivable system. And it was precisely because he was of that opinion that he had insisted that DEFA participate in the Mannheim Festival.[30] Diplomatic differences, however, trumped individual commitments, and the Leipzig Festival, once again, did not take place in 1959.

The Bitterfeld Way

In April 1959, the city of Bitterfeld, hitherto known mainly for its chemical industry, hosted the SED's first cultural conference, which gathered 150 professional writers and some 300 "worker writers" (*Schreibende Arbeiter*). The socialist cultural revolution was launched here, setting in motion the cultural movement known as the Bitterfeld Way (*Bitterfelder Weg*). Intellectuals and artists were to visit factories to observe and report on working conditions, while the workers were to "take up the pen" to describe the daily progress being made in East German production (Emmerich 2000). The conference itself primarily addressed writers, painters, sculptors, composers, actors, and fictional feature film directors, however. Documentary film was no more mentioned at the Bitterfeld conference than it had been at the cinema conference held in November 1958. Documentarists were still not considered filmmakers and artists, and their work continued to be widely equated with that of journalists and newsreel directors (Gass 1995).

DEFA documentary filmmakers had hoped that by establishing the Leipzig Festival they would gain some recognition, both in the eyes of those in power in East Berlin, who seemed to have pushed documentary filmmaking into the background, and on the international scene. They had also regarded the festival as a way to become better informed about what was happening beyond their borders and thus avoid isolation from the world at large and the pitfalls of provincialism. Returning delegates who had been sent to festivals and conferences abroad were often concerned about DEFA lagging behind.

In December 1958, the Second Conference on the Cinema of Socialist Countries in Romania brought together delegates from twelve countries. Moscow's objective was to compare policies and cinematographic production in these countries and to impose a single interpretation of cinema's role in constructing socialism. An account given by one of the East German participants, addressed to the minister of culture, stressed that the delegation had proven itself politically more mature, more determined, and more active and combative than it had at the First Conference, held in Prague in December 1957. The fact remained, however, that the delegation was still insufficiently prepared, especially with respect to films from some problematic countries, notably the Polish, Hungarian, and Czechoslovakian feature films.[31] At the Third Conference, held in Bulgaria in November 1960, Klaus Wischnewski, at the time chief dramaturg at the DEFA Feature Film Studio, remarked on how unaware of global trends in film production the East German delegates were, whether from the socialist or the Western camp: "We are submerged in a deep-seated provincialism, which allows us neither to work at the national level, nor to assert ourselves internationally, as our Soviet comrades have clearly demonstrated."[32]

This echoes a concern widely shared by intellectuals and those active in East Germany's cultural world, who were increasingly aware of the separate paths being taken by the two German societies and the countries in the two blocs.[33] It was a concern that those in high places were aware of. In March 1957, the ZK internally circulated the future policy to be adopted with regard to documentaries, which particularly recommended organizing screenings of the "best films from friendly countries, but also the best progressive documentaries from other countries, to be followed by discussions."[34] In this light, the Leipzig Festival now appeared to be one of the rare opportunities, in East Germany, for people to watch and discover certain noteworthy films produced abroad.

Meanwhile, new film festivals were beginning to emerge in the East. In 1956, the International Federation of Film Producers Associations (FIAPF) ranked the Karlovy Vary Festival in the prestigious Category A, on par with the festivals in Venice, Cannes, and the Berlinale.[35] The first festival in the East to receive such international recognition, Karlovy Vary had to swiftly come to grips with its Soviet big brother, which established the Moscow International Film Festival (MIFF) in 1959. Because FIAPF, dominated by Western countries, had decided that there would be only one Category A festival in the East per year, from its inception the MIFF alternated with the Karlovy Vary Festival. Establishing MIFF was part of a thaw in cultural policy enjoyed by Soviet cinema after 1956. Soviet filmmakers had succeeded in forming a filmmakers' union in 1957, and the festival was experienced as an additional achievement by filmmakers and enthusiasts alike (Eisenschitz 2000). MIFF became a very important fixture in the festival calendar, presenting both feature films and documentaries with a resonance that extended well beyond the confines of the East Bloc. It became a model for East Berlin's leaders, who understood the significance of its creation.

The support of prominent international figures and the founding of MIFF gave East German professionals hope for a change in East Berlin policy.[36] The main objective of VVB Film for 1960 was to intensify international cooperation, with particular attention paid to preparing festivals and conferences on film.[37] It was an incident at the Mannheim Festival, however, that made it possible to revive the Leipzig project.

Internationalizing the Festival: 1960–1961

Developments accelerated over the course of the spring of 1960. The challenges of 1955 remained: to demonstrate how far the GDR was ahead of the FRG, which was depicted as a regime steeped in censorship and hostile to progressive cinema. National and international contexts had changed, however, and the 1960 Leipzig Festival differed greatly from the template of its first two years.

Here again, German-German relations lay at the core of what was at stake and led to a dramatic reversal of position by East German leaders. Since 1955, the two West German documentary festivals had continued to mature. Mannheim awarded its first official prizes with an international jury in 1958. The

Figure 2.2. Poster for 1960 Leipzig Festival. © Bundsarchiv-Filmarchiv, Archiv der Leipziger Dok-Filmwochen GmbH.

same year, Oberhausen chose a new motto, which was to become identified with the festival: *Weg zum Nachbarn,* the "Way to the Neighbor." The presence of Czechoslovakian film director Jiří Trnka beginning in 1955, along with the participation of DEFA, justified setting a program policy that was willing to open up to certain countries, including countries against which Bonn had taken a position (Holloway and Holloway 1979). In 1959, the festival was rechristened as the West German Short Film Days and a year later was recognized by FIAPF.

As of 1954, programming any film from the GDR or other socialist country in the FRG had to be authorized by an interministerial assessment panel established by Bonn. This measure also affected film festivals. Furthermore, given that the GDR was not recognized as a country by the FRG, it was forbidden to officially announce DEFA films as originating in the GDR. In 1958, East Germany thus refused to participate in the Mannheim and Oberhausen Festivals, which could not accord the East German delegation a status equal to that of its West German counterpart. Protracted negotiations eventually resulted, however, in the participation of DEFA at Mannheim in 1959 (Kötz and Minas 2001). First and foremost, everything hinged upon the issue of nomenclature.

At the Oberhausen Festival in February 1960, as well, delicate negotiations were necessary to find a solution for how to refer to the East German films that were to screen at the festival. During an initial trip to West Germany by Werner Rose, secretary of the East German Filmmakers' Club, in late November 1959, Hilmar Hoffmann,[38] the director of Oberhausen, declared that he could not use the term "GDR" in the festival program; the Federal Ministry of the Interior categorically forbade it. "He himself knew that the GDR existed, but he would inevitably incur disciplinary measures [should the term appear]. Government officials in Bonn were already deeply suspicious about Oberhausen; at confidential meetings they dubbed it the 'red festival,' because in recent years most prizes had been awarded to socialist countries."

This was also one of the reasons Bonn refused to provide financial assistance at the last minute. A solution, however, had to be found—for, as Hoffmann judged at the time, "it would be absurd for our very nearest neighbor not to participate in a festival whose stated aim is to open the Way to the Neighbor."[39] In January 1960, he traveled to East Berlin and proposed to bill West German films as being "from Germany," followed by the name of the production company concerned, thus clearly indicating that it was a West German production, and East German films as being "from Germany" followed by "DEFA Studios." A month later, Oberhausen ultimately programmed two hours of films from the DEFA Documentary Studio. This was not simply a question of details but of essential terminology in the Cold War between the two German states. Both were extremely anxious to be clearly differentiated from one another; in addition, the GDR was adamant that it be treated as an independent and legitimate state. Bonn even set up a special commission to follow nomenclatural issues concerning East and West German delegations at international gatherings.[40]

In May 1960, an incident occurred at Mannheim that more seriously compromised collaboration between DEFA and the West German festival, however. At the request of the FRG's Interior Ministry, the mayor of Mannheim banned the screening of two DEFA films, *You and Some Comrade* and *Ein Tagebuch für Anne Frank* (1958, *A Diary for Anne Frank*),[41] which had been programmed for a special session. According to an official report of the East German Filmmakers' Club in 1962, the GDR delegation reacted to this by departing from the festival.[42]

The festival program was in fact modified at the last minute due to pressure from the West German federal government, which partially financed the Mannheim Festival.[43] Both documentaries were turned down on the grounds that they depicted a partisan history of Germany in which Bonn appeared as the sole heir of the Nazi past. On 30 May, the board of VVB Film demanded that the Filmmakers' Club "immediately" hold a press conference and that an article devoted to the subject be published in the GDR journal *Deutsche Filmkunst* to expose "the manner in which the West German interdepartmental commission operates." An assessment of the situation was to be addressed to the socialist countries and a collective protest was to be issued at the Karlovy Vary Festival.[44]

Meanwhile, in East Germany the idea of organizing an annual exhibition of documentary films had never been completely abandoned by films directors or the supervisory authorities. The question remained as to what approach such a project would take, however. In December 1959, VVB Film stated that "despite delays and hesitations" the Documentary and Educational Film Week would take place as resolved by the Ministry of Culture in November 1959.[45] This, however, referred to a weeklong event devoted exclusively to films from socialist countries, which was to take place after Leipzig's spring fair in March 1960. The director of HVFilm regarded the project as a "necessary counterweight in inter-German relations" such that plans for a festival in 1961 should already be in place.

Director of the DEFA Documentary Studio Günter Klein was granted the largely honorific title of president of the Film Week.[46] In mid-January 1960, it was decided that the festival would not take place until September.[47] On 16 May 1960, a further meeting postponed the project until October and decided that it ought to focus on the theme of agriculture.[48] The GDR was then in the throes of its final, very radical phase of agricultural collectivization, which had been instigated by Ulbricht at the end of 1959 (Schröder 1998). The intention was to circulate images of the agrarian revival and the world of socialist farmers.

As this sequence of events makes apparent, the concept of the festival was still very flexible, and its organizers hesitated until the last minute. It quickly became clear, however, that internationalizing the event would be an asset. In August 1959, the organizers of the Film Week noted that "capitalist countries would most likely be strongly represented." It thus became imperative to make every effort to ensure at least equivalent participation on the part of the socialist camp, and they undertook to write to the ministries of culture in the socialist states to convince them of the festival's significance.[49] Moreover, it was essential to meet the expectations of an international audience by addressing significant themes. "This is how we altered the concept of the festival, albeit a bit too much at the last minute," admitted Klein (1961: 38).

The Leipzig Film Week finally took place from 13 to 19 November 1960; its slogan was: "Film at the service of scientific, technical, and cultural progress—for peace and the well-being of all peoples." The East German regime had accepted a slogan mirroring its priority themes: economic progress and social modernization. Two "experts" sat on the jury, an agronomist and the vice-president of the Chamber of Technology.[50] Their presence drew the following remark from documentary director Karl Gass, the jury president: "In the future, we should recruit them at the next level up, because Professor Wunderlich and Dr. Otto allowed themselves to be unduly swayed by the technical processes being shown. For them, documentary films were a discovery."[51] As of the following year, there were no more outside experts on the jury.

A week before the Leipzig Film Week, the instant discontent that was felt owing to censorship exerted by the FRG against the two DEFA documentaries programmed for Mannheim was skillfully exploited by East Berlin. On 6 November 1960, the SED's Central Committee announced:

> The Leipzig Week is of the utmost importance for the GDR and for the entire socialist camp. It is the only one of its kind in the socialist camp and contributes to exerting influence on documentary filmmaking internationally. . . . It acts as a counterbalance to the Mannheim Film Week, the nature of which is increasingly dependent upon the psychological warfare conducted by West Germany and helps us to unmask and isolate Bonn.[52]

At the opening of the festival in Leipzig, the Mannheim incident was still on everyone's mind, and East German newspapers referred to it directly: "Leipzig topples Mannheim!" ran the headline in the daily *Mitteldeutsche Neueste Nachrichten* on 15 November 1960. In the end, the previous May's events seemed to have turned in favor of the GDR. The director of the Mannheim Festival, Kurt Joachim Fischer, stepped down from his post. According to the mayor and co-organizer of the festival (Kötz and Minas 2001), there were too few quality films for the program and too many competing festivals. In December 1960, the press announced that the new festival would henceforth be called Mannheim International Film Week (Internationale Filmwoche Mannheim), that it would take place in October instead of May, and that programming would include feature films.

When asked whether organizing the Leipzig Festival was linked to events that had taken place in Mannheim earlier that year, Günter Klein replied, "Absolutely. . . . The Mannheim Film Week no longer exists. We feel all the more obliged to create a new tradition, distinct from Mannheim's, a tradition that is open to the world. . . ." His assessment of Oberhausen was equally harsh:

> The Oberhausen Festival has no great prospects. Until now, the organizers have spread the idea that they have supposedly organized a festival in the heart of the Ruhr region, where socialist countries would not only participate, but also have a forum, where the workers of the region, as well as intellectuals, technicians, and engineers could get to know the filmmakers of the socialist countries. . . . It remains to be seen whether they will live up to their mission. (Klein 1961: 39)

This extended confrontation with West Germany ultimately played a decisive role in tipping the balance in favor of the Leipzig Festival's fully fledged internationalism.

The Wall

The Second Leipzig International Documentary and Short Film Week took place from 11 to 19 November 1961, three months after the construction of the Berlin Wall on 13 August and in the midst of the ensuing radical shift in East-West relations and policy. Leipzig was henceforth destined to become an even more significant meeting place in the attempt to maintain communication channels open on either side of the Iron Curtain. Festival organizers festooned a new slogan, "Films of the World—for Peace in the World," throughout the city streets and on all its posters.

In 1960, on the list of "foreign and West German" participants, seventeen had come from the FRG (*Protokoll 1960* 1961). The following year, twenty-four participants defied the West German Film Producers' Union and crossed the Wall. These guests merit closer examination; among the West Germans attending in 1961, seven had attended in 1960, including Will Wehling, program director at Oberhausen, and the cinematographer Peter Hellmich, who actually worked jointly with DEFA. Moreover, the number of visitors from the FRG easily increased as, for the most part, they brought their spouses. The West German delegation thus represented the second largest delegation after the GDR, followed by Czechoslovakia, the USSR, and Poland.[53]

The participation of "West German colleagues" had been warmly welcomed in 1960. "They demonstrate [by their presence] just how conscious they are of their national and cultural responsibility," remarked East German actor Harry Hindemith on opening night.[54] As the West German jury member, producer, and director Walter Leckebusch recalled, they were not an official delegation "but some . . . had gladly accepted the invitation . . . in the hope that German film production might appear as one, united whole."[55] Will Wehling, invited this year as a reporter for the West German daily *Die Welt*, even noted that the West German selection was a success, not because of its quality per se but rather because of "the yearning of the [East German] public to gain insight into Germany as it [was], and not as the press, radio, and television represent[ed] it, with every conceivable distortion" (Wehling 1960). Here Wehling was advancing an argument in favor of more active participation on the part of West German producers and documentary filmmakers, which ran counter to the stance advocated by the Film Producers' Union.

A year later, the issue of participation by West German directors, producers, and journalists was raised even more critically. As in 1960, the Film Producers' Union refused to send either delegates or films to Leipzig. "The Union has allowed itself to rally to Cold War tactics," remarked a West German director, and "to the applause of the public," emphasized Hans Rodenberg, deputy minister of culture.[56] As not one West German sat on the jury in 1961 or subsequent years, the festival's organizers de facto gave up on the original goal of East-West parity (*Protokoll 1961* 1962).[57] In some sense, the Wall had thus reached as far as Leipzig.

In introducing the Free Forum at the fourth Leipzig Festival in November 1961, director Andrew Thorndike stated:

> These last twelve months have not been uneventful ones in the history of humanity. . . . For the first time, two men . . . have left the earth, two communists. . . . Thanks to a heroic struggle, the Cuban people have repelled an invasion. . . . On 13 August, the peace-loving forces of the German people said there is "a clear limit, not to be exceeded" and thus proved that, today, the forces for peace of our people represent a real power. (Thorndike 1962: 13)

Apart from this statement, no other official speech mentioned the construction of the Wall the previous summer. The subject of the Wall was equally muted in terms of the program.

Among the DEFA films selected, two were animation films and two were documentaries. One, *Allons enfants . . . pour l'Algérie* (1961, *Arise, You Children . . . for Algeria*), was a three-part film by Karl Gass that dealt with Algeria.[58] The other, a fifteen-minute short film titled *Das Ganze halt* (1961, *It Stops Here*), had been directed by DEFA's Augenzeuge newsreel collective and was the only piece about the Wall. "The film justifies the measures taken by the GDR on 13 August 1961 to maintain peace" was how the catalogue soberly summarized the film (*Protokoll 1961* 1962: 57): no big name director, then, but rather an immediate reaction to the event.

As a comment on the quality of the film, and a reminder of the mindset prevailing in the USSR following Khrushchev's thaw, it is worth noting that Soviet director Roman Grigoriev expressed regret that the film had not turned out to be "a combative reportage, that gets an overview, a veritable document about the period, a testimony to the indefatigable work of cameramen, invariably on the front line, never shrinking before any difficulty" (Grigoriev 1962: 54). Film scholar Matthias Steinle argues that the film was a "minimalist legitimation of the Wall" (Steinle 2003: 193). A classic montage of archival and newsreel footage, the film drew a parallel between "Henlein's fascists"—who had infiltrated Czechoslovakia before 1939 and prepared the entry for Hitler's troops—and generals in the West German Bundeswehr—who were former Wehrmacht officers under the Nazis.

The conclusion of the film led to the necessary outcome: the construction of an "antifascist protection wall on the border of the GDR," to use the official phrase (Steinle 2003: 194). A jury established in 1961 by the German Film Journalists Association (Deutsche Journalisten-Verband, DJV) awarded its prize to a documentary by Pavel Haser, produced by the Czechoslovakian army studio. According to the jury, *Das Zeugnis* (1961, *The Testimony*),[59] a montage of archival footage on the history of Czechoslovakia from 1929 to 1941, was awarded the prize because "the lessons of history thus presented encourage the men and women of today to conscientiously defend peace" (*Protokoll 1961* 1962: 10). The example of neighboring Czechoslovakia thus served as a common thread in the historical legitimization of the Wall, which was thereafter regarded—officially, at least—as firmly rooted in the antifascist struggle and cause of peace that had been waged against the Nazis by the communists and was being carried on by the GDR.

A year later, the festival screened a full-length justification of the Wall at a special session, out of competition. Karl Gass's *Schaut auf diese Stadt* (1962, *Look at This City*) traces the history of Berlin after 1945 by means of a compilation of archive footage, newsreels, and television reports from the period, from either side of the Wall. The project predated the Wall's construction, so Gass had to entirely reedit the film to accommodate the events of 13 August. Ultimately, the Wall itself and its construction appeared in only three very short sequences of a few seconds each. Even in such a polemical, purely propagandistic film, it was difficult to show the Berlin Wall.

Instead, the audience was accosted by an extremely tight montage of images showing West Berlin occupied by Allied troops, with street names in French and English, and a militarized society where violence reigned and revanchism loomed large under the influence of NATO; in the East, in contrast, lessons had been learned from the war, and Germany's classical cultural heritage was preserved from American influence. A jazzy soundtrack and snippets from Allied radio news bulletins—citing stock prices, for example—were dubbed over images of West Berlin, whereas German classical music served as the musical backdrop to sequences devoted to the GDR highlighting the Buchenwald concentration camp monument, the nation's industrial infrastructure, universities, and so on. In terms of official discourse, the documentary offered no analysis; it essentially limited itself to setting the two Germanys against each other by juxtaposing them through commentary and images. The screening of the film at the Leipzig Festival was thus inscribed within the regime's offensive against both the East German public and international opinion.

Behind the Scenes

As of 1960, the festival effectively became an important element in East German propaganda vis-à-vis foreign nations. Its internationalization transformed the character of the event, offering fresh perspectives but also creating new needs. While in 1956 forty-eight films were shown in competition, by 1960 this figure had risen to ninety-one films representing twenty-three countries, with twenty-seven different nationalities invited. The official number of spectators remained at around 30,000 (*Protokoll 1960* 1961). In preparing for such an event, the organizers faced a number of logistical problems and constraints tied to tight deadlines and the still experimental nature of the festival. The festival's organizational and management structures depended on personalities and institutions that were themselves embedded in the East German state system. From now on, the Film Week was co-organized by the Filmmakers' Club and Progress Filmverleih, East Germany's sole film distribution company.

Wolfgang Kernicke, vice-president of the Filmmakers' Club, became "secretary of the Organizing Committee," responsible for the practical implementation of the Film Week. The presidium—an honorary committee in support of the festival, in place since 1956—remained a supervisory body.[60] It was chaired by Günter Klein, former director of the News and Documentary Studio, and a new member of the State Broadcasting Commission.[61] Kernicke gave a bitter account of the 1960 festival. In January 1960, he had sent the first invitations to socialist countries for September, the month initially set aside for the Film Week. Posters and advertising materials were ready. In March, the Ministry of Culture approved sending the first press releases to media outlets. On 1 June, however, following the Mannheim Festival, VVB Film and the Ministry of Culture of the GDR decided that the Film Week would finally be internationalized, that it should have an overarching theme

Figure 2.3. Poster for 1962 Leipzig Festival. © Bundsarchiv-Filmarchiv, Archiv der Leipziger Dok-Filmwochen GmbH.

and would take place in November. New plans, along with fresh invitations, had to be swiftly prepared.

Kernicke received very little support for this demanding assignment, however. Among other things, he continued working at the DEFA Synchronization Studio, where he was reproached for spending too much time at VVB Film preparing for the festival. As for the authorities in Leipzig, he recalled, "There was no support." The festival presidium also proved ineffective, as its members were either overworked elsewhere, on leave, or otherwise unable to do what had been assigned to them. On 1 October, work began on the ground in Leipzig. Material support—office space, accommodation, cars—was insufficient. There had been scarcely any replies to invitations and very few films had been submitted.

Werner Rose, of the Filmmakers' Club, was "in West Germany on special missions" and could be of no assistance. Klein, the president of the festival, "was unreachable for days at a time" and was replaced by Kernicke in 1962. Visas and residence permits for a hundred foreign guests had to be organized in just two weeks, without any interpreters. The first press conferences had to be organized without the press officer, who only arrived on 5 November. The Leipzig fairs administration did not provide staff for things like buffets, cleaning, and toilets as it had promised; yet again, members of the organizing bureau had to cope with these matters. As Kernicke recalled:

It was a constant struggle against incomprehension and a lack of interest on the part of the City Council and the Ministry of Culture with regard to financial issues, as well of the Synchronization Studio. . . . Only thanks to the support of SED municipal leadership and the local authorities of the Ministry of State Security [secret police] was it consistently possible to overcome the bureaucracy, . . . including for booking hotel rooms.[62]

Such an intervention on the part of the secret police (*Staatssicherheitsdienst,* Stasi) in this sphere is rather surprising and indicates the breadth of its missions. This document, moreover, presents one of the rare direct mentions of the Stasi's role in preparing and running the Leipzig Festival. It thus communicates a sense of the tensions between institutions, and especially between local authorities and the central authorities in East Berlin.

New Stakes

Given the undue haste and lack of cooperation, the 1960 Film Week proceeded in a largely improvised manner; and yet, it was hugely ambitious. The primary challenge for the organizers was to present Leipzig as the "place where, every year, documentary filmmakers from every country meet on an equal footing" ("Ansprache des Vorsitzenden" 1961: 5), irrespective of origin or nationality. This meant establishing an international meeting place that would give voice to all cinematic traditions, whether established or still developing. Western European nations were well positioned in Leipzig, with delegates from Great Britain, France, Denmark, Sweden, Belgium, the Netherlands, Austria, and West Germany. Even though all the socialist countries had sent delegates and films,[63] East German documentarist Andrew Thorndike (1962) regretted all the more the lack of big names from the Soviet documentary world, such as Roman Karmen.

The GDR was particularly interested in the newly decolonized or decolonizing countries of the Third World.[64] Asia was in attendance at Leipzig, represented by delegates from Korea, Vietnam, and China. From Africa, there were Algerian and Ghanaian films ("Im Wettbewerb gezeigte Filme" 1961). Algeria's participation, in particular, garnered attention. Unlike the FRG, East Berlin had been denouncing the war being waged by France in Algeria for six years; as Klein remarked (1961), neither Oberhausen nor Mannheim had as yet screened any Algerian films. Two Algerian producers and one director were invited to the festival, which had selected Djamel Chanderli's documentary *Notre Algérie* (1959, *Our Algeria*) for the program.[65] There were even films from the United States, although the "interesting documentary productions of 'outsiders'" were only shown at film club screenings or to narrow circles of interested parties (*Protokoll 1961* 1962: 38). Finally, Latin America was represented not only by a guest and three Cuban films but also by the outstanding Brazilian filmmaker Alberto Cavalcanti.

Third World cinema would quickly assert itself at Leipzig. The festival organizers regarded the participation of these countries as a diplomatic and political victory over Mannheim and Oberhausen. Hadn't the British documentary filmmaker Paul Rotha regretted, on behalf of the jury over which he presided at Mannheim in 1959, that not a single Asian or African film had been selected?

The participation of filmmakers, journalists, and foreign dignitaries at the festival was certainly an asset in creating an image of the regime's openness. Their attendance, however, was also regarded as a disruptive element in a system where communication between East German citizens, let alone between East Germans and foreigners, was supposed to take place within prescribed frameworks that posed clear limits on the exchange of views. Supervising foreign guests during the festival thus presented a twofold challenge. In the first place, it was necessary to assist delegates in finding their way around Leipzig and the festival. In the majority of cases the newcomers did not speak German, necessitating the continued presence of translators and interpreters. Behind the willingness to guide guests, however, lurked other motives that enable us to guess at measures taken during the preparations. Supervisory personnel were carefully vetted and chosen, certainly to ensure a warm welcome but also to provide the most reliable information at the close of the festival.

Karl Marx University in Leipzig, where journalism and languages were prominent in the curriculum, was one of the main sources of staff for the festival. The directors of the film academy in Babelsberg were also tasked with providing the "best qualified [students], both politically and professionally" for the festival.[66] Local businesses, too, were to choose people capable of overseeing the various delegations. Considered a separate case, West German guests required designated "comrades from the studios, particularly experienced and qualified." In theory, solid ideological training as well as language skills were required. On top of this, there were additional constraints. To be avoided, for example, was the supervision of male guests, especially from Africa and Asia, by women.[67]

Although expectations were clearly expressed in writing, on the ground things were often vaguer. In fact, there was a consensus that those attending the visitors were most often not up to the job and manifestly underinformed about the task awaiting them in Leipzig.[68] This particularly necessitated ensuring a better standard of translation for future festivals.[69] The overriding problem was with supervisory personnel, who were often very arrogant and cold. In 1964, a report from the directors thus noted that the Chinese and Vietnamese delegates had felt they had not received adequate support, while the Swedes, the Dutch, and some West Germans had even complained about the rudeness with which they were treated when crossing the border.[70]

In December 1966, the director of the East German State Film Archives again noted that "the hosting of foreign guests has gotten worse." It was at least necessary to plan to take care of the guests, not just until their departure from Leipzig but until they left the GDR. According to him, this would have prevented the "utterly needless incident" to which a group of French guests were exposed on the morning they left Berlin.[71] Guests should be treated on a more individual basis and in keeping with basic rules of politeness. According to the director of the Documentary Studio, future festival employees should be identified early on, so that over the course of the year they could familiarize themselves with the films from the delegation's country of origin or visit these countries in order to nurture personal contacts. In any case, Polish and Czechoslovakian colleagues, at least, had expressed such wishes.[72]

In terms of gleaning information from those who had attended the delegations, results proved equally unsatisfactory. Though reports were to be submitted at the close of the festival, they usually arrived in a trickle. This was considered all the more regrettable given that "those responsible for delegations [were] best placed to gather the opinions of our foreign guests."[73] Politically, such a barometer of the immediate response to the festival was very important. Unfortunately, the festival management's request fell on deaf ears, and no trace remains of any such report summarizing the work done by and experience of those responsible for foreign delegations.

Nevertheless, in the early 1960s, the Leipzig International Documentary Film Festival did, by means of gradual adjustments, succeed in establishing itself. Although it still encountered numerous organizational problems, it rapidly became a vibrant meeting place for discussion and meetings between filmmakers with very diverse experiences. The enthusiasm of these early years also undoubtedly reflected the long-awaited fulfillment of the creation of the festival at a juncture at which documentary filmmaking was evolving internationally.

Notes

1. Anton Ackermann, Vorlage für das Ministerium für Kultur zur Sitzung am Montag, 27 June 1955, SAPMO-BArch DR1/4194.
2. Christiane Mückenberger records the dates as 11–18 November 1955; my research, however, has revealed only the dates listed here.
3. The festival was officially put on by a committee, which in turn was led by an executive committee made up of a president, two vice-presidents, and a secretary. One of

the vice-presidents was also the director of the festival and, as such, was responsible for organization.
4. Statistics published on the occasion of the festival's twentieth anniversary, BArch-FArch, Leipzig, 1977.
5. J. R. Becher, Vorlage zur Beschlussfassung im Politbüro des ZK der SED, Thematische Pläne des DEFA-Studios 1955, SAPMO-BArch DR1/4194.
6. For more, see chapter 1.
7. As director Karl Gass recalled with irony during a workshop focusing on his œuvre organized during the 2002 Leipzig Festival.
8. The image of the Peasants' Revolt against the occupying nobility combined with the burlesque quality of the main character inspired DEFA twice more: in the 1957 French-GDR coproduction *The Adventures of Till Eulenspiegel*, with Gérard Philipe, and in Rainer Simon's 1975 *Till Eulenspiegel*, based on a scenario by Christa et Gerhard Wolf.
9. Statistics published on the occasion of the festival's twentieth anniversary, BArch-Farch, Leipzig, 1977.
10. Letter from Will Wehling to Wolfgang Kernicke, 9 August 1955, BArch-FArch, Filmmakers' Club. Cited in Mückenberger 1996: 367.
11. Author's interview with Erika Richter, Berlin, Germany (1 November 2000).
12. Motto of the 1956 Festival, BArch-FArch, Leipzig, 1977.
13. II. Kultur- und Dokumentarfilmwoche in Leipzig, press release by Günter Klein, undated, SAPMO-BArch DR1/1663.
14. Statistischen Angaben zur Internationalen Leipziger Dokumentar- und Kurzfilmwoche, 1955–1986, BArch-FArch, Leipzig, 1987.
15. BArch-FArch, Leipzig, 1977.
16. Festival program January 1956, BArch-FArch, Leipzig, 1956. The Information Program provided an arena for presenting more problematic films, without the chance of winning a prize.
17. II. Kultur- und Dokumentarfilmwoche in Leipzig, press release by Günter Klein, undated, SAPMO-BArch DR1/1663.
18. A journalist before the war, then exiled, Jerzy Bossak (1910–1989) returned to Poland in 1945 and set up the Warsaw Documentary Film Studio, which was part of Film Polski.
19. BArch-FArch, Leipzig, 1956.
20. Also from the FRG were the film critic Heinz J. Furian from Göttingen, the composer Fritz Wenneis from Munich, and the producer Hubert Schonger.
21. BArch-FArch, Leipzig, 1956.
22. It was composed of eight members: directors and cinematographers from DEFA; Gerhard Klein, the Director of the Documentary Studio; Wolfgang Kernicke, First Secretary of the Filmmakers' Club; and the Deputy Mayor of Leipzig. BArch-FArch, Leipzig, 1956.
23. We can cite the court case of the philosopher Wolfgang Harich, who had advocated a German path to socialism and non-Stalinist Marxism-Leninism.
24. From the ZK to HVFilm, Zu einigen Fragen des gegenwärtigen Standes und der Weiterentwicklung des Dokumentarfilms in der DDR, 12 March 1957, SAPMO-BArch DR1/4194.
25. Letter from Günter Klein to Werner Rose, 7 July 1957, BArch-FArch, Leipzig, 1957.

26. HVFilm, Sektor Kulturelle Arbeit mit Westdeutschland, signature illegible (Kehler?), undated, probably spring 1958, SAPMO-BArch DR1/7878.
27. In March, the government in Bonn had decided to furnish the West German army with atomic weapons (Mückenberger 1997).
28. Section leader to the Minister of Culture, Gen. Alexander Abusch, Kulturelle Arbeit mit Westdeutschland, Berlin, 21 December 1959, SAPMO-BArch DR1/7878.
29. Werner Rose, Günter Klein, Gespräch mit dem Verantwortlichen der Mannheimer Woche, Dr. K. J. Fischer, über den Entwurf eines Friedensvertrages, den Deutschlandplan der SED und den Brief unseres Zentralkomitees an den Parteivorstand und die Organisationen der SPD, Berlin, 16 April 1959, SAPMO-BArch DY 30/IV 2/2.026/79, p. 2.
30. He had declared, "Even without being communist, one had to admit there were a lot of possible topics of conversation, including with the delegates of the GDR," SAPMO-BArch DY 30/IV 2/2.026/79, pp. 13–15.
31. Bericht zu der II. Internationalen Konferenz der sozialistischen Länder, VVB Film, Gen. Donner, Büro des Hauptdirektors, an den Minister für Kultur, Ernst Hoffmann, Berlin, 7 January 1959, SAPMO-BArch DR1/4610.
32. Bericht des III. Konferenz der Filmschaffenden aus den sozialistischen Ländern in Sofia, 15–22 November 1960, SAPMO-BArch DR1/4610.
33. For more on the situation of authors, see Emmerich 2000; Kunert 1997; and Wolf 2003.
34. Zu einigen Fragen des gegenwärtigen Standes und der Weiterentwicklung des Dokumentarfilms in der DDR, Zentralkomitee der SED, 12 March 1957, SAPMO-BArch DR1/4194.
35. That same year, in 1956, the West Berlin film festival—the Berlinale—became a Category A festival.
36. Gérard Philipe, Georges Sadoul, Joris Ivens, and Nikolai Cherkasov (title role in Eisenstein's masterful *Ivan le Terrible*) were honorary members of the Filmmakers' Club (Mückenberger 1996: 370).
37. Jahresarbeitsplan der VVB Film 1960, SAPMO-BArch DR1/7721.
38. As an official, because he was the director of the Volkshochschule Oberhausen.
39. Aktennotiz, Werner Rose, 15 January 1960, SAPMO-BArch DY 30 IV/2.906/248.
40. Jens Niederhut also emphasizes this in his work on scientific exchanges and international scientific colloquia where the FRG and GDR were both represented (Niederhut 2007).
41. *You and Some Comrade:* a composite film, this documentary traces fifty years of German history in an effort to show that the GDR represented continuity with the history of German socialist and democratic struggle. *A Diary for Anne Frank:* starting with the fate of Anne Frank, the documentary warns viewers that the executioners are still present in West Germany; the film was banned in France and Great Britain.
42. Bericht über die Internationale Filmwoche Mannheim 1962, Club der Filmschaffenden, 29 October 1962, SAPMO-BArch DY 30 IV 2/906/248.
43. It is interesting to note that this incident, central from the East German perspective, is not even mentioned in Kötz and Minas's 2001 volume on the history of the Mannheim Festival.
44. Protokoll der 19. Leitungssitzung der VVB Film, 30 May 1960, SAPMO-BArch DR1/4380.

45. Protokoll der 41. Leitungssitzung der VVB Film, 14 December 1959, SAPMO-BArch DR1/7721.
46. Protokoll der 42. Leitungssitzung der VVB Film, 21 December 1959, SAPMO-BArch DR1/4380.
47. Wolfgang Kernicke, Hans Wegner, Bericht über die Arbeit des Organisationsbüros der III. Leipziger Kurz- und Dokumentarfilmwoche (13–19 November 1960), Berlin, 29 November 1960, SAPMO-BArch DY 30 IV 2/9.06/228, p. 168.
48. Protokoll der 17. Leitungssitzung der VVB Film, 16 May 1960, SAPMO-BArch DR1/4380.
49. Protokoll der 29. Leitungssitzung der VVB Film, 8 August 1960, SAPMO-BArch DR1/4380.
50. Information zur Leipziger Woche, SAPMO-BArch DY 30 IV 2/9.06/228, p. 48.
51. Karl Gass, Bemerkungen zur III. Leipziger Kurz- und Dokumentarfilmwoche, Potsdam-Babelsberg, 24 November 1960, SAPMO-BArch DY 30 IV 2/9.06/228, p. 145.
52. Letter of the SED ZK to the Leipzig district SED leadership, 6 November 1960, SAPMO-BArch DY 30 IV 2/9.06/228, p. 41.
53. There were sixteen Czechoslovakian participants, ten Russian and Polish (*Protokoll 1961* 1962).
54. Ansprache des Vorsitzenden des Clubs der Filmschaffenden der DDR, Harry Hindemith, zur Eröffnung der III. Leipziger Woche (*Protokoll 1960* 1961:5–6), SAPMO-BArch DY 30 IV 2/9.06/228, p. 5–6.
55. Walter Leckebusch, Zum Programm der Deutschen Bundesrepublik, SAPMO-BArch DY 30 IV 2/9.06/228, p. 306.
56. Address by Professor Hans Rodenberg at the close of the fourth Leipzig Festival (*Protokoll 1961* 1962).
57. To clarify this and upcoming citations, the festivals regularly published a newsletter called the *Festival Bulletin*. These newsletters, along with other documents, such as reviews, were collected after the festival and published under the title *Protokoll*, which appeared the following year.
58. Gass gave this film a French title.
59. *Das Zeugnis* was directed by Pavel Haser for the Army Film Studio in Prague. Reviewing the history of Czechoslovakia, two parts were filmed—one covering 1929–1941, the second 1941–1945—but only the first part was shown at Leipzig.
60. It was composed of about ten members, DEFA collaborators and a representative of the City of Leipzig, Barch-FArch, Leipzig, 1956/1.
61. This organization had two names: das Staatliches Komitee für Rundfunk (StKfR) and Staatliches Rundfunkkomitee (SRK).
62. Wolfgang Kernicke, Hans Wegner, Bericht über die Arbeit des Organisationsbüros der III. Leipziger Kurz- und Dokumentarfilmwoche (13–19 November 1960), Berlin, 29 November 1960, SAPMO-BArch DY 30 IV 2/9.06/228, pp. 168–69, 171–72.
63. List of guests and films shown at the third Leipzig Festival, SAPMO-BArch DY 30 IV 2/9.06/228.
64. Coined in 1952 by French economic historian Alfred Sauvy, the term "Third World" referred to countries that were not part of the First World—the industrialized "West"— or the Second World, which consisted of socialist and communist countries. The Third World included countries in Asia, Africa, and Latin America that had been or were still colonies; the Non-Aligned Movement, articulated at the Bandung Conference, in part

represented this bloc. Later, as international development theory gained in currency, the term was increasingly considered synonymous with "underdeveloped" or "developing" countries and was thus derogatory. The term appears here in its original sense.
65. Directed by Chanderli, one of the first important Algerian directors (along with René Vautier and Lakhdar Amina), the film was shot by cinematographers of the Algerian National Liberation Front (FLN). Chanderli completed a first version in 1959 but then revisited it in 1960–1961 and renamed it *Voix du peuple* (*Voice of the People*). (See *Kirche und Film* 1960)
66. Hans Bentzien, 1964, SAPMO-BArch DR1 4272, p. 15.
67. Hinweise für die Gestaltung künftiger Kurz- und Dokumentarfilmwochen in Leipzig, betrachtet vom Gesichtspunkt der Entwicklungsländer Afrikas und Asiens, Berlin, 19 December 1964, SAPMO-BArch DR1/4272.
68. Kosielski, *chargé* of the Polish delegation, Stellungnahme zum Problemspiegel für die Auswertung der VII. Leipziger Woche, 26 November 1964, SAPMO-BArch DR1 4272.
69. Bauer, coordinator with the protocol service of the festival, Auswertung der VII. Leipziger Woche, 26 November 1964, SAPMO-BArch DR1 4272.
70. Internationale Repräsentanz, Zu konzeptionellen Fragen der VIII Leipziger Woche. November 1964, SAPMO-BArch DR1 4272.
71. The incident remains mysterious; there is no further mention anywhere. Hoffmann, Auswertung der IX. Leipziger Woche, 7 December 1966, SAPMO-BArch DR1/4331.
72. Director of the DEFA Studio for Newsreels and Documentary Film, Bericht über Erfahrungen auf der diesjährigen Dokumentarfilmwoche und Vorschläge für kommende Festivals, 1966, SAPMO-BArch DR1/4331, p. 4.
73. Belling, Einschätzung der VII Internationalen Dokumentarfilm-und Kurzfilmwoche in Leipzig, 1964, SAPMO-BArch DR1/4272.

CHAPTER 3
|||||||||||||||||||||

Between Propaganda and *Cinéma Vérité*

In the East, as in the West, the 1960s were a period of considerable political, social, and cultural tumult. Cinema was one of its richest expressions. In just a few years, the world of filmmaking experienced profound changes, symbolized by the New Waves of different countries, which varied profoundly (Douchet 1998).[1] Parallel to developments in fiction films, documentary filmmaking experienced significant mutations with the emergence of *cinéma vérité* — sometimes associated with "observational" or "direct" cinema (Gauthier et al. 2003; Marsolais 1974). Given that as of 13 August 1961 a wall "protected," according to the official discourse, East Germans from pernicious Western influences and given that filmmaking in the GDR was closely scrutinized by the regime, how did DEFA documentary films interface with the international ferment of the 1960s?

The Leipzig Festival undoubtedly played a pivotal role in this, particularly after its internationalization in 1960. The motto chosen for the 1961 festival, "Films of the World—for Peace in the World," which remained unchanged until 1989, clearly expressed the festival's aspirations. The construction of the Berlin Wall made Leipzig the sole venue where most East German filmmakers could come into contact with foreign filmmakers. Here, East met West and North met South. In this respect, the Leipzig Festival offers an excellent vantage point from which to observe the formative period of the global 1960s. By retracing the evolution of the festival's program over time and the debates of the first half of the 1960s, we can follow the complex relationships between film production and innovation in various parts of the world.

The Old Guard of International Documentary Filmmaking

The list of filmmakers and critics that participated in the Leipzig Festival during this period of its history is both lengthy and undoubtedly international. It reveals common political affiliations, uniting leftist sympathizers and Communist Party members. In 1960, the hundred-some guests attending the festival came from twenty-four different countries; the following year, the figure rose to forty countries.[2] Among the many viewers attending screenings, some personalities stood out. They were among the pioneers of the documentary genre, whose engagement in the "antifascist struggle" during World War II had mostly united them behind a single cause.

In 1964, festival director Andrew Thorndike referred to the "political bureau [politburo] of documentarists from around the world" that gathered at the Leipzig Festival (*Protokoll 1964* 1965). Nine years after the Leipzig Festival's launch, organizers could boast of a prestigious photograph in which leading documentarists from East and West are featured, thus encapsulating, as it were, the various schools and tendencies of documentary filmmaking at that juncture. They were primarily members of the avant-garde generation of the interwar years, with a place of honor reserved for the retrospective of works by the American director Robert Flaherty, best known for the silent documentary *Nanook of the North* (1922). His widow, Frances Flaherty, attended the festival for the occasion, thereby underlining the significance of the event and the exceptional nature of the festival.

Among the well-known people in attendance, we should distinguish between festival regulars and occasional guests. As seen above, the Dutch director Joris Ivens unquestionably dominated the festival in the 1960s. He was a leading participant who had been very active in establishing an international festival in Leipzig. Given that his birthday coincided with the Film Week, he was the guest of honor at the festival virtually every year—at any rate before his pro-Maoist positions led him to distance himself from the GDR at the end of the 1960s. His extensive travels enabled him to establish contacts worldwide, which he used to the festival's benefit. Thanks to his efforts, several renowned documentarists traveled to Leipzig to participate in the fledgling festival in East Germany.

Alberto Cavalcanti—who was born in Brazil in 1897 and disappeared in Paris in 1982—thus started attending the festival in 1960 and was a member of Leipzig's honorary presidium. The 1962 retrospective was dedicated to his work. His international experience, relatively common for that generation, was invaluable to festival organizers, particularly in helping them establish links to Latin America. Cavalcanti had begun his career in France in 1917, making silent films with social themes. Moving to Great Britain in 1934, he participated in the British Documentary School and joined the General Post Office Film Unit

Figure 3.1. 1964 gathering of important documentarists at the Leipzig Festival. First row (*left to right*): Jean Lods, Santiago Álvarez, Basil Wright (*seated in front*), Paul Rotha, Frances Flaherty, Richard Leacock, Alberto Cavalcanti, Sara Gómez Yera, and Bert Haanstra. Second row (*left to right*): Andrew Thorndike, Henri Storck, Gian Vittorio Baldi, Goverdhandas Agarwal, John Grierson, Ivor Montagu, Karl Gass, Bruno Sefranka, Joris Ivens, Walter Heynowski, Annelie Thorndike, Vaclav Táborský, Chris Marker, Saad Nadim, Gerhard Scheumann, and Dušan Vukotić. © Filmmuseum Potsdam, Bundesarchiv-Filmarchiv.

at Grierson's invitation. He was unsuccessful in his attempt to establish a National Institute of Cinema in his native Brazil in the 1950s. Returning to Great Britain, he directed numerous films. During public debates or in interviews given during the Leipzig Festival, Cavalcanti did not conceal his rather critical view of films made in East Germany and throughout Eastern Europe.

Another central figure in the history of documentary filmmaking was the Scotsman John Grierson (1898–1972), who first attended Leipzig in 1960 and returned in 1964. While not as committed to the Leipzig Festival as Ivens, Grierson also participated at other German documentary festivals; he became the president of the international jury at Oberhausen in 1959 and 1960 before becoming its honorary president. In 1964, he duly noted, "Through my weekly commentaries on Scottish television, I have done far more for Eastern Europe than any English daily newspaper in a single year" (Herlinghaus 1982: 55).

"Constantly in search of inspiration," Grierson attended the Leipzig Festival because of the opportunity it presented to view many films from socialist countries. His colleagues and compatriots Basil Wright (1907–1987) and Paul Rotha (1907–1984) also traveled to Leipzig. The producer Stanley Forman (1921–2013) served as the intermediary between this elite of British documentary filmmaking and the festival. His distribution company, Plato Films, which had been founded in 1950 and only distributed films from socialist countries, acted as a kind of cultural center for the GDR in Great Britain (Forman 1997). It was through this venture that Forman met Andrew Thorndike and learned about the birth of the international film festival. Without too much difficulty, he then arranged for British participation.

Danish filmmaker Theodor Christensen (1914–1967), a member of the Danish resistance movement during World War II, took an active part in the festival until his disappearance in 1967. His political engagement took him to Cuba in 1964 to help develop a film industry there. As a member of the honorary presidium and international jury of the Leipzig Festival on several occasions, he, like Grierson and Cavalcanti, maintained a critical perspective on the documentaries screened at the festival.

From the East Bloc countries, the presence of the prominent Soviet war correspondent and documentarist Roman Karmen (1906–1978) was especially significant.[3] He, too, had traveled the world, filming the Spanish Civil War and the beginnings of the conflict in China. He was among the cameramen sent to the front by the Red Army and went to Vietnam in 1954–1955, to India, and to Cuba. He first attended the Leipzig Festival in 1961 and became a member of the honorary presidium and the jury in 1963, 1967, and 1970. In 1971, the festival devoted the retrospective to his work. Poland was also well represented, with the regular attendance of the director, critic, and teacher Jerzy Bossak (1910–1989), who had a great influence on Polish documentary filmmaking, and of film historian Jerzy Toeplitz.[4]

Other figures from cinema circles who were not documentarists also accepted invitations to the festival. This was the case for Ivor Montagu (1904–1984), "aristocrat and communist, journalist, biologist, filmmaker, and friend of George Bernard Shaw, Sergei Eisenstein and Charlie Chaplin" (Hogenkamp 2000: 286), who organized the distribution of DEFA films in Great Britain with Stanley Forman. Vladimir Pozner (1905–1992), writer and author of screenplays residing in France, regularly attended the Leipzig Festival as of 1960, even after the number of French delegates decreased following 1968 (Gass 1995; Jordan and Schenk 1996).

As fellow travelers and members of communist parties, the documentary filmmakers who were present all advocated political and social engagement anchored on the left. It should also be noted that these people continued to participate in festivals of either side of the Iron Curtain as well. During the first half of the 1960s, Jerzy Bossak, Jerzy Toeplitz, Kazimierz Karabasz, Roman Karmen, Richard Leacock, John Grierson, and even Joris Ivens were on the guest lists at all three German festivals: Leipzig, Mannheim, and Oberhausen (Holloway and Holloway 1979; Kötz and Minas 2001).

According to Karl Gass, then the festival president, the participation of such renowned foreign directors on the jury at the 1960 Leipzig Festival, comprising no fewer than fourteen members, was not always easy: "The jury's final meeting suffered greatly from the attitude of Messrs. Cavalcanti and Grierson, whose contributions to the discussion were very brusque, very obtuse and very undisciplined, talking very loudly and without tact. Both of them ... were clearly under the influence of alcohol."[5] The fact remains that the presence on the guest list of these leading figures of documentary filmmaking enabled the festival to acquire legitimacy and an excellent reputation beyond its initial circles of support. As Günter Klein (1961: 41) noted, "The achievement of these masters is to have contributed to what exists today: a left-wing of documentary filmmaking that does not just include communists. It goes beyond that."

In fact, most participants, directors, and journalists did consider the 1960 Leipzig Film Week a success; they lauded its international character and encouraged the project of creating a world federation of documentary filmmakers.[6] During a public discussion, Joris Ivens traced the different attempts to found such an international movement since World War II. There had in fact been a meeting of film directors in Brussels in 1948, at which Henri Storck, Basil Wright, and Paul Rotha were present (Hahn 1997). The project did not get off the ground: "It was a private circle," Ivens noted, "the world has progressed since then and we can be more ambitious." And, he added, "It is almost inconceivable to imagine that an international congress of documentary film might take place next year in Leipzig!" (Ivens 1961: 26).

It remained to be determined which countries and personalities to bring together on a founding committee. Ivens's observations testify to a certain geography of documentary filmmaking in the early 1960s: "Denmark, which initiated this project; possibly France, which introduced major advances in the documentary genre; Poland which showed us a lot of films; the GDR, because our organization must remain linked to this wonderful festival in Leipzig; and England, too. These, I think, have their place." As it transpired, the committee mandated to prepare the creation of the federation brought together the Pole Tadeusz Makarczyński, the Frenchman Jean-Jacques Languepin, the Briton Anthony Simmons, and Karl Gass representing the GDR. Theodor Christensen became its president. A rendezvous was set for the following year, at the fourth Leipzig Festival.[7]

Although the International Documentary Association (IDA) was eventually founded, it did not materialize until 1964 and it did so in the West, at

Mannheim (Aitken 2013). Renamed the Mannheim International Film Week in 1961—and now organized by the Association of German Film Clubs and scheduled for October rather than May—the festival gathered fresh impetus and experienced growing international success (Kötz and Minas 2001). The quality of the Oberhausen Festival improved during this period as well, and it succeeded in creating its own distinctive profile. As of 1962, Leipzig Festival organizers could congratulate themselves on hosting representatives of both West German events (*Protokoll 1961* 1962), and they welcomed leading figures from the world of international documentary filmmaking, thus participating in the period's dynamics surrounding East-West circulation.

The Case of French Documentarists

To what extent, however, did the Leipzig Festival reflect the dynamism of the so-called golden age of documentary from the late 1950s to the early 1960s? A close examination of French participation at the festival can help us explore this question. From its creation until the 1960s, the Leipzig Festival was a key witness to the rapid expansion of French documentary cinema. Wolfgang Kernicke, festival director until 1963, spoke French and was one of the major ambassadors in developing a strong web of friendships between the festival and French filmmakers and enthusiasts (Becker and Petzold 2001).

In the early 1950s, documentary filmmaking experienced a very fruitful period in France. A declaration of the Groupe de Trente (Group of Thirty)[8] was published on 20 December 1953 in response to a series of legislative texts, including a decree that would have waived the requirement for movie theaters to screen a short film produced within the previous decade before French feature films (Odin 1998b). The group was not made up of film directors seeking to improve the conditions of production but was rather a movement of filmmakers rallying around a specific concept of documentary film. Thanks to ensuing debates in the press, as well as to the films produced and screened at movie theaters and festivals, their action was ultimately effective, for it resulted in increased recognition on the part of both the general public and the French state, which launched a new system to subsidize French film production.

Leipzig programmed several films by members of the group, for whom the issue was to create quality documentaries with educational and cultural goals and to distribute them as extensively as possible. In 1956, the festival screened *Guernica,* by Alain Resnais, a film he shot in 1950[9] inspired by Picasso's works and by Paul Éluard's poem "Victory of Guernica." In 1960, it screened Pierre Prévert's *Paris la belle* (1960, *Paris the Beautiful*), which contrasted nostalgic black-and-white images of Paris in 1928 with color images of Paris shot in 1959. The documentaries of the Group of Thirty most often resulted from institutional commissions; the social dimension was highly important and was often expressed in a style evoking Socialist Realism (Caron et al. 1998). Edouard Luntz's *Les enfants du courant d'air* (1959, *Children Adrift*), for example, which virulently decried the plight of children living in Paris's slums, was selected and awarded a prize at the 1961 Leipzig Festival (*Protokoll 1961* 1962).[10] Other films presented positive appraisals of technical progress and scientific research. An example was Henri Fabiani's short *Tu enfanteras sans douleur* (1956, *Birth without Fear*), programmed in 1956, which created a sensation by grappling directly with the issue of painless childbirth.

While such social themes were consistent with issues raised in DEFA documentaries, the theme of war and antifascism proved a double-edged sword in the eyes of the East German authorities, as the fate awaiting Alain Resnais's *Nuit et brouillard* (1956, *Night and Fog*) indicates. *Night and Fog* is a documentary about Nazi concentration camps during World War II. Drawing on multiple sources, the film is a montage of archival materials—photographs and film footage of diverse provenance—and color sequences shot by Resnais in the ruins of the Auschwitz concentration camp. The text was written by the author and camp survivor Jean Cayrol and the score was by German composer Hanns Eisler; both Cayrol and Eisler regularly collaborated on films produced by members of the Group of Thirty.[11]

The film was partially censored by French authorities,[12] and its scheduling for the Cannes Festival in May 1956 provoked a sharp response from the West German embassy in France; it was supported in this by the Quai d'Orsay (the French Ministry of Foreign Affairs), which advanced the baffling argument that the Cannes Festival, according to its own statutes, was not to program any film that might hurt the national sentiment of another people. At the end, *Night and Fog* was projected, but in a private screening. A few weeks later, after much heated discussion, the Berlinale festival decided to project Resnais's film at three special screenings in accordance with the wishes of the West Berlin Senate, thus opposing Bonn. Willy Brandt, then president of West Berlin's Chamber of Deputies, declared, "We must not forget, so that others can forget" (Jacobsen 2000: 67–68). The Berlinale thus managed to set itself apart from Cannes and, equally significant, vis-à-vis Bonn. In that same spring of 1956, *Night and Fog* received an award at Oberhausen, thereby becoming one of the first French films to enter the festival's archives (Holloway and Holloway 1979).

In November 1956, *Night and Fog* also screened at the Leipzig Festival, out of competition. Resnais, who had been invited, canceled his visit because he had a shoot in Tunisia.[13] It was only two years later, however, at the end 1958, that there was any discussion of a general release in East German movie theaters, and only on condition that the film's closing credits "link the film's theme with current political events and strengthen [viewers'] willingness to take an active part in the struggle against fascism and war, for peace and socialism."[14] Günter Klein, director of the DEFA Documentary Studio, felt that such a text would be in conflict with the remainder of the film and negatively affect the effectiveness of Resnais's theme.

Instead he proposed to produce a short film showing East German audiences that the release of *Night and Fog* had not been permitted in the FRG, thus exposing the influence of former Nazis at the heart of the West German state.[15] Only in 1960 did Resnais's film get the green light for projection at rare screenings and to be broadcast on East German television—with German voice-over that drastically modified Jean Cayrol's original commentary.[16] The time lag between the film's initial screening at the festival and its general release reflects not only the debates that were prevailing in the GDR about how the war should be depicted but also the specificity of the Leipzig Festival, which remained a privileged social occasion for invited East German journalists and documentary filmmakers to discover foreign films.

Figure 3.2. Award ceremony on stage at the Capitol Theater, the Leipzig Festival's main venue, in 1963. © Filmmuseum Potsdam, Reinhard Podszuweit.

Upon her return from France in May 1957, the DEFA documentarist Annelie Thorndike spoke to her colleagues of a "renaissance of the French documentary" and encouraged them to foster links with France.[17] Jean-Jacques Languepin, vice-president of the Group of Thirty, was thus invited to sit on the Leipzig Festival's first international jury in 1960 and became a member of the honorary presidium in 1962 (*Protokoll 1962* 1963). Film director Jean Lods attended as a guest in 1963 and then sat on the jury in 1964. Among other luminaries present at Leipzig from the intellectual and cinema worlds close to the group were Vladimir Pozner and his wife, Ida Pozner. The journalist and historian of French cinema Georges Sadoul, who had translated Dziga Vertov's writings into French and was an active member of the French Communist Party, sat on the jury at Leipzig in 1961. Most French guests at Leipzig were members of the French Communist Party, including the activist Robert Menegoz, who collaborated on two DEFA documentaries, in 1954 and 1957. Others, such as the director Henri Fabiani, were merely fellow travelers.

The official French selections, for example, for 1963—*Algérie, année zéro* (1962, *Algeria, Year Zero*) codirected by Jean-Pierre Sergent and Marceline Loridan, wife of Joris Ivens; *Salut les Cubains* (1963, *Greetings, Cubans*) by Agnès Varda in collaboration with Chris Marker and Anne Philipe, wife of Gérard Philipe; and Jean Lods's *20,000 matins* (1964, *20,000 Mornings*), about the domestic distribution of *L'Humanité*, the French communist daily — also fell within the scope of this circle of professional friendships based on political engagement.

From Kino-Pravda to Direct Cinema

The festival unquestionably demonstrated openness and insight by disseminating the French documentary movement, one of the most interesting trends in documentary production of the period. Western filmmakers also expressed opinions that provoked heated debate during public discussions at Leipzig. As indicated by discussions about the prospects of documentary cinema, not everyone identified with the communist or orthodox Soviet position. The Leipzig Festival was thus not only a meeting place for filmmakers and film enthusiasts from diverse backgrounds or an opportunity to watch films for an entire week. It was also a forum for professionals eager to exchange ideas and their conceptions of documentary. In the first half of the 1960s, the Documentary and Short Film Week hosted—often unwittingly—most of the major debates that were agitating international film production at the time.

In March 1957, the Central Committee (ZK) of the SED, seeking to understand the inferior quality of DEFA output, particularly deplored the studios' lack of "an artistic atmosphere that, through discussions, confrontations, and collaborations between artists, would allow individual creative capabilities to blossom. ... The sterile imitation of models, ... the routine" were the principal shortcomings constraining production.[18] And yet, as film scholar Erika Richter recalls, even if the discussions of 1958–1959 were still marked by extremely dogmatic positions, later much more open discussions were possible.[19]

The Free Forum

In 1960, the ZK decided to initiate a "forum" at Leipzig.[20] According to Klein (*Protokoll 1960* 1961), the Free Forum, where everyone could speak of what was of interest and concern to them, was established in a somewhat vague and improvised fashion, which the large number of participants only accentuated.[21] In the year of its founding, no fewer than twenty prominent personalities from the world of cinema participated in the four-hour debate. In subsequent years, the number of participants decreased slightly, but the forum was spread over several days.

Director Andrew Thorndike opened the first Free Forum in 1960. He stressed the "immense power of documentary," citing Dziga Vertov, Jean Vigo, Joris Ivens, John Grierson, and Alberto Cavalcanti, whose films had had an impact "on hundreds of millions of people." Once again, Thorndike raised the question of the responsibility borne by many German documentary filmmakers who had more or less consciously contributed to Nazi propaganda, and he revisited his own track record (*Protokoll 1960* 1961: 12–13). In 1961, Thorndike again opened the proceedings and sought to channel debates around a single theme to provide a theoretical basis for discussion. The East German critic Hermann Herlinghaus gave a presentation on "prospects for documentary film" (*Protokoll 1961* 1962), revisiting the controversy of the late 1920s between the Soviet filmmakers Dziga Vertov and Sergei Eisenstein.

In the fledgling Soviet Union, Vertov had devoted himself to an avant-garde approach to documentary filmmaking that he referred to as Kino-Pravda, which explored capturing reality "firsthand" during shooting—without anything fictional and by means of an impartial *kinoglaz* (cine-eye)—then editing the footage as expressively as possible through montage. The idea was that the spontaneity of shooting would generate emotions, which the montage would then shape into a discourse (Ferro 1989). Eisenstein, in contrast, considered it a shortcoming that Vertov's Kino-Pravda did not carry out a clear political concept formulated before shooting began. Ultimately, Vertov became a victim of the Stalinist system and of the doctrine of Socialist Realism, imposed from above, which rejected his avant-garde approach to documentary. Because the festival's debut retrospective in 1960 had been consecrated to Vertov's opus, it was important to revisit this choice, which was not exactly obvious from a political perspective (*Protokoll 1961* 1962).

In 1962, two topics were chosen for the Free Forum: "The role of documentaries in educating the masses," with an introductory speech by the Soviet filmmaker Ilya Kopalin, which turned into a history of Soviet film production (*Protokoll 1962* 1963); and "reality in documentary film," presented by the Polish filmmaker Jerzy Bossak, who emphasized the commonality of approach of Vertov and Grierson—the idea that a documentary ought to present a conscious and critical representation of reality—despite their very different backgrounds (*Protokoll 1962* 1963). If we are to believe eyewitness accounts, the Free Forum was often more a series of sleep-inducing monologues than real exchanges alongside theoretical presentations and introductory talks. Debates became more intense, however, whenever it came to discussing concrete examples or specific films that allowed participants to raise essential questions, both ideological and technical, about what documentary filmmaking should and could be.

Aesthetic questions immediately entered the political debates between filmmakers and journalists who were left leaning but not necessarily orthodox communists. They revolved around one critical issue: can you be a poet if you are a militant? In the words of Joris Ivens:

> There are some apples there and I want to show them. As an artist, I have to show them so that they appear beautiful, appetizing, so that their arrangement has the same charm as a still life. But this is not enough. As a documentary filmmaker, I want to show that we use them, that men worked for them, that fruits and vegetables form part of people's everyday needs and that they have become a commodity. Let's say at times I see apples as Cézanne would have, and at times like Grierson sees herrings in *Drifters* (1929).[22] (Herlinghaus 1982: 43)

The comparison drawn by Ivens reflects the ambiguity inherent within politically and socially engaged documentary. What place is left for aesthetic experiment, art, and poetry?

At the Leipzig Festival in 1960, Ivens presented *La Seine a rencontré Paris* (1957, *The Seine Meets Paris*), a highly personal portrayal of the river and its banks with a text by the poet Jacques Prévert. The film observes all aspects of life on the banks of the Seine—lovers, fishermen, artists, workers, flaneurs—most often avoiding clichés or cleverly diverting from them. The documentary received a prize at Cannes in 1957 and the third prize at Oberhausen in 1959. As Guy Gautier described it, "*The Seine Meets Paris* introduces us to French documentary film, more enticed by the margins and poetic glimpses than its British and American counterparts" (Gauthier 1995: 65–66)—and than East German film as well, we might add.

Ivens contrasted orthodox documentary, which he associated with newsreels, with a broader conception of the documentary genre. The former corresponded to the notion that what was filmed was contingent upon only the event to be filmed, whereas the latter implied an attempt to film an event with the maximum expressive force possible (Brandt 1987). Grierson, for his part, warned against "tedious films," devoid of all poetry. "In today's documentaries, we think far too much and follow our feelings far too little" was how he summed up his position (*Protokoll 1960* 1961: 14).

Faced with documentarists like these, most DEFA directors defended the need for documentaries that were solely and explicitly combative and militant. Karl Gass regretted not seeing a "raised fist" in *The Seine Meets Paris*, going so far as to predict that the film would have no place in the annals of documentary cinema (*Protokoll 1960* 1961: 16). Three years later, in an interview with the film critic Hermann Herlinghaus during the 1963 festival, Ivens revisited the controversy triggered by his film. He questioned his interlocutor—as a "representative of the Marxist youth at Leipzig"—regarding his personal opinion on the issue: had he not himself written a booklet titled *Dziga Vertov—Journalist and Poet of the Documentary World* on the occasion of the Soviet avant-gardist's 1960 retrospective?

Herlinghaus was clearly torn between his respect for Ivens and his adhesion to the stance taken by the majority of East German filmmakers, replying, "I think we must understand these criticisms in the specific context of our documentaries, conceived as a weapon against West Germany's revanchism. Here, in our country, documentaries have a highly political profile." In the eyes of many of the "more or less young" East German documentary filmmakers, *The Seine Meets Paris* lacked a clear exposition of the class struggle. In contrast to the powerful *Song of the Rivers*, directed by Ivens for DEFA in 1954, the observations made in *The Seine Meets Paris* remained too much on the surface. According to Herlinghaus, the lofty lyricism of the 1954 documentary corresponded more closely to the expectations of GDR documentary filmmakers than the sensitive paean Ivens later paid to the Seine (Herlinghaus 1982: 37).

Festival organizers and DEFA filmmakers were thus fundamentally in agreement that documentaries should primarily be political objects. They did not express their disagreement with Ivens and Grierson on this particular point, but rather on the form documentary filmmaking ought to take as a propaganda weapon. Here again, however, it was necessary to come to an agreement on what the term "propaganda" actually meant. The Free Forum in 1963, devoted to the topic of the documentary filmmaker's responsibility toward his or her era, enabled participants to revisit this question.

Devoting his contribution to the works of Ivens, the historian of Polish cinema Jerzy Toeplitz made a point of emphasizing the importance of *Pierwsze lata* (1947, *The First Years*), which Ivens had shot in Czechoslovakia, Bulgaria, and Poland in 1946–1947. Though it had screened at Leipzig in 1956, *The First Years* was actually censored east of the Iron Curtain. Shot before the communist takeover, the film painted a picture that scarcely corresponded to what was now required by the new regimes in the socialist republics: Bulgarian peasants looked too miserable; Polish reality too bleak. Toeplitz regretted this turn of events and said, "We are at fault for not having had the courage to show our audiences the film as Joris Ivens actually shot it." Many grave mistakes had been committed in the preceding years, he continued, and the filmmakers had let them pass; now, however, they should at least have the courage to acknowledge those made in the cultural domain. Ending his scathing tirade, patently demarcating the line dividing Stalinists and non-Stalinists, Toeplitz concluded, "And Marxist dialectic is on the side of Joris Ivens" (*Protokoll 1962* 1963: 25).

Free Forum discussions in the early 1960s thus revealed profound differences between documentarists not only from the East and the West but also from different East Bloc countries. At Leipzig, a critical approach was primarily articulated by the Polish participants, who were always at the forefront of reformist movements in their country. In fact, Toeplitz was dismissed in 1968 as rector of the Polish Film School in Łódź, in the wake of the wave of anti-Semitism launched by a government eager to find a scapegoat for unrest primarily provoked by students and workers (Michalek 1992).[23]

Such criticisms were voiced by participants from the West in equal measure. Grierson, however, never disavowed the function of documentaries as propaganda. "Basically, I have never been a documentary filmmaker. . . . I'm nothing but a propagandist—a propagandist for film, television, and the press, for my country and against fascism," he remarked in 1964. Grierson had developed his concept of documentary film and democratic propaganda based on the research of American thinkers, such as Walter Lippmann, and political scientists, notably at the University of Chicago.[24] According to Grierson, in the context of a modern society that was increasingly difficult to grasp and understand, it was the duty of a democratic government to explain its policies to its citizens in the most transparent, engaging, and clear way possible.[25] He further argued that the documentary had become an indispensable tool to convey to audiences a sense of global thinking and a determination to cooperate internationally (Hahn 1997).

Grierson also stated, however, that "anything to do with self-reflection, . . . or that suggests a tedious formal report is foreign to me," thereby criticizing the official selection at the Leipzig Festival. To his way of thinking, the films produced by DEFA documentarists did not mirror the reality that East Germans faced every day. Depicting the reality of East German society in its current state was the weak spot of these documentaries. All was not lost, however, as Grierson summed up: "In the meantime you have shot some fine documentaries like the one about the furnace builders. But it's still not enough. You could and should film more about what you do and produce in your life" (Herlinghaus 1982: 55–56).

Renewing East German Documentary Film

Grierson thus paid tribute to a young documentary filmmaker, Jürgen Böttcher, who had indeed garnered everybody's attention when *Ofenbauer* (1962, *Furnace Makers*) was screened at Leipzig in 1962. It attested to a possible resurgence of documentary filmmaking at DEFA in connection with what was happening elsewhere. Within DEFA, some young filmmakers showed their longing to innovate. Freshly graduated from the film school in Babelsberg, they were soon able to shoot their own films. This generation experienced a real opportunity after the erection of the Wall in August 1961, which made working conditions for DEFA employees residing in West Berlin virtually impossible and their resignation less than voluntary (Junge 2000).

Born in 1931, Jürgen Böttcher was among the first to offer a fresh perspective on East German documentary filmmaking. Trained as a painter, he had to abandon his studies at the Dresden Academy of Fine Arts in 1953 after being accused of "cosmopolitanism, existentialism, and formalism." From 1953 to 1954 he taught classes as an independent artist (Blume and März 2003).[26] Increasingly faced with difficulties in practicing his art, in 1955 he began studies at the newly established film school in Potsdam-Babelsberg and joined the DEFA Studios in 1961.

Released in 1962, *Furnace Makers* was Böttcher's fourth film. He inherited the project from the former director, who had fallen ill (Böttcher 2000). Typical for the time, the film focused on a technical challenge in the context of a unified action, time, and place. In the ironworks at Eisenhüttenstadt, a newly constructed town built between 1951 and 1954 on the border with Poland, the task was to film a spectacular operation due to take place at the steel complex: a fifty-six-meter tall blast furnace weighing 2,000 tons had to be moved eighteen meters (Moine 2002). The film crew moved its equipment onto the site during the initial stages of the operation in order to familiarize itself with the universe of the steel mill.

The project was conceived in the spirit of the aforementioned Bitterfeld Way—the new trend in East German cultural policy whereby intellectuals were supposed to reach out to the working classes and testify to their working and living conditions (Emmerich 2000). Significantly, the film's commentary was written in the first-person plural: "We have only eight short meters ahead of us." Collective work had become a central theme in all cultural output.[27] The documentary thus inscribed itself within the prevailing official discourse

Figure 3.3. Jürgen Böttcher (*center*) and crew shooting *Furnace Makers* (1962). © DEFA Stiftung.

in which the artist appeared as observer and witness of the modernization of East German society.

Furnace Makers differed from other propaganda films of the time, however, in part because the task at hand evolved into a pretext to experiment with a new style. All the technical means available at the time were deployed to recreate the atmosphere and difficulty of the work. The director reduced the commentary to an absolute minimum, preferring to use direct audio takes; the soundtrack thus conveys the harsh din produced by steel ropes and machines under tension. The filmmaker imposed his vision of constant struggle: "I had to hold my ground to the very end to retain the ambient sound of the working conditions just as they were . . . and those alone: they were determined to add . . . as an illustration . . . segments of Beethoven's [Sonata] Pathétique, as was the convention at the time" (Böttcher 2000: 12). So as to film "from within," the highly mobile crew integrated itself into the group of workers, despite the reluctance of plant officials to allow them to stand directly under the colossus while it was being moved (Böttcher 2000). The crew was thus able to shoot close-ups of the workers' precise gestures and their tense and concentrated faces. Some fleeting shots even reveal a cinematographer with a handheld camera and a soundman squatting beside the workers.

Even if at this juncture the worker still occupied the role of iconic figure in the socialist-humanist community—the positive hero of Socialist Realism—the director's gaze was becoming more personal, trying to break away from a style that until then had been more like a hieratical staging. *Furnace Makers* won the first prize at the 1962 Leipzig Festival and Böttcher became one of the chosen; but this triumph also gave the young filmmaker an opportunity to make a name for himself outside of the GDR and to attempt to claim his place in an international world of filmmaking that was experiencing a fresh impetus.

Direct Cinema

In France during the summer of 1960, the filmmaker and anthropologist Jean Rouch, the sociologist Edgar Morin, and the Québécois cameraman Michel Brault shot *Chronique d'un été* (1960, *Chronicle of a Summer*), a documentary that described itself as an "essay in *cinéma vérité*." Aside from the film's sociological aspirations, the lightweight equipment employed, still in its experimental phase, represented a break with existing documentary production methods. The new 16mm cameras and a new type of sound recorder simultaneously gave birth to both the recording of synchronized sound and greater mobility during the shoot. The profound changes generated a new approach to filmmaking, first called "*cinéma vérité*" and then, after 1963, "Direct Cinema" (Marsolais 1974).[28] This approach was particularly noticeable in Canada,[29] the United States, and France, where filmmakers and technicians enjoyed access to good technology, high-quality documentary traditions, and freedom of movement and expression (Gauthier 1995). But what role could documentary filmmaking in other countries play within this trend, which entailed both technical and ideological stakes?

The Leipzig Festival welcomed leading filmmakers from "the direct generation," in the words of Guy Gauthier (1995: 266). The American School was very well represented. Richard Leacock, for example, attended the festival in 1964, and his film *A Happy Mother's Day* (1963)—which documented the life of the middle-class family with the first surviving quintuplets in US history—was awarded second prize in the full-length features category. Born in 1921, Leacock, who had been Robert Flaherty's assistant, played a vital role in the development of Direct Cinema in the United States.

Albert Maysles also came to Leipzig in 1964. He and his brother David worked from 1954 to 1963 with Robert Drew, founder of Drew Associates, where American Direct Cinema directors gathered before forming their own production company in 1962. Two of their works screened at Leipzig in 1964. The first, *Showman* (1963)—also known as *Mr. Levine*—is the portrait of a businessman and had screened at UNESCO in 1962 during a debate about Direct Cinema (Rouch 1963). The second, *What's Happening! The Beatles in the U.S.A.* (1964), was screened in a shortened twenty-minute version adapted for theatrical release, having initially been shot for television; indeed, the American directors quickly transitioned to working primarily for television, which ensured both broadcasting and funding (Herlinghaus 1982).

The presence of these Americans at Leipzig was paramount for DEFA documentary filmmakers. As the East German director of photography Werner Kohlert, born in 1939, declared in 1984, "In my youth, Eisenstein served as a model for all my work. Then, about twenty years ago, I saw the *cinéma vérité* films that Richard Leacock brought to Leipzig, and from that moment on my camera work blended Leacock's freedom of style and Eisenstein's stylistic formality!"[30]

Obviously, this diverse group of documentarists did not fit into the political schema of the orthodox Marxists. Soviet documentaries had deeply marked many of them, however. According to Jean Rouch, Leacock had been impressed by Victor Tourine's *Turksib* (1929), which was about the Turkestan-Siberian railroad, even before discovering Flaherty's films (Devarrieux and Navacelle 1988; Gauthier 1995). Even Rouch, like other French Direct Cinema directors, aligned himself with Soviet role models such as Dziga Vertov and Aleksandr Medvedkin. And Albert Maysles, in 1955, had devoted his first documentary to the USSR. In an interview at Leipzig in 1964, Maysles commented that his feature-length *Showman* attempted to present both the positive and the negative aspects of a businessman: a paragon of success, but also an individual swept along by a capitalist system that was rejected elsewhere. Maysles concluded that, although he was by no means a Marxist, he did think that documentaries had to be dialectical (Herlinghaus 1982). Year after year, Direct Cinema documentarists seemed primarily to find common ground in their desire to represent the social and political reality around them as directly as possible.

It was, however, Chris Marker, a French filmmaker of the Direct generation with a highly individual cinematographic style and screen-writing method, who opened the debate on *cinéma vérité* at Leipzig in 1963. Marker, then about thirty, swiftly attracted attention at Leipzig. He was among the first guests, attending the festival regularly from 1960 to 1968. His career trajectory was of particular interest to the organizers. He had collaborated with Alain Resnais in 1953 on *Les statues meurent aussi* (1953, *Statues Also Die*), an essayistic film denouncing colonialism that was heavily censored in France for about ten years. They had also worked together on *Night and Fog* in 1955. His paean to the Chinese communist regime shot in 1955, *Un dimanche à Pékin* (1956, *Sundays in Peking*), was also censored, as was his *¡Cuba, Sí!* in 1961. In 1963, Leipzig finally could program one of his films, *Le joli mai* (1963, *The Lovely Month of May*).

Two years after *A Chronicle of a Summer*, as the war in Algeria was winding down, Marker and his cameraman Jean Lhomme undertook a similar project.

Taking to the Parisian streets, they randomly interviewed passers-by or persons with whom they were acquainted, asking them questions about, for example, their idea of happiness. Marker and Lhomme shot *The Lovely Month of May* with a prototype of the lightweight Éclair film camera. The use of the freely moving handheld camera along with synchronized sound gave the film a new lightness and visual acuity, to which was added Marker's commentary. Considered "a philosophical essay, an ironic chanson, a social testimony, a sociological test" (Gehler 1963), *The Lovely Month of May* made a strong impression on East German filmmakers and journalists. The West German critic Enno Patalas (1964) observed, "For young East German documentarists, Marker's film contains numerous references to their own attempts. Some of them even saw it as a manifesto for what they want to attain. For them, the fact that Marker was awarded the Golden Dove unquestionably represents encouragement." Jürgen Böttcher was among those East German documentary filmmakers profoundly influenced by Marker. The particular impact of *The Lovely Month of May* came from the original sound and the extended interviews with authentic heroes from the streets.[31]

Böttcher's latest film was also in competition at Leipzig in 1963. *Stars* (1963) depicted a collective portrait of a team of young women working at a lightbulb plant in East Berlin. The ironic title alluded to the glitz and glamour of the cinema, in contrast to the severe and tedious job done by these factory workers. Shot at the workshop, during both working hours and breaks, over the course of the film the members of the team gradually become individuals. According to Böttcher's cinematographer, Christian Lehmann, conditions on location were challenging: while the camera they used did allow them to shoot with synchronized sound, it wasn't silent, and they had to wrap it in blankets to reduce the noise it made.

During editing they also had to remix the sound takes with other ambient noises.[32] The snippets of conversation captured are thus more or less audible to the public, something that critics made sure to point out at the time. Because *Stars* was filmed by a crew that was more mobile than usual, with equipment that was substantially less imposing than the big cameras on stands, however, the workers don't come across as intimidated or wooden. As he had in *Furnace Makers*, Böttcher demonstrated a deep respect for those being filmed and their work, and yet further de-mythicized the conventions set by official propaganda for representing the working class. After having watched the documentary at Leipzig, Chris Marker (1964: 201) declared:

> Before I conclude, allow me to mention one more film, which seems to me to admirably represent the new trend, which reflects reality as it is and ushers the viewer towards a better understanding of reality. I am referring to the film *Stars*, by Jürgen Böttcher, and in this way I would like to publicly tell him that I consider his film to be one of the best.

Böttcher's international reputation, which had been tentatively proffered the previous year with *Furnace Makers,* was thus sealed.

Patalas (1964) greeted the record of achievements of the 1963 festival warmly in an article symbolically titled "Leipzig: A Path toward the Neighbor." He regarded the conferral of the Golden Dove on Marker's *The Lovely Month of May* as a "joyful indicator" and went on to conclude:

> Bearing in mind the past practices of East Bloc festivals, we might well expect that the first prize would go to a masterful piece from the "socialist camp"—for example, to *The Russian Miracle*—and a second prize to a militant film from the West. . . . Admittedly, we heard the usual tirades whenever Mr. von Schnitzler[33] appeared in the Hotel Astoria bar. And yet, we also heard very different things, and not just from young filmmakers and enthusiasts. The Cold War did not take place at Leipzig.

Other films, aside from *Furnace Makers,* also set out to address "the tendency to embellish without having anything to say, which paralyzed documentary production" (Gass 1982: 405). In 1963, during a seemingly never-ending shoot,[34] Karl Gass directed *Feierabend* (1964, *Leisure*).[35] It was shot on location at Erdölleitung Freundschaft, a new facility at the petrochemical combine in Schwedt/Oder that went into production in the winter of 1963–1964. The plant mobilized nearly 9,000 workers, who lived away from their families in temporary barracks—a truly forlorn town in the midst of a no man's land that the workers quickly dubbed the "taiga." For the directors, Schwedt presented a socially sensitive zone: how were workers to occupy themselves after their long day's toil?

Leisure presents all the activities offered to the workers: music and painting classes, ping-pong matches, chess, dancing, and so forth. But Gass's ironic gaze swiftly challenges the idyllic portrait of this community of workers engaged in healthy pursuits. Scenes shot at the company canteen introduce a strikingly different tone: the workers, still in their work clothes, their faces and hands blackened, avidly drink beer after beer and sing and play cards in an increasingly pernicious atmosphere, while in the background spirited music intermingles with the ambient din. The camera captures comic impersonations, words exchanged, and even a few steps of the twist at the end of the evening, depicting a moment of pure relaxation that contrasts with the other recreational venues shown, such as the library, where silence and concentration reign.

Leisure's highly idiosyncratic style is primarily based on a new relationship between the camera and the people filmed. "It was a matter of finding a link to Schwedt's reality (= a piece of the truth about the GDR)" was how the film's authors explained it (Biegholdt et al. 1964: 265). To achieve this, the crew split into two or three groups. The technology had to be as unobtrusive as possible: "We were in the background, discreet, patient" (267). Many of the workers already knew the crew members, who had been living in Schwedt for months. While in the canteen it was feasible to shoot with a handheld camera thanks to the prevailing background noise that was loud enough to muffle the sound of the camera; other sequences, shot in silent places, had to be filmed with much less handy cameras, or even with hidden cameras, like the scenes shot in the library (Biegholdt et al. 1964).

Leisure was acclaimed as an East German version of Direct Cinema: the BBC broadcast it, and the British Film Institute listed it among the best documentaries of 1964. In the GDR, in contrast, it was screened out of competition at Leipzig and not widely distributed. Starting from a theme that corresponded to the concerns of the authorities, Gass—only two years after making his virulently polemical *Look at This City* about the Berlin Wall—had made a film that really displeased them, for it revealed the inherent limits of that branch of public policy not regulated by law. The workers, in contrast, reacted enthusiastically to the documentary when it was screened in Schwedt.[36]

Leisure remained a relatively isolated example among DEFA productions and within the œuvre of Karl Gass, who never again attained such freedom of tone and perspective. The political context, like working conditions in the GDR, did not foster the development of Direct Cinema.

A Window (Slightly) Open to the World

In the early 1960s, the Leipzig Festival was thus a venue for debates at which distinguished film directors and film enthusiasts from the East and West took opposing positions. The participation of such renowned figures of the film world seemed to ensure the festival's international success, notwithstanding dissension and tensions that rapidly emerged concerning political and aesthetic approaches to documentary cinema. What impact did all these debates and screenings have within East Germany?

In East Germany in the early 1960s, the "communists who'd been in exile and the camps" were starting to be replaced in the positions in which they had exercised political, cultural, and economic responsibilities in the GDR (Kott 2000: 207). The new generation, comprising young people who had grown up in the "new socialist Germany," took over in part. In 1961, Hans Bentzien became minister for culture at the age of thirty-four; Jochen Mückenberger took the reins at the DEFA Feature Film Studio at thirty-two; and director Konrad Wolf, at thirty-nine, was elected president of the GDR's Academy of Arts (AdK; Agde 1991).

While pioneers of documentary cinema were certainly in the spotlight at Leipzig, the younger generation from the Babelsberg film school was also well represented; its members were eager to attend the festival to absorb all that was being discussed and screened in its enthusiastic atmosphere and to attempt to find their own niche. The DEFA Studio for Documentary Film welcomed its first batch of graduates from the film school. Like Jürgen Böttcher, they upheld concepts of documentary film that differed from those of their elders and were curious to explore all the possibilities offered by evolving technology. As such, these up-and-coming directors represented a challenge to the system implemented by the founding generation.

For them, Leipzig offered an opportunity. "Leipzig's Capitol Cinema was a classroom for a week, for the forty students from the Babelsberg film academy," rejoiced Winfried Junge at the age of twenty-one, when he participated in the festival for the first time, in 1956 ("Joris Ivens und Joop Huisken" 1956). At a later stage, Junge recollected, "I belong to the generation that personally knew the 'elders.' Sometimes friendships even developed, as was the case with Karabasz, with the Pozners, with Erwin Leiser. We didn't want to miss out on this window onto the world" (Gass et al. 1997: 31).

In 1963, a special session was organized around student films from the film schools in Babelsberg, Prague, Budapest, Belgrade, Paris, and Vienna (Ebbrecht-Hartmann 2017); 150 students and teachers from some twenty nations then gathered to discuss their respective experiences. The model of the Balázs Béla Studio (BBS) in Budapest was discussed at length (Lehmann and Wiehring von Wendrin 1997). Founded in 1958, the BBS as of 1960 functioned as an autonomous association, offering graduates from the Budapest film school the material support needed to produce their films, be they documentary, fiction feature, or experimental. In 1961, the BBS had twenty-six members; in 1965, the number had already tripled, a sign of the dynamism and success it represented, in keeping with Hungarian film production (Jeancolas 2001). Foreign critics always closely scrutinized the screenings of films from the Babelsberg film school that followed and were often warm in their praise.

Retrospectives: A Major Asset

For young DEFA directors, not only did the Leipzig Festival represent an invaluable meeting place, it also enabled them to discover or to review the classics, thanks to its retrospectives. The idea of having retrospectives originated with Wolfgang Kernicke, the representative of the Filmmakers' Club. "The backdrop for that impetus is readily understandable: the fear of losing our success and our international reputation in the wake of the construction of the Wall" was how Wolfgang Klaue (1997: 33) described it in hindsight.[37] The project corresponded perfectly with the agenda of Herbert Volkmann, the director of the State Film Archive of the GDR as of 1959.[38] Founded in

October 1955, the archive was still finding its feet and needed to establish contacts with foreign institutions.

Organizing retrospectives required relying upon a network including nonstate institutions—film societies, film clubs, and certain cinematheques—as well as state-run structures, such as the various national film archives. Personal connections played a paramount role, given that at the time the GDR neither enjoyed diplomatic recognition nor had a sufficient budget at its disposal.[39] When it came to organizing the Alberto Cavalcanti retrospective in 1962, for example, none of the documentarist's works were to be found in East German archives. Putting on the retrospective—and avoiding shipping and rental costs—required the help of John Grierson, Paul Rotha, and Cavalcanti himself (Klaue 1997). The organizers generally overcame the challenges, for the retrospective series represented a trump card for the festival that attracted foreign cinephiles; the catalogues published to coincide with the retrospectives were in themselves an event, as publications dealing with documentary film were a rarity at the time.

The early retrospective programs were devoted to genre pioneers acclaimed in both East and West: Dziga Vertov (1960), Alberto Cavalcanti (1962), and Joris Ivens (1963). At the end of 1960, Karl Gass, the chairman of the jury, expressed his wish to organize a retrospective featuring French or British films.[40] Organizing such an ambitious program still represented too formidable a task for the organizers, however, and the 1961 retrospective was based on the theme of the festival's new slogan, "Films of the World—for Peace in the World." The Flaherty retrospective in 1964 was instrumental in drawing numerous filmmakers and critics, from East and West alike. Some theoretical adjustments were still called for, however, as can be gleaned in a text from the East German Ministry of Culture:

> To date, [Flaherty's œuvre] has only been fully appreciated by bourgeois filmgoers. However, it is essential to judge the humanistic and democratic tendencies present in Flaherty's work in terms of the aesthetics of Marxist-Leninist film. Consequently, it seems of the utmost importance, within the framework of our cultural policy and on the occasion of such a major international event in the GDR, to present Flaherty as the "good American," the friend of F. D. Roosevelt.[41]

Aside from perseverance and patience, organizing the retrospective demanded diplomatic skills and a thorough awareness of politically sensitive subjects that divided filmmakers, critics, and politicians, such as *cinéma vérité*.

Technological and Other Handicaps

The international cinematic effervescence of the 1960s was based on technical advances in filming techniques and more sensitive film that enabled filming outdoors without recourse to artificial lighting, as well as a political era that was putting existing cultural and political systems into question in more or less radical and social ways. The GDR was one of the first regimes in the East Bloc where the development of a new documentary style butted against both political and technical constraints, which were difficult to disentangle from one another. In 1960, Hermann Herlinghaus was hailing the prevailing dynamism in French, Polish, and Czechoslovakian short films, which "were undertaking fresh approaches, surprising us with original works where human faces and social reality were exposed in a highly impressive manner and in an innovative formal language" (*Protokoll 1960* 1961).

The program at the Leipzig Festival made little room for those Czechoslovakian, Hungarian, and Polish documentaries, which reflected the reforms under way in their respective countries. Jürgen Böttcher and the film critic Erika Richter recall having seen Polish films and Czechoslovakian feature films by Miloš Forman and Jiří Menzel—not in movie theaters, where they were rarely programmed, but at private screenings organized by the Filmmakers' Club or the cultural institutes of the respective countries in East Berlin. "All the filmmakers and critics attended those screenings."[42] With their freedom of expression and tone, often insolent and showing little respect for official morality, and offering a more accurate representation of daily life, these films left a profound impression[43]—but they were only available to the privileged few.

The specific phenomenon of *cinéma vérité*, which formed part of this larger movement, perturbed partisans of a form of cinema in keeping with the dominant ideology. It was, of course, necessary that "bourgeois documentarists in capitalist countries" be able to question conditions existing in their societies: "the problem of racism and the Algerian question in France, the fate of those deprived of their human rights—the excluded, the Blacks, and the young—in the United States, . . . the housing conditions of workers in the suburbs in England" (Baumert 1964: 310).

On a broader level, filmmakers such as Roberto Rossellini discredited the very concept of *cinéma vérité*. During a debate at UNESCO in 1962, the Italian director virulently criticized the emphasis placed on new technological conditions of shooting. "There is no technique to grapple with reality. Only a moral stance can do this. . . . Your fascination with the camera is a sick fascination of the weak-willed, that serves no purpose" (Rouch 1963). It is noteworthy that Gass himself rejected the term *cinéma vérité*; he underlined that he had shot *Leisure* in 1963 before seeing *The Lovely Month of May* at Leipzig and thus refuted the notion that he had in any way been influenced (Gass 1982). There remained, however, a formidable challenge for Gass: acquiring better equipment in order to improve the quality of DEFA productions. Notwithstanding Rossellini's utterances on the subject, technical developments did play a vital role in carrying the seeds of a new language.

The improvement of film sound through direct recording on location utterly changed the work of documentary filmmakers in the 1960s, just as studio sound technology had revolutionized feature films around 1930. In France, the camera Éclair 16 (or Éclair Coutant), a 16mm camera invented by André Coutant and produced by Pathé, was used as a prototype in filming *A Chronicle of a Summer* and *The Lovely Month of May* (Pinel et al. 2009). Lightweight and silent, this camera synchronized sound by means of a cable connected to the sound recorder before becoming fully independent.

DEFA documentarists, however, had only technically flawed equipment at their disposal. In 1964, in talking about making *Stars*, Böttcher remarked, "Here we still don't have very advanced equipment that would be easy to handle and technically perfect" (Böttcher 1964: 7). He thought that a rapid improvement of sound-recording technology was badly needed. In fact, as of about that time the montage depended on the utterances of those interviewed on the street. "The character of the image has changed, the rhythm of the scenes and the cuts must adapt to the breath of the narrator on the street" (Böttcher 1964: 8). The young man's dissatisfactions echo those of a more battle-hardened director; by the time he finished filming *Leisure*, Gass came to the same conclusions: "Our determination to achieve international standing in documentary filmmaking is equally dependent on technical challenges. Smaller! Lighter! Quieter! Discreter! This ought to be our motto" (Biegholdt et al. 1964: 275). His appeal largely fell on deaf ears.

Cinematographer Christian Lehmann provides some background on the two directors' comments. It was actually possible to film with lightweight equipment in the GDR, but only on condition of working for television, which had the financial wherewithal to purchase the latest model cameras from West Germany. Those who opted to work exclusively in cinema had less effective equipment at their disposal.[44] It seemed as though the situation was deadlocked. In 1964, Böttcher had to admit:

> [*The Lovely Month of May*] is unquestionably a work of genius. . . . But the comparison is of little use to us. On a number of counts the standard is completely different. Quite frankly, the plea for us to produce films of a similar quality—which is indirectly directed at us by most critics, and at times nearly turned into a reproach for not yet having done so—both astonishes and bewilders me. (Böttcher 1964: 11)

The personal contacts established at Leipzig with foreign filmmakers, East and West, thus exposed even more clearly the limits placed on East German filmmakers and critics when it came to openness toward the world. In a long account of the 1964 festival, written for the Ministry of Culture, critic and journalist Hermann Herlinghaus painted a rather gloomy picture of the situation:

Compared with their foreign colleagues, the [East German] documentarists and critics are the most uninformed about current problems in international documentary production.... Hence, while no example of *cinéma vérité* has yet reached us, our Soviet, Czechoslovakian, Polish, and Hungarian colleagues have long known at least two or five.[45]

Film directors from other Eastern European countries were often more in touch with what was then happening in the West. Hungarian director András Kovács, for example, attended—"as luck would have it," as he put it—the 1963 congress held in Lyon, France by the research unit of the French RTF broadcaster, during which the term "Direct Cinema" first surfaced.[46] Problems related to distribution and access to foreign films, especially documentaries, were therefore central in the GDR. When the couple Erika and Rolf Richter interviewed Richard Leacock in 1964, they confessed that they had not yet seen *Primary* (1960)—a documentary following John F. Kennedy and Hubert Humphrey during the Wisconsin primary, which was already widely known and screened, especially in Europe (Herlinghaus 1982).

Herlinghaus continued his report by deploring the fact that no film scholar had as yet had the opportunity to travel to festivals in the West, notably to Oberhausen and Mannheim. Leipzig remained the sole international meeting place for filmmakers and film professionals from East Germany. Filmmakers could only attend foreign festivals if their films were selected, and only if the East German authorities allowed them to travel abroad. Herlinghaus's account represented a warning shot in which he ultimately questioned the meaning of Leipzig: "The Festival finds itself at a juncture where it is difficult to define what its specific character is."[47]

In fact, the festival was still in the process of changing. After 1955, and especially following its internationalization in 1960, the festival was attracting leading names in documentary filmmaking and thus allowed a glimpse of the innovative global trends prevailing at the turn of the 1960s. Conversely, Leipzig also facilitated making a new generation of East German filmmakers known abroad. Around 1964, a transitional phase was initiated. It is important to try to fathom the shift that resulted in terms of East German cultural policy.

Notes

1. What they had in common was that they all were trying to assert themselves against existing production systems: auteurist cinema in France, the more politically and socially engaged Free Cinema in Great Britain, and independent cinema in the United States. In the East as well—in Czechoslovakia, Poland, Hungary, and the USSR—

young feature film directors questioned official artistic conventions and changed tone and themes; the films of the Prague Spring are the best known examples.
2. For 1960, see SAPMO-BArch DY 30 IV 2/9.06/228, p. 208; for 1961, *Protokoll 1961* 1962.
3. See, for example, the forthcoming history thesis of Victor Barbat at the University Paris 1 Panthéon-Sorbonne, tentatively titled "Roman Karmen, la vulgate soviétique de l'Histoire. Stratégies et mode opératoire d'un opérateur-documentariste au XXe siècle."
4. Jerzy Toeplitz (1909–1995) is the author of the classic *History of Cinema Art*, translated from Polish into several languages.
5. Karl Gass, Bemerkungen zur III. Leipziger Kurz- und Dokumentarfilmwoche, Potsdam-Babelsberg, 24 November 1960, SAPMO-BArch DY 30 IV 2/9.06/228, p. 146.
6. Protokoll der 41. Leitungssitzung der VVB Film, 28 November 1960, SAPMO-BArch DR1/4380.
7. Bericht über die Durchführung der III. Leipziger Woche, 13–19 November 1960, SAPMO-BArch DY 30 IV 2/9.06/228, p. 213.
8. This text was signed by forty-three directors and later by many others.
9. This film thus precedes the Group of Thirty, but the director was active in this group.
10. This film had been awarded the Jean Vigo Prize and selected at Cannes in 1960.
11. For an analysis of the genesis of this film and its reception, see Lindeperg 2007.
12. The cap of the guard at the Pithiviers camp had to be hidden, as it allowed viewers to identify him as a French policeman and thus too clearly revealed the responsibility of the French Vichy government for internment on French territory. See Delage and Guigueno 2004.
13. II. Kultur- und Dokumentarfilmwoche in Leipzig, Press Release by Günter Klein, SAPMO-BArch DR1/1663.
14. SAPMO-BArch DR 117/vorl., p. 100. The author thanks Günther Jordan for indicating this source.
15. SAPMO-BArch DR 117/vorl., p. 100. It was not possible to determine whether the explanatory short film was ultimately produced or not (Lindeperg 2007; Mückenberger 2000).
16. The text for the East German edition was written by Henryk Keisch, who had been in the French Resistance during the war. Protokoll 0386/60, *Night and Fog:* projection for the commission on 13 June 1960, decision made on 15 July 1960, SAPMO-BArch DR1/4356.
17. Aktennotiz, Vorbereitende Besprechung zur 3. Leipziger Kulturfilmwoche am 3 May 57, signed by Kurt Herlinghaus, BArch-FArch, Leipzig, 1956.
18. From the SED ZK to HVFilm, Zu einigen Fragen des gegenwärtigen Standes und der Weiterentwicklung des Dokumentarfilms in der DDR, 12 March 1957, SAPMO-BArch DR1/4194.
19. Author's interview with Erika Richter, Berlin, Germany (1 November 2000).
20. Information for Comrade Alfred Kurella. Betrifft die Durchführung der III. Leipziger Woche, November 1960, office of Alfred Kurella, Cultural Commission of the Politburo, SAPMO-BArch DY 30 IV 2/9.06/228, p. 40.
21. In order to reconstitute the content and atmosphere of discussions, it is important to compare written archives and oral sources. Although transcripts of debates appeared in the minutes published by the festival from 1960 to 1964, after this they were not.

As a result, we must excavate the echoes in the press, reactions in various accounts of the festival, and memories of participants.
22. *Drifters* (1929) was the first documentary shot by John Grierson; it was dedicated to the hard work of herring fishermen in the North Sea. The film made a big impact, as much for its style—which was similar to that of Soviet documentarists—as for its subject matter.
23. For more, see chapter 5.
24. On the work and thought of John Grierson, see Hörl 1996.
25. In Great Britain, Grierson worked for the Ministry of Commerce and the Post.
26. The first film made by Jürgen Böttcher, *Drei von vielen* (1961, *Three of Many*), is a documentary short about three young men who studied with him as amateur artists at the Volkshochschule in Dresden: Peter Hermann, engraver; Peter Graf, truck driver; and Peter Makolies, stone carver. The film shows them painting, talking, playing jazz, taking walks—conveying the atmosphere in which Böttcher worked in Dresden and his circle of friends and colleagues. The well-known painter A. R. Penck, a friend of Böttcher, also appears in the film and Manfred Krug narrates it—neither are mentioned in the credits. *Three of Many* ended up being banned; the representation of these amateur artists, who were too bohemian, did not correspond closely enough to the official discourse, especially right after the Wall went up and given that the paintings produced by Böttcher under the name Strawalde (which he uses as a painter) were under renewed critique for their "formalism."
27. For more on this topic, see Damus 1991.
28. During a colloquium on *cinéma vérité* organized in Lyon, director Mario Ruspoli proposed the more neutral term "Direct Cinema."
29. It was namely in Canada—at the National Film Office, which John Grierson had founded—that such important advances were made in film equipment in the late 1950s.
30. Stephen Peet, "Documentaries, The Leipzig Festival," newspaper and date not indicated, BArch-FArch, Leipzig, 1984.
31. Author's interview with Jürgen Böttcher, Berlin-Karlshorst, Germany (31 October 2000); Herlinghaus 1982.
32. Author's interview with Christian Lehmann, Berlin, Germany (22 August 2000).
33. Karl-Eduard von Schnitzler was a polemical Cold Warrior who hosted the East German TV show *Der schwarze Kanal* from 1960 to 1989. He was also the narrator in Karl Gass's 1962 documentary *Look at This City*.
34. The film *Asse*—the name of the brigade to which he belonged—came out in 1966.
35. On the term *Feierabend*, see Korff 2009.
36. Author's interview with Karl Gass, Berlin/Kleinmachnow, Germany (18 August 2000).
37. Wolfgang Klaue, born in 1935, directed the GDR State Film Archive from 1969 to 1990 and the International Federation of Film Archives (FIAF) from 1979 to 1985.
38. Herbert Volkmann (1901–1983), a member of the SED as of 1946, was the finance director of the DEFA Feature Film Studio and then director of the GDR State Film Archive from 1959 to 1969. The archive became the sole organizer of the retrospectives starting in 1962.
39. Author's interview with Wolfgang Klaue, Berlin, Germany (30 June 1999).
40. Karl Gass, Bemerkungen zur III. Leipziger Kurz- und Dokumentarfilmwoche, November 1960, SAPMO-BArch DY 30 IV 2/9.06/228, p. 151.

41. Concept for the seventh Leipzig Festival, Minister Hans Bentzien, Minister of Culture for the secrétariat of the ZK of the SED, SAPMO-BArch DR1/4272.
42. Author's interview with Erika Richter, Berlin, Germany (1 November 2000).
43. Author's interview with Jürgen Böttcher, Berlin-Karlshorst, Germany (31 October 2000).
44. Author's interview with Christian Lehmann, Berlin, Germany (22 August 2000).
45. Hermann Herlinghaus, summary of the Free Forum of the sixth International Festival in Leipzig, 13 January 1964, SAPMO-BArch DR1/4272, p. 14–16.
46. Back in Hungary, Kovács shot *Nehéz emberek* (1964, *Difficult People*). Except that he did not use a light camera with synchronous sound, the director followed the same method of investigation. In the field, he questioned and filmed people to highlight the blockage of a system: an engineer had designed a revolutionary plow, but the invention was not picked up (Jeancolas 2001).
47. H. Herlinghaus, Summary of the Free Forum of the sixth International Festival in Leipzig, 13 January 1964, SAPMO-BArch DR1/4272, p. 19.

PART II

Between Provincialism and International Dialogue (1964–1973)

CHAPTER 4
When the Tide Turns . . .

"The years from 1961 to 1965, as I remember them, were full of energy, years when we took risks and had great confidence in ourselves. We gained a lot in those years, in theory as well as in practice. And at the same time, in hindsight, we were of a staggering naïveté," recalled journalist and critic Klaus Wischnewski (1990: 35), reflecting the state of mind among East German intellectuals during the period of uncertainty following the construction of the Berlin Wall in August 1961. His statement attempts to explain the vast discrepancy between the high hopes that were entertained for a while by East German filmmakers and the abrupt and violent rupture of 1965–1966; this rupture was tied to the SED party's Eleventh Plenum, which effectively put an end to the phase of cultural renewal present during the first half of the 1960s.

Professionalizing the Festival

While the awarding of the 1963 Golden Dove to Chris Marker's *The Lovely Month of May* met with satisfaction in some quarters, it antagonized ideologues who felt that some members of the festival Selection Committee had been too lax about the official line. Signaling a tightening of control over the festival, new actors appeared and new rules were imposed in an effort to avoid an excessive openness toward innovative films from countries to the West. As of 1964, even before the tide began to turn,[1] the Leipzig Festival entered a new phase marked by several significant changes. A new festival director, the emergence of the new medium of television, and an increased commitment on the part of the regime were all meant to contribute to professionalizing the festival, which had become a key element in the cultural offensive of the GDR and the communist world in the international arena.

Although no one could predict in which direction the balance of power would ultimately shift, the Leipzig Festival was at the confluence of two currents within the regime: the reformist wing and the conservative wing, which was dominant at the state television station, Deutscher Fernsehfunk (DFF).

Change in Leadership

Wolfgang Kernicke, vice-president of the GDR Filmmakers' Club, had directed the Leipzig Festival since 1960, assisted by Hans Wegner. Although Günter Klein had been honorary president of the two earlier editions of the Leipzig Festival in 1955 and 1956, Kernicke had also been in charge of its practical implementation during these years. In the summer of 1964, however, Wolfgang Harkenthal (1922–2006) was tapped to become the new festival director; his career path helps shed light on the fresh direction being taken by the festival.[2]

Specializing in film distribution and programming, Harkenthal had worked in the film industry for many years. During the war, he had been sent to the Eastern Front, before being taken prisoner by the Americans. Upon his release in 1946—the year he joined the SED—he began working for the Soviet film distribution company Soyuz-Intorgkino, which would become Sovexportfilm. In August 1950, he then became the head of press and advertising for the new East German film distribution company, Progress Filmverleih. On 1 January 1956, Progress became a publicly owned enterprise (VEB) and subsequently exercised a monopoly on films distributed to East German movie theaters until 1990. Among his numerous functions at Progress, Harkenthal had co-organized screenings of documentary and educational films in the Soviet pavilion at the Leipzig Trade Fair as well as the "Film Weeks of the Popular Democracies,"[3] which took place in Berlin, Erfurt, and Leipzig. He had also been in charge of presenting new DEFA films to a chosen circle of people from the diplomatic corps and other official representatives to the GDR.[4]

In January 1954, Harkenthal was sent to complete his ideological and political training for a year at the Central School of Art and Literature in Erfurt. Earmarked for functionaries in the cultural sphere, the training was both strict and intensive, and all students were members of the SED. Harkenthal returned to Berlin in February 1955, this time as deputy director of the Central Administration for Film (HVFilm), where he was responsible for movie theaters.[5] His successive positions enabled Harkenthal to establish a broad network of contacts at both the central and local levels—that is, in East Berlin and the East German provinces—and, above all, to prove his ideological loyalty to his superiors. The fact that his duties had led him to travel to Moscow regularly, where he worked with members of Soviet film studios as well as Soviet film archives and the ministry in charge of film, was particularly helpful in this regard. These good personal relations with Soviet partners led Andrew Thorndike to propose, in 1963, that Harkenthal become the production director for his film *The Russian Miracle*.[6]

Coinciding with this, Harkenthal was given another assignment, which he could not refuse. In July 1958, as part of a vast reform package aimed at further centralizing the GDR's various economic sectors, a new association of all VEBs involved in film (VVB-Film) was created within HVFilm to manage film production and distribution. In charge was Ernst Hoffmann. When Hoffmann's relationship with Harkenthal swiftly deteriorated, the latter had to quit his post and was sent to Leipzig to be in charge of culture on the Regional District Council. While sending Harkenthal to the provinces was intended as a form of banishment, the new position actually turned out to be an opportunity in disguise. Arriving in Leipzig on New Year's Day in 1960, Harkenthal developed an important sphere of activity over the ensuing three years, thereby acquiring extensive knowledge of cultural life in the region of Saxony: "In Leipzig, my horizons broadened, I had to learn to respond to problems, to talk with artists, to help and support them whenever possible."[7]

In January 1963, with his penitence behind him, Harkenthal returned to East Berlin to become the deputy director of Progress, responsible for programming, press, and advertising. The following year, he actively participated in preparing a Gathering of German Youth (Deutschlandtreffen der Jugend), organized in East Berlin by the GDR's official youth movement, the Free German Youth (FDJ) and held from 16 to 18 May 1964.[8] For this occasion, East Berlin opened its borders to 25,000 participants from the FRG and West Berlin. The GDR presented the image of a more self-confident regime, ready to open up to the West and to address the younger generation's expectations. Pop music concerts and cultural events filled the three days, with more than 500,000 young East Germans in attendance. DEFA filmed the event, and the resulting documentary, *Drei Tage im Mai* (1964, *Three Days in May*), was publicly screened at the Leipzig Festival in November 1964. Having definitively proved himself, Harkenthal was appointed director of the Leipzig Festival, a position he held until 1973.

Well acquainted with Leipzig and the region, Harkenthal had already taken part in the festival as a member of the Selection Committee, as a delegate from Progress, in 1961. He was also aware of the vital role the festival was playing in the GDR's endeavors to acquire international recognition. From a more practical standpoint, his predecessor Wolfgang Kernicke greatly helped Harkenthal understand the festival's inner workings. They traveled together to the Karlovy Vary Festival and to Budapest to facilitate making contact with partners abroad. A self-confessed Russophile and loyal to the SED party, Harkenthal possessed the ideal background to ensure clearer ideological control over the festival.

According to Harkenthal, Kernicke neither knew, nor understood what had instigated his replacement. For the incoming festival director, however, the reason for this personnel change was clearly due to friction between Kernicke and Andrew Thorndike on the topic of Chris Marker's *The Lovely Month of May*, which Kernicke had initially discovered and subsequently championed. Thorndike was indeed against selecting Marker's film. It epitomized a form of cinema diametrically opposed to his conception of what a documentary should be. Thorndike had spent millions of East German marks trying to develop 70mm filmmaking in the GDR, even though it was obvious that this widescreen format had no future for documentaries.[9] Young filmmakers, in the West as in the East, were striving to find a cinematic language that could achieve greater proximity to the world and the society in which they were living.

In contrast, Thorndike was seeking a technique that augmented, rather than diminished, a film's distance from reality (Rother 1996). Gisela Harkenthal—at the time not yet married to the future festival director—sat on the Selection Committee and recalls heated discussions about *The Lovely Month of May*.[10] In the end Kernicke prevailed, and Marker's film was selected in competition. Thorndike's setback, notwithstanding his key position at Leipzig, clearly explains Kernicke's removal. Harkenthal, in whom Thorndike had already discerned a fine connoisseur of Soviet partners and an assertive proponent of the regime's cultural policy, was thus a natural choice as the next festival director.

The Advent of Television

The change in leadership made in 1964 was not as much a case of changing personnel as a settling of personal scores. At the heart of ongoing discussions lay the very spirit of the festival, however. Although none of the filmmakers or functionaries from the supervising institutions questioned the festival's essentially political stakes, there remained the question of which path the festival ought to take with respect to two opposing trends, one championed by the DEFA Film Studios and the other by DFF television.

While Soviet authorities had initially focused their attention on radio, they had also encouraged the establishment of an East German television station, following the sharpening of positions in the Cold War and the birth of two German states in 1949. In 1950, construction began on the Adlershof Studios in southeastern Berlin. On 21 December 1952—Stalin's birthday and a year after the maiden broadcasts of the West German station Nordwestdeutscher Rundfunk, based in Hamburg—DFF started its public programming (Laser 2001).[11] Although DEFA had remained the principal site for producing films in the early 1960s, television was becoming a medium to reckon with, in the

GDR as elsewhere. DFF had also begun to play a burgeoning role with respect to movies, at first commissioning DEFA to produce programs for broadcast, and increasingly exerted influence on government decision making.

In 1954, Heinz Adameck became the director of DFF, a position he held until the GDR collapsed in 1989. An apparatchik, Adameck had been in charge of training party functionaries in Thuringia before specializing in radio broadcasting. He professionalized the institution, clearly imposing the primacy of politics and ideology and enforcing strict discipline among his colleagues. Starting in early 1956, DFF broadcast on a daily basis (Heimann 2003). By the fall of that turbulent year, which saw the Suez Crisis and the Hungarian Uprising, the regime thought that DFF had not sufficiently defended the official line—especially as West German media outlets had proven to be reliable mouthpieces for the conservative Adenauer administration.[12] DFF henceforth became a focal point for the attention of the East German authorities, now aware of its national and international impact during the Cold War. In 1962, Adameck stated, "DFF broadcasts into West Germany the image of a new world, of a new society . . . , the image of peace, democracy, and socialism. It is an effective tool against the provocations of Bonn's policy" (Klessmann 1997: 393).

In addition to Adlershof, DFF appropriated the Johannisthal Studios, which hitherto had been earmarked for DEFA, whose employees were showing increasing concern about the competition.[13] In 1963, the Sixth SED Congress underlined the ideological function of DFF, which depended on the Agitation and Propaganda Department of the SED's Central Committee (ZK; Glatzer 1977). Documentary film, in contrast, was assigned to the Ministry of Culture and the Culture Department of the ZK.

The Leipzig Festival was to become one of the zones of friction between DEFA and DFF. In 1964, an additional milestone in bringing the festival under state control was reached, in accordance with a precise hierarchy. Within this constellation, television was the new stakeholder. Henceforth, the Leipzig Festival was to have three official organizers: the minister of culture, the first secretary of the GDR Filmmakers' Club, and the managing director of DFF.[14] The festival's practical implementation was to involve DEFA, Progress, the East German Film Archive, the Leipzig District and City Councils, the company managing movie theaters in the Leipzig district, and, lastly, DFF.[15] Significantly, the Free Forum debate at the Leipzig Festival in 1964 focused on the topic "Documentary—between Cinema and Television."[16] In that year, the festival also established an Egon Erwin Kisch Prize, named after the prominent German journalist of the interwar years and intended to honor films produced by DFF.[17] At the organizers' meeting following the 1964 festival, the second item on the agenda was about the need to enhance the "role of East German Television within the festival."[18]

Filmmakers, meanwhile, multiplied their attempts to reduce their rival's leverage. In 1964, the Selection Committee comprised its president, film historian Heinz Baumert; a secretary; and representatives from DFF, the Ministry for Foreign Affairs (MfAA), the Filmmakers' Club, and the DEFA Documentary Film Studio. These members were appointed by the festival's Organizing Committee, which was dependent upon the festival director who, ultimately, had the final say on internal disagreements.[19] It was only the following year, however, that the Selection Committee's specific status was clearly defined, when HVFilm and the Filmmakers' Club jointly decided that the selection of the festival's DEFA program would henceforth be discussed by a larger group, including the Filmmakers' Club, the East German Journalists Union and Artists Association, Ciné club management, and so on.[20] Thus squeezed into a minority position, DFF was the intended and direct target of this decision.

In addition to the 124 documentaries selected in 1965, 22 television productions and reports were included in the festival program. This number remained essentially the same over subsequent years, reflecting in part the still rather limited number of television productions. This was the case in the GDR as well as abroad, especially in Southern Hemisphere countries, which still represented a significant number of the films submitted to the Film Week. The balance of power would not undergo a change until 1968, when the festival decided to organize another competition solely confined to films produced by DFF.

The official arrival of the new broadcast medium into the festival's organization was also reflected in a substantial increase in budget, a development not to the liking of all institutions concerned. Thanks to this, DFF rapidly began to overshadow the DEFA Documentary Studio, even in terms of the established code of procedure. DFF director Adameck organized large receptions, where the buffet was noticeably more lavish than on the festival's opening night. In its diplomatic quests, the regime often made choices that, while politically advantageous, were rarely economically or financially so (Siebs 1999; Wippel 1996). Similarly, at the festival the regime's financial interests did not necessarily align with its political and diplomatic interests.

The ZK supported increasing the budget for the Leipzig Festival, in this case reaching a decision that was detrimental to the Finance Ministry, which was reluctant to increase its contribution to the festival yet again.[21] According to the ministry, considerable efforts had already been made to ensure an organizational structure commensurate with the festival's objectives.[22] In 1965, it proposed to contribute 550,000 East German marks, as had been apportioned the previous year. Expressing concern about improved control over spending, the ministry demanded among other things that the festival no longer underwrite the accommodation of guests from so-called capitalist countries and the FRG. The organizers' attention was drawn to the fact that the twelve East German delegates, who had attended the Oberhausen Festival, had had to pay not only their own travel costs but also their living expenses, as had the four delegates sent to the Edinburgh Festival; accordingly, the GDR should not hesitate to have guests from the West cover their own costs. The ZK, however, disagreed and requested an increase of 60,000 marks for 1965.[23]

The budget had to cover not only expenses tied to the ever-increasing participation of foreign guests—which there was absolutely no question of relinquishing—but also those for all the public relations work required to reach an ever-wider circle of filmmakers. This included overseas travel for the festival management, press conferences, and meetings to negotiate with potential partners, printing costs for advertising, and so forth. Such expenditures were also meant to keep the festival in the international arena, which was becoming increasingly competitive.

The Krakow Festival: Competitor and Model

As the Director of HVFilm Günter Witt said to delegates in closing the Film Week in November 1964, "Many of you will surely meet again soon in Oberhausen, Mannheim, Krakow, Venice, or Tours. But in 1965 you are all warmly awaited back in Leipzig, where you will be welcome! *Auf Wiedersehen!*" (*Protokoll 1964* 1965: 31).

Krakow's Polish Film Week, established in 1961, indeed represented a new competitor with the East. Initially conceived exclusively for Polish films, it opened up to international competition in 1964 under the motto "Our Twentieth Century." Despite tough competition, Krakow's international success was almost instantaneous. The festival was held in June, a favorable time of year for such cultural events, and in 1966 it was recognized by the International Federation of Film Producers Associations (FIAPF) as a Category A event—unlike the Leipzig Festival.[24] Poland generally enjoyed much broader diplomatic recognition than the GDR, in large part because West Germany was much less strict about participation in cultural events in Poland than in East Germany.[25] Furthermore, Poland's reputation for high-quality documentary filmmaking meant that audiences had seen Polish films at international festivals in the West, in particular at Oberhausen (Holloway and Holloway 1979). Lastly, the organization of the Krakow Festival was professional and efficient, which duly impressed its East German counterparts.

The Leipzig Festival organizers had demonstrated an awareness of everything they had to learn from other festivals on the international circuit as early as 1960.[26] Krakow immediately became a model. A report on the 1966 Krakow Festival was decidedly complimentary: the festival program had been distributed on opening day, the press kits for films in competition contained summaries in five languages, and the graphic design of the whole was highly successful.[27] Another positive aspect mentioned—one that gives us a reverse glimpse into screenings at Leipzig—was that the public was forbidden to enter the movie theater once a screening had commenced. Televisions in the foyer indicated what film was being screened. Organizers envisioned building a theater large enough to hold a thousand spectators in which 70mm movies could be projected. Lastly, the festival management met every morning to coordinate the day.

The contrast with the Leipzig Festival was stark. In 1964, both the organization and the day-to-day running of the festival still undeniably suffered from substandard coordination and a lack of experience on the part of most of the collaborators.[28] Film Week planning remained faltering, impaired by the competition between DFF and DEFA. The program and invitations to the opening ceremony had only arrived on the morning of opening day.[29] The master of ceremonies complained about the lack of a set schedule of events earmarked for foreign guests and the delay in receiving the instructions of the Ministry of Culture, which arrived three days before the close of the festival![30] The first time the printed program was ready for the opening ceremony was 1966.[31]

The International Cultural Offensive

While efforts to professionalize the festival were thus halting, it is clear that they began in earnest only once the East German authorities were fully persuaded of the festival's strategic role in international cultural policy. Throughout the 1960s, an international communication policy was being put in place around the Leipzig Festival, which was based on a highly structured network and a mechanism that combined the work of institutions, organizations, and individuals, who thus served as more or less official channels and messengers.[32] This policy manifested itself at different stages of the festival. As a first step toward winning diplomatic recognition for the GDR, the Foreign Ministry argued that East Berlin had to "popularize the Leipzig Festival abroad" in order to fight against the ideological and political embargo imposed by the FRG.[33]

As of 1960, the Central Committee (ZK) of the Socialist Unity Part (SED)—which decided the direction of East German foreign policy—considered the Leipzig Festival to be of vital strategic importance, for it offered an "invaluable opportunity to transmit images of life, production and creation in the socialist camp, as well as to enhance the GDR's prestige abroad."[34] The leadership set out the festival's broad outlines, presented in its "annual resolution about the Documentary Film Week," in which the "preparations for the festival in the domain of foreign policy" were always given priority.[35]

In 1962, an SED Party Group, similar to what existed in every institution and administrative structure in the GDR, was established within the festival organization. This group's function was to "take charge of the Film Week's political and ideological leadership"[36] — a broad enough objective to secure it a substantial margin for maneuver behind the scenes at the festival. It brought together representatives of the Departments of Culture, Propaganda, and Foreign Policy of the ZK, as well as the managing directors of HVFilm and the various DEFA Studios.[37] In addition to other suggestions, in 1962 the ZK advocated expanding the Selection Committee to include those with a minimum level of experience and knowledge in the field of foreign policy.[38]

In 1960, a subcommittee on cinema was established within the Committee on Cultural Relations at the MfAA, a sign of the growing importance of film in the GDR's cultural policies abroad.[39] Though not an official organizer, from the outset the Foreign Ministry provided the festival with essential financial and logistical support, particularly prior to its launch,[40] when it primarily assisted by helping to establish contacts abroad.[41] It also organized cocktail receptions intended to introduce DEFA films and the Leipzig Festival to various members of the diplomatic corps wherever the GDR was represented on a diplomatic level. Overall, the results were fairly satisfactory.

While the reception and film screening held in Prague had been a success in 1962, it did not meet expectations the following year. In 1963, efforts to organize a similar cocktail reception in Belgrade were unsuccessful, due to both "objective reasons — Khrushchev's visit to Yugoslavia and the large trade fair being held in Belgrade — and subjective reasons — insufficient leadership on the part of the Foreign Ministry and lack of initiative on the part of embassy staff."[42] A year later, in 1964, the outcome was more favorable, with receptions held in May and June preceding the festivals in Moscow and Prague, as well as at the East German consulate in Belgrade.[43] Every year the attention and interest of their foreign partners, who were highly sensitive to unexpected changes, had to be regained.

Where the absence of formal diplomatic relations prevented organizing such receptions in a given country, the MfAA took advantage of film festivals for cocktail parties organized in the embassies of other socialist countries, especially the Soviet Union.[44] For the Moscow receptions, usually held at the Hotel Rossia, the GDR Embassy provided "money, a couple of interpreters, and a suitable number of cases of Radeberger or Wernesgrüner beer," recalls Wolfgang Harkenthal, for whom the Moscow and Karlovy Vary Festivals represented one of the year's highlights.[45] Finally, in order to maintain international contacts with foreign delegates, the MfAA was also represented by numerous delegates at the Leipzig Festival.[46]

For its part, the Ministry of Culture, an organizer of the Leipzig Festival until 1973, arranged meetings in East Berlin between the festival director and international cultural attachés or government representatives responsible for cinema in other socialist countries.[47] During the festival, delegates from the ministry discussed potential coproductions and film exchanges with both state and nonstate partners. In addition to these GDR state support mechanisms, Günter Klein (1961) had already made an appeal for participants to mobilize all personal contacts and existing communist networks in his concluding remarks at the 1960 festival.

A Showcase for Communist Internationalism

In its attempt to represent the "true face of communism" abroad, East German cultural diplomacy relied on the Soviet model of the All-Union Society for Cultural Relations with Foreign Countries (VOKS), which was founded in 1925 and dissolved in 1957.[48] As of 1952, the GDR counterpart of this organization was the Society for Cultural Relations with Foreign Countries (Gesellschaft für kulturelle Verbindungen mit dem Ausland).[49] In December 1961, the International Friendship League of the GDR (Liga für Völkerfreundschaft) was founded to counteract the negative effects of the Berlin Wall. According to the deputy foreign minister at the time, Otto Winzer, it was meant to "publicize the case for recognition of the GDR abroad" (Troche 1996: 30). Regional and national friendship committees (such as the US Committee for Friendship with the GDR) acted as go-betweens.[50]

For the first time in November 1961, the Society for Cultural Relations with Foreign Countries awarded a prize at Leipzig. The prize went to Karl Gass's documentary about the Algerian war of independence, *Arise, You Children . . . for Algeria,* "because the film was able . . . to foster a sense of solidarity with the Algerian people . . . by using three narrative forms: the story, the portrait and the battle song" (*Protokoll 1961* 1962: 9). The Leipzig Festival thus became a significant moment in the annual calendar of these East German cultural associations. As early as 1962, the league also willingly became a generous donor. In exchange for the forum that the league thus obtained, it advertised the festival in its publications abroad.[51] Its scope of influence, however, remained confined to circles already favorable to the GDR, which constituted the readership of these magazines.

Other international associations also helped consolidate the image of a festival that was open to the world and primarily focused on international peace and solidarity. In 1949, following the World Congress of Partisans for Peace, held concurrently in Paris and in Prague, a German Committee for Peace was launched in the GDR; in 1963 it was renamed the GDR Committee for Peace.[52] Peace was a central mobilizing theme for the international communist movement, which in terms of the intellectual Cold War counteracted the theme of freedom brandished by Western countries (Bois 2003).

The Committee got involved in the festival from early on: in 1961, it awarded a prize to the Cuban program presented at the festival as a whole "for the high ideological and artistic level of young Cuban cinema, which through its films conveys such a moving image of the revolution, so deeply rooted in the Cuban people" (Protokoll 1961 1962: 9).[53]

In 1964, other prizes and diplomas started being conferred by international organizations closely linked to the East Bloc and Moscow: the World Federation of Trade Unions, the Women's International Democratic Federation, and the World Federation of Democratic Youth (Bois 2003). From one year to the next, a rapid increase in the number of prizes and diplomas ensued, despite the risk of devaluing the rewards (Gehler 1997). It was a matter of pleasing as many participants and nationalities as possible, however. In 1964 alone, the festival bestowed no fewer than eighteen awards and five honorable mentions (Protokoll 1965 1966).

Other awards, such as the aforementioned Egon Erwin Kisch Prize, facilitated a certain inclusiveness with respect to the West. Selected by a jury from the International Radio and Television Organization (OIRT) — which, since 1959, had included countries from both the East and the West[54] — prize winners represented the best reports and documentaries on television networks affiliated with Intervision,[55] which had been established in 1960 and was the Eastern counterpart to Eurovision, which had been in existence since 1954. Until 1963, this competition took place at the Moscow Film Festival; the following year, OIRT decided that the prize would be bestowed at the Leipzig Festival. This indicated recognition of the festival not only by its television colleagues in the East but also by colleagues in the West, who undoubtedly seized the opportunity to distance themselves, albeit symbolically, from Moscow.

Opening Up to the West

While it was dependent upon the support of the East German government and international networks in the East, the Leipzig Festival also strove to continue developing progressive contacts in the West. Several professional groups and public figures were mobilized to develop a network around the festival. Journalists, in particular, were a focus of attention. The number of journalists attending the Leipzig Festival quickly grew, and, as elsewhere on the international festival circuit, an international film critic's prize, awarded by a jury from the International Federation of Film Critics (FIPRESCI), was created ("Arbeitsordnung der Jury" 1961). An international festival of such caliber involved year-round preparation. The GDR Journalists' Association (VDJ) was in fact tasked with sending articles about the Leipzig Festival to foreign newspapers all year long, as well as with inviting journalists or recognized film critics, such as the Pole Jerzy Toeplitz and the Frenchman Georges Sadoul.[56]

Reviews in major "bourgeois" newspapers in the West were highly sought after and especially encouraged. The festival organizers eagerly hailed a success whenever *Le Monde*, *The Times*, or other big names of the Western press—"progressive" or not—printed "broadly positive" reviews.[57] Here too, however, they were primarily left leaning and communist press outlets, or film magazines anchored on the left.[58] The interests of the festival organizers often coincided with those of numerous journalists and critics in the West. After the Wall was built, the festival became de facto one of the rare opportunities for them to visit the GDR. In 1962, forty-two foreign journalists attended the festival, including those from West Germany; a year later the number had risen to seventy, and it continued to increase over subsequent years.

The desire to use the festival in a large-scale seduction campaign required working with yet other networks. In 1962, the Filmmakers' Club advised inviting well-known public figures from neutral countries and Western Europe.[59] According to Wolfgang Harkenthal, these ambassadors for the Leipzig Festival contributed "to the influence of the GDR's humanist and pacifist foreign policy."[60] Often bypassing traditional institutions and diplomatic channels, their presence at Leipzig was very useful for East Berlin. Certain success was thus achieved in 1962, when Pablo Picasso gave his consent for his Dove of Peace to become the festival's emblem and decorate the medals that were awarded by the international jury and created at the East German State Mint[61]: the Golden Dove and the Silver Dove.[62]

Over time, however, the standing and role of these public figures waned. While the overall number of guests increased and their geographical origins multiplied, the spirit of the early editions of the festival could not continue very long. Initially, at least, the festival was partly permeated by a quite convivial atmosphere, with invitations extended to friends and personal contacts among East German and foreign professionals, but the 1960s saw new practices coming into being. In December 1966, the director of the East German State Film Archive (SFA) criticized the new prohibition against sending personal invitations to certain renowned documentarists. Instead, preprinted, impersonal invitations had been sent. Some regarded this as a deviation that no longer con-

Figure 4.1. The Golden Dove grand prize medal, with the festival motto and Picasso's dove (1963). © Filmmuseum Potsdam, Reinhard Podszuweit.

sidered culture a question of people, of individuals, but merely as a question of ideology and structure. What was supposed to demonstrate the professionalization of the festival thus became, for some, a regrettable flaw that explained the decrease in attendance of international figures at Leipzig.[63]

Such disaffection, however, can be explained by citing other, arguably more decisive factors. Generational issues deserve mention, with the advancing age and death of those who had been among the festival's earliest and most stalwart supporters: Theodor Christensen passed away in 1967, John Grierson in 1972, and Roman Karmen in 1978. The rupture after 1968, following the departure of Joris Ivens, was also essential.[64] One of the major objectives facing the festival in the 1960s, even before 1968, was to succeed in positioning itself within a context of significant political fluctuations on a national and international scale.

Negotiating De-Stalinization

While the GDR had remained impervious to changes in policy announced by Khrushchev at the Twentieth Congress of the Communist Party of the Soviet Union (CPSU) in 1956, the same cannot be said of the Twenty-Second Congress in 1961, which triggered a second wave of de-Stalinization in the USSR. Changing Soviet policies were not without consequence for domestic and cultural policy in the GDR (Grunert 1991). East German policy remained ill defined, however, and the departure of Khrushchev in October 1964 called into question de-Stalinization processes that were already under way (Werth 2010). Torn between the contradictory influences in documentary film of the period in the GDR and abroad, the Leipzig Festival experienced contrary movements, striving with difficulty to stay on course and follow a clear political line.

De-Stalinization Onscreen in the East

In the first half of the 1960s, the second thaw of de-Stalinization allowed young filmmakers east of the Iron Curtain to engage in the new cultural and political momentum of the period. It presented each country the opportunity to rework its past and its representations—with similarities but also differences between countries. While the prevailing tense political and economic situation severely affected Polish documentarists,[65] Hungarians of the "Generation of 1956" made Direct Cinema their own, working as sociologists of their time and their collective memory.[66] In the USSR, documentarists working during the second wave of de-Stalinization preferred portraits of individuals captured in their daily lives over monumental cinematic frescoes.[67] In the GDR, the issue assumed entirely different dimensions from elsewhere in the East Bloc. In 1965, the year marking the twentieth anniversary of the victory over fascism and Nazism, the problem was to disentangle the antifascist struggle, which was at the heart of East Germany's grand narrative, from an apologia for Stalinism. This delicate question, to which the Leipzig Festival had to respond, was not without challenges and tensions.

Organizing the festival retrospective that year turned out to be highly contentious. In the spring of 1965, Wolfgang Klaue, director of the Research Department at the GDR Film Archives, assessed preparations for the festival planned for November, indirectly revealing tensions he encountered with the Ministry of Culture.[68] According to Klaue, the retrospective, which had hitherto mostly been devoted to "progressive [documentarists] from capitalist countries," was finally to pay tribute to Soviet documentary filmmaking. The difficulties associated with this, however, were not negligible. After a series of screenings organized by Soviet archives, it became clear that films from the 1930s and the war period, overly marked by Stalin's cult of personality, were "no longer suited for public screenings." The selection process then turned to the 1920s and the *kinoglaz* (cine-eye) movement, pioneered by Dziga Vertov. Unfortunately, initial communications with the USSR's Central State Film and Photo Archive in Krasnogorsk fell on deaf ears, as the avant-garde documen-

Figure 4.2. Wolfgang Klaue at the festival in 1970. © Filmmuseum Potsdam, Reinhard Podszuweit.

tarist had as yet to be rehabilitated in the USSR. Again the festival retrospective had to search for a new theme.

Eventually, a compromise was arrived at around the theme of "Films against Fascism," which was thought might be of interest to foreign guests. Tensions were not allayed, however, and the final selection met with reluctance in high places (Klaue 1998). The image of a single victorious coalition led by the USSR was undermined, for instance by American films shot during the war by Frank Capra. *Den Blodiga Titen* (1959, *Mein Kampf: A Blueprint for the Age of Chaos*), a Swedish documentary directed by Erwin Leiser, had already screened at Leipzig in 1960; a press release had expressed regret that the film did not sufficiently showcase the "role of the German Communist Party as a driving force in the multilateral fight against Hitler" or the "responsibility of capitalism in the Nazi rise to power," however, and noted that "many of the fascists and militarists shown in the film [were] once again in power in West Germany."[69] Another American film also incurred disapproval: Louis Clyde Stoumen's *Black Fox: The True Story of Adolf Hitler* (1962), with a commentary narrated by Marlene Dietrich, who, according to some, was settling scores with her country of origin.

Romm's Ordinary Fascism

The retrospective, originally meant to honor Soviet documentary film, thus wound up taking another direction. And yet, the big event of 1965 turned out to be a Soviet film. *Obyknovennyy fashizm* (1965, *Ordinary Fascism*) by Mikhail Romm (1901–1971), struck viewers with its intensely personal tone and a form of reflection hitherto never undertaken in documentary filmmaking (Moine 2005b). Born in 1901 in Siberia to a Jewish family that had been banished by the tsarist regime, Romm was part of the second generation of Soviet filmmakers.[70] He shot his debut work, *Pyshka* (*Boule de suif*), a silent feature-length film, in 1934. Stalin greatly appreciated his work. In the wake of Stalin's death in 1953 and Khrushchev's report in 1956, Romm entered a profound crisis (Klejman 2000). In the same period, his denunciation of anti-Semitism at a conference on theater bolstered his popularity among Soviet intellectuals but lost him leverage with the authorities (Turovskaya 1998).

It was at this juncture that two young authors, Maya Turovskaya and Yuri Chanjutin, approached Romm. They proposed he join them in studying how ordinary citizens responded in the face of authoritarian power, modeled on the example of Nazism (Turovskaya 1997); the principal protagonist was to be the "petty bourgeois German" (Romm 1981).[71] Over a two-year period, the three authors viewed more than two million meters of German film—newsreels, documentaries, and feature films—from the period.[72] According to the American critic and film historian Jay Leyda (1967), the documentary became

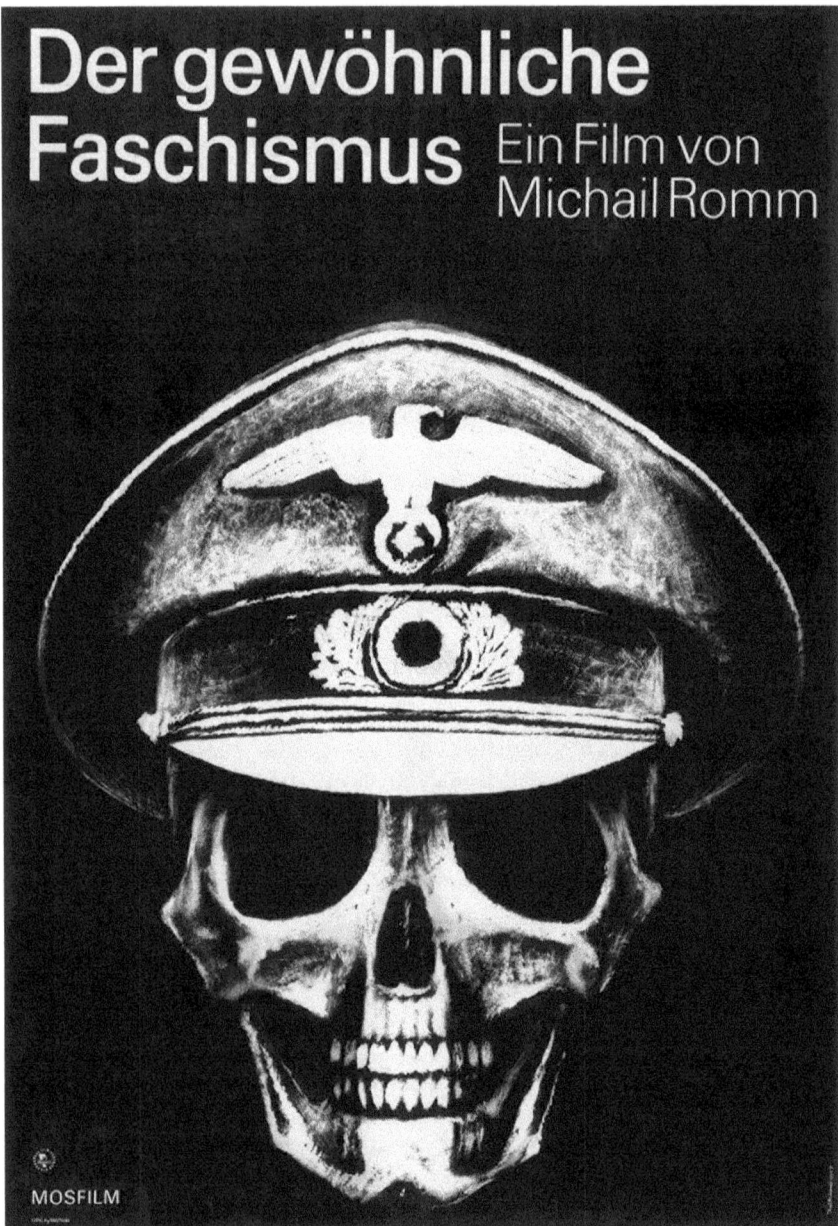

Figure 4.3. GDR poster for M. Romm's *Ordinary Fascism* (1965). © DEFA Stiftung, Axel Bertram.

a compilation film, often including unedited footage that went much further than anything seen up until that point.

Ordinary Fascism comprises sixteen segments, each heralded by a quotation from *Mein Kampf*, in what, at first sight, seems a random order. "The film has the logic of a nightmare," noted a West German critic (Kurowski 1970). In reality, Romm disassembled the stylization and transmission of media images exploited in the service of propaganda. He made signature use of his commentary—alternately funny, ironic, or filled with pathos—to reach a new dimension in documentary filmmaking (Gregor 1966a), as though he were inviting the viewer to converse with him.[73] His goal was to describe Nazism in such a way as to get audiences to reflect on the roots of fascism and to question the past, primarily through the prism of the present (Leyda 1967). Unlike his two coauthors, who "as typical young people in the 1960s" longed to make something very intellectual, Romm made the film in the hope of reaching a very wide audience (Turovskaya 1998: 47). The reception of the film is thus an essential part of its history, in which the Leipzig Festival played a key role.

Romm had produced *Ordinary Fascism* with the support of a Jewish, former antifascist combatant at Goskino, the USSR State Committee for Cinematography. There remained the question of distribution and reception. "We were warned it would be a disaster," Romm (1981) recalled. For the preview screening, he opted to send the documentary to the Leipzig Festival, where a large international audience could see it. If it were acceptable to Walter Ulbricht, the first secretary of the SED and leader of the GDR, it would make it easier to subsequently insist on its release in the USSR (Turovskaya 1997).

The first challenge was to get the documentary on the program at Leipzig. The film's selection and Romm's appearance at the festival caused a sensation, recalls Wolfgang Harkenthal with enthusiasm.[74] A preliminary discussion was held by Günter Witt, deputy minister of culture responsible for cinema, and Vladimir Baskakov, a deputy managing director at Goskino who arrived in East Berlin two days before the festival opened.[75] The Soviets were reluctant to accept the selection of Romm's film in competition, as it might overshadow Roman Karmen's entry *Velikaya otechestvennaya* (1965, *The Great Patriotic War*), which was intended to mark the twentieth anniversary of the end of the German-Soviet War. Witt came up with a compromise that ensured that Karmen's film would receive at least one award, namely the FIPRESCI Prize.

The fourteen jury members[76] somewhat foiled this plan, however. *Ordinary Fascism* won the Special Jury Prize, which placed it *hors catégorie* (out of competition), while Karmen's *The Great Patriotic War* was awarded the Silver Dove. But as the FIPRESCI Prize also went to Romm's documentary, he was transformed into the star of the festival (Leyda 1967). "It was one of those magical moments at Leipzig; there was a standing ovation of almost fifteen minutes," reported East German journalist Hans-Dieter Tok (1997: 75).

Romm's film was passionately discussed throughout the week. "Was he not speaking in veiled terms about Stalinism as well?," wondered West German journalist Wilhelm Roth (1997: 86). Admittedly, an East German critic discerned in the film a condemnation of "imperialist barbarity in Vietnam and elsewhere" (Lohmann 1972) Yet, as Harkenthal acknowledged,[77] parallels with policies of the party and the Soviet state were patently obvious to everybody. Significantly, the opening and closing segments of the documentary were street scenes shot in Moscow in 1964.

Ordinary Fascism by necessity struck the audience in Leipzig as extraordinary, noted a West German journalist: "Those who find [socialist political documentaries] depressing, now understand that it is not the only genre that exists. And those who consider them excellent can now see how they pale beside Romm's film, whose significance, however, goes far beyond this dual challenge" (Färber 1966). Romm (1981) declared in 1968, "*Ordinary Fascism* is the upshot of bitter losses and lost illusions." Aside from denouncing how images are manipulated, this documentary revisited a theme dear to Romm, who felt that the masses strip away every vestige of humanity from individuals. That a Soviet documentary would champion such a position could not be overlooked.

Notwithstanding the success of the approach toward Nazism proposed by *Ordinary Fascism* at the Leipzig Festival, the issue of collective and individual responsibility and the theme of Stalinism remained taboo in the GDR. After the 1965 edition of the festival, the freedom of speech that had been accorded during the screening of Romm's film was swiftly quelled.

Rupture: The Eleventh Plenum

As we have seen, technological advances, such as synchronized sound, were essential to the cultural liberalization of cinema in the early 1960s, in East as in West. The resulting direct speech corresponded in particular to the younger generation's need to express itself, thus assuming a more or less subversive character. In the GDR, the political environment directly influenced the stakes of using unfiltered speech in documentary film. Documentary film produced in the GDR during the 1960s allowed increasingly more room for direct speech, not so much through the use of voice-over commentary, but rather in the form of interviews.

Youth, Politics, and Documentary

After completing *Stars*, director Jürgen Böttcher tried something new. In the summer of 1964 he shot *Barfuß und ohne Hut* (1964, *Barefoot and without a*

Hat), a film meant to give voice to East German youth. It was a fairly ambitious project. "I wanted to tackle several themes: old age and youth, generational issues, love, the past, dreaming about the future," recalls Böttcher.[78] In choosing to focus on young East Germans, the documentarist was casting his eye over a social group that was a core concern of the regime at the time. A few months earlier, in September 1963, the government had issued a "communiqué to young people" that accorded them absolute freedom with respect to music, clothes, and hairstyles and in return called on them to engage in the country's political and professional life (Krenzlin 1991: 150–51). In May 1964, two related events then took place: the People's Chamber (Volkskammer) passed legislation that would involve youth more in the "general construction of Socialism," and the aforementioned Youth Gathering brought young people from West and East Germany together in East Berlin (Schröder 1998: 152–53). Such initiatives and events indicate the extent of the campaign designed to bring young people on board.

For the evocatively titled *Barefoot and without a Hat*, Böttcher filmed a group of university students on vacation at a Baltic Sea beach, far away from educational and social pressures. We see them playing the guitar—blues, jazz, and some airs by Django Reinhardt. In swimsuits or jeans they dance the twist, and a few of them spontaneously improvise a pop band. Their evening is spent dancing and eating a huge roast cooked over an open campfire. Between swimming and flirting, the young people respond to the film crew's questions. They describe their studies, their plans for the future: to join the navy or work at a nuclear plant. Amid stereotyped formulas, we at times hear scathing critiques—of a teacher deemed too boring, uninspiring military service, working conditions that will undoubtedly be harsh. With such nuances, the film succeeds in capturing the spirit of a generation. And this is precisely what it was accused of.

Böttcher's documentary projected an accurate image of a portion of young people in the GDR, as tastes in popular music show. In the early 1960s, young East Germans were primarily listening to pop music. After the construction of the Wall, many East German pop bands emerged, both professional and amateur. The Sputniks, for example, played pop hits from the West, primarily in instrumental versions with a predilection for guitars, which were often "improved" with whatever means were at hand (Hintze 1999b). The Beatles were a huge success in the GDR as well, thanks to access to Western media sources. The radio program DT 64—originally launched to accompany the 1964 Youth Gathering (the Deutschland Treffen, or DT)—was such a success that it became a regular broadcast, focusing on culture, politics, sports, and music (Hintze 1999a).

While editing the film, Böttcher found himself at a critical juncture, as the regime was not sure what stance to adopt toward young people attracted to the West. While *Barefoot and without a Hat* was not officially banned, the projected full-length feature film was cut down to a twenty-minute version after protracted and difficult negotiations between the film crew and HV-Film. Authorities deemed that the young people portrayed in the film in no way represented East German reality and resembled young vacationers on the French Riviera more than on the Baltic (Böttcher 2000). The film was also not approved for as wide a distribution as had been expected.

Böttcher's documentary had already been announced for the November 1964 Leipzig Festival. Several weeks before the festival opened, a journalist divulged this: "In his lyrical chronicle, filmed at a campsite and using direct sound, Jürgen Böttcher will reveal the zest for life, the opinions, projects, and dreams of young people in our Republic" (Albrecht 1964). Ultimately, however, *Barefoot and without a Hat* was not selected for Leipzig. Instead, following a typical strategy deployed by the regime, it was sent abroad, without Böttcher being informed, to the Short Film Festival held in Tours, France (1955–1971; Böttcher 2000). In the eyes of the orthodox faction of the regime, the documentary's caliber and the accuracy of its representation of young people's desires and expectations rendered it dangerous for East German consumption. Conversely, it conveyed an image of a modern and up-to-date GDR that was perfectly suited for dissemination in the West.

Cinematographer Christian Lehmann still maintains that shooting *Barefoot and without a Hat* was one of his best experiences, despite challenging technical conditions on location due to the wind.[79] The images indeed divulge a pleasure in filming the carefree spirit of these young people on vacation, like seashells undulating beneath the water's surface, a freedom of tone and gesture. But it was a carefree spirit that abruptly came to an end in the winter of 1965–1966.

Censorship and Documentaries

The regime's internal struggles pitted supporters of the economic reforms that had been enacted against those anxious to meet the expectations of the new Soviet leader, Leonid Brezhnev.[80] In early 1963, the SED launched its New Economic System (NÖS); it was to replace the system of Five-Year Plans in an effort to end the economic crisis, which had led to partial rationing at the turn of the 1960s, and thereby stabilize the regime. After Brezhnev became first secretary of the CPSU in November 1964, however, the new leadership in Moscow began to lose interest in the new system, which had not yielded the hoped for results.

Despite the liberalizing tendencies toward young people outlined above, other factions in the SED continued to speak out against the "immorality" of the current pop music and the prevailing fashion of long hair and Western clothing.[81] In the fall of 1965, a combo group concert was banned in Leipzig, provoking sharp public protests that were violently repressed. This was a mere foretaste of what was to happen several weeks later.

In December 1965, the Eleventh Plenum of the SED's Central Committee heralded the victory of conservatives within the party and government. "Our GDR is a clean state," declared Erich Honecker, who emphasized that ethics, morality, and concern for social mores ought to prevail in the GDR, as opposed to the pernicious influences originating in the West (Honecker 1965). If anything, the arguments deployed to condemn cultural productions loosely considered "modernist," "skeptical," "anarchist," "nihilistic," or even "pornographic" bespoke the accusers' anxieties more than their values.

The ensuing censorship, which affected the entire spectrum of cultural life in the GDR,[82] saw to it that twelve DEFA feature films were banned, including Gerhard Klein's *Berlin um die Ecke* (1965, *Berlin around the Corner*), which drew inspiration from two Böttcher films—*Furnace Makers* and *Stars*—and mixed fictional and documentary aspects of the lives of young workers in East Berlin (Richter 1994). Another victim of censorship was Böttcher's one and only feature film, *Jahrgang 45* (1966, *Born in '45*), a fragment in the life of the twenty-year-old protagonist who wanders aimlessly through East Berlin's streets, unable to communicate with his parents or his wife. This portrait was deemed anticonformist and overly gloomy (Heimann 2000). In 1966, Böttcher was even barred from attending the Leipzig Festival.[83] This setback had a lasting effect on Böttcher, one of the most inventive and promising figures in East German cinema, as he never made another feature film.

Heads also rolled. Deputy Minister of Culture Günter Witt, responsible for cinema, was removed from office, as were Jochen Mückenberger, DEFA's managing director, and Heinz Baumert, president of the Selection Committee at Leipzig (Baumert 1991). Editor in chief of the film journal *Filmwissenschaftliche Mitteilungen,* Baumert was accused of "inciting filmmakers in their attempt to produce films critical of the socialist social order, our life, and our state."[84] Denounced by the Thorndikes, Christiane Mückenberger—who would later direct the Leipzig Festival, after the fall of the Wall—and Günter Dahlke were fired from the Film Research Institute (Institut für Filmwissenschaft), which Heinz Baumert directed and which published *Filmwissenschaftliche Mitteilungen* (Kötzing and Schenk 2015). In reality, however, Baumert had displayed genuine open-mindedness on the committee—for example, toward *Ordinary Fascism,* which he had been instrumental in programming at Leipzig.

Cinephiles against Ideologues

Documentary film—which reached a smaller audience and had been less critical of the system and the hypocrisy of official morality than fictional feature films[85] — was initially sheltered from the wave of censorship. The consequences of the ideological hardening, however, were eventually felt in the documentary realm, just slightly later. By early 1966, a political and cultural freeze was in full force. In the USSR, the public trial of the dissident authors Yuli Daniel and Andrei Sinyavsky heralded the end of Khrushchev's cultural thaw (Vaissié 1999). Numerous films were banned. Studios, magazines, and film education became victims of cultural purges (Fomin 2000). While forty million viewers had seen *Ordinary Fascism* in movie theaters, it was not broadcast on television, and the book the authors wrote about the documentary was censored at the last minute (Turovskaya 1998). Once again, the GDR followed the Soviet about-face. In May 1967, *Ordinary Fascism* disappeared once and for all from East German movie theaters, following a decision made by Kurt Hager, who was responsible for culture at the SED Politburo, "based on the subjective observation of certain details of the evolution of fascism."[86] Given the enthusiastic reception that Romm's documentary had received at Leipzig, however, it was impossible to completely suppress it, and it continued to be screened at the Babelsberg film academy and at special sessions, pending official permission (Jordan and Schenk 1996).

Control exerted over the Leipzig Festival was to become even stricter, including with regard to the retrospectives. The retrospective program devoted to French documentary film being planned for the festival's 1966 edition illustrates the kinds of difficulties that emerged. Ultimately it only took place as the result of a series of compromises that were reached following renewed battles between the SFA and the Ministry of Culture. In December 1965, the director of the archive had proposed a retrospective on the "evolution of French documentary filmmaking,"[87] fortifying his proposal by means of a diplomatic argument. During a trip to Paris, he had observed how much more favorable to socialist countries the French Foreign Ministry had become. HV-Film, however, hesitated, and in February 1966, one of its officials deemed that many French films had absolutely no place at Leipzig.[88]

Alternative proposals were mooted, including one for a retrospective devoted to Polish film. Wolfgang Klaue, who was responsible for the Leipzig retrospectives at the SFA, was against this idea: whereas no retrospective devoted to French documentary cinema had screened at any film festival, Polish documentary was now too well-known on the international circuit, thanks to retrospectives previously organized in London and Brussels (Klaue 2015). The Leipzig Festival would lose the advantage of exclusivity, which it had enjoyed. Furthermore, opting for a Polish program ran the risk of giving the impression that the festival focused exclusively on documentaries from socialist countries.[89] Klaue stressed the diplomatic context as well: France, in breaking away from NATO, was seeking a rapprochement with East Bloc countries.

Such a retrospective could well provide an opportunity for the Union of French Producers to participate in the competition at Leipzig. This was key, as the union played a key role in FIAPF and the festival was still waiting to be granted Category A status. Lastly, he argued, it would serve as an opportunity to invite many French filmmakers and critics, even if France did not participate officially—a development that in itself could only enhance the festival's prestige.[90] Klaue's arguments won the day. Finally, the Ministry of Culture agreed to cohost a retrospective of French documentary filmmaking.

Producing the catalog to accompany the retrospective was the source of renewed tensions with the Ministry of Culture. Klaue reported that the selection focused on the period from 1920 to 1950 as a way to integrate films shot immediately after the war and exclude more recent—namely, *cinéma vérité*—productions, "it being assumed," the ministry argued, "that these are already internationally well-known."[91] Those at the SFA were not pleased with this chronological truncation, however, and a first draft of the introductory text, penned by Klaue, hinted at their disappointment. A copyeditor at HVFilm did not hide his irritation, remarking, "Why such reservations? Who has ever done better?"[92]

He moreover expressed his devotion to the themes of antifascism and the Vietnam War, which should be omnipresent, and his distrust of any film that did not seem sufficiently politically engaged. Why screen *Toute la mémoire du monde* (1957, *All the Memory of the World*), he quipped? This early work by Alain Resnais about the Bibliothèque nationale in Paris, filmed in collaboration with Chris Marker, delivers with humor and sensitivity a masterful reflection on literature and the connection between a book and its readers. The cinephiles working at the SFA were surprised and dismayed by such remarks, and, at the end, Resnais's film was kept in the program, thanks to an interpretation of the film aimed at the HVFilm censors.

It was argued that, in reality, Resnais was exerting a critique "against bourgeois society, which buried its spiritual riches" and did little to pass them on (*Protokoll 1961* 1962: 29). The Film Research Institute (Institut für Filmwissenschaft), affiliated with the Babelsberg Academy, also had to get in on the critique of the catalog. Did not the complete absence of Marxist analysis in its presentation run the risk of transforming the retrospective into a "party for cinephiles," which had little to do with the festival? Although they had admittedly not seen most of the films, the film synopses led them to anticipate "unbounded realism."[93]

Notwithstanding that the festival was due to open on 12 November, repeated corrections and reformulations meant that the retrospective catalogue was not ready for printing before early November. Ultimately, with about forty films programmed,[94] the retrospective was a success. Although West German journalists bemoaned the inferior quality of the festival as a whole—an "exhausting monotonous propaganda" — they applauded the retrospective.[95] The SFA even dared point out that many viewers, and East Germans in particular, regretted the absence of *cinéma vérité* documentaries.[96] Furthermore, Herbert Volkmann,[97] director of the SFA, demanded that a representative from the SFA join the SED Party Group at the heart of the festival, so that the retrospective would no longer be considered a mere appendage to the Film Week. By playing on the festival's diplomatic and international dimension, the SFA had thus cleverly succeeded in getting closer to the festival organizers — and in retaining a margin for action — while fully respecting the rules of the game.

Following the Eleventh Plenum of the ZK in 1965, East Germany thus embraced a new political line, in order to satisfy the new master in the Kremlin (Eckert 1991; Steiner 2004), and thereby sacrificed its most promising cultural productions. The momentum of the New Wave remained strong and vibrant, however, in other Eastern countries (Segert 2003). Developments abroad, especially in neighboring Czechoslovakia, were closely monitored in the GDR, be it with hope or trepidation, depending on whose interests were at stake. Once again, the Leipzig Festival was at the heart of debates and exchanges involving East German and foreign actors, from the East as well as the West.

Notes

1. Or, as DEFA feature film director Frank Beyer — who experienced both great successes in the GDR and censorship, notably in 1966 — put it in titling his 2001 autobiography, *Wenn der Wind sich dreht* (When the Wind Turns).
2. Hermann Schauer became Harkenthal's deputy director; he had been the deputy director of VBB Film since 1959 (see below). Discussion with Comrade Minister Witt on the topic of the Leipzig Week, 3 July 1964, SAPMO-BArch DR1/4272.
3. Here this term refers to the European countries in the so-called East Bloc.
4. For Soviet officials who were real cinephiles, special screenings were even organized over the weekend. Harkenthal went to West Berlin on the Saturday to pick up prints of three or four Western films, such as Marcel Carné's *Les enfants du paradis* (1945, *Children of Paradise*) and David Lean's *The Bridge on the River Kwai* (1957), which he projected one after the other overnight, before taking them back to the West in the morning.
5. Author's interview with Wolfgang Harkenthal, Murchin, Germany (7 August 2000). The following Harkenthal citations are all from this interview.
6. For more, see chapter 1.
7. Author's interview with Wolfgang Harkenthal, Murchin, Germany (7 August 2000).
8. This Youth Gathering was the third and last of its kind.
9. On the history of 70mm films in the West and East, see the catalogue of the 2009 retrospective organized during the Berlinale (Deutsche Kinemathek 2009).
10. Author's interview with Gisela Harkenthal, Murchin, Germany (7 August 2000).

11. Several technicians and experts who had contributed to the development of radio in Germany since the 1930s came to help set up the facilities at Adlershof. See, for example, Lektorat Rundfunkgeschichte 1985; Müncheberg 1984.
12. Protokoll Nr. 36/56 of the extraordinary meeting of the Secretariat of the ZK on 5 November 1956, SAPMO-BArch DY 30/J IV 2/3 534. See also Gumbert 2006.
13. I should note that Willi Zahlbaum—who would later become the director of the DEFA Documentary Studio from 1960 to 1962—was one of the people close to Heinz Adameck in these first years.
14. HA Programmaustausch und Film, Zum Leipziger Festival 1965, Zur Information aus Beschlüssen des Sekretariat des ZK und des Komitees, SAPMO-BArch DR1/4276.
15. Hans Bentzien, Vorlage an das Sekretariat des ZK der SED, SAPMO-BArch DR1/4272.
16. Zu konzeptionnellen Fragen der VII. Leipziger Dokwoche, November 1964, SAPMO-BArch DR1/4272.
17. HA Programmaustausch und Film, Zum Leipziger Festival 1965, Zur Information aus Beschlüssen des Sekretariat des ZK und des Komitees, SAPMO-BArch DR1/4276.
18. This meeting was organized by HA Programmaustausch und Film, HVFilm, December 1964, SAPMO-BArch DR1/4276.
19. Statute of the Selection Committee for the Eighth Leipzig Festival, 1965, SAPMO-BArch DR1/4276.
20. Letter from Hermann Schauer to Günter Klein, 24 September 1965, SAPMO-BArch DR1/4276.
21. Ministry of Finance, signed by Sandig, Stellungnahme zum Finanzplan der VIII. Internationalen Leipziger Dokumentarfilm- und Kurzfilmwoche, 9 October 1965, SAPMO-BArch DY 30/J IV 2/3A/1238. I thank Günter Jordan for showing me this reference.
22. In 1962, the minister financed Leipzig with 200,000 East German marks; in 1963, it was 300,000; and in 1964, it was 550,000.
23. ZK-Sekretariat, Protokoll Nr. 83, Finanzplan der VIII. Internationalen Leipziger Woche, 3 November 1965, SAPMO-BArch DY 30/J IV 2/3A/1238.
24. Category A—which included internationally recognized festivals, such as those at Cannes and Venice—conferred an unmistakable prestige, not only on the festival itself but also on the city and country in which it took place. If it became a Category A festival, Leipzig could expect to see an increase in the number of official national participants.
25. Auswertung des VII Leipziger Festivals, 26 November 1964, Protokollabteilung der HVFilm, annex 2, SAPMO-BArch DR1/4272.
26. Wolfgang Kernicke, Bericht über die Arbeit des Organisationsbüros der III. Leipziger Kurz- und Dokumentarfilmwoche 13–19 November 1960, SAPMO-BArch DY 30 IV 2/9.06/228.
27. In 1966, the principal East German review of film criticism—*Filmwissenschaftliche Beiträge*—published an account of the Krakow Festival that was just as positive.
28. Hans Belling, deputy director of the festival, Einschätzung der VII. Internationalen Dokumentar-und Kurzfilmwoche in Leipzig, December 1964, SAPMO-BArch DR1/4272.
29. Braune, colleague in the protocol service of the festival, Auswertung des VII. Leipziger Internationalen Dokumentarfilm- und Kurzfilmfestivals, 26 November 1964, SAPMO-BArch DR1/4272.
30. Deckers, responsible for the protocol service, Evaluation of the Leipzig Week, 26 November 1964, SAPMO-BArch DR1/4272.

31. Kurzinformation über die IX. Leipziger Woche, addressed to HVFilm, author unknown, 23 November 1966, SAPMO-BArch DR1/4331.
32. See Berghahn 2004; Caute 2003; Grémion 1995.
33. Abteilung Kultur des ZK der SED, Aussenpolitische Gesichtspunkte für die Konzeption der VII. Leipziger Dokumentarfilm- und Kurzfilmwoche, SAPMO-BArch DR1/4272, p. 4.
34. Culture Department of the ZK of the SED, letter to the SED leadership in Leipzig, 6 November 1960, SAPMO-BArch DY 30 IV 2/9.06/228, p. 41.
35. See, for example, HVFilm, Zu konzeptionnellen Fragen der VII. Woche, Erster Entwurf, unsigned, November 1964, SAPMO-BArch DR1/4272, p. 1.
36. Letter from Kimmel, Deputy Director of the Culture Service of the ZK of the SED, to Dr. Wilfried Maaß, Director of HVFilm, Berlin, 6 April 1966, SAPMO-BArch DR1/4331.
37. Club der Filmschaffenden, Bericht über den Stand der Vorbereitungen für die V. Dokumentar-filmwoche von 1962 an das Ministerium für Kultur, SAPMO-BArch DY 30 IV 2/2.026/84, p. 19; Protokoll der 1. Sitzung der Parteigruppe für die IV. Dokumentarfilmwoche, 20 October 1961, BArch-Farch, Leipzig, 1961.
38. Vorlage für das Kollegium des MfK zur Vorbereitung und Durchführung der Leipziger Dokumentar-film Woche, unsigned, 15 July 1966, SAPMO-BArch DR1/4331.
39. Incomplete MfAA archives and the thirty-year time lapse make it impossible to undertake a more in-depth study of the role played by this subcommission. Protokoll der 3. Sitzung der Unterkommission Film bei der Kommission für kulturelle Beziehungen zum Ausland beim MfAA, 18 October 1960, PA/AA, Fond MfAA/A 17387, pp. 26–30.
40. See, for example, Kulturabteilung des MfAA. Massnahmepläne und Orientierung für die Gestaltung der kulturellen Auslandsbeziehungen der DDR zu nord- und westeuropäischen Staaten. Politische und fachliche Orientierung für die Planung der kulturellen Auslandsarbeit, Berlin, 5 June 1965, PA/AA, Fond MfAA/A 16870, p. 106.
41. Bericht über den Stand der Vorbereitung vom 1 November 1960, SAPMO-BArch DY 30 IV 2/9.06/228, p. 1.
42. Zetek, Bemerkungen zur VI. Leipziger Woche, Kulturabteilung MfAA, SAPMO-BArch DR1/4272.
43. Vorlage an das Sekretariat des ZK der SED, Minister für Kultur, Hans Bentzien, Konzeption der VII Leipziger Woche, SAPMO-BArch DR1/4272.
44. Letter from Wolfgang Harkenthal to Inge Kleinert, 18 March 1965, SAPMO-BArch DR1/4276.
45. Author's interview with Wolfgang Harkenthal, Murchin, Germany (7 August 2000).
46. On average, there were just under ten delegates. In 1972, there were 6 (*Protokoll 1972* 1973).
47. For an example from 1964, see Zu konzeptionnellen Fragen der VIII Leipziger Woche, November 1964, SAPMO-BArch DR1/4272.
48. On the history of the VOKS, see: Cœuré 1999; Fayet 2002; Fox 2011.
49. See Mallinckrodt 1972.
50. See, for example, Badia 2000.
51. Abteilung Kultur des ZK der SED, Aussenpolitische Gesichtspunkte für die Konzeption der VII. Leipziger Dokumentarfilm- und Kurzfilmwoche, DR1/4272, p. 4.
52. Deutscher Friedensrat, then Friedensrat der DDR. The committee claimed to represent the entire German nation—thus excluding all West German participation in the movement (Mallinckrodt 1972).

53. In 1962, it was the World Congress of Partisans for Peace that gave a prize, again to a documentary about Cuba.
54. In 1946, the International Broadcasting Organization (IBO), or in French Organisation Internationale de Radiodiffusion (OIR), was established in Geneva; in 1959, it expanded to include television and became OIRT. OIR had been formed on the initiative of the USSR but included members from nonsocialist and capitalist countries, such as France and Italy.
55. Created by the GDR, Hungary, Czechoslovakia, and Poland, to which were later added the USSR, Bulgaria, and then Romania.
56. Abteilung Kultur des ZK der SED, Aussenpolitische Gesichtspunkte für die Konzeption der VII. Leipziger Dokumentarfilm- und Kurzfilmwoche, SAPMO-BArch DR1/4272, p. 4.
57. See, for example, from 1962, Bericht über den Stand der Vorbereitungen für die V. Internationale Leipziger Dokumentar-und Kurzfilmwoche vom 9–18 November 1962 an das Ministerium für Kultur, SAPMO-BArch DY 30 IV 2/2.026/84, p. 18.
58. With respect to the French press, *L'Humanité-Dimanche, La Vie ouvrière, Les Lettres françaises,* and *Jeune Cinéma* as well as the important cinema reviews *Positif* and *Image et Son.*
59. Club der Filmschaffenden, Bericht über den Stand der Vorbereitungen für die V. Internationale Leipziger Dokumentar- und Kurzfilmwoche vom 9–18 November 1962 an das Ministerium für Kultur, SAPMO-BArch DY 30 IV 2/2.026/84, p. 20.
60. Author's interview with Wolfgang Harkenthal, Murchin, Germany (7 August 2000).
61. Club der Filmschaffenden, Bericht über den Stand der Vorbereitungen für die V. Internationale Leipziger Dokumentar- und Kurzfilmwoche vom 9–18 November 1962 an das Ministerium für Kultur, SAPMO-BArch DY 30 IV 2/2.026/84, p. 20.
62. In 1960 and 1961, the prizes awarded included a "grand prize"—a copper cup decorated with amber and the arms of the City of Leipzig—and three "principal prizes" given in the name of the minister of culture, the City of Leipzig, and Progress Film-Verleih.
63. Herbert Volkmann, director of the Film Archives, Evaluation of the Ninth Leipzig International Film Week, Berlin, 7 December 1966, SAPMO-BArch DR1/4331, p. 4.
64. For more, see chapter 5.
65. This period witnessed tensions, compromises, and arrangements; see Szczepanska 2011.
66. In an interview in Budapest in February 1985, film director Ferenc Kósa declared, "In the Stalinist years we were innocent adolescents. It was the drama of 1956 that made us adults" (Jeancolas 2001: 62–65).
67. Viktor Lissakowitch's *Katjuscha* (1964), for example, was very successful in the USSR and at festivals, including Leipzig. The viewer sees a nurse who had fought in the navy during the war—and who was not depicted as a determined heroine, but rather as a sensitive woman. (For more on this film, see Klaue and Lichtenstein 1967.) The director denounced the Stalinist lies of the 1940s and 1950s by reusing propaganda films of the period and exposing their manipulation of information (Engel 1999).
68. Wolfgang Klaue, Information über die Retrospektive zur diesjährigen Dokumentarfilmwoche, undated, probably between March and May 1965, SAPMO-BArch DR1/4276.
69. Pressebüro, Einige Hinweise zum schwedischen Film *Die blutigen Jahre,* DY 30 IV 2/9.06/228, p. 142.

70. Conversations in Moscow, July 1965 (Schnitzer et al. 1966; Lohmann 1972).
71. Although published in 1981, Romm wrote this text in 1968.
72. This material had arrived in the USSR as war booty.
73. The German version was read by Hermann Herlinghaus, who was perfectly bilingual, having been born in Russia, where his father, a German engineer, had worked; according to contemporary witnesses, he knew how to translate and best convey the nuances and effects in the Russian text.
74. Author's interview with Wolfgang Harkenthal, Murchin, Germany (7 August 2000).
75. Conversation between Minister Günter Witt and Minister Baskakow, 11 or 12 November 1965, BArch-FArch, festival de Leipzig, 1965.
76. The jury that year was top-notch, with the Pole Jerzy Bossak, the Swede Theodor Christensen, the Frenchman Marcel Martin, the Brit Ivor Montagu, and Gerhard Scheumann from DEFA.
77. Author's interview with Wolfgang Harkenthal, Murchin, Germany (7 August 2000).
78. Author's interview with Jürgen Böttcher, Berlin/Karlshorst, Germany (31 October 2000).
79. The wind posed problems with respect to recording the synchronized sound. Author's interview with Christian Lehmann, Berlin, Germany (22 August 2000).
80. For more on power plays among members of the regime leadership in this period, see Kaiser 1997.
81. For an analysis of how the concept of "glorification of dances in the occidental style" has been used, see Lindenberger 2003: 49.
82. In music, see Hintze 1999b; Rauhut 1991. And more widely, see Agde 1991.
83. "Böttcher question: Banned from travel to Leipzig. But remains in the Doc Film Studio." Handwritten notes, probably by Schauer (HVFilm), on the back of the DEFA Documentary Studio's production plan for 1967, late 1966, SAPMO-BArch, DR1/4322, p. 24.
84. Decision of the leadership of the SED Party Group at the German Academy for Filmmaking (HFF) in Potsdam-Babelsberg from 19 January 1966.
85. For examples, such as Kurt Maetzig's *Das Kaninchen bin ich* (1965, *The Rabbit Is Me*) and Frank Vogel's *Denk bloss nicht, ich heule* (1965, *Just Don't Think I'll Cry*), see Wichnewski 1991.
86. Letter from Ernst-Joachim Herrmann to Ursula Ragwitz, 19 October 1977, SAPMO-BArch DY 30 IV B 2/9.06/81.
87. Letter from Herbert Volkmann to Günter Witt, 14 December 1965, SAPMO-BArch DR1/4331.
88. Zetek, Opinion Concerning the Ninth Leipzig Week, 21 February 1966, SAPMO-BArch DR1/4331.
89. Wolfgang Klaue to HVFilm, Vorschlag für die Veranstaltung einer Retrospektive "Französische Dokumentarfilme aus drei Jahrzehnten" während des Internationalen Leipziger Dokumentar- und Kurzfilmfestivals 1966, 19 April 1966, SAPMO-BArch DR1/4331.
90. Ibid.
91. Ibid.
92. Wolfgang Klaue, program text, 15 October 1966, SAPMO-BArch DR1/4331. The text was addressed to a certain W. Geier at HVFilm; it is Geier's annotations that are cited and referred to here.

93. Rabenalt, Head of the Theory and History Department at the Deutsche Hochschule für Filmkunst, Institut für Filmwissenschaft, to HVFilm, Film Production Department, "Stellungnahme zum Manuskript des Filmarchivs," SAPMO-BArch DR1 4331.
94. These included *À propos de Nice* (1929, dir. Jean Vigo); *Aubervilliers* (1946, dir. Eli Lotar); *Cuba sí!* (1961, dir. Chris Marker); *Du côté de la côte* (1958, dir. Agnès Varda); *Les enfants des courants d'air* (1960, Children Adrift, dir. Edouard Luntz); *Espagne 1936* (1937, produced and cowritten by Luis Buñuel); *Farrebique* (1944–1945, dir. Georges Rouquier); *Finis Terrae* (1928–1929, End of the Earth, dir. Jean Epstein); *Goëmons* (1948, Wrack, dir. Yannick Bellon); *La grande pêche* (1954, dir. Henri Fabiani); *Guernica* (1950, dir. Alain Resnais); *Hôtel des Invalides* (1951, dir. Georges Franju); *Lettre de Sibérie* (1958, Letter from Siberia, dir. Chris Marker); *Le monde du silence* (1955, The Silent World, dir. Jacques-Yves Cousteau); *Nogent, Eldorado du dimanche* (1929, Nogent, Marcel Carné); *Night and Fog*; *L'Opéra Mouffe* (1958, Diary of a Pregnant Woman, dir. Agnès Varda); *Le retour* (1945, The Return, dir. Henri Cartier-Bresson); *Rien que les heures* (1926, Nothing but the Hours, dir. Alberto Cavalcanti); *The Seine Meets Paris*; *Terre sans pain* (1932, Land without Bread, dir. Luis Buñuel); *Toute la mémoire du monde* (1956, All the World's Memories, dir. Alain Resnais); *Vivent les dockers* (1950, dir. Robert Ménégoz); *Le voyage au Congo* (1925, Travels in the Congo, dir. Marc Allégret); *La zone* (1928, The Zone, dir. Georges Lacombe).
95. See the reviews of Roth 1966 and Harmssen 1966.
96. Herbert Volkmann, Auswertung IX. Internationale Leipziger Dokumentar- und Kurzfilmwoche, Berlin, 7 December 1966, SAPMO-BArch DR1/4331.
97. Volkmann was director of the SFA from 1958 to 1968. He had come from the DEFA Studio for Feature Films, where he had been the economic director. At the SFA, he favored the international opening of the GDR's Film Archives. The Leipzig retrospectives were a sure means to achieve this goal.

CHAPTER 5

Toward Documentaries with a Human Face

Developments taking place in Czechoslovakia in early 1968, referred to as the Prague Spring, incorporated elements of international movements, de-Stalinization, and popular protest movements in the West but was rooted in Czechoslovakia's national specificity. The unique dynamics emerging from this constellation of elements made Czechoslovakian developments particularly alarming to East German political leaders, who closely monitored all existing contacts between the GDR and its southern neighbor (Bollinger 1995). And yet, during this period many East Germans traveled to Czechoslovakia, where censorship was less strict and exchanges with the West easier, particularly in the cultural sphere (Neubert 1997).

Culture, particularly cinema, was a highly effective vehicle to spread awareness of the Czechoslovakian revival in the international arena. Filmmakers knew how to make use of the platform afforded them by their success at film festivals and in movie theaters throughout the West. But, given the position of East German authorities, would documentaries aspiring to "socialism with a human face" find a place at the Leipzig Festival? An examination of the eleventh festival, held in November 1968, reveals the extent to which this particular year was a key juncture, allowing tensions that had accumulated over the previous years to crystallize.

The Prague Spring and Its End

The Czechoslovakian example dominated the period of liberalization that had swept across Central and Eastern Europe during the mid-1960s. The reform movement in Prague went much further than its counterparts in Hungary and in the GDR. It resonated remarkably in the West, as in the East, and was not without ramifications on East German culture. In the East, culture acted as a privileged vehicle of de-Stalinization. Along with authors, filmmakers were among Czechoslovakia's most proactive ambassadors, and these supporters of reform knew how to effectively use their connections to contacts abroad and benefit from the positive reception they found in the West.

A Cultural New Wave

In May 1963, an international conference on Franz Kafka, on the occasion of the eightieth anniversary of the novelist's birth, was held in Lidice, near the site of the World War II massacre (Mittenzwei 1991). This conference became a catalyst for the European left, at a time when both a new culture of thought and a new political culture were taking shape. Through debates on Kafka, highly topical political issues were actually being aired (Neubert 1997). A consideration of the work of a modernist, nonsocialist author in itself represented a challenge to authorities. Kafka's legendary parables, which describe a system whose absurdity crushes the individual, were now applied not only to the capitalist world but also to countries vaunting "real existing socialism." The historical import of the Kafka conference lay in the fact that it took place in the East but contained an international dimension that integrated it into the European context. One of the key hopes of reformers in the East was to bring an end to the cultural autarchy of the socialist countries (Langermann 2002).

The conference immediately provoked an increased hardening of policy in the East German literary domain. After the construction of the Berlin Wall in 1961, young East German authors had expressed their yearning for greater subjectivity and radicalism in the treatment of German history, as well as for an aesthetic modernity tied to a reinterpretation of Marxism (Emmerich 2000). This revival had assumed multiple forms of expression. In December 1962, author Stephan Hermlin organized a public reading of young authors at East Berlin's Academy of the Arts, followed by a public discussion, the reading featured Volker Braun, for example, and the singer-songwriter and poet Wolf Biermann.

In contrast to the official emphasis on the socialist community, the individual, the *ich*, lay at the heart of the works presented, thus instigating a "truly Copernican revolution" (Jordan 2003: 46). Hermlin had to resign from his position as assistant secretary of the academy (Emmerich 2000). The Second Bitterfelder Weg Conference, held in April 1964, represented a counterattack against such subjectivist tendencies; five years after the initial conference, it sought to reaffirm and implement the "principles of a socialist working class culture and to oppose any Western or modernist temptation" (Emmerich

2000: 181). The final blow was then delivered at the Eleventh Plenum in December 1965.

In Czechoslovakia, in contrast, international responses to artistic experimentation represented a veritable windfall for authors such as Milan Kundera and Bohumil Habral. At least initially, their newfound fame protected them from both censure and the risk of provincialism, things equally dreaded by East German artists. The success of the Kafka Conference also augured well for Czechoslovakian cinema, which was experiencing a significant period of renewal.

Socialist Realism had become the official artistic doctrine in Czechoslovakia, just as in the GDR, at the country's Ninth Party Congress in 1949. In the late 1950s, however, international acclaim for Soviet films produced during Khrushchev's thaw, as well as for Poland's Black Series documentaries, caused those in charge of Czechoslovakian filmmaking to reevaluate the conservative line. Author Jiří Marek was appointed the new managing director of the Central Administration for Film, thereby emphasizing the ties between literature and cinema, and Prague's Barrandov Film Studios offered several fledgling directors their first breaks. The top specialist journals welcomed theoretical debates. As early as 1958, Czechoslovakians enjoyed tremendous success at the Brussels World's Fair.

In 1964, a young Miloš Forman attracted international attention at the Locarno Film Festival with his fictional feature film *Cerny Petr* (1963, *Black Peter*), which depicts the gray daily life of a sixteen-year-old far more interested in love than political ideology.[1] In 1965, *Obchod na korze* (1965, *The Shop on Main Street*), by Jan Kadár and Elmar Klos — which explores bystander complicity in the anti-Semitic persecutions during World War II — won the Academy Award for Best Foreign Language Film. The films of Forman, Ivan Passer, and Jiří Menzel were warmly applauded on the festival circuit and released in movie theaters in a great number of countries (Kopaněvová 1996). These feature films — which advocated an end to all dogmatism and also displayed a strong documentary dimension — touched a wide audience by virtue of their impertinent tone. They turned an ironic gaze, with nothing spectacular about it, on daily life or the history of their country, and their documentary touch in fictional films involved successfully using both professional actors and amateurs. The international resonance of these films also resulted in great part from the place accorded to the real and sometimes futile interests of young people.

The Karlovy Vary Festival, which continued to take place in June, alternating years with the Moscow International Film Festival, played a key role in offering Czechoslovakian cinema an opening to the world at large. In 1962 and 1964, for example, Lindsay Anderson and Tony Richardson, two of the "angry young men" responsible for the emergence of a British New Wave in literature and filmmaking in the late 1950s, attended the festival.[2] In the tradition of John Grierson, they made short films rooted in the realities of the day, closer to underprivileged milieus and those living in the provinces. Also among the cinematic luminaries in attendance at Karlovy Vary in 1962 and 1964 were Richard Attenborough, Henry Fonda, Elia Kazan, Alain Resnais, and more.

Spotlight on The Russian Miracle

At their annual congress in June 1967, the Union of Czechoslovakian Writers openly expressed discontent with the Communist Party of Czechoslovakia (KSČ), thereby reviving the progressive vanguard role played by intellectuals there since the nineteenth century (Reichardt 2003). The Czechoslovakian crisis then erupted and culminated in major demonstrations and strikes in fall 1967, followed by the ascent of the reformist Alexander Dubček to become first secretary of the KSČ in January 1968. This was the harbinger of the Prague Spring. Given this context, the organizers of the upcoming Karlovy Vary Festival—which Tony Curtis, Ken Loach, and Cesare Zavattini were to attend in June—proposed new reforms: instead of a single jury, three independent international juries awarded three prizes—for best film, which went to Jiří Menzel for *Rozmarné léto* (1968, *Capricious Summer*), as well as for acting and for technical excellence.

The films of the Czechoslovakian New Wave sought to break taboos that the East German regime was unwilling to call into question, starting with the relationship with the Soviet big brother. The overriding Czechoslovakian demand was to develop an independent national path toward socialism, as this was the only basis for reform. This implied reexamining the role played by the USSR in establishing the Communist regime in Prague. Whereas in Germany, Soviet military presence and the relations between the GDR and the USSR had been a natural outgrowth of the defeat and occupation of Germany, the situation was quite different for its southern neighbor (Reichardt 2003).

The release of Andrew and Annelie Thorndike's documentary *Das russische Wunder* (1963, *The Russian Miracle*) in the GDR in 1963 embodied the opposite approach to the issue. Mixing archival footage and material shot by the Thorndikes in the USSR, the film depicts the first forty-five years of Soviet history—from the underindustrialized and undemocratic tsarist regime to Yuri Gagarin in outer space in 1961—as a continuous ascent toward ever-increasing progress. The average Soviet citizen rarely appears or speaks, however, and the film ignores the Russian Civil War, Stalin's cult of personality, and the purges. Officially approved by Khrushchev, in the GDR *The Russian Miracle* benefited from a major propaganda campaign that attempted to show it to the entire population, including blue- and white-collar workers and all schoolchildren older than thirteen.³ At the Leipzig Festival⁴—at which the Thorndikes' documentary was screened as the opening title—the town of Schwerin, in the northern State of Mecklenburg-Vorpommern, was announced to be the winner of a contest for the district that attracted the largest audiences.

Among the articles and reviews lauding the film, a few discordant voices were heard in the Czechoslovakian press. In the quarterly journal *Film á doba*, critic Antonín Navrátil denounced the film as a historical falsification, with facts and images used to underpin a preexisting line of argument. The response was swift. Navrátil's critique was translated into German and published in the East German periodical *Filmwissenschaftliche Mitteilungen*, where Hermann Herlinghaus, custodian of the orthodox line, refuted every point with praise he gleaned from the Soviet, Polish, and Hungarian press (Herlinghaus 1964; Navrátil 1964).

Divergences became increasingly clear, between the freedom of speech championed on the Czechoslovakian side and the attitude of East German colleagues, who, for the most part, were extremely reluctant to go so far. The managing director of the DEFA Feature Film Studio remarked on this during a trip to the Barrandov Film Studios in May 1968. His counterpart at the Prague studio sought to reassure him: East German communists had nothing to fear from policy changes that were committed to the fundamentals of Marxism-Leninism, while seeking to free Czechoslovakia from dogmatic positions; relations with the USSR would only deteriorate if Moscow repeated the mistakes it had committed with respect to Yugoslavia.

The East German visitor expressed his doubts concerning the reforms under way, but he had to admit how determined his partners were: "I was extremely taken aback at how naively . . . and how casually the comrades responded to the designs of our opponents, and to witness to what extent they showed themselves . . . reluctant to consolidate our ideological positions."⁵ Viewed from East Berlin, the Yugoslav precedent was seen as a deviation that had to be condemned, as indeed had been the call for a German route to socialism that Anton Ackermann had advocated in 1946. Compromise was thus ruled out.

Impact on the Festival Circuit

After Warsaw Pact tanks crushed the Prague Spring on 21 August 1968, the situation became increasingly tense. Though East German troops did not cross the Czech-German border for fear of rekindling war memories,⁶ from the outset the East Berlin regime had participated in condemning Dubček's political reforms (Tantzsche 1994), as, along with other perceived threats to the GDR, they envisaged Czechoslovakia normalizing diplomatic relations with the FRG (Klessmann 1997). The developments of 21 August did not immediately settle the problem for East Berlin, however; how were East German intellectuals and filmmakers going to react?[7]

The invasion of Czechoslovakia unleashed widespread emotion in the East as in the West. Czechoslovakian intellectuals made use of the international forum of film festivals, in which they had defended the Prague Spring and their desire for independence from Soviet control (Moine 2014b). A report from November 1968, submitted to HVFilm in East Berlin, recorded various public utterances and forms of action.[8] According to it, Czechoslovakian filmmakers had mostly sought to boycott the five Warsaw Pact nations whose troops had participated in the invasion. At the Venice Film Festival in late August, already deeply shaken by student protests (Pisu 2017), ten Western journalists had signed on to this boycott, some of whom—for example, the American critic Gideon Bachmann and the West Berliner Ulrich Gregor—were regular visitors to the Leipzig Festival. The call, however, produced no concrete results. At the Locarno Film Festival in Switzerland in late September, the Czechoslovakian New Wave film director Jiří Menzel, who was a member of the jury, refused to watch the Soviet, Hungarian, and East German entries in competition. When the organizers refused to change the program, the jury resigned, and an unofficial jury ultimately conferred the awards.

The Mannheim Festival planned for 7–12 October 1968 was awaited with bated breath in the East German film world. There, the film director Pavel Juráček adopted a new approach, issuing a personal statement in his own name, in which he condemned the events of 21 August but clearly separated art from politics. He did not call for a boycott: he had many friends among filmmakers from other socialist countries and did not wish to see these relationships undermined by political events. East German observers saw in this an attempt to spread "revisionist views" among filmmakers from other countries. They were equally taken aback by the attitude of Antonin Liehm,[9] critic and historian of Czechoslovakian cinema, who was to moderate festival discussions: "He remained silent during the discussion on East German film, visibly unhappy to witness participants analyzing the film in a thorough and reasoned way, without posing provocative questions on the Czechoslovakian issue. Thereafter, Liehm did not attend any further discussions."[10]

Elsewhere, and again according to the East German delegates, Jan Němec's entry, *Oratorium pro Prahu* (1968, *Oratorio for Prague*)—a short film about pop music groups confronted with political and cultural reforms and culminating in images of 21 August—was reported by the Stasi to have been booed during its screening for being so bad. The Czechoslovakian participants apparently then left the movie theater. The film must have appealed to some, however, for it received the FIPRESCI Prize. Some months later, in spring 1969, the Oberhausen Festival's Grand Prize was, significantly, bestowed on Karel Vachek's and Joszef Ort-Šnep's *Spřízneni volbou* (1968, *Elective Affinities*), dedicated to one of the crowning moments in the evolving Czechoslovakian political developments, when hardline president Navotny stepped down in March 1968 and was replaced by Ludvík Svoboda (Müllerová 1996).

Overall, the report asserted, Czechoslovakian participants had pointedly ignored their East German colleagues. At the Carthage Film Festival in Tunisia, a Czechoslovakian journalist even asked the West German film director Ulrich Schamoni, who had just been conversing with DEFA director Konrad Wolf, "how he could talk to a German fascist."[11] The attitude of the East Germans baffled them. For the most part, in fact, intellectuals in socialist countries responded to the invasion of Czechoslovakia with silence.[12] In the GDR, the Writers' Union, under the presidency of Anna Seghers, even published a statement welcoming the invasion on 26 August.

At the GDR's DEFA Feature Film and Documentary Film Studios, the general attitude was one of resignation, if not an outright sanctioning of the invasion. The attitude of feature film director Frank Beyer is instructive here. Born in 1932 and a former student at FAMU, the Prague film school where he studied from 1952 to 1955, Beyer was deeply upset by the violence of the repression—all the more so as he had kept in regular contact with Czechoslovakian colleagues, sitting on the jury of the 1964 Karlovy Vary Festival. And yet, Beyer did not publicly air his profound disagreement with the East German authorities.

After his film *Spur der Steine* (1966, *Trace of Stones*) was banned, Beyer had become persona non grata at the DEFA Studios and was engaged as a stage director at the Dresden Theater: "Cowardice? Yes, certainly. Opportunism in a hopeless situation? I wanted to get back to exercising my profession as a film director as soon as possible, and any public statement in support of the Prague political reforms would have seriously jeopardized such a comeback" (Beyer 2001: 165). Indeed, many who had been stung by the Eleventh Plenum followed this line of reasoning. Only a handful, including Wolf Biermann and the scientist Robert Havemann, audibly voiced their opposition (Neubert 1997).

Czechoslovakian filmmakers chose to break off all relations with their East German colleagues. The East German Film Days in Prague, scheduled for October 1968, were canceled. In November, the Czechoslovakian Barrandov Studios did not participate in the Eleventh Leipzig Festival: "The Czechoslovakians initially gave as an excuse, somewhat demagogically, that the [Leipzig] Selection Committee had not come to Prague in late August, as planned. The fact is that, given the circumstances, comrade Harkenthal postponed the meeting until the end of September."[13] But those in Prague fixed no fresh date, and on 24 September they were informed that the Barrandov Studios were withdrawing via telegram. The East Germans, subtly, noted, "In our view, the withdrawal is a reaction to the events of August."[14] In contrast,

Czechoslovakian State Television (ČST), which had immediately followed the lead of those now in power and was closer to the regime than the film studios, did attend. This is a clear indication that the prevailing rift between film studios and television networks witnessed in the GDR was playing out in Czechoslovakia as well.[15]

A year of pledges, scissions, and fierce disappointments, the events of 1968 crystallized the internal tensions and paradoxes of the communist systems—set up on a Soviet model that was now being deeply challenged—throughout Eastern Europe. The Leipzig Festival was one of the rare places on East German soil where this challenge was openly expressed and offered one of the rare opportunities to publicly voice strong criticism. In fact, according to the Cuban filmmaker Octavio Cortázar (1997: 41), the "last Leipzig Festival that was really good" was precisely the 1968 edition:

> It was a festival replete with discussions, confrontations, marked by everything that had happened in Paris in May and in Czechoslovakia in August. . . . There were violent critiques, starting with the important dissident movement around the university in Leipzig. And many visitors from West Germany fueled the debates. For many of us, the violence of the conflicts thus exposed made us think that the festival would not survive so much criticism.

Repercussions for the Festival

Among East Germans, the main questions of the post–Eleventh Plenum period was how to reform an ossified system that focused on a single ideological, political, and aesthetic line. While censorship was still on everyone's mind in the postplenum period, developments in the West and in Czechoslovakia encouraged some to call for dialogue and a margin of freedom. To this end, they tried to encourage debate and to arrange screenings at Leipzig that would air the entire gamut of documentaries being made at the time, while remaining, we should note, within a legal framework. It was not a case of radical opposition against the system, but rather the expression of a will to see "socialism with a human face" applied in the GDR as well.

Leipzig 1967: A Too Human Secretary?

In 1967, this approach had provoked a scandal at the festival, around a documentary by Jürgen Böttcher screened outside the official program. The incident underlines attempts made by the younger generation to use the festival as a forum for open exchange. As noted in chapter 4, in 1965 both Böttcher's documentary, *Barefoot and without a Hat,* and his feature film, *Born in '45,* had been censored. Unlike Frank Beyer, for whom censorship had resulted in exile from the DEFA Feature Film Studio, Böttcher received a new commission from the DEFA Documentary Film Studio on the occasion of the SED's Seventh Party Congress. This assignment—to film a portrait of a district party secretary—gave him a renewed opportunity to prove his credentials. The subject, Gerhard Grimmer, who had been the SED secretary at the Schkopau Buna chemical complex near Halle since 1961, was not chosen by Böttcher, but rather by Horst Sindermann, an SED stalwart and first secretary of the party for the Halle district. Initial contacts between Grimmer and Böttcher took place during the spring of 1967, with two representatives of the party present. In his own words, Böttcher had "nothing to lose."

Der Sekretär (1967, *The Party Secretary*) opens with a shot of Grimmer arriving at the factory on a bike. Viewers then follow him through a series of encounters with factory workers and colleagues, in his office, and on the shop floor, where he gladly helps out. Various testimonies round off the portrait of this local party secretary. The women factory workers say they appreciate Grimmer's work: he understands their concerns and was able to improve communications between them and their superiors. There is certainly no shortage of people who feel that Grimmer, with his cap always on his head, his raincoat and a scarf around his neck, does not correspond to what you'd expect of such a functionary. As the commentary notes, however, "This captures Grimmer's distinguishing feature: he doesn't attach any importance to appearances, but rather to what he says and does." A longtime activist of humble origins, differing little from the workers, in his mid-fifties Gerhard Grimmer embodied what socialism with a human face could have been.

The documentary's premiere was scheduled for opening night at the Leipzig Festival in November 1967. Contrary to all expectations, however, the film was not included in the selection of films that DEFA sent to the festival. It appeared that, by the time the film was finished, Grimmer no longer represented the image of a party secretary that the SED wanted to put on view. Although the GDR's New Economic Policy (NÖS) had been called into question following the Eleventh Plenum, the Communist regime had launched a process of economic modernization that resulted in a growing role for engineers and technicians. Henceforth, according to Böttcher, a party secretary was to resemble "an economic strategist, no longer a trade unionist in short-sleeves" (Deutscher Bundestag 1993: 551). In other words, he should be a white-collar employee rather than a blue-collar worker.

The film, however, did have advocates who made it possible for *The Party Secretary* to screen at the Leipzig Festival. A recurrent issue at the festival had to do with the selection process for DEFA films. Documentaries were selected, as we have seen, based on a proposal from DEFA, with the agreement of HVFilm and the culture department of the SED's ZK. If the authorities didn't accept a film, it was impossible to screen it at Leipzig. In December

1966, however, Herbert Volkmann, director of the State Film Archive (SFA), criticized the selection criteria for both East German and foreign films, which, in his opinion, did not sufficiently take into consideration the diversity of national production. He requested that the competition be given less prominence, in favor of parallel programs in which nonselected films would screen.[16] While Volkmann's plea was a blatant attack upon HVFilm and the festival director, it reflected the expectations of numerous filmmakers and film enthusiasts, as well as devoted festivalgoers, such as Fred Gehler.

In 1967, Fred Gehler (b. 1937) was the head of Leipzig's Film Club. He was also in charge of *Film*, a cinema journal with very limited circulation published from 1964 to 1968 by the Association of GDR Film Clubs, which had published texts on the Czechoslovakian literary and cinematic New Wave (Gehler and Schenk 2001). Film clubs played a key role in the GDR, particularly during this period, as they made it possible to see films that did not appear in theaters and offered a space for rich discussions and exchanges (Becker and Petzold 2001).[17] Director of photography Christian Lehmann, for example, recalls taking a group tour with his local film club in 1964 to Munich, in West Germany.[18] In August 1967, in view of its scheduled screening at Leipzig, *Film* had interviewed Jürgen Böttcher about *The Party Secretary*. The interview took up no fewer than ten of the fall issue's forty pages. Gehler was summoned by Werner Rose, secretary of the new Filmmakers' Association, established in January 1967. Rose reprimanded Gehler for having accorded such prominence to Böttcher and for publishing an interview that was ideologically unsatisfactory, playing as it did with allusions and innuendos. Furthermore, Böttcher's printed filmography listed his feature film *Born in '45*, which had been banned.

Lastly, and above all, Gehler was accused of having deceived and doublecrossed the organizers of the Leipzig Festival (Gehler 2001). When it became clear that *The Party Secretary* had been withdrawn from the festival program, the Leipzig Film Club took the initiative to organize a screening in its own venue, the Casino art house theater, at 10 PM, after the official screenings were over. Word of mouth did the rest and Böttcher's film was shown to a packed house. Many foreign guests were in the audience, including Chris Marker. It was here that the West German journalist Wilhelm Roth discovered Böttcher—of whom he had never heard—for the first time. Being familiar with other DEFA documentaries, Roth (2001: 12) detected in *The Party Secretary* a "new tonality, tinged with humanism, but also with humor and at times almost intimate." Once again, and apart from his own actions, the festival played a key role in consolidating Böttcher's international reputation.

The festival director had been unable to react in time to prevent the screening, but it was difficult to speak of real wrongdoing on Gehler's part. After all, *The Party Secretary* had been issued a certificate of general release, and, as an autonomous institution, the Leipzig Film Club was allowed to organize screenings as it saw fit. Following a decision made by the festivals' party group, Gehler was nevertheless barred from attending the festival and even forcibly expelled by Wolfgang Harkenthal. Harkenthal afterward regretted this incident,[19] but Gehler (1997: 7) recalls the episode with irony: "Wolfgang Harkenthal, a new cherub, guardian of the heavenly kingdom, armed with his blazing sword, hounded me out of the festival's sublime halls."[20] Böttcher was summoned to present his version of the events at HVFilm, but without further consequence.[21] This episode demonstrates that, even after 1965, there were ways to push the limits, if someone dared try, although they could not be made to vanish entirely (Lindenberger 1999b). It also reveals just how vague (and changeable) the limits actually were: two years later, *The Party Secretary* was included in a festival retrospective devoted to East German documentary film.[22]

Leipzig 1968: The End of Innocence

Over the months following the Böttcher debacle, tensions continued to mount, with street protests in Poland and the invasion of Czechoslovakia in summer 1968. Another unofficial screening then triggered a serious crisis during the 1968 Leipzig Festival—although the East German critic Hartmut Albrecht (1969: 255) chose to ignore it in his assessment: "The year began with a deafening bang for international film festivals: the festival calendar set off one crisis after another. Many festivals in the West were affected. The social role of film in decadent capitalism was revealed to be in a full-blown crisis. Despite this, the Leipzig Festival took place calmly." The festival had by no means been spared the unrest unleashed by protests in the West, however. For numerous contemporary witnesses, the 1968 edition represented a moment of crisis and rupture that shaped how they subsequently depicted the festival. In the words of documentary directors Walter Heynowski and Gerhard Scheumann (1997: 93), it was when the Leipzig Festival "lost its innocence." Personal recollections, which intersect, complement, and at times even contradict each other, allow us to catch a glimpse of the festival as a concurrently political and human experience.

In 1968, while the Communist Bloc found itself weakened by internal tensions, which became increasingly violent, opposition grew in the West as well. Relations between Moscow and Beijing—which had been deteriorating since 1963 and more intensely since 1966 and China's Cultural Revolution—served as the backdrop for a growing craze for Maoism within the extreme left in the West. The May 1968 movement in France had already presented an opportunity for an increasing number of left-wing voices to speak out against Communist regimes in Eastern Europe and the Soviet Union (Grémion 1985).

Figure 5.1. 1968: Streamers, posters, and the flags of all countries represented at the festival decorated the center of Leipzig. © Filmmuseum Potsdam, Reinhard Podszuweit.

Student movements, but also workers throughout Western Europe and the United States, contributed to intensely animated discussions among leftists. The Prague Spring and its subsequent suppression by the Soviet-led invasion exacerbated internal dissension, causing deep rifts within both the Western left and Communist circles. The Communist Parties of France, Italy, and Romania—on whose behalf Ceaucescu had refused to send troops for the invasion of Prague—notably voiced their disapproval, as did a great many communist intellectuals (Courtois and Lazar 1995). Beijing, too, condemned the invasion.

Leipzig and Western Protest Movements

As the Eleventh Leipzig Festival opened in November 1968, the year's developments were naturally on everyone's minds. Discussion of Western opposition—notably in West Germany—was almost taboo in the GDR, however, where the protests of the West German extraparliamentary opposition were rarely covered by the press, unless they were against the Vietnam War. Vietnam had indeed been the unifying theme behind the first large student demonstrations in West Berlin as of February 1966 (Gilcher-Holtey 2001; Görlich 2002). But Western activists soon became involved in other issues as well.

In June 1967, a state visit to the FRG by the Shah of Iran triggered a renewed wave of protests, during which the student Benno Ohnesorg was fatally wounded by a policeman. Protests spread throughout West Germany. In April 1968, Rudi Dutschke, a leading figure in the student movement, survived an assassination attempt, setting off a series of protests that turned Easter 1968 into one of the most violent moments of the period. Protesters also vehemently attacked the Emergency Acts that were passed in West Germany in May 1968. What had started as condemnation of US policy in Vietnam was now bundled with Third World issues and questions about the older generation's role under Nazism. These last issues were above all taken up by students, intellectuals, and artists who were equipped with an education and privileged access to information (Klessmann 1997).

In 1967, the Leipzig Festival had screened only one documentary from the FRG: a West Berlin film shot and produced by AStA, the General Student Council at West Berlin's Free University, and titled *Berlin—2 Juni 1967* (*Berlin, 2 June 1967*).[23] The AStA film focused on police violence during student demonstrations protesting against the shah's visit to West Berlin. In fall 1968, just one DEFA documentary broached the subject of West German unrest: Harry Hornig's *Ostern 68* (1968, *Easter '68*). Screened out of competition at Leipzig, the film showed a sequence of shots of young West German protesters confronting the police with slogans calling for the recognition of the GDR and denouncing rampant fascism in the FRG.

The film depicts the current political climate in the FRG by focusing on the coalition between the conservative Christian Democratic Union and the Social Democratic Party and the Emergency Acts that had been implemented, which the left suspected was a means to establish a fascist government. It then draws a parallel between this contemporary climate and the chaotic crisis situation that reigned during Weimar Republic Germany's 1923 inflation (Klessmann 1997). *Easter '68* did not reflect the anarchist leanings of some protesters, however, or their often highly critical stance with regard to Communist regimes in Eastern Europe, as exemplified by Rudi Dutschke.

Following on what had taken place in France in May 1968, French participants at the Leipzig Festival were determined to discuss the demonstrations agitating Western industrial societies. As a result, filmmaker Marceline Loridan, the companion of Joris Ivens, had come to Leipzig with seven films. These were short films focusing on strikes and other events in France in May 1968 that were directed by either Chris Marker or collectives of which Loridan herself was a member.[24] The importance of these shorts, according to Loridan, was that they gave a voice to workers, who otherwise had little opportunity to express themselves publicly. Upon arriving at the festival, Loridan went to drop off the films with the Selection Committee, which was used to receiving such so-called suitcase films at the last minute. The following day, however,

Figure 5.2. Joris Ivens (*left*) with festival director Wolfgang Harkenthal at the 1968 Leipzig Festival. © Filmmuseum Potsdam, Reinhard Podszuweit.

she was informed that the committee had already disbanded and that, as they had been unable to view the films, the shorts could not be screened.

Loridan grasped what was really at stake: although the regime that had been shaken by crisis in May 1968 was a capitalist one, such freedom of speech and such reformist and revolutionary aspirations could only be viewed with grave concern by East German political leaders. In response, she decided to rent, for a day, all the small projection booths normally reserved for the festival's "trade show," during which they were used to screen films during negotiations between film producers and distribution companies. Loridan drummed up interest in the screenings, especially talking to students at the film academy in Babelsberg, and word of mouth did the rest. The projection booths were overflowing. Loridan acknowledged that, although she had been deliberately very provocative, "The real outrage, however, was that the films could not be shown. The outrage I provoked was merely a response to that!" (Loridan-Ivens 1997: 57–58). As Wolfgang Harkenthal recounts, these screenings were a godsend for journalists.[25] At the formal discussions, where the officially selected films were usually debated, the French films were the sole topic of discussion.

The screenings made a strong impression on East German audiences; it was entirely new for them to see French workers taking the floor, expressing their demands for self-management and challenging the existing system. A young filmmaker, who congratulated Loridan and asked her if he could hold on to the films, turned out to be Jürgen Böttcher,[26] who recalls the 1968 festival as being one of the rare occasions when the real issues of the day were at the heart of discussions—precisely thanks to Loridan's screenings.[27]

Although Western protest movements were the subject of considerable scrutiny by the East German authorities, much stricter control was exercised over information on the Warsaw Pact invasion of Czechoslovakia, which East Berlin had accepted without the slightest misgiving. In November 1968, however, the topic remained more controversial than ever at Leipzig.

The Briton Stanley Forman, for example, who had supported the festival since its inception, found himself in a difficult and painful quandary and refused to translate an English voice-over for a film that legitimized the invasion of 21 August 1968. His decision was made, in part, because an "upright Marxist he knew"—Eduard Goldstücker, who had been victim of Stalinist purges in Czechoslovakia and then rehabilitated and released in 1955[28]—was violently attacked in the film. Goldstücker had been among the co-organizers of the 1963 conference on Franz Kafka—the "master," as he put it, "of the destruction of illusions" (Barck and Münz-Koenen 2002: 40).

Forman (1997) even wondered whether it still made sense to send British filmmakers to the Leipzig Festival at all. Cuban delegates, of whom there were many, also actively participated in discussions and supported the French in their revolt against festival organizers. A documentary by the Cuban filmmaker Santiago Álvarez, who had previously won several awards at Leipzig, was put on the back burner and received no awards—presumably because his film showed Fidel Castro, who, while he did not condemn the invasion of Czechoslovakia, did declare it to be illegal (Jordan 2007).

Criticism did not come solely from foreign guests. According to the official report on the festival, "Young filmmakers, probably on the initiative of students at the [Babelsberg] film academy," wanted to circulate a petition protesting against such indirect censorship of Álvarez's film (Forman 1997: 55). The prompt intervention of festival management prevented the petition from being circulated, however, and the attitude of the students was strongly condemned. A resolution denouncing the suppression of the Prague Spring had also been signed by these same students. This protest resulted in, among other things, the expulsion of students and the arrest of author Thomas Brasch, at the time a student at the film academy and the son of Deputy Minister of Culture Horst Brasch (Löser 1996).

Initially taken aback by this event, festival organizers swiftly evaluated the incident and opted to counterattack. The reassuring accounts of the festival organizers were not enough to convince them that the danger was past, however, and the SED's ZK felt it was necessary to once again take control of the situation. Following the festival, a virulent text was drawn up within the ZK. It claimed that the failure of "counterrevolutionary plots" had caused, particularly in "West Germany's ruling circles, hatred and anger at seeing their political maneuvering undermined." A "flood of calumnies" then came crashing down, especially on the GDR,[29] which led to a call to boycott international events in socialist countries. First and foremost, according to the text's authors, it was necessary to hail as a success the fact that the Leipzig Festival had even taken place, let alone in such a controlled manner.

Nevertheless, it was imperative to take some political-ideological action with respect to festival guests. It must be clearly explained that the 21 August 1968 intervention had been a "genuine expression of humanism and human dignity," and it must be stressed that the Bonn government had supported counterrevolutionary forces in Czechoslovakia. For Latin American guests, it was particularly important to emphasize that "proletarian internationalism was fundamentally different from a movement of rabble rousers [*Revoluzzertum*]."

In focusing on foreign guests, it seemed that the ZK did not to want to acknowledge that criticism was also coming from within East German society. The West German film critic Ulrich Gregor (1967b) spoke of "the festival's schizophrenia" during those years, when both official and unorthodox discussions mingled in the corridors. Where were the opposition voices coming from? What were they critiquing? And how did the regime seek to silence them?

Cuba and Others: Neither Oppositional nor Orthodox

In the opinion of festival director Harkenthal, the 1968 edition signaled that the Leipzig Festival was truly an international forum, where one could exchange highly diverse opinions, outside of official doctrine, and even at the expense of the festival.[30] He seems to have quickly forgotten his own attitude toward those seeking to express themselves outside of the official lines— even though he subsequently expressed reservations or regret, particularly about having thrown Fred Gehler out of the festival in 1967. But it was no easy feat to disseminate a different perspective from the one advocated on the rostrum at Leipzig—making it all the more important to follow the rare individuals who did so.

The career of critic Fred Gehler accurately illustrates the ways in which a number of East German artists and intellectuals were trapped in the middle. While a student at the University of Leipzig, Gehler had started writing for the GDR's culture magazine, *Sonntag*. He soon made his mark with articles calling for greater openness to films from the West (Buñuel, Bergman etc.) in GDR movie theater programs. He himself had discovered German and foreign classics while working at the SFA during his studies; this had also enabled him to travel to Prague and Warsaw, making contact with cinephiles sensitive to new trends in their respective countries. One of his articles, however, did lead to his expulsion from the University of Leipzig in the summer of 1965, well before the Eleventh Plenum.

Unable to continue his academic studies, Gehler became an independent journalist and worked at *Film*, the Film Club magazine launched in 1964. The growing discontent of the Filmmakers' Union with the tone and themes of the journal, however, resulted in its being banned in 1968. That same year, Gehler published an interview in his own name, with the highly acclaimed film critic and historian Enno Patalas, about Konrad Wolf's DEFA feature film *Ich war neunzehn* (1967, *I Was Nineteen*) in the West German magazine *Filmkritik*. Not only had Gehler failed to receive official permission to publish in the West, something he did regularly, but he also slipped in some unorthodox remarks about Wolf's film, to the effect that the autobiographical tale about the liberation of Berlin in 1945 avoided the prevailing East German cliché of happy Soviet liberators and a welcoming German populace (Gehler and Schenk 2001). This time, Gehler was banned from publishing in *Sonntag*. He nevertheless continued working on editing a history of film and at the Leipzig movie theater affiliated with the SFA; his lack of high visibility and the solidarity of his colleagues undoubtedly helped Gehler through this challenging period.[31]

Gehler thus built his career mostly on the margins, testing the limits, but never slipping into illegality. A mixture of enthusiasm for the films being championed, but also a streak of naiveté or lack of awareness explains such a trajectory, which was embraced by several filmmakers, critics, and journalists at that time. As a consequence, they did not immediately perceive the significance of the wave of censorship unleashed in 1965. "Most did not grasp how deep the hole would be. I think there were many illusions. [For many] a chapter had simply ended, and it was now necessary to reach another summit, but by means of other paths" was how Gehler evaluated the situation in hindsight (Gehler and Schenk 2001: 94). Despite all this, it remained possible in the meantime to continue expressing such positions at certain venues and spaces at the Leipzig Festival.

In 1968, West German journalist Wilhelm Roth was not invited or allowed to travel to the festival because he had been the one to conduct the *Filmkritik* interview with Gehler.[32] When he returned the following year, he was struck by the mediocrity of the program. In his estimation, only the midnight discussions continued to be of interest. With less strict supervision, animated discussions still took place here, and contrary and opposing positions were still articulated. The presence of Cuban guests further accentuated the attraction of these evenings and debates.

Among Communist nations beginning to voice criticism against the system that the Soviet Union was imposing in Eastern Europe, the countries from the

Southern Hemisphere were the most virulent. Unquestionably, Cuba was the least compliant acolyte in the communist camp. The specificity of Cuban communist thinking and of the ideology and style of Fidel Castro's approach emphasized essential differences within what was called the Bloc. In the 1960s, tensions around these differences became particularly acute, especially as many Cuban documentary filmmakers had a close relationship with Czechoslovakia, where they had undertaken part of their studies.[33]

As early as 1961, documentarist Octavio Cortázar experienced internal opposition at the festival between supporters of radical politics, primarily represented by the Cubans, and the more clear-cut positions of the "officials." As a member of the jury, Cortázar clashed fiercely with Polish member Tadeusz Makarczynski over Karl Gass's *Arise, Childern . . . for Algeria*. In this film, the Cuban saw a people's unavoidable guerilla struggle for its independence and the construction of socialism. Makarczynski, on the other hand, preferred a film on extracting gas in Siberia, which, in his opinion, symbolized peaceful coexistence by emphasizing progress achieved through peaceful means. Such tensions were not unknown to Cortázar; he had also experienced them elsewhere in Eastern Europe, such as when he served on the jury for the Moscow Festival in 1963. But at least at Leipzig, he remarked, there were those midnight discussions, where participants could hold informal discussions (Cortázar 1997).

In 1969, Roth recalled heated debates on a related subject that, for many, remained taboo—namely, the issue of depicting the USSR without recourse to the myths and gilded memories of the "Great Patriotic War."[34] Once again, the Leipzig Festival, despite itself, was echoing international developments. The events of 1968 had accelerated the increasing autonomy and distancing of some Communist parties from their Soviet elder brother, following the example of the Italian Communist Party (Courtois and Lazar 1995). Thus, when the International Meeting of Communist and Workers Parties took place in Moscow in June 1969, with seventy-five of ninety-two existing Communist parties in attendance, the Communist Party of the Soviet Union (CPSU) no longer played the role of the center, let alone of the leader or guide of the international communist movement.

A Younger Generation under the Influence

In addition to the oppositional voices we have just mentioned, other voices among the younger generation were raised. To those of Karl Gass and Andrew Thorndike, and then of Jürgen Böttcher and cinematographer Christian Lehmann, were added those of the generation of film directors that experienced the events of 1965 and 1968 as students at Babelsberg and Leipzig.

They saw New Wave films from the West and East, felt themselves akin to young people in the West, and had matured both personally and politically with each successive political crisis. The role played by this generation of young East Germans at Leipzig cannot be overlooked and, indeed, was one that troubled orthodox forces in East Berlin.

The Festival On and Off Stage

These young cinephiles and filmmakers quickly grasped the festival's dual nature, its official and less conformist sides, and sought to navigate it to their advantage Volker Koepp (b. 1944) recalls that there were even three distinct Leipzig Festivals: "For me, as for some friends, there were three parts to Leipzig. The first was the films. From around the world. The second was the weeklong party. Meeting people, moments of happiness. The third was the political spectacle. An atmosphere like the 'Kaiser's birthday'" (Koepp 1997: 99).

We will focus on the second aspect: the desire to reappropriate a place for discussion and exchange, free from pomp and official speeches. A geography of the festival emerges, in which one can distinguish places within the official festival and places on its fringes, at various unofficial locations. Jürgen Böttcher provides us with an overview of this:

> First, there was the Capitol [movie theater], an enormous complex used for the city's trade fairs. It was hard to find something to eat, but there were always small sandwiches. And we used to move around from one table to the next. After the screenings, we continued on to the festival's Club. Then to the Astoria Hotel, near the railway station, where the festival celebrities stayed. That lasted all night, a party until dawn. And there was also the [university's] student club, in vaulted cellars from the Middle Ages, beautifully reconstructed after the war. We would all get together in this grotto. It was fantastic. Or we'd sit all night with friends in the waiting areas of the train station, until six in the morning.[35]

A geographical hierarchy unfolds, from the festival's principal movie venue to the railway station, a transit zone, at a distance from overly tight controls. On the way were the hotels, where the festival management lodged all its distinguished and important guests—still in the official zone, but with the ability to speak more freely. It was up to participants to find their way around these various sites, to capture the different ambiences of the festival.

In addition, younger participants, be they students at the film academy or the University of Leipzig or others, formed their own separate group. Volker Koepp, a budding documentarist in the late 1960s, mixes irony and emotion in his recollections of the festival:

It was during the sad month of November. The first snow often fell during the Leipzig Festival. The cold wind swept through the plaza in front of Central Station. For many years, this is where we got together after the screenings. We took refuge there, away from the third part [the official festival], often until the next morning. Mitropa—East Concourse. Mitropa—West Concourse. After a slight hesitation, the Saxon waiters greeted us like a welcome distraction. . . . At around five in the morning, we moved from the East Concourse to the West Concourse: they had to clean. Above our heads, the lofty domes of Europe's largest railway station. Leipzig, a festival of life. The drink was called The Grey Monk, our favorite dish, oatmeal. (Koepp 1997: 99)

Koepp's recollections show that, even in the wake of the crises of 1965 and 1968, the festival remained an exciting destination for young East German filmmakers and enthusiasts.

Relations between the festival and the younger generation had nevertheless been strained. As we have seen, a large gathering of teachers and students from film schools in the East and the West had taken place at the festival in 1963. Given its success and the enthusiasm it generated, a second meeting was envisaged. It did not take place until 1992, however (Wiedemann 1998). There were obstacles to arranging a sequel. In 1965, John Grierson felt obliged to advise, "Do not bestow prizes on elderly, veteran filmmakers, and don't even select them in the competition."[36] For his part, the year after the Eleventh Plenum the rector of the Babelsberg Academy wrote an article in the festival's *Protokoll* highlighting the importance of Leipzig in the students' political and cinematographic training, and in favor of reestablishing a place for the younger generation at the center of the Documentary Week.[37] The events of 1968 demonstrated to what extent the young East Germans at the festival did not feel understood or listened to by the responsible authorities.

The festival's setting in a university city, moreover, provided an audience with a considerable potential for unrest (Wierling 1994). A great number of students from the university's German Institute for Literature were, in fact, excluded from the festival during the fall of 1968, after having actively participated in gestures of support for Czechoslovakian reformers and subsequently protesting against the Soviet-led invasion of August 1968. They had created a literary circle, aligning themselves with the ideals of the Prague Spring (Neubert 1997). The destruction, on 30 May 1968 of the university church—the Paulinerkirche, dating back to the thirteenth century—had already affected the citizens of Leipzig deeply. Ultimately, the years of struggle by those opposing the church's demolition had been unsuccessful, but once again they had revealed the potential for resistance among city residents and the Saxon city's deep sense of identity.[38] Wolfgang Harkenthal recalls experiencing the tensions surrounding the church's destruction "only from afar," but he is well aware that a considerable proportion of the city's population opposed the decision.[39]

The events unfolding in Prague, Paris, and West Berlin also exposed this younger generation to fresh perspectives. In the words of one member of that generation: "The beach was not only under Parisian cobblestones,[40] but also under Wenceslas Square in Prague, under the Free University's Otto Suhr Institute in West Berlin, and under Schönhauser Allee in East Berlin" (Kleinert 1998). The Babelsberg film academy soon joined these hotbeds of protest.

The HFF under Surveillance

In an attempt to keep the HFF film school in Potsdam-Babelsberg under tight control, two ministerial decisions, issued in December 1966 and December 1967, modified the structures of the institution. In order to consolidate and support the development of a second state television channel, from now on the academy was to train students qualified to work at DFF. On one hand, this entailed integrating technical training for the medium of television; on the other, it brought with it the close monitoring of the HFF film school by DFF (Wiedemann 1998).

In December 1968, an inspection brigade came to monitor the implementation of reforms at the HFF.[41] Their report was clear and recommended rectifying a situation deemed critical, for disorder reigned. They ascertained that Marxist-Leninist aesthetics, a mandatory subject irrespective of the degree pursued, was no longer being taught at the academy; the professor had fallen ill more than a year earlier and had not been replaced.[42] The report underlined that the carelessness of school management was reflected in the absence of any control over "discipline and respect for socialist norms of behavior on the part of students." It noted that students arrived late, smoked, and drank coffee during some lectures.

Apart from such disciplinary issues, it was apparent—be it in relation to the films produced or the courses pursued—that "too many concessions were made with respect to phenomena drawn from decadent capitalism," that "many students did not grasp the importance of Marxism-Leninism in their artistic formation," and, lastly, that the "lessons of the Eleventh Plenum had not been sufficiently integrated." The students' enthusiasm for the films of Jean-Luc Godard and François Truffaut, "representatives of a decadent, petty-bourgeois cinema," also demonstrated the students' lack of political and ideological maturity.[43]

The report also referred to debates concerning the invasion of Czechoslovakia, claiming that academy management had not dealt with events as they ought to have and had been far too chaotic in their approach: discussions had mostly been conducted "by those groups of students who had no clear idea of the GDR's cultural policy, or had been influenced by the ideology of the class enemy."⁴⁴ Finally, according to the report, Rector Konrad Schwalbe was in no small way responsible for the "unhealthy atmosphere" that reigned at the academy. He had proven himself incapable of directing the institution with authority, and, above all, he did not seem to grasp why DFF was partnering with the academy. In conclusion, the report demanded that Schwalbe quit his post,⁴⁵ which he did. In 1969, a new rector took charge of the academy. Lutz Köhlert came from television, as did Karl-Eduard von Schnitzler, who was appointed to assist him.⁴⁶ Once again, DFF came to the rescue of orthodox forces in the regime. In light of the success, from the point of view of the authorities of adjustments implemented by the academy's new directorate, as of 1971 the Leipzig Festival was permitted to organize a special selection of films newly returned to the fold from the Babelsberg Academy.

Von Schnitzler, who as of 1968 had occupied a tenured and pivotal position at DFF, ensured that students' films were formatted to fit official policy requirements. He himself had been involved in making documentaries, mostly writing and narrating voice-over commentaries.⁴⁷ Well-known for his aggressive and rarely subtle Cold War stance, he also got attention for his "ten reasons against growing beards" (Wiedemann 1998: 62); at DFF it was advisable to appear beardless if you didn't want to come across as a dangerous leftist or deviant.⁴⁸ In 1972, he served as jury president at the Leipzig Festival.

A Sea Change

Director Karl Gass thinks that the festival lost its true identity with the arrival of DFF, which he recalls as being a zealous servant of the political authorities.⁴⁹ The influence of the film professionals who had facilitated the birth of the festival and its revival in 1960–1961 was thus limited. After 1964, Gass (1998) felt that Leipzig was merely a ceremonial affair—the "Kaiser's birthday" to which Volker Koepp alluded. The new line thus instilled in the festival primarily came down to the influence of director Andrew Thorndike. In 1963, his *The Russian Miracle* had positioned him favorably in the corridors of power. He perfectly understood how the Leipzig Festival could bolster the GDR's authority in the international arena and what a technical as well as financial asset television represented, essential for both documentary filmmaking and the festival.⁵⁰ Thorndike's triumph meant the decline of his rival, Karl Gass, whose documentary *Leisure* had screened at the festival in 1964, but out of competition in the Information Program. Gass had to wait until 1978 before his work would again be shown at Leipzig, and he was not president of the jury again until 1980.⁵¹

Thorndike's open hostility toward Gass did not escape the attention of their superiors, who were aware of how to benefit from such rivalries. According to

Figure 5.3. 1967: Rooms with televisions now supplemented the main screening venue and projection booths—here a television film competition. © Filmmuseum Potsdam, Reinhard Podszuweit.

a note drafted by the Central Committee of the SED in 1964, "[Andrew and Annelie] Thorndike clearly believe themselves to be almost alone, among filmmakers, to represent the party's cultural policy and they lambaste everything that does not correspond to their idea of documentary film. On the other hand, we have just as much need of the Thorndikes as of Karl Gass."[52] To compensate for his loss of influence at Leipzig, in 1965 Gass became director of the class on documentary filmmaking at the film academy; the subsequent overhaul of the academy in 1968, however, led to his departure.

After having trained several filmmakers, who then became his associates, he devoted himself increasingly to directing films.[53] Among the new generation arriving at the DEFA Studio for Documentary Films were directors who later played a significant role at DEFA. These included Volker Koepp and Konrad Weiss (b. 1942), who had been Gass's students at Babelsberg; Gitta Nickel (b. 1936), who did not attend the academy, was also mentored by Gass and shot her debut documentary around then in 1970. In the late 1960s, Gass thus enjoyed some influence at the studio, ensconced in his group working at Kleinmachnow, while Andrew and Annelie Thorndike were asserting themselves at Leipzig and among the upper echelons of the regime.

Karl Gass's character is particularly interesting because he had a certain allegiance to the regime, but also a relatively individualistic attitude. The first trait earned him persistent antagonism from some quarters, including from Jürgen Böttcher; the second took the form of setting up this group of young documentary filmmakers around himself and thus standing apart from other directors. Gass's significance for these young filmmakers, as well as the influence he exerted becomes clear below, as we follow the contrasting trajectories of filmmakers such as Winfried Junge, Volker Koepp, and Gitta Nickel.

The Leipzig Festival in 1968 must thus be considered in the context of the entire decade of the 1960s. Furthermore, as of the end of 1965 the attitude of East German authorities, filmmakers, and critics can only be understood in relation to the Eleventh Plenum and its ramifications. The idea of the "1968 years" (Dreyfus-Armand et al. 2008) at Leipzig also raises the issue of modernization in the GDR (Engler 1999). East German leaders encouraged technological advances in order to increase, as they saw it, productivity and enhance the quality of life. Once the government's economic reforms targeting improved working conditions were launched, however, no other reforms could be contemplated, particularly if they aspired to develop socialism with a human face (Steiner 2004).

Ideologically rigid, the East German regime thus missed the opportunity for renewal that was being offered in the cultural sphere, especially in the cinematic domain. It did not know how to take advantage of the seeds of modernization and the fresh impetus brought by a new generation of East Germans and DEFA filmmakers, which echoed developments that reached far beyond East Germany and the East Bloc. Proponents in favor of orthodoxy had succeeded, at least temporarily, in neutralizing influences they deemed harmful, be they internal or external, coming from the West and the Southern Hemisphere.

Aside from the question of the regime's legitimacy among the East German population, the country's isolation in the international arena persisted.[54] To try to offset this dual deficit, the national grand narrative focusing on antifascism gave way to the clarion call of international solidarity. This new theme was to become ubiquitous. As of the mid- to late 1960s, it took hold of the world of documentary filmmaking, and the Leipzig Film Week presented it with a perfectly suited venue.

Notes

1. These themes reappear in Forman's second feature film, *Lásky jedné plavovlásky* (1965, *The Loves of a Blonde*), which became a huge international hit, remaining in theaters for twenty-five weeks in Paris and twenty-seven in New York (Douchet 1998).

2. Tony Richardson made one of the principal films of the movement, *The Loneliness of the Long Distance Runner*, in 1962 (Pilard 2010).
3. Letter from the Municipal Council of the City of Gera, 19 April 1963, SAPMO-BArch DR1/4579.
4. Protokoll, Auswertung des Wettbewerbs mit dem Film *Das russische Wunder*, HV-Film, Berlin, 14 November 1963, SAPMO-BArch DR1/4579.
5. Letter from Franz Bruk, general director of the DEFA Studios, to Siegfried Wagner, director of HVFilm, Report on my trip to Prague on 18 and 19 May 1968. Confidential! 20 May 1968, SAPMO-BArch DY 30 IV A2/9.06/28.
6. The East German army took part in the operation but was just in charge of provisioning and the rear of the invasion (Wenzke 1995).
7. For more on the East German reaction to the Prague Spring, see Priess et al. 1996.
8. International Relations section of HVFilm, on foreign appearances of Czechoslovakian filmmakers after 21 August 1968, Berlin, 13 November 1968, SAPMO-BArch DY 30 IV A2/9.06/28.
9. He was the author, with Mira Liehm, of numerous works of film history, such as their pioneering work *Les cinémas de l'Est de 1945 à nos jours* (1989), which was reissued several times.
10. International Relations section of HVFilm, on foreign appearances of Czechoslovakian filmmakers after 21 August 1968, Berlin, 13 November 1968, SAPMO-BArch DY 30 IV A2/9.06/28.
11. International Relations section of HVFilm, on foreign appearances of Czechoslovakian filmmakers after 21 August 1968, Berlin, 13 November 1968, SAPMO-BArch DY 30 IV A2/9.06/28.
12. See Fejtö and Rupnik 1999; Krause 2002.
13. HV Film. Sektor Kulturelle Beziehungen, Bericht. Erfüllung der Vereinbarungen mit der CSSR im Jahre 1968, 14 November 1968, SAPMO-BArch, DY 30 IV A2/906.
14. Ibid.
15. For insight into the politics of Czechoslovakian television during the "normalization" period, see Bren 2010.
16. Herbert Volkmann, Auswertung IX. Internationale Leipziger Dokumentar- und Kurzfilmwoche, Berlin, 7 December 1966, SAPMO-BArch DR1/4331.
17. Director Tamara Trampe remembers having been able to organize screenings of classic films in Rostock. Author's interview with Tamara Trampe, Berlin, Germany (23 August 2004).
18. Author's interview with Christian Lehmann, Berlin, Germany (22 August 2000).
19. Author's interview with Wolfgang Harkenthal, Murchin, Germany (7 August 2000).
20. (Author's trans.) "[In meiner Erinnerung ist die Anekdote aufbewahrt, wie dereinst] Wolfgang Harkenthal mich aus den hehren Hallen des Festivals verwies, ein neuer Cherubin mit dem Flammenschwert."
21. Minutes of the conversation conducted at HVFilm with Jürgen Böttcher about the screening of the film *Der Sekretär* during the tenth Leipzig Festival, 21 December 1967, SAPMO-BArch DR1/4267.
22. See the brief allusion to the film screening in Voigt 1969.
23. AStA stands for Allgemeiner Studentenausschuss. The Free University of Berlin, founded in 1948 in the American sector of the city as the counterpart to Humboldt University in East Berlin, was one of the first sites of contestation of students in the 1960s.

24. Among these were a ten-minute film made by Pierre Bonneau, Liane Estiez-Willemont, and Jacques Willemont—*La reprise du travail aux usines Wonder* (*The Return to Work at the Wonder Factory;* Iskra)—and another ten-minute film by Michel Andrieu and Jacques Kébadian—*Le droit à la parole* (*The Right to Speak*)—both made in 1968.
25. Author's interview with Wolfgang Harkenthal, Murchin, Germany (7 August 2000).
26. In 1989, when she returned to Leipzig for the first time, Böttcher told her how the students at the film school and, more generally, East German documentarists had often watched these films (Loridan-Ivens 1997).
27. Interview by the author with Jürgen Böttcher, Berlin/Karlshorst, Germany (31 October 2000).
28. Eduard Goldstücker (1913–2000), born in Slovakia into a Jewish family, became committed to the communist movement very early. After his exile in London during the war, he returned to Czechoslovakia in 1945 and worked in the diplomatic corps. In 1953, he was condemned to life in prison but then freed in 1956. He was a professor of German literature at Charles University in Prague and president of the Writers' Union during the Prague Spring. After 21 August 1968, he went back to Great Britain.
29. Concept for the Twelfth Leipzig Festival, BArch-FArch, Leipzig, 1968.
30. Author's interview with Wolfgang Harkenthal, Murchin, Germany (7 August 2000).
31. Andreas Kötzing has offered yet more evidence of the difficulty of tracing neat boundaries in the political and cultural landscape of East Germany in his research in the Stasi archives, which seems to indicate that Fred Gehler was enrolled as an informant (IM, informelle Mitarbeiter) from 1968 to 1976. Gehler denies, however, having ever cooperated with the Stasi. See Kötzing 2012.
32. Author's interview with Wilhelm Roth, Berlin, Germany (9 March 2003).
33. Octavio Cortázar, who studied directing at Charles University in Prague from 1963 to 1967, thus lived through the intense atmosphere that led to the Prague Spring (Cortázar 1979).
34. Author's interview with Wilhelm Roth, Berlin, Germany (9 March 2003).
35. Author's interview with Jürgen Böttcher, Berlin/Karlshorst, Germany (31 October 2000).
36. Protokoll der Tagung des Ehrenpräsidiums in Wiepersdorf, 2–5 May 1965, SAPMO-BArch DR1/4276.
37. Article by Rector Schwalbe, written 17 October 1966 and published in the *Protokoll* of the ninth festival, SAPMO-BArch DR1/4331.
38. See Erich Loest's (2001) beautiful description.
39. Author's interview with Wolfgang Harkenthal, Murchin, Germany (7 August 2000).
40. This refers to a well-known slogan coined during the unrest in Paris in May 1968: "Under the cobblestones, the beach!"
41. Report on the brigade inspection at the German Academy for Film Arts in Potsdam-Babelsberg from 9 to 19 December 1968, Culture Department of the SED's ZK, Berlin, 8 January 1969, annex 1, SAPMO-BArch DY 30 IV A2/9.06/43, p. 3.
42. Ibid., 4.
43. Ibid., 4, 8. This illustrates the privileged status of students at Babelsberg Academy, where recent films from the West, which did not appear in movie theaters in the GDR, were screened.
44. Ibid., 12.
45. Ibid., 9–10, 21.

46. On television during this period, after 1968, see Heimann 2002.
47. Notably, for Karl Gass's *Look at This City.* For more, see chapter 3.
48. A historical irony: Karl-Eduard von Schnitzler later had a prosthesis for his jaw and had to opt to wear a beard himself.
49. Author's interview with Karl Gass, Berlin/Kleinmachnow, Germany (18 August 2000).
50. Author's interview with Wolfgang Harkenthal, Murchin, Germany (7 August 2000).
51. Gass was president of the jury in 1960, 1962, and 1963; Andrew Thorndike in 1961, 1965, and 1966.
52. SAPMO-BArch DY 30 IV A2/9.02/69. See Steinle 2003.
53. Author's interview with Karl Gass, Berlin/Kleinmachnow, Germany (18 August 2000).
54. At this point in time, it must be remembered that only the twelve socialist countries maintained diplomatic relations with the GDR.

CHAPTER 6

Documentaries in the Service of International Solidarity

Following the construction of the Berlin Wall in August 1961, and lasting until 1973, the GDR enjoyed greater latitude in the so-called Third World than anywhere else on the globe (Siebs 1999).[1] As East German leaders increasingly bet upon cultural policy in their fight against American and other Western influences in the Southern Hemisphere, cinema provided a particularly favorable field of action for implementing such a strategy. With its motto "Films of the World—for Peace in the World," the Leipzig Film Festival thus set out to link the three fundamental ideological strands upon which the GDR's foreign policy rested: socialist internationalism, anti-imperialist solidarity, and peaceful coexistence (Jacobsen 1980; Siebs 1999).

The festival became a key moment in staging support for "peoples in struggle against imperialism" and for fledgling nation-states in the making. Although the concept of the Third World had made its political entry onto the international stage at the Bandung Conference in 1955, the same year as the Leipzig Festival, the commitment of the East German government and the DEFA Film Studios as advocates for films produced by newcomers from the South took shape only gradually and against a backdrop of international cultural rivalry. To examine the reality upon which broad expressions of solidarity were founded thus requires that we compare such public discourse with actual events and measure the impact of each on both foreign and East German guests at the festival.

Cold War Cultural Offensive in the Global South

Over the course of the 1950s, the Third World increasingly became an explicit object of desire over which Moscow and Washington competed, each seeking to expand its sphere of influence into new regions without endangering the principle of peaceful coexistence (Soutou 2001). At Bandung in 1955, Nikita Khrushchev made a pivotal decision, offering to provide military and technical support to both communist and nonaligned Third World countries. The United States launched its cultural offensive in the early 1960s, as evidenced by the establishment of the Peace Corps in March 1961, allowing the American government to send young American volunteers into developing countries in the name of "peace and friendship in the world" (Westad 2006).

The two Germanys did not remain on the sidelines in this competitive, soft power arena. The FRG pursued a proactive cultural policy in the Third World by dint of initiatives undertaken by the ministries for Foreign Affairs and Economic Cooperation, as well as by the West German radio station *Deutsche Welle*. The worldwide network of the Goethe Institute (Kathe 2005), as well as several foundations that were more or less closely aligned to political parties, also played an instrumental role in the Adenauer administration's foreign policy, in particular by investing in the development of diverse media and means of mass communication.[2]

The foreign policy vehicles related to the Third World in the GDR were equally diverse: dispatching experts, initiating trade missions, and launching Radio Berlin International.[3] In July 1960, the Solidarity Committee with the Peoples of Africa was established; gradually broadening its scope, it subsequently became the Solidarity Committee of the GDR (Herbst et al. 1994; Mallinckrodt 1972). From school to the workplace and leisure activities, members of the East German public were regularly called upon to express their solidarity through campaigns for cash donations, blood drives, etc. These gestures and acts of solidarity were part of the social ritual that punctuated everyday life (Vorsteher 1997).

Training and Support for Third World Documentarists

In the West as in the East, education played a key role in cultural policy aimed at the Southern Hemisphere. President John F. Kennedy encouraged the establishment of an educated elite in the countries of the Global South.[4] In the USSR, the opening of the Patrice Lumumba People's Friendship University in 1960 epitomized its determination to train and educate students from Asia, Africa, and Latin America (Coumel 2001). In the GDR, a Solidarity School was established in 1963 with the express purpose of training journalists and media representatives from the Third World (Hillebrand 1987; Lamm and Kupper 1976). The HFF film academy in Babelsberg, no exception to this trend, also admitted many students from the Southern Hemisphere. The results were tangible: the Commission for the Establishment of Film Production, founded in Algiers in the newly independent country of Algeria in 1962, included two members who had been trained at the HFF film academy (Kerzabi 1963).

This much-vaunted openness, however, concealed a less rosy reality.[5] In general, the welcome awaiting foreign students in the GDR was not always the warmest (Brunner 2015; Müller and Poutrus 2005; Slobodian 2015). This is illustrated by the daily life of foreign students at Babelsberg, who were actually kept apart—and not only because of difficulties in following courses in German. In fact, foreign students posed potential dangers in the eyes of the East German authorities. Because they were not East German citizens, they could repeatedly visit West Berlin, bring books back from the West, and travel in "imperialist countries"; they also possessed valuta—foreign currencies that were very rare in the GDR.[6]

Before he became a persona non grata at the Leipzig Festival, the documentarist Joris Ivens sought to put an end to the exclusion of these budding filmmakers, establishing a foreign students' group at DEFA (Jordan 2018).[7] The intervention remained timid, however, and ended in failure as soon as Ivens left the GDR.[8] Training young filmmakers nevertheless remained an important calling card for the East Berlin government overseas. It formed part of a broader policy of material assistance to documentarists from the South, who, once in the GDR, would also serve as interpreters at the Leipzig Festival.

In her study of state-run enterprises in the GDR, historian Sandrine Kott (2000) builds on Marcel Mauss's classic work on gift giving to highlight the importance of "donor rhetoric."[9] Indeed, the economic dimension of the gift—as "antimarket"—as well as tensions arising between generosity and the obligatory act, were particularly relevant in the East German context (Kott 2000). Applying the concept of donor rhetoric to the case of the GDR underlines the country's desire to find ways to get around the lack of hard currency in order to finance international projects. In terms of film production, gift giving as a token of international solidarity was primarily inscribed in the practice of what Sandrine Kott calls the "socialist gift from afar" (Kott 2000: 273–74),[10] here highlighting attempts to apply what worked within the GDR to the international scale.

The state-directed Solidarity Fund, which along with the GDR Solidarity Committee was responsible for financing aid to the Third World, was a key player in enacting this practice.[11] It decided to invest in the Leipzig Festival, in particular, which offered it a valuable international platform. In 1964, it established a working committee comprising representatives of festival management, the GDR Filmmakers' Club, and the "young film industries" of Asia, Africa, and Latin America.[12] In 1964, the committee initiated the Joris Ivens Award, a continuation of the short-lived Dziga-Vertov Prize, and three film directors (a Bolivian, a Cypriot, and a South Vietnamese) received a cash prize,

Figure 6.1. Collecting for International Solidarity at the Leipzig Festival, soon after the coup d'état in Chile in 1973. © Filmmuseum Potsdam, Günter Linke.

black-and-white film stock, and an 8mm movie camera. In 1971, however, the Ivens Award abruptly vanished. Wolfgang Harkenthal justified this measure in the following terms:

> Joris Ivens now has an extremely radical attitude vis-à-vis socialist countries and the GDR, and he has fallen under the influence of the extreme left and Maoist radicals. It is no longer appropriate to envisage a Joris Ivens Award in the festival statutes. This is why I proposed to transform it into a Combatant Camera (Kämpfende Kamera) Prize, endowed with the same funds.[13]

The Combatant Camera Prize remained a stable feature at the festival until 1990 (Mauersberger 1997). The prize brought with it material support. In 1976, for example, the Portuguese anticolonial author José Luandino Vieira left Leipzig with rolls of film stock and a camera purchased thanks to a donor campaign. In exchange for material assistance, the festival could expect political support from foreign participants, even if this merely extended to spreading a positive image of the Leipzig Festival and East German society. Numerous producers and film directors from the South grasped the value of this quid pro quo. In 1965, the Uruguayan president of the Independent Union of Latin American Producers agreed to send films to Leipzig in exchange for film stock.[14] In terms of the GDR's international communication policy, the results were, on the whole, positive. Festival directors Wolfgang Harkenthal and Ronald Trisch recall with pleasure the pride they felt upon seeing diplomas and awards received at Leipzig on the walls of producers and film directors worldwide.[15]

Competition for Third World Filmmakers?

In addition to the image carefully cultivated by festival management—for example, in events including Solidarity Bazaars[16]—we have recourse to personal recollections. Colombian documentarist Marta Rodríguez de Silva recalls winning the Golden Dove of Peace prize at Leipzig in 1972 for the debut film by her and her husband, Jorge Silva.[17] The prize opened the door to French television networks, thus enabling them to purchase their own film equipment and make more films. Admittedly, the young woman had already had contacts in France, as she had studied anthropology at the Musée de l'Homme in Paris in 1963, in the midst of the debates on *cinéma vérité*. According to Rodríguez de Silva, however, it was the Leipzig Festival that allowed them to continue working independently. Furthermore, the invitation to attend the festival enabled them to view films not programmed elsewhere and to meet other Latin American documentary filmmakers impossible to meet in Colombia, including

Santiago Álvarez, one of their role models; Jorge Sanjinés from Bolivia; and Patricio Guzmán from Chile (Rodríguez de Silva 1997).

For filmmakers who, in their native countries, had little or no access to what was happening elsewhere, the Leipzig Festival thus offered a window on to the world. As an Algerian guest remarked in November 1962, "Those of us with no experience had the opportunity here, in Leipzig, to meet Cuban friends. At the outset they had to confront the same problems as we had and they thus provide the most interesting example for us" (Kerzabi 1963: 84). The Leipzig Festival's specific focus on the Third World, initiated in 1961, eventually faded over time, however.

Despite such positive recollections, the Leipzig Festival was not the only platform for documentary filmmakers from the Global South.[18] Under the influence of Jean Rouch, for example, French film festivals — such as the one in Tours (Mazany 2015) — had access and a greater openness to young, mostly African film productions. As of the late 1960s, the East German festival was suddenly faced with stiff competition from festivals in West Germany, especially Oberhausen.

In 1969, the Oberhausen Festival turned its attention toward Latin America, with the selection of *LBJ* (1968) by Santiago Álvarez; and in 1970, its retrospective was dedicated to Cuban documentary — four years before Leipzig (Holloway and Holloway 1979). Cuban filmmakers did not hesitate to attend other film festivals. Álvarez notes that those films that were not selected by the GDR were simply sent to Oberhausen: "The Ruhr Festival, without being on the left, was more open for us Latin Americans and everything could be discussed there. In comparison, Leipzig seemed more closed-minded than its West German rival" (Álvarez 1997: 65–66). Álvarez's colleague, the filmmaker Octavio Cortázar, however, preferred to emphasize that Leipzig, in turn, remained more open-minded than the Moscow Festival: at Leipzig it was at least possible to discuss matters, particularly within the jury (Cortázar 1997).

The shift of interest toward Latin America on the part of the Oberhausen Festival is in part explained by West Germany's new Ostpolitik, the policy of openness toward the East embraced under Chancellor Willy Brandt, who came to power in 1969 (Miard-Delacroix 2013).[19] Once the Treaty of Warsaw was signed in December 1970 — with Brandt's celebrated "Warsaw Genuflection" before the monument to the victims of the Warsaw ghetto — culture was no longer the only bridge connecting Poland and West Germany. In one sense, then, the motto "A Path toward the Neighbor" — which Oberhausen had been using since 1958 — had indeed served its purpose and procured a political victory. As a result, Oberhausen was free to find another space to conquer; the departure in 1969 of one of its founders, Hilmar Hoffmann, only accelerated the turnaround (Holloway and Holloway 1979).

The Leipzig Festival between North and South

The Leipzig Festival nevertheless continued to champion its particular conception and geopolitical understanding of international solidarity. John Grierson and Joris Ivens (1997) had insisted on the need for East Germany to assist developing countries and encouraged the festival to open to the Global South as early as 1960. While the festival did become a point of contact between North and South, however, it is clear that some countries benefited more than others from the platform it afforded them; apparently, each Third World country involved in a struggle did not require the same degree of solidarity. Selected on the basis of their potential importance to the diplomatic recognition of the GDR, the organizers divided the countries invited to the festival into two groups. The first group comprised those countries whose national film industries had already attained a certain level of development in the 1960s: India, Egypt, Indonesia, Ceylon (now Sri Lanka), Algeria, Morocco, Lebanon, Ghana, Mali, and Nigeria. In the second group of countries, national cinema production was still weak, as in Guinea, Cambodia, Iraq, and Syria.[20]

In general, India and a few African nations were particularly receptive to the GDR's diplomatic outreach, but this hardly translated to the sphere of documentary film.[21] In general, Africa lagged behind in this respect, except for the regular participation of members of and films produced by the African National Congress. Following the Suez Crisis in 1956, it was the 1967 Six Day War that effectively revived contacts between Arab nations and the GDR, which had shown itself very hostile toward Israel.[22] The Palestinian Liberation Organization first participated in the festival in 1973, as of which point the Palestinian struggle became key at Leipzig.[23]

Cuban Cinema and Santiago Álvarez

Starting in the 1950s, Latin America attracted more interest than any other part of the Third World in East Germany. For DEFA, which sought to participate in non-European festivals starting early on, Latin America swiftly became a priority destination; in May 1956, for example, DEFA presented sixteen documentaries at the Montevideo Festival in Uruguay.[24] Finally, among the extremely wide range of foreign guests attending the festival, it was the Latin Americans who garnered the most attention. Their critical point of view demonstrates the extent to which the exchanges taking place at Leipzig were by no means unambiguous.

Cuba played a pivotal role in the evolution of East German international relations. The first major East German delegation to Cuba traveled soon after Fidel Castro came to power in 1960. Among the delegates was Hans Rodenberg, the deputy minister of culture, who immediately invited Cuban filmmakers to

Leipzig. As early as 1960, three Cuban documentaries were shown in competition, including *Por qué nació el Ejército Rebelde?* (1960, *Why Was the Rebel Army Born?*) by José Massip (1926–2014), who first attended the Leipzig Festival in 1962 (Massip 1997; *Protokoll 1960* 1961).[25] Massip, had helped found the Cuban Institute of Cinematographic Art and Industry (Instituto Cubano del Arte e Industria Cinematográficos, ICAIC) in March 1959, along with Tomás Gutiérrez Alea, Julio García Espinosa, and Alfredo Guevara. In 1961, there were five Cuban films, including one by Alea and *Carnet de viaje* (1961, *Travel Notebook*), directed by Joris Ivens.[26]

Contacts were indeed quickly established with other documentarists and directors, such as Joris Ivens and Chris Marker, who went to Cuba early on to chronicle the young, triumphant revolution.[27] Documentarist Octavio Cortázar admits that the documentaries Ivens shot in Cuba were not among his finest; but Cubans were undoubtedly helped by the interest of Western filmmakers in their struggles and their filmmaking. The Cubans also knew how to maximize the benefit they received from being represented at the Leipzig Festival. The platform that the festival afforded them effectively made them known in Europe and allowed them to make essential contacts. It was at the Leipzig Festival, for example, that Cortázar—who would be awarded the Golden Dove in 1968[28]—first made the acquaintance of film director Theodor Christensen; he invited Christensen to Cuba, where the Danish director subsequently played a pivotal advisory role for Cuban filmmakers.

Cuba's presence at Leipzig was thus a long-lasting and uninterrupted success. The presence of Cuban guests, as well as guests from Chile and Brazil, was often more highly anticipated than that of their West German colleagues.[29] In 1986, Cuba thus ranked as fourth among the most often awarded countries at the festival, with forty-two awards in all, tied with Czechoslovakia and slightly ahead of Vietnam, with its forty-one awards.[30] If only first prizes were taken into consideration, Cuban films ranked in third place. Although they often won prizes, Czechoslovakian and Polish entries seldom obtained the Golden Dove. This indicates both the highly symbolic value of this first prize and the fact that it was more readily bestowed on friendly Third World countries and progressive filmmakers from capitalist countries than to entries from Warsaw Pact countries. The symbolic hierarchy among communist countries that thus emerged reserved indeed a special place for Cuba.

A close examination of the pioneering figure of Santiago Álvarez (1919–1998), one of the great international documentarists, allows us to evaluate the influence and role of Cuban documentary filmmaking at Leipzig. Born in Havana, Álvarez, starting very early on, actively took part in the Cuban revolution: "Cinema is an ideological and cultural product. We are a country at war—not that we chose to be at war, but because of it, we are committed" (Gauthier 1995: 266–67). Fidel Castro, using Lenin as his model, paid particular attention to cinema, establishing ICAIC three months after his victory, which thereafter played a central role in Cuban film production. Although he had no experience in the field, Álvarez became responsible for the Noticiero Newsreels—produced by ICAIC for all of Latin America—thus becoming the chronicler of the Cuban Revolution and its leader. In his career, Álvarez devoted himself primarily to the documentary genre and filmed extensively in the Americas, Africa, and Asia.

It was thanks to the Leipzig Festival that Álvarez became known in Europe. He sat on the festival's international jury, first in 1964 and on four subsequent occasions, thus becoming the foreigner who was invited most often to be on the jury.[31] As a member of the honorary presidium of the Leipzig Festival in 1965 and 1966, he became the key figure in the animated discussions that followed screenings. Álvarez affected proceedings through his force of character and personal flair, embodying a Cuban identity, in sharp contrast to European and East German practices. Witness accounts regularly evoke Cuban and other Latin American guests launching into passionate dances to liven up parties that then lasted all night.

Cuban documentaries generally impressed festival audiences, who received them enthusiastically.[32] "Cuban films have yet again clearly demonstrated their tendency to develop a uniquely national style in the documentary

Figure 6.2. Cuban documentarist Santiago Álvarez at the festival's opening gala in 1983. © Filmmuseum Potsdam, Reinhard Podszuweit.

genre," noted the deputy director of HVFilm, Hermann Schauer, in 1966.³³ West German journalist Wilhelm Roth observed that Cuban films were invariably the highlight of the festival.³⁴ It was primarily Álvarez's films, however, that contributed a distinctive tenor to the festival. From 1964 to 1973, seven of Álvarez's works received awards at the Leipzig Festival. His singular output is illustrated by his outstanding short documentary *Now* (1965), which was both selected and awarded at Leipzig. *Now* is a searing indictment of racial discrimination in the United States.

The title is taken from the 1963 song upon which the entire documentary rests; it features new words set to the melody of "Hava Nagila" and was recorded by the American jazz singer Lena Horne. The film's montage of archival and contemporary images and footage unfolds in perfect harmony with Horne's interpretation, adapting to its duration and especially to its rhythm, and transforming *Now* into a masterful example of particularly powerful editing. While some commentators compared it with Dziga Vertov's work, precisely for this editing, Álvarez replied that he had not known the Soviet documentarist's works when he started shooting, but that the comparison did not surprise him: "We are both working in the midst of a revolution—he a few years after the Russian October Revolution, and I a few years after the Cuban January Revolution" (Gauthier 1995: 267).

The Cubans, like the Algerians, certainly represented a revolutionary Third World; but they were reluctant to blindly embrace the Soviet model, and rather more inclined to champion their own identity. On the occasion of the death of Ho Chi Minh, and at the height of the Vietnam War, Álvarez shot *79 Primaveras* (1969, *79 Springs*), which was selected at Leipzig. One particular scene aroused a lot of emotion. The critic Wilhelm Roth (1998: 20–21) recalls:

> On screen appears the phrase, "Let the division of the socialist camp not darken the future," and Álvarez makes this threat patently clear. The sentence breaks, the image dissolves, the film seems to burn and destroy itself (should we exit the movie theatre?); but we can breathe again: Álvarez slowly reconstructs the phrase, which reappears on screen. . . . An outstanding moment.

Álvarez indeed borrowed from the classic Soviet documentary tradition—from Eisenstein to Vertov—the method of metaphorical montage, of visual effects, without recourse to an offscreen voice over, but instead employing intertitles that provide a form of explanation (Labaki 1998). Álvarez moreover integrated, as we observed in *Now*, equally compelling sound and music editing.

In the 1970s, Álvarez continued attending the festival. He sat on the jury, an internationally recognized guarantor of high-quality documentary films, but his own films no longer enjoyed the official resonance they had aroused earlier. In 1968, it was a sign of the times that his short documentary *LBJ* (1968), about US President Lyndon B. Johnson, was not screened in competition, but rather in the Information Program.³⁵ Álvarez had committed the faux pas of shooting Fidel Castro denouncing the illegal entry of Soviet tanks into Prague on 21 August 1968 for a Noticiero Newsreel.[36]

Vietnam on Screen

If Cuban films revealed flaws in the Communist world, documentary films championing the Vietnamese cause enabled the forging of a sense of global solidarity that went beyond the East-West Bloc rift. The Vietnamese conflict was triggered after the United States dispatched military advisers to South Vietnam in 1961—the year the Leipzig Festival embraced an international dimension—and the Vietnam War effectively took center stage for the ensuing decade (Soutou 2001). The Vietnamese cause permeated the entire festival space—at screenings and numerous symbolic protests in the form of petitions, cash donations, and blood drives, as happened in 1970.

Informing the public about developments on the ground in Vietnam was a major challenge to the festival. Leipzig thus programmed films shot by the Vietnamese themselves and hosted several Vietnamese film directors, who were feted as true heroes. A first wave of Vietnamese films arrived in 1961; then, once the war began in earnest, came the aforementioned "suitcase films," transported and personally delivered by their creators after perilous journeys.[37] As of 1976, the festival finally started programming entries produced in a Vietnam now reunified after the entry of North Vietnamese forces into Saigon in late April 1975. As seen above, among the numerous Vietnamese documentaries selected for Leipzig, forty-one received awards, of which six won the Golden Dove.[38] In terms of festival politics, this gave Vietnam an average ranking approaching those of Cuba, Czechoslovakia, and Poland.

In 1966, the international jury decided to bestow an honorable mention on all eighteen documentaries that focused on Vietnam in all categories (*Protokoll 1966* 1967). Four were East German productions, including the 1966 documentary *400 cm,*[3] by Walter Heynowski and Gerhard Scheumann. With a score by composer Paul Dessau and shot by Werner Bergmann, one of DEFA's finest cameramen of fiction feature films, the film is a six-minute-long montage that alternates images of the war and blood donation campaigns in the GDR.

American opponents to the Vietnam War were also in attendance at Leipzig. In 1966, the Golden Dove was awarded to the American film director Peter Gessner for *Time of the Locust*, a "terse and precise shock montage" lasting ten minutes, which juxtaposed the pacifist statements of American politicians with the realities of the war (Roth 1998: 15). In 1974, Leipzig enjoyed a Cannes-worthy moment of mediated emotions, when Jane Fonda attended the festival to present *Vietnam Journey: Introduction to the Enemy*, which chronicles her travels through Vietnam. Following the screening, the actress even answered questions for a quarter of an hour (Tok 1997).

Figure 6.3. Jane Fonda visits the 1974 Leipzig Festival. Besides unidentified Vietnamese guests, the group includes (*left to right*): Soviet director Roman Karmen (*front row, profile*), Annelie Thorndike, journalist Karl-Eduard von Schnitzler, festival director Ronald Trisch (*flanking Fonda*), and documentarist Gitta Nickel. © Filmmuseum Potsdam, Reinhard Podszuweit.

Communist propaganda was further radicalized in 1966, as announced at the Tricontinental Conference in Havana in January. An appeal, the first of many, was issued for "international solidarity with the Vietnamese people in their liberation struggle." It was also suggested to the documentarists concerned that they submit their films to the Nobel Laureate Bertrand Russell, who had just called for the constitution of an international commission to investigate war crimes committed in Vietnam.[39] The Russell Tribunal, chaired by Jean-Paul Sartre, met once in Stockholm and once in Roskilde, Denmark.[40] It referred explicitly to the Nuremberg Trials, at which documentary footage and newsreels shot during the liberation of the concentration camps and ghettos were screened in the courtroom as evidence for the prosecution (Delage 2006).

By condemning the Vietnam War so actively, Leipzig Festival organizers hoped to win over Western peace activists, within the context of international mobilization efforts. In France, Chris Marker brought together filmmakers, artists, and intellectuals to produce an omnibus documentary, *Loin du Vietnam* (1967, *Far from Vietnam*), with part of the profits to be donated to the Committee to Aid the Vietnamese. Still unique in its genre, *Far from Vietnam* encapsulates all the features of activist or militant documentary (*cinéma militant*) and even served as a template for many, heralding a type of collective production that emerged subsequently.[41] The nearly two-hour-long documentary film essay, shot over the course of 1967, opens with a prologue and is followed by eleven discrete episodes directed by many of the big names in cinema.[42] They were thus simultaneously making a militant documentary and an auteurist film, mixing documentary and fiction, black-and-white archival footage, and sequences in color.

Far from Vietnam was mainly shown at festivals and at screenings organized at universities, especially on North American campuses. Its release in movie theaters was banned by Franco's Spain and Cambodia alike; it was not released in the United States; and far-right activists interrupted its release in France. In November 1967, a month before its Paris premiere, the film was programmed and received an award at the Leipzig Festival. There, the film was an instant sensation. Thanks to the contributions of an outstanding group of film directors, it shed a new and nuanced light on the Vietnamese problem, depicted in all its complexity.

The segment directed by William Klein about the massive pro- and antiwar demonstrations in New York contradicted the idea of an American government waging a war against the will of its people. By means of a monologue by a fictional leftist intellectual, Alain Resnais decried the proliferation of images about the conflict; festival audiences, for years overwhelmed with films about the Vietnam War, could not remain indifferent to such rhetoric. At Leipzig, these arguments were even perceived as provocative (Gregor 1967b). At the same time, this example reveals to what extent the Leipzig Festival could, on occasion, echo the zeitgeist; with this film, it opened itself up to a critically militant cinema that demonstrated that, in the words of Laurent Véray (2004), "aesthetics and politics are not mutually exclusive."

Anti-Imperialist Propaganda: Studio H&S

International solidarity was also on view at Leipzig in a series of films, principally devoted to the Vietnamese theme, produced at Studio H&S in the GDR. Unquestionably, the H&S acronym was among the most successful East German brands internationally. Behind these initials are the names of Walter Heynowski and Gerhard Scheumann, who as of 1965 formed a close-knit team within GDR documentary production. The two filmmakers met each other in the early 1960s and were soon able to gather a devoted team of collaborators in the service of a specific conception of documentary film. Their trajectory is remarkable: they were the only East German filmmakers ever to have their own studio, completely independent of DEFA; they also engaged in a highly controversial investigative and directorial style. And yet, had it not been for the network of international festivals that existed across Europe and elsewhere, their documentaries would never have had such widespread distribution or resounding success.

Born in Bavaria in 1927, Heynowski was a soldier and assistant at the Luftwaffe at the end of World War II before being captured and detained in a prison camp south of Mainz (Heynowski 2007). In 1945, he studied Catholic theology and then political economy at the University of Tübingen, all while getting his start as a journalist. In late 1948, he moved to Berlin, where he started contributing to the *Berliner Zeitung*, a newspaper circulated in the Soviet zone. He penned articles and news columns in satirical newspapers until 1955. In 1956, Heynowski was hired by DFF television, where he became vice-intendant and program director from 1959 until 1963, when he joined the DEFA Documentary Studio as an author and film director. Two years later, he began collaborating with another documentarist at the studio, Gerhard Scheumann.

Also born in 1927, in East Prussia, Scheumann grew up in Saxony-Anhalt, where he began working at the local *Thüringer Volk* newspaper. Karl Gass, while still a radio journalist, brought Scheumann to Berlin in 1949, where he specialized in economic and domestic policy issues. Scheumann subsequently taught at the specialized school for radio broadcasting in Weimar, before going on to edit cultural and scientific reportages for East German Radio. From 1960 to 1962, he directed television programs; in 1963 he created the domestic political magazine *Prisma*, which he also moderated (Steinle 2003). In 1965, while working for DFF, Scheumann began collaborating with Heynowski. It is noteworthy that both their careers passed through both written and broadcast journalism, an experience that significantly influenced them.

For Heynowski and Scheumann, the challenge was to depict events "according to the yardstick of the century" (Michel 1977: 93). Their method proved to be radical: "Film and television documentarists must not hesitate to fight—perhaps in different divisions, yet nevertheless as members of the same army" (Scheumann 1962: 464). Their combativeness thus fully appropriated the notion of a movie camera as at the service of propaganda, a veritable weapon in the fight against the enemy. This enemy—primarily represented by Bonn and Washington—was violently attacked in films that were percussively edited and underpinned by commentary that left neither room for doubt nor any recourse for their targeted opponents.

Early Festivals

Heynowski received his first award at Leipzig in 1961 for *Aktion J*. The documentary—produced for DFF and made in a similar vein to earlier works by Andrew and Annelie Thorndike—went in search of former Nazi criminals among those working closely with FRG Chancellor Konrad Adenauer.[43] Heynowski then directed two films commissioned by DFF, which were devoted to atrocities committed in the Congo by West German mercenary soldiers in Commando Unit 52. Interviewed in person by the filmmakers, mercenary leader Major Siegfried Müller—nicknamed "Kongo-Müller"—confesses his past and present actions in Africa in front of the camera without remorse. Müller appears as though in court—seated in a small space and shot straight on—and becomes increasingly inebriated over the course of the interview, thanks to the attentions of the crew.⁴⁴

In 1965, *Kommando 52* won the Golden Dove at Leipzig; the following year, *Der lachende Mann—Bekenntnisse eines Mörders* (*The Laughing Man*, 1966), made with Scheumann, was awarded the Special Jury Prize. Released in nearly forty countries, *The Laughing Man* had toured the international festival circuit before screening at Leipzig ("Behörden. DDR-Film: Lachender Mann" 1967; Steinle 2003). When it became clear that the Mannheim Festival would not program the film, students there organized a private screening.⁴⁵ Its subsequent screening at Leipzig thus only served to confirm a success already celebrated elsewhere, and the public greeted the film with such enthusiasm that a second screening was held. Some West German film critics, such as Ulrich Gregor (1966b), condemned the film's spirit and tone, however.

Following this initial success, in 1966 Heynowski and Scheumann proposed establishing an independent production group within the DEFA Studios, which came into existence on 1 March 1967; on 1 May 1969, Studio H&S became entirely independent of DEFA.⁴⁶ They wanted to have means proportionate to their ambitions: "The group's objective is to represent the GDR at international festivals with its films."⁴⁷ They were already working with a West German cinematographer, Peter Hellmich, "who, as a citizen of the FRG, [had] permission to work with DEFA" and opened many doors for them abroad. Because of strong reticence on the part of the institutional partners involved, it took three years and the support of Erich Honecker for Studio H&S to finally come into being in 1969. It was thus under this label that Heynowski and Scheumann pursued the frontal attack initiated by *The Laughing Man*.

For Heynowski and Scheumann, the anti-imperialist struggle entailed denouncing the neocolonial policies of the United States and its allies. Vietnam and Chile became the central symbols of Third World liberation struggles in their productions. In the context of numerous other productions about these two countries, Studio H&S's documentaries could be distinguished primarily by their signature tone and style.

H&S Vietnam Films

The Thirty Years War in Indochina—a proxy war primarily concerning Vietnam—inspired Studio H&S to produce a series of documentaries between

1968 and 1977, with the documentarists taking particular care to monitor developments in Vietnam once hostilities with the United States ceased. Once again, international success awaited them.

Piloten im Pyjama (1968, *Pilots in Pyjamas*),[48] a new commission from DFF, was shot during the summer of 1967 and won the Golden Dove at Leipzig in November 1968. This four-part interview film was made possible by the North Vietnamese authorities, who authorized the film crew to interview ten American bomber pilots whose planes had been shot down by North Vietnamese forces and were being held in the "Hanoi Hilton" POW camp. Accompanying the film, Studio H&S published a book featuring all ten transcribed testimonies, as well as an interview with Heynowski and Scheumann that had appeared in the West German magazine *Der Spiegel* (Heynowski and Scheumann 1968). As in *The Laughing Man*, the staging is deliberately biased against the American POWs; aged twenty-five to forty-two, they are filmed under the stark light of studio projectors and must answer a barrage of questions posed by the two directors from the depths of the room. Once again, West German critic Ulrich Gregor (1968b) castigated the methods employed, which, in his eyes, discredited the film's message, as viewers were confronted with assertions that offered no reflection upon the reason for the guilt of these irrevocably condemned people.

This frontal approach differentiated the Studio H&S films from other DEFA documentaries, which concentrated more on victims of conflict and the consequences of war than on the "enemies of the Vietnamese people." This was the hallmark of Studio H&S films. In addition to appealing for international solidarity and eliciting an emotional response, triggered by witnessing war atrocities, their true goal was to condemn American imperialism. The fact that *Pilots in Pyjamas* won the Golden Dove also reminded the public in the GDR and abroad where the priorities of international solidarity lay in 1968: in Hanoi, not Prague.

Eight years later, the documentarists revisited a unified Vietnam to observe the beginnings of the newly established republic.[49] Again, Leipzig warmly welcomed the films they shot during their visit: *Vietnam 4—Die eiserne Festung* (1977, *The Iron Fortress*) received the Golden Dove in 1977; and *Phoenix* (1979), a film assembled around the declarations of a CIA agent sent to Vietnam during the war, was awarded the Silver Dove in 1979.

Chile at the Leipzig Festival

As the leader of the Popular Unity Coalition (Unidad Popular), which united Socialists, Communists, and Christian Democrats, Salvador Allende's victory in the Chilean presidential election of September 1970 raised great hopes among leftist activists worldwide. Starting only a few weeks after Allende's victory, Chilean documentaries reflecting the new policies were programmed and awarded at the Leipzig Festival. In 1970, the festival opened with Pedro Chaskel's and Héctor Rios's ¡Venceremos! (1970), showing demonstrations of joy after the electoral victory; Reportaje a Lota (1970, Report to Lota), by Diego Bonacina and José Román, showed the terrible living and working conditions at a coal mine; and Brigada Ramona Parra (1970), by Alvaro Ramirez and Samuel Carvajal, followed a Santiago mural painting brigade during the campaign. All three were awarded the Golden Dove. In 1971, the top prize was awarded to Pedro Chaskel and Luis Alberto Sanz's No es hora de llorar (1971, No Time for Tears), on Brazilian political refugees in Chile.

Unsurprisingly, then, the subsequent rightwing putsch of General Pinochet in Chile on 11 September 1973 unleashed a surge of emotion and indignation in both the East and the West (Compagnon and Moine 2015).[50] For the Communist Bloc, the coup d'état offered the opportunity to spotlight the imbrications of the CIA, "American imperialist policy," and Third World dictatorships such as those in Latin America. As part of a broad, international mobilization, numerous activists and artists worldwide joined in condemning the military junta and organizing support for its victims (Moine 2015).

When the Leipzig Festival opened in November 1973, everybody was still in shock about the coup in Santiago. In her opening address, Annelie

Figure 6.4. The Free German Youth (FDJ) call for International Solidarity at the 1975 festival, with posters and music against the Chilean coup and apartheid. © Filmmuseum Potsdam, Reinhard Podszuweit.

Thorndike, president of the festival's International Committee, gave an impassioned assessment of the importance of documentary filmmaking:

> This, our kind of documentary, was borne of the socialist October Revolution. It enabled a proudly burgeoning branch of political art to flourish out of newsreels, and breathed the spirit of the revolution into this branch, once and for all. Since then, it lives on in documentary film, and no Hitler, no Franco can extract it—no Diem or Thieu, no junta, be it Chilean, Greek, Portuguese, or military, can crush it! (*Protokoll 1973* 1974: 7)

The Chilean playwright and singer-songwriter Víctor Jara, who helped establish the Nueva Canción Chilena, had been invited to Leipzig before he was arrested in September 1973 with thousands of others and killed in Santiago's National Stadium. After his death, his wife, Joan Jara, came to the festival several times as part of her international advocacy campaign to perpetuate the memory of her husband and contribute to the mobilization of collective action.

The American singer Dean Reed (1938–1986), nicknamed the "Red Elvis," was among the most popular figures at these solidarity actions (Ernstring 2006). He had gone on a wildly successful tour of Latin America in 1961 and

Figure 6.5. Dean Reed's debut at the Leipzig Festival in 1971; the translator to the right is American expat and author Victor Grossman. © Filmmuseum Potsdam, Reinhard Podszuweit.

settled in Italy in 1966; in 1970, he was invited to the investiture of Salvador Allende in Chile. Reed participated in the Leipzig Festival for the first time in 1971 and settled in the GDR in 1973. His concerts drew a lot of media attention and was a high point in the festival's cultural and musical programming. In 1975, a delegation of Chilean documentary filmmakers—in exile in different countries—came to Leipzig, where they could meet again. Salvador Allende's widow had them read these words: "I would like to warmly greet the people of the German Democratic Republic, who have been so generous and helped the cause of the Chilean people in their struggle against fascism" (Allende 1974: 12)

Leipzig's support for Chile was not just staged on the festival's podiums but also projected on its screens. The situation in Chile inspired numerous documentary filmmakers the world over (Roudé and Barbat 2013), of which audiences at Leipzig were able to view several. *Septembre chilien* (1973, *Chilean September*), by French directors Bruno Muel and Theo Robichet, and *Chili—L'heure de la lutte, l'heure de l'agitation* (1973, *Chile: Time to Fight, Time to Agitate*), by Soviet directors Roman Karmen, D. Barsceski and O. Trifimova, screened in 1973 (Barbat 2013). In 1974, there was *Compañero: Víctor Jara of Chile* (1974), by the British director Stanley Forman. Of special importance were screenings of the first two parts of *The Battle of Chile*, by the Chilean filmmaker Patricio Guzmán, who lived in exile in Cuba. The first, titled *La insurrección de la burguesía* (1975, *The Insurrection of the Bourgeoisie*), received wild applause in 1975; the second, *El golpe de estado* (1976, *The Coup d'État*), received the Special Jury Prize in 1976.[51]

Studio H&S was also very active in condemning the military junta, with three principal feature-length films on the topic: *Der Krieg der Mumien* (1974, *The War of the Mummies*), a chronicle of the years preceding the coup that condemned the support provided by industrialists, who were opposed to the Allende government because their enterprises had been nationalized; *Ich war, ich bin, ich werde sein* (1974, *I Was, I Am, I Will Be*), devoted to the military junta's political prisoners; and *El golpe blanco* (1975, *The White Coup*), documenting the hostility of the Chilean bourgeoisie toward Allende's policies.

I Was, I Am, I Will Be screened at Leipzig in 1975 and won the Special Jury Prize. It is framed as a police investigation. An offscreen voice-over narrates how the filmmakers sought to find traces of their missing "friends" and "comrades" by visiting one of the junta's prison camps; they succeeded in doing so by posing as West Germans and obtaining the permission, in person, of none other than General Pinochet. Years later, however, Heynowski (2013) admitted that he had never set foot in Chile after 11 September 1973, contrary to what the film's narration would have us believe and contrary to the marketing of and propaganda on screenings of the film in the GDR and abroad. Instead, the images were shot by West German cameraman Peter Hellmich, who did not speak Spanish, and the interviews were organized and conducted by Miguel Helberg, a Spaniard whose name does not appear in the credits.[52]

I Was, I Am, I Will Be shows us prisoners at the Chacabuco and Pisagua prison camps in northern Chile. The commentary explains that it was impossible to make clear to the prisoners that the intent of the East German film was "to espouse their cause." Men and women who claim to be communists or leftist sympathizers answer brief questions on camera, as does the general in charge of the camp, who makes much of what he considers its very humane conditions. A few furtively taken photos indicate the exhausting physical exercise regime that prisoners are forced to follow in this desert region of Chile (Moine 2011b). Close-ups of somber, tired faces alternate with more general scenes, showing the barracks and, at the end of the film, Allende singing before a large audience. Several shots from this H&S film, such as the aerial view of the Chacabuco camp, were later used by other documentary filmmakers, including Patricio Guzmán.

Among the prisoners filmed was Allende's personal physician, Danilo Bartulin. In 1975, following his release, Bartulin traveled to the Leipzig Festival and, from the podium, greeted Peter Hellmich, who had proven that he was still alive and thus enabled the organization of an international campaign to free him. At such moments, the Leipzig Festival attained a unique dimension: international solidarity became embodied in individual trajectories, and documentary film provided an invaluable witness (Schlegel 1975) — even though this mise-en-scène rested on a lie: the supposed presence of Heynowski and Scheumann in Chile by the sides of Peter Hellmich and Miguel Herberg.

Studio H&S films were regularly broadcast in East Germany on DFF television, which most often also coproduced them. Even though their documentaries were made in the service of an ideology deeply rooted in East German realities of production, Heynowski and Scheumann skillfully wielded emotional impact, cinematic effectiveness, and appeals to internationalism (Moine 2011b). At Leipzig, they received no fewer than twelve awards from 1966 to 1988. The Chilean cycle was shown at international events in Paris, Athens, Mexico City, and Rome, before gatherings at the United Nations, at twenty-two film festivals, and on television in twenty-two countries. In 1980, five hundred copies of the films were sent abroad for screenings.

Studio H&S also received prizes at festivals in the East, West, North, and South, including in Krakow (1971, 1974, 1978); Prague (1970); Moscow (1965, 1971, 1977); Nyon, Switzerland (1975); Grenoble (1975, 1976) and Lille (1978) in France; Fondi, Italy (1987); Bilbao (1976, 1978, 1979, 1980); Benalmadena (1978) and Huesca (1981) in Spain; Tampere, Finland (1978); and Ho Chi Minh City (1983) and Hanoi (1988) in Vietnam. The two documentarists were even welcomed at the West German Oberhausen Festival, which proved more interested in their later films than in those about the Congo. From 1974 to 1977, Studio H&S films received a prize every year, including the festival's Prize of the Ecumenical Jury for their film *Psalm 18* (1974) about Chile. Their films were selected for the 1979 Oberhausen retrospective, titled "Possibilities of Documentary Film," and were thereby featured alongside works by the luminaries of documentary film, including John Grierson, Joris Ivens, Henri Storck, Roman Karmen, Santiago Álvarez, and Chris Marker (Holloway and Holloway 1979).

Over the course of the 1970s, Heynowski and Scheumann's documentaries succeeded as propaganda for international and anti-imperialist solidarity for East Berlin. By broadly disseminating this solidarity-driven narrative, the two documentarists actively aided the regime, which wanted to distract East German as well as international public opinion away from domestic policy issues and toward more distant horizons.

1973

At the end of his influential monograph on antiquity, *Le pain et le cirque. Sociologie historique d'un pluralisme politique,* historian Paul Veyne (1976: 692) concludes:

> The State apparatus felt, or believed itself to be threatened by certain interests of those governed, who longed for pleasures and bread. . . . For this problem, several solutions could be envisaged. . . . Festivals: you satiate satisfactions during certain, limited moments. . . . It is [also] good, in the interest of the authority itself, to occasionally let the childlike population play. . . . Rulers [thus] had to symbolically demonstrate that they remained at the service of the governed.

Veyne's musings help us shed light on parallels in the policies of the East German regime in the early 1970s.

Erich Honecker, the GDR's new leader as of June 1971, had only one aspiration: international recognition of the GDR. To achieve this end, he had to jettison the GDR's hitherto purely offensive approach and play a game of seduction vis-à-vis the outside world as well as within East German society. The theme of international solidarity effectively concealed key challenges facing the GDR's domestic policy. The socialist equivalent of "bread and circuses" was meant to bring citizens closer to the regime (Schröder 1998), while growing international prestige helped persuade East German citizens that they were governed by a "normal state power" (Bleek and Bovermann 1995b: 1154).

The 1973 World Youth Festival

The tenth World Youth Festival (Weltfestspiele der Jugend und Studenten, WYF) proves illustrative of the ambiguity of Honecker's international and domestic cultural policies.[53] From 28 July to 5 August 1973, more than 25,000 delegates and guests from 140 countries gathered in East Berlin, during a week in which temperatures soared. The city's streets were thronged with lively, young, and colorful crowds, who participated in over 1,500 political, cultural, and sporting events, day and night. Documentary film was mobilized in the service of this self-congratulatory moment of festive political staging, and the Leipzig Festival was transformed into a key element of the government's new seduction policy. Images of enthusiastic crowds masked a much starker reality, however (Moine 2010b).

The context could not have been more auspicious. In the months following December 1972 and the signing of the Basic Treaty between East and West Germany—which normalized political relations between the two nations— sixty-seven countries accorded diplomatic recognition to the GDR (Bleek and Bovermann 1995). On 8 July 1973, international détente was achieved with the opening of the Conference on Security and Co-operation in Europe in Helsinki, organized on the initiative of the USSR.

Although preparations for the 1973 WYF had commenced well before Honecker came to power—including at a meeting of the WYF Organizing Committee and representatives of East Bloc broadcasters at the Leipzig Festival in November 1972 (*Neues Deutschland* 1973a)—Honecker knew how to make his mark. International coverage of the WYF monopolized all East German television and radio stations, which offered daily reports filmed in color that were relayed to Intervision and Eurovision and broadcast to the other continents via satellite (*Protokoll 1972* 1973). According to official figures, 1556 accreditations were issued to various print and broadcast media from eighty-nine countries (*Neues Deutschland* 1973b).

East Berlin, capital of the GDR since 1949 and a symbol of a divided Germany and Europe, offered an ideal setting for the occasion and was duly transformed for the duration of the festival (Rostock 1999). Multiple stands and outdoor stages were erected in the streets. Alexanderplatz—with its recently built television tower, symbolizing the GDR's modernity—was a major center of attraction. Festival emblems were ubiquitous: a stylized flower with five colored petals whose core was the Earth; and the terrestrial sphere carried by outstretched white, black, and yellow arms, with a dove of peace flying above it—an image Picasso conceived for the first WYF in 1947. Here we rediscover the core elements of the official staging of a modern and outward-looking East Germany.

The festival's slogan, "For Anti-Imperialist Solidarity, Peace and Friendship!" was everywhere to be seen—on badges, posters, banners, podiums—and was translated into English, French, Russian, Spanish, and Arabic. The choice of honored guests also illustrated the broad outlines of the festival's diplomatic thrust: the African American philosopher and political figure Angela Davis; Yasser Arafat, the chairman of the PLO executive committee; and the first ever woman cosmonaut, Valentina Tereshkova from the Soviet Union. The idea of solidarity addressed struggling peoples in the Third World, as well as the peoples of the USSR.

Nearly everything was permitted during the nine days of the WYF. No participant was reprimanded by police for looking "decadent and hostile"—terms usually employed to characterize those with long hair or wearing jeans. Young people could flirt in peace, enjoying a sexual freedom that in other circumstances would have been severely chastised.[54] Young people from all around the world held animated discussions late into the night in encounters that opened new horizons. For many young East Germans, particularly those from the provinces, the WYF truly had the "effect of a cultural upheaval" (Wolle 1998: 164).

During festival preparations, however, authorities had feared that West Berlin might be used as a rear base for movements hostile to the festival. On 25 June 1973, Honecker approved "measures proposed to ensure security [in preparation for and] during the tenth festival," which had been fleshed out by Erich Mielke, head of the Stasi.[55] In the provinces, repression was very harsh. In the capital, however, where more than 20,000 Stasi collaborators and as many policemen mingled with the crowds, few incidents were reported (Wolle 1998).[56] Even so, zealous members of the FDJ at times swiftly broke up spontaneous public discussions (Rexin 1973). Differing recollections of the summer 1973 festival overlap with one another. In the collective memory of numerous East Germans, especially Berliners, the festival week remains a luminous moment, where a spirit of freedom, exchange, encounters, and openness reigned. On the other hand, the recollections of victims—such as the author Reiner Kunze, who was barred from entering East Berlin because he had long hair—remind us of the other side of events.[57]

The government planned to continue holding the youth festival. DEFA accordingly produced a documentary about the 1973 edition of the WYF, whose budget was commensurate with the scale of the event. *Wer die Erde liebt* (1973, *Those Who Love the Earth*) is a feature-length film in color, shot with the help of five sound engineers and thirteen cinematographers, including star cameramen such as Christian Lehmann and Hans-Eberhard Leupold.

The film opens with shots of the Earth taken from outer space, accompanied by Richard Strauss's *Also Sprach Zarathustra*, followed by the opening title and the motto "Peace for all. And by every means!" The following sequence alternates between crowd scenes—multicolored and with raised fists—and aerial views of the Earth. The universalist nature of the theme is then tinged by a revolutionary note, as "La Marseillaise" is sung by the French delegation at the opening ceremony. Black-and-white photos of police and clashes in Paris in May '68 open the next sequence, which introduces the various countries represented at the event and the struggles being waged on the different continents. For the Soviet delegation, images of Lenin and Honecker appear in turn—after which the image of the SED first secretary becomes omnipresent. Pigeons in flight end the opening sequence, thus reintroducing the leitmotiv of the dove of peace.

The film then shows aerial views of postwar Berlin and pays homage to Soviet soldiers. Festival banners in every language reintroduce the theme of internationalism and international solidarity, as does the presentation of invited celebrities. Shifting the focus to the streets of East Berlin, the camera captures glimpses of city life during the festival: couples gathering in the evening near the Worldtime Clock at Alexanderplatz, concerts, FDJ parades, lively discussions in the streets. The documentary culminates with Angela Davis speaking a few words in German to the crowd during the closing ceremony,[58] and the final fireworks display reawakens the image of a multicolored festival, while a solidarity song commissioned for the occasion is sung offscreen: "Solidarity! It's never too late!"

The lyricism of the film is built around this recurring combination of motifs throughout the documentary: on one hand, the international diversity of the participants, diversity of language, skin color, traditions; and, on the other hand, the sense of community joined in the struggle "for democracy and peace, against imperialism." Like the festival, the documentary intended to demonstrate to East German youth that, thanks to the ideological struggles they had espoused, they had earned their place in the international arena and that their horizons extended far beyond the limits, rendered invisible in the film, of the Berlin Wall and the East Bloc.

Five years after an East German team first participated in the 1968 Olympics and a year after the 1972 Summer Olympics in Munich,[59] the 1973 WYF helped show the entire world a modern East Germany. With the Basic Treaty and, on 18 September 1973, the admittance of two German states into the United Nations, Erich Honecker had achieved his objectives. A month later, *Those Who Love the Earth* opened the Leipzig Festival in celebration of these diplomatic triumphs. "We've been too long on the threshold!" Annelie Thorndike (1974: 8) exclaimed triumphantly in her opening address, while the new festival director, Ronald Trisch, warmly greeted members of the diplomatic corps who were present, including a UNESCO delegate (Bhowhagary 1974; Trisch 1974).

Transitions at the Leipzig Festival

Conscious of a changing international climate, the authorities had already begun to adapt the festival's organization a few years earlier. In 1966, the festival's honorary presidium had been dissolved and replaced by an international committee, which, notwithstanding its name, exclusively comprised East German cinema and television professionals. The festival committee really only came into its own in 1973, when it became the sole official organizer of the festival, and the Ministry of Culture was in effect no longer involved.

At this point, after heading the honorary presidium from 1963 to 1966, Annelie Thorndike became its de facto permanent president. Festival director Trisch now became the vice-chairman of the committee, further consolidating the various organizational bodies involved. Above all, the renewed emphasis on the committee was meant to mitigate the image of a festival under state control (Steinmetz 1998). In a sign of continued tight control, however, Jürgen Böttcher and a television journalist, who were deemed too nonconformist with respect to the official line, were excluded from the festival committee in summer 1973.

The institutional reorganization of the festival also involved a change of personnel. The 1973 Leipzig Festival opened with a new director, Ronald Trisch, then aged forty-four. The similarities and differences of his professional trajectory, in comparison to that of his predecessor Wolfgang Harkenthal, help illuminate both the rationale behind how key positions were filled in the GDR and the new role now being assigned to the Leipzig Festival.

Born in Thuringia in 1929, Trisch joined the Hitler Youth at the age of fifteen and was taken prisoner by American forces at the end of the war. Upon returning to eastern Germany—the Soviet Occupation Zone—in summer 1945, he trained as an electrician and became politically engaged. At first close to the Social Democrats, Trisch built his career in the East German SED's youth group, the FDJ. In 1950, he took courses at the FDJ's political school near Berlin; the following year he moved to East Berlin and, in 1952, he worked in the cultural department of the FDJ's Central Council, which involved him in the international youth festivals it co-organized. From 1961 to 1971, Trisch was responsible for organizing trips abroad for East German artists and preparing tours for foreign artists visiting the GDR. An East German artists' agency—the Deutsche Künstler-Agentur GmbH Berlin (as of September 1968, Künstler-Agentur der DDR)—had been established in May 1960 ("Künstler Agentur der DDR" 2010). The construction of the Wall in August 1961 led the East German government to encourage such structures to maintain contacts between artists in the East and West. Trisch, here in charge of "entertainment" as opposed to "serious art," notably organized travel arrangements for the Italian actress Sophia Loren and the French singer Juliette Gréco.

In 1973, Werner Lamberz—as of 1966 head of the Agitation Department in the SED's Central Committee and previously in charge of information disseminated abroad (*Auslandspropaganda*)—became president of the newly founded Entertainment Arts Committee in 1973 (Wicke and Müller 1996). Werner had already had occasion to collaborate with Trisch and appreciated his work; he asked Trisch to take charge of the cultural program for the WYF to be held in summer 1973. As Harkenthal had with the German Youth Gathering in 1964, Trisch now underwent the trials and tribulations of co-organizing a major event of international and cultural significance. This parallel between the two festival directors underlines to what extent East German leaders regarded the Leipzig Festival as a prime vehicle to advance their diplomatic policy of openness. The diplomatic character of Trisch's previous functions, which had made him an insider in the system, most likely facilitated his nomination. His knowledge of the world of cinema and its workings remained very limited, however. Harkenthal did not hide his unkind verdict on his successor: "He knew nothing about cinema."[60] Trisch himself admits that he had much to learn upon becoming festival director, a position he held until 1989.

The diplomatic recognition of the GDR did not substantially alter the role of the festival, however. Now, more than ever, it had to create an image of modernity and openness by attracting young people, playing the culture card, and developing contacts to the West, the East, and the South. Appealing to international solidarity enabled it to integrate all these aspirations.

Gaining diplomatic recognition did have the particular advantage of pushing questions of internal order into the background. One incident nevertheless illustrates the essential insecurity of individuals. At the congress of the Filmmakers' Association in 1982, Gerhard Scheumann of Studio H&S—someone who could not be more closely aligned with the regime's international solidarity policies and rhetoric—spoke out about what he saw as a full-blown rift between the East German public and its media. He considered this rift symptomatic of the society's lack of maturity, which affected its ability to discuss its problems publicly.[61] As a result, Scheumann was expelled from the Filmmakers' Association and had to resign as president of the international jury at Leipzig.[62] Studio H&S was also immediately dissolved, thus bringing the curtain down on a unique experiment in the GDR.

This incident underlines how intellectuals—including even those most favored by and closest to those in power—could never be sure of their status. It also illustrates how—despite projecting itself to the world as a more self-confident country, which had attained a certain diplomatic and political maturity—under the leadership of Erich Honecker the GDR went through moments of violent rupture between intellectuals and the regime.

Notes

1. The use of the term "Third World" allows direct reference to the rhetoric and concepts used in the Cold War period. For more detail, see chapter 2, note 64.
2. In terms of foundations (Stiftungen), we can cite the Friedrich-Ebert-Stiftung (tied to the Social Democratic Party of Germany, or SPD), the Konrad-Adenauer-Sitftung (tied to the Christian Democratic Union, or CDU), and the Friedrich-Naumann-Stiftung (tied to the FRG's liberal party (the Free Democratic Party, or FDP; Dakowska 2014).
3. This station first broadcast in 1955—first in French, then in eleven languages—to Europe and the rest of the world. It depended on the GDR's State Committee for Radio Broadcasting (Staatliches Rundfunkkomitee, SRK), and thus on the ZK of the SED (Klessmann 1997; Lamm and Kupper 1976).
4. See the article by White House counselor John Galbraith (1961).
5. See the work of Constantin Katsakioris (2008) on the physical violence against Third World students in the USSR from 1960 to 1991.
6. Bericht über den Brigadeeinsatz an der Deutschen Hochschule für Filmkunst Potsdam-Bablesberg in der Zeit vom 9–19 December 1968, Berlin, 8 January 1969, SAPMO-BArch DY 30 IV A2/9.06/43, p. 14.
7. One of its members was Otto-René Castillo, a Guatemalan poet who returned to his country in 1965 to join the guerrillas and who was arrested, tortured, and killed in 1967 (Jordan 2017).
8. Filmed interview with Karl-Heinz Mund conducted by Ralf Schenk and produced by the DEFA-Stiftung.
9. Anthropologist Marcel Mauss (1999) presents the gift as, at once, a wholistic social fact and individual act, which is conceived of as voluntary but also reflects social, political, and economic constraints.
10. Sandrine Kott (2000: 271–93) distinguishes between the "socialist (or official) gift," the "paternalistic gift"—specific to business enterprises—and the "community gift" among people who are close to one another.
11. Konzeption für den Solidaritätsfonds zur Unterstützung junger Kinematografien, Hermann Schauer, 17–18 November 1964, Spenden für den Solidaritätsfond, SAPMO-BArch DR1/4272.
12. Ibid.
13. Letter from Wolfgang Harkenthal to Hermann Herlinghaus, Berlin, 13 October 1971, BArch-FArch, Leipzig, 1971.
14. Ruff, Hauptreferent der Abteilung Kulturelle Beziehungen Sektor III, HVFilm, an Günter Witt, 19 October 1965, SAPMO-BArch DR1/4276.
15. Author's interview with Wolfgang Harkenthal, Murchin, Germany (7 August 2000); Author's interview with Ronald Trisch, Berlin, Germany (11 March 2004).
16. Such bazaars were also organized in West Germany, for example, in churches that served as sales points for products coming from developing countries.
17. This documentary presented the very difficult work done by brickmakers.
18. Andreas Harkenthal, Zur Arbeit des Solidaritätsbasars, Leipzig, 3 December 1985, BArch-FArch, Leipzig, 28/1985.
19. Willy Brandt established a "North-South" commission within the Socialist International in order to discuss possible means of aid to struggling economies in the Global South.

20. Hinweise für die Gestaltung künftiger Kurz- und Dokumentarfilmwochen in Leipzig, betrachtet vom Gesichtspunkt der Entwicklungsländer Afrikas und Asiens, Berlin, 19 December 1964, SAPMO-BArch DR1/4272, p. 2.
21. The Leipzig Festival retrospective was first devoted to Indian cinema only in 1988.
22. While the FRG established diplomatic relations with Israel in 1965, five Arab countries recognized the GDR as the second German state in 1969.
23. Kurt Tetzlaff received the PLO Prize at Leipzig in 1980 for *Die Kinder Palästinas* (1980, *The Children of Palestine*); he had visited one of the refugee camps in Lebanon and filmed a conversation with Yasser Arafat.
24. Author's interview with Wolfgang Harkenthal, Murchin, Germany (7 August 2000).
25. The film shows how a rebel army emerged under the dictatorship of General Batista.
26. *Travel Notebook* was on daily life in Cuba compared to the prerevolutionary period before 1959. Tomás Gutiérrez Alea filmed *Assemblea General* (1960, *General Assembly*), a reportage on Fidel Castor's Declaration of Havana on 2 September 1960.
27. Ivens also made *Pueblo en armas* (1961, *People at Arms*), and Chris Marker made *Cuba sí!* (1961).
28. It was awarded for Cortázar's very beautiful film *Por Primera vez* (1967, *For the First Time*) on the discovery of cinema by the inhabitants of a provincial Cuban village.
29. The author's interviews with East German directors, critics, and authors indicate this. See, for example, the interview with Gitta Nickel—Werder, Germany (3 August 2000)—and Tamara Trampe—Berlin, Germany (23 August 2004).
30. Statistische Angaben zur Internationalen Leipziger Dokumentar- und Kurzfilmwoche, 1955–1986, BArch-FArch, Leipzig, 1986. See Appendix IV, Figure A.1.
31. Statistische Angaben zur Internationalen Leipziger Dokumentar- und Kurzfilmwoche, 1955–1986, BArch-FArch, Leipzig, 1986.
32. West German critic Ulrich Gregor (1968a) even evokes the frenetic jubilation of the public for the 1968 programming.
33. Hermann Schauer, Information über die IX. Internationale Leipziger Dokumentar- und Kurzfilmwoche, Berlin, 25 January 1967, SAPMO-BArch DR1/4331.
34. Author's interview with Wilhelm Roth, Berlin, Germany (9 March 2003).
35. See also chapter 2, note 16. The Information Program allowed more problematic films to be screened, but outside of competition.
36. For more, see chapter 5.
37. In 1966, director Vu Nam explained the epic effort required to get to the festival; at one point, he had to stay in water up to his chin for several hours under heavy bombing, holding the case with his film reels above his head. Bulletin der Dokwoche 1966, BArch-FArch, Leipzig, 1966.
38. Statistische Angaben zur Internationalen Leipziger Dokumentar- und Kurzfilmwoche, 1955–1986, BArch-FArch, Leipzig, 1986.
39. Information über die IX. Internationale Leipziger Dokumentar- und Kurzfilmwoche, HVFilm, SAPMO-BArch DR1/4331, p. 2.
40. For transcriptions of the sessions, see Dedijer and Sartre 1967–1968.
41. This examination of the film is largely drawn on the analysis proposed by Laurent Véray (2004).
42. Alain Resnais, Jean-Luc Godard, William Klein, Claude Lelouch, Agnès Varda, Joris Ivens, and Michèle Ray.
43. The documentary accuses Hans Globke—at the time secretary of state at the Chan-

cellerie in Bonn, close to Adenauer—of having been a Nazi "bureaucrat of death" participating in organizing the genocide.
44. The viewer knows nothing precise about his background—first with the Wehrmacht, then with the Americans, and then sent to Korea and South Africa before arriving in the Congo. Images from the preceding film and photographic documents serve as pieces of evidence against him.
45. Entwurf für einen Artikel des Genossen Wagner für das Bulletin der Dokwoche 1966, SAPMO-BArch DR1/4331.
46. See, in particular, Steinmetz and Prase 2002.
47. Beschlussvorlage zur Gründung der DEFA-Gruppe Heynowski&Scheumann, 17 January 1967, SAPMO-BArch DY 30 IV A2/2024/35, p. 12.
48. The four episodes of *Pilots in Pajamas* are *Yes, Sir; Hilton-Hanoi; Der Job (The Job)*, which was awarded the Golden Dove, and *Die Donnergötter (The Thundergods)*.
49. *Die Teufelsinsel* (1976, *Devil's Island*), *Der erste Reis danach* (1977, *And Then the First Rice*), *Ich bereue aufrichtig* (1977, *I Sincerely Repent*), and *Die eiserne Festung* (1977, *The Iron Fortress*).
50. See also Soutou 2001; Labin 1980.
51. In the German-language version of Guzmán's documentary, the commentary was revised and partially changed.
52. See the work of Jean-Noël Darde (2017) on this topic. While some of the results of Darde's research on the work of Heynowski and Scheumann around the Chilean military junta are worth noting here, the tone and method of his blog do not follow the conventions of scholarly historical inquiry and debate.
53. The first youth meetings took place in Prague in 1947. They were organized by the World Federation of Democratic Youth, founded in November 1945 in London, which, it soon became clear, was a communist organization under strict Soviet control. The meetings became the International Festival of Youth and Students in 1951. The FDJ—the East German youth organization—participated in the second meetings in Budapest in 1949, then in Bucharest (1953), Warsaw (1955), Moscow (1957), Vienna (1959), Helsinki (1962), and Sofia (1968). East Berlin first hosted the festival in 1951.
54. The official iconography of the festival extensively utilized images of young couples kissing in front of the Alexanderplatz fountains.
55. The festival served as a pretext for the Stasi to intensify its actions on society as a whole. Those the regime considered to be "asocial"—those without work, the mentally handicapped, and even prostitutes—were questioned in great numbers. On 23 July 1973, 19,779 people across the country were interrogated and prevented from going to East Berlin. Only those who were authorized could go.
56. Wolle mentions twenty-four arrests among festival goers.
57. In a text titled "Element," Kunze humorously evokes his unsuccessful attempts to get to East Berlin by train and hitchhiking. With his long hair and guitar, he raised police suspicions, however, and was always stopped. The text was published in the West in the collection *Die wunderbaren Jahre: Ausgewählte Gedichte* (Kunze 1976). Kunze left the GDR for West Germany in 1977, after the Wolf Biermann affair.
58. Angela Davis had studied for a while at the University of Frankfurt in West Germany before moving to East Berlin to earn her Ph.D. in philosophy from Humboldt University.

59. A comparison also picked up by the *Frankfurter Allgemeine Zeitung* on 30 July 1973.
60. Author's interview with Wolfgang Harkenthal, Murchin, Germany (7 August 2000).
61. Speech by Gerhard Scheumann, Berlin, 16 September 1982, SAPMO-BArch DY 30 vorl SED/32718.
62. Gerhard Scheumann to Annelie Thorndike, Berlin, 30 September 1982, SAPMO-BArchq DY 30 vorl SED/32718.

PART III

A Trompe L'Oeil Mise-en-Scène? (1973–1983)

CHAPTER 7
IIIIIIIIIIIIIIIIIII
Wide Angle on Socialist Society

Once East Germany had achieved international diplomatic recognition in 1973, the East Berlin government sought to enlist the support of its population by focusing on improving their everyday life; socialism must draw its legitimacy not just from the hope of a utopian future, but also from the present and tangible social gains (Meuschel 1992; Staritz 1990).[1] Daily life thus became a prominent theme in official discourse, as well as onscreen. This trend was accompanied by an international dynamic in the realm of documentary cinema.

In the wake of the effervescent 1960s, documentary as a genre continued going through changes in the 1970s — less marked but introducing trends that would endure over time (Gauthier 1995). In the East Bloc as in the West, the 1970s witnessed the emergence of a sociological form of documentary film that was committed to depicting social realities more profoundly. In the West, the documentaries of the 1970s assigned a large role to politically engaged and militant cinema imbued with a strong sociological dimension. In some eastern countries, at least, constricting of the political realm did not impede the development of cinematographic productions that also sought to express the complex experience of people in societies that were at the crossroads of state-mandated technological modernization and economic scarcity.

DEFA documentary filmmakers were actively involved in this international development, as evidenced by two long-term documentary series: Winfried Junge's *Die Kinder von Golzow* (*The Children of Golzow*) and Volker Koepp's *Wittstock Zyklus* (*Wittstock Cycle*), for which filming began in 1961 and 1974, respectively. Though the Leipzig Festival acknowledged the trend, it only did so to a limited extent, and the role it played with respect to the diffusion and reception of these two seminal documentary cycles was complex. A closer examination of this history reveals which particular images of East German society were presented to the court of international opinion and highlights two quite distinct conceptions of documentary film. It also raises questions about the role played by international public opinion in the transformations that East German society underwent during the 1960s and 1970s.

In the West, a Field Camera

Undoubtedly, sociological audiovisual media and social documentary are rooted in the very origins of cinema. *La sortie de l'Usine Lumière à Lyon* (1895, *Workers Leaving the Lumière Factory in Lyon*), the debut motion picture of the Lumière brothers, can be considered quite akin to empirical sociology.[2] The role played later by Soviet documentarists Dziga Vertov and Aleksandr Medvedkine, too, is paramount. They served as a benchmark for numerous documentarists in the 1960s and 1970s at a time when the trend was to champion an investigative and immersive[3] cinema.

French Labor Activist Cinema at Leipzig

Once again, the French example illustrates the stakes involved in programming at Leipzig. Echoing the antiestablishment movements of 1968, the handheld field camera acquired an essential emancipatory and revelatory role for some filmmakers in France. It was, in the words of Guy Gauthier (1995: 82), the "intermediary of interventionist cinema." Some documentarists positioned the world of work at the core of their plan, giving voice to workers. Such an approach assumed a particular significance in the East German context.

The Leipzig Festival timidly served as a forum for this trend in documentary filmmaking, branded as progressive (*fortschrittlich*) in capitalist France.[4] Although it remained taboo to denounce the crushing of the Prague Spring, after the festival's November 1968 crisis the mobilization of workers in the West managed to find a place in the program. In 1969, *Classe de lutte* (1969, *Fighting Class*), by the Medvedkin Group collective in Besançon, was awarded the World Federation of Trade Unions Prize. This film is in line with the critical vein of *À bientôt, j'espère* (1968, *Until Soon, I Hope*), shot in 1967 by Chris Marker and Mario Marret, and has an interesting story (Stark 2012). The Marker-Marret film documented the December 1967 workers' strike at the Rhodiaceta textile factory in Besançon. At its subsequent screening at the factory, however, the workers were highly critical, condemning its overly intellectual perspective on their work. They, in turn, then took the camera and shot their own film: *Fighting Class*.

In 1971, *Le Train en marche* (1971, *The Train Rolls On*) was also programmed at Leipzig. The film was produced by the Société de Lancement des Oeuvres Nouvelles (SLON), a production and distribution collective created in 1967 by Chris Marker[5]; it was a tribute to the Soviet Russian filmmaker Aleksandr Medvedkin, who had traveled the length and breadth of the Soviet Union during the 1930s on board his ciné-train, which he'd equipped with facilities to develop and project films he'd made during the trip for people encountered along the way, in the spirit of agitprop. Medvedkin's adventures inspired many filmmakers, as far away as Algeria and Latin America (Graham 1999). Throughout the 1970s, the festival's official selection often contained films produced by other collectives close to SLON—which in 1974 changed its name to Image, Son, Kinescope et Réalisations Audiovisuelles (ISKRA; Guyot-Bender 2014)—such as Dynadia and Unicité, both linked to the French Communist Party.[6] In 1976, René Vautier, a leading figure in French documentary and militant Breton filmmaker—who campaigned against colonialism, the war in Algeria, and France's nuclear arsenal in turn—became a member of the festival's international jury.[7]

These French participants, the majority of whom were closely linked to the French Communist Party, were moreover unlikely to criticize the festival's orthodox line, in contrast to Joris Ivens and Marceline Loridan-Ivens, whose

Figure 7.1. French documentarist René Vautier (*seated, with cap*) at a festival discussion in 1976. © Filmmuseum Potsdam, Reinhard Podszuweit.

Maoist leanings excluded them from the guest list as of the turn of the 1970s. By the time Chris Marker finished making *Le fond de l'air est rouge* (1977, *A Grin without a Cat*), however, the limits to the inclusivity of the East German festival were exposed once again. Marker's lucid and disillusioned cinematic essay about the previous decade and its social and political commitments (Gauthier 2004) could not be accepted in the original at Leipzig. Festival director Ronald Trisch went to France to ask Marker to alter certain passages that were considered too critical of the Communist Party or the USSR — all to no avail. This, like Marker's subsequent work, was not screened at Leipzig.[8]

Journalist Wilhelm Roth is of the opinion that, among all the left-leaning international documentary festivals of that epoch, the Leipzig Festival was ultimately the most reactionary, as it did not present the entire spectrum of leftwing filmmaking, with all its various subdivisions and currents. In contrast, Oberhausen, Mannheim, and Nyon in Switzerland,[9] for example, paid more attention to documentaries of the extreme left, which was critical of Moscow's doctrine.[10]

Sociological Essays from Other Countries

The Leipzig Festival was even more reserved with regard to social and sociological documentary films from other Western countries, especially the United States and FRG. American entries — of which there were few, averaging only one film in competition per year — focused primarily on films about the Third World made by collectives. This was the case despite the fact that some American documentarists at the time were producing critically important films about American society. A case in point was Frederick Wiseman (b. 1930), whose works were never screened at Leipzig. In 1967 Wiseman, then a law professor, shot his first documentary, conceiving of it as an extension of his teaching. His work offers a precise and profound observation of American society through its institutions — psychiatric hospital, university, ballet company, and so on.[11] No doubt his penetratingly critical and insightful view of American society, at once exacting and profound, appeared insufficiently militant, and was, above all, disconnected from the network of documentarists associated with the Leipzig Festival.

As for West German documentaries, the picture is somewhat more mixed. In the late 1960s and throughout the 1970s, several projects emerged in the FRG that reflected a growing interest in the world of labor and, in a broader sense, in West German society (Jordan 2000; Roth 2000). A few directors conducted long-term observations, such as those by Wilhelm Bittorf, director of *Der Untergang der Graf Bismarck* (1967, *The Sinking of the Count Bismarck*), which dealt with the dismissal of minors, and Christian Weisenborn and Michael Wulfes, whose *Profis — Ein Jahr Fußball mit Paul Breitner und*

Uli Hoeneß (1979, *Professionals: A Year of Soccer with Paul Breitner and Uli Hoeneß*) chronicled a year of crisis for the Bayern München soccer team. To shoot his documentary *In der Fremde* (1967, *Far from Home*), Klaus Wildenhahn lived with a group of construction workers for ten weeks, documenting the working conditions of these men living far from their families and mounting tensions with management.

These documentaries were not screened at Leipzig, most often on the grounds that they were produced by West German television channels that were not officially represented at the festival.[12] Of course, because they were broadcast on West German television, these documentaries could be viewed in the East. Ultimately, the West German documentaries selected and present at Leipzig represented a very small circle of directors. About ten names surface over the course of the 1970s, often belonging to Das Team production group in Munich. Their films addressed anti-imperialist struggles in the Third World or focused on a few specific social problems in the FRG, such as the 1972 Anti-Radical Decree (*Berufsverbot*), which excluded certain people, on political grounds, from employment in given professions.

New Images of Society in Eastern Europe

The assessment of the selection of films from Eastern Europe is even more severe. The political hardening that affected all the East Bloc countries during the Brezhnev era forced those wishing to make documentaries—often people who had participated in movements for social and political renewal during the 1960s—to explore new avenues. The Hungarian and Polish examples demonstrate divergent routes taken, during the 1970s, to capture everyday life as accurately as possible in these societies.

Hungary: Sociological Cinema, Direct Cinema

Already recognized internationally for its feature films of the 1960s, over the following decade Hungarian cinema also attracted attention for its high-quality documentary output. The term "Budapest School" appeared relatively late, in the context of a 1980 symposium, "Fiction and Documentary Film in Today's Cinema," organized by FIPRESCI, the International Federation of Film Critics in Budapest.[13] This label referred to a group of documentaries made during the 1970s in the tradition of sociological cinema. It should be noted that Hungarian cinema had always striven to be a vector of social criticism and to initiate debate beyond official ideology (Madeline 2004). It now aspired to document the state of society by drawing upon scientific methods, especially meticulous fieldwork.

This approach naturally went against the grain of a top-down and totalitarian vision of society, which had hitherto consisted—in Hungary, as elsewhere in the East—of invariably tacking a rigid vision, inspired by a form of Marxism that was set in stone through its Stalinist reinterpretation, on to the village, the cooperative, or the factory. Although the practice of sociological and anthropological investigation was just beginning in the Soviet Union and the East (Matthews 1978), Hungary was ahead of the game, thanks to Béla Bartók and Zoltán Kodály, who had collected Magyar folk melodies at the turn of the twentieth century. In response to the wishes of young Hungarian documentarists, the Balázs Studio in Budapest thus launched a five-year program for sociological documentary in 1969.

The documentaries of Judit Elek (b. 1937) attracted particular attention. After four years of fieldwork and tens of hours of footage, Elek came out with a two-part, three-hour long chronicle that began in 1971. *Istenmezején 1972–73-ban* (1973, *A Hungarian Village*) was followed in 1975 by *Egyszerű történet* (*A Commonplace Story*). *A Hungarian Village* opens with festivities surrounding the graduation of a group of teenage girls in a village in northern Hungary; for the sequel, Elek returned to the village to see what had happened to these girls in the meantime. The assessment is bleak: worn down by social pressures and constraints, the erstwhile vibrancy of the girls has vanished. Conscious of the reality her film exposed, Elek refused to show the documentary to the villagers. "The film director is vested with inhuman responsibility, not knowing how personal secrets revealed during filming today might affect the person's life, let's say ten years down the road. It's impossible to take it on" (Jeancolas 2001: 161).[14] In 1971, Elek also shot *Találkozunk 1971-ben* (*We Met in 1971*), a medium-length film about miners forced into retirement. She juxtaposed her footage with 1950s documentary footage glorifying these same workers at the height of the Stalinist era. The film remained on the shelf for a year.

Another filmmaker, Márta Mészáros, also directed a short film in 1971—*A Lörinci Fonóban* (*At the Lőrinc Spinnery*), portraying a spinning mill with an almost exclusively female workforce (Jeancolas 2001). With her films Mészáros, who worked in both features and documentaries, illustrated the feminist wave of the 1970s—which, to a certain extent, affected cinema in socialist countries. Very few of the sociological documentaries from Hungary were programmed at Leipzig. *At the Lőrinc Spinnery* was one of the few documentaries in the series we can verify was actually screened; it received a special mention from the jury in November 1972 (*Protokoll 1972* 1973).

The designation "Budapest School" may perhaps artificially and retrospectively unite film productions that, in reality, were diffuse and splintered, without any real conceptual unity.[15] It nevertheless encapsulates the expression of a particularly prolific and innovative period in Hungarian documentary filmmaking. Only glimpses of this diversity were offered at the Leipzig Festival, which opted for films depicting a less complex image of Hungarian reality. The extent to which the themes addressed by filmmakers like Elek and Mészáros would become central in East German sociological documentary is nevertheless striking.

A New Generation of Polish Documentarists

Among the other socialist countries in the East, we should also mention Polish documentary, which, as of the 1950s, had sought to show Polish society as it was, refusing to smooth the rough edges of everyday reality. In the mid-1960s, Poland, like Czechoslovakia, had seen the emergence of a reform movement. The student protests of March 1968 were repressed, however, and the participation of Polish troops in marching into Prague on 21 August 1968 confirmed the tougher line being taken by Gomułka, which was marked by a strong wave of anti-Semitism. People left Poland by the thousands; among these were two well-known figures of the film world. Film historian Jerzy Toeplitz, the rector of the Łódź Film School, emigrated to Sydney, where he became the founding director of the newly established Australian Film, Television and Radio School, while in the meanwhile, the documentarist Jerzy Bossak accepted an offer from the Copenhagen School of Cinema/Danish Film Institute. Given their international reputations, these two Poles in exile did nonetheless continue to be invited to both to Leipzig—Bossak was even a member of its international jury in November 1970—and to Oberhausen.

A group of young Polish filmmakers was the focus of particular attention at the 1971 edition of the Krakow Documentary Festival: Krzysztof Kieślowski (1941–1996), Tomasz Zygadlo (1947–2011), Marek Piwowski (b. 1935), and not forgetting Marcel Lozinski (b. 1940), the nephew of French filmmaker Jean Vigo (Wach 1998). Along with Kieślowski, Lozinski succeeded in circumventing censorship by agreeing to a deal with their unit managers: in exchange for making films complying with the desiderata of the regime, they would be allowed to make a few more provocative documentaries. In a country where dramatic reversals in domestic and foreign policy were legion, the tactic paid off. Kieślowski, who had graduated from the Łódź Film School in 1969, was thus able to direct a series of critical films. *Fabryka* (1970, *The Factory*) revealed the absolute absurdity of an economy of scarcity and its devastating impact on production conditions. The short film *Spzital* (*Hospital*), shot in 1976 and released in 1977, chronicles the night shift in the surgical ward of a Warsaw hospital. While the scenes taken from life are reminiscent of *cinéma vérité*, this approach was not consciously undertaken by Kieślowski, who sought above all to formulate a social critique of the situation in Poland (Michalek and Turaj 1992).

Following the announcement of further price hikes, in June 1976 workers and intellectuals had joined forces, something quite remarkable in the East; in September, intellectuals created the Workers Defense Committee to give aid to prisoners and their families after the ensuing government crackdown. These events were also pivotal for young filmmakers, and a Polish revival emerged, in which documentaries played a vital role and exerted influence on feature films (Michalek and Turaj 1992). Director Andrzej Wajda, for example—whose feature film *Czlowiek z marmuru* (1977, *Man of Marble*) focused on a television journalist investigating the fall from grace into obscurity of a 1950s proletarian hero—encouraged filmmakers to tackle social and moral questions more boldly.[16] Feliks Falk paid tribute to his fellow documentarists, who, "without the slightest compromise, exposed us to as much as possible about Polish reality" (Michalek and Turaj 1992: 114). Reflecting the reputation thus acquired by Polish documentary on both international and national stages, young Polish filmmakers won a number of prizes at Oberhausen, as well as at Krakow—as was the case for Kieślowski's *Hospital* in 1977. Their documentaries, however, were never selected for the Leipzig Festival.

The distrust of East German authorities was long standing, as evidenced by their strained relationship with the Krakow Film Festival.[17] At the close of the Polish festival in June 1976, the GDR Foreign Ministry complained of errors committed by HVFilm that had seriously compromised DEFA's participation at Krakow.[18] The director of the Polish festival, Henryk Zielinski, even observed that cinematic relations between the two countries had deteriorated since 1975. The director of the international relations department at HVFilm replied that if there were problems, these were primarily due to Polish colleagues; for example, film reels sent by express train from East Berlin to Warsaw arrived at the wrong station.

Despite such logistical problems on either side, HVFilm noted that the atmosphere had quickly become more relaxed over the course of the festival. In particular, a discussion between Ronald Trisch and his Polish counterpart smoothed over the fact that two Polish documentaries that had been initially selected for the competition ultimately disappeared from the 1975 Leipzig Festival program. HVFilm was making efforts to ease tensions, without being able to deny that they did actually exist; indeed, within the East German government, many wanted to ensure that East German film production remained free from all external influences deemed to be harmful.

Tentative Sociological Experiments at DEFA

In the early 1970s, small art galleries, meeting places between artists and the general public, developed in the GDR. Literary circles were formed in East Berlin, Jena, and Leipzig (Neubert 1997). The prevailing cultural liberalization benefited artistic spheres such as painting (Blume and März 2003; Damus 1991) and literature, more than cinema, although feature films were undergoing a revival and enjoyed box office successes.[19] In effect, documentary films did not seem to be part of the artistic dynamic observable elsewhere in society (Schreiber 1996). A new trend, however, was tentatively emerging, which had to do with focusing more on questioning and observing reality. This approach paralleled the growth of sociology in the GDR (Schreiber 1996); the first big comprehensive empirical fact–based investigation into the working and living conditions of East Germans took place in 1973.[20] It is worth noting, however, that in East Germany, unlike in Hungary or Poland, most documentaries claiming to take a sociological approach stuck with the prevailing party line.

In the early 1970s, Karl Gass launched a series of projects chronicling the technical and technological modernization of East German industry. He gathered the Effekt artistic group around him—a reference to the Party's new guidelines that touted, inter alia, "greater efficiency and increased labor productivity" to ensure better living standards for the East German population.[21] Documentaries made by Effekt enabled their filmmakers to introduce the use of 16mm film techniques at the DEFA Documentary Studio (Jordan 2000).

A special session focusing on Effekt films was held at the 1970 Leipzig Festival, featuring screenings of "films about the organizational and management problems in a firm" (*Protokoll 1970* 1971: 62) All these overly verbose documentaries were built around interviews with scientists and managers of the factories under review,[22] as indicated by the explicit title of Volker Koepp's 1970 film, *Die Rolle des Meisters im System der sozialistischen Betriebswirtschaft* (1970, *The Role of the Foreman in the Management System of the Socialist Enterprise*). Most of these films did not present shortcuts, or offscreen images that might have helped shed new light on East German reality. Only two long-term documentaries delved deeper. From today's perspective, Winfried Junge's *The Children of Golzow* and Volker Koepp's *Wittstock Cycle* make an indispensable contribution to research into the history of both East German society and documentary cinema. A detailed look at these two film cycles illustrates their impact.

The Golzow Cycle

The cycle began in 1961 with *Wenn ich erst zur Schule geh* (*Some Day, When I Go to School*).[23] Born in 1935, the director of this film cycle, Winfried Junge, stopped studying educational science at the Humboldt University in East Berlin in order to enter the Babelsberg film academy in 1954 and, four years later, he became assistant director to Karl Gass. It was this young documentarist's mentor who had the idea, in 1961, of filming the first school year of children in Golzow, whose population was 1,300 at that time (Zimmermann 2000).

The initial project was perfectly in tune with SED policy, which aspired to create a "socialist human community" (*sozialistische Menschengemeinschaft*). As Junge recalled in 1993: "We actually wanted to chronicle the construction of socialism, . . . through the changes in human beings and the education of a generation growing up in a socialist context" (Rother 1996: 116). This socialist context took a dramatic turn even before filming got under way. Scheduled for mid-August 1961, the beginning of the shoot had to be postponed until the end of the month, because cinematographer Hans Dumke was called with his combat group to guard the "antifascist protective bulwark" starting 13 August, the day work on building the Wall was begun (Klunker 1993: 20). The project would thus unfold in the shadow of a wall that fenced in and isolated East German society. The cycle's first two episodes also represented a turning point in DEFA documentary production. Devoid of spectacular effects or dramatic impact, their very titles heralded a new direction now being taken by young documentarists, who were more interested in issues concerning East German society than the recurrent denunciation of fascism and the FRG (Mückenberger 2000).

The authorities approved the choice of location for this long-term observation project, for, after protracted consultations, Golzow clearly came out on top (Rother 1996). One overriding argument was its proximity to the film studios: the town was within an hour of Berlin and thus easily accessible for the film crew. Furthermore, the Oderbruch region had suffered particularly badly from the war and symbolized that border zone with Poland where many Germans from East Prussia and German enclaves even farther east had taken refuge. For the regime, integrating these newcomers into the new society remained an outstanding challenge to be tackled — one the documentary was meant to bear witness to. The observation of young children as they first enter school naturally afforded Junge all the requisite symbolism needed to begin his chronicle on the prospects of a socialist future. The challenge of the film was to bear witness to how these seven-year-olds would grow up within the socialist community in both private and professional terms, that is, to observe the birth of "socialist personalities."[24] It was up to the crew to optimally capture the fate of these young citizens.

Didactic Ambition and the "Aesthetic of Trust"

Like most DEFA documentaries, each film episode in the cycle was shot on 35mm film; this especially involved the use of imposing and cumbersome equipment that, during every shoot, literally transformed the school into a studio set and turned the presence of the DEFA crew into a veritable event (Voss 1993). In 1966, the fixed cameras used in 1961 gave way to more manageable, albeit still noisy, cameras. In 1975, shoulder-mounted cameras were introduced that recorded synchronous sound and were equipped with highly sensitive lenses, thereby enabling the crew to limit the need for projectors and artificial light. In the late 1970s, color film made its appearance, and audio recording became more easily manageable as it shifted from using a boom to wireless microphones (Junge 1982). Aside from taking these technical constraints and advances into consideration, Junge and cinematographer Hans-Eberhard Leupold upheld a certain ethics of documentary filmmaking, refusing as early as 1962 the practice of employing a hidden camera.

The camera itself thus played a vital role in the direct confrontation with those being filmed. The chronicle, in fact, represents the intertwining of two viewpoints—those of director Junge and cinematographer Leupold. Throughout their collaboration, however, disagreements emerged, reflecting two opposing concepts of documentary film. For Leupold,[25] who ended up withdrawing from the project in 1985, Junge could not appreciate the significance of details captured by the camera. As he said, "Often it's about small details that nevertheless play a big role in the documentary. . . . It might be a gesture, a glance, the connection between this gesture and glance that suddenly reveal something unforeseeable" (Voigt 1981: 5). From Leupold's point of view, Junge could not accept the unexpected—he who determined the script in advance and, in the cutting room, sought to rectify the sense of the story by means of his voice-over to bend images that too often resisted him. More often than not they resisted his attempts (Roth 2000). The commentary was a constant attempt to link Jung's two aspirations: to remain faithful to the children of Golzow, to what the camera captured of their lives, and yet, at the same time, to remain equally loyal to the regime, by showing a generation reaching adulthood and fulfillment within socialist society.

Junge (1995: 134) effectively lays claim to an "aesthetic of trust," thus posing a question of ethics—as did the Hungarian Judit Elek—but with different conclusions. According to him, it is not a question of taking advantage of the trust of the young people of Golzow to deceive them, but rather to get them to feel sufficiently confident in his integrity to be able to reveal a part of their lives and their emotions on camera. In hindsight, Junge remarked, "My way of talking with [the children of Golzow] is a document of that era, with its faults and weaknesses, which must be taken into account" (Schieber 1996: 184). The entire chronicle does, in fact, constitute a truly precious document, not only with respect to a director's professional evolution but also on individual trajectories that, in turn, cinematically convey the history of East German society.

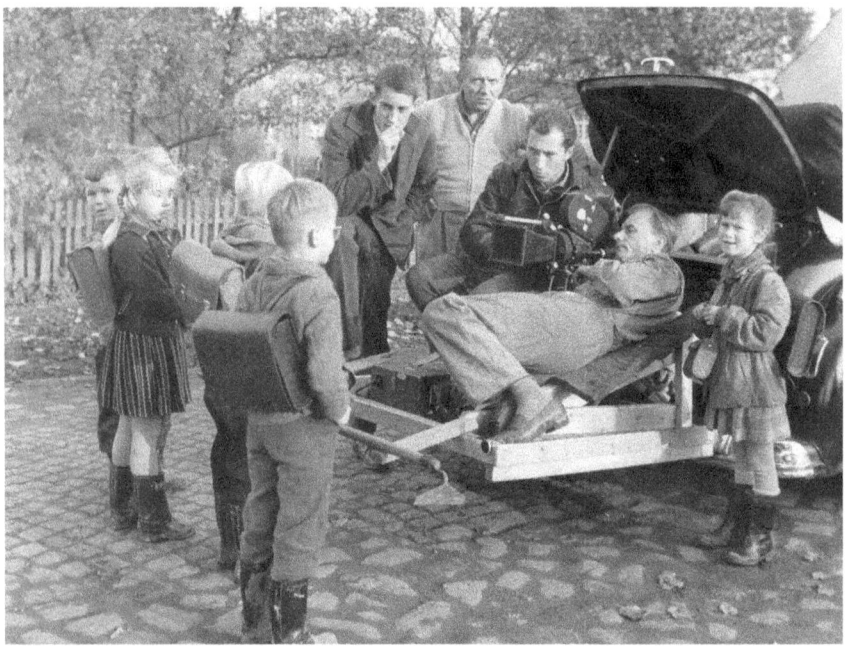

Figure 7.2. Winfried Junge (*left*) and cinematographer Hans-Eberhard Leupold (*third from left*) shooting first film in the Golzow Series, as the children start school in 1961. © DEFA Stiftung.

Growing Pains

As Junge (1995: 142–43) later put it, "What objective was I sure I'd reach, when I started shooting the first film at twenty-six? Obviously I thought that when my work was finished, in around the year 2000, I would have filmed the achieving of socialism — so it was worth filming the stages of this development," but, he continued, "the dream had shattered in the GDR well before the fall of '89."

As the scope of the project gradually expanded — from the school to the village of Golzow and then from the village to the entire country — and as the children grew into teenagers and adults, the tenor grew more somber, and the social issues became graver. While shooting the third documentary in the cycle, *Eleven Years Old,* the film crew increased its commitment to the project by staying in Golzow, thereby making it easier to get better acquainted with the children's families and community. This 1966 film, the lightest and most upbeat in the series, thus widened the perspective and gained in depth, while the children became more active in the filming process (Junge 1995).

The camera captures the children in groups, without yet focusing on specific individuals. Viewers discover Gudrun, daughter of the cooperative's director, Brigitte, with her round face, and blond-haired Jürgen, who is easily distracted, as well as many others. In 1969, as the GDR commemorated it twentieth anniversary, the children were celebrating their *Jugendweihe*—the socialist coming-of-age ceremony adopted by the state in 1955, which involved taking an oath to integrate into East Germany's socialist society—in *When You Are Fourteen*.[26] In retrospect, Junge felt that "none of the other films in the chronicle bears the traces of official influence to such an extent" (Junge 1995: 139).

The subsequent episodes, as of the early 1970s, enable us to discern how the children's individual destinies are increasingly anchored in a restrictive social context, creating tensions that Junge sought to solve or to circumvent. As soon as the students left school, the crew was no longer faced with a class but with a group of teenagers who had distinct individualities and who seemed to want to avoid the gaze of the camera and to control their own images. The documentaries thus became progressively more talkative, featuring extensive conversations with young people in semistaged situations at work or at home. The project simultaneously gained observational depth, as the discussions

Figure 7.3. Shooting *Eleven Years Old* in Golzow in 1966. © DEFA Stiftung.

finally allow a glimpse of the characters' aspirations and feelings. As of this time, the documentaries of the series were only broadcast on television and no longer played in movie theaters; this form of filmed interview, the so-called talking head, was part of a general trend in televised reports.

In the late 1970s, Junge had reached the limits of observation (Voss 1993). He called on author Uwe Kant and, in 1979, directed *Anmut sparet nicht noch Mühe (Spare No Charm and Spare No Effort)*,[27] which seeks to take stock of the project by integrating and referring to sequences in the various films in the cycle. HVFilm, however, reduced the film's message to a harmonious portrayal of a socialist village.[28] A decade later, journalist Margit Voss (1993: 13) listened "to the commentary more carefully"; now she discerned "the demagogy" in it and could no longer understand "the euphoric response at the time." West German critic Heinz Klunker (1993: 23) is equally harsh: "The text is a handicap for the images, forcing them into an ideological framework instead of allowing them to unfold."

In 1981, Junge directed a second omnibus film that encapsulated his original series. *Lebensläufe* (1980, *Children of Golzow: Individual Portraits*) lasted more than four hours, fleshing out the portraits of nine children, while recapitulating the seven previous Golzow films. What is most striking across the nine destinies intersecting in this documentary is the diversity of these individual portraits.

Gudrun is unquestionably the chronicle's model character, who best meets official expectations, even though she does not marry; leaving school after tenth grade, she trains as a cook before she goes on to study political science and becomes the mayor of a neighboring village. As for Marieluise, she exemplifies a completely different character type; her father is employed at the local cooperative and, born into a practicing Protestant family, she receives a religious education, which distinguishes her from her peers. She then pursues her studies in Frankfurt (Oder) and becomes a lab assistant at a semiconductor factory. In 1979, she marries a military officer—relatively late compared to her former classmates—and they settle near Berlin and have two children. Fragments of the puzzle are reconstituted from one film to the next, as though the film director is gradually daring to reveal the full picture. Only in *Individual Portraits*—in which viewers witness her church wedding—is it explicitly stated that Marieluise has taken Confirmation.

As for Elke, she leaves the village for Frankfurt (Oder) at an early age, where she studies industrial design. She becomes pregnant at eighteen, soon marries, and divorces a year later; she has a second child with an engineer, from whom she also separates. Elke's life story and the issues it raises introduce a certain feminism into the cycle, of the sort that existed in the GDR. Coming from a humble background, Brigitte leaves school after eight years of study in order to undergo training as a poultry breeder; divorced, she lives alone in difficult conditions with her son and dies prematurely. Her short life cuts through any optimistic rhetoric.

The professional lives of the men are equally varied, even though a shared sense of frustration is discernable. Jürgen's trajectory testifies to the gap between reality and his initial ambitions; the bright and dreamy boy of the earlier documentaries is forced to confront scholastic failure and quits school at fourteen. In *Individual Portraits*, Jürgen is twenty-four, marries, fathers a son, and works as a house painter—a profession no one imposed upon him, as he himself likes to reiterate, but one he doesn't want to pursue very long, as the work is tedious.

Like the women, the men experience break-ups and divorces in their private lives. Junge's frequently posed questions—attempts at persuading the young singles to marry—opened him to accusations that he wanted to play at being the right-minded, petit bourgeois thinking uncle from Berlin. His questions were nonetheless emblematic of cracks in East German society, as the young people from Golzow did not escape the marital crises being experienced by the majority of East German couples.[29] Choosing one's life partner was one of the rare decisions one could freely make in the GDR; on the other hand—given the ban on travel abroad, general feelings of deprivation, and the recurrent confrontation with restrictions—married life became the crux of all of life's frustrations

In concluding his documentary, Junge had to acknowledge, "Now, the community only exists on film." The commentary can no longer dress up what the faces, words, and silences allow us to see and to hear. The disillusionment experienced over the years by the children born in 1961 dissolves the optimistic and confident portrayal of everyday life and the future of East German society.

From Leipzig into the Wider World

Individual Portraits garnered public acclaim at the Leipzig Festival in November 1981, where foreign guests, including film enthusiasts and journalists from both East and West, had nothing but praise for the work. For West German journalist Wilhelm Roth (1995: 179), a great connoisseur of both DEFA and the Leipzig Festival, it remains the "most complete self-representation of the GDR." The documentary was greeted with excitement and enthusiasm at its screening at the Leipzig Festival precisely due to its role as a societal mirror. It projected a familiar image not only to citizens of the GDR but to foreign audiences as well (Klunker 1993). The Leipzig Festival played a vital role in transforming Winfried Junge into an acclaimed film director and his longitudinal chronicle into an international success. As early as 1962, *Some Day, When I Go to School* had received the festival's Silver Dove; chaired by Karl Gass, the jury also selected *Furnace Makers*, by Jürgen Böttcher, thereby bringing two young DEFA documentarists out of virtual anonymity. In 1966, *Eleven Years Old* was also awarded a Silver Dove, and public acclaim soon followed.

The *Children of Golzow* documentaries became favorites of East German audiences, who could watch trailers for them in movie theaters before the feature film screened. Even more spectacular was the regime's embrace of the cycle. The small town in the Oderbruch effectively saw a stream of visiting diplomats and luminaries—including Erich Honecker, who was accompanied by Kim Il Sung, supreme leader of North Korea. After viewing one film in the cycle, the then GDR prime minister Willi Stoph spontaneously decided to award the Order of Karl Marx to the town of Golzow (Junge 1995). For his Golzow project, Winfried Junge also earned national awards in 1967 and again in 1981.

In 1973, the Leipzig Festival programmed *Nyolc év után* (1973, *After Eight Years*), a Hungarian documentary that revisited children—who had originally been filmed upon starting school eight years earlier—when they graduated. Junge's project had thus effectively set a precedent, in the East as in the West, although these replicas never attained the scale of the East German model. At the end, *Individual Portraits* was awarded only an "honorary" Golden Dove at Leipzig in 1981—because the documentary's running time, of four hours and seventeen minutes, far exceeded the prescribed duration of films selected for competition. Conferred by the festival's international jury, the prizes naturally reflected not only the regime's support for the project but also the enthusiasm among foreign audiences for the project. It was the Leipzig Festival that enabled Junge's documentaries to cross East German borders and acquire an international profile.

Though Junge's *A Year Later* had received an honorary commendation at the West German Oberhausen Festival as early as 1963, the fate of the eighth film in the cycle, *Individual Portraits*, is more illustrative of this dynamic. It garnered a great deal of attention at Leipzig in November 1981. West German journalist Wilhelm Roth (1995) recalls how West German journalists reacted after the film screened at Leipzig. It was obvious that those being filmed seemed neither personally fulfilled nor happy, forced to live hemmed in by constraints, both in the professional sphere and in their private lives. And yet, the overall impression at the time was less gloomy than it might seem to viewers today. This portrait of East German society was actually regarded as a rather positive sign, which showed that East German documentarists were now presenting a less distorted view of their fellow citizens and seemingly offering the hope that, moving forward, East German society could change, as long as it continued to take stock of its own limitations.

After seeing the film at Leipzig, West Berlin–based critics Erika and Ulrich Gregor selected Junge's documentary for the Berlinale Forum in February 1982. The couple had already singled out *Spare No Charm and Spare No*

Effort in 1979, but the film's narration had made it impossible to screen in the FRG (Junge 2000). At the Berlinale in 1982, *Individual Portraits* received the FIPRESCI Prize, granted by a jury of international journalists and film critics, as well as the Otto Dibelius Prize, granted by an international Protestant jury.[30] Junge (2000: 383–85) and his cinematographer had asked themselves, "Where did we go wrong, to make our film please the class enemy so much?"

The day after the award ceremony, the managing director of HVFilm summoned the filmmakers to his office; both men wondered whether they were going to be rebuked for having accepted the award or whether they were suspected of wanting to defect to the West with the prize money they were to receive. Though warmly welcomed, they learned that they would have to hand over the prize money they would receive—60 percent in East German and 40 percent in West German marks; this meant that directors reaped none, while the East German authorities reaped all the benefits of receiving the prize: political, symbolic, and financial. Once again, in contrast, the East German authorities were able to reap the benefits, and not only political ones, of a DEFA film winning an award abroad.

The critical reception of *Individual Portraits* at the Berlinale Forum also led to West German television buying the right to broadcast the film.[31] After airing on East German television in October 1982, it was broadcast over two evenings on West Germany's ARD channel in June 1983. The "Dallas of the East," as *Spiegel* magazine called it, caused a sensation. Suddenly, West German viewers saw men and women leading a regular life "on the other side," far from the propaganda and customary slogans emanating from the East Berlin regime: the film showed "faces [that were] difficult to forget afterwards" (Umbach 1983). Critics concentrated on highlighting commonalities between the two societies, the proximity of their professional and private trajectories (Grüning 2010). It was in this light that the Golzow Cycle garnered the attention of critics and historians outside of the Germanys.

Post-Wall Impact

A clear sign of the significance of *The Children of Golzow* cycle is unquestionably the place it has taken in research by film historians since 1990. Winfried Junge's documentaries are not merely considered in terms of being DEFA productions but are also studied in and for themselves, as landmarks in the history of international documentary filmmaking. In comparing *The Children of Golzow* with similarly oriented projects—such as the British longitudinal documentary series *7 Up*, directed by Michael Apted starting in 1964—the American researcher Barton Byg (2000, 2001) examines the commonalities that exist between the two cycles, despite very different sociopolitical contexts. He approaches them as experiments in critical sociological documentation that construct characters between continuity and the freedom to contradict. Byg (2000: 361) offers an account of his impressions on first discovering *Individual Portraits* in 1982:

> For me, this film was very impressive because it showed the transition from village life to modern industry and the large agricultural corporations such as [I] had experienced in the region where I come from, in South Dakota in the United States. This film made me aware of the similarities that exist between people's destinies under capitalism and socialism, and it represented, for me, a great intellectual achievement.

In 1993, a preview of a new episode in the cycle, *Drehbuch: Die Zeiten. Drei Jahrzehnte mit den Kindern von Golzow und der DEFA* (1993, *Screenplay: The Times. Three Decades with the Children of Golzow and the DEFA Documentary Film Studio*), screened at the Berlinale. For over four and a half hours, the tenth film in the series—which now competed under the label "Germany," instead of "GDR"—presents the ramifications of the collapse of the Wall upon the lives of the inhabitants of Golzow and the project itself. It mostly follows individual trajectories, an approach that started with *Individual Portraits* and made the group concept obsolete. Junge appears highly critical of his earlier approach and methods—in particular, his highly subjective way of asking questions—while in no way renouncing his work, which he presents as a document. Just as the chronicle had broken through the Wall, it now survived East Germany itself.

The Young Women of Wittstock

The Children of Golzow, however, was not the only attempt to observe East German society from a long-term perspective. Across the 1970s and 1980s, director Volker Koepp shot a long-running series of documentaries devoted to a group of young female factory workers in the East German heartlands. In 1984, three years after Junge's *Individual Portraits* had drawn attention at the Leipzig Festival, it was Koepp's *Leben in Wittstock* (*Life in Wittstock*) that received the Silver Dove. It was the next in Koepp's *Wittstock Cycle*, which—while the GDR was in existence—also included: *Mädchen in Wittstock* (1975, *Wittstock Girls*), *Wieder in Wittstock* (1976, *Back in Wittstock*), *Wittstock III* (1978), and *Leben und Weben* (1981, *Living and Weaving*). In 1990, Koepp then returned to Wittstock in response to the women's request and shot *Neues in Wittstock* (1992, *Modern Times in Wittstock*) and *Wittstock, Wittstock* (1997).

The *Wittstock Cycle* differs fundamentally from the Golzow project, not least due to its initial aspirations. When he began shooting in 1974, Koepp did not have the slightest intention of undertaking a long-term observation. *Wittstock Girls* was meant to be a short, stand-alone film dealing with a team (or brigade) of young women starting to work at a textile factory that had just opened in the East Prignitz area of the GDR. This first encounter, however, paved the way for an in-depth observation of the factory and its women workers.

Koepp (2004: 42) likes to tell how when crisscrossing the East German countryside in search of subject for a documentary, he stumbled upon across the hosiery factory in Wittstock at an Autobahn exit: "Once again drifting around in my car. Like a ping-pong ball between the Oder and the Elbe. Preferably somewhere north of Berlin, along the byways of Brandenburg and Mecklenburg. . . . Between the barracks [of the Soviet Army], the signpost: Wittstock 44 km. Why not toward Woodstock?" Although the film director emphasizes that he stumbled upon it by sheer coincidence in his wanderings, theoretically the choice of this small provincial town, with its 10,000 inhabitants, was a perfect place to highlight the official political and economic objectives of the time. In fact, in the late 1960s, the government had decided to give a fresh impetus to industrializing the GDR, in particular by establishing new factories in deeply remote rural areas such as East Prignitz, then one of the least densely populated regions in the country (Ansorg 1999). Part of this initiative, the Obertrikotagebetrieb (OTB), had commenced production in Wittstock in 1971.

Filming at OTB should therefore have been considered a way to enhance the industrialization policies being spearheaded by the company and region. OTB factory management, however, expressed dissatisfaction with the first film, *Wittstock Girls*, where viewers could easily discern future problems. It was precisely the latent discontent of the workers, however, that had attracted Koepp in the first instance and brought him back in 1976 to see what had happened to the workers whose outspokenness he had witnessed.[32] The film cycle thus gradually fell into place, following, as we have seen, a trend that captured the spirit of the times that was in the air.[33] Unlike Junge's cycle *The Children of Golzow*, Koepp's long-term documentary project did not proceed from a preliminary decision reached at an early stage but imposed a discourse that was to be justified by the acts and words of protagonists chosen for the purpose.

Here, the deterministic reading discernable in *The Children of Golzow* is absent. Instead, Koepp paid close attention to the things revealed by conversations with the young women and shooting on location. However, Koepp did not shoot an industrial film. He provides data on the factory's progress and the town's development and films the workers at their sewing machines or the endless assembly line on which the sweaters circulate. But beyond the firm, what interested him most were three individual lives, three women who fought for and committed themselves to what had become "their factory."

Living and Working in Wittstock

Koepp's film crew was truly fortunate in the girls they singled out during the first shoot in 1974: Renate, Edith, and Elsbeth, known as Stupsi, were among the very few workers who remained all those years at a factory where the majority, discouraged by difficult working conditions, quit after just a few months. The *Wittstock Cycle* constitutes a document of great value on women in the East German workplace, a theme that was important to the ideals of the communist state and had been represented in a wide range of art forms (Clemens 1998; Kott 2000).

At the turn of the 1970s, the factory had been expected to achieve two objectives: (1) the industrialization and the establishment of new business operations in the region, and (2) the integration of the surplus workforce that was no longer needed in the agricultural sector. Women were most affected, for their rate of participation in the workforce remained extremely low in this region compared to the GDR average.[34] In 1974, the team of young workers that the film crew followed comprised girls who, for the most part, actually came from the region. Among them, still inexperienced in this trade, was eighteen-year-old Stupsi, born in Wittstock, and nineteen-year-old Edith, who lived in a neighboring village. Renate came from Saxony, to the south, where the factory's parent company works was located in Karl-Marx-Stadt

Figure 7.4. Volker Koepp (*facing away*) shooting in Wittstock in 1975; here the crew films Edith (*left*) walking with friends. © DEFA Stiftung.

(now Chemnitz). Thirty years old and more experienced, Renate was meant to advise the young teams of workers in Wittstock.

In the first film, Edith seems the most committed of the three. We often see her surrounded by other colleagues, speaking on their behalf at the plant's general meeting and discussing things with them in smaller groups. The local FDJ secretary, Edith becomes the spokeswoman for the workers grievances. In 1974, she appears determined to defend their rights, including the right to be heard whenever the production norms are not appropriate. She acknowledges, however, that her task is difficult, for there are few that are willing to utter, or even to hear, the truth, beginning with management. She nevertheless articulates her concerns loud and clear: "It's from above, and not below that improvements must come." In 1977, her erstwhile smiling face has become gloomier, more resigned.

Working night shifts and living with her mother at some distance from the plant, Edith is thinking of quitting. She undertakes an advanced additional training program, however, thus becomes a supervisor, and decides to stay put "for the time being"—despite the disappointments and resistance she has encountered. In 1983, Edith has been promoted to director of the clothing department. The situation seems to be improving; things are working better since the arrival of a new director; he is the first to agree to be filmed and exudes confidence that he will do better than his predecessors. When Koepp asks Edith, "Have things improved?" the young woman replies, "Yes. . . . We'll see," smiling and turning away.

Interviewed in 1974 about her first impressions, Stupsi seems disappointed: the shop floor is noisy and windowless, and there's no feeling of solidarity among the workers. Four years later, in 1978, Stupsi still finds the working conditions to be bad; with a sigh of resignation, she explains that a wall was to have been built to separate her area from the loud machines of the ironing section, but management never followed through on their promises. Six years later, she is filmed in front of new, large windows. "You see, there are windows now. Is that because you went and demanded them?" enquires Koepp; "I don't know, can't say," replies Stupsi laconically, avoiding the camera's gaze. The poor quality sweaters are also mentioned, ironically, by Stupsi in 1975, who herself was responsible for quality control of the finished knitted products. She displays the sweater to the camera, without comment, just smiling. In 1984, Koepp asks her if she now finds the sweater up to scratch. Lifting one of the pullovers, the young woman, with the same gesture she used a decade earlier, smiles ironically, "It'll do," while casting a wry glance at her comrades off camera.[35]

The editing of the 1984 documentary *Life in Wittstock* clearly demonstrates problems with the factory's functioning. Problems highlighted by the girls starting in 1974–1975 remained unresolved in 1984: difficult working

Figure 7.5. *On the right:* Elsbeth—nicknamed Stupsi—at work in Wittstock in 1984. © Filmmuseum Potsdam, Gerhard Niendorf.

conditions in the vast, enclosed, windowless, and noisy facilities; lack of confidence on the part of management; irregular deliveries; ten years waiting for windows; the sweaters still not up to snuff. It is hard to stay motivated. Are they resigned to it? It is not their fault if they seem resigned, objects Stupsi in 1978; if management only trusted and listened to them more, the workers would find more satisfaction in their work.

The Filmmaker's Craft

In an attempt to alleviate their disappointments, the young women opt for humor. In 1983 a fourth woman, the new party secretary, explains that she has been at the factory for three years. Laughing, she exclaims that she has held on and resisted even longer than the factory directors! In the same year, the workers are "technically" laid off—due to problems procuring the sweater pieces they need. In response, Edith mockingly parodies an official slogan: "They were needed in the USSR!" Such scenes, revealing the confidences and attitudes of the women, testify to the complicity that exists between them and the film crew.

In fact, a sense of mutual respect and trust are discernable throughout the film cycle. For viewers, the ties between the young Wittstock workers and the

DEFA film crew are manifestly of a different order than in the Golzow Cycle. Koepp's films simply show how workers lived and worked, without trying to conceal or diminish their problems or to preach or draw a moral from their stories. The manner in which the questions are posed, the way Koepp and his crew direct and film the series, thanks in large part to cinematographer Christian Lehmann, all say a lot about the relationship between the protagonists in front of and behind the camera. The shots are often static; the young women look straight into the camera lens. "Out of respect for the people we were interviewing, I always refused to move around them with my camera," explains Lehmann, who worked on the entire cycle and considers the ethical question paramount.[36] A frank look into the camera or eyes that avoid the lens can immediately communicate to viewers the state of mind of the young women. By 1983, they indeed appear less talkative, less willing to confide in others, as though weary of confirming the same situation, the same stalemates over and over again.

Koepp was privy to secrets and comments from the young women that surprised him and exceeded the political limits that people usually observed. This meant he was burdened with an even greater responsibility than usual in the cutting room. Could he, should he retain all these utterances? Choices also had to be made while filming. When should he stop the camera? Take, for example, the following scene: In 1984, Stupsi, married and the mother of two children, is living in a new apartment in Wittstock. Filming her at home, Koepp asks whether she recalls her dream of eventually moving away from the little town, which she found boring. The young woman calmly replies that she now has no desire to leave, that she is doing well in Wittstock. Nearly all her childhood dreams have been realized, she adds, with her habitually discreet smile. Stupsi is amused that the camera continues to roll; but then her smile starts to fade, leaving only a face with sad and tired eyes, lost in memories or regrets—up to the viewer to decipher. No commentary comes to her assistance.

In 1984, Koepp's *Life in Wittstock* thus offered a sensitive portrayal of life and work practices at the OTB factory. Viewers were invited to step back in time, with the help of chronological editing that combined freshly shot sequences with excerpts from previous films in the cycle. The overall impression was one of bittersweet halftones, like the closing smile of Stupsi, although the girls had by now become young women—married, mothers—and the factory the largest consumer goods industry in the area. In addition, the documentary showed time itself at work: it was a process taking place before the eyes of the viewers, which highlighted opposing forces in motion and conflict, the women's energy against a system's inertia, a system running out of steam. East German audiences of the time would catch all of it; all they had to do was find a way to see Koepp's film.

Figure 7.6. Poster for the 1975 Leipzig Festival. © Bundsarchiv-Filmarchiv, Archiv der Leipziger Dok-Filmwochen GmbH.

Documentaries in Search of Their Audience

From East German film clubs to the Berlinale, the trajectory of the *Wittstock Cycle* zigzagged, to say the least: yet another sign of the complex and shifting, even if not unpredictable, government policies. Without censoring Koepp's documentaries per se, the regime did try to limit their reach to a domestic distribution, all while simultaneously playing the "Wittstock" card with respect to international audiences.

While the first three films in the *Wittstock Cycle* had not been selected for the Leipzig Festival, other documentaries by Koepp had been programmed, such as his series focusing on landscapes—which included *Das weite Feld* (1976, *The Vast Field*), which earned a Silver Dove[37]—and *Hütes-Film* (1977, *Dumplings*), which subsequently took the Grand Prix at the Oberhausen Festival in 1978.[38] Koepp was thus by no means blacklisted at the Leipzig Festival. His portraits of Stupsi, Renate, and Edith could not be accommodated, however, at a festival that sought to show the "evolution of socialist society" in an exclusively optimistic light.

According to the rationale that had prevailed since the end of 1965, films deemed undesirable were rarely censored outright. Instead, they obtained the censor's approval—but only one or two copies were printed, thereby limiting the number of places the documentary was shown, the length of its run, and the extent of programming in movie theaters. This is what happened to the earlier episodes of Koepp's cycle. A parallel circuit for screening their works existed for filmmakers who wanted to circumvent this indirect form of censorship, however, thanks to the film club networks and various locally organized private soirées and events.[39] Koepp thus crisscrossed the GDR with a portable 35mm projector and his film reels under his arm (Hübner 1996). As he saw it, it was part of the director's job to go to meet the public and start stimulating discussions that soon went beyond the subject of the projected film.[40] Lehmann, however, recalls how at times they felt discouraged at making films that they knew the public would only see with difficulty and rarely.[41]

It is thus no wonder that the filmmaker experienced going to the International Festival of Leipzig as a breath of fresh air. The first presentation of a Wittstock film to an international audience took place at Leipzig in 1981. *Living and Weaving* was programmed in competition, but there was no mention in the program that it was the fourth in a running documentary series that had commenced in 1974 (*Protokoll 1981* 1982). Furthermore, the screening of Koepp's documentary was overshadowed by Winfried Junge's *Individual Portraits*. In contrast, in 1984 *Life in Wittstock* was explicitly presented as the "adventure of the growth and transformation, over a ten year period, of a large industrial company, its staff, and its landscape" (*Protokoll 1984* 1985: 43). The screening was a success, and met with loud applause, and the film won a Silver Dove (*Neuer Tag* 1984). "The documentary is full of accurate valid observations that East German citizens, judging from reactions in the theatre, can expand upon from their own experiences," noted a West German journalist (*Deutsche Volkszeitung* 1984).

Journalists from East and West alike underlined the film's "startling frankness" (*Mitteldeutsche Neueste Nachrichten*, 1 December 1984)—without, however, drawing the same conclusions, even among East German journalists. The very fact that the film raised "unpleasant questions without always providing answers" demonstrated for those on one side the refusal to "play the schoolmaster" (*Thüringer Landeszeitung*, 29 November 1984); in contrast, others, such as the SED newspaper *Neues Deutschland*, saw in it a "too subjective" approach (Berger and Meves 1984), a weakness. At the same time, the party newspaper hailed the film for documenting "girls becoming women, dreams reality, the workplace the place of one's identity (*Heimat*), a new factory becoming 'our enterprise.'" West German critics were predictably more skeptical. As Wilhelm Roth (1984) observed, "The factory . . . is now a model. But, what has become of the women? Have they become reasonable, or have they adapted? Are they happy or have they abandoned their desires? The film offers no clear answer to these questions." Heinz Kersten (1984) even pointed out, "Stupsi assures [us] that she is happy, but this does not exactly correspond with the tired expression on her face."

Whether a tale of success or resignation, the censors—who had learned their lesson from the success of *Individual Portraits*—had finally decided that, because of its cinematic quality, *Life in Wittstock* could only serve the image of DEFA and hence the GDR. Thanks to Erika and Ulrich Gregor, who once again served as intermediaries, the film was allowed to be sent to the Berlinale's Forum in February 1985. There, broadcast rights to the film were sold to Bayerischer Rundfunk (Bavarian Broadcasting; Nowak 1995), a development that led to fresh tensions. Horst Pehnert, managing director at HVFilm, inquired of Heinz Adameck, intendant of DFF, whether it might not be judicious to broadcast Koepp's documentary on DFF before it was shown in West Germany.

But, unlike the protagonists in Golzow, the young women of Wittstock never appeared on television in the GDR. Following the Leipzig Festival in November, East German newspapers had announced that *Life in Wittstock* would have its theatrical release in January 1985 and would soon be shown on television (*Junge Welt* 1984; *Märkische Union* 1984). Nevertheless, the DFF answer to HVFilm was no. Their representatives had viewed the film at the East German National Festival in Neubrandenburg and, in reference to the Solidarity labor union that was daring to challenge the Polish regime, concluded, "It's a Solidarność film!"[42]

This episode with Volker Koepp's film vividly illustrates the diversity of opinions within the East German regime. In particular, it reveals how, in the GDR, new DEFA documentary films were seen and perceived as an echo chamber created by what was unfolding on the world stage. As we have seen, the combination of these two dynamics repeatedly led to paradoxical situations.

While Winfried Junge and Volker Koepp, in comparison to their counterparts in other countries east of the Iron Curtain, can by no means be considered "dissidents" seeking to distinguish themselves from the system and the dominant order, they nevertheless contributed, almost despite themselves, to providing audiences with a fresh take on their societies. Echoing the outstanding popularity of the 1973 DEFA feature film *Die Legende von Paul und Paula* (*The Legend of Paul and Paula*), for example, the success of *The Children of Golzow* demonstrated that the general public was no longer interested in the political sphere or a utopian horizon, but rather in everyday life (Segert 2003; Feinstein 2002). These cycles offered an "unofficial cartography" of public sentiment that sufficed for their most conservative critics to equate Volker Koepp's new film with what was unfolding in neighboring Poland—developments they found deeply threatening (Jeancolas 2003).

And yet, despite everything, HVFilm grasped the exceptional nature of these films and played the card of international openness, albeit partial, to take advantage of the resonances they engendered. From this perspective, it is clear that programming parts of the two cycles at the Leipzig Festival effectively allowed the government to showcase the sheer normalcy and universality of life in East Germany. At the same time, these screenings allowed international audiences in the East as in the West to register how the fault lines gradually appearing on the hitherto smooth façade of East German society were becoming increasingly visible at the close of the 1970s.

Notes

1. New slogans proclaimed the "unity of economic and social policies" (*Einheit der Wirtschafts- und Sozialpolitik*) and the institution of consumer socialism (*Konsumssozialismus*). See Ina Merkel's work (1999) on consumer product design.
2. These remarks on sociological documentary owe a great deal to Yvonne Mignot-Lefebvre's 1994 article.
3. This term refers to the immersion of the long-term documentary crew—in a place, a group of people, etc.—in order to go deep into how things functions.
4. In 1971, there were approximately forty French guests: directors, journalists, and critics, as well as two delegates from the Cinema Bureau of the communist trade union, the CGT.

5. In English, Society for Launching New Works. In Russian, the word *slon* means "elephant." See Roudé 2017.
6. In Russian, the word *iskra* means "spark." This was also the name of a political newspaper, published by exiled socialist Russians starting in 1900 and managed for a time by Vladimir Lenin.
7. Author's interview with René Vautier, Montreuil, France (30 November 1999). DEFA had produced the documentary *Flammendes Algerien* (1958, *Algeria in Flames*); Vautier was credited as director, although the film was made by a collective under his initiative. In such cases, it was the practice at DEFA to choose which directors to credit based on the political advantage such credit offered. Vautier (1970) published a long article on engaged and militant documentary filmmaking in France in the GDR's principal scholarly film journal, *Filmwissenschaftliche Beiträge*.
8. Author's interview with Robert Grélier, Paris, France (15 January 1999); author's interview with Ronald Trisch, Berlin, Germany (11 March 2004).
9. The festival in Nyon, Switzerland, was established in 1969, part of the ciné-club movement.
10. Author's interview with Wilhelm Roth, Berlin, Germany (9 March 2003).
11. These include *Titicut Follies* (1967), *High School* (1968), *Hospital* (1970), and *Welfare* (1975). See, in particular, Pilard 1979.
12. Author's interview with Heinz Klunker, Berlin, Germany (15 September 2004).
13. Concerning remarks on and analysis of Hungarian documentary film of the period, see Jeancolas 2001.
14. This is a moral and ethical question that also arose, as we shall see, for DEFA long-term documentarists Winfried Junge and Volker Koepp.
15. According to Jeancolas (2001), Hungarian documentary filmmakers themselves rejected this designation.
16. It is interesting to note that *Man of Marble* features a documentary filmmaker trying to make a movie about Stalinism. On Polish cinema of this period, see Szczepanska 2011.
17. For more, see chapter 5.
18. From the Director of Cultural Relations at the East German Foreign Ministry to the Director of International Relations at the Ministry of Culture, Dr. H. Tautz, Berlin, 23 June 1976, SAPMO-BArch DY 30 IV B2/9.06/107.
19. Such as Heiner Carow's *Die Legende von Paul und Paul* (1973, *The Legend of Paul and Paula;* Schenk 1994).
20. Although the results were not made public, this study attests to a characteristic of the period, which sought an improved understanding of social structures. See Engler 1999.
21. Resolution of the SED's Eighth Party Congress in June 1971, cited in Schröder 1998: 219.
22. Among the films made by the Effekt group are Karl Gass's *Mit Netz und Spinne* (1971, *With Web and Spider*—a reference to spider-dial watch faces), commissioned by the state watchmaking company in Ruhla, as well as Peter Ulbrich's *Erfolge sind Pflicht* (1970, *Successes Are Duty*) and Gitta Nickel's *Zum Beispiel . . . Silbitzer im Wettbewerb* (1971, *For Example . . . Silbitzers in Competition*), both commissioned by the Central Institute for Socialist Economic Management of the SED's central committee, a center for research and education.
23. This was followed by *Nach einem Jahr—Beobachtungen in einer 1. Klasse* (1962, *One Year Later: Observations in a First Grade Class*), *Elf Jahre alt, Teil 3* (1966, *Eleven*

Years Old), *Wenn man vierzehn ist* (1969, *When You Are Fourteen*), *Die Prüfung/ Chronik einer Schulklasse* (1971, *The Exam*), *Ich sprach mit einem Mädchen* (1975, *I Spoke with a Girl*), *Anmut sparet nicht noch Mühe* (1979, *Spare No Charm and Spare No Effort*), *Lebensläufe—Die Geschichte der Kinder von Golzow in einselnen Porträts* (1981, *Children of Golzow: Individual Portraits*), and *Diese Golzower—Umstandsbestimmung eines Ortes* (1984, *These Golzowers*).

24. On the influence of school on the formation of East German youth, see Droit 2013.
25. Born in 1937, Leupold started at the DEFA Documentary Studio in 1961, after training at the HFF in Babelsberg from 1955 to 1960. The first Golzow film was his first assignment at the studio.
26. On the importance of the *Jugendweihe* in the GDR, see the work of Albrecht Döhnert (2009) and Marina Chauliac (2006).
27. The title is a citation from *Kinderhymne* (Children's Hymn) by Bertolt Brecht and Hanns Eisler.
28. A screening was organized for Erich Honecker, who decided to have it broadcast on television (Schieber 1996).
29. In 1960, the GDR counted 25,640 divorcées; in 1989, there were 50,063. Also in 1989, 69 percent of divorces were on the woman's initiative, and 340,000 women were raising their children alone. See Kott 2000; Hellwig and Nickel 1993.
30. This West German prize, with a purse of 2,500 deutschemark, had been created in honor of Dibelius (1880–1967), the council president of the Protestant Church of Germany, who was always against a rapprochement with the East German Protestant Church.
31. GDR television (DFF) was thus obliged to broadcast the documentary in October 1982, so that *The Children of Golzow* would not make its debut in the West on the small screen.
32. Author's interview with Volker Koepp, Nyon, Switzerland (2002).
33. Neither Christian Lehmann nor Volker Koepp remember having seen Márta Mészáros's *At the Lőrinc Spinnery*, even though it had been awarded a prize at Leipzig in November 1972.
34. In order to study the political and economic evolution linked to female employment, historian Leonore Ansorg (1999) focused on the eastern Prignitz district, looking at the industrialization of agriculture, as well as at the knitting factory in Wittstock. A comparison of her study and Koepp's *Wittstock Cycle* would certainly be very pertinent.
35. Everyone had a different explanation for the poor quality of the knitwear. The party secretary who was filmed in 1976 chalked it up to worker inexperience, while the women themselves attributed it to unrealistic and vague production quotas, which made them work too fast and less carefully.
36. Author's interview with Christian Lehmann, Berlin, Germany (22 August 2000). According to Lehmann, the films were shot in black-and-white for technical reasons. The color film stock used in the GDR in the 1970s, which was not yet very sensitive, would have made it too complicated to shoot on the factory floor with artificial lighting. This bias also corresponded to an aesthetic choice to ensure the photographic quality of the 35mm film.
37. In this film, the author Gotthold Gloger guides viewers through a village in Brandenburg, retracing a history that is local, regional, even national, because one of the members of the Red Orchestra anti-Nazi resistance movement, Libertas Schulze-Boysen, was a child here.

38. While preparing dumplings, two sisters talk about the history of their village and region, the Rhön, in southwestern East Germany bordering Bavaria.
39. Each year, for example, a "cinema springtime" (*Filmfrühling*) took place in the Mecklenburg region, which multiplied the screenings that took place in districts independent of the usual movie theater circuit (Becker and Petzold 2001).
40. To put this in context, in East Germany, filmmakers often met with audiences for discussions of their films after screenings in noncommercial venues, such as film clubs, factories, and union halls. The same was true in France in this period.
41. Author's interview with Christian Lehmann, Berlin, Germany (22 August 2000).
42. Reported by Volker Koepp during a discussion organized in the context of the twenty-fourth Leipzig International Film Festival in November 2004.

CHAPTER 8

Don't Wait for Better Times

At the Eighth SED Congress in June 1971, Erich Honecker had announced a policy of cultural détente and encouraged artists to create a "truthful and even critical representation of socialist reality." "If we rely on socialism's firm positions, in my opinion there can be no taboos in either the artistic domain or literature," Honecker (1971) had declared. Many writers, painters, filmmakers, and playwrights had seen in this statement genuine hope for renewal and change. Some uncertainty persisted, however: how should "socialism's firm positions" be interpreted?

Two crises—the Wolf Biermann affair in 1976 and the European missile crisis and peace movements at the turn of the 1980s—crudely exposed the irresolvable contradiction inherent in this policy of détente. Contrasting these two crises, both of which emerged in an international context of major upheavals, enables us to grapple with the complex forms assumed by both contestation and repression during this period of East Germany history. Albert Hirschmann (1993) distinguishes two possible routes people could take: leaving the country or publicly voicing dissatisfaction, alone or as a group. Focusing on the case of a specific social group, namely, documentary filmmakers, and within the specific context of the Leipzig International Film Festival, we can clearly see how these two approaches intertwined in a complex power struggle between authorities, intellectuals, and the rest of the population.

The Biermann Affair

On 16 November 1976, news that the East German government had stripped singer-songwriter Wolf Biermann of his citizenship set off a series of chain reactions within the country. It deeply altered the relationship between East

German artists and intellectuals, on one hand, and the regime, on the other. It also affected relationships between artists, many of whom had felt that they were united in solidarity until people started going their separate ways on the crucial question of whether to stay or leave. The stripping of Biermann's citizenship, finally, also had repercussions abroad, thus assuming proportions that the regime had in no way envisaged. The increasingly strained power struggle between Biermann and the regime that eventually came to a climax in the fall of 1976 afforded, in turn, many East Germans the opportunity to articulate their discontent.

A Communist Becomes a Pariah

And yet, in biographical terms, Biermann had possessed perfect political legitimacy. His father, a Jewish worker, died during deportation to Auschwitz; his mother, a lifelong communist, decided to leave Hamburg for the GDR in 1953, when her son was thirteen. Biermann, however, was to become one of those figures who most perturbed the East Berlin regime. As yet hardly known in the early 1960s, the lyrics of the young singer and poet, who declared himself a Marxist and communist, would later be deemed too critical by the authorities. His poems, in which a hint of aggressiveness intermingled with gentleness, were prone to vulgarity, poetic metaphors, and crude expressions, were scarcely the stuff of Socialist Realist dogma (Emmerich 2000). In 1963, Biermann was expelled from the SED; yet he could still tour throughout the GDR and travel to West Germany.

Through his wife, the actress Eva-Maria Hagen (1998), he established relationships with many other artists and intellectuals, especially filmmakers. In 1965, film director Frank Beyer asked him to compose a song for the credits of *Trace of Stones*.[1] When the humorous and provocative lyrics were banned, Beyer wanted to use another Biermann song, "Don't Wait for Better Times."[2] At the Eleventh Plenum of the SED in December 1965, however, the singer was denounced for "petty bourgeois" and "anarchist attitudes," as well as for his "skepticism" and "cynicism" (Agde 1991: 142).

Biermann was banned from publishing and performing in the GDR.[3] He continued to publish in the FRG, however, and maintained his contacts with the West, particularly at the Leipzig Festival, which he attended in a private capacity, not as an official guest. At the festival, Biermann actively participated in discussions—remember Chris Marker's (1997: 64) evocation of the 1967 festival and "East German dissidents hollering (Biermann among them)." Alongside scientist Robert Havemann and author Stefan Heym,[4] he became a leading proponent for democratizing socialism. He was among the few intellectuals in East Germany to openly denounce the August 1968 invasion of

Czechoslovakia. He enjoyed a faithful following among leftists in the FRG and elsewhere in the West, who saw in him an alternative to the existing system. In fact, censorship assured him increased visibility, especially among young people; notwithstanding his "internal emigration," he sought to be heard as widely as possible, constantly playing with the regime's limits. But how far could such transgressions go?[5]

In June 1976, the aspirations expressed by the French, Italian, and Spanish Communist parties for greater independence vis-à-vis Moscow gave rise to fresh hopes. As Biermann (2001) recalls, "It had the disturbing scent of the Prague Spring." On 11 September 1976, the singer gave his first concert in eleven years at a church in the East German provinces. From the regime's point of view, the threat that various opposition movements, both inside and outside the Church, would unite was becoming real.

When, in November 1976, Biermann received permission to travel to the West for a series of concerts, many mistakenly saw this as a sign that the government was liberalizing its policies. The first concert took place in Cologne on 13 November and was broadcast on West German television. In a highly charged atmosphere, before some 7,000 enthusiastic spectators and fans, he critiqued the regimes on either side of the Wall, while emphasizing, yet again, that he was a child of socialism and the East German republic. Three days later, a dispatch from the East Berlin news agency announced that "Wolf Biermann, who crossed over from Hamburg to the GDR in 1953," no longer had the "right to remain in the GDR." The singer, it continued, had shown contempt for his civic duties during his stay in a capitalist country, engaging in violent critiques of the regime that made this decision inevitable (Neubert 1997). Karl-Eduard von Schnitzler set the tone with the title of his weekly program, *Schwarze Kanal,* on 22 November—"Biermann, or Ordinary Anti-Communism"—which twisted the title and intention of Mikhail Romm's groundbreaking documentary *Der gewöhnliche Faschismus* (1965, *Ordinary Fascism*).[6]

The Biermann affair provoked a wave of protest in the GDR, the likes of which had not been seen since the invasion of Czechoslovakia. It was a reaction the East German leaders had not expected.[7] As Stefan Heym (1996: 21) noted in his diary, when West Berlin's *New York Times* correspondent informed him of the news over the telephone, "Don't those who made this decision have any idea of the storm they will unleash—and not only within the Republic? Every author here . . . will oppose this decree, for he cannot but feel personally affected: today Biermann, tomorrow him." Robert Havemann, four actors, the author Stephan Hermlin,[8] and nine other celebrities of the East German literary world[9] wrote protest letters, which appeared in *Der Spiegel,* a Reuter's news agency communiqué (Geiss 1997) and various print media titles throughout the West.[10] Ordinary citizens also voiced their disagreement and were met with a violent crackdown, especially in the provinces.[11]

Fallout at the Festival

The authorities attempted to counter Western reactions to news of the crisis.[12] On 20 November, *Neues Deutschland* published a series of accounts by artists and intellectuals who defended the action taken against Biermann. Among the numerous signatories were the principal members of the Leipzig Festival Committee: Annelie Thorndike, Karl-Eduard von Schnitzler, and Ronald Trisch. On this same day, the nineteenth edition of the Leipzig Festival opened. Naturally, the ghost of 1968 was on everyone's mind. Authorities had little time to prepare and were concerned about how the Biermann affair would reverberate during the Leipzig Festival and how East German festival participants and filmmakers would interact with foreign guests, especially West Germans. Rarely did those at Leipzig speak "with so many convolutions as this year," and every effort was made "so the Biermann bomb would not detonate," reported a West German journalist.[13]

The affair took place amid an ideological hardening instigated by the desire of the authorities to regain control over a situation they felt had become unduly liberal. Despite the recent international recognition of the GDR and the staging of the big Youth Festival in East Berlin in the summer of 1973—events meant to present an image of openness—at home in the GDR, the atmosphere became increasingly tense as of 1974–1975. This even led the Stasi to establish an operative group wholly dedicated to monitoring the East German intellectual and artistic scene (*Operativgruppe der HA XX*). Among the numerous persons placed under surveillance in 1974–1978, we find documentary filmmakers Karl Gass and Jürgen Böttcher.[14] In spring 1976, the decision was made to transform the Leipzig Festival's habitual "midnight discussions," in which open debate had often reigned, into more traditional "Leipzig beer tables" (*Leipziger Biertische*), similar to press conferences, during which "only the films of the day" were to be discussed.[15]

FRG journalist Wilhelm Roth (1976) denounced, in the strongest terms, the official silence imposed on the Biermann affair during the festival. Where was that spirit of solidarity that had been mobilized for the likes of Angela Davis? Roth's tone and message cost him, for he was not invited back in 1977—concurrently, it should be noted, with the release in West Germany of his book on DEFA, which criticized documentarists Heynowski and Scheumann, yet defended the films of Jürgen Böttcher and Volker Koepp, both of whom were considered "dissidents" by the East Berlin authorities, "whereas of course they weren't."[16] In 1978, Roth was allowed to return to Leipzig, where he became the most well-known self-funded visitor (*Selbstbezahler*) to attend. Among accredited foreign journalists, there were those whose expenses were covered by the festival, while others paid their own way; relegating a journalist to this second category was a means of exerting pressure against those deemed disobedient and inconvenient.

Sanctions linked to the Biermann affair thus did affect some West German participants at Leipzig. Even though Biermann was not alluded to in official speeches or press conferences, the authorities, for all their efforts, did not succeed in containing the issue. In private discussions, supporters and opponents of Biermann vehemently clashed. Even high-ranking officials seemed to feel that the problem could only be resolved head on.[17] The crisis highlighted the essential fear of the East German regime that a localized conflict might spill over and contaminate other places and social groups.[18] The terms of the problem were therefore immediately reformulated. No longer was the issue whether or not to support Biermann (many who had signed the petition persisted in backing his cause); it was rather to acknowledge the error petitioners had made by sending their text to foreign news agencies and, most egregiously, to those in the West.

With this line of argument, the authorities managed to recruit the support of several intellectuals, including from among the first signatories. Stephan Hermlin unwittingly opened a breach in the apparent solidarity of the protesters; on 4 December, he signed a declaration acknowledging it had been wrong to contact Agence France-Presse (AFP). Though it had only been intended for members of the politburo of the ZK (Heym 1996), the statement was immediately used as leverage over the other signatories of the petition (Emmerich 2000). The first cracks were appearing. In this context, feature film director Frank Beyer (2001) submitted a self-critique; as a result, he received only a severe reprimand and was able to return to work at DEFA. In contrast, those protesters who were members of the SED and refused to recant, such as author Jurek Becker, were judged guilty of disobedience and excluded. Many of those intellectuals who did recant tacitly decided to primarily focus on their individual freedom of expression and criticism and on the need to consolidate relations with the authorities, ignoring the broader problems posed by East Germany's inexistent public opinion and inadequate political participation (Neubert 1997).

To Stay or to Leave

The petition protesting Biermann's expatriation did not ally itself with all of his public pronouncements, but rather criticized the procedure followed by the East German government. Nearly all those who had signed the petition on 17 November 1976 came from the world of literature and theater. Most filmmakers had preferred to keep their own counsel, including documentarist

Gerhard Scheumann. As head of Studio H&S and vice-president of the East German Academy of Arts (AdK), Scheumann might have been in a safe enough position to impose his views; he did not attend the Leipzig Festival in November 1976, however, ostensibly on health grounds.[19] This behavior echoed that of Konrad Wolf eleven years earlier; president of the AdK, Wolf had not attended a Party meeting about Frank Beyer's film *Traces of Stones*. Beyer (2001) supported his decision: it was better for filmmakers, he argued, that Wolf retain his post, even if it entailed this silence.

Among the six filmmakers who originally signed the petition, documentarists were much more implicated than feature film directors. These filmmakers included Frank Beyer at the DEFA Studio for Feature Films and Jürgen Böttcher, Heinz Brinkmann, Richard Cohn-Vossen, Werner Kohlert, and Heiner Sylvester from the DEFA Studio for Documentary Films. The diversity of responses to the Biermann affair also tended to reflect personal position and individual trajectories, more than ideological commitments. Among the five documentarists listed, generational differences are key.

In theory Cohn-Vossen, born in 1934 in Switzerland, had a spotless family and seemingly orthodox trajectory, just like Biermann. The family fled from the Nazis to Moscow, where they lived from 1943 to 1953. He arrived back in the GDR in 1955, when his mother married Alfred Kurella, who had just been appointed director of the Johannes R. Becher Institute of Literature in Leipzig (Brandt 1995). Cohn-Vossen was Andrew Thorndike's assistant from 1960 to 1965—a period including the making of *The Russian Miracle*—before starting to make his own films and develop a more personal look and tone. In 1967, Cohn-Vossen's portrait of composer Paul Dessau was very warmly received at the Leipzig Festival and was awarded a prize in Mannheim. In 1976, he shot *Abgeordnete in Rostock—Im Vorfeld* (*Deputy in Rostock;* Cohn-Vossen 1976).[20] In this film, parliamentary representatives of the port city of Rostock, on the Baltic Sea coast, question shipyard workers about what they would like to see improved. What follows is a litany of complaints—about inconvenient public transportation schedules in the morning, inadequate childcare for those working nightshifts, mediocre food at the canteen, and so forth. The film was never screened publicly (Brandt 1995). When Biermann was expatriated, Cohn-Vossen was thus already in a prickly situation.

Werner Kohlert (b. 1939) had worked as a cinematographer at the Documentary Film Studio as of 1966 and had shot several films, including *Für Angela* (1972, *Angela*), a tribute to Angela Davis; in 1976, he worked with Jürgen Böttcher on his commissioned films. In 1976, Heinz Brinkmann (b. 1948) had just finished his training at the Babelsberg film academy; in 1974, however, he had participated in the collective film produced for the twenty-fifth anniversary of the founding of the GDR, *Weggefährten (Traveling Companions)*, alongside Jürgen Böttcher and Richard Cohn-Vossen, among others. Finally,

Heiner Sylvester had just shot *Rosenthaler Str. 51* (1976),[21] about a choir of veterans and retired workers—a film completely devoid of ideology, notwithstanding its subject matter, according to the critic Eduard Schreiber (1996).

All four of these young filmmakers were connected through Jürgen Böttcher, the first documentarist to sign the petition, who had known Biermann since the early 1960s. The crossed, or entangled trajectories of these two central figures in the cultural history of the GDR merit closer examination. Bound in part by a sense of solidarity, the two friends and artists both faced censorship as of the early 1960s and were subsequently victims of the Eleventh Plenum in December 1965.[22] As Biermann found himself stripped of his citizenship, Böttcher naturally signed the petition.

In November 1976, critic Wilhelm Roth regretted that Böttcher had no new film to present at Leipzig. Böttcher, however, was working on a project, *Im Lohmgrund* (1976–1977, *In the Lohm Valley*), about sculptor Peter Makolies, who he knew from his time in Dresden.[23] The documentarist simply observed his friend working on impressive sculptures, outdoors in a sandstone quarry. "I was once a painter," lets slip Böttcher in the beginning, as though thumbing his nose at the authorities. Viewers pick up on the close rapport not only between the filmmaker and the sculptor but also between the director and cameraman Thomas Plenert, who was filming his first DEFA documentary. Each shot reflects a shared happiness, observable in the long, calm, fixed nature shots and in seeing the workers strenuously tackle the walls of the quarry and the emerging sculptures, filmed in a light that emphasizes their forms and contours.

The film does not set out to demonstrate anything. As Roth (2000: 146) pointed out in 1976, this free play was, in its way, "a provocation, an act of resistance." It is a judgment that may seem extreme but makes complete sense once set in its historical context. *In the Lohm Valley* was programmed at Leipzig in November 1977, although out of competition and with no publicity; the venue was quickly filled to the rafters, however, with participants wishing to watch the film (Roth 1977).

It was the opinion of documentary director Karl Gass that Böttcher's problems were not due to his films but solely to the fact that he had signed the Biermann petition.[24] This perspective overlooks the harsh criticism and censorship Böttcher suffered for his films, as well as his paintings, before 1976. As Biermann, already settled in the FRG, wrote of his friend at the end of 1976:

> What a shame, what a crime that a filmmaker as great as Jürgen should have to eternally contend with adversity and the primitive stupidity of the studio! Here [in the FRG], he is known to many of the finest and he could certainly work here as never before in his life. But, of course, it would be in a society that is foreign and perhaps uninteresting to him, which means that the effort involved would outweigh the benefits and that he'd still be standing there, his hands full of nothing.

At least he should know that many people here admire him and would like to work with him. He should bear that in mind, in case they ever pull the plug on him. (Löser 2001: 7)

During the spring of 1977, the Biermann affair took on a new dimension. In the face of the regime's lack of openness and internal rifts within intellectual circles, some felt the only solution was to leave East Germany. Those who decided to emigrate did so after being more or less explicitly pushed into the decision by the authorities. The actor and popular singer Manfred Krug is a case in point. He requested an exit visa on 19 April 1977, saying that his mother and brother lived in the FRG; but his letter was, in fact, a long argument outlining the political and ideological reasons, both private and social, why he wanted to leave. For months, he had been suffering the direct consequences of signing the petition (Krug 1996). Others who were close to or sympathized with the signatories were also bullied in their professional lives.

Between 1977 and 1982, Böttcher witnessed the departure of some thirty authors as well as stage directors and actors; in 1979, it was Ralf Winkler—alias A. R. Penck—Böttcher's former student and friend from his years in Dresden. Of the filmmakers who signed the petition, only one departed for the West; in 1979, Cohn-Vossen was fired from the Documentary Studio and went to West Germany.[25] This striking imbalance between film directors and writers can, in large part, be explained by the economic constraints of the film industry (Beyer 2001). In comparison to the system in the West, whereby directors must raise funds to make a film, the fixed employment and opportunities to make films that DEFA offered represented an advantage, despite issues with on set working conditions and other limitations.

Böttcher decided to stay put: "I was unable to go to the West. Because of my friends, and my elderly parents who were in their nineties at the time. . . . There was no question for me of going to the West. And that's how I lost my shirt in the East and was also responsible for what happened there."[26] Family ties often played a role in addition to policy arguments for not leaving. As critic Fred Gehler explained in 2001, "I never considered leaving. At the latest, the issue was resolved with my second marriage in 1970. Had I remained single longer, everything might have worked out differently. I can't rule that out" (Gehler and Schenk 2001: 96).

Those who stayed had to cope with the system. Heinz Brinkmann, for example, had to wait until the latter half of the 1980s to produce documentaries other than commissioned titles.[27] Böttcher chose to follow a middle path between compromise and aesthetic radicalism. The culmination was *Rangierer* (1984, *Shunters*), a film he shot with cinematographer Plenert in the railway yards in Dresden. For twenty minutes, viewers witness a squad of shunters working the night shift. This film of great visual beauty shot in winter offers a highly contrastive black-and-white palette, in which the rails trace abstract designs on the snow. The passing wagons, the shunters' movements, the airborne birds over the tracks set the scene for a spare ballet. The film foregoes commentary and music but is not mute: creaking wagons, shunters' tools striking the rails, the crunch of footsteps in the snow, and snippets of rare verbal exchanges create a soundtrack at once discrete, natural, and yet deeply expressive of the difficult work. Böttcher does not opt for extreme aestheticism, however; the challenge remained to bear witness to highly demanding work, filmed in all its physicality.

In November 1984, *Shunters* was selected at Leipzig, where it caused a sensation. It had the merit of offering an original take on the world of work—a theme that was omnipresent in DEFA documentaries—while making a contribution to the evolution of the language of documentary filmmaking. The people represented were deeply rooted in East German reality, even as they acquired a universal dimension.[28] The film received several awards in the West, as in the East.[29] Through his films, Böttcher succeeded in pursuing a dialogue on an international scale. To whatever extent the regime, anxious to retain its domestic policy prerogatives, sought to control the cultural sphere, the Leipzig Festival remained a place where the rules could be, at least somewhat, questioned and sidestepped. The growing integration of the GDR into the international arena rendered it increasingly difficult to maintain a dichotomy between the foreign and domestic policy.

Figure 8.1. Still from J. Böttcher's *Shunters* (1984). © DEFA Stiftung, Thomas Plenert.

Opposition Movements in the East

The Biermann affair corresponded to a new phase of opposition on the part of intellectuals throughout Eastern Europe. Notably the creation of Charter 77 in Prague, an upshot of Czechoslovakia ratifying the 1975 Helsinki Accords, led to a solidarity movement in Hungary, which in turn served as a transition to the organizing of various citizens' movements (Dalos 1995). Such initiatives surfaced amid unfavorable conditions for the Soviet authorities and people's democracies, mired in a series of crises as of the late 1970s—the war in Afghanistan, starting in 1979, and the series of strikes and protests in Poland, which culminated in the founding of the Solidarność (Solidarity) labor union. In East Germany, the authorities and public alike followed events unfolding in neighboring countries very closely.

The first trade union in a Warsaw Pact country not controlled by a Communist party, Solidarność was declared legal by the Polish Supreme Court in October 1980; union membership swiftly reached almost ten million and its ideas spread even further, becoming a nationwide social protest movement. Although there was no way for Solidarność to become a political party, the trade union did represent a major political victory, in that it succeeded in earning full recognition both of workers' right to strike and of a union that was independent of the powers that be. The Polish working class had stood up to the Communist system and won (Schröder 1998). Reforms to "real-existing socialism" were thus being successfully implemented in a country neighboring the GDR.

The East German opposition was highly receptive to what was happening on the other side of the Oder. For them, as for numerous intellectuals internationally, Solidarność was a "motivating factor" (Soutou 2001: 627): a new impetus to reach out to East German as well as international public opinion. This turn of events signified real danger to the SED,[30] however, as it demonstrated the possibility of a very large cross-section of the population turning against the government. The SED was convinced that the Polish situation was worse than 1968 in Czechoslovakia. As of September 1980, the Stasi and the East German army were swiftly mobilized, and Stasi members were sent to Poland to monitor and contain the risk of the movement spreading to the GDR (Neubert 1997).

Solidarność and Polish Cinema

GDR authorities had considered the Polish filmmakers to be especially dangerous since the 1950s, when they had not shied from social and political critique.[31] In November 1981, the Polish delegation to the Leipzig Festival was particularly large, comprising more than fifty delegates. The Stasi had taken preventive measures,[32] and, even before their departure, the Polish delegates had received specific instructions. The result was judged "satisfactory" by the Stasi department responsible for culture and media at Leipzig: the Polish guests had caused no "incidents" during the festival, and the visiting journalists had been "disciplined." Similar precautions had been exercised in selecting the Polish documentaries. Festival leadership congratulated themselves that the programming had broached "some substantive issues that Polish society was facing," but without giving the floor to representatives of Solidarność.[33]

East German authorities regarded the eventuality of Polish filmmakers gaining influence in the GDR with grave concern: these filmmakers had gotten involved with Solidarność very rapidly. In August 1980, for example, on the initiative of the Polish Filmmakers' Association, the documentarists filmed the last phase of negotiations between representatives of the workers and the Polish government—a truly remarkable feat. In no time, *Robotnicy '80* (1980, *Workers '80*), directed by Andrzej Chodakowski and Andrzej Zajaczkowski, became widely known. With the Gdańsk Agreement signed on 31 August, ten days before the seventh Polish Film Festival opened in the city, the documentary premiered on opening night, in front of the events' protagonists. During the annual forum of the Polish Filmmakers' Association, its president, feature film director Andrzej Wajda, read a report entitled "Reflections on our profession's duties vis-à-vis our country and our time:"

> In today's world, cinema is the only place where equal access to culture becomes more real each day, where a real debate on Poland and the contemporary world takes place. No other media can replace it, not even television. It is up to us to decide whether we want to see a new consciousness for Poland emerge from movie theatres, and under what conditions. (Michalek and Turaj 1992: 120)

For sixteen months, a great wave of hope raised Polish society. The Polish state, however, dragged its feet as much as possible in implementing the Gdańsk Social Accords. The Soviet regime became increasingly menacing, relying on the Polish army, the best controlled institution in the country and favored by the Soviets. The Kremlin thus intervened in Poland without having to deploy its own tanks, as it had done thirteen years prior in Czechoslovakia. A state of emergency was declared on 13 December 1981; General Jaruzelski established martial law, conducting numerous arrests, and Solidarność was banned. During the first months of martial law, director Krzysztof Kieślowski received permission to film the trial of the striking workers; while filming, however, he realized the risk of being manipulated and decided to stop (Wach 1998). The state of war did not succeed in neutralizing social tensions; on the contrary, it provoked a general, if peaceful resistance. Myriad forms of an underground cultural life were established: self-education, press, literature, plastic arts, and even radio broadcasts (Michalek and Turaj 1992).

The Polish documentaries programmed at the Leipzig Festival in no way reflected this social and cultural dynamic. They were essentially productions made by Polish state television, devoted to sports or social topics that carefully avoided any critical dimension. Instead, the Polish Cultural Center of East Berlin served as intermediary between film productions connected with Solidarność and an increasingly interested East German public. The film clubs also sought to act as a relay, although local authorities monitored their screenings very closely (Becker and Petzold 2001). Both these outlets focused more on feature films than documentaries, however, which East German audiences could only access with difficulty.

There was always West German television, however. In November 1981, Christa Wolf (2003: 302) noted in her diary: "Television evening. . . . A forum on film, entitled 'We saw reality,' featuring an interview with Andrzej Wajda and excerpts from his film *Man of Iron*.[34] Finally, Polish filmmakers allied with workers. That will never happen here. 'Never' is a heavy word." Even though critical Polish cinema clearly resonated among intellectuals and a section of the population in the GDR, the East German opposition movement assumed different forms from in Poland. This is illustrated by the growth of the peace movement in early 1980s East Germany, and its complex appropriation by citizens and intellectuals.

Pacifism and the Two Germanys

As the most advanced outpost bordering the West, the GDR represented one of the bastions most tightly controlled by the USSR, which deployed the most troops and tanks there (Hirschman 1993). In 1977, the Soviets replaced the old medium-range missiles in Eastern Europe with the SS-20 Saber, with a more limited range, but more modern and virtually invulnerable. Countries in Western Europe were apprehensive because the United States did not have equivalent arms on European soil, capable of responding in case of attack. The arms race thus started up again.

In December 1979, NATO adopted a "double-track decision," whereby it proposed to redeploy missiles in Western Europe in 1983, while at the same time launching negotiations with Warsaw Pact forces. In November 1981, Ronald Reagan proposed the "zero option" to Leonid Brezhnev, whereby Washington would refrain from deploying missiles in Europe if Moscow withdrew its arsenal. The USSR refused. As of 1983, more than 5,000 U.S. vehicles and cruise and Pershing 2 missiles were installed in Great Britain, West Germany, and Italy. The Euromissile Crisis of 1981 to 1983 was a major new international crisis with high technical and military stakes; but, perhaps above all, it also constituted a "great battle for influence" (Soutou 2001: 646) that revived the Cold War.

Against this very tense background, mass pacifist campaigns were organized in Great Britain, Italy, the Benelux countries, and the FRG. The USSR had every interest in these burgeoning movements, which enjoyed broad support among the public. Meeting in Moscow in October 1981, the assembled Communist parties decided that the Social Democratic political parties in Western Europe could be considered "strategic allies" in this campaign (Miard-Delacroix 2010). From the perspective of the SED, a rapprochement with the West German Social Democratic Party (SPD) should enable them to circumvent the threat posed by Solidarność in Poland.

As this extensive peace movement emerged throughout Europe, it also gained momentum in the GDR. Erich Honecker, who had opted for the hardline approach in 1976, was still reluctant to entertain a different pacifist discourse from the one propagated by the regime, however. The East German government thus pursued its proclaimed offensive for peace, hoping to be able to exploit the West German peace movement. From 1982 onward, an annual event called "Rock for Peace," which featured West German and foreign rock groups, took place at the Palace of the Republic, East Berlin's principal cultural center (Hintze 1999b). In April 1983, Moscow hosted the Karl-Marx Conference, organized by the SED to mark the centennial of Marx's death. Secretary of the SED Erich Honecker wanted to avail himself of this venue to present the GDR as the principal defender of détente and of peace and security in Europe and the East Bloc: "Peace and again peace is the utmost guiding principle of our policy," he asserted (Siebs 1999: 242–43).

The SED-led campaign condemning the arms race caused a great stir among East Germans, for whom pacifism was a deeply entrenched principle, and artists and intellectuals were particularly active in disseminating this message. The cause of peace, an invariable theme at the Documentary Studio since its inception, enjoyed a major revival there. As usual, pacifism was closely associated with the denunciation of American imperialism and Washington's foreign policy, which were often linked to the nuclear threat, as exemplified by the U.S. atom bombs that had devastated Japan in August 1945.

Particularly focused on the tragedy that had befallen Hiroshima and Nagasaki, contacts between Japanese and East Germans filmmakers had been growing since the 1950s. Japanese film directors and independent producers had been involved in the Leipzig Festival every year since 1960 and actively took part in the various appeals for the cause of peace. Japan had also been the guest of honor at Leipzig in 1976, when the retrospective was dedicated to Japanese cinema. In 1980, Gitta Nickel shot *Verbrennt nicht unsere Erde (Do Not Burn Our Earth)*, having traveled to Japan in search of victims of the 1945 bombings; thirty-five years after the disaster, the film was more broadly situated within an exploration of the situation of workers in one of the world's most industrialized nations. With witness accounts in the background, the film's commentary launched a moving appeal against nuclear weapons and war. A whole series of events had been envisaged to coincide with the documentary's release. In August 1980, the film was screened as part of an exhibition on Hiroshima in the Palace of the Republic, before it was released in movie theaters. Finally, in November 1980 the documentary featured in the "Fight for Peace and Disarmament" program at the Leipzig Festival, where it received the International Journalists' Union Prize.

As an East German film director noted at the Leipzig Festival in 1981, Reagan's rearmament strategy had united Marxists, Christians, and pacifists in the same struggle (Hornig 1982). Numerous West German film directors and producers hostile to NATO missiles in Europe traveled to Leipzig as well, seemingly in confirmation of the festival's slogan: "Films of the World—for Peace in the World." At Leipzig in 1982, Karl Gass revisited the bombing of Japan with *Zwei Tage im August* (1982, *Two Days in August: Reconstruction of a Crime*), which was awarded the Golden Dove. Shots retracing preparations for the aerial attacks alternated with footage of the two devastated cities, highlighting the bomb's savagery and irreparable nature in a tightly edited whole. Mingling Japanese traditional melodies, American jazz standards, and originally scored contemporary music, built around a skillfully exploited storyline, the film's sound montage contributed to its effectiveness. The documentary in effect represented Gass's return to favor at Leipzig, at a juncture when he was focusing on a series of historical films.[35]

A New Take on Pacifism in the GDR

Such manifestations, featuring the official pacifist discourse focused primarily on anti-American propaganda, were also useful to the regime. The GDR also experienced the growth of a significant parallel peace movement from 1979 on. This movement, connected to the Protestant Church and primarily targeting policies pursued by Moscow and East Berlin, eventually won over nearly all East German political opponents. It was rooted in a reaction against the growing militarization of East German society and the desire to become part of the growing European peace movement (Schröder 1998).

Now that the GDR was internationally recognized, oppositional pacifists argued, it ought to respect the democratic rules of the international community—starting with the "third basket" of the 1975 Helsinki Conference on Security and Cooperation in Europe, which addressed human rights, including freedom of emigration. The Soviet Union had pledged to respect human rights and freedoms and not to meddle in the internal affairs of other sovereign nations. Nevertheless, in his own backyard Erich Honecker sought to completely stifle the opposition peace movement (Neubert 1997). Although initially backed by Moscow, the international peace movement provoked by the European Missile Crisis ultimately proved to be disadvantageous to the Kremlin's policies.

In 1983, emerging from it strictly underground status, the East German peace movement demonstrated how much it had grown by starting to organize public protests throughout the country. Several confrontations took place, notably in Jena, in which members of a peace community stood up against Stasi forces (Bensussan 2007); in April and May, however, the Stasi launched a counteroffensive that temporarily put an end to demonstrations in the region. The West German press reported these incidents, a development that was considered a small victory, after all, for the opposition.

In February 1983, the Peace Forum, founded in Dresden in 1982, enjoyed another success during commemorations of the city's aerial bombing in 1945, for which it had organized events and meetings in the city's churches. Even though the Stasi had prevented hundreds of young people from traveling to the city, these attracted thousands of people; hence, on the evening of 13 February, numerous participants holding candles assembled at the ruins of the Frauenkirche, the symbol of the destruction caused by the firebombs. Candles were to become the signature symbol of the peace initiative demonstrations calling for nonviolence. Peace demonstrations also sought to derail Easter parades and meetings organized by the Free German Youth (FDJ), who were eager to take over and monopolize the peace movement.

Among the oft-repeated slogans of the peace protests were those denouncing the partition of the two Germanys by the Wall and those claiming the right to refuse military service in the NVA (National People's Army) as a conscientious objector. Thus, little by little, demonstrators were demanding not only peace but also freedom and democracy. West German journalists and pacifists were becoming increasingly aware of the significance of the peace movement and its widespread dissemination throughout East German society; in July 1983, significant numbers traveled to East Berlin to attend the second Peace Workshop (Friedenwerkstatt) organized by the Erlöserkirche (Church of the Redeemer). With 3,000 people in attendance, the Stasi did not succeed in diminishing the impact of the event. In late summer, however, the repression became more systematic, announcing a "hot fall" (Neubert 1997: 491).

World Peace Day, announced for 1 September 1983, and Ten Days for Peace, scheduled from 6 to 16 November, only ramped up tensions throughout the GDR. In Leipzig, several Catholic and Protestant churches organized daily prayer meetings for peace and other events that attracted a public beyond the habitual circle of believers (Feydt et al. 1990). In the evenings, following the prayer for peace, thirty to fifty protesters gathered in silence at the city's busy intersections, holding candles. The Stasi sought to convince the religious authorities to assist them in preventing such "symbolic acts," but to no avail. Tensions increased even more in Leipzig because the Ecumenical Days—which marked the end of the Luther Year and attracted prominent international religious guests to the city—were taking place at the same time.

It was in this context that the Leipzig Festival was to open on 18 November. Half an hour before the opening ceremony, twenty to fifty[36] mostly young people holding candles gathered in silence in front of the Capitol movie theater, where the event was taking place. Local police and Stasi members promptly intervened, and seventeen people were arrested, six of whom were detained for several days (Neubert 1997). The incident was not a new development; several days earlier demonstrators had also been arrested. On this occasion, however, festival guests witnessed the forceful intervention of security forces firsthand. There were immediate repercussions, which were monitored closely by the local Stasi. The festival leadership, East German and foreign guests, and even the Stasi each reacted in their own way, perfectly reflecting the stakes that the festival represented to each of these groups. The confrontation also showed to what extent Leipzig could or could not be used by the opposition as a platform for reaching international public opinion.

Collision Course at Leipzig

The crackdown on demonstrators clearly exposed the close Stasi surveillance going on behind the scenes at the festival, as well as the polarity between two pacifist discourses—one official, destined for consumption by foreign public opinion, and the other presented by those challenging the existing system (Kötzing 2014). Guests at Leipzig were deeply divided about the incident. Informed by "unofficial and official sources," the Stasi learned that festival participants were talking about the "measures taken by the People's Police on November 18th."[37] Emotions were indeed running high, among German and foreign guests alike.

Stasi Gatecrashers

On Sunday, 20 November, Christian Lehmann-Peddersen, a West German producer from Hamburg and a regular at the festival, handed festival director Ronald Trisch a letter from "members of the Unidoc delegation[38] and other festival guests" who had "witnessed the incident or heard about it." "Deeply upset by the manner in which the security forces acted," they demanded a meeting as soon as possible, as well as information about the identity and fate of the ten to twelve people who had been "beaten and taken away" by the police.[39]

That evening at 7 PM, Trisch, accompanied by Karl-Eduard von Schnitzler, received four foreign guests in his office: West German independent director Christoph Boekel and producer Joachim Winterlich; Karl Saurer, a Swiss teacher at the German Film and Television Academy of West Berlin (dffb); and Werner Gensch, an Austrian director living in London. The discussion lasted a good half hour, allowing Trisch to present the official position, which saw the incident of 18 November as a "provocation organized by enemy forces" aiming to "disrupt the festival." According to Trisch,[40] nobody had been arrested but only taken to the police station to verify their identities.

Nevertheless, according to the Stasi informer's report, "Werner Gensch reacted very angrily to the events, for he was at the scene during the intervention of the People's Police [Volkspolizei] and, what is more, of a very sensitive disposition." Above all, he condemned the "disproportionate method deployed" and demanded that they exercise more "tact." Notwithstanding this, the four "representatives from the FRG, Switzerland, and Austria"[41] stated that it was necessary to try to calm the situation, and that they would convey the festival director's arguments to the other members of their delegations, although they couldn't say how they would react.

The discussion had proven successful for Trisch, who had followed instructions of the festival's SED party group: "Filmmakers at Leipzig from around the world had gathered together against imperialism and rearmament, and would not allow themselves to be manipulated and led into actions directed against living conditions in East German society."[42] It was unclear, however, whether the discontent would remain limited to just a few people without descending into a larger act of protest.

The festival director sought to reassure the Stasi: "Comrade Trisch believes that Unidoc did not consciously intend a provocation and that there was no intention to create a conflict with the festival board."[43] The protesters seemed willing to accept the leadership's explanations. Unofficial sources, however, had informed the Stasi that around forty people had gathered in the Unidoc screening booth during the meeting to await the outcome of the discussion; among them were West German journalists, who remain unidentified in the report.

What the authorities and festival leadership feared was to see contacts develop between displeased guests from the West and East German oppositional circles. The Stasi was thus informed that the Quebec-Canadian director Martin Duckworth had gone to the Nikolaikirche on 20 November, where he'd had a conversation with an "as yet unidentified" pastor. He had specifically asked the pastor about who had been arrested, if they had since been released from police custody, and what coercive measures were to be prepared for. According to "inside information," the pastor gave him the addresses of those still in police detention and informed him that their apartments had been sealed.[44]

Duckworth attempted to take to the floor on the evening of the closing ceremony, but a Stasi agent stopped him from getting on the stage. This measure was denounced by an East German attendee, a young woman who was the deputy director of a youth center near Leipzig. In a "face-to-face" discussion with the Stasi informant, who wanted his or her identity to remain fully protected, this young woman, speaking of the West German filmmakers at the festival, was of the opinion that "the reds were pigs, really were redder than the Stasi!"[45] The attitude of West Germans indeed became the subject of quite considerable controversy.

Response of Participants from the West

"Despite a common language, we have to get used to the idea that we are in a foreign country, with a completely different social system," remarked a West German journalist (Pfister) at the festival in 1979. Not all his colleagues were of a similar opinion. In 1983, serious disagreements erupted in a West German delegation that was particularly sizable. For West German journalist Heinz Klunker, the incident was a litmus test to distinguish between those West Germans willing to report what the opposition was up to in Leipzig, and the others, who were anxious to please the festival leadership to ensure that they would be invited back.[46]

A member of the Festival Committee warned journalists from the West that they had been accredited in order to report on the festival, and only the festival. The message was clear: if they broached the incident of 18 November, it could result in canceling their press accreditation for the following year ("Leipziger friedensfilmfestival" 1983; "Zahnbürste mitnehmen" 1983). FRG film director Manfred Vosz, recipient of numerous awards at Leipzig,[47] showed particular zeal in favor of the festival leadership. He was of the opinion that the letter addressed to Trisch represented, "consciously or otherwise, a provocation."

On his own initiative, he had met many "comrades in the West German Communist Party (DKP) and other representatives from the FRG" and had urged them not to go to Trisch's office, arguing that "11/21/1983 [sic],[48] the day on which the Bundestag was due to vote on whether to station rockets in the FRG, was more important than any other issue for the West German delegation." Vosz stated that he had not witnessed the incident but had been told about it by a third party. Finally, the aforementioned Stasi informant reported that Vosz said, "So much attention should not have been paid to the people who had gathered on Petersstrasse." To quote Vosz verbatim, "They should have burned their fingers on their candles."[49]

Though the rapid spread of the news could not be prevented, the festival was not unduly disturbed. Some participants from the West, such as Heinz Klunker, had briefly considered leaving Leipzig in protest but decided to stay.[50] While some journalists—such as Heiko R. Blum, or Doris Schmidt-Blum (1983) in her account in the *Stuttgarter Zeitung*—did not mention one word about the incident, others did, playing a key role in disseminating the news to the West. In fact, the West German news agency Deutsche Presse-Agentur (DPA) issued a communiqué on 25 November, a week after the fact. Novelist Günter Grass confirmed that he was aware of the incident. The exact number of arrests, among the "some twenty-five young people" who had assembled on 18 November, was not specified, but it was stated that "based on information available in West Berlin, two women and three men" had not yet been released.[51] The deputy director of the youth club near Leipzig was suspended.

In the *Tagesspiegel*, a West Berlin daily, Heinz Kersten (1983) wrote of the "unpleasant situation" in which some festival guests—who kept asking for news about the young people who had been arrested, some of whom had been in prison for several days—found themselves. According to the alternative paper, the *Tageszeitung* of 29 November 1983, the young people still held in detention were struggling to find their place in "petty bourgeois" East German society; the exception was 53-year-old film director Klaus Fiedler, from Dresden—who had just been passing by but was imprudent enough to disagree with police methods. Among the young people were five whom the Stasi had been monitoring for quite some time: two were half–East German and half-African, both about twenty years old; there was Patrice Castillo, twenty-one and son of René Castillo, the Guatemalan poet and resistance fighter, and his German wife; and also a twenty-year-old pregnant woman.

The article sparked a controversy in the daily paper that revealed internal tensions within the West German left, which had also been expressed behind the scenes at the festival. The newspaper opined that a committee formed by eight festival guests had contributed to preventing any public debate on the issue and had even accepted that East Germans would not be allowed to attend the briefing organized by the festival. The daily's editorial board thus asked, "Has the peace of real-existing socialism won over the minds of Western filmmakers and accredited journalists?" (*Tageszeitung* 1983).

Ciril Vider, a filmmaker from Cologne, sent a strongly worded letter to the *Tageszeitung*. He repeated the arguments put forward by Director of HVFilm Horst Pehnert, according to whom the demonstrators included people who had applied for exit visas to leave the GDR and sought to get themselves arrested in order to expedite their departure for the West. Vider (1983) moreover stressed that the committee organized by festival guests had simply preferred dialogue about the "shocking developments of 18.11," judging it to be "more politically effective" than the "blind activism" of a few. His letter ended on a sarcastic note: "To conclude, I consider [this article] a contribution to the Cold War and congratulate you on having served the cause of Kohl and Reagan."

The sharp divisions that set West German guests against each other during the festival reflected tensions within the peace movement in the FRG. Since 1981, lively discussions—fueled by new momentum in the West German peace movement following the massive demonstration in Bonn in October— had been taking place about the East German movement. While the peace movement's popular success had encouraged the West German Social Democratic Party (SPD) to adopt a pacifist stance in June 1982, West German communists, who retained a prominent role in movement leadership, sought to block all support to opposition movements in the East—including the GDR opposition and, unsurprisingly, Solidarność in Poland (Neubert 1997).

East Germans between Censorship and Self-Censorship

East German responses to the Leipzig incident on 18 November 1983 laid bare the extent of internal divisions in the GDR as well as the limits on possible forms of protest. Isolated figures attempted to publicly voice their disagreement with the consequences that had been brought to bear on protesters, but there were no group protests. Among those who had witnessed the Stasi's forceful intervention on 18 November was DEFA dramaturg Tamara Trampe, a regular festivalgoer since the early 1970s. She had just arrived in Leipzig and wanted to leave right after the events, but Jürgen Böttcher, who had also been present at the Capitol theater, suggested she stay so she could testify: "Stasi, everywhere! They were well able to observe. But, I can observe even better," he reputedly said (Voigt et al. 1998: 79).

The following Wednesday, a committee of eight guests from the West met with Ronald Trisch; Peter Ulbrich, director of the GDR Filmmakers' Union; and Deputy Minister of Culture Horst Pehnert, who was also the managing director of HVFilm. The visiting committee announced that it would report on the meeting at an informal gathering at the Hotel Astoria. Trampe recalls that only a few East Germans wanted to attend the gathering at the Astoria; others, including Böttcher, preferred to go to the press conference against the Bundestag vote allowing the installation of missiles on West German soil. Trampe and her East German colleagues were turned away, however, by two gentlemen in civilian attire, who indicated that only foreign guests were invited to the meeting of the festival directors. When Trampe complained about being excluded, Böttcher retorted that the key issue was not the fate of those arrested at the Capitol, but rather the rearmament policy of the FRG and the West; for him, this was a higher priority.[52]

Böttcher's attitude reveals the atmosphere that prevailed among the majority of East German intellectuals, who were clearly aware of the hardening of government policies but still considered the West German and Western threat to be a sufficient reason to relativize violations against freedom of speech in East Germany. This internalized hierarchy of national and international issues was skillfully exploited by both the authorities and the festival organizers. And indeed, between 1980 and 1983, the issue of internal social tensions took a backseat for East German artists and intellectuals, who were more concerned with fears raised by the arms race between the superpowers. The majority of GDR authors were also still in shock in the wake of the departure of a series of friends and acquaintances for the West, following the Biermann affair. Nonetheless, the threat of a third world war or nuclear conflict became the overriding issue — not so much in literary works per se as in the literary politics of the period (Emmerich 2000).

In December 1981, GDR author Stephan Hermlin thus initiated a "Berlin meeting to maintain peace" in East Berlin. With significant media coverage, well-known public figures of all persuasions participated in very open discussions and debates. From the FRG came Günter Grass as well as Jurek Becker and Thomas Brasch, two East German authors who had recently emigrated to the West. What was remarkable about these debates was that they rejected both Moscow and Washington. The Berlin meeting exemplified, yet again, the dual game of GDR leader Erich Honecker; ever ready to play with international public opinion, he allowed such opinions to be expressed in front of journalists, while simultaneously orchestrating an intensifying crackdown on East Germany's pacifist opposition movements.

Among the few East Germans who, like Tamara Trampe, wanted to publicly condemn the police and Stasi actions against the peaceful demonstrators in 18 November, were two other young women: the one in charge of the aforementioned youth center and one who ran a movie theater in the region. Turned away from the official meeting, they joined the spontaneous gathering in the Hotel Astoria lobby. Bringing together the eight guests from the West, who were to report on the meeting with festival directors, and East German festival participants, the discussion was intensely heated and the comments very harsh. Someone was heard to say, "Now you can see how they treat us, we citizens of the GDR! We are nothing but a herd [of animals] that has no right to do anything!"[53]

Several days earlier, Trampe had been proposed for a trip abroad to select films for the Leipzig Festival. Now her name vanished from the list of proposed travelers.[54] When she went back to work, one of the other young women was summoned by her superior, who condemned her attitude in Leipzig and prohibited her from any future participation in the festival. She showed no remorse, however, and stated — in a private discussion with the anonymous Stasi informant—that "Leipzig was the grubbiest quagmire of espionage she had ever come across in the world."[55]

Aside from such isolated individual actions, some East Germans sought to express their strong reservations about the arrests within their professional institutions. The incident did not seem to have triggered any disturbance at DFF, the film academy in Babelsberg, or the DEFA Studios. Things were different within the GDR Filmmakers' Union, however, where about ten members had, in fact, expressed incomprehension at the methods employed and the Stasi's intervention. These included the film directors Joachim Tschirner and Günter Jordan, the journalist Regine Sylvester, and the cinematographer Christian Lehmann, all present at the festival.[56] Lehmann admits that he regrets to this day having done nothing when the incident occurred; at the time he justified his lack of action by the fact that he had not been a direct eyewitness but had merely heard about it from inside the movie theater.[57]

The Stasi's forceful intervention and the ensuing debates were spontaneously mentioned by all of the witnesses whom I interviewed. The incident made a lasting impression, even though its exact date is not always remembered. It represented a break from what had hitherto been the rather smooth progress of the festival. Certainly, the significance and interpretation of the incident vary somewhat from one witness to the next—how many people demonstrated? Were arrested? Who were they, in fact? Agitators seeking to be expelled from the GDR, or opponents wishing to reform society from within? Either way, for many the festival's lofty official pacifist rhetoric sounded particularly hollow from that point on.

Increasingly Visible Contradictions

At the festival's opening ceremony in 1983, shortly after the arrest of protesters outside the Capitol theater, festival director Ronald Trisch read a letter aloud. It was from the American singer and activist Harry Belafonte, who wrote: "I think there is no more convincing evidence than this festival to prove that cinema can serve the pacifist cause. . . . I am fighting at your side for peace!" (*Protokoll 1983* 1984: 12).

The theme of peace and international détente dominated the entire festival that year, which was taking place during an extremely tense period in the Cold War (Soutou 2001). In August, a Soviet fighter plane had shot down a Korean Air passenger jet when it strayed, without permission, into Soviet airspace over the Kamchatka Peninsula. Washington, perhaps behind the changed trajectory of the Korean jet, vociferously condemned the incident. On 25 October, American forces landed on the island of Grenada for fear that it would fall under Cuban influence. In response to this incident, the Leipzig Festival leadership organized a minute's silence dedicated to Grenada, while Cuban filmmakers lodged an official protest against the American intervention. During his speech about the Bundestag vote in Bonn, Karl-Eduard von Schnitzler opposed the "minority" Bonn government to the West German "people," whose "anger" had been expressed in the towns, villages, and streets of the country (*Protokoll 1983* 1984: 12). And Leipzig's first prize was awarded to a West Berlin film on the peace movements.

When the Berlin meeting for peace had taken place in December 1981, East German authors Stefan Heym and Günter de Bruyn had denounced the schizophrenia of East Berlin leaders, who actively encouraged the pacifist movement in the West and yet opposed establishing a civilian service (*Zivildienst*) for pacifists being demanded by young people in the GDR (Emmerich 2000). Now, two years later, the discrepancy was becoming increasingly untenable and seemed to be undermining even the most unconditional support for the regime abroad. The Stasi was concerned when an Austrian filmmaker expressed that participants at Leipzig would have a hard time reporting on the situation facing the East German peace movement to "progressive forces" back home: "It would be complicated to explain that people fighting for peace in the GDR were being arrested by the police."[58] The ramifications of the 18 November incident were thus felt far beyond Leipzig, and the festival did not escape unscathed.

In contrast to isolated reactions in response to the wave of censorship set off by the Eleventh Plenum in 1965, the Biermann affair had given rise to a widespread, collective movement of solidarity. Many intellectuals started leaving the GDR in 1976, but the hardening of regime policies and the ensuing crackdown on opposition and peace movements in 1983 prompted a massive upsurge in departures, well beyond intellectual circles.[59]

While documentarists were more numerous than feature filmmakers to support Biermann, nearly all of them chose to remain in the GDR, often taking refuge in internal exile. At the same time, however, they managed to create a new space for dialogue and exchange. This was the case with the establishment of a national documentary festival in 1978. The idea had dated back to 1966, and this annual gathering was intended to enable the DEFA Documentary Studio, the Army Film Studio,[60] and State Television to show each other their latest productions.[61] The city of Neubrandenburg, north of Berlin, hosted the event, which became a sort of preliminary venue for Leipzig.

As the Leipzig Festival made its way through the late 1970s and the early 1980s, Ronald Trisch had to contend with this moderate competition, not to mention a progressively acute financial crisis, as the regime found itself in increasingly dire economic circumstances. As the festival's budget diminished significantly, fewer posters and *Festival Bulletins* were printed, support for guests was reduced,[62] and the festival was shortened by one day. Naturally, this altered the profile of Documentary Week. In an attempt to create new dynamism, Trisch sought to open up the festival politically and appointed Richard Ritterbusch, who had participated in writing Volker Koepp's documentary *Wittstock Girls*, as the new head of the Selection Committee (Ritterbusch 1998).

From 1979 onward, the committee also enjoyed greater flexibility. It launched a selection called "Trade-Show, or the Committee Presents . . ." that allowed the screening of films that could not be in competition—whether due to their duration or on political grounds. An "Ad Hoc Selection" was also initiated for films that arrived too late to be entered in competition but that deserved to be screened (Jordan 1998a). In an international context favoring this renewed dynamism, the new sections breathed fresh life into the festival.

Notes

1. A translation of Biermann's lyrics: "Here is a DEFA film! / . . . A cop lands in manure. / A bureaucrat's doublespeak / jeopardizes the state. / An anarchist / becomes a communist."
2. "Wartet nicht auf bessere Zeiten . . ." (Don't Wait for Better Times) is the title of one of Wolf Biermann's most well-known lyrics, which he sang in Cologne on 13 November 1976.
3. We must remember that *The Trace of Stones* was also a victim of the Eleventh Plenum, withdrawn from theaters in January 1966, and that Frank Beyer had to stop working at DEFA.
4. Stefan Heym (1913–2001) was one of East Germany's most important literary and cultural figures. Born into a Jewish family in Germany, during the war he left Germany for Prague and then the United States, where he began his career as an author. He returned to Germany as a member of the U.S. armed forces and settled in the GDR.
5. For more, see Lindenberger 1999a.
6. For more, see chapter 4.
7. For Wolf Biermann's own version of the affair, see Biermann 2016.
8. Stephan Hermlin (1915–1996) went to Palestine briefly in 1936 and then France, before fleeing to Switzerland in 1943. He returned to Frankfurt am Main in 1945, before moving to the Soviet Occupation Zone two years later.
9. These were Sarah Kirsch, Christa Wolf and her husband Gerhard, Volker Braun, Franz Fühmann, Stefan Heym, Günter Kunert, Heiner Müller, and Rolf Schneider.
10. The text of the petition appears in Biermann and Pleitgen 2001.
11. As in Jena, where fifty people were arrested on 18 November 1976 and then stripped of their East German citizenship (Neubert 1997).
12. In France, for example, a Biermann Committee was formed, initiated by the newspaper *Allemagnes d'aujourd'hui* (Pfeil 2004).
13. Bericht von Peter B. Schumann, WDR Köln, BArch-FArch, Leipzig, 1976/33.
14. *Operativvorgang "Spezialist"* for Karl Gass. See Walther 1999.

15. Konzeption zur Gestaltung des "Leipziger Biertisches" im Festivalklub des XIX. Festivals, Leipzig, 25 October 1976, BArch-FArch, Leipzig, 1976/30.
16. Author's interview with Wilhelm Roth, Berlin, Germany (9 March 2003).
17. Report of Peter B. Schumann, WDR Köln, BArch-FArch, Leipzig, 1976/33.
18. See Thomas Reichel on this culture of conflict, examined on the scale of the enterprise, in Hürtgen and Reichel 2001.
19. Letter from Eva-Maria Hagen to Wolf Biermann, 22 November 1976 (Hagen 1998).
20. Cohn-Vossen's article is also cited in Jordan 2000.
21. This film was also known as *Chor Berliner Parteiveteranen*.
22. In October 1966, Wolf Biermann wrote, "That B[öttcher's] inoffensive film should now be liquidated confirmed what no longer needed confirmation: those in power today will no longer permit even a meter of film that does not serve their narrow-minded interests" (Hagen 1998: 81).
23. Sculptor Peter Makolies had been one of the central characters in *Three of Many*, Jürgen Böttcher's first documentary, made at DEFA in 1961 and immediately banned. Since then, the director had devoted no film to the plastic arts, a theme that was nevertheless dear to him.
24. Author's interview with Karl Gass, Berlin/Kleinmachnow, Germany (18 August 2000); Gass 1995.
25. There, he was immediately hired by the NDR television station in Hamburg (Roth 1995).
26. Author's interview with Jürgen Böttcher, Berlin/Karlshorst, Germany (31 October 2000).
27. For more, see chapter 10.
28. According to West German critic Wilhelm Roth, the shunters were "perfect specialists, with precise gestures, professionals, like Howard Hawks' cowboys (Roth 2001: 13–14).
29. At Leipzig, the film won the Ministry of Culture Prize; at Oberhausen in 1985, it won the International Federation of Ciné-Clubs Prize; an award at the festival in Melbourne in 1986; and the Grand Prix of Brioude in France in 1987.
30. See Kubina and Wilke 1995.
31. For more on this, see chapters 2 and 7.
32. Sicherungsbereich Kultur/Massenmedien, Die Leipziger Dokwoche, 1981, BStU BVfS Leipzig Abt. XX/278/02, p. 203.
33. Report of the Director of National and International Festivals of the GDR, Leipzig, 3 November 1981, BArch-FArch, Leipzig, 1981/46.
34. *Człowiek z żelaza* (1981, *Man of Iron*) is the continuation of *Man of Marble* from 1977. For more on this, see chapter 7.
35. For more on this, see chapter 10.
36. Sources are contradictory with respect to the number of demonstrators. Erhart Neubert (1997) refers to about fifty people, the ADP West German press agency mentions around twenty-five participants, and the West German daily *Tageszeitung* describes a group of about forty people.
37. Captain Heinig, Information, Leipzig, 20 November 1983, BStU BVfS Leipzig XX/269/01, p. 46. All the reports and information concerning the 1983 incident and gathered by the Stasi come from this dossier in the BStU archive.
38. Unidoc was a distribution company in Munich. Its films, which were judged to be "progressive," made it a partner of the Leipzig Festival.

39. An das Komitee der Internationalen Leipziger Dokumentarfilm und Kurzfilmwoche, BStU BVfS Leipzig XX/269/01, p. 2.
40. Captain Heinig, Information, Leipzig, 20 November 1983, BStU BVfS Leipzig XX/269/01, p. 47
41. The guests were not considered professionals, deserving a personal invitation, but rather were invited as national representatives, ambassadors of their countries.
42. Captain Heinig, Information, Leipzig, 20 November 1983, BStU BVfS Leipzig XX/269/01, p. 6.
43. Ibid., 48.
44. Ibid., 5.
45. Second Lieutenant Stadelmann of the Kreisdienststelle Greiz: Information, Leipzig, 4 January 1984, concerning information transmitted on 1 December 1983 and signed « Source » BStU BVfS Leipzig, XX/269/01, p. 39.
46. Author's interview with Heinz Klunker, Berlin, Germany (15 September 2004).
47. Among other awards, Vosz received a Silver Dove for his documentary *Deutsche Kirchweih* (1968, *Church Anniversary*). He shot many films about the Palestinians. In 1976, he was a member of the international jury.
48. The vote did not take place on 21, but rather on 22 November 1983.
49. Captain Heinig, Information, Leipzig, 20 November 1983, BStU BVfS Leipzig XX/269/01, p. 48.
50. Author's interview with Heinz Klunker, Berlin, Germany (15 September 2004).
51. ADN-Information, nur Zur Information. Interne Dienstmeldung, "dpa: Festnahme nach Friedensaktion in Leipzig, Berlin, 25/11/83," BStU BVfS Leipzig XX/269/01, p. 10.
52. Author's interview with Tamara Trampe, Berlin, Germany (23 August 2004).
53. Second Lieutenant Stadelmann of the Kreisdienststelle Greiz: Information, Leipzig, 4 January 1984, concerning information transmitted on 1 December 1983 and signed "Source," BStU BVfS Leipzig, XX/269/01, p. 39.
54. Author's interview with Tamara Trampe, Berlin, Germany (23 August 2004).
55. Second Lieutenant Stadelmann of the Kreisdienststelle Greiz: Information, Leipzig, 10 January 1984, concerning information received on 20 December 1983 from an unnamed source, BStU BVfS Leipzig, XX/269/01, p. 40–41.
56. Captain Heinig, Information, Leipzig, 20 November 1983, BStU BVfS Leipzig XX/269/01, p. 43.
57. Author's interview with Christian Lehmann, Berlin, Germany (22 August 2000).
58. Captain Heinig, Information, Leipzig, 20 November 1983, BStU BVfS Leipzig Abt XX/269/01, p. 5.
59. In 1983, 11,343 people left the GDR; in 1984, it was 40,974. These figures include refugees, official émigrés, and exchanges made by the two regimes (Hirschman 1993).
60. The Army Film Studio was founded in the National People's Army (Nationale Volksarmee, or NVA) in 1960.
61. Kurzinformation über die IX. Leipziger Woche, 23.11.1966, to HVFilm, SAPMO-BArch DR1/4331.
62. In 1983, the flights of only seventeen foreign guests were covered, in contrast to one hundred in 1972.

PART IV
Toward New Horizons (1984–1990)

CHAPTER 9

An Opening in the East?

> Paradoxical as it may seem, Gorbachev, Poland, Hungary, and all those who, over the years, abandoned the GDR—angry and helpless, grief stricken, anguished, resigned, or nostalgic—they are the ones who actively participated in the process that culminated here in the cry, "We are the people."
> —Jörg Foth, "Forever Young"

In the midst of the GDR's historic turning point, feature film director Jörg Foth succinctly summed up the difficult and complex process, initiated by Mikhail Gorbachev, that was perestroika. Reforms from Moscow enabled the development far beyond the borders of the USSR of an extensive liberalizing movement that engulfed Eastern Europe. Documentary filmmaking of the period was not immune to these developments. Critical documentary, in particular, was part of a dynamic that had taken shape earlier in the East Bloc but remained repressed until reforms were under way in the USSR.

The Leipzig Festival offers an ideal perspective from which to grasp, in all its complexity and specificity, how East German society experienced perestroika before the GDR collapsed in the 1989 revolution—as it offers a multilateral framework that is well suited to tracking different phases of a dynamic that was both national and international.[1] First and foremost, festival history enables us to compare documentary films made in the various socialist countries during this period, a topic on which little, if any, other research has been done to date.[2] Documentary films provide an ideal prism through which to study problems related to the glasnost process, not just in the USSR[3] but also in other East Bloc countries. The festival also concentrated the diverse reactions to the discovery of critical documentaries from the East; the multiple stances taken on the subject of glasnost brought to light serious divergences within the East German cultural system. On a broader level, this moment of crisis raises the key question of whether the movement for liberalization in the GDR was caused by glasnost coming from Moscow or whether reforms emanating from the East merely accelerated profound changes that had already been in process for years.

Lessons in Truth: Leipzig 1987

The reforms originating in Moscow accelerated the development of a formidable liberalization movement that spread across Eastern Europe from the mid-1980s. Contemporary documentary film did not remain insensitive to this dynamic, as an examination of programming at the 1987 Leipzig Festival illustrates.

Soviet Reforms and Documentary Film

After Gorbachev came to power in March 1985, the new cultural policy—which instantly reverberated beyond its borders of the USSR—ensured the dissemination of ideas and films that broke sharply with the hitherto dominant narrative. In May 1986, little over a year later, the founding event for new Soviet policies on culture and cinema took place in Moscow. The 1986 Congress of the Soviet Filmmakers' Union effectively constituted a historical rupture with the past, with ramifications that participants and outside observers recognized immediately, even though the international press had not been allowed to follow the proceedings.

A delegation from the GDR Filmmakers' Union represented East Germany at the congress.[4] Its report reflects the impression made by the debates and prevailing anarchic atmosphere, emphasizing "the heated controversy, the passionate arguments, the brilliant rhetoric, statements often based on indisputable examples."[5] One by one, the official directors of the Soviet Filmmakers' Union were booed offstage. Speakers condemned the disastrous economic and social conditions facing the vast majority of filmmakers, as well as film studios that offered no real opportunities to a younger generation of artists. A sign of the extent of changes underway was that film director Elem Klimov—himself a former victim of censorship—was chosen as the new president of the Soviet Filmmakers' Union. During the proceedings, documentary production was explicitly called into question: "It has sunk very low, has lost all meaning, due to lack of communication with the public and as a direct consequence of declining quality."[6]

The leadership of the Communist Party of the Soviet Union (CPSU), which welcomed the decisions made by the congress, asked the delegations from its brother countries in Eastern Europe to widely disseminate what they had

Figure 9.1. Poster for 1987 Leipzig Festival. © Bundsarchiv-Filmarchiv, Archiv der Leipziger Dok-Filmwochen GmbH.

heard there.[7] The significance of the event did not escape the government in East Berlin. In November 1986, Kurt Hager, responsible for culture within the SED's politburo, noted with relief in his report on the Leipzig Festival, "Problematic trends, such as surfaced at the congress of Soviet cinema, have not appeared on the [festival] program."[8] The following year, however, the floodgates opened. Documentary filmmaker Oleg Uralov (b. 1943), secretary of the new board of the Soviet Filmmakers' Union and a member of the 1987 Leipzig Festival jury, drew the following conclusion:

> We are living in a time that requires documentaries. To state it more bluntly: an era that needs truth. People line up outside movie theaters to watch such films. We are experiencing a real boom. Lenin [acknowledged] the importance of the documentary genre. This privileged place was conserved until the 1930s. Then came a time in which we were more in need of mythology than truth. . . . Following the 20th Congress [of the CPSU], we witnessed a return of the genre. And now, . . . interest is particularly strong again. This reflects shifts in society as a whole; once again, people are more interested in what is happening around them. And having information, knowing the truth is an important element in the mobilization of people. (Uralov 1987)

The films selected at Leipzig in 1987 reveal the latest trends in Soviet documentary filmmaking, which prized an unvarnished depiction of society. This was particularly true for films produced at the USSR's most politically and aesthetically progressive studios: the studios producing the documentaries that best captured an unvarnished version of reality. Of the eight Soviet films produced by film studios (not television) selected across categories, three came from the Central Studio for Documentary Film (CSDF) in Moscow, while the remainder were produced "on the periphery," in Leningrad, Sverdlovsk, Riga, Tallinn, and Kiev. Each entry directly addressed the shortcomings of the Soviet system. The title of the Ukrainian documentary *Uroki Pravdy* (1987, *Lessons in Truth*) perfectly epitomized what everybody aspired to in this uncertain, but exciting period.

Among the documentarists "overturning the construction of socialism" (Niney 1990a), filmmakers at the Lenfilm Studio in Leningrad (now St. Petersburg) represented a school that had long been deeply incisive in its observation of daily life and had cultivated a unique identity, quite distinct from Moscow's. Pavel Kogan,[9] a leading figure in this group, directed a gem of humor and impertinence, *Skoro Leto* (1987, *Summer Will Soon Be There*), which was selected for competition at Leipzig. The film focuses on "the working conditions, lifestyle, and morale of employees at a chocolate factory in Leningrad" (*Protokoll 1987* 1988: 97). It shows young employees who prefer to smoke cigarettes and tell each other funny stories than to work, while colleagues at their workstations also show scant enthusiasm for their work.

Among other things, the camera documents the stages involved in confecting pralines and chocolates; with ramshackle machinery and difficult working conditions, the setting is uninviting, to say the least.

Films from the Baltic republics were also a highlight at the 1987 Leipzig Festival. In competition, for example, was Mark Soosaar's *Musiikki s ostrava Kihnu* (1986, *Man of Kihnu*), made at the Estonian studio in Tallinn. It presents a deeply somber portrayal of this island in the Baltic Sea, where the disappearance of traditional trades has destroyed the social cohesion of a population whose rate of alcoholism is constantly on the rise. Notwithstanding, a journalist noted, "The film does not limit itself to a mere observation of multiple dysfunctions. . . . It drafts solutions . . . : excessive centralization must be corrected, and Kihnu's specific problems must be recognized for what they are" (Mäde 1987).

The other Baltic entry, *Vai viegli but jaunam?* (1986, *Is It Easy to Be Young?*) by Juris Podnieks, a Latvian director working in Riga, was screened in a session devoted to films that had already received awards at other festivals. Podnieks's documentary had received an award in the USSR, where it enjoyed tremendous success: it attracted some eleven million spectators, who formed long lines in front of movie theaters following its release in Moscow in the fall of 1987 (Roberts 1999). It also struck a chord abroad, where it furnished living proof that glasnost was well and truly under way.[10] Is it easy to be young? "No" is the answer of the film, which shows distraught and alienated youth indulging in drugs and susceptible to the arguments of spiritual movements akin to sects (Lawton 1992). "We lost our illusions incredibly fast and, at seventeen or eighteen, we feel completely disempowered. What can we change?" asks one of the young people interviewed by Podnieks.

In Moscow, the CSDF did not distance itself from the wave of liberalization. Rollan Sergiyenko's *Kolokol Chernobylya* (1987, *The Bell of Chernobyl*), also on the program at Leipzig in 1987, addressed the burning issue of the environment, which was close to the heart of the new freedom of expression. Shot during the summer and fall of 1986, Sergiyenko interviewed inhabitants of the region where the nuclear disaster had occurred on 26 April. He summed up his project thus: "Anyone who thinks about what has happened at Chernobyl is led to reflect on humanity's core values. . . . Today, we must remember the values that have been neglected for decades" (Sergiyenko 1987). The project's universality was clearly understood: *The Bell of Chernobyl* won the prize of the International Association of Film Journalists and Critics.

These films caused a sensation because they reinvigorated Soviet documentary production, not only thanks to their tenor and subject matter but also because they were largely supported by the new cultural policy in Moscow, whose influence on the Leipzig Festival was still considerable. The major themes of the glasnost era films, however—which called work practices into question, condemned social and human misery, and expressed young people's disillusionment—were attacks on the very foundations of long-dominant orthodox discourse, whose central tropes included the working-class hero, socioeconomic progress, and the radiant future borne by younger generations. Indeed, in his festival report for the politburo, Kurt Hager deplored the fact that "many films shown at Leipzig at times represent[ed] socialist daily life from an extremely critical angle."[11]

Films from Eastern Europe

In Eastern Europe, a particularly incisive form of documentary was burgeoning—often encouraged by new cultural policies and structural reforms within the film studios, but at a pace that was different from one country to the next. Polish cinema, financially dependent on the state, had suffered particularly badly under martial law, decreed by General Jaruzelski in December 1981; but after it was lifted in 1983, production of critical documentaries picked up again. Documentary production in Poland, which had been imbued with a subversive spirit since the 1930s, now also succeeded in reaching a wider audience (Wach 1998). The Solidarność movement was mobilizing support far beyond intellectual circles (Dalos 1995), and many hitherto "undesirable" films were screened in churches, which had been transformed into unofficial cultural centers (Michalek and Turaj 1992). For the Polish opposition movement, the Catholic Church constituted a powerful institutional framework, drawing its legitimacy from a long history of resistance against communism, as well as against its Russian and then Soviet neighbor dating to well before 1945.

In 1986, Hager had condemned "problematic" Polish films, including one that recognized the "Catholic Church as sole social authority" and "rejected the role of women's emancipation."[12] In 1987, however, six Polish films were shown in competition at Leipzig, including a film from the experimental Irzykowski Documentary Film Studio: a montage of 8mm amateur movies[13] offering a nonorthodox perspective on the "man in the street confronted by politics and history."[14] The *Festival Bulletin* gravely described it as "An essay on the relativity of truth" (*Protokoll 1987* 1988: 127). This surprise discovery— Marcel Łozinski's *Cwiszenia Warsztatowe* (1984, *Workshop Exercises*)—was unobtrusively screened in the festival's Information Section.

The film's opening sequences show bystanders being interviewed on Warsaw streets and expressing their mostly negative opinions on young people. For subsequent sequences, the preceding montages were manipulated and reshown with freshly synchronized commentaries, written by the film crew, that made the people stopped on the street say the contrary of what they had originally said (Wach 1998). In this way, Łozinski called into question media representations of Polish society as living harmoniously, although it was under siege.

This film, which had waited three years to be selected, revealed the extent to which Gorbachev's perestroika had provided a necessary impetus for the international dissemination of critical documentaries. Not all documentaries from other East Bloc countries selected for the Leipzig Festival were deemed problematic by officials, however—far from it, in fact. Hungarian productions, for example, lagged behind. This may be due to issues facing the Hungarian film industry, which was undergoing profound structural changes in the mid- to late 1980s.[15] This alone, however, cannot explain why Hungarian entries at Leipzig in 1986 and 1987 did not have the subversive force of the Polish documentaries. While we might suspect that this reflected a less discerning selection process, historian Jean-Pierre Jeancolas has another explanation. In 1985, the economic crisis in Hungary assumed such dramatic proportions that no sector was spared; Jeancolas (2001: 211) remarks that Hungarian filmmakers regard it as the "year of 'stalemate' and 'closure' for Hungarian cinema, following the golden years of 1980–1985."

In Czechoslovakia from 1985 to 1988, in contrast, the tone was extremely strident. Social critique was at the heart of both feature and documentary films, which often treated similar themes. Several feature film directors had started making documentaries in the 1970s, finding the expressive field more suited to portraying daily life.[16] In the 1980s, cinema "represented the favorite medium for collective gatherings, and movie theaters a good venue for exchanges, where we could express our revolt in the dark of projections," recalls Jan Lukeš (1996: 141). At Leipzig in 1986, two Czechoslovakian documentaries screened in competition, aside from television and animated film productions such as Pavel Koutecký's *Maximaliste v mikrosvete* (1985, *Maximalists in a Microcosm*). Dedicated to a scientist working on the invention of an electric lithograph machine, this film was brimming with murderous quips against the regime for its failures in every sphere.[17]

Brother Countries . . . or Enemies?

It is clear, then, that in 1986 and 1987 audiences at the Leipzig Festival were able to watch numerous films from socialist countries that more or less directly denounced the political, social, economic, and moral situation in their respective societies. This triggered considerable concern among East German advocates of the orthodox line. As we have seen, the principle behind selecting Eastern European films for the Leipzig Festival had been laid out in 1980 and then reviewed on several occasions, without finding a satisfactory solution. Fundamentally, this reflected insufficient mutual trust between the GDR and other socialist countries; while they maintained contact with one another, it was often in an atmosphere of deep mistrust, as evidenced in the spring of 1987 by two meetings in preparation for the festival.

In March 1987, the culture department of the SED Central Committee sent a delegation to Hungary to study "the results . . . and problems encountered . . . in the cultural domain."[18] Their Hungarian counterparts spoke out very openly. A profound crisis of values was destabilizing society, as shown by "suicides, crime, alcohol, and drugs." The number of visitors to cultural institutions was declining. As for artists, the regime was "on the defensive"; only 10 to 20 percent of members of the various artist unions were in the Hungarian Communist Party. In their view, films ought to avoid two pitfalls: being reduced to a "single ideological function" and being considered a "mere market commodity." The "independence" of the studios should be increased, following the new Soviet model. They hailed the choice of Elem Klimov as president of the Soviet Filmmakers' Union, and his film *Agoniya* (1973–1975, *Rasputin*)[19] was shown in a private session at the Hungarian Filmmakers' Union.

The East German delegate hastened to add that "this film [had been] released in GDR theaters in 1983."[20] This remark clearly reveals that most East German leaders were still trying to convince others, as well as themselves, that the situation in the GDR was much better than in its socialist brother countries. It contrasted all the more with the Hungarians' lucid analysis. This divergence characterized the distinct developments in each country. As Hungarian author and historian György Dalos (1995: 557) concluded in his April 1994 address to the Bundestag in Berlin, "Just as the GDR was isolated within the 'socialist camp,' its opposition movement remained relatively distant from those in other countries in Central and Eastern Europe"—thereby establishing a causal link between the regime's attitude and the situation of its domestic opponents.

The particularly delicate relationship with Poland also came into play. Ever since martial law had been lifted in 1983, the East Berlin government had anxiously monitored Jaruzelski's ambiguous policies, which turned out to be far less orthodox than the line taken by Honecker, especially in cultural affairs. In May 1987, a delegation from the Polish United Workers' Party (PZPR) undertook a study tour in the GDR and met Kurt Hager of the SED Central Committee.[21] According to the delegation, the Polish opposition was not as entrenched as some would have the world believe; the impending visit of Polish-born Pope John Paul II, in contrast, posed a more concrete threat and was being given the full attention of Polish leaders.[22] With respect to cultural policy, the delegation explained that the party had gone on the offensive. The most progress had been achieved in the fields of theater and film; the situation was proving to be more complex for the visual arts and literature.[23] Hager replied that in the GDR, in contrast, "the political situation in the cultural domain [was] stable," in particular because the regime was applying the system of "democratic participation of the cultural intelligentsia."[24]

In fact, East German intellectuals differed substantially from their Polish counterparts as regarded their relationship to power. In the GDR, intellectuals remained heavily imbued with the Marxist ideal,[25] most often because of their visceral opposition to West Germany, which they considered as the successor to Nazism (Meuschel 1991). Indeed, the very existence of the FRG and the possibility of relocating there, voluntarily or not,[26] implied that those who remained in the GDR accepted its politics. Another distinctive feature, which might help explain the East German intelligentsia's ambiguous relationship with the state, was its elitist attitude "vis-à-vis a population who had elected Hitler" (Reichardt 2003: 72). The opening up and liberalization of cultural policy taking place in East Bloc countries thus collided in the GDR with social and ideological structures that were distinct from those existing in the other socialist countries.

Another factor might also have contributed to the GDR's isolation among East Bloc countries. Unlike those in other countries, East German workers and intellectuals did not have the foundational experience of widespread and dramatic events—such as had occurred in Hungary in 1956, in Prague in 1968, and in Poland throughout the 1970s and 1980s—to help forge a collective awareness vis-à-vis the dominant regime (Bispinck et al. 2004). Even if these dates were significant outside the countries directly concerned, they primarily represented national crises that triggered changes in government and formed new generations of opponents, for whom the system could no longer be changed except from within (Reichardt 2003). These numerous factors thus explain the GDR's isolation in the reform movement, which was then being launched—an isolation that the German-German problem only accentuated.

The 1987 Berlinale: Risk of Contagion from the West?

Meanwhile, every year programming for the West Berlin film festival—the Berlinale—was closely monitored and analyzed on the other side of the Wall. In February 1987, the Berlinale's theme was the cultural thaw between East and West. A "reliable and verified source" furnished a detailed account of the festival to the Stasi.[27] The author of the report underlined the pivotal role played during the Berlinale by those socialist countries that were embracing Gorbachev's reform strategies. Márta Mészáros's *Napló gyermekeimnek* (1984, *Diary for My Children*), for example, screened as the Hungarian entry at the Berlinale before its official world premiere; spanning the period from 1950 to 1956, this "very provocative and highly personal confrontation with the Stalinist era"—as conceded by the Stasi source—was a resounding success.

Films from the USSR dominated the Berlinale program, however. Soviet feature films and documentaries that had been censored came off the shelves for the first time. The exiled Andrei Tarkovsky, who had died in Paris in 1986, and the Armenian director Sergei Parajanov were among those on the long list of rehabilitated filmmakers—not to mention Alexander Sokurov, whose latest film, *Skorbnoye beschuvstviye* (1984, *Mournful Unconcern*), was deemed "partly incomprehensible" by the Stasi informant. The jury bestowed the Golden Bear on Gleb Panfilov's *Tema* (*The Theme*), which had been banned since its production in 1979; in this critique of apparatchik writers who toe the party line, the heroine wants to go to Israel, saying she prefers "to die of homesickness abroad, rather than die of hate here."

Elem Klimov's *Proshchanie* (1981, *Farewell*), which screened out of competition, tells of the destruction of a village after the construction of a dam. Klimov was greeted "with thunderous applause" at the press conference and was the "undisputed star of the festival." The Stasi was particularly interested in the contacts Klimov made with official American representatives, with a view to preparing a cultural meeting between the two countries. The highlight of the Berlinale was undoubtedly when Klimov, as the newly elected president of the Union of Soviet Filmmakers, shook hands with Jack Valenti, the powerful president of the Motion Picture Association of America (Jacobsen 2000).

With "all this drama" surrounding films from East Bloc countries, entries from the GDR and the FRG were relegated to the background.[28] DEFA films, in particular, were booed by the audience, or viewers simply left the movie theater. The press conference for Heiner Carow's feature film *So viele Träume* (1986, *So Many Dreams*)[29] was an "outright fiasco," with no one except East German journalists in attendance. The Berlinale thus triggered genuine fears among East German officials, and not without good reason.

Rollan Sergiyenko's *The Bell of Chernobyl*, which screened in West Berlin in February 1987, was then chosen to screen in Leipzig a few months later.[30] At Leipzig, this documentary—which the Soviets had greatly hesitated to send to the West—hence not only screened in a brother country but was also bestowed with the FIPRESCI Prize. Such circulation between the Leipzig and Berlin festivals provoked a strong reaction among East German partisans of a strict separation between the cultural policies of the two Germanys, however. Over the ensuing months, in preparation for the 1988 Leipzig Festival, animated debates took place between those supporting a cultural policy of withdrawal and those championing a greater openness to the reforms that were taking place in the East.

Inner Conflicts: Leipzig 1988

Documentary director Günter Jordan (1998b: 127) noted that the Leipzig Festival Selection Committee was:

incorporated into the system; it never enjoyed the slightest autonomy. And yet, it knew how to develop initiatives and its own identity, and for this it found allies. The fault line separating stupidity and intelligence, openness and withdrawal into oneself . . . did not run between those above and those below, but right through society itself.

In 1993, documentarist Jochen Wisotzki, who had been "in charge of the *Festival Bulletin* and a member of the Selection Committee from 1986 to 1988," described the atmosphere within the Selection Committee: "I found myself in the midst of trench warfare . . . between the people from state television (DFF) and those from DEFA" (Wisotzki 1993: 264). As he then remarked, however, "The Committee was my first democratic experience in the GDR" (128). The tensions that had hitherto more or less been contained ended up exploding while preparing for the 1988 festival, as is clear in reports on meetings and in the Stasi archives. These documents make it possible to trace an institutional history of developments in East Germany in the wake of glasnost.

Division in the Ranks

The camps consolidated following the thirtieth edition of the Leipzig Festival in 1987. On 9 February 1988, the Organizing Committee convened in the presence of representatives of the main institutions involved in the festival. Hans-Joachim Seidowsky was the associate director of DFF and a member of the Festival Party Group for over a decade.[31] The discussion pitted those from DFF, who were shocked by the festival's program, against the majority of others present, who supported more nuanced positions.

Seidowsky's intervention was notably virulent.[32] In an intensely aggressive tone and manner, which betrayed a deep sense of anxiety, even panic in face of the new situation, his criticisms targeted almost everybody: "For a long time now, there has been talk about the weakness of the socialist entries; but this time the socialist films have impassioned minds, . . . attracting media attention particularly in the West. It is now our duty to respond to this."[33] He violently denigrated the content of incriminated documentaries: "Films with serious intentions must be presented at Leipzig, not just journalism eager for revelations, or a revisiting of the past along the lines of 'Trotsky was there, too.' Such films have no place at an international festival."

According to Seidowsky, the image they depicted of everyday life was false: "Is socialism really the socialism we see on Kichnu Island, or in the Leningrad confectionery factory?"[34] He utterly failed to grasp the relevance of the environmental theme: "Films on the environment and other such green stuff [*solches grünes Zeug*] have cropped up in the program; if we observe the regulations, they have no place at Leipzig."[35] What struck Seidowsky as most inconceivable, however, was that the USSR was on the side of the deviants. Henceforth, the only thing that mattered was the line advocated by the East German government. He concluded, "We have a completely different point of view, . . . and the festival takes place on our turf."

Reactions to the Soviet documentaries were thus commensurate with the seismic political shift in the balance of power between the GDR and the USSR that was taking place. On 25 February 1988, a fresh meeting was held in the office of Seidowsky, who had lost none of his vigor. To his thinking, "the festival had deviated from its true purpose, and 'a bunch of halfwits [*Halbidioten*] who were rising up against socialism in their own countries' had found their way into the program." He concluded that everything must be done to prevent Leipzig from turning into a "Herz Frank festival"[36] — referring to the Latvian auteurist filmmaker who was one of the key exponents of the Baltic vein of documentary, which harshly critiqued Soviet society.[37] The festival thus had to be reorganized, Seidowsky reasoned, starting with the Selection Committee: "At present, we must see whether there aren't a few loafers [*Faulpelze*] on the committee, or whether it is not so overwhelmed by its tasks that it must be enlarged."[38] Members of the committee in question, however, refused to be challenged in this manner by someone from DFF — an institution that, after all, was merely one among many organizing the festival.

Selection criteria remained at the heart of the debate, however.[39] The Selection Committee comprised eight members: four from the DEFA Documentary Studio,[40] two from DFF, and one each from the Babelsberg film academy and the East German State Film Archive (SFA). Members shared the task of seeking out suitable films when traveling abroad and attending festivals on the international circuit. The ultimate selection, however, was not theirs to make.[41] Eberhard Ugowski, from HVFilm, thus felt obliged to respond to Seidowsky's attacks, pointing out that Seidowsky himself had been "in Moscow in the company of Trisch and Ritterbusch[42] for the pre-selection."[43] As documentarist Günter Jordan (1998a: 113) recalls, word of mouth played an equally vital role: "I was one of the first Germans to view the new films produced in the USSR . . . (*The Bell of Chernobyl*; *Is it Easy to be Young?*) and I informed my colleagues about them . . . in order to put pressure on Moscow to have the films sent to the Leipzig Festival."[44]

The line of defense chosen in answering Seidowsky followed three rationales. The first clearly distinguished the categories in which films were programmed in order to try to diminish the importance of certain selections. Ugowski thus rebutted any accusation of having "failed politically." *Is it Easy to be Young?* had been programmed out of competition.[45] The second argument denounced a policy that aimed to silence and repress problems by censoring the incriminated documentaries. Ugowski again took the lead, asking,

"Should we no longer screen any films from socialist countries?" And festival director Ronald Trisch warned, "We certainly have not finished with critical films; if anything, the number of such documentaries will increase in the future." Finally, the third argument built on unanimous encouragement for developing the theme of ecology. Richard Ritterbusch emphatically declared, "We absolutely cannot accept the term 'green stuff.' . . . This is precisely the domain in which the program can be expanded."

Peter Ulbrich summed up the position of the majority of committee members thus: "Under current conditions, the selection was as good as it could be." After these very animated discussions in February 1988, those in favor of openness to the new trends seemed to have prevailed. The concept for the thirty-first Leipzig Festival endorsed the course chosen in 1987; in addition to the program's "political objectives and strengths" were added the "problems posed by safeguarding the diversity of nature and by the protection and conservation of the environment."[46] A film night was planned, devoted to films in the Information Section, but also to "films outside the norm [*Aussergewöhnliche Filme*]"[47] Audiences were thus able to watch the American documentaries *Chuck Berry, Hail! Hail! Rock'n' Roll* (1987) and *Sign o' the Times* (1987),[48] celebrating an unorthodox musical culture. Seidowsky found himself isolated in his call for the ideological retrenchment of the festival.

In early 1988, the festival thus found itself at a critical juncture, where each participating institution had taken a stand. These debates affected not only the Leipzig Festival but also the entire cinematic milieu that, echoing East German society as a whole, aspired to greater freedom of speech. Over the course of 1986 and 1987, filmmakers, including documentarists, had protested a great deal, demanding the right to openly discuss problems posed by the prevailing situation in the GDR and reform movements in the East (Beutelschmidt 1998). The fifth GDR Filmmakers' Congress would, they assumed, present an opportunity to openly discuss cultural policy in the GDR.

Originally scheduled for the spring of 1987, the congress had been deferred for a year, as authorities feared a repeat in the GDR of the debates that had animated the Soviet Congress in May 1986. It eventually took place from 19 to 21 April 1988. According to a note addressed to Kurt Hager, Secretary of the Central Committee, several documentary filmmakers were particularly virulent during the congress, going so far as to encourage the "use of the terms 'glasnost' and 'perestroika' in speaking of the evolution of society in the GDR."[49] Film director Dieter Schumann spoke enthusiastically in favor of developing a public sphere, the sole means to "create relationships of trust, the foundations of social life and the sense of belonging to a country [*Heimatgefühl*]" (Verband der Film- und Fernsehschaffenden 1988: 104). The debates, however, were sheltered from excessive publicity, taking place on the outskirts of East Berlin, where the foreign press had no access.

Ultimately, the congress represented a missed opportunity for the regime to initiate a public discussion with film directors. The documentary filmmakers nevertheless continued their attempts to engage in dialogue with the party. In July 1988, Erwin Burkert, president of the Documentary/Television Production Section of the Filmmakers' Union, invited Hager to discuss "international developments."[50] "Socialist film is on the move," he said. "Are we, too, moving in the same direction, or shall we remain apart?" More and more documentarists were eager to participate in the reforms set in motion in the Soviet Union and sought to convince their superiors.

The Stasi at the Festival

The 1988 edition of the festival took place under the strict control of state security organs—in accordance with measures set in 1985, regarding the "political and operative security of the Leipzig Week"—in order to prevent a repetition of incidents such as those of 1983.[51] The objective was to coordinate between the Leipzig branch of the Stasi and festival organizers. A liaison officer was appointed for the duration of each festival, in order to centralize information collected and orders given.[52] In addition to uniformed and plain clothes Stasi officers, unofficial collaborators and other temporary informants were mobilized. Orders were also issued to maintain "continual contact with key figures of the festival office."[53] Every day of the week, from 9:00 AM to 1:00 the next morning, a Stasi "operative"[54] manned a small projection booth located in the Petershof movie theater, on the same floor as the festival office.[55]

The Stasi paid particular attention to venues where public debates took place: the Petershof, the Capitol and Casino movie theaters, the Festival Club, the Thüringer Hof restaurant, and the Moritzbastei. Any "sudden irruption of activists or demonstrators" and all "writings or hate literature against the [East German] state" were to be prevented at these venues. The objective was to detect "the enemy's" plots as well as schemes to "disturb the festival." Western journalists were particularly affected and were well aware of it. Wilhelm Roth (1997: 88) recalls, "Whenever we wanted to discuss really important matters, we did it while walking or in a café, where we weren't at risk of meeting anyone from the festival leadership." This monitoring also affected the West German ARD/SFB and ZDF television and radio stations, which were covering the festival for only the second time, with some twenty delegates per channel.[56]

The Stasi's overriding fear, after all, was that contacts would be established between West and East Germans. They had to preempt groups linked to the "nonstate peace movement" from assembling.[57] Ten Days for Peace, focusing on prayers and meetings, again took place in Leipzig and elsewhere in the

GDR from 6 to 16 November 1988. Although the festival was not starting until 23 November, the specter of 1983 was on everybody's mind. The Stasi was also fearful that protest movements in East Berlin would spread to Leipzig; several opposition movements had launched an appeal for a day of action on 27 November as a gesture of solidarity with the students who had been arrested in the north of East Berlin.[58]

This appeal, however, risked diverting attention from the commemoration of the fiftieth anniversary of the Nazi pogrom known as *Kristallnacht* (the Night of Broken Glass), scheduled at the festival for the morning of 28 November.[59] In addition, this year weekly Monday prayers for peace would also coincide with the festival.[60] Finally, the Stasi seriously considered the possibility of physical attacks against leading East German political figures in attendance at the festival. In the end, such dreaded incidents did not take place—evidence either of the Stasi's effectiveness or of an overestimation of the risks posed, or most likely both. Above all, such protective measures reflected the deep anxiety and paranoia of the authorities, a fact that could hardly go unnoticed.[61] The Stasi's control over the festival did not, however, succeed in silencing discordant voices.

Selection Scandal

In 1988, the Stasi also closely monitored the unfolding of an overt crisis.[62] During a trip to Moscow, festival director Ronald Trisch had been presented with a selection of films chosen by Soviet documentary filmmakers and destined for the Leipzig Selection Committee. This time, all the films had been previewed beforehand at the SED ZK in the presence of Kurt Hager. Of the twenty-two documentaries proposed, only half remained after this preview; these were then handed over to the festival Selection Committee. Unaware that the films had been prevetted, the committee viewed them and retained ten of the eleven for the festival program.

The matter might well have ended there if, the day after the festival opened, eight of the twenty-seven Soviet delegates in attendance had not denounced the selection.[63] They even threatened to make the affair public: to write a dispatch to the Soviet news agency, TASS, and appear on a program on the West German ZDF television channel. The festival organizers were gravely concerned, and the programming director commented that they couldn't rule out an escalation of the affair—not only on the Soviet side but also on the part of the Selection Committee. In fact, committee members did denounce the maneuver and some resigned upon learning what had happened (Wisotzki 1993). The affair hardly remained a secret. West Berlin *Tageszeitung* correspondent Hans-Michel Peters went to the Selection Committee office to inquire whether the rumors circulating—that several Soviet films had been censored by authorities other than the Selection Committee—were true.⁶⁴ The committee members present reiterated the official version of events, according to which the rules had been respected.

This anecdote reveals that it was becoming increasingly difficult to turn a deaf ear to internal conflicts and debates. It also illustrates the importance of the presence of Western journalists at the festival, as well as the critical role they played in disseminating and publishing information that some wanted suppressed. In 1988, the West German media presence at the festival was indeed very substantial. ZDF television showed itself to be particularly aggressive, seeking to make as many contacts as possible among East German film directors and producers present at Leipzig, and they went so far as to demand that the festival board allow it to view one of the censored Soviet documentaries, for which it wanted to purchase broadcast rights.⁶⁵

Nor did diplomats remain indifferent to developments that were now clearly apparent. Information from the Stasi reported discussions in November 1987 between the West German government in Bonn and its permanent mission in East Berlin about policies to be followed with respect to the festival.⁶⁶ In concrete terms, the question for Bonn was whether or not to include the Leipzig Festival in the federal film funding law that was due for renewal.⁶⁷ The cultural attaché at the Permanent Mission of the FRG to the GDR had been attending the festival regularly since 1973.⁶⁸ In 1988, however, the Stasi attentively monitored the arrival of other FRG diplomats,⁶⁹ who not only attended screenings but also met artists who were part of Leipzig's "alternative scene." Most notable among these was a gallery opening organized at EIGEN+ART, one of the city's prominent art venues, launched in 1983.⁷⁰

The festival was thus increasingly attracting the interest of foreign observers. According to Stasi sources, the press attaché at the American embassy in the GDR spoke with festival director Ronald Trisch in an attempt to envisage the broader participation of American documentary filmmakers, such as Emile de Antonio, beyond the limited circle of independent filmmakers at Leipzig.⁷¹ The festival had indeed become one of the places where outside observers could get a sense of the atmosphere prevailing in the GDR, and hard-liners had to concede that they had not succeeded in regaining control over the festival in November 1988.

Programming: A Gaping Breach

Notwithstanding the dirty trick played on the Selection Committee, a new work by Estonian filmmaker Mark Soosaar, *Zhizn'bez* . . . (1987, *A Life Without* . . .), about one of the sixty-eight teen suicides in Estonia in 1987—was featured among the Soviet films in competition (Horton and Brashinsky 1992). This was sufficient to reveal that the breach that had been opened at the 1987 festival was far from sealed. Selections from other countries in the East Bloc bore witness to this as well. The Czechoslovakian entry was *Obrazy Stareho Sveta* (1972, *Images of the Old World*), by Slovak director Dušan Hanák,[72] which for many years had been censored for daring to expose an area and culture ignored by the rest of society.[73]

This documentary, of outstanding artistic quality, refuses to embellish the portrait of a mountain village abandoned by the world, where only elderly people live as the younger generation heads to the cities to work in factories. A remarkable montage alternates photographs and filmed sequences over a soundtrack that blends interviews and classical and contemporary music. This film received several awards at Leipzig, including the FIPRESCI Prize, which lauded the aesthetic quality with which "a world in the throes of extinction [is] revealed in all its beauty and all its horror" (*Protokoll 1988* 1989: 267) Screening this film in 1988 obviously had very special significance in that it revealed to what degree things had shifted, so that now this film could focus on the regime's failures and not its successes.

A short Vietnamese documentary, *Chuyen Tu Te* (1985–1987, *The Story of Kindness or How to Behave*), also made its mark at the 1988 festival. In this highly personal film essay, director Tran Van Thuy (Kersten 1995) pays tribute to his closest friend, a terminally ill cameraman who, over the course of his life, had to learn to distinguish "between the morality of the Party and a humanist morality" (Thuy 1988). The film had enjoyed great success in Vietnam, and the simplicity and clarity of its message also touched the public at Leipzig. When the commentary stated, "Many film directors do not care so much about truth and honesty in their films; they are more concerned about not shocking their superiors," a thunder of applause and calls of approbation swept through the Capitol theater (Evangelische Pressedienst 1988). The international jury did not remain indifferent either, for *The Story of Kindness* was awarded the Silver Dove (Dalos 1991).

Subversive Images of the GDR

In 1988, the leaders in East Berlin had wanted to prove that the GDR had, against all the odds, maintained its course and kept better control over the situation than its neighbors. The impact of developments in neighboring socialist countries, however, could only be partially curbed. In 1991, the former Hungarian opposition activist György Dalos observed, "In comparison with the SED regime, which propagated the most blatant lies until its collapse, Kádár's Hungary went from pure and simple non-truth to a tranquil half-truth." Nonetheless, as of the early 1980s DEFA documentaries contributed to the process that called the prevailing official discourse into question in the

GDR. Indeed, faced with the regime's rigidity, East German documentary film proved to be so dynamic and in the midst of such evolution that it succeeded in piercing the lead box in which the authorities were seeking to contain it. The program at the 1988 edition of the Leipzig Festival was the culmination of this process.

German History Revisited

Václav Havel commented in 1984 that, in the context of a totalitarian system, reflecting on the past in itself constituted an act of dissent, for it contributed to exposing the regime's foundation as mythological (Havel et al. 1989). In search of renewed legitimacy with respect to its population, the East German regime took advantage of the opportunity afforded in 1983 by the commemoration of the 500th anniversary of the birth of Martin Luther—also being celebrated in West Germany—to present a new reading of German history and a new patrimonial policy (Chaix 2009; François 2009). Certain documentaries also contributed, in their own way, to revisiting the GDR's national narrative.

In the GDR in 1985, commemorating the fortieth anniversary of the end of World War II represented an opportunity to revisit the official narrative, although this did not take place without animated discussion. In 1984, Karl Gass released *Das Jahr 1945* (*The Year 1945*), a project he had been planning for a long time but had shelved following the release of Mikhail Romm's *Ordinary Fascism* in 1965.[74] The film chronicles the year 1945, often using previously unreleased footage from Soviet archives. The impressive montage work is set off by a commentary by Klaus Wischnewski, one of DEFA's leading dramaturgs, who, like Gass, had survived the war. The seriousness of the subject matter does not lend itself to a heroic or enthusiastic presentation of the end of the war and the arrival of Soviet troops; the commentary sums it up: "Germany 1945—it is pure contradiction: mourning and hope, tragic and grotesque."

Reacting strongly to the film's tone and certain sequences, DFF cancelled the broadcast originally scheduled for 8 May 1985.[75] Specifically, Gass was accused of emphasizing the 11 June 1945 founding statement of the German Communist Party (KPD), which acknowledged the KPD's responsibility for having undermined the creation of an antifascist union against the Nazis before 1933. Under pressure from Erich Honecker and Kurt Hager, Gass had to agree to cut this offending sequence; *The Year 1945* was programmed for general release and viewed by two million viewers between May and November 1985.[76] Screened at Leipzig, it received the Silver Dove; according to Gass, it would have been awarded the Golden Dove, had it not been for DFF's intervention.[77]

While it is striking that *The Year 1945* does not touch upon the fate of the Jews, other film directors seized upon Jewish memory. In 1988, the festival organized an event commemorating *Kristallnacht*, despite protests by representatives of the Palestinian Liberation Organization (PLO). Three DEFA documentaries were screened: two devoted to the war and a third by Róza Berger-Fiedler,[78] titled *Erinnern heißt leben* (1987–1988, *Remembering Means Living*),[79] which proposed that the GDR undertake a renewed and more extensive reflection on the history of the Jews in Germany (Offenberg 1998).

Uprooted: East German Identity

In a similar vein, reflecting on the meaning of East German history and identity, other documentarists examined the ties binding the East German population to the GDR. Even though deeply imbued with elements of Nazi ideology, the concept of *Heimat*[80] had not entirely vanished in the GDR. During the 1970s, it even became something of a challenge for the regime to forge a sense of belonging in an East German *Heimat* (Wierling 2000). The gap between the manner in which people were experiencing this relationship and how the regime depicted it became increasingly pronounced, however.

A highly personal project, Kurt Tetzlaff's *Erinnerung an eine Landschaft— für Manuela* (1983, *Memory of a Landscape*),[81] powerfully illustrated this gap and struck a chord with contemporary viewers. Shot near Leipzig, the documentary explores the sprawling open-pit mining of a vast lignite basin, a "large field of ruins" (Spindler 1998; Tetzlaff 1984). To get the mine in place, the government had razed entire villages and relocated the residents to large, high-rise apartment complexes in the Leipzig suburbs. Following these residents over the course of two years, the film unambiguously bears witness to the suffering and upheaval wrought by the ravaged landscape and enforced departures. The new urban housing developments, one of the regime's flagship projects, appear sterile and bereft of life. *Memory of a Landscape* brought to light the fact that an ever-growing number of citizens was disposed to express its dissatisfaction in front of a camera. It was also the first DEFA documentary that jettisoned all symbolism and explicitly dared to broach the question of ecology and pollution in the GDR.[82]

Programmed at Leipzig even out of competition, films such as Tetzlaff's, which contributed to a rereading of the core themes in the official legitimization discourse, could find an audience—both East German and foreign—and timidly initiate debate on the issue.[83] More broadly, they helped to return the documentary genre to favor with East German cinemagoers. During the 1980s new spaces had emerged for socializing and self-expression, notably affiliated with Protestant churches at which screenings were organized.[84] Film clubs also experienced a resurgence starting at the end of the 1970s. From 1979 to 1989, no fewer than seventeen new film clubs opened in East Berlin, and documentary films were increasingly shown on their screens (Fritzsche

1994). Now films that the authorities refused to release in movie theaters or broadcast on television could sometimes still be screened for an increasingly eager public.

Youth on the Margins: whisper & SHOUT

The developments of 1988 thus only confirmed this trend, as well as the place that DEFA productions could assume in the new global landscape. The period's effervescence and people's desire to shatter their shackles, to transgress imposed limits, and open up to the world beyond were captured in two groundbreaking documentaries that won prizes at Leipzig in 1988: Dieter Schumann's[85] *flüstern & SCHREIEN* (1988, *whisper & SHOUT*), focusing on the East German rock scene, and Helke Misselwitz's *Winter Adé* (1988), a series of portraits of women from across the GDR.

Nearly two hours long, Schumann's *whisper & SHOUT* benefited from a large production budget from the DEFA Documentary Studio. The objective was to produce a film that would entertain the public and attract younger audiences to movie theaters.[86] With a freedom of speech and tone never before witnessed, Schumann's report covered concerts, followed young fans and musicians—from various rock groups, including Silly, Feeling B, Chicoree, and Sandow—and engaged them in conversation. Some of the groups were formally recognized in the GDR, while others—such as Feeling B—belonged more to an underground punk scene that was increasingly heard in the late 1980s, especially in Thuringia, Saxony, and East Berlin (Hintze 1999b). Conspicuous for the time was how frankly musicians, singers, and fans spoke on camera about their circumstances, their feelings, and their views on society. A young band member of Feeling B, complaining about the administrative procedures required to get married, concludes, "It's as hard to get married as it is to travel abroad. . . . [A smile.] Nooo, not that hard!" The long concert excerpts were also an event, testifying to an alternative and nonconformist music scene.

It was no secret that the regime was having trouble convincing young people to participate in mainstream East German society. In the 1970s and 1980s, not only the official FDJ youth group but also the trade unions and the SED found it increasingly difficult to integrate young employees and apprentices into the structures of the socialist enterprise. This disquiet was reflected in widespread professional instability, as well as in musical and fashion countercultures (pop music, discos, jeans, etc.; Kott 2000, 2001). Young women who did not stay long at the Wittstock textile factory, young punks crisscrossing the GDR from one concert to the next—in their own ways, all of these expressed their rejection of the imposed order and their determination to choose their own paths.

Figure 9.2. GDR rock icon Tamara Danz and director Dieter Schumann shooting *whisper & SHOUT* (1988). © DEFA Stiftung, Michael Lösche.

Previously, several DEFA films had also documented the malaise experienced by young people in East German society. Six years before Schumann's film, for example, documentarist Günter Jordan had made the short film *Einmal in der Woche schrei'n* (1982, *Yell Once a Week*). It is about young East Berliners—"aged eleven-, twelve-, thirteen-years-old. Old enough to understand," in the words of the commentary—who clandestinely attend a Pankow concert in a tiny venue. The rock group Pankow, formed in 1977, was noted for their provocative texts: "Always asking for permission, we no longer dare do anything, who wants to be kept on a leash? I want to think for myself, see for myself!" Jordan's documentary was immediately banned and not released until October 1989.

In an opening sequence in *whisper & SHOUT,* Schumann follows a group of punks in East Berlin and the concert that follows. A young punk in the audience, a hairdresser with oversized glasses, answers his questions very seriously: "I think it's good that our Minister of Culture allowed this concert to take place," she remarks. At the end she slips in, "I'd also like to add that we're not against this society, or against socialism. We're on the left. But we still don't always agree with everything." Schumann wanted to show that punks were not rightwing, as well as differentiate groups such as the self-styled "Red Skins"—who walked a line between leftwing and neo-Nazi thinking—from the others.

The young people in *whisper & SHOUT* long to express themselves without constraint, to dress and live as they wish, without straightaway being regarded as dangerous elements. In another sequence, a group of young people that the director runs into at a concert is filmed in the backyard of one of their parent's houses, drinking beer and playing croquet. Schumann is astonished: notwithstanding their leather jackets and mohawk hairstyles, he does not find them "very rebellious." The teenagers say that what they want above all is peace and to enjoy life. Their parents went through the war, had a tough life, another form of education. For them now, things are different; their ideology isn't the same. The film's penultimate sequence shows a girl returning home late from a Silly concert; she remarks that now that she's going to start

Figure 9.3. Still from D. Schumann's *whisper & SHOUT* (1988). © DEFA Stiftung, Michael Lösche.

working, she'll have to limit herself to going out only on Friday nights and weekends.

Throughout the film, morality thus remains intact. When *whisper & SHOUT* was released in movie theaters, its subject matter—which allowed it to attract fans of all the groups involved—and, more broadly, its freedom of tone assured it of a resounding success. And yet, the ideological shackles are still there, reining in every subversive and transgressive impulse.

Women's Words: Winter Adé

Schumann's documentary encapsulated the desire to break with the conformity of socialist society and to flout the codes imposed by the regime. The same year, Helke Misselwitz's[87] *Winter Adé* also raised themes of social marginality and exclusion, this time by giving voice to anonymous women throughout East Germany. Misselewitz went even further than Schumann, however, expressing a desire for liberation—first by granting women a platform to articulate their views, then by demanding, in the same breath, an opening up of East German society, and finally by inscribing her purpose within a universal dimension.

Misselwitz sets out her project in the opening sequence:

> At age forty, I once again leave the place of my childhood, to go see how other women have lived and what kind of life they would like to have. We will talk together, at their workplace, in their homes, or during random encounters. At times we will only get a glimpse of them, the women and girls of this country.

Misselwitz crisscrossed the country from south to north, shooting an authentic East German road movie. In contrast to Volker Koepp—who stayed in a single location for the duration of a shoot—she, like Schumann, chose this movement-based narrative form. The freshness of their films thus used a suitable formal structure, which symbolized their longing to bring an end to the stagnation of a system and push it to evolve. Misselwitz exhibited an intensely personal commitment as well. Her use of the first-person singular in the commentary and the parallel posed, from the start, between herself and the women she meets create a sense of strong complicity.

In the film, Misselwitz collects testimonies from women of different backgrounds and ages.[88] Each portrait helps to further reveal the deep fissures that cross East German society. Through these life stories—about family and professional lives, the place of women in "real existing socialism," the sense of political engagement, the reality of solidarity within society—the system itself is called into question. These women's critical utterances, not without humor, drain the regime's ideological foundations and dare to evoke taboo subjects, such as sexuality. Here, *Winter Adé* returns to a hallmark of DEFA documentary filmmaking.[89] The difficulties these women face in harmonizing their professional and private lives seem to make them more prone to testify to the shortcomings of the "advanced socialist society" touted by Erich Honecker. Whether in front of or behind the camera—even though women documentarists were rather scarce—it was women who ventured the most direct judgments about society.[90]

The portrait of Christine in *Winter Adé* is particularly illustrative of the significance of the film. The third stage of her journey brings the director to a coal briquette factory in Meuselwitz, where 37-year-old Christine Schiele has been working for a decade. In long, fixed shots, Thomas Plenert's camera captures the woman's work and then hesitatingly follows her along the factory corridors. Here, work is not an action embedded in a logical and dynamic process; rather, it dissolves in repetitive gestures whose meaning eludes us.[91] Christine, chained to a thankless task, does not meet a living soul at work. The factory is almost empty, sinister; the only sound is of hammers banging on pipes.

No spectacular action, just the daily reality of many women in the GDR. Although 80 percent of East German women of working age were employed in 1989, they were in the least skilled trades; despite the rhetoric in favor of gender equality, proclaimed in the GDR's various constitutions, their wages were also lower than those of men.[92] Misselwitz succeeds in desacralizing the image of the female worker in the sequence in which the camera lingers on the tired bodies of Christine and her co-workers taking a shower at the end of their workday. Without a word being uttered, the viewer feels how utterly exhausted these women are. Christine does not seem to feel fulfilled, either at work or in her private life: married at eighteen, divorced at twenty-three, the mother of two children. Christine was by no means exceptional in the GDR, where the divorce rate was remarkably high, and it was difficult to raise children alone on such a meager salary.

Misselwitz's documentary is somber, at times even despairing. And yet, it is precisely this despair, thus exposed in front of the camera, that gave the film its full force and revealed the changes taking place in East German society. It gripped the foreign critics and journalists who attended its preview screening at Leipzig; as West German critic Ulrich Gregor recalls, "It revealed that things were on the move" (Freunde der Deutschen Kinemathek 2000: 123).

"My mother gave birth to me in front of a closed street-level crossing barrier. In the ambulance." These words, with which Misselwitz opens her film, refer to the memory of a birth, a liberation, but are also immediately associated with an image of closure. On screen a street-level crossing barrier rises, allowing Misselwitz to set out on her journey toward new horizons. Images of trains accompany viewers through the entire film; railroad tracks cross, bifurcate, mirror the trajectories of women encountered over the course of this journey that ultimately leads to the edge of the Baltic. Erika, fifty-five years old and unmarried, lives alone with her two children. Deputy mayor of her district, she is in charge of a residential school for children with difficult family circumstances.

The cinematic perspective then widens little by little, to shots taken from the deck of a boat. The camera shoots a series of postcards, lined up on the windowsill of the cabin, that depict well-known portraits of women from art history, which are now added to the faces of Christine and Erika. The daily lives of these East German women are thus inscribed within a historical and geographical continuity, and their destinies assume a universal dimension. Underlining this new perspective, the camera pans toward the sea, toward an infinite horizon without barriers. Janis Joplin's rendition of "Summertime" accompanies these closing shots, hinting at the film's ultimate wish: a farewell to winter.

The documentary screened in competition at Leipzig in the large hall of the Casino Theater, with seats for a thousand. There it deployed its full force. Laughter erupted as audiences grasped the film's various ironic remarks.[93] That evening in 1988—one year before the collapse of the regime—the East German authorities suffered a serious defeat (Roth 1998). The Golden Dove was not bestowed on *Winter Adé*, however, but rather to *Kamerad Krüger* (1988, *Comrade Krüger*), a portrait of a former SS officer by Gerhard Scheumann and Walter Heynowski. This was the ultimate, heavy-handed attempt of orthodox forces at the festival to restrict the impact of films such as *Winter Adé*. The audience was not taken in, however, and gave Misselwitz a triumphant welcome when she went onstage to receive the Silver Dove.

The jury of the FIPRESCI Prize also bestowed an award on *Winter Adé* at Leipzig; and after the festival, the Academy of Arts awarded it the Konrad Wolf Prize (Heynowski and Scheumann 1997). The success of the film was thus established, and it reverberated strongly once it was released in theaters in January 1989, with over a million tickets sold in the first few weeks.[94] The documentaries of Misselwitz and Schumann were also singled out by West Berlin critics Ulrich and Erika Gregor and programmed as part of the Berlinale Forum in February 1989 (Freunde der Deutschen Kinemathek 2000). As history would have it, they also completed and virtually brought to a close the list of DEFA documentaries that would be hailed abroad.

The liberalizing perestroika movement, which permeated Eastern European socialist countries as of 1985, was rooted in developments initiated several years prior, which had as yet to find their true expression and their public. By dint of the global echo they afforded, the political, economic, social, and cultural upheavals of 1986–1988 made existing fault lines more visible, both nationally and internationally. Agitated by conflicting and intensifying tenden-

Figure 9.4. Helke Misselwitz awarded the Silver Dove in 1988; behind her stands Annelie Thorndike. © Filmmuseum Potsdam, Günter Linke.

cies, 1988 ended in great confusion in the GDR. On one hand, more and more voices aspiring to democratize society were emerging, while on the other, Erich Honecker continued to attempt to hamper any influence of Soviet glasnost. This led to odd contradictions: although East Berlin's USSR House screened Tengiz Abuladze's *Pokayaniye (Repentance)*, a reflection on Stalinist terror shot in 1984 and not released until 1986,[95] the Soviet Feature Film Festival—which had been held every October since 1973—was canceled. In November the Soviet magazine *Sputnik*—which devoted articles in its German edition to crimes perpetrated during the Stalinist era—vanished from the list of postal subscriptions.

The regime's attitude was incomprehensible to a very large portion of the population, reaching well beyond circles in opposition to the regime. For example, film historian Erika Richter was soon sporting a pro-Gorbachev sticker on her handbag[96]—although she admits to having been among those whom the system privileged, thanks in particular to her position in the International Federation of Film Societies (IFFS).[97] Indeed, the refusal of East German leaders to participate in the reform movement taking place to the East was becoming intolerable for an ever-growing number of people. It threatened to lead not only artists, who were increasingly impatient to express themselves and learn from major international developments, but also society itself into a deadlock. The success of films such as Misselwitz's *Winter Adé* could be a wake-up call for a regime finally willing to open its eyes to society's profound disillusionment, as easily as proclaiming the end of a depleted system.

Notes

1. The approach remains largely bilateral among studies devoted to the glasnost years and the liberalization of East Bloc societies—both in excellent works comparing different national processes (Deppe et al. 1991; Garton Ash 1989; Görtemaker 1994) and in those analyzing opposition developments and movements by means of an intertwined historical approach to different national experiences (Lutz 1999; on the GDR and Hungary, see Dalos 1995).
2. Aside from the reference work compiled by Liehm and Liehm (1989), works promising a comparative approach are largely nonexistent, and monographs are too often consecrated to fictional feature films. Exceptions include Hadeln 1990; Jeancolas 2001; Michalek and Turaj 1992; Tchernava 2014; Wach 1998; Zaoralová and Passek 1996.
3. See, in particular, *Aspects du cinéma soviétique 1987–1988*; Galichenko 1991; Godet 1991; Lawton 1992; Martin 1993; "Spécial cinéma soviétique" 1990.
4. The delegation was made up of Lothar Bellag, president of the GDR Filmmakers' Union; Hermann Herlinghaus, the vice-president; and Peter Ulbrich, first secretary.

5. Peter Ulbrich, Bericht über den Kongress des Filmverbandes der UdSSR, Moskau, May 1986, 30 May 1986, SAPMO-BArch DY vorl. SED/42307, p. 8.
6. Ibid.
7. Bericht über den Kongress des Filmverbandes der UdSSR, Moskau, May 1986, 30 May 1986, annex, SAPMO-BArch DY vorl. SED/42307.
8. Kurt Hager, Information für das Sekretariat des ZK, über die 29. Internationale Leipziger Woche vom 21. bis 27. November 1986, Berlin, 12 December 1986, SAPMO-BArch DY 30/J IV 2.906/35, p. 3.
9. Pavel Kogan (1931–1998) shot his first film in 1965. As a whole, his documentaries form an inviting gallery of portraits of Leningrad residents filmed in their daily surroundings.
10. In France, it was broadcast on television and shown in a few theaters. See Niney 1990b.
11. Kurt Hager, Information for the ZK Secretariat about the 29th International Leipzig Documentary and Short Film Week from 21 to 26 November 1987, Berlin, 8 December 1987, SAPMO-BArch DY 30/J IV 2.906/35, p. 3.
12. Ibid., 4.
13. Such as Jacek Skalski's *Portret Własny (Autoportrait)*.
14. It was shown in the Information Section (*Protokoll 1987* 1988).
15. Since January 1963, Hungarian production had been divided between four studios (or production units), which were called Budapest, Dialóg, Hunnia, and Objektív and mostly produced fictional feature films. From 1981 to 1985 a fifth studio also existed; Studio Társulás brought together filmmakers and social science researchers to develop documentary production. The reorganization of 1985 put an end to this studio. Beginning on 1 July 1985, a reorganization of production granted film studios more autonomy vis-à-vis the Ministry of Culture, paving the way for competition between them (Jeancolas 2001). Two years later, the studios became financially independent enterprises, in keeping with economic reforms being enacted in the country (Görtemaker 1994).
16. In 1984, Fero Fenič saw two films censored: his comedy *Dzusový román (Les années Schweppes)*, on the immobility of time fixed by socialism, and his documentary *Dedinský sen*, which focused on an older couple and was selected to screen at Leipzig.
17. "Order is made for idiots; an intelligent man would know how to handle chaos itself" (Müllerovà 1996).
18. Bericht über den Aufenthalt der Studiendelegation der Abteilung Kultur des ZK der SED vom 9. bis 13. März 1987 in der Ungarischen Volksrepublik, SAPMO-BArch DY 30/J IV 2.906/24, p. 1. The following citations are from the same document, pp. 4, 5, and 7.
19. *Rasputin* is about the considerable influence exerted by the famous monk from Siberia upon the family of Tsar Nicolas II. Made and immediately censored in 1975, the film was not released until 1981 at the festival in Moscow.
20. Bericht über den Aufenthalt der Studiendelegation der Abteilung Kultur des ZK der SED vom 9. bis 13. März 1987 in der Ungarischen Volksrepublik, SAPMO-BArch DY 30/J IV 2.906/24, p. 7.
21. Bericht. Aufenthalt einer Studiendelegation der PVAP unter Leitung des Genossen Andrzej Wasilewski, Sekretär des ZK der PVAP, vom 11. bis 13. Mai.1987 in der DDR, SAPMO-BArch DY 30/J IV 2.906/24.

22. On the distinctive role of the Church in the two countries, see Dalos (1995) and Tatur (1991).
23. Bericht. Aufenthalt einer Studiendelegation der PVAP unter Leitung des Genossen Andrzej Wasilewski, Sekretär des ZK der PVAP, vom 11. bis 13. Mai.1987 in der DDR, SAPMO-BArch DY 30/J IV 2.906/24, p. 4.
24. Ibid., 6.
25. See Jäger and Villinger 1997.
26. On the expatriation of intellectuals, see Dalos (1995).
27. The following citations come from the archival document BV Leipzig Abt II/6, Information 163/87, Inoffizielle Einschätzung zum Verlauf der Berlinale in West-Berlin, signed Schönley, Department Chief II/6, Leipzig, 12 March 1987, BStU BVfS Leipzig, Abt XX/269/04, p. 126–27.
28. From the FRG, there were Jean-Marie Straub's *Der Tod des Empedokles* (1987, *The Death of Empedocles*) inspired by Hölderlin, and Jeanine Meerapfel's *Die Verliebten* (1987, *Days to Remember*).
29. Even East German critics were not very kind to the film (Habel 2001).
30. The film print did not arrive for its first screening outside of the GDR until the day before the end of the Berlinale (Jacobsen 2000).
31. Komitee-Vorlage, BArch-FArch, Leipzig, 34/1977.
32. He repeated the conclusions about the festival of the State Committee for Television.
33. Protokoll der Komiteesitzung am 9 February 1988, Leipzig, BArch-FArch, Leipzig, 31/1988, p. 1.
34. Here he was alluding to the aforementioned films by Mark Soosaar and Pavel Kogan (Protokoll der Komiteesitzung am 9 February 1988, Leipzig, BArch-FArch, Leipzig, 31/1988, p. 2).
35. Ibid.
36. Gedächtnisprotokoll der Beratung am 25 February 1988, Berlin, 23 March 1988, BArch-FArch, Leipzig, 31/1988, p. 1.
37. Herz Frank's (1929–2013) documentary *Bez leģendām* (1967, *Without Legends*), which denounced the lies of official films, had been banned until 1970. *Augstākā tiesa* (1987, *The Supreme Judgment*) is about a prisoner on death row, whose fate, at the end, is more moving than that of his victim; is not the criminal essentially a victim of the society that formed him (Lawton 1992)?
38. Protokoll der Komiteesitzung am 9 February 1988, Leipzig, BArch-FArch, Leipzig, 31/1988, 7.
39. The Selection Committee was formed on the basis of the proposal presented to the Organizational Committee by the festival director; the list of people was then approved by the institutions that had to delegate someone to the task for a period of six weeks.
40. In 1987, Petra Tschörtner (b. 1958) replaced Rainer Ackermann (b. 1946), who had participated in the two preceding festivals.
41. The final choice fell to the Organizational Committee and the festival director, who could be pressured; see the case of films withdrawn from the program mentioned in previous chapters.
42. Richard Ritterbusch, author and dramaturg at the DEFA Documentary Studio, was president of the Selection Committee in 1978 and 1979 and then from 1983 to 1987.
43. Protokoll der Komiteesitzung am 9 February 1988, Leipzig, BArch-FArch, Leipzig, 31/1988, p. 3.

44. Jordan (b. 1941), who had been at DEFA since 1969, was a member of the Selection Committee in 1980.
45. Protokoll der Komiteesitzung am 9 February 1988, Leipzig, BArch-FArch, Leipzig, 31/1988, p. 2. The following citations are excerpted from the same document.
46. Klausurtagung des Komitees am 9./10.2.1988 zur Vorbereitung der 31. Internationalen Leipziger Dokumentar- und Kurzfilmwoche, BArch-FArch, Leipzig, 1988.
47. Ibid.
48. Taylor Hackford's *Chuck Berry* was also shown at West Berlin's Berlinale in February 1988.
49. Office of Kurt Hager, summary of the congress, unsigned, May 1988, SAPMO-BArch DY 30 vorl. SED/42307.
50. Erwin Burkert to Kurt Hager, 5 July 1988, SAPMO-BArch DY 30 vorl. SED/42314. The following citations are from the same document.
51. Dienstanweisung 1/85, VVS MfS 00008-5/85 über die politisch-operative Sicherung der Internationalen Dokumentarfilm- und Kurzfilm Woche, BStU BVfS Leipzig Abt XX/487.
52. BVfS Leipzig Abt. XX, Leiter der Abteilung, Wallner, Oberstleut., Massnahemplan zur Sicherung der 31. Internationalen Woche für Dokumentarfilm und Fernsehen, 1988, 18 November 1988, BStU BVfS Leipzig Abt XX/487, pp. 3–11.
53. In 1998, however, Ronald Trisch maintained that there was no "specific location reserved for the Stasi as such" during the festival (Gehler and Steinmetz 1998: 80).
54. BVfS Leipzig Abt. XX, Leiter der Abteilung, Wallner, Oberstleut., Massnahemplan zur Sicherung der 31. Internationalen Woche für Dokumentarfilm und Fernsehen, 1988, 18 November 1988, BStU BVfS Leipzig Abt XX/487, p. 11.
55. In an overview of a meeting in September 1989, Trisch gave assurances that the booth on the fourth floor would be reserved for the Ministry of Security. (Barré [IM de la Stasi], Information zur Vorbereitung und Durchführung der 32. Internationalen Dokumentar-und Kurzfilmwoche in Leipzig, 19 September 1989, BstU BVfS Leipzig Abt XX/489, p. 2.)
56. Abt. XX /7 [ge-ehr] an Abt. II, Journalistische Aktivitäten von BRD-Medien zur 31. Woche, Leipzig, 14 November 1988, BStU BVfS Leipzig Abt XX/487, pp. 62–63.
57. The author of the Stasi text uses quotation marks to define exactly the people and actions deemed to be "enemy."
58. High school students in Pankow had suffered extreme repression after having publicly expressed their hostility to the military commemorations of 7 October (Neubert 1997).
59. Every year the festival organized guided tours parallel to screenings. Foreign guests could thus visit sites such as model factories or the different memorial sites in the region, including the Buchenwald and Sachsenhausen concentration camp sites.
60. BVfS, Abt XX, Operative Lageeinschätzung im Vorbereitung der 31. Woche 1988, Leipzig 22 November 1988, BStU BVfS Leipzig Abt XX/487, pp. 55–56.
61. Stellv. Aufklärung, AKG, Oberst Brüning, Leipzig, 5 December 1988, BStU BVfS Leipzig Abt XX/487, p. 228.
62. Oberstlt. Wallner, Information zu Problemen und Aktivitäten mit Mitgliedern der sowjetischen Delegation zur 31. Internationalen Dokumentar- und Kurzfilmwoche, Leipzig, 28 November 1988, BStU BVfS Leipzig Abt XX/7, pp. 85–86.
63. All of them came from the Kiev region, which was very active in the perestroika movement.

64. Aktenvermerk, AWK, Leipzig, 30 November 1988, BArch-FArch, Leipzig, 31/1988.
65. Oberstlt. Wallner, Information zu Problemen und Aktivitäten mit Mitgliedern der sowjetischen Delegation zur 31. Internationalen Dokumentar- und Kurzfilmwoche, Leipzig, 28 November 1988, BStU BVfS Leipzig Abt XX/7, p. 86.
66. Information A/039962/20/11/87/Leipzig. Informationen aus Äusserungen von Holter, BMB, Ref. 5; Eilers, StV, BStU BVfS Leipzig Abt XX/00269/04.
67. According to this law, winning an award at an officially recognized festival qualified a West German director for federal support, as long as the film received the backing of the evaluation office in Wiesbaden.
68. Author's interview with Ronald Trisch, Berlin, Germany (11 March 2004).
69. BVfS Abt. II/3, Oberstlt. Schönley, Teilnahme von Diplomaten an der Leipziger Dokumentar- und Kurzfilmwoche, Leipzig, 23 November 1988, BStU BVfS Leipzig Abt XX/487, p. 90; Information 751/88. Einreise von Mitarbeitern der Ständigen Vertretung der BRD in den Bezirk Leipzig, Leipzig, 29 November 1988, BStU BVfS Leipzig Abt XX/487, pp. 97–98.
70. See Blume and März 2003.
71. Wallner, Leiter der Abt., Aufenthalt eines USA-Diplomaten im Bezirk Leipzig am 10. 11. 88, Leipzig 24.11.88 Abt II, BStU BVfS Leipzig Abt XX/487, pp. 88–89.
72. Hanák (b. 1938), a graduate of the FAMU film academy, was one of the main directors involved in the Prague Spring.
73. "In 1972, when a general apathy had overcome our country . . . , I found . . . creativity and an internal liberty in those older people whom the rest of society ignored. . . . Despite extreme social misery, they lived in real harmony with themselves and nature," recalled Hanák (1993: 43).
74. Author's interview with Karl Gass, Berlin/Kleinmachnow, Germany (8 August 2000).
75. Zum DEFA-Dokumentarfilm *Das Jahr 1945* von Karl Gass. Eindrücke von Genossen des Fernsehens und der Abteilung Agitation des ZK, die ihn gesehen haben, Berlin, 4 March 1985, unsigned, SAPMO-BArch DY 30 vorl. SED/42314.
76. To put this number in context, it is important to remember that the film was often projected as part of official and organized events commemorating the end of the war.
77. Author's interview with Karl Gass, Berlin/Kleinmachnow, Germany (8 August 2000).
78. Róza Berger-Fiedler was born in 1940 in Béziers in southwestern France. Her family, Polish Jews, had settled in Berlin after fleeing the pogroms at the turn of the twentieth century and left Germany in 1933. As a child, she was in an internment camp before being hidden in a Catholic cloister. In 1948, she was repatriated to Poland, but following a wave of anti-Semitism in 1957 she gained asylum in East Germany, where she studied German in Berlin. At DEFA as of 1966, she made her film debut in 1976.
79. Reading the different names on the tombstones in the Jewish Cemetery in East Berlin's Weissensee district brings to life the complex history of the centuries-old integration of Jews in Berlin. It was hard to get the project made; finally shot in 1987, it still had to wait until 1988 to be screened publicly. Correspondence between Róza Berger-Fiedler and Kurt Hager, SAPMO-BArch DY 30 vorl. SED/42314.
80. In German, this word conveys the deepest sense of home and belonging; it is usually translated as "home" or "homeland," or possibly "hometown."
81. Kurt Tetzlaff (b. 1933) worked as a dramaturg from 1952 to 1955 at the DEFA Studio for Educational Films. He then studied directing at the HFF from 1955 to 1960 and began at the DEFA Documentary Studio in 1961. A member of the Leipzig Festival

278   *Screened Encounters*

Committee from 1973 to 1984, he had already won several awards, including for *Die Kinder Palästinas* (1980, *The Children of Palestine*) in 1980.

82. Lignite mining made the Leipzig area one of the most polluted in the GDR, alongside Bitterfeld (Hofmann and Rink 1990).
83. Gitta Nickel had less success with *Manchmal möchte man fliegen* (1981, *Sometimes You'd Like to Fly*), shot in 1979 at the vast model construction site in the East Berlin suburb of Marzahn, which came across as an empty propaganda vehicle. The film was hardly screened at all.
84. The Association of GDR Film Clubs had been part of the International Federation of Film Societies since 1965 (Becker and Petzold 2001).
85. Dieter Schumann (b. 1953) worked as a sailor until 1976. He then worked in television, before studying to become a director at the HFF from 1978 to 1983, after which he worked at DEFA.
86. Abteilung Künstlerische Produktion, Zur Kinofilmproduktion 1988 im DEFA-Studio für Dokumentarfilme, Berlin, 3 March 1989, SAPMO-BArch DR1/4716, p. 3.
87. Helke Misselwitz, born in Thuringia in 1947, first trained as a physiotherapist from 1966 to 1969, then worked as a production assistant for television, then trained at the HFF from 1978 to 1982, before joining the DEFA Documentary Film Studio in 1983.
88. Hildred Kulmann (forty-two), economist in Berlin; Liselotte Schaller (seventy-three), dance school director in Altenburg, Saxony; Christine Schiele (thirty-seven), worker near Altenberg; Anja and Kerstin, two teenagers moving from one reformatory to another; Margarete Busse (eighty-five), living in a village in the Uckermark; Erika Banhardt (fifty-five), deputy mayor of a town on the Baltic coast; and others, who remained anonymous.
89. We can think of the women workers of Wittstock, or those in Jürgen Böttcher's films *Stars* and *Martha* (1978; Richter 2000).
90. We can cite Annelie Thorndike, Gitta Nickel, and Petra Tschörtner.
91. For eight hours a day, Christine knocks on the conduits that cross the factory in order to loosen any deposits that might block the evacuation of smoke.
92. See Kott 2000.
93. For example, when Hildred ironically describes the official meeting in which she discovered she was one of the only women present.
94. In 1989, the population of the GDR had reached 16.4 million inhabitants.
95. See Feigelson 2005; Lawton 1989.
96. Author's interview with Erika Richter, Berlin, Germany (1 November 2000).
97. In charge of Eastern Europe within the IFFS since 1978, Richter traveled a lot in socialist countries but also to Paris and Tunisia. In East Berlin, she worked with the cultural centers of different countries. The authorities were more willing to assign her such privileges given that she was openly supportive of the GDR and spoke English.

CHAPTER 10

Revolution on the Screen, on the Street

> On 10 November, the Wall had become a dance floor, a picture gallery, a bulletin board, a movie screen, a videocassette, a museum, . . . nothing but a heap of stone.
>
> —Robert Darnton, *Berlin Journal, 1989–1990*

The decade-long expression of protest movements contesting the official discourse reached its apogee during the summer and fall of 1989. The East German population then made its demands and its hostility to the existing system heard loud and clear. The city of Leipzig hosted the largest peaceful demonstrations in the country, echoing those in Dresden and East Berlin. East German intellectuals, including filmmakers, played an active role in this citizens' movement. Unlike the revolutions taking place in neighboring socialist countries, however, the collapse of the Berlin Wall on 9 November 1989 and the end of the SED regime did not bring an end to the upheavals in the GDR. The question of German-German unification arose very quickly, lending a new dimension to what, for most demonstrators, had been aspirations for reforms. The rapidity of this shift in perspective bewildered many East Germans, but most notably those very same intellectuals who had not considered that they might lose their country and were, for the most part, hostile to the intensifying process that led to German unification on 3 October 1990.

The Leipzig Festival was thus at the very heart of the tumultuous turning point—*Die Wende*—in the history of East Germany and Europe. Documentary filmmakers were swept up in the challenge of capturing history, of which they were a part, in the making. Comparing the 1989 and 1990 editions of the Leipzig Festival, however, allows us to grasp the prevailing dynamics of different stages in the final months of the East German state.

Figure 10.1. 1989: Street scene before the Capitol Theater. © Filmmuseum Potsdam, Reinhard Podszuweit.

"The peoples' struggles for their social and national liberation have finally caught up with the city that, for over thirty years, has offered them a platform to reach the entire world. Leipzig itself has become the center of a revolutionary movement," noted the Selection Committee for the thirty-second festival in 1989 ("Leipzig 1989" 1990). The organization of international events, such as the trade fair and film festival, as well as the city's highly dynamic alternative cultural scene also favored the political mobilization fueled by the region's particularly acute economic and social crisis.

Leipzig, Symbol of Peaceful Protest

Over the course of 1989, independent parties and organizations emerged against the backdrop of massive demonstrations and protest movements throughout the country. Public opinion was now being expressed outside of the official sphere (Feinstein 2002). Leipzig[1] became one of the most dynamic centers of protest.

St. Nicholas Church (Nikolaikirche) in the heart of Leipzig had been hosting Monday afternoon prayer meetings for peace since the early 1980s.[2] On 15

January 1989, an unauthorized silent march took place across the city on the occasion of the seventieth anniversary of the 1919 assassinations of Karl Liebknecht and Rosa Luxemburg, who had become emblematic figures among the opponents of the regime. Coming two days before a march planned in East Berlin, 160 people were arrested before the demonstration even started (Neubert 1997).

On 7 May 1989, municipal elections were held throughout the GDR. When the official results attributing 98 percent of the votes to the SED were released, a series of protests broke out countrywide. Over the course of May and June, Leipzig's weekly Monday gatherings increasingly turned into protest meetings. One slogan was to be heard everywhere: "We want out!" (*Wir wollen raus*). During the summer, the mass exodus of East Germans to Austria, via Hungary, assumed mammoth proportions. In April 1989 5,887 East Germans left the GDR, in May it was 10,640, and in August the figure rose to 20,955, with no fewer than 600 crossing into Austria on 16 August alone (Wendt 1991).

Following a brief recess during the summer, the Nikolaikirche meetings resumed on 4 September 1989. A new slogan emerged—"We're staying here" (*Wir bleiben hier*)—and the demonstrators were divided between those seeking reforms and those favoring the exodus. Among other changes, they left the shelter of the church and gathered in the adjoining streets. Numerous arrests were made.

In early October, public attention shifted from Leipzig to Dresden. Many East Germans, en route from the north and west of the GDR to cross into Czechoslovakia, found themselves stranded there on 3 October, when the East German authorities closed the border with its neighbor. Following violent clashes with the police, thousands of people demonstrated daily throughout the city. As tensions were reaching a bursting point on 7 October—which was the fortieth anniversary of the East German state—the police refrained from intervening. The demonstrators took advantage of this window of opportunity, and negotiations began. In a few days, the situation had shifted, and some felt the *Wende* began on 8 October in Dresden.[3]

In East Berlin, in which protests had been less active, several hundred demonstrators gathered in front of the Palace of the Republic on 7 October to applaud Mikhail Gorbachev during the official national commemorations. "Gorbi, help us!" could be heard from among the crowd. The following Monday's demonstration, in Leipzig on 9 October, was thus anticipated with great trepidation, as many feared a bloody government crackdown, like the one that had taken place in Beijing's Tiananmen Square just a few months earlier. It became the largest demonstration of all, bringing together 70,000 people.[4] The march proceeded along Leipzig's ring, which bypasses the city center, with participants chanting a new slogan—"We are the people" (*Wir sind das*

Volk) — and calling for nonviolence (Zwahr 2009). Against all expectations, the police and armed forces did not intervene; growing internal dissent within the SED leadership and government largely explains the attitude of the Leipzig Stasi. The significance of this event was beyond dispute; the way forward now seemed free, and the ensuing weeks saw the pace of the movement accelerate. In mid-October, the border with Czechoslovakia was reopened and the flow of emigrants started up again.

On 18 October, the SED's ZK relieved Erich Honecker of his duties — but this maneuver was not enough to prevent the regime's collapse. On 4 November, 500,000 people demonstrated peacefully at East Berlin's Alexanderplatz, representing the culmination of the protest movement that had chosen to give voice rather than exit the country (Hirschman 1993; Pfaff 2006). The author Christoph Hein (1990) paid tribute to Leipzig, calling it a city of heroes (*Heldenstadt*). Five days later, at a press conference on 9 November, Günter Schabowski, the politburo's secretary for political information and media, announced that GDR citizens wishing to cross into the West could obtain a visa to do so; improvising the rest in response to a journalist's question, he clarified that this should be possible as of the following morning. This announcement had an immediate impact: East Berliners rushed to checkpoints all along the Wall and, in the ensuing confusion, made their way to West Berlin by means of a simple stamp in their passport or identity card. The Wall had finally been breached.

Why Leipzig?

In February 1997, writer and publisher Erich Loest[5] sought to understand the role played by the Saxon city of Leipzig in the tumultuous events of 1989:

> As the beginning of an answer, one cannot but observe how much [Leipzig's] trade fairs, particularly the book fair, enabled the musty smell to disperse; the guests and their hosts would talk all night long about German topics, over a local beer or imported whiskey. . . . There the Wall had a crack. (Loest 2001: 51)

The fairs clearly played a significant role in creating a unique atmosphere in Leipzig. Other long-term developments, as well as social and economic factors, must also be taken into account, however.

The heavy industry that had been prioritized in Leipzig had not been accompanied by the requisite modernization. As early as the 1950s the city saw several publishers and printers, who constituted one of its traditional economic pillars, relocate to the West.[6] Leipzig topped the list of East German regions in terms of numbers requesting to leave for the West (Wötzel 1989). Finally, as Kurt Tetzlaff had highlighted in his 1983 documentary, *Memory of a Landscape,* environmental protection — a theme so central to the political demands of the 1980s—took on a special dimension in this particularly polluted and disaster-stricken area (Hofmann and Rink 1990).

Leipzig's potential for protest had also manifested on several occasions, for example, in demonstrations in favor of pop music in 1965 and in opposition to the destruction of the university chapel in 1968. The leaders of these protest movements, like those of 1989, were mostly young people, mainly students and intellectuals, whose field of experience was precisely Leipzig's specific cultural and artistic scene. The artistic milieu was indeed highly complex, at once recognized by the regime—in terms of painting, the Leipzig School had acquired an international reputation—but also a nexus for dissent, as well as with a hidden agenda in their dealings with local functionaries. From 15 November to 7 December 1984, in the midst of the documentary festival, the First Leipzig Autumn Salon was held in the trade fair's Ring-Messehaus Building, directly opposite the Capitol Cinema.

This first self-organized and self-financing exhibition to take place in such a prominent location allowed young artists to protest against the impossibility of expressing themselves within the officially sanctioned Association of Visual Artists (Verband Bildender Künstler der DDR, or VBK). Playing their hand very skillfully, the young painters had hoodwinked the authorities.[7] As Karl Gernot Kuehn (1997: 133) shows, the artists, especially photographers, discovered ways to increasingly circumvent the constraints imposed by the regime; "They used their imagination to that end. This is how the silent revolution took shape in the 1980s." In 1984, the SED retaliated by excluding two of the painters from decision-making bodies in the VBK; three other painters left the GDR soon thereafter (Blume and März 2003).

The Leipzig Documentary Film Festival, for its part, represented a much-anticipated rendezvous for the city's youth and students from Karl Marx University, who experienced it as a unique opportunity to come together, discuss issues at the students' club at the Moritzbastei for hours on end, and discover images of countries that remained inaccessible to them. The festival also offered the opportunity to work for a few weeks, all while coming into contact with foreigner visitors. In 1988, when the regime decided to drop public debates following screenings, it was precisely to put an end to a practice that contributed, even minimally, to the creation of a space for self-expression and public communication.

It should be noted, however, that in real terms the film festival solely concerned intellectual and student circles in Leipzig and across the nation: the working class was absent from festival venues. It was only with the development of the Monday demonstrations that the protest movements integrated workers; until then, they had had nowhere to express themselves, given that the once powerful Social Democratic trade union movement had been crushed under Nazism and then again under the Stalinization of the 1950s.

Once the demands of oppositional forces united within religious movements merged with those of workers, the situation became very critical for the regime (Hofmann and Rink 1990).

Filmmakers Face the Wende

In this chain of events, the vast majority of East German intellectuals—such as Kurt Masur, Kappellmeister of the Gewandhausorchester in Leipzig—were quite active, lending their voices to the population's demands and participating in the demonstrations. Many theaters opened their doors to debates at a time when the official media still remained tight-lipped about what was happening (Segert 2003). Writers, in particular, enjoyed a renewed popularity and regularly participated in various demonstrations and public discussions, such as the one that took place in East Berlin on 4 November; but filmmakers were not to be outdone.

In January 1989, the SED secretary at the DEFA Documentary Studio sent a letter to Ronald Trisch, informing him of discussions in Babelsberg concerning the November 1988 festival.[8] The tone was very critical. The competition program had been of scant political or artistic interest. Moreover, given that in recent years the festival had demonstrated that documentary films were attracting a growing number of young viewers, it was all the more regrettable that discussions and round tables had been discontinued; it was a "politically questionable decision." Demands were not only for a "more democratic and more transparent" allocation of seats but also for greater participation of members of the studio. The party secretary did welcome the fact, however, that these internal conflicts had not been made public in a strained atmosphere following the East German ban of the Soviet magazine *Sputnik* and of five Soviet feature films.[9]

On 21 and 22 October 1989, the GDR Filmmakers' Union leadership made a series of decisions, which it then transmitted to the East German news agency ADN ("VFF" 1989). Following nine hours of intensive discussion regarding the political situation, particularly having to do with the media, the union called for an extraordinary congress; this was a follow-up to the proposal put forward by the Association of Theater Workers (Verband der Theaterschaffenden), a union of artists and scholars working in theater, to form working groups in order to discuss new functions for artistic unions in a society expressing new expectations. Moreover, they demanded that the interests of the party and those of society be considered as distinct. Freedom of the media needed to be applied by implementing instruments of democratic control.

DFF had to open a direct dialogue with those who desired it and to immediately give national and foreign documentaries access to its channels. DEFA and the Film and Television Academy in Babelsberg (HFF) should encourage the production of programs on current affairs and events in the country. Finally, the Filmmaker's Union demanded a series of rehabilitations, notably that of Walter Janka, who had been managing director at DEFA from 1948 to 1950 and a victim of the GDR's Stalinist show trials in 1956; in a similar vein, a working group was tasked with identifying censored movies and television films, which should be brought into circulation.

As a hopeful sign that their demands would be met with openness, union leadership decided to organize an international documentary film symposium in the GDR. Glasnost—the transparency sought by their Soviet colleagues— directly inspired East German documentarists, ever eager to participate in the international process. In the USSR, however, documentary film played an important role in the formation of civil society and free public opinion, which was under way. On 23 March 1989, the first International Documentary Film Festival in the USSR had been organized by the Soviet Filmmakers' Union (Roberts 1999). The gold medal was awarded to *Vstrechnii isk* (1989, *The Meeting Campaign*), which documented Belarusian writer Ales Adamovich's campaign for a public monument to the victims of Stalinism.

With emotions running high, the intense debates at DEFA sought to determine what attitude to adopt in face of the prevailing upheaval. On 11 October 1989, upon their return from the National Documentary Festival in Neubrandenburg, some documentary filmmakers took the initiative to go film the events that were turning their country upside down (Hecht 1996). It was a question of refuting the silence of DFF state television, which was refusing to cover the demonstrations. The attitude of this group of documentarists represented a veritable revolution within the studio, which had made no move in response to the 1953 uprising, the construction of the Wall in 1961, or events in Prague in 1968.

Finally—and this was perhaps the clearest sign of the profound changes that were taking place—the managing director of the DEFA Documentary Studio gave permission to different crews to go film events live. In question was the practice of documentary filmmaking in the original sense of the term: to produce documents that witnessed the times in which they were living. For these DEFA filmmakers, the Soviet example—which many had discovered at the 1987 Leipzig Festival—was ultimately decisive in convincing them to undertake such an initiative. Only ten or so of them made this choice, however; the overwhelming majority of their colleagues decided to continue working on ongoing projects, irrespective of current events.

Students in the Field

At the HFF, a "euphoric" phase had begun in 1986 with the appointment of Lothar Bisky as rector (Löser 1996). Bisky was among those who spoke in front of an enormous crowd, at Alexanderplatz in East Berlin on 4 November 1989. He had advocated developing teaching methods that would stimulate and not hinder students' creativity. Encouraged by Gorbachev's reform policies, he in fact implemented numerous fundamental changes at HFF. In concrete terms, thematic constraints were no longer imposed on students, and they were now allowed to attend the international festivals for which their films had been selected. Freedom of creation and movement, ensuring freedom of communication with foreign colleagues—the significance of such reforms was paramount. Bisky also pledged to personally defend two students threatened by the Stasi.

In an interview conducted at the end of November 1989, Bisky (1989) stated that he had learned a great deal about East German society through his contact with students, who had introduced him to novel aesthetic perspectives, among other things. He also noted that East German media production and research risked no longer having a role in the international arena, unless policies were altered. The first challenge was to revive trust between the viewer and various media; unless the media swiftly gained credibility and effectiveness, socialism would be in grave danger. A socialist policy in this field should be as follows: the media should consider viewers to be rational people and seek to steer them toward humanist, democratic, and socialist values—without hesitating to also produce pure entertainment.

Over the course of the summer and fall of 1989, students mobilized. On 9 October, in a resolution made public, a general assembly demanded freedom of the press, opinion, and assembly; the release of prisoners; public debate; and media freedom (Jäger and Villinger 1997). HFF crews were given permission to film the events that were unsettling the GDR. Three films captured images from this epoch-making fall: *Zehn Tage im Oktober* (1989, *Ten Days in October*), by Thomas Frick; *Makulatur 7/10/89* (1989, *Waste Paper 10/7/89*), by Kerstin Süske; and *Deutschland ist so gross und so schön* (1989, *Germany Is So Big and So Beautiful*), by Jana Püchner. Televised images, however, remained under the tight control of regime hard-liners until 7 November.

On 17 November 1989, Hans Modrow became the premier of a new government, comprising seventeen ministers affiliated with the SED and eleven belonging to other parties within the national bloc. Demonstrations in Leipzig did not cease, however, and on 18 November, the New Forum (Neues Forum) organized its first meeting there. On 23 November, Frank Beyer's 1966 feature film *Trace of Stones* was screened in public—some twenty-three years after it had been banned—at the spacious International Cinema on Karl Marx Allee. At the screening, Egon Krenz—Erich Honecker's successor as head of the SED—saluted Beyer and the film's leading actor, Manfred Krug, who was in the GDR for the first time in thirteen years. The following day, on 24 November 1989, the thirty-second edition of the Leipzig Festival opened.

The 1989 Leipzig Festival amid Turmoil

At the 1989 festival, East German documentaries garnered attention as never before, and the city of Leipzig, which had mostly served as a backdrop in the past, now occupied center stage. Audiences discovered the latest DEFA films, some still unfinished due to the acceleration of events. On screen there suddenly appeared what had previously been lacking in DEFA documentaries: a sense of insolence and aggressiveness (Roth 1995). Discussions centered on the reforms that had led to the opening of the Wall on 9 November and the highly controversial prospect of German unification.

The festival itself was experiencing the uncertainties of transition, trying to adapt to events that each day brought new elements to the debate and new images of a society in turmoil. Decisions were made in a hurry, indicating a certain confusion within the festival leadership, which was overwhelmed by all that was happening just meters away. At the same time, the festival's program represented a culmination of trends that had been under way for several years.

Instead of the usual interminable official speeches at the opening of the festival, festival director Ronald Trisch read a brief statement, written the day before by the ten members of the Organizing Committee.[10] In it, the committee announced its collective resignation at the end of the current edition, in the wake of internal disagreements about the history and future of the Leipzig Festival: "The history, situation, and prospects for the Documentary Week are perceived and evaluated differently by given committee members. Their request to resign must leave the organizers free to find a structure which, freed from past political constraints, will ensure the future of this important festival" (*Festival Bulletin* 1989).

Internal tensions—which had coexisted within the festival leadership in recent years, triggering both the opening up of 1987 and the ensuing nervous retreat of 1988—became increasingly radical. Now a choice had to be made as to which path to follow. The committee brought together different factions: DEFA directors who, through their respective films, had demonstrated an engagement with the social role of documentary film—Kurt Tetzlaff, Gitta Nickel, Roland Steiner—DFF directors, who obeyed an entirely different rationale; critics such as Horst Knietzsch; and well-known public figures who were closely associated with the festival—such as Annelie Thorndike and Ronald Trisch, who had themselves advocated both openness and withdrawal at different moments.

In fact, however, the festival that opened in November 1989 had already undergone several revolutions that were far from insignificant. Not a single member of the SED politburo attended the opening evening.[11] For the first time, the president of the jury was not an Eastern German, but rather the

French film director Jean-Daniel Simon, former president of the French Filmmakers Union and the Lille International Film Festival. Films from the HHF film academy were finally integrated into the festival's main program, with the exception of the documentaries dealing with the latest events in the GDR.[12] The retrospective also constituted another first: it was devoted to a DEFA documentary filmmaker, Karl Gass, a cofounder of the festival who had been quickly relegated to the backseat by his rival Andrew Thorndike.[13]

Konrad Weiss's Tribute to Karl Gass

As with all the festival's retrospectives over the years, a catalog was published devoted to the work of Karl Gass and featuring testimonials of those who had worked with him. The text by film director Konrad Weiss (1989) — which was not selected for inclusion in the catalog — was nevertheless distributed to festival participants with the following comment: "In light of political developments in recent days, this contribution strikes us as being of such importance in characterizing Karl Gass that we decided to print and distribute it separately."

In order to grasp the significance of this text, we must revisit the trajectory of its author. Born in Silesia in 1942, Weiss belonged to the populations of German origin who lived in territories to the east of current-day Germany and were displaced toward the west at the end of the war. He grew up in the southern part of the GDR. Raised by his mother, who made a living cleaning houses, Weiss was classified as part of a bourgeois social element, due to the fact that his father, who had died in 1945, had been a functionary. As a young man Weiss, a committed Christian, was forbidden from enrolling in high school and from taking the baccalaureate exam.[14] He trained as an electrician, but in 1962 enrolled in a lay program at the Görlitz seminary, after which he worked at the Catholic Office for Pastoral Counseling (*Seelsorgeamt*) in Magdeburg until 1965. In the evenings, he attended adult education classes and passed his baccalaureate in 1965. Then he applied to the film school in Babelsberg.

In the fall of 1965, the documentary filmmaker Karl Gass was just arriving at the HFF himself, with the intention of implementing a project that was close to his heart: a special curriculum for documentarists that included training as both film directors and cinematographers.[15] Among the students who were to form this class, Gass chose Volker Koepp and Konrad Weiss. According to Weiss (1989), it was his tortuous journey that convinced Gass to choose him — as well as the ambition he clearly expressed during their first interview: "to make films as a Christian under a socialist regime."[16] Courses began in January 1966, just after the Eleventh Plenum of December 1965 had set off an extensive wave of censorship that marked the first years of the young filmmaker's studies.

Gass ensured that his students enjoyed a highly privileged situation within HFF, enabling them—unlike other students—to shoot their own short films and to participate as of 1966 in the making of *Vietnam,* produced by the GDR Solidarity Committee; Weiss shot an episode titled *Vietnamese Passion,* with explicitly Christian undertones. Bringing his colleagues from the studios to the film school, Gass also had his students meet with experienced professionals. Winfried Junge showed them the first episode of the *Children of Golzow,* and Jürgen Böttcher *Barefoot and without a Hat.* Gass also accompanied them to the Leipzig Festival, where, thanks to him, they could talk with the likes of Joris Ivens or the Estonian playwright and scientist Alexander Dymschitz. "No taboos and no apprehension, despite the rules at the time," observed Weiss.

After the intense collaboration of the first year, relations between Gass and his students became more strained. In 1968, most of them found themselves under close surveillance by the Stasi. Koepp, for example, was among those students accused of internal agitation and had his diploma film banned. In 1995, he quoted from his Stasi file:

> We suspect some students of wanting to create a platform to impose their demands against socialist democracy and socialist cultural policy. A close relationship exists between Thomas Brasch and students Roland Bischoff, Volker Koepp, Alexander Ziebell, and the Catholic student Konrad Weiss, with whom they ideologically agree to a significant degree. (Koepp 1995: 152–53)

That Gass's experiment was not renewed after 1969 can undoubtedly be put down to the forceful personalities of his students; the crushing of the Prague Spring in 1968, which led to a hardening of regime policies, did not help matters. Gass subsequently returned to his artistic production group (KAG), Gruppe Effekt.[17] East German documentary filmmaking thus did not benefit from a privileged training facility, such as the Béla Balász Studio in Budapest, which greatly affected Hungarian cinema from 1961 onward.

Weiss's 1989 accolade for Karl Gass drew a sensitive and nuanced portrait that could never have been published before 1989. It reflected not only the profound diversity that existed among DEFA documentarists but also the sense of complicity and respect that brought many of them together amid complex relationships. Gass, the director of *Look at This City* and *Oktober kam ...* (1969–1970, *October Came ...*)[18]—films at the service of the regime's offensive discourse—but also of *Leisure,* was thus shown, in the end, to have enabled a critical generation of DEFA documentarists to assert themselves.

Weiss subsequently directed documentaries that conveyed a sensitive image of East German society, without concealing its fault lines or weaknesses.[19] As of 1985, he articulated his political commitment outside the studio, writing for the West German daily *Die Zeit,* Polish publications such as *Polityka,* and various samizdat—underground publications distributed by hand—in the

GDR. Weiss started actively participating in the East German protest and opposition movements in 1988,[20] and in September 1989 he helped found the Democracy Now citizens' movement, whose objective was to think through the democratic evolution of the GDR (Neubert 1997). Twenty-one years later, at the end of a protracted process, the Catholic student at the Babelsberg film school, placed under surveillance by the Stasi in 1968, thus participated in the transformation of the regime.

Images of the Revolution

In the festival program of November 1989, the theme that attracted the largest audiences was undoubtedly this mobilization of the East German population to overthrow a forty-year-old system. The festival's opening night featured a screening of *Leipzig im Herbst* (1989, *Leipzig in the Fall*), with its images of a revolution in process, a mere stone's throw away from the movie theater. As of 11 October, a group of young DEFA documentarists received permission to take part in the ongoing revolution, forming three production units: Andreas Voigt and Gerd Kroske went to Leipzig and Lew Hohmann and Joachim Tschirner went to East Berlin, as did Hans Wintgen and Jochen Denzler. Meanwhile, documentarist Róza Berger-Fiedler filmed alone in Dresden, as did Georg Kilian in Leipzig. Their films were to become valuable audiovisual records of East Germany in the fall of 1989.

Figure 10.2. Still from A. Voigt and G. Kroske's *Leipzig in the Fall* (1989). © DEFA Stiftung, Sebastian Richter.

Directors Andreas Voigt and Gerd Kroske thus took to the streets of Leipzig, as well as those of Dresden and Berlin, with a cameraman, microphones, and cameras, during the massive Monday demonstrations from 16 October to 7 November. Shot with 35mm cameras in black-and-white, *Leipzig in the Fall* is striking for the energy that emanates from it. A broad section of society spoke in front of the cameras: anonymous demonstrators, a city councilor, a street sweeper, the founders of the New Forum, theologians, young police conscripts and police officers, a SED functionary, and so on. "Leipzig in the fall: the silence is over!" was how the article on the film in the festival's *Bulletin* summed the matter up (Lux 1989).

The image is certainly bewildering: the film was shot mostly at night, with dim lighting, and under constant threat of a possible crackdown by the police. The sound quality is poor: interviewee responses and slogans were caught on the fly. These imperfections, however, only augment the emotional force created by the images. The anguish and hope, the courage of the demonstrators, as well as of the film crews in these extraordinary moments are delivered to us in an unadulterated state. During the animated public discussion that followed the festival screening, the audience was divided. Some confessed an impression of utter turmoil in the face of developments. Others felt the film had tried too hard to furnish an objective point of view, suffocating the emotion that was still palpable in the streets of Leipzig.[21]

Lothar Bisky (1989) — who was still rector of the Babelsberg film school but had in mid-November also become the director of the Culture Department of the SED ZK — commented, "At this point in time, classes are mainly taking place in the street." He accompanied to Leipzig a series of films shot by his students, to which a special session was devoted. In early October, three films crews had formed at the school, which had access to the equipment best adapted to shoot the demonstrations: one unit shot a video in Leipzig, and the two other units went with 16mm cameras to East Berlin and Dresden, respectively (Rümmler 1990).

Interventionist video — a genre often overlooked in the history of cinema — played a crucial role in activist documentary media of the late 1970s and early 1980s (Fleckinger 2011; Löser 2011; Mignot-Lefebvre 1994). While the Leipzig Festival had heralded the way forward in the GDR by organizing the first "video workshop," this only took place in 1985 and was only on a modest scale.[22] The delayed emergence of video as a documentary tool in the GDR was a result of the mistrust felt by the authorities and certain film directors accustomed to another cinematographic language.[23]

Nevertheless, the emergence of video as an audiovisual medium at the festival offered hope to champions of a form of documentary that fostered reflection, as well as to defenders of a festival conceived as a space for individual expression and collective dialogue within East German society. Video experiments gathered momentum as of 1987, when, faced with a growing number of foreign films shot on video, the festival included the format in their selection of competition entries.[24] In 1988, the East German videos programmed ranged from commissioned works to artistic ciné-essays.[25] A year later, spectators could watch East German videos shot predominantly by students from the HFF or young East German journalists. Finally unshackled from any aesthetic and ideological restraints, they filmed events that were about to engender political and social turmoil throughout their native land. A history of the video format in the GDR that would connect the pre- and post-1990 periods remains to be written.

In contrast to *Leipzig in the Fall,* which seemed much more level, *Aufbruch '89 Dresden* (1989, *New Beginning Dresden '89*), *10 Tage im Oktober* (1989, *10 Days in October*), *Es lebe die R . . .* (1989, *Long Live the R . . .*), and the other student films stood out for their energy and their extreme rawness; *Waste Paper 10/7/89* was even screened despite being unfinished. In these films, students had dared ask inconvenient, disturbing questions, for example about the fate of arrested protesters, at a moment when Erich Honecker was still in office and the outcome of events was still highly uncertain.

Long Live the R . . . was shot on video under the direction of Jörn Zielke. Students received authorization to shoot on 13 October. They were the first East German film crew to shoot inside the Gethsemane Church in East Berlin, a meeting place for many protesters and members of the opposition. On 16 October, the crew set out for Leipzig. SED and FDJ functionaries, a professor of philosophy, a co-organizer of the Monday prayers for peace—each spoke in front of the camera, each offering a distinct reading of the situation. On 18 October, permission to film was suspended, as Egon Krenz became the new leader of the SED and the regime. Notwithstanding, the students continued to shoot. At Leipzig in November, the International Jury awarded an honorary Golden Dove to *New Beginning Dresden '89, Long Live the R . . .* and *Ten Days in October.* The international jury also unanimously decided to award a "symbolic prize"—the Leipzig Dove '89—to *Leipzig in the Fall,* which was programmed out of competition—thereby seeking to express "its solidarity and empathy toward the people of the GDR, who are undergoing a process of revolutionary renewal" (*Special Festival Bulletin* 1989).

Echoes of Other Revolutions

These films reminded Western journalists and critics of documentaries of 1968 (Roth 1995). Whereas 1968 had been inspired—notably in its documentary expression—by its anticapitalist tenor, 1989 in the GDR articulated a more or less acknowledged attraction to the capitalist society of Western neighbors. Nevertheless, the political, ideological, and artistic effervescence of 1968 was an important precursor to the 1989 movement (Arrighi et al. 1997). The activists of 1968 had condemned not only the capitalist system but also the old entrenched left: the Social Democrats in the West and the Communists in power in the East. None other than Alexander Dubček, the Czechoslovakian leader during the Prague Spring, emphasized the similarities he observed between Gorbachev's policy reform and the policy that he himself had sought to implement in 1968. However, the particularly deep economic and financial crisis facing the GDR in 1989 clinched a radicalization of the situation that had not occurred in 1968. Above all, this time the desire for change originated within Soviet society and not in a satellite country—a very big difference, particularly for the reach of national movements.

In Leipzig, the East German revolution did not entirely overshadow the upheavals taking place in other socialist countries. During this unsettled and unsettling period, contacts with other countries in Eastern Europe assumed an even greater importance, in particular with regard to the exchange of experiences and ideas. The Leipzig Festival hosted the meeting of the Central European Regional group of the International Federation of Film Societies (IFFS).[26] Eva Kacerová, a Czechoslovakian, was elected as the new secretary, replacing Erika Richter, who had held the post since 1978 (Becker and Petzold 2001). Nevertheless, the festival program rarely included images from the revolutions going on to the east.

A report from Czechoslovakian Television, *Prague, Day of Filming 23.11.1989*, was screened as part of the festival's video workshop.[27] It retraced the latest developments in Czechoslovakia's "Velvet Revolution," which succeeded in bringing down the communist regime in less than a fortnight. On 17 November 1989, riot police had brutally suppressed a demonstration on Wenceslas Square in central Prague, triggering the increased mobilization of the population (Reichardt 2003; Segert 2003). On 21 November, Václav Havel—the spokesperson of the newly established Civic Forum—was received by the prime minister. The remainder of the televised report covered events still taking place as the Leipzig Festival opened: on 24 November the Central Committee of the Communist Party of Czechoslovakia resigned; on 27 November all political prisoners were released; and, on 29 November 1989 the principle of party monopoly was removed from the constitution, and reforms were announced.

Intellectuals played a pivotal role in this chain of events and the ensuing democratization of Czechoslovakia. The Civic Forum had been founded in a Prague theater around the figure of the internationally renowned author and playwright Havel; one of the leading opposition figures against the regime, he was subsequently elected president of Czechoslovakia in December 1989. In the GDR, the role of intellectuals—who since 1945 had conceived of their function as highly political but who were also closely aligned with the official themes of antifascism and pacifism—was also very critical during the upheavals in the fall of 1989. After the Berlin Wall opened, they maintained a greater distance from political events, however.

In contrast to their Polish and Czechoslovakian neighbors, the ouster of Erich Honecker and the collapse of the government in fall 1989 did not signify the end of the transition for East Germans. The national question remained unresolved, giving rise to the possibility of the unification of East and West Germany. The issue was particularly debated at Leipzig—in part because of when it was being held at the point that the dissident slogan "We Are *the* People" became "We Are *One* People"—but also in relation to certain documentaries that prolonged debates that had started on the city streets.

The Challenging Question of German Unity

The problem posed by the national question raised as many hopes as fears among Germans in both the East and the West. The festival was profoundly riven on this subject. A documentary by Roland Steiner[28] most clearly addressed the issue, which had been suppressed for forty years. *Unsere Kinder* (1989, *Our Children*), broke one of the dominant taboos in the GDR by focusing on people excluded from mainstream East German society: rightwing radical punks and skinheads who had been excluded from the media. They were not unfamiliar to the population, however; in 1987, Konrad Weiss had written an article in the underground paper *Kontext,* titled "The New Age-Old Threat: Young Fascists in the GDR," which had evoked a strong response in circles sensitized to the subject (Weiss 1989).

In the early 1980s, Steiner shot several films about young people that the authorities disapproved of, due to their freedom of tone, most notably on the issue of the Wall. These films ultimately had to be reedited, and Steiner went through a profound crisis (Schieber 1996). With the support of Horst Pehnert, director of HVFilm, in 1986 he started work on a new project devoted to neo-Nazis. It was difficult to film skinheads: they did not always agree to speak in front of the camera, and the authorities did not recognize their existence. While filming, the crew was thus placed under surveillance and they sometimes arrived to find that streets had suddenly been blocked off (Steiner 1989). Steiner nevertheless succeeded in completing the film, with support from the minister of culture—a turn of events that indicated that party hard-liners were no longer all-powerful.

The film's very title, *Our Children,* appealed to viewers to no longer close their eyes to a phenomenon that was an integral part of East German society. "This film is a plea to encourage listening better, seeking to understand, discussing things openly before it is too late," announced the commentary. The film attempted to show a complex situation: the punk band Rote Front

Pankow had proclaimed itself in favor of Gorbachev's perestroika policy and denounced the GDR's lack of freedom of the press; their terribly extreme remarks—such as calling for "incinerating foreigners in the ovens, like the Jews"—were presented as an ultimate attempt to express their radical opposition to the regime. Steiner invited viewers to consider that not just young people but society at large was responsible for this violence.

In this sense, *Our Children* joined several Soviet glasnost films, such as the Latvian documentary *Is It Easy to Be Young?* by Juris Podnieks, which had screened at Leipzig in 1987.[29] *Our Children* did not confront the problem of physical violence, however, limiting itself primarily to the verbal violence of these young people. In general, racism leveled against foreigners in the GDR remained one of the most taboo topics in the land of international solidarity and was studied only later, as part of GDR history (Behrends et al. 2003; Müller and Poutrus 2005). At Leipzig, *Our Children* was awarded a Silver Dove, tying with Michael Moore's documentary *Roger & Me* (1989).[30] Discussions following the screening revealed anxieties felt by many spectators at the festival.

On 20 November 1989, as mentioned above, participants in the regular Monday demonstration introduced the first slogans in favor of German unification to the Leipzig streets, as "We Are *the* People" became "We Are *One* People." On Wednesday, 29 November, "in anticipation of discussions" about the film *Our Children*, a declaration was published in the festival's newsletter, *Bulletin*. The signatories, predominantly West Germans but also some East Germans, welcomed the changes toward "openness and democratization" initiated in the GDR. They did note with concern, however, that the Monday demonstration had "conveyed an impression of nationalistic undertones [*nationalistische Töne*]." "Progress in the GDR [should] not signify a return to a Germany of the past" (*Festival Bulletin* 1989, vol. 5).

The festival Organizing Committee declared that it shared the concerns expressed. Steiner, himself a member of the committee, did not share this view; as he saw it, the slogan "We Are One People" was not a step backward, but was instead directed at the "policies, at best insufficient, of the social forces still in command." He continued:

> For me, it is part of a realistic assessment of things in the GDR to observe that not everyone in the country places hope in a reform of socialism. We should take note of the fact that here, in our population, nationalist tendencies exist. . . . Only by doing so will we be able to mount an offensive confrontation.

Ronald Trisch recalls very heated discussions between West German guests and participants, hostile to any idea of German unification, and East Germans who were mostly more open to such an eventuality.[31] The ensuing months, however, would prove that the line separating partisans and enemies of unification did not pass only between East Germans and leftwing West Germans,

Figure 10.3. Poster for R. Steiner's *Our Children* (1989). © DEFA-Stiftung, Detlef Helmbold.

who were critical of the West German system; instead it divided the entire German population, beginning with its intellectuals and filmmakers, in a more complex and winding manner. In early 1990, Konrad Weiss wrote:

> I lost my *Heimat:* this gray, narrow, ugly country [*Land*]. This beautiful country.... This is [the] country in which I grew up, it was the country where I first fell in love, the country of my dreams, the country of my anger.... And now, it's a rugged, screaming, familiar homeland [*Vaterland*] that assails us.

1990: A Unified German Festival?

On 3 October 1990, as a new Germany was coming into being, a state was disappearing. It was now time to take stock of the GDR's legacy. For the past year, East German documentary filmmakers had been faced with a major challenge. They had had to find their place in the face of ubiquitous international television stations that overwhelmed spectators with images of the GDR. A certain number chose to distance themselves from events and devote themselves to the gray zones of East German society that had escaped the attention of other media (Müller 1992). The November 1990 Leipzig Festival once again centered on the fate of Germany, relinquishing its international dimension for a time; it was critical to assess the lessons of history in order to better conceive of an uncertain future.

What Remains

As a sign of the confusion that gripped most East Germans in the months between the breaching of the Wall and German unification, more and more voices were raised in an attempt to rehabilitate the cultural life of the GDR (Corbin-Schuffels 1998; Muschter and Rostock 1992). In this spirit, the Leipzig Festival sought to pave a way between a past worthy of rejection and values to be safeguarded.

One of the most violent moments of the period was what was called the German-German literary battle (*deutsch-deutsche Literaturstreit*), which erupted when Christa Wolf published her novella *Was Bleibt* (*What Remains*) in June 1990 (Deiritz and Krauss 1991; Emmerich 2000). Initially drafted in the summer of 1979 and reworked in November 1989, the text depicts a day in the life of a writer being surveilled by the Stasi. In a period of transition and confusion during which it was better to present oneself as a longtime opponent of the East German regime, the novella struck many as Wolf's attempt to position herself as a victim. Many West German public figures reproached the author for trying to make the reader forget the very close relations that she—like most other East German artists and intellectuals—had nurtured with the authorities. The sense of loyalty that kept them bound to the regime had certainly been the source of profound dilemmas, yet had nevertheless been central to their attitude for the forty years of the state's existence.[32] It was proving difficult to save the slightest positive aspect of a society that had been assimilated into its regime, including in the cultural sphere, from the overall debacle.

The situation for East German filmmakers seemed no more favorable than for their literary counterparts. In early 1990, the DEFA Documentary Studio employed 877 people in East Berlin and Potsdam-Babelsberg, including eighty film directors (Burkhardt 1995). In July of the same year, it was privatized and became a joint stock company (DEFA Studio für Dokumentarfilm GmbH). This triggered a wave of layoffs, which overnight affected filmmakers such as Karl Gass, who had been at DEFA for decades; without any prior notice, they were informed of their dismissal by letter in December 1990.[33]

The Leipzig Festival also underwent profound changes. In April 1990, a new committee replaced the previous one, which had collectively resigned as announced in November 1989. Among its eleven members were festival stalwarts, as well as new members, all from the GDR. Ronald Trisch reappeared, this time as the festival director. Documentarists Winfried Junge and Ralf Marschalleck,[34] the author and playwright Klaus Wischnewski, and the cinematographer Julia Kunert represented DEFA. Journalist Barbara Cantow represented DFF television. Journalists, critics, and film historians Bernd Burkhardt, Klaus Schmutzer, and Norbert Wehrstedt completed the list. The Filmmakers' Union proposed that Christiane Mückenberger chair the committee, replacing Annelie Thorndike, who had occupied the post since 1973.

Mückenberger's professional and personal trajectory had undergone numerous ruptures under the East German regime. Born on the German-Polish border, she studied Slavic languages and culture before going on to teach at HFF, where she was head of the Cinema Theory and History Department. In 1965, she was among those dismissed following the wave of censorship triggered by the Eleventh Plenum. The leadership of the SED party group within HFF accused her of "using her position as director [of the department] to propagate ideas foreign to Socialist Realism" and of having thus encouraged censored filmmakers to shoot films "against our way of life and our state."[35] In 1969, after having been strictly forbidden to attend the festival for four years, she was again able to attend the Leipzig Festival, in a private capacity and with the personal support of Wolfgang Harkenthal and then Ronald Trisch (Mückenberger 1997). In 1975—after being forbidden to work in her profession—Mückenberger resumed teaching at HFF.

For the committee's new chairperson, it was not a question of settling old scores; it was time, however, to draw lessons from the past. "Ahead of the festival we asked ourselves which traditions we should maintain and what we had to definitively set aside," summarized Mückenberger (1990: 5). Rather than change everything, the committee sought what it felt was essential to conserve. This approach was not common at the time, but it seemed to work (Mückenberger 1998). The structures in fact remained the same. The festival was allocated the budget that had been determined the year before by the East German government; the DEFA Documentary Studio was still operative, although it had been privatized in March; and there was still talk of "East German" documentary filmmakers.

One of the committee's initial measures was to modify its motto—not to deny it, but rather to restore accurate meaning and legitimacy. "Films from Around the World—for Peace in the World" now became "Films from Around the World—for the Dignity of Humankind" (*Filme der Welt—für die Würde des Menschens*). The pacifist mission, which had turned out to be hollow official propaganda, was now jettisoned in favor of the festival's enduring commitment to politically engaged documentary film. But what remained of the festival's international dimension?

From International Solidarity to National Retrenchment?

"The internationalist drug of recent years is no longer effective. From now on we are looking at what is happening in our country," remarked an East German journalist in 1989 (Voigt 1989). The German-Argentine film director Jeanine Meerapfel (1990: 5), a regular at the festival and a jury member in 1990, regretted the almost complete absence in the program of films from the Southern Hemisphere, breaking with the long tradition that had rendered Leipzig a "meeting place and a home [*Heimat*] for filmmakers from the so-called Third World." Of the 600 films sent to the festival, 200 were German productions, explained Mückenberger. In its final report, however, the Selection Committee criticized the lack of "openness to the world" (*Weltoffenheit*) evident in films from Eastern Europe (Abschlussbericht der Auswahlkommission 1990); they accused them of addressing the problems of Latin American and Africa from a "provincially narrow perspective," in complete ignorance of the real problems on the ground and their inherent complexity.

Concerned by such a turn of events, on 23 November 1990 the committee published an open letter addressed to "political leaders in Germany and friends and partners of international documentary" (*Festival Bulletin* 1990, vol. 2: 1–2). It reiterated the mission of the festival as a venue for "the exchange of social, humanitarian, and aesthetic information between individuals, peoples, and the continents." Although the international context had changed, Leipzig remained of paramount importance "because, after the walls, the relics of the Cold War that remained in people's minds [needed] to fall, the many other barriers and chains that [weighed] upon so many people, wounding them and destroying their dignity."

It was clear, however, that very few participants from the Global South were able to attend due to the severely reduced budget, and, apart from the festival's organizational and diplomatic intermediaries, had virtually disappeared. Several public figures showed their solidarity by establishing a group called the Friends of the Festival, whose mission was to support the festival. Beside Marceline Loridan-Ivens—who wished to remember the discovery and encounters that took place at Leipzig and no longer censorship as in 1968—there were the East German author Stefan Heym, the British film producer Stanley Forman, the Polish film director Kazimierz Karabasz, and the French literary couple Vladimir and Ida Pozner (*Festival Bulletin* 1990, vol. 1: 2, 7). Their backing, however, was not enough to fill the void brought about by the disappearance of the ideological and material support of the East German government, which had been so vital in maintaining international solidarity with countries in the Global South. The festival now found itself facing the concrete consequences of the termination of the state's commitment.

The 1990 edition thus marked a critical turning point in the Leipzig Festival's history. The freedom of speech and expression that had finally been won primarily resulted in turning the festival away from the rest of the world and focusing its program on Germany. Evidence of this shift in perspective was that, on the heels of the Karl Gass retrospective in 1989, the 1990 retrospective was devoted to West German director Klaus Wildenhahn. In this sense, unification had gained traction. For the organizers, Wildenhahn, an internationally recognized documentarist, had the advantage of being one of those rare West German filmmakers who had quite early become interested in the working class, which he approached in a more or less sociological manner. Symbolically, however, the retrospective opened with *Der König geht* (1990, *The King Goes*), not with one of the films Wildenhahn had shot in West Germany. In May and June 1990, he had filmed the restoration of the Royal Palace in Dresden. His observation of daily progress on the site offered a framework for chronicling the final months of the GDR; epoch-making events take place only in the background, punctuated by news bulletins heard on the radio and newspapers read in the canteen.

Requiem for a Nation: **The Wall**

In reality, however, the latest upheavals that had been taking place in Germany's cities and streets continued to be ubiquitous on Leipzig's screens. In 1990 the festival featured no fewer than twenty documentaries on the collapse of the GDR and its ramifications, almost exclusively German productions from both sides of the border. Following *Leipzig in the Fall*—the visual log of the ongoing revolution that had opened the 1989 festival—Jürgen Böttcher's *Die Mauer* (1990, *The Wall*) opened the festival in 1990 (Pusch 2000; Richter 2001). Shot during the winter of 1989–1990, the film presented a sort of chronicle of the Wall's destruction (Wolfrum 2009). With it Böttcher—now fifty-nine and having worked at DEFA for nearly thirty years—offered a visual reflection in the form of an overview that ultimately belonged to an entire generation.

Throughout the ninety-minute documentary, the public's boisterous joy alternates with prolonged periods of silence. The crowd shots contrast with scenes where silhouettes intertwine, in tears, or isolated, pensively observing a breach in the Wall. Pickaxes attack the reinforced concrete. Clouds of birds cross the Berlin sky, an open space that dominates the site on the ground where segments of the Wall still stand, obstacles that are no longer menacing but nonetheless very present. Highly crafted color images play with the daylight and sudden transformations of the landscape as sections of the Wall are knocked down. No commentary, no music is added to the images and diegetic sound of different scenes. Long panning shots, fluid camera movements imbue the documentary with a calm pace, inviting the viewer to meditate on the event, in the face of the fast pace of actual events.

Böttcher projects iconic scenes from German history on one section of the Wall: the kaisers, Hitler, Nazi torch-lit processions, women clearing rubble (*Trümmerfrauen*), 13 August 1961, and so on. The rough surface of the concrete serves as a backdrop for the "ghosts of twentieth-century German history" (Roth 1991) made of ruptures and violence. The documentarist becomes a painter once again, introducing himself into the scene by installing these images in a sequence that he considers the "core of the film" (Genth 1992 : 21). In this landscape that's disintegrating piece by piece, the multifaceted artist—who loves to play with surfaces, with different types of images[36]—discovers the pleasure of playing with these visual scraps, these bursts of memory.

The camera plunges underground, into the Berlin subway and the long-closed station under Potsdamer Platz; behind the scenes is a vanished world where soldiers are still on patrol, though they no longer bear arms. It's a nod in the direction of film history; forty-four years earlier, in January 1946, cameraman Reimar Kuntze shot the first DEFA footage in this flooded Berlin subway tunnel (Jordan 1996). In 1989, the Wall looks like a set in the process of being dismantled, bringing down the curtain on an episode that seems to have become unreal.

In the face of the overwhelming inflation of images shot by television crews from around the globe, gathered at Potsdamer Platz and in front of the Brandenburg Gate, Böttcher and the cinematographer, Thomas Plenert, had deliberately chosen a contemplative rhythm and kept a certain distance. This decision to remain in the background articulated the profound uncertainty in which millions of East Germans found themselves. From adjacent rooftops, the two men thus filmed the New Year's fireworks of 1989–1990 and the outdoor Roger Waters concert in 1990, where he and others performed Pink Floyd's *The Wall*. Thousands of people stand below, while the soundtrack mingles the blows of pickaxes against the Wall with music from the concert; the whole thing is shot from a rooftop where two chimneysweeps do their work, virtually indifferent to the spectacle that is unfolding at their feet. Böttcher thus links the symbolic force of a unique moment in history with the banality of the everyday, the gaze of the historical witness and the filmmaker's own, more intimate gaze. Böttcher professed that he was full of hope of what tomorrow would bring but also conscious of the end of an era, which was giving way to the unknown.[37]

In *The Wall*, Böttcher doubled up as a documentarist and chronicler of his time and society—not only in documenting events but also in allowing viewers to step back and reflect upon the acceleration of history and the incoming tide of images. More than simply recording history that was unfolding, he sought to impose order on a reality that was becoming more and more complex.

Figure 10.4. Jürgen Böttcher, Thomas Plenert, and Gerd Kroske (*left to right*) shooting *The Wall* (1989–1990). © DEFA Stiftung.

Portraits of an Era

Most DEFA documentarists embraced an even more radical stance than Böttcher, filming East German society far from spectacular venues and staging. The Leipzig Festival echoed this trend, seeking in this way to offer different images of what was happening in the GDR from those being broadcast on television. The festival committee organized two series of screenings, one titled "Stalin's Legacy" and the other "The Past Year," about the end of the GDR; the goal of the second program was to present differentiated views of the situation and, above all, the views of young directors (Mückenberger 1990).

Across the fifteen films,[38] a series of portraits testified to the deep and intimate wounds inflicted by the policies of the East German regime. Karlheinz Mund thus retraced the life of Walter Janka (1914–1994) in *Aufgeben oder neu beginnen* (1989–1990, *Give Up or Start Anew*). Roland Steiner's *La Rotonda/Vicenza* focused on suicide, another taboo subject in the GDR; it is the story of a Marxist architect who believed in socialist society his whole life but, realizing the GDR had failed, killed himself in 1985. Another life of heartbreaks, bitter compromises, and disillusionment—that of the GDR's first minister of culture and expressionistic poet Johannes R. Becher—is portrayed by Konrad Herrman in *Die Angst und die Macht* (1990, *Fear and Power*). In *Ich war ein glücklicher Mensch* (1990, *I Was a Happy Person*), Eduard Schreiber sought to understand how the staunch communist Tilbert Eckertz—who, despite being innocent, was arrested in 1953 and sentenced to three years for espionage, and whose daughter was incarcerated for attempting to flee to the West—could not only remain in the GDR but also address a reproachful letter to his daughter and then in 1990 write, "I was a happy man. Despite everything."

In her autobiographical film *Verriegelte Zeit* (1991, *Locked Up Time*), DEFA directors Sibylle Schönemann and her husband retrace their own trajectory. They had refused to sign a petition condemning Wolf Biermann at the 1976 Leipzig Festival, which only accentuated the bullying they experienced at the studio and caused them to go through a protracted period of personal crisis (Schönemann 1990). The couple subsequently filed several visa applications to leave the GDR, all of which were denied. They were then arrested in November 1984. After they'd spent a year in prison, West Germany "bought" them out, and they settled in Hamburg. To make the film, Schönemann went to meet those who had accused her, condemned her, and kept her in prison. Executioners against victims? The contrast between the two turned out to be not so obvious. Yesterday's culprits repeatedly gave way to new culprits, imposing the need for this confrontation with the past to constantly shift perspective. For Schönemann, filming was a painful process but also a liberation (Pusch 2000). After it premiered at Leipzig, where it received the Silver Dove, the film went on to enjoy great success in German movie theaters of the unified country.

Such individual portraits thus sketched out the individual dimension of the failure of the communist project, as well as the personal injuries inflicted by the system. Faced with the magnitude of the catastrophe, these documentary directors had chosen to film it on a human scale.

Other documentary filmmakers, in contrast, opted to present group portraits that offered a bittersweet image of the situation in the face of unification. In *Berlin–Prenzlauer Berg* (1990, *Berlin, Prenzlauer Berg*), Petra Tschörtner, one of DEFA's few women documentarists, focused on residents of Prenzlauer Berg, a section of East Berlin, filming there between 1 May and 1 July 1990. On the eve of the monetary union between the two Germanys, the mood was gloomy. People were divided between the joy of having seen the regime collapse and the anguish of an unknown future. Workers at a clothing factory, so much like the young women of Wittstock, admitted they did not like what they were producing and yet worried about the coming competition from the West. You could hear "Not everything was bad in what we had." After the complete rejection of a system, there thus appeared to be a longing to salvage a part of the past as if it would help them confront the future.

Komm in den Garten (1990, *Come into the Garden*), codirected by Heinz Brinckmann and Jochen Wisotzki, screened in competition during the Leipzig Festival. It obtained the Silver Dove for feature-length films and a "recommendation" from the festival's Ecumenical Jury, which wrote, "The film shows people we don't usually come across, how they really are, and a place in society where they can live and love." A journalist, an economist, and a painter form a small group in which each tries to regain a sense of balance in their lives. All three had suffered various failures in the GDR due to their political stance or alcoholism, and even found themselves in prison or psychiatric institutions. Having never contemplated leaving the GDR, the three men gathered together and continue to help each other out. For Brinckmann and Wisotzki, the destiny of these three men show that there was resistance to the communist regime, but a "nonspectacular" resistance (Brinckmann 1990). History's upheavals will not alter their situation in the slightest; they will remain on the margins of society, ideologically and socially.

By 1990, the revolution of 1989 had thus become a revolution without illusions, the last of which vanished into thin air the previous winter. The raw and enthusiastic character of the documentaries of November 1989 had disappeared. The documentaries of 1990 carry in seed form the difficulties of unification and constitute valuable documents of the crucial period between the demonstrations of 1989 and German unification on 3 October 1990. Within a single year, the perception of East German society and the function of the documentary filmmaker had been utterly transformed.

Notes

1. See Jessen 2009.
2. In 1988, these gatherings became a rallying point for people who had applied for an exit visa and were waiting for permission to leave the GDR (Ausreiser, Ausreisewillige; Feydt et al. 1990).
3. See Richter 2004.
4. From 25 September to 6 November 1989, more than 900,000 people marched in Leipzig.
5. Author Erich Loest (b. 1926) grew up in Leipzig and worked there as a journalist. He was one of the victims of trials that started at the end of 1956 against those working for reforms and de-Stalinization in the GDR, including W. Janka and W. Harisch. He was condemned to seven years of prison from 1958 to 1965. He emigrated to the West in 1981. Very attached to Leipzig, the author returned there in 1998 (Emmerich 2000).
6. On the mutations of Leipzig and the surrounding region, see the thesis of Agnès Labrousse (2003), especially chapter 8.
7. Bernhard Heisig, one of the principal painters of the GDR and a member of the SED's directorate in the Leipzig district, had been an intermediary between the authorities and six painters of the Leipzig School. One of these, also a member of the SED, had rented this space privately, giving the impression that it was for an official exhibition.
8. Letter from Dr. Georg Hentschel, Party Secretary, to Ronald Trisch, Festival Director, Berlin, 11 January 1989, BArch-FArch, Leipzig, 1988/31.
9. For more on this, see chapter 9.
10. Author's interview with Ronald Trisch, Berlin, Germany (11 March 2004).
11. Komitee des Festivals, Konzeption und Rahmenprogramm des 33. Festivals, 14 November 1989, BStU MfS HA XX/2085, p. 2
12. Author's interview with Ronald Trisch, Berlin, Germany (11 March 2004).
13. For more on this, see chapter 3.
14. In 1952, the regime had in fact launched an offensive against the Protestant church (Mählert 1998).
15. Author's interview with Karl Gass, Berlin/Kleinmachnow, Germany (28 July 2000).
16. Unless noted otherwise, the following citations are all from the same text.
17. For more on this, see chapter 7.
18. *October Came* . . . is a chronicle commemorating the twentieth anniversary of the GDR.
19. Whether on Chile, on Africa, on the destiny of a little Polish Jewish boy murdered with his parents in Treblinka in 1942, or on the taboo subject of handicapped youth.
20. He became one of the leaders of Aktion Sühnezeichen in East Germany—an ecumenical religious movement seeking to expiate the crimes committed during World War II—as well as a member of the GDR Union of Evangelical [Lutheran] Churches council for ecclesiastical radio.

21. Interventions by the Swiss journalist Lorelan Matthias and the East German critic Sybille Licht (Thieme 1989).
22. Reserved for accredited guests at the festival, the workshop only drew 200 viewers, in contrast to the 10,500 tickets sold for the rest of the festival program (Beutelschmidt 1995; Fritzsche and Löser 1996; *Protokoll 1985* 1986).
23. Video technology did, in fact, raise important political issues, as it offered a way to make films inexpensively and, thus, independently and in a decentralized fashion. Video was not adopted by the DEFA Documentary Studio until 1988.
24. In November 1987, the fifth Colloquium of the Filmmakers' Union was dedicated to video (Becher 1987).
25. These were music videos and other video essays supported by a project of the FDJ — a sign of the organization's attempts to open and modernize.
26. Also known as the Fédération Internationale des Ciné-Clubs (FICC).
27. Tomás Bilý, Martin Clupác, and Karel März were the directors.
28. Steiner (b. 1949), who had trained as a pipe fitter, joined DEFA as an assistant cameraman in 1968. He studied film directing at the HFF from 1970 to 1974 and worked as an assistant director for two years at the Feature Film Studio, before moving to the Documentary Studio in 1976.
29. For more on this, see chapter 9.
30. Among the documentaries selected at Leipzig that did not have to do with events in Eastern Europe, we should also mention Marcel Ophüls's *Hôtel Terminus* (1988, *Hotel Terminus: The Life and Times of Klaus Barbie*), devoted to the activities of Klaus Barbie in Lyon during the German occupation.
31. Author's interview with Ronald Trisch, Berlin, Germany (11 March 2004).
32. See, in particular, Schirrmacher 1990.
33. Author's interview with Karl Gass, Kleinmachnow, Germany (8 August 2000).
34. Ralf Marschalleck participated in the takeover of the Stasi building in East Berlin by demonstrators on 15 January 1990. In *Streng vertraulich oder Die innere Verfassung* (1990, *Strictly Secret or the Inner Condition*), the director evokes the delicate question of collective responsibility on the part of the East German population during the forty years of the GDR.
35. Decision of the leadership of the SED-Grundorganisation of the HFF Potsdam-Babelsberg on 19 January 1966 (quoted in Baumert 1991).
36. In 1981, the documentarist shot three short films in which he filmed his process of drawing on postcards of classic paintings — *Frau am Klavichord* (*Woman at the Clavichord*), *Venus nach Giorgione* (*Venus after Giorgione*), and *Potters Stier* (*Potter's Bull*) — published on DVD by the DEFA Film Library as *Transformation Trilogy*. These films were not selected at Leipzig.
37. Author's interview with Jürgen Böttcher, Berlin/Karlshorst, Germany (31 October 2000).
38. Thomas Heise shot *Imbiss Spezial* (1990, *Snack Bar Special*) on 7 October 1989 in the basement of a train station in East Berlin, far from the big official parades commemorating the fortieth anniversary of the country. The regime's propaganda is heard on the radio, interrupted by advertisements; customers seem to be quite indifferent to this official speech.

CONCLUSION

Beyond the Cold War
A Memory in the Making

The Leipzig Festival was, and remains, a milestone in the transnational circulation of films, film directors, producers, and critics. From its inception until 1990, the history of the Leipzig Festival reveals the singularity of an event that, while certainly an officially staged venue controlled by the East German state and party, was also a site of encounters and exchanges that were central to the relationship between cinema and the Cold War. A distinct periodization emerges from the festival's trajectory in these years, revealing multiple nonlinear and sometimes contradictory evolutions. Its history exposes mechanisms that comforted the GDR regime, as well as impasses that ultimately led to its downfall. These salient characteristics of the Leipzig Festival clearly make it a rich and pertinent object of study into the social and cultural dynamics of the Cold War period.

This study has striven to offer an in-depth analysis of the political, social, economic, and cultural stakes involved in the festival during the Cold War by tracing the different stages of its organization as well as local and international reception. In order to avoid a narrative that focuses exclusively on the festival's institutional aspects, special attention has been paid to the biographical trajectories of people, German or otherwise, closely connected with the festival: film directors, critics, political leaders, and producers (film and television studios). Of course, the documentaries selected and screened at Leipzig—both German and foreign—are given center stage in this history, as are the animated and sometimes heated discussions they provoked. Presented in their aesthetic, political, and social dimensions, these films from around the world open up a new, comparative perspective on the history of European and non-European documentary cinema from the 1950s through the 1980s.

Inevitably, a history ending in 1990 prompts the question of what has taken place since the fall of the Wall. In November 2017, twenty-eight years later, DOK Leipzig—the festival's rebranded name, as of 2005—celebrated its sixtieth anniversary. It has become an important event, on a German, European, and international scale, within a new global geography of festivals.[1] But what traces remain in this new landscape of the singular past of the oldest documentary film festival in the world?

Shifting Chronological Frames

The case of the Leipzig Festival bears witness to the importance of film festivals as observational posts from which we can identify the cultural policies of given political systems, including their manifold challenges, and how stakeholders interact at national and international levels. In the case of the GDR, this observational post allows us to trace five basic shifts in power relations and international trends. From the turn of the 1950s until 1964, the festival gradually took shape and evolved into an international cultural event under the intertwined influences of East-West German relations, the politics of the two power blocs, and East German intellectuals intent on fighting cultural autarky in the emerging Cold War climate. Directors and journalists from East and West came together at Leipzig, which, for a while, aspired to become *the* tribunal of international documentary filmmaking. In effect, in those years the festival welcomed pioneers of the documentary film world, such as the Dutchman Joris Ivens, the Frenchman Chris Marker, the Scot John Grierson, and the Russians Mikhail Romm and Roman Karmen, all of whom had championed the festival's beginnings.

The emergence in 1964 of television as an official organizer ushered in the increasing professionalization of the Leipzig Festival, which was concurrently called to contribute more actively to the regime's cultural and diplomatic offensive in the international arena. In the international political and cultural effervescence of the 1960s—dominated by artistic New Waves and the aftereffects of de-Stalinization—the festival became a nexus of both animated debate and recurrent censorship.

Algerian and Cuban filmmakers (with Santiago Álvarez at the forefront) greatly contributed to breathing new life into festival programming and discussions during this period. As Walter Heynowski observed in 1997: "In the early years, the Leipzig Festival was an elixir of life. It took a stand against our own form of provincialism. It was created in this spirit, at least. And then the authorities arrived on the scene, with their provincialism" (Heynowski and Scheumann 1997: 93). This statement, issued in retrospect by a principal of the H&S Studio—one of the most militant practitioners of offensive cultural politics, loudly celebrated by the East German regime for his contributions to "international solidarity" — aptly reminds us how crucial it is to consider the festival's history as a series of complex evolutions within shifting frames of reference.

Once the GDR had obtained international diplomatic recognition in 1973, it was necessary to reassess the challenges facing the Leipzig Festival in a new era. On one hand, with the development in the GDR as elsewhere of sociologically oriented documentaries, the border dividing East German society and cinema was becoming increasingly permeable. On the other were ongoing political and cultural developments. The call for international solidarity with those fighting against imperialism in Asia, Africa, Latin America, and Palestine resonated particularly strongly on screen, as well as at concerts and other artistic events at the festival.

In the early 1980s, DEFA documentaries started undergoing profound changes, caught up in international dynamics that, as of 1985, were accelerated by glasnost reform policies in the USSR. On festival screens, the topics of the day were now the environment, the malaise felt by younger generations, the place of women in society — subjects that, until then, had remained almost completely off camera. As the decade came to a close, the Peaceful Revolution of 1989 took place both out on the streets of Leipzig, as well as in the theaters and other venues of the festival.

Beginning with the collapse of the Berlin Wall and the privatization of the DEFA studios in June 1990 and culminating with the end of the GDR regime the following October, the rupture of 1989–1990 was earthshaking. Over the space of eleven short months in 1990, the working and living conditions of Jürgen Böttcher, like all East German documentarists, changed dramatically. Three years later, he explained, "Curious — we used to be the westernmost ones in the East, and now we are the easternmost in the West" (Deutscher Bundestag 1995: 555). In this way, he expressed the widely felt shock of such a sudden change of perspective, which was as radical as it was unexpected. And yet, in the rapidly altering landscape of a reunified Germany and Europe, a few landmarks — such as the Leipzig Festival — were to become enduring points of reference.

Mirroring Changing Realities

This cursory overview of the different phases of the festival during the Cold War highlights a fundamental contradiction: East German culture is often misleadingly pictured as utterly dependent upon the East and a Soviet model, itself presented as frozen in time. The film screenings at the Leipzig Festival, in contrast, attest to the production of varied and changing documentary films, which reflected domestic, as well as international, realities that were constantly changing.

Cinematic portrayals of the GDR screened at the Leipzig Festival, for example, clearly evolved between 1955 and 1990. More importantly, the films that were the most critical of the regime garnered the most attention from foreign guests and ultimately contributed—in the aftermath of the *Wende*—to the forging of a collective and international memory of social change in East German society. As examples, we can cite the films of Jürgen Böttcher, Volker Koepp, and even some by Winfried Junge. Junge's and Koepp's documentary cycles—clearly overarching in scope—played a critical role in shaping a specific, imaginary social world for those who had never lived in the GDR.

Not even remotely related to the GDR's early explicitly staged and propagandistic productions, these homegrown documentaries made it possible to at once grasp and safeguard a realer image of everyday East German life, which simultaneously substantiated how contradictory the system under which people were living was. Paradoxically, the Janus-like quality of the regime's cultural policy—which opted to be strict with regard to internal affairs and more open toward international public opinion— also enabled certain documentary filmmakers to enjoy an international reputation abroad before 1990, from which they were subsequently able to benefit. Jürgen Böttcher's 1964 film *Barefoot and without a Hat* was not shown in the GDR, for example, but it was allowed to screen at a film festival in France. In 2000, Böttcher acknowledged that, after 1990, the censoring of some of his earlier works had actually helped him "rise like a phoenix from the ashes."[2]

Besides illustrating the evolution and diversity of East German documentaries, Leipzig Festival programming allows us a glimpse of which foreign documentary productions attracted the most attention from East German film directors. An overview of themes selected for the retrospectives—which were the highlight of the festival for international visitors—reveals the international documentary tradition with which the festival wanted to be associated.[3] Far from focusing on the Soviet documentary tradition, retrospectives during the festival's first decade were devoted to the classics and the pioneers of the genre—the international documentary avant-garde of the 1920s and 1930s. Unquestionably, the Soviet director Dziga Vertov had set the projectors rolling; but then came the Brazilian Alberto Cavalcanti, who settled in France; Joris Ivens from the Netherlands; and the American Robert Flaherty. Even in 1966, the retrospective devoted to French documentaries included works from documentary's nascent phase during the interwar years.

Finally, we should not overlook the tastes and demands of the public, which has its part to play in social evolution—although the East German example reveals just how slow the evolution of public consciousness really was. Audience reactions in movie theaters, which are recalled in various personal accounts, as well as the midnight discussions during the festival, contributed in their own way to the very specific atmosphere at Leipzig. In 1972, film director Károly Makk (1972: 96), one of the instigators of the revival of Hungarian cinema in the 1960s, remarked:

> What, in my opinion, determines the true nature of a country's cinema is not the number of prizes obtained at a festival, but rather the relationship between the people and its films. The question is to know whether people rediscover their lives on screen and whether the films reveal something about their lives to them. . . . Just as Italian Neorealism was closely related to Italian reality at the time.

The different phases of East German cultural openness in the 1960s and early 1970s enabled the development of an audience that evolved within a society that was itself changing, modernizing, and gradually circumventing the regime and its systems. Audiences learned to watch films differently, to grasp the importance of a smile, of a nuance in the voice but also to decipher a sense of silences and of what was happening offscreen. Eventually the phenomenon of glasnost revealed the audience's expectations, which had hitherto not been explicit.

Successive crises ended the quest for documentaries with a human face in the mid-1960s and short-circuited attempts to publicly express critical views of society after 1976. In response, East German documentary filmmakers learned to speak a language other than the one imposed by officially sanctioned Socialist Realism. There thus emerged an increasingly distinct East German identity over the course of the 1970s, which was not anchored in the image of the present leading to a promising socialist future but rather in everyday life, independent of all ideological stakes.

This mutual evolution of audiences and filmmakers, without a doubt, culminated in the box office successes of *Winter Adé* and *whisper & SHOUT* in 1988–1989. These resided, in part, in the fact that the directors and film crews felt directly concerned by what and who they were shooting. The engagement was real and enabled a unique encounter between those in front of and behind the camera—a coming together that was one of the driving forces behind the revolutionary upheaval of 1989.

Shifting Roles of Festival Stakeholders

As we have seen, the Leipzig Festival was not merely a representational event at which films were screened and discussed but also—despite the profound divisions engendered by the Cold War—a nexus for encounters and exchanges between individuals, whose dynamics were regularly reconfigured. To revisit the complexity of these encounters, it helps to recall the three groups of East

German stakeholders involved in the Leipzig Festival introduced at the start of this volume. Official stakeholders—regime officials, festival directors, and other representatives of the supervisory authorities—formed the first circle; the second circle consisted of film professionals: directors, technicians, and others who contributed to making the films; and the third group comprised individuals in East Germany's cultural sphere, such as journalists, critics, students, and teachers at the HFF film academy.

Throughout the history of the Leipzig Festival, each of the three circles followed its individual trajectory, while at the same time intersecting with the other two. Events—such as the Biermann Affair in 1976, the 1983 arrests in Leipzig, and even the 1989 revolution and question of German unity—divided members of East Germany's professional and artistic circles. The emergence of glasnost themes at the festival provoked tensions even within officialdom, notably between those at DFF television, who were vehemently against all forms of opening up, and those who supported a more flexible cultural policy.

Over the course of the festival's history, rifts and tensions—both internal and in relation to one another—also demonstrate how questions of culture were constantly coupled with questions of dominance. If we focus on the case of East German documentary filmmakers, for example, we see that they were invariably part of the system, which paid them and gave them the opportunity to work. Like Hungarian writers, East German intellectuals thus participated in devising the constraints and subjugations that affected their lives.[4] And yet their relationship with the regime was by no means ossified: one need only evoke, for example, the reactions following the Biermann Affair and the ensuing hesitation exhibited on both sides. Renowned scriptwriter Yevgeni Gabrilovich divided Soviet filmmakers into three categories: those who glorified the regime, eating salmon and caviar during cocktail receptions at the Kremlin; those who denounced Communist reality and were beaten and bloodied; and those who were willing to accept glorification but with certain misgivings (Shlapentokh 1993: 23).

In practice, of course, it was professionally and politically viable for documentary filmmakers in the GDR to belong to each of these three categories during a single career. The sense of unity associated with belonging to the same film studio apparently did not stifle the political vision or professional ambitions of filmmakers. This makes it crucial that we observe individual trajectories closely. When we do, it emerges that precisely those individuals whose career trajectories were not linear in the GDR ultimately survived the collapse of the country—even as DEFA's documentary group itself disappeared from the public sphere.[5] After 1990, in addition to the overwhelming majority of DEFA documentary filmmakers, the circle of officials and administrators also vanished from the festival podium. The regime's collapse had thus dragged down two of the three main circles of festival stakeholders.

Representatives of East Germany's cultural sphere, however—especially those who had maintained a relatively independent stance—were able to remain involved longer. The trajectories of Christiane Mückenberger and Fred Gehler illustrate this. Before 1989, both had been among the journalists and film critics who had sought to create a forum for public discussion at the festival, as well as at other venues, such as the HFF and film clubs. Both of them had been banished from the festival for a time, yet nevertheless attempted to return to it, as they had no desire to leave the GDR. Refusing both orthodoxy and dissidence, they had thus had to execute a balancing act in the GDR—which was sometimes very tricky, as evidenced by later debates about Gehler and his possible role as an informal Stasi collaborator. It is therefore not insignificant that both played vital roles in the post-unification history of the festival: Mückenberger served as its director from 1990 to 1993, during the tensest period of the post-*Wende* transition; and Gehler served as director from 1994 to 2003.

Finally, in the debates that raged on the subject of "inter-German" memory after unification, it was such stakeholders in East German public life that played a major role in disseminating a certain discourse about the GDR, in historiography as in the media. With the exception of some thorny moments in East German history where gray zones dominated, they insisted on a narrative that portrayed East German society as full of niches where it was possible to find refuge and engage in a different mode of sociability, free of state control.

The International Dimension

Of course what made the Leipzig Festival unique in East Germany was its international openness and the fact that foreign guests participated in the festival. Beyond the official trumpeting and staging of international openness, by means of mottos, posters, and prizes and awards, it seems clear that the festival was truly considered a venue that enabled an openness that went beyond contacts with Eastern European popular democracies. East German filmmakers felt just as close to the directors of Italian Neorealism, the Dutch director Joris Ivens, and the French innovator Chris Marker as to their Polish counterparts. East German guests did not so much keenly await the delegations from the East, which in the main comprised officials from Moscow and Prague, as filmmakers and films from Cuba, Brazil, Chile, and the Palestinians. Latin American cinema was long a stalwart of the festival, constituting a major attraction for audiences. The attitude of these guests—notably the Cubans, whose public statements often sharply contrasted with official East German and Soviet rhetoric—paved the way for fresh perspectives, both aesthetic and political.

The dance, music, and other cultural events that accompanied the arrival of South American delegations also added highly appreciated folkloric and exotic touches to the proceedings. While deeply rooted in the local German and European context, the Leipzig Festival, in its fashion, offered a concrete manifestation of the global Cold War, in which countries in the Southern Hemisphere were integrally involved, sometimes even playing the East and West Blocs off against each other.[6]

As time progressed, however, the tastes of festival guests shifted, and this eventually became a game changer. As glasnost reforms accelerated the dissemination of new Soviet documentaries on the international scene—a development that scared orthodox SED leaders in East Berlin—the attention of some documentary filmmakers turned less to the West and South and more to the East. The overview of Soviet selections at Leipzig clearly shows how, far from being stagnant across the decades, Soviet cinema actively influenced and contributed to the profound political, cultural, and social changes taking place in Moscow and, as a result, in all East Bloc countries.

For many East German moviegoers and filmmakers, the festival was more about learning from international experiences and traditions beyond the deep divisions of the Cold War than about promoting DEFA films to foreign audiences. We know that in the GDR profound contradictions encompassed and complicated the image, so often portrayed of a festival with a "window open onto the world." At the same time, enthusiastic accounts of encounters and discoveries of other aesthetic and political cinemas and narratives are reflected in many interviews and testimonies of participants. The festival's call for international openness, together with the social and political mobilizations that accompanied it, continue to hold a privileged place in the collective memory of erstwhile guests and organizers of the festival. Such apparent contradictions suggest it would be important to further explore East Berlin's policy of international solidarity—which has come under increased scrutiny in recent years—in an attempt to discern the daily reality of these mobilizations beyond the official speeches and enactments.[7]

Finally, we must remember that the international dimension of the Leipzig Festival also evolved in reaction to increasingly stiff competition with other festivals—whether with documentary festivals in the West (Kötzing 2013) or those in the East, such as in Krakow. Within the international festival geography—however strongly influenced by the Cold War context—Leipzig won itself a unique place. After 1990, the social arena in which filmmakers worked and their films were being produced and circulated had changed dramatically. The challenge for the Leipzig Festival was to maintain its reputation and niche in a transformed festival landscape. Now, the challenges brought about by international openness had utterly altered the stakes involved.

Tracing the Past

In exploring the history of the Leipzig Festival, we are led to reflect upon what endures of the Cold War festival years, which are now between history, memory, and oblivion. Here is how Claas Danielsen opened a round table discussion in October 2013:

> It is important to reveal to what extent the state's intrusion into the running of the festival directly impacted many people. And, for us, the current organizers of the festival, it is all the more important to be conscious of this history, of which we can see the traces to this very day. We are, effectively, working in spaces and places that are in no way devoid of memories or outside of time.[8]

Thirty years later, the roundtable was focusing on the Stasi intervention of 18 November 1983 against the peaceful demonstrators gathered in front of the Capitol Cinema, where the festival's opening ceremony was unfolding. During his tenure from 2004 to 2014, Danielsen actively contributed to preserving the traces of the past, initiating a clear commitment to do so among festival organizers.

The fiftieth anniversary celebrations of the festival in 2007 bore witness to this project. Four events in the program were devoted to the anniversary: a retrospective, a symposium, a book publication, and the release of a DVD boxed set.[9] The retrospective, titled "Tracing the Past: Film Perspectives over Five Decades," was originally conceived by Grit Lemke. Born in the GDR in 1965, Lemke had been part of the festival team since 1991 and embodied, as it were, a living memory of all the years since the break represented by the *Wende*. With the retrospective, she hoped to trace "the political topography of an event that was much more than a film festival" (Lemke 2017: 122). The symposium Identities of a Festival explored the inheritance represented by the festival's first four decades.

The retrospective—which spanned the gamut from avant-garde films to films touting the East Berlin orthodoxy—succeeded in showing the political, aesthetic, and geographical diversity of perspectives screened and discovered at Leipzig. The edited volume *Bilder einer gespaltenen Welt* (Images of a Divided World) compiled by film historian Ralf Schenk (2007) assembled former protagonists of the festival—including Christiane Mückenberger, Fred Gehler, Ronald Trisch, and journalists Wilhelm Roth and Margit Voss—and researchers of different generations and nationalities. Their diverse standpoints offer a differentiated, chronological, and thematic panorama of cultural policy iterations implemented at Leipzig.

This series of events and publications, at the core of the 2007 festival, were aimed at a broad audience in Germany and abroad and demonstrated a longing to nourish a pluralistic and open reflection on the festival's history—crucially, in association with its former protagonists. Lemke's initiative, with the support of Claas Danielsen, was pivotal here and continued after she became head of film programming in 2010. Danielsen's departure in 2014 and Lemke's in 2016, however, marked the end of a phase in the festival's history that prioritized maintaining ties between the past and present, all while undertaking transformations necessary for DOK Leipzig to continue to thrive among other German and international film festivals.[10]

In November 2017, the sixtieth edition of the festival took place with a thoroughly new team. In acknowledgment of the festival's anniversary, Ralph Eue, the new head of film programming, developed a series of three screenings-cum-discussions titled "Then and Now. Now and Then," intended to highlight "themes, cinematographic languages, and ideological changes of atmosphere that will not only bring out ruptures and continuities from sixty years of film, cultural and social history but form a comprehensive moving image of the history of DOK."[11] As it was scheduled during the weekend prior to the festival opening, this historical segment seems to have been intended more for the inhabitants of Leipzig than for festival goers from elsewhere in Germany and abroad.

Over three evenings, six participants from the festival's past and researchers specializing in the history of documentary, the GDR, and the festival held informal conversations covering the GDR and ensuing eras in the same narrative embrace on the following: politics and history, youth in film festivals, and the art of documentary addressing other arts. During the festival itself, the sixtieth retrospective was devoted to the other notable 2017 anniversary—the Soviet October Revolution and its aftermath—and titled "Commanders—Chairmen—General Secretaries. Communist Rule in the Visual Languages of Cinema."

Twenty-eight years after German unification, the festival's East German past, while not forgotten, no longer seemed central to the identity of a Leipzig Festival in the midst of changes. Perhaps tellingly, for the first time the new festival director—Leena Pasanen, who took up the post in 2015—is not from Germany but rather Finland. Born in 1965, Pasanen worked as a journalist, film director, and director of television programming in Helsinki before moving to the European Documentary Network in Copenhagen; she was then head of the FinnAgora Cultural Institute in Budapest from 2011 to 2014. Upon taking up the reins in Leipzig, she said, "DOK Leipzig has a long history and a firm place in Eastern European film culture, so it was an exciting challenge for me to take over as its director and try something new" (Prahs 2015). By highlighting the festival's past and its regional roots in a geography inherited from pre-1990 Eastern Europe, Pasanen seems to understand that the festival's roots in the Cold War still have meaning in the present; yet, at the same time, her call for renewal is very clear. How this internationalization of the directorship of the Leipzig Festival will play out, the future alone will tell.

Notes

1. According to its website, it is second in size only to the Amsterdam Documentary Film Festival, with an average of over 45,000 viewers and over 300 films from around the world every year.
2. Author's interview with Jürgen Böttcher, Berlin/Karlshorst, Germany (31 October 2000).
3. See Appendix III, Leipzig Festival Retrospectives.
4. See Krause 2002. For a recent reflection on the nature of dissidence in the GDR from a comparative perspective, see Eichwede et al. 2017.
5. The decisive factor in this disappearance was the privatization of the studio in June 1990, which provoked a wave of dismissals. Of 877 employees on 1 January 1990, only 660 remained on 1 January 1991, and the following April, only 330 (Radevagen 1992).
6. For an overview of this historiographical debate, see Romero 2014.
7. See Slobodian 2015; Emmerling 2013; for Chile, Maurin 2003; Düfner 2008.
8. Claas Danielsen's introductory speech for an evening titled "Kerzen vor dem Capitol. Kritische Jugend, Dokwoche und Stasi." Zeitgeschichtliches Forum Leipzig, 29 October 2013. The taped debates are online at: http://www.dok-leipzig.de/industry-training/industry-offers/panels/kerzen.
9. The DVD boxed set, put out by Icestorm Entertainment in 2007, is called *Spurensuche—DDR-Dokumentarfilme im Abseits*. It is different from the other commemorations of the fiftieth anniversary of the Leipzig Festival in that it represents a very selective vision—highlighting "unusual films that recall the history of a wholly unusual festival"—and runs the risk of erasing all too soon the memory of all the other films, which nevertheless dominated East German production and, thus, the festival (Edition DOK Leipzig, *Spurensuche—DDR-Dokumentarfilme im Abseits*, Berlin: Icestorm Entertainment, 2007).
10. In addition to the change of logo and name to DOK Leipzig in 2005, we should note the launching of DOK Markt in the same year, which sought to attract the documentary industry to Leipzig.
11. See: https://www.dok-leipzig.de/en/dok/dokarchiv/2017/festival/jubilaeum/programm.

APPENDIX I

Archival Sources

East German archives were almost completely opened following German unification in fall 1990. In addition to routine regulations limiting access to archives less than thirty years old, certain judiciary archives have not yet been made entirely accessible, however (Mouralis 2008). The bulk of archival documents used in this history of the Leipzig Documentary Film Festival reside in a handful of archives, all in Berlin.

The Bundesarchiv (BArch, the FRG's Federal Archive) was established in 1919 and incorporates a wide range of collections. Several former East German archives were integrated into it after unification, two of which are of primary importance here. The records of the Ministry of Culture and its Central Administration for Film (HVFilm) make it possible to follow the evolution of the GDR's cultural policies. The Stiftung Archiv der Parteien und Massenorganisationen der DDR (SAPMO-BArch, Foundation Archive of the Parties and Mass Organizations of the GDR) houses records related to the SED Party and other mass organizations in the GDR. In combination, these two archives make it possible to trace areas of dissension between the government and the party in matters related to film and the Leipzig Festival.

The holdings of the GDR's State Film Archive (SFA) were integrated into the Bundesarchiv-Filmarchiv (BArch-FArch, Federal Archive-Film Archive). It houses an enormous collection of German and foreign documentary films as well as production documents, stills, and film negatives of DEFA productions. Not all DEFA films are included, however, as some disappeared during the GDR or in the tumultuous period encompassing the opening of the Wall (1989), German unification (1990), and the privatization (1992) of the studios. In 2004, records related to the Leipzig Festival (BArch-FArch, Leipzig) were moved to the archive's site in Berlin-Lichterfelde. These make it possible to document the different stages of the festival in depth, from organization to reception. Although not always exhaustive, records include minutes of meetings of the Organizing Committee, *Festival Bulletins* published during the festival, annual reviews of the prior year's festival (*Protokolle*), lists of films and invited guests, international press coverage, photographs, and so on. Correspondence—only partially conserved—offers important insights into the types of relationships and contacts existing within the festival and with officials of the regime.

While the archives of the Behörde des Bundesbeauftragten für die Unterlagen des Staatssicherheitsdienstes (BStU, Federal Agency in Charge of the Archives of the State Security Service [Stasi] of the Former GDR) attracted a great deal of attention as soon as the Wall opened, they have not been central to this study. Records concerning the Leipzig Festival can be found in both the central site in Berlin and Leipzig's local Stasi archive. Only one set of documents, related to the spectacular incident involving the Stasi in 1983, was required.[1]

Finally, the Politisches Archiv für Auslängische Angelegenheiten (PA/AA, Political Archive for Foreign Affairs) houses the records of the Ministerium für Auslängische Angelegenheiten der DDR (MfAA, Ministry of Foreign Affairs of the GDR); these make it possible to explore decisions and debates related to the GDR's international relations as well as international visitors and filmmakers who participated in the Leipzig Festival.

Note

1. See Chapter 8. I thank Günter Jordan for helping me gain access to this archive.

APPENDIX II

List of Interviews

Böttcher, Jurgen, DEFA documentary director, painter. Berlin-Karlshorst: 31 October 2000, 2 hours.

Danielsen, Claas, Leipzig Festival director 2004–2014. Leipzig: 24 October 2004, ½ hour.

Gass, Karl, cofounder of the Leipzig Festival, DEFA documentary director. Berlin-Kleinmachnow: 28 July 2000, 3 hours; 8 August 2000, 3½ hours.

Grélier, Robert, French journalist. Paris: 15 October 1999, 3½ hours.

Harkenthal, Gisa, East German journalist. Muchin (Anklam): 7 August 2000, 5 hours.

Harkenthal, Wolfgang, Leipzig Festival director 1964–1972. Muchin (Anklam): 7 August 2000, 5 hours.

Heise, Thomas, East German documentary director. Nyon: 25 April 2002, 1 hour.

Jordan, Günter, DEFA documentary director, film historian. Berlin-Kleinmachnow, multiple discussions.

Kersten, Heinz, West Berlin journalist. Berlin: 24 November 2002, 1 hour.

Klaue, Wolfgang, responsible for Leipzig Festival retrospectives, GDR State Film Archive director 1969–1990, DEFA Foundation director 1998–2003. Berlin: 30 June 1999, 2 hours.

Klunker, Heinz, West German journalist (left GDR in 1955). Berlin: 15 September 2004, 1½ hour.

Koepp, Volker, DEFA documentary director. Nyon: 24 April 2002, 1 hour.

Lehmann, Christian, DEFA cinematographer. Berlin: 22 August 2000, 3 hours.

Nickel, Gitta, DEFA documentary director. Werder: 3 August 2000, 3½ hours.

Pawloff, Niko, DEFA cinematographer. Berlin: 9 August 2000, 5 hours.

Richter, Erika, GDR representative to the FICC, film historian. Berlin: 1 November 2000, 1½ hour.

Roth, Wilhelm, West German journalist. Berlin: 9 March 2003, 2 hours.

Schwarze, Wolfgang, DEFA scriptwriter and dramaturg. Berlin-Pankow: 15 August 2000, 1½ hour.

Trampe, Tamara, DEFA scriptwriter and dramaturg. Berlin: 23 August 2004, 1½ hour.

Trisch, Ronald, Leipzig Festival director 1973–1989. Berlin: 11 March 2004, 4 hours.

Vautier, René, documentary director. Montreuil: 30 November 1999, 2 hours.

Zaoralová, Eva, critic and film historian. Prague: 21 August 2007, 2 hours.

APPENDIX III

Leipzig Festival Retrospectives

Chronological Overview

Films of the World for Peace in the World, 1961
The Films of Cavalcanti, A. (Brazil/France), 1962
The Films of Ivens, J. (Netherlands), 1963
The Films of Flaherty, R. (USA), 1964
Films against Fascism, 1965
Films from France, 1966
Fifty Years of Soviet Documentary Film, 1967
Films from Poland, 1968
GDR Documentary Cinema and Television Journalism, 1969
Documentaries in the Age of Lenin, 1970
The Films of Karmen, R. (USSR), 1971
Films from Latin America, 1972
Traditions of the Proletarian Film Movement in Germany before 1933, 1973
Films from Cuba, 1974
Leipzig Prize Winners 1956–1974, 1975
Films from Japan, 1976
New Soviet Documentary Films, 1977
Animation Films from Socialist Countries, 1978
HFF Films (Babelsberg Film Academy), 1979
Films from Czechoslovakia, 1980
Films from the USA, 1981
Trailblazers, 1982
Films from Chile, 1983
Films from Great Britain, 1984
Animation Films for Peace, 1985

Films from Spain (1936–1939), 1986
Documentary Films of the Central Asian Soviet Republics, 1987
Films from India, 1988
The Films of Gass, K. (GDR), 1989
The Films of Wildenhahn, K. (FRG), 1990

Thematic Summary of Retrospectives

Based on Mauersberger 1997: 215.

National and Regional Cinemas (non-USSR) (11)

France, 1966
Poland, 1968
Latin America, 1972
Cuba, 1974
Japan, 1976
Czechoslovakia, 1980
USA, 1981
Chile, 1983
Great Britain, 1984
Spain (1936–1939), 1986
India, 1988

Portraits of Documentary Filmmakers (7)

Vertov, D. (USSR), 1960
Cavalcanti, A. (Brazil/France), 1962
Ivens, J. (Netherlands), 1963
Flaherty, R. (USA), 1964
Karmen, R. (USSR), 1971
Gass, K. (GDR), 1989
Wildenhahn, K. (FRG), 1990

Transnational Themes (6)

Films of the World for Peace in the World, 1961
Films against Fascism, 1965
Leipzig Prize Winners 1956–1974, 1975
Animation Films from Socialist Countries, 1978
Trailblazers, 1982
Animation Films for Peace, 1985

USSR / Soviet Union (4)

Fifty Years of Soviet Documentary Film, 1967
Documentaries in the Age of Lenin, 1970
New Soviet Documentary Films, 1977
Documentary Films of the Central Asian Soviet Republics, 1987

GDR, FRG and Germany (5)

GDR Documentary Cinema and Television Journalism, 1969
Traditions of the Proletarian Film Movement in Germany before 1933, 1973
HFF (Film Academy), 1979
Gass, K. (GDR), 1989
Wildenhahn, K. (FRG), 1990

APPENDIX IV
Leipzig Festival Statistics

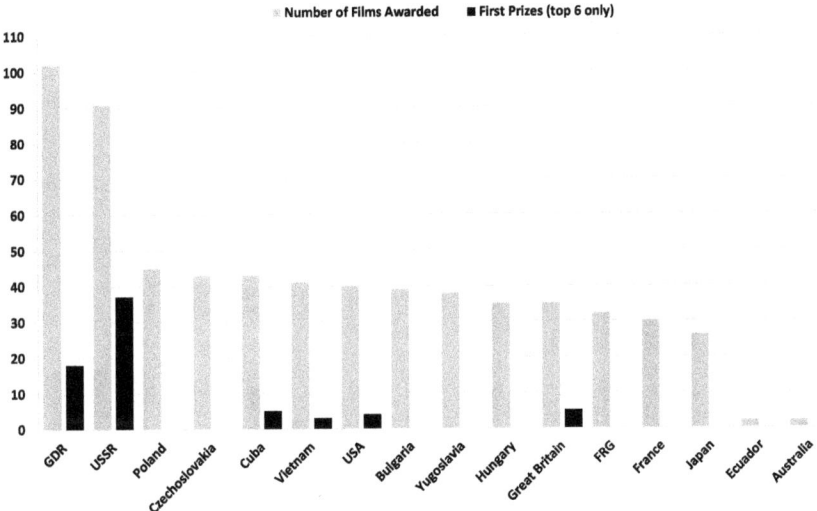

Figure A.1. Number of awarded films by country, 1955–86

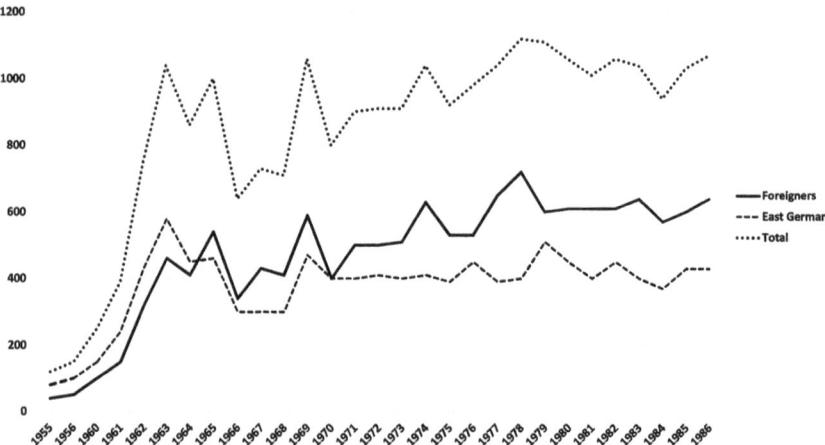

Figure A.2. Invited GDR and foreign guests

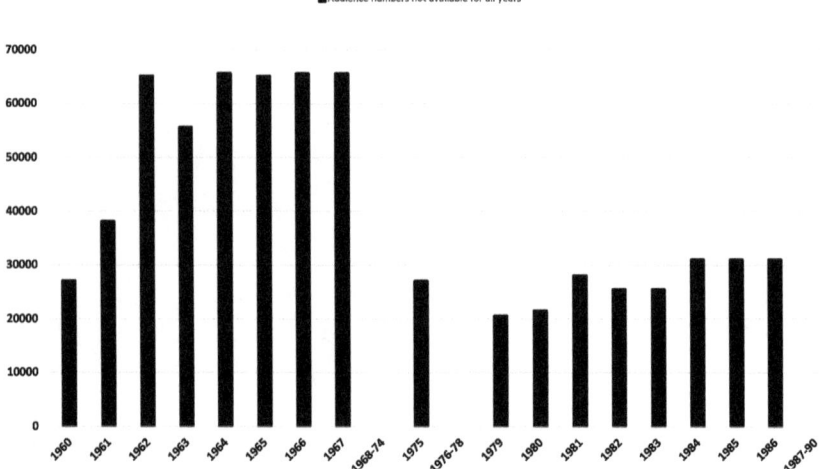

Figure A.3. Audience numbers

Source: The information represented in these graphs was taken from Statistische Angaben zur Internationalen Leipziger Dokumentar- und Kurzfilmwoche 1955–1986 (BArch-FArch, Leipzig Festival Collection, 1986). Calculations made by the author.

Glossary of Acronyms and Organizations

AdK: Akademie der Künste der DDR—GDR Academy of Arts

BArch: Bundesarchiv—German Federal Archive (FRG)

BArch-FArch: Bundesarchiv-Filmarchiv—Film Archive of the German Federal Archive (FRG)

BBS: Balázs Béla Studio, Budapest (Hungary)

BStU: Behörde des Bundesbeauftragten für die Unterlagen des Staatssicherheitsdienstes der ehemaligen DDR—Federal Agency in Charge of the Archives of the State Security Service (Stasi) of the Former GDR (FRG)

CGT: Confédération générale du travail—General Confederation of Labor (France)

CPSU: Kommunistícheskaya pártiya Sovétskogo Soyúza—Communist Party of the USSR

CSDF: Tsentral'naya studiya dokumental'nykh fil'mov—Central Studio for Documentary Film (USSR)

ČST: Československá televize—Czechoslovakian State Television

DEFA: Deutsche Film Aktiengesellschaft—State-owned film studios of the GDR

DFF: Deutsche Fernsehfunk—German Television Company (GDR)

dffb: Deutsche Film- und Fernsehakademie Berlin—German Film and Television Academy Berlin (FRG)

DJV: Deutsche Journalisten-Verband—German Film Journalists Association

DPA: Deutsche Presse-Agentur—German Press Agency (FRG)

DSV: Deutscher Schriftstellerbund—German Authors' League

FDGB: Freie Deutsche Gewerkschaftsbund—Free German Trade Union Federation (GDR)

FDJ: Freie Deutsche Jugend — Free German Youth (GDR)

FIAPF: Fédération Internationale des Associations de Producteurs de Films — International Federation of Film Producers Associations

FIPRESCI: Fédération Internationale de la Presse Cinématographique — International Film Critics Federation

FRG: Federal Republic of Germany (West Germany; since 3 October 1990, united Germany)

GDR: German Democratic Republic (East Germany)

HFF: Hochschule für Film und Fernsehen — Academy for Film and Television (GDR, in Potsdam-Babelsberg)

HVFilm: Hauptverwaltung Film — Central Administration for Film in the Ministry of Culture (GDR)

IDA: International Documentary Association

ISKRA: Image, Son, Kinéscope et Réalisations Audiovisuelles — Image, Sound, Audiovisual Cinescope and Creations

KAG: Künstlerische Arbeitsgruppe — Artistic Production Group (DEFA Film Studios)

KPD: Kommunistische Partei Deutschlands — Communist Party of Germany

KSČ: Komunistická strana Československa — Communist Party of Czechoslovakia

MfAA: Ministerium für Auswärtige Angelegenheiten der DDR — GDR Foreign Ministry

MIFF: Moskóvskiy myezhdoonaródniy kinofyestivál — Moscow International Film Festival

NÖS: Neues Ökonomische System — New Economic Policy (GDR)

NVA: Nationale Volksarmee — National People's Army (GDR)

OIRT: Organisation Internationale de Radiodiffusion et de Télévision — International Radio and Television Organization

PA/AA: Politisches Archiv für Ausländische Angelegenheiten — Political Archive for Foreign Affairs

PZPR: Polska Zjednoczona Partia Robotnicza — Polish United Workers' Party

SAPMO-BArch: Stiftung Archiv der Parteien und Massenorganisationen der DDR — Foundation Archive of the Parties and Mass Organizations of the GDR

SBZ: Sowietische Besatzungszone — Soviet Occupation Zone

SED: Sozialistische Einheitspartei Deutschlands—Socialist Unity Party of Germany (GDR)

SFA: Staatliches Filmarchiv der DDR—State Film Archive of the GDR

SFP: Stowarzyszenie Filmowców Polskich—Polish Filmmakers' Association

SLON: Société pour le lancement des oeuvres nouvelles—Society for Launching New Works

SPD: Sozialdemokratische Partei Deutschlands—Social Democratic Party of Germany (FRG)

Stasi: Ministerium für Staatssicherheit, Staatssicherheitsdienst—Ministry for State Security, Service for State Security (GDR secret police)

VBK: Verband Bildender Künstler der DDR—GDR Association of Visual Artists

VDJ: Journalists' Association (GDR)

VEB: Volkseigener Betrieb—Publicly owned company (GDR)

VFF: Verband der Film- und Fernsehschaffenden—Association of Film and Television Workers (GDR)

VGIK: Gerasimov Institute of Cinematography, Moscow (USSR)

VOKS: Vsesoiuznoe Obshchestvo Kul'turnoi Sviazi s zagranitsei—All-Union Society for Cultural Relations with Foreign Countries (USSR)

VVB: Vereinigung Volkseigener Betriebe—Association of Publicly Owned Enterprises (GDR)

VVB-Film: Association of State Owned Film Enterprises (GDR)

WYF: Weltfestspiele der Jugend und Studenten—World Youth Festival

ZDF: Zweites Deutsches Fernsehen—Second German Television Channel (FRG)

ZK: Zentralkomitee der SED—Central Committee of the SED

Bibliography

Primary Sources

"Abschlussbericht der Auswahlkommission der 32. Leipziger Woche." 1990. *Beiträge zur Film- und Fernsehwissenschaft* 38: 165–66.
Ackermann, Anton. 1951. *Auf neuen Wegen: 5 Jahre fortschrittlicher deutscher Film*. Berlin: Deutscher Filmverlag.
Albrecht, Hartmut. 1964. "Warum Ulrich Thein nicht sprechen wollte." *National-Zeitung* (Fall).
———. 1969. "Leipzig 1968." *Filmwissenschaftliche Beiträge* 10: 255.
Allende, H. B. de. 1974. [At the Leipzig Festival]. In *Protokoll 1973*: 12.
"Ansprache des Vorsitzenden des Clubs der Filmschaffenden der DDR, Harry Hindemith, zur Eröffnung der III. Leipziger Kurz- und Dokumentarfilmwoche, 1960." 1961. In *Protokoll 1960*: 5–6.
"Arbeitsordnung der Jury." 1961. [Leipzig, 12 November 1961]. In *Protokoll 1965*: 6.
Baumert, Heinz. 1964. "'Cinéma-vérité'—das Problem des sprechenden Menschen vor der Kamera." *Filmwissenschaftliche Mitteilungen* no. 5: 306–37.
Becher, Uta. 1987. "Video—Möglichkeiten eines neuen Mediums." *Podium und Werkstatt* 27: 79–80.
"Behörden. DDR-Film: Lachender Mann." 1967. *Der Spiegel* 24: 70.
Berger, Peter, and Ursula Meves. 1984. "Was Arbeiter können—in einem Staat, in dem Arbeiter regieren." *Neues Deutschland*, 29 November.
Bhowhagary, Jehange. 1974. [Interview]. In *Protokoll 1973*: 67.
Biegholdt, Michael, Werner Wüste, and Karl Gass. 1964. "Unsere Arbeit an dem Dokumentarfilm *Feierabend*." *Filmwissenschaftliche Mitteilungen* 2: 264–75.
Biermann, Wolf. 2001. "Die Ausbürgerung." *Der Spiegel* 46 (12 November): 60–68, 76–78.
———. 2016. *Warte nicht auf bessre Zeiten! Die Autobiographie*. Berlin: Propyläen.
Biermann, Wolf, and Fritz Pleitgen. 2001. *Die Ausbürgerung: Anfang vom Ende der DDR*. Berlin: Ullstein.
Bisky, Lothar. 1989. "Medien, Konzepte, Positionen." [Interview with Manuela Thieme]. In *Festival Bulletin* vol. 3.
Böttcher, Jürgen. 1964. "Bemerkungen zu meinem Film *Stars*." *Filmwissenschaftliche Beiträge* 1: 1–12.

Böttcher, Jürgen, and Erika Richter. 2000. "Filmsplitter. Fragmentarisches über die Anfänge." [Interview with Erika Richter, 16 March 2000]. In *Apropos: Film 2000*, ed. Ralf Schenk, Erika Richter, and Claus Löser. Berlin: Neue Berlin. 10–16.

Brinckmann, Heinz. 1990. In *Festival Bulletin* vol. 4: 2.

Cahiers du cinéma. 1990. Special issue, "Spécial cinéma soviétique" (September).

Cohn-Vossen, Richard. 1976. "Als Mensch zum Menschen werden." *Film und Fernsehen* 2.

Cortázar, Octavio. 1979. "Por primera vez." *Film und Fernsehen* 5.

Danielsen, Claas. 2004. "Wandel und Beständigkeit." In *Katalog des 47. Internationalen Leipziger Festivals für Dokumentar- und Animationsfilm: 19. bis 24. Oktober 2004*, ed. Patricia Steer. Leipzig: Leipziger Dok-Filmwochen. 4–5.

Darde, Jean-Noël. 2017. *Chili 73, 74, Chacabuco, Pisagua* . . . Accessed September 2017. http://cluster014.ovh.net/~chilirda/chili73/?page_id=304 on 27.

Dedijer, Vladimir, and Jean-Paul Sartre, eds. 1967–1968. *Le tribunal Russell*. Paris: Gallimard.

Deutsche Volkszeitung. 1984. 21 December.

Deutsche Zeitung und Wirtschaftszeitung. 1961. 20 December.

Djagalov, Rossen, and Masha Salazkina. 2016. "Tashkent '68: A Cinematic Contact Zone." *Slavic Review* 75, 2 (Summer): 279–298.

Evangelische Pressedienst, ed. 1988. "Lahme Taube." *Die Welt*, 3 December.

Färber, Helmut. 1966. *Filmkritik* 1.

Festival Bulletin. 1987. Vols. 2–3; 1988, Vol. 3; 1989, Vols. 1–5; 1990, Vols. 1–4.

Frankfurter Allgemeine Zeitung. 1973. 30 July.

"Für den Aufschwung der fortschrittlichen deutschen Filmkunst. Resolution des Politbüros des ZK der SED." 1952. *Neues Deutschland*, 27 July.

Gass, Karl. 1982. "Näher an das Leben, an die Menschen heran." In Herlinghaus 1982: 399–408.

Gehler, Fred. 1963. "Le joli mai." *Sonntag* 49.

———. 1964. "Authentizität und Wahrheit." *Sonntag* 49.

Genth, Johanna. 1992. "Zwischen den Zeiten. Ein Festival auf Reisen. Filme von DEFA-DokumentarfilmregisseurInnen: November 1989/1990." [Conversation with Jürgen Böttcher]. *Informationsblatt*. Filmtheater Babylon / Dokfilmstudio Babelsberg.

Gregor, Ulrich. 1966a. [Introduction]. Special issue, "Obyknowennyj faschism/The Land/Point of Order," *Kinemathek*, 24 February.

———. 1966b. *Die Welt*, 26 November.

———. 1967a. "Kulturelles Wort: Kulturpolitik, Atelier am Sonntagabend." *RIAS Berlin Radio*, 3 December.

———. 1967b. "Leipzig: im Zeichen Vietnams." *Filmkritik* 1.

———. 1968a. *Filmkritik* 1.

———. 1968b. *Filmkritik* 5: 318.

Grigoriev, Roman. 1962. "Mich begeisterte die Dramaturgie des Lebens." In *Protokoll 1961*.

Harmssen, Henning. 1966. *Der Tagesspiegel*, 24 November.

Hein, Christoph. 1990. "Der alte Mann und die Strasse: Ansprache zur Demonstration der Berliner Kulturschaffenden." In *Als Kind habe ich Stalin gesehen: Essais und Reden*. Berlin: Aufbau-Verlag. 175–77.

Herlinghaus, Hermann. 1964. "Eine notwendige Erwiderung." *Filmwissenschaftliche Beiträge* 2: 439–70.
———. 1982. *Dokumentaristen der Welt in den Kämpfen unserer Zeit (1960–1981)*. Berlin: Henschelverlag.
Heynowski, Walter, and Gerhard Scheumann. 1968. *Piloten im Pyjama*. Berlin: Verlag der Nation.
Honecker, Erich. 1965. "Bericht des Politbüros an das XI. Plenum des ZK der SED, Dezember 1965." *Neues Deutschland*, 16 December. Reprinted in Judt 1997: 326–27.
———. 1971. "Zur Verwirklichung der Beschlüsse des VIII. Parteitages." *Berliner Zeitung*, 18 December.
Hornig, Harry. 1982. "Tendenzen." In *Protokoll 1981*: 24.
"Im Wettbewerb gezeigte Filme." 1961. In *Protokoll 1960*: 43–44.
Ivens, Joris. 1961. [Conference at the Freies Forum.] In *Protokoll 1960*: 26.
"Joris Ivens und Joop Huisken waren Trumpf." 1956. Forum, 2 November.
Junge, Winfried. 1982. "Die Geschichte der Kinder von Golzow." In Herlinghaus 1982: 459–66.
———. 1986. *Filmspiegel* 19: 10–11.
———. 1995. "Ästhetik des Vertrauens." In Zimmermann 1995: 133–49.
———. 2000. "Das Ding mit dem Preis." In Jacobsen 2000: 383–85.
Junge Welt. 1984. 4 December.
Karabasz, Kasimir. 1997. "Von Publizistik halte ich gar nichts." In Mauersberger 1997: 42–44.
Kersten, Heinz. 1983. "Zwischen Krieg und Frieden." *Tagesspiegel*, 27 November.
———. 1984. *Frankfurter Rundschau*, 3 December.
Kerzabi, Ahmed. 1963. [Interview]. In *Protokoll 1962*: 84.
Kirche und Film. 1960. No. 12.
Klaue, Wolfgang. 1997. "Etwas Zivilcourage, etwas Abenteuerlust." In Mauersberger 1997: 33–37.
———. 1998. "Retrospektiven in Leipzig." In Gehler and Steinmetz 1998: 25–30.
———. 2015. "PS zu den Retrospektiven." In *Bilder des Jahrhunderts. Staatliches Filmarchiv der DDR 1955–1990. Erinnerungen*, ed. Eva Hahm, Hans Karnstädt, Wolfgang Klaue, and Günter Schulz. Schriftenreihe der DEFA-Stiftung. Berlin: DEFA-Stiftung. 179–81.
Klaue, Wolfgang, and Manfred Lichtenstein. 1967. *Sowjetischer Dokumentarfilm*. Berlin: Staatliches Filmarchiv der Deutschen Demokratischen Republik.
Klein, Günter. 1961. "Bemerkungen zur Durchführung der Woche." In *Protokoll 1960*.
Koepp, Volker. 1995. "Meine Arbeit bei der DEFA." In Zimmermann 1995: 151–54.
———. 1997. "Reiseziel Leipzig." In Mauersberger 1997: 99–100.
———. 2004. "Notizen aus Tagebüchern." In *Volker Koepp, Menschen—Landschaften Filme von Wittstock bis Czernowitz; eine Retrospektive des Bundesarchiv-Filmarchivs während des 47. Internationalen Leipziger Festivals für Dokumentar- und Animationsfilm*, ed. Bundesarchiv-Filmarchiv. Berlin: Bundesarchiv-Filmarchiv. 41–44.
Kunze, Reiner. 1976. "Element." In *Die wunderbaren Jahre: Prosa; Ausgewählte Gedichte*. Frankfurt am Main: S. Fischer. 38–42.
Krug, Manfred. 1996. *Abgehauen: ein Mitschnitt und ein Tagebuch*. Düsseldorf: Econ.

Kunert, Günter. 1997. *Erwachsenenspiele*. Munich: Carl Hanser.
Kurowski, Ulrich. 1970. *Jugend Film Fernsehen*: 4–5. Quoted in "Bundesarbeitsgemeinschaft e.V. der deutschen Jugendfilmclubs." 1977. *Regisseur-Biographien*, vol. 11, Aix-La-Chapelle: 182.
"Leipzig 1989: Abschlussbericht der Auswahlkommission des 32. Internationalen Dokumentar- und Kurzfilmwoche für Kino und Fernsehen." 1990. *Beiträge zur Film- und Fernsehwissenschaft* 38: 161.
"Leipziger friedensfilmfestival." 1983. *Tageszeitung*, 29 November.
Lemke, Grit. 2017. "Die Spuren des Politischen. Zur Filmauswahl der internationalen Retrospektive." *Katalog des 50. Festivals* : 122–124.
Loest, Erich. 2001. *Träumereien eines Grenzgängers: Respektlose Bemerkungen über Kultur und Politik*. Stuttgart: Hohenheim-Verlag.
Lohmann, Hans. 1972. "Michail Romm." In *Regiestühle*, ed. Fred Gehler. Berlin: Henschelverlag. 83–97.
Lux, Petra. 1989. "Leipzig im Herbst." In *Festival Bulletin* vol. 1.
Mäde, M. 1987. "Und nur die Birke ist mir geblieben . . . " In *Festival Bulletin* vol. 2.
Maetzig, Kurt. 1946. "Vom Wesen des Dokumentarfilms." In Mückenberger and Jordan 1994: 256–57.
Makk, Károly. 1972. "Le cinéma hongrois est en bonne santé." *Cinéma 72* 165: 91–96.
Marker, Chris. 1964. "Beitrag auf dem Freien Forum in Leipzig." Film Wissenschaftliche *Mitteilungen* 1: 201.
———. 1971. "Le ciné-ours." *La revue du cinéma. Image et son* 225 (December): 4–5.
Märkische Union. 1984. 1 December.
———. 1997. "Doppelte Verwirrung." In Mauersberger 1997: 63–64.
Massip, José. 1997. "Eine ganz besondere Bindung." In Mauersberger 1997: 45–47.
1990. In *Festival Bulletin* vol. 1: 5.
Mauersberger, Kerstin, ed. 1997. *Weisse Taube auf dunklem Grund*. Berlin: Henschel.
Michel, Robert, ed. 1977. *Dokument und Kunst: Vietnam bei HeJS*. Arbeitsheft 27. Berlin: Akademie der Künste den Deutschen Demokratischen Republik.
Mitteldeutsche Neueste Nachrichten. 1956. 9 November.
———. 1984. 1 December.
Mückenberger, Christiane. 1990. [Interview]. In *Festival Bulletin* vol. 1: 5.
Navrátil, Antonín. 1964. "Wertow, die Thorndikes und das *Russische Wunder*." *Filmwissenschaftliche Beiträge* 2: 432–38.
Neuer Tag. 1984. 12 December.
Neues Deutschland. 1973a. 29 June.
———. 1973b. 6 August.
Patalas, Enno. 1964. "Leipzig: Ein Weg zum Nachbarn." *Filmkritik* 1.
Pfister, Thomas. 1979. *Film-Korrespondenz* 12, 18 December.
Pilard, Philippe. 1979. "Wiseman ou la découverte de l'Amérique." *La Revue du cinéma* 337 (March).
Prahs, Madeleine. "DOK Leipzig 2015. Seeing the World More precisely." [Interview with Leena Pasanen, Goethe-Institut Online, November 2015]. Accessed 15 June 2018. https://www.goethe.de/en/kul/flm/20649652.html.
Protokoll 1960–1988. [Annual publication, published the year following the festival]. Berlin.
Richter, Michael. 2004. "Der letzte Tag der DDR." *Tageszeitung*, 9–10 October.

Ritterbusch, Richard. 1998. "Das Festival öffnen: die Programmauswahl." In Gehler and Steinmetz 1998: 119–24.
Rodríguez de Silva, Marta. 1997. "Die eigenen Bilder." In Mauersberger 1997: 69–70.
Romm, Mikhaïl. 1981. "Von den Zweifeln und der Qual des Suchens." *Filmwissenschaftliche Beiträge* 3.
Roth, Wilhelm. 1966. *Süddeutsche Zeitung*, 24 November.
———. 1976. "Der trügerische Frieden von Leipzig." *Süddeutsche Zeitung*, 1 December.
———. 1977. "Mit kleinen Kühnheiten die Ecke glätten. Zum 20. Mal: die Leipziger Dokumentarfilmwoche." *Süddeutsche Zeitung*, 12 December.
———. 1984. *Süddeutsche Zeitung*, 5 December.
———. 1991. "Leipzig 1990: Zwischen den Zeiten." *epd Film* 1: 4.
Rouch, Jean. 1963. [Transcription]. *Arsept* 2 (April–June).
Rümmler, Klaus. 1990. "Ein Zeitdokument entstand." *Beiträge zur Film- und Fernsehwissenschaft* 38: 170–71.
Schehufer, Klaus. 1955. *Sonntag*, 2 October.
Scheumann, Gerhard. 1962. "Das Fernsehen—die Chance des Dokumentarfilms." *Filmwissenschaftliche Mitteilungen* 3: 444–64.
Schirrmacher, Franz. 1990. *Frankfurter Allgemeine Zeitung*, 1–2 June.
Schlegel, Hans-Joachim. 1975. "Leipziger Filmbilanz: Bonn vor der Anerkennung." *Berliner Extra-Dienst*, 9 December: 14–17.
Schmidt-Blum, Doris. 1983. "Von der Vorsicht gegenüber Menschen." *Stuttgarter Zeitung*, 26 November.
Schönemann, Hannes. 1990. [In a conversation with Steffi Grünewald]. In *Festival Bulletin* vol. 3: 13.
Sergiyenko, Rollan. 1987. "Jedes Wunder dauert nur neun Tage." In *Protokoll 1986*.
Special Festival Bulletin. 1989. (31 November).
Steiner, Roland. 1989. [Interview with Norbert Wehrstdt]. In *Festival Bulletin* vol. 2.
Tageszeitung. 1983. 29 November.
Tetzlaff, Kurt. 1984. *Film und Fernsehen* 10.
Theuerkauf, Herbert. 1956. "Vier Preise und drei Gartenzwerge." *Junge Welt*, 15 November.
Thieme, Manuela. 1989. "Na endlich!" In *Festival Bulletin* vol. 3.
Thorndike, Andrew. 1956. "Le court métrage est plus aimé qu'on ne le pense." *Sonntag*, 18 November.
———. 1962. "Den Menschen die Wahrheit sagen." In *Protokoll 1961*.
Thorndike, Annelie. 1974. "Discours d'ouverture du festival." In *Protokoll 1973*: 8.
Thüringer Landeszeitung. 1984. 29 November.
Thuy, Tran Van. 1988. [Interview with Oksana Bulgakowa]. In *Festival Bulletin* vol. 2.
Trisch, Ronald. 1974. "Willkommen" In *Protokoll 1973*: 6.
Umbach, Klaus. 1983. "Alltag im Oderbruch, ein Lehrstück für Macher." *Der Spiegel* (20 June): 135–40.
Uralov, Oleg. 1987. "Eine Zeit, die Wahrheit braucht." [Interview with Petra Lux]." In *Festival Bulletin* vol. 3.
Vautier, René. 1970. "Die zwei Kulturen und die Entwicklung des französischen Films seit Mai 1968." *Filmwissenschaftliche Beiträge*: 337–48.
Verband der Film- und Fernsehschaffenden, ed. 1988. *V. Kongress. Protokoll 2; Schriftlich eingereichte Diskussionsbeiträge; Grussadressen an den V. Kongress;*

Beschlüsse und Festlegungen. Berlin: Verband der Film- und Fernsehschaffenden der DDR.
"VFF, Veränderungen in der Medienpolitik erörtert." 1989. *Leipziger Volkszeitung,* 27 October.
Vider, Ciril. 1983. *Tageszeitung,* 10 December.
Voigt, Jutta. 1969. *Sonntag,* 7 December.
———. 1981. "Eins plus eins: Winfried Junge und Hans-Eberhard Leupold im Gespräch." *Sonntag* 47: 5.
———. 1989. "Wenn Stuyvesant kommt." *Sonntag* 51.
Wehling, Will. 1956. "Viel Zelluloïd — wenig Licht." *Die Welt,* 20 November.
———. 1960. "Auch im Osten ist man gegen Experimente." *Die Welt,* 26 November.
Weiss, Konrad. 1987. "Die neue alte Gefahr: Junge Faschisten in der DDR." *Kontext,* 5 March, 3–13.
———. 1989. *Lehrjahre bei Karl Gass.* Leipzig: Komitee Internationale Leipziger Dokumentar- und Kurzfilmwochen.
———. 1990. "Der Heimatverlust schmerzt." *Der Spiegel* 8 (19 February): 27–28.
Wischnewski, Klaus. 1990. "Hoffnungen, Illusionen, Einsichten." *Film und Fernsehen* 6: 35.
Witt, Günter. 1965. "Rede zur Abschlußeranstaltung." In *Protokoll 1964*: 31.
"Zahnbürste mitnehmen." 1983. *Tageszeitung,* 10 December.

Secondary Sources

Agde, Günter. 1991. *Kahlschlag. Das 11. Plenum der ZK der SED 1965. Studien und Dokumente.* Berlin: Aufbau Taschenbuch Verlag.
Aitken, Ian, ed. 2005. *Encyclopedia of the Documentary Film.* New York: Routledge.
———, ed. 2013. *The Concise Routledge Encyclopedia of the Documentary Film.* New York: Routledge.
Allan, Seán, and John Sandford, eds. 1999. *DEFA East German Cinema, 1946–1992.* New York: Berghahn Books.
Álvarez, Santiago. 1997. "Aus einem anderen Stoff gemacht." In Mauersberger 1997: 65–67.
Ansorg, Leonore. 1999. *"Irgendwie war da eben kein System 'drin'": Strukturwandel und Frauenerwerbstätigkeit in der Ost-Prignitz (1968–1989).* In Lindenberger 1999b: 75–117.
Arrighi, Giovanni, Terence K. Hopkins, and Immanuel Wallerstein. 1997. "1989 — die Fortsetzung von 1968." In *1968 — Ein europäisches Jahr,* ed. Étienne François, Matthias Middell, Emmanuael Terray, and Dorothea Wierling. Leipzig: Leipziger Universitatsverlag. 147–64.
Aspects du cinéma soviétique. 1987–1988. Vol. 9.
Autissier, Anne-Marie, ed. 2008. *L'Europe des festivals. De Zagreb à Édimbourg, points de vue croisés.* Paris: Editions de l'attribut.
Badia, Gilbert. 2000. "L'association France-RDA." In *La RDA et l'Occident (1949–1990),* ed. Ulrich Pfeil. Asnières: Presses Sorbonne Nouvelle. 453–64.
Baecque, Antoine de, and Emmanuelle Loyer. 2007. *Histoire du festival d'Avignon.* Paris: Gallimard.

Barbat, Victor. 2013. "Roman Karmen, un soviétique au Chili: campagne de tournage et solidarité à l'Est autour du film Le Coeur de Corvalán." In Roudé and Barbat 2013.

———. Forthcoming. "Roman Karmen, la vulgate soviétique de l'Histoire. Stratégies et mode opératoire d'un opérateur-documentariste au XXe siècle." Ph.D., University Paris 1 Panthéon-Sorbonne.

Barck, Simone, and Inge Münz-Koenen, eds. 2002. *Im Dialog mit Werner Mittenzwei: Beiträge und Materialien zu einer Kulturgeschichte der DDR*. Berlin: Trafo-Verlag.

Barnouw, Erik. 1993. *Documentary: A History of the Non-Fiction Film*. Oxford: Oxford University Press.

Bartie, Angela. 2013. *The Edinburgh Festivals: Culture and Society in Post-war Britain*. Edinburgh: Edinburgh University Press.

Batančev, Dragan. 2017. "The Belgrade FEST, or What Happened When Peckinpah Met Wajd." In Kötzing and Moine 2017: 153–65.

Baumert, Heinz. 1991. "Das verbotene Heft: film-wissenschaftliche mitteilungen, 2/1965." In Agde 1991: 189–200.

Bazin, Jérôme. 2015. *Réalisme et égalité. Contribution à une histoire sociale de la peinture en RDA (1949–1990)*. Dijon: Presses du Réel.

Becker, Wieland, and Volker Petzold. 2001. *Tarkowski trifft King Kong: Geschichte der Filmclubbewegung in der DDR*. Berlin: Vistas.

Behrends, Jan C., Thomas Lindenberger, and Patrice G. Poutrus, eds. 2003. *Fremde und Fremd-Sein in der DDR: Zu den historischen Ursachen der Fremdfeindlichkeit in Ostdeutschland*. Berlin: Metropol.

Bensussan, Agnès. 2007. "La répression de la déviance politique en RDA (1971–1989)." Ph.D., University of Picardie Jules Verne.

Berger, Peter, and Ursula Meves. 1984. "Was Arbeiter können — in einem Staat, in dem Arbeiter regieren." *Neues Deutschland*, 29 November.

Berghahn, Volker. 2004. *Transatlantische Kulturkriege: Shepard Stone, die Ford-Stiftung und der europäische Antiamerikanismus*. Geschichte; Transatlantische historische Studien 21. Stuttgart: Franz Steiner Verlag.

Berry, Chris, and Luke Robinson, eds. 2017. *Chinese Film Festivals*. New York: Palgrave MacMillon.

Bessel, Richard, and Ralph Jessen. 1996. *Die Grenzen der Diktatur. Staat und Gesellschaft in der DDR*. Göttingen: Vandenhoeck & Ruprecht.

Beutelschmidt, Thomas. 1995. *Sozialistische Audiovision: Zur Geschichte der Medienkultur in der DDR*. Potsdam: Verlag für Berlin-Brandenburg, 1995.

———. 1998. "Dokfilm und Video: Wahrnehmung neuer Gestlatungs-formen und themen ab Mitte der 80er Jahre am Beispiel des Festivals." In Gehler and Steinmetz 1998: 83–104.

Beyer, Frank. 2001. *Wenn der Wind sich dreht*. Munich: Econ.

Bispinck, Henrik, Jürgen Danyel, Hans-Hermann Hertle, and Hermann Wentker. 2004. "Krisen und Aufstände im realen Sozialismus. Einleitung." In *Aufstände im Ostblock: Zur Krisensituation des realen Sozialismus*, ed. Henrik Bispinck, Jürgen Danyel, Hans-Hermann Hertle, and Hermann Wentker. Berlin: Ch. Links Verlag. 9–22.

Bispinck, Henrik, Dierk Hoffmann, Michael Schwartz, Peter Skyba, Matthias Uhl, and Hermann Wentker. 2005. "Die Zukunft der DDR-Geschichte. Potentiale und Probleme zeithistorischer Forschung." *Vierteljahrshefte für Zeitgeschichte* 4: 547–69.

Blahova, Jindriska, ed. 2014. "Filmove festivaly." [Film Festivals]. Special issue, *Iluminace: The Journal of Film Theory, History, and Aesthetics* 26: 1.
Bleek, Wilhelm, and Rainer Bovermann. 1995. "Die Deutschlandpolitik der SPD/FDP Koalition 1969–1982." In *Deutschlandpolitik, Innerdeutsche Beziehungen und Internationale Rahmenbedingungen.* Baden-Baden: Nomos.
Blume, Eugen, and Roland März, eds. 2003. *Kunst in der DDR. Eine Retrospektive der Nationalgalerie.* Berlin: Nationalgalerie.
Bois, Pierre du. 2003 "Guerre froide, propagande et culture (1945–1953)." *Relations Internationales* 115: 437–54.
Bollinger, Stefan. 1995. *Dritter Weg zwischen den Blöcken? Prager Frühling 1968: Hoffnung ohne Chance: mit einem Anhang bisher nicht veröffentlichter Dokumente zur Haltung der SED-Führung zum Prager Frühling.* Berlin: Trafo-Verlag.
Borchmeyer, Dieter. 2009. "Goethe." In François and Schulze 2009: 1:187–206.
Boym, Svetlana. 1994. *Common Places: Mythologies of Everyday Life in Russia.* Cambridge, MA: Harvard University Press.
Brandt, Hans-Jürgen. 1987. *NS-Filmtheorie und dokumentarische Praxis.* Tübingen: Max Niemeyer Verlag.
———. 1995. "Was aber bleibt? Ein Rückblick auf die Dokumentarfilme der DDR." In Zimmermann 1995: 161–76.
Bren, Paula. 2010. *The Greengrocer and Its Television: The Culture of Communism after the 1968 Prague Spring.* Ithaca: Cornell University Press.
Brunner, Detlev. 2015. "DDR 'transnational': Die 'internationale Solidarität' der DDR." In *Deutsche Zeitgeschichte—transnational*, ed. Alexander Gallus, Axel Schildt, and Detlef Siegfried. Göttingen: Wallstein Verlag. 64–80.
Buffet, Cyril. 2008. *Défunte DEFA. Une histoire du cinéma allemande.* Paris: Cerf-Corlet.
Buffet, Cyril, and Laurent Maguire, eds. 2014. *Cinéma et guerre froide. L'imaginaire au pouvoir.* Paris: Charles Corlet Eds.
Burkhardt, Bernd. 1995. "Die Abwicklung des DEFA-Studios für Dokumentarfilme durch die Treuhand." In Zimmermann 1995: 217–22.
Byg, Barton. 1999. "DEFA and the Traditions of International Cinema." In Allan and Sandford 1999: 22–41.
———. 2000. "Die Kinder von Golzow und die Porträtphotographie." In Zimmermann and Moldenhauer 2000: 361–79.
———. 2001. "GDR-Up: The Ideology of Universality in Long Term Documentary." *New German Critique* 82: 126–44.
Byg, Barton, and Betheny Moore, eds. 2002. *Moving Images of East Germany: Past and Future of DEFA Film.* Harry & Helen Gray Humanities Program series 12. Washington, D.C.: American Institute for Contemporary German Studies.
Camarade, Hélène, and Sibylle Goepper. 2016. *Résistance, dissidence et opposition en RDA (1949–1990).* Villeneuve-d'Ascq: Presses Universitaires du Septentrion.
Caron, Estelle, Michel Ionascu, and Marion Richoux. 1998. "Le cheminot, le mineur et le paysan." In Odin 1998a: 1:63–98.
Carter, Erica. 2001. "Culture, History and National Identity in the Two Germanies." In *Twentieth-Century Germany: Politics, Culture and Society, 1918–1990*, ed. Mary Fulbrook. New York: Oxford University Press. 247–69.
Caute, David. 2003. *The Dancer Defects: The Struggle for Cultural Supremacy during the Cold War.* Oxford: Oxford University Press.

Chaix, Gérald. 2009. "Die Reformation." In François and Schulze 2009: 2:9–27.
Chapman, James. 1998. *The British at War: Cinema, State, and Propaganda, 1939–1945*. London: I. B. Tauris Publishers.
Charnay, Amélie. 2003. "Le festival de Salzbourg: un lieu de médiation culturelle internationale (1917–1938)." *Relations internationales* 116 (Winter): 549–58.
Chauliac, Marina. 2006. "Die Jugendweihe zwischen familialem und politischem Erbe der DDR: zur Erfindung einer neuen Tradition." In Droit and Kott 2006: 198–215.
Chomentowski, Gabrielle. 2016. *Filmer l'Orient. Politique des nationalités et cinéma en URSS (1917–1938)*. Paris : Éditions Pétra.
Clemens, Petra. 1998. "Les femmes de l'usine de drap: Contribution à l'histoire du travail féminin en RDA sur la base de sources biographiques." *Annales, histoire, sciences sociales* 53, no. 1: 69–89.
Cœuré, Sophie. 1999. *La grande lueur à l'Est. Les Français et l'Union soviétique, 1917–1939*. Paris: Seuil.
"The Cold War and the Movies." 1998. Special issue, *Film History* 10, no. 3.
Compagnon, Olivier, and Caroline Moine, eds. 2015. Special issue, "Chili 1973, un événement mondial." *Monde(s)* 8 (November).
Corbin-Schuffels, Anne-Marie. 1998. *La force de la parole: Les intellectuels face à la RDA et à l'unification allemande*. Paris: Presses universitaires du Septentrion.
Cortázar, Octavio. 1997. "Alles sehr naïv aber sympathisch." In Mauersberger 1997: 38–41.
Coumel, Laurent. 2001. "Moscou, 1960: La création de l'UDN." *Bulletin de l'Institut Pierre Renouvin* 12 (Autumn): 53–71.
Courtois, Stéphane, and Marc Lazar. 1995. *Histoire du Parti communiste français*. Paris: Presses universitaires de France.
Dagnaud, Monique. 2011. "Le cinéma, instrument du soft power des nations." *Géoéconomie* 3, no. 58: 21–30.
Dakowska, Dorota. 2014. *Le pouvoir des fondations: Des acteurs de la politique étrangère allemande*. Rennes: Presses universitaires de Rennes.
Dalos, György. 1991 "Über die Verwirklichung der Träume." In Deppe et al. 1991: 182–207.
———. 1995. "Der politische Umbruch in Ost- und Mitteleuropa und seine Bedeutung für die Bürgerbewegung in der DDR." In *Materialien der Enquete-Kommission: Aufarbeitung von Geschichte und Folgen der SED-Diktatur in Deutschland*, ed. Deutscher Bundestag. Frankfurt am Main: Suhrkamp. 541–57.
Damus, Martin. 1991. *Malerei der DDR. Funktionen der bildenden Kunst im realen Sozialismus*. Reinbek: Rowohlt.
Darnton, Robert. 1991. Berlin Journal, 1989–1990. New York: Norton.
Deiritz, Klaus, and Hannes Krauss, eds. 1991. *Der deutsch-deutsche Literaturstreit: Analysen und Materialien*. Hamburg: Luchterhand.
Delage, Christian. 1989. *La vision nazie de l'histoire. Le cinéma documentaire du Troisième Reich*. Lausanne: L'Âge d'Homme.
———. 2006. *La vérité par l'image: De Nuremberg au procès Milosevic*. Paris: Denoël.
Delage, Christian, and Vincent Guigueno. 2004. *L'historien et le film*. Paris: Gallimard.
Deppe, Rainer, Helmut Dubiel, and Ulrich Rödel, eds. 1991. *Demokratischer Umbruch in Osteuropa*. Frankfurt am Main: Suhrkamp.
Deutsche Kinemathek, ed. 2009. *70 mm — Bigger than Life*. Berlin: Bertz+Fischer.

Deutscher Bundestag, ed. 1995. "Protokoll der 35. Sitzung, 5. Mai 1993, Kultur und Kunst in der DDR." In *Materialien der Enquête-Kommission: Aufarbeitung von Geschichte und Folgen der SED Diktatur in Deutschland. Vol. 3, Rolle und Bedeutung der Ideologie, integrativer Faktoren und disziplinierender Praktiken im Staat und Gesellschaft der DDR*. Baden-Baden: Nomos.

De Valck, Marijke. 2007. *Film Festivals: From European Geopolitics to Global Cinephilia*. Amsterdam: Amsterdam University Press.

De Valck, Marijke, and Skadi Loist. 2009. "Film Festival Studies. An Overview of a Burgeoning Field." In *Film Festival Yearbook, 1: The Festival Circuit, St. Andrews Film Studies*, ed. Dina Iordanova and Ragan Rhyne. St. Andrews: St Andrews Film Studies. 179–215.

De Valck, Marijke, Brendan Kredell, and Skadi Loist, eds. 2016. *Film Festivals: History, Theory, Method, Practice*. New York: Routledge.

Devarrieux, Claire, and Marie-Christine de Navacelle. 1988. *Cinéma du réel: avec Imamura, Ivens, Malle, Rouch, Storck, Varda et le ciné-journal de Depardon*. Paris: Editions Autrement.

Dimou, Augusta, Stefan Troebst, and Maria N. Todorova. 2014. *Remembering Communism: Private and Public Recollections of Lived Experience in Southeast Europe*. Budapest: CEU Press.

Döhnert, Albrecht. 2009. "Die Jugendweihe." In François and Schulze 2009: 3: 347–60.

Douchet, Jean. 1998. *Nouvelle vague*. Paris: Cinémathèque française.

Dreyfus-Armand, Geneviève, Robert Frank, Marie-Françoise Levy, and Michelle Zancarini-Fournel, eds. 2008. *Les années 68: Le temps de la contestation*. Brussels: Editions Complexe.

Droit, Emmanuel. 2013. *Vers un homme nouveau? L'éducation socialiste en RDA (1949–1989)*. Rennes: Presses universitaires de Rennes.

Droit, Emmanuel, and Sandrine Kott, eds. 2006. *Die ostdeutsche Gesellschaft: Eine transnationale Perspektive*. Berlin: Ch. Links Verlag.

Dubosclard, Alain, Laurent Grison, Laurent Jeanpierre, Pierre Journoud, and Dominique Trimbur. 2002. *Entre rayonnement et réciprocité: contributions à l'histoire de la diplomatie culturelle*. Paris: Publications de la Sorbonne.

Düfner, Georg. 2008. *"Chile als Bestandteil des revolutionären Weltprozesses." Die Chilepolitik der DDR im Spannungsfeld von außenpolitischen, ökonomischen und ideologischen Interessen 1952–1973*. Sarrebrücken: VDM Verlag Dr. Müller

Dulphy, Anne, Robert Frank, Marie-Anne Matard-Bonucci, Pascal Ory, eds. 2010. *Les relations culturelles internationales au XXe siècle. De la diplomatie culturelle à l'acculturation*. Brussels: Peter Lang.

Ebbrecht-Hartmann, Tobias. 2017 "Socialist Competition or Window to the World? East German Student Films at International Festivals in the Context of the Cold War." In Kötzing and Moine 2017: 15–29.

Eckert, Detlef. 1991. "Die Volkswirtschaft der DDR im Spannungsfeld der Reformen." In Agde 1991: 20–31.

Eichwede, Wolfgang, and Jan Pauer, eds. 2017. *Ringen um Autonomie. Dissidentendiskurse in Mittel- und Osteuropa*. Münster: Lit Verlag.

Eisenschitz, Bernard. 1999. *Le cinéma allemand*. Paris: Nathan Université.

Eisenschitz, Bernard, ed. 2000. *Lignes d'ombre: Une autre histoire du cinéma soviétique (1926–1968)*. Milan: Mazzotta.

Elsaesser, Thomas. 2005. "Film Festival Networks: The New Topographies of Cinema in Europe." In *European Cinema: Face to Face with Hollywood*, ed. Thomas Elsaesser. Amsterdam: Amsterdam University Press. 82–107.

Emmerich, Wolfgang. 2000. *Kleine Literaturgeschichte der DDR*. Berlin: Aufbau Taschenbuch Verlag.

Emmerling, Inga. 2013. *Die DDR und Chile (1960–1989)*. Berlin: Ch. Links Verlag.

Engel, Christine, ed. 1999. *Geschichte des sowjetischen und russischen Films*. Stuttgart: J. B. Metzler.

Engler, Wolfgang. 1999. *Die Ostdeutschen: Kunde vom verlorenen Land*. Berlin: Aufbau-Verlag.

Eppelmann, Rainer, Bernd Faulenbach, and Ulrich Mählert, eds. 2003. *Bilanz und Perspektiven der DDR-Forschung*. Paderborn: Verlag Ferdinand Schöningh.

Ernstring, Stefan. 2006. *Der rote Elvis*. Berlin: Aufbau Taschenbuch Verlag.

Espagne, Michel, and Michael Werner, eds. 1988. *Transferts: les relations interculturelles dans l'espace franco-allemand (XVIIIe et XIXe siècle)*. Paris: Editions Recherches sur les Civilisations.

Ethis, Emmanuel, ed. 2001. *Aux marches du Palais: Le festival de Cannes sous le regard des sciences sociales*. Paris: La Documentation Française.

Fayet, Jean-François. 2002. "La VOKS, entre culture, politique et lobbying diplomatique." In *Relations internationales, échanges culturels et réseaux intellectuels*, ed. Hans-Ulbrich Jost and Stefanie Prezioso. Lausanne: Antipodes. 97–113.

Feigelson, Kristian. 2005. "Le repentir ou l'inquiétante étrangeté." Special issue, "Cinéma et stalinisme." *Théorème* 8: 269–77.

Feinstein, Joshua. 2002. *The Triumph of the Ordinary. Depictions of Daily Life in the East German Cinema, 1949–1989*. Chapel Hill: University of North Carolina Press.

Fejtö, François, and Jacques Rupnik, eds. 1999. *1968: le printemps tchécoslovaque*. Brussels: Editions Complexe.

Ferro, Marc. 1989. "Le cinéaste dans la cité." In *Culture et révolution*, ed. Marc Ferro and Sheila Fitzpatrick. Paris: Éditions de l'École des Hautes Études en Sciences Sociales. 83–89.

Feydt, Sebastian, Christiane Heinze, and Martin Schanz. 1990. "Die Leipziger Friedensgebete." In Grabner et al. 1990: 123–35.

Fink, Carole. 2009. "1958 – The Prague Spring Music Festival Joins Europe." In Fleury and Jilek 2009: 345–63.

Finke, Klaus, ed. 2001. *DEFA-Film als nationales Kulturerbe?* Berlin: Vistas.

Flacke, Monika, ed. 1995. *Auftrag: Kunst 1949–1990. Bildende Künstler in der DDR zwischen Ästhetik und Politik*. Berlin: Deutsches Historisches Museum.

Fléchet, Anaïs, Pascale Goetschel, Patricia Hidiroglou, Sophie Jacotot, Caroline Moine, and Julie Verlaine, eds. 2013. *Une histoire des festivals. XX–XXIe siècle*. Paris: Nouveau Monde.

Fleckinger, Hélène. 2011. "Cinéma et vidéo saisis par le féminisme (France, 1968–1981)." Ph.D., University Sorbonne Nouvelle-Paris 3.

Fleury, Antoine, and Lubor Jilek, eds. 2009. *Une Europe malgré tout, 1945–1990. Contacts et réseaux culturels, intellectuels et scientifiques entre Européens dans la guerre froide*. Brussels: Peter Lang.

Fleury-Villatte, Béatrice. 1995. *Cinéma et culpabilité en Allemagne, 1945–1990*. Paris: Institut Jean Vigo.

Fomin, Valerij. 2000. "Le cinéma du dégel, naissance et disparition." In Eisenschitz 2000: 151–54.
Forman, Stanley. 1997. "Die Wärme der internationalen Solidarität." In Mauersberger 1997: 53–56.
Foth, Jörg. 1993. "Forever Young." *Kinemathek* 83 (December): 29.
Fox, Michael David. 2011. *Showcasing the Great Experiment Cultural Diplomacy and Western Visitors to the Soviet Union, 1921–1941.* Oxford: Oxford University Press.
François, Étienne. 1995. "Les 'trésors' de la Stasi ou le mirage des archives." In *Passés recomposés,* ed. Jean Boutier and Dominique Julia. Paris: Autrement. 145–51.
———. 2009. "Die Wartburg." In François and Schulze 2009: 2:154–70.
François, Étienne, and Hagen Schulze, eds. 2009. *Deutsche Erinnerungsorte.* 3 vols. Munich: C. H. Beck.
Frank, Robert. 2003a. "Introduction." *Relations internationales* 116 (Winter): 319–23.
———. 2003b. "Penser historiquement les relations internationales." *Annuaire français des relations internationales* 4: 42–65.
———. 2012. "Culture et relations internationales: les diplomaties culturelles." In *Pour l'histoire des relations internationales,* ed. Robert Frank. Paris: Presses universitaires de France. 371–86.
Freunde der Deutschen Kinemathek, ed. 2000. *Zwischen Barrikade und Elfenbeinturm: Zur Geschichte des unabhängigen Kinos. 30 Jahre Internationales Forum des Jungen Films.* Berlin: Henschel.
Fritzsche, Karin. 1994. "Was tut man im Filmclub? Sehen-Gucken-Gaffen = GAFF." *Fiklmclub-Kurier* 1: 12.
Fritzsche, Karin, and Claus Löser, eds. 1996. *Gegenbilder. Filmische Subversion in der DDR 1976–1989. Texte, Bilder, Daten.* Berlin: Janus Press.
Galbraith, John. 1961. "A Positive Approach to Economic Aid." *Foreign Affairs* 39, no. 3: 444–57.
Galichenko, Nicholas. 1991. *Glasnost—Soviet Cinema Responds.* Austin: University of Texas Press.
Gallinari, Pauline. 2007. "L'URSS au festival de Cannes 1946–1958: Un enjeu des relations franco-soviétiques à l'heure de la guerre froide." *1895* 51: 22–43.
Garton Ash, Timothy. 1989. *The Uses of Adversity: Essays on the Fate of Central Europe.* New York: Random House.
Gass, Karl. 1995. "Von der filmischen Hymne zur realistischen Dokumentation." In Zimmermann 1995: 77–106.
———. 1998. In Gehler and Steinmetz 1998: 28.
Gass, Karl, Winfried Junge, and Klaus Wichnewski. 1997. "Generationen." In Mauersberger 1997: 26–32.
Gauthier, Guy. 1995. *Le documentaire. Un autre cinema.* Paris: Nathan.
———. 2004. "Cinéma, vidéo, militantisme et participation." Special issue, "Le cinéma militant reprend le travail." *CinémAction* 110: 59–65.
Gauthier, Guy, Simone Suchet, and Philippe Pilard. 2003. *Le documentaire passe au direct.* Montréal: VLB.
Gehler, Fred. 1997. "Vorwort. Filmszenen, Filmrisse." In Mauersberger 1997: 7–8.
———. 2001. "Über die Anmassung des Künstlers." In Gehler et al. 2001: 4–6.
Gehler, Fred, Claus Löser, and Peter Nau. 2001. *Seismogramm(e) des Augenblicks: Texte zu Jürgen Böttcher.* Leipzig: Leipziger Dok-Filmwochen.

Gehler, Fred, and Ralf Schenk. 2001. "Ich war nicht subversiv. Ein Gespräch mit Fred Gehler über Filmkritik in der DDR und die Auf- und Einbrüche der 60er Jahre." In *Apropos: Film 2001*, ed. Ralf Schenk and Erika Richter. Berlin: Neue Berlin. 87–97.

Gehler, Fred, and Rüdiger Steinmetz, eds. 1998. *Dialog mit einem Mythos: ästhetische und politische Entwicklungen des Leipziger Dokumentarfilm-Festivals in vier Jahrzehnten: Vorträge und Diskussionen des Symposiums anlässlich des 40. Festivals 1997, zugleich VII. Hochschultage fur Medien und Kommunikation.* Leipzig: Leipziger Universitätsverlag.

Geiss, Axel. 1997. *Repression und Freiheit. DEFA Regisseure zwischen Fremd- und Selbstbestimmung*. Potsdam: Brandenburgische Landeszentrale für Politische Bildung.

Geiss, Axel, ed. 2001. *Filmstadt Babelsberg*. Berlin: Nicolai.

Gerull, Brigitte, and Hannelore Grusser, eds. 1996. *DEFA-Dokumentarfilm 1946–1992: Bestandsnachweis, Zeitungsausschnittarchiv*. Potsdam-Babelsberg: Hochschule für Film und Fernsehen "Konrad Wolf," Bibliothek/Zeitungsausschnittarchiv.

Gienow-Hecht, Jessica. 2009a. "Cold War." In *The Palgrave Dictionary of Transnational History*, ed. Akira Iriye and Pierre-Yves Saunier. Basingstoke: Palgrave Macmillan. 174–77.

———. 2009b. *Sound Diplomacy: Music, Emotions, and Politics in Transatlantic Relations 1850–1920*. Chicago: University of Chicago Press.

Gilcher-Holtey, Ingrid. 2001. *Die 68er Bewegung; Deutschland-Westeuropa-USA*. Munich: Beck.

Gili, Jean, ed. 1981. *Recherches sur l'histoire du cinéma italien*. Brussels: Groupe européen de recherche et d'information sur l'Italie contemporaine.

Glaessner, Gert-Joachim, ed. 1988. *Die DDR in der Ära Honecker*. Wiesbaden: VS Verlag für Sozialwissenschaften.

Glatzer, Dieter. 1977. *Die Entwicklung des Fernsehens der DDR. Eine Zeittafel*. Berlin: Fernsehen der DDR.

Godet, Martine. 1991. "Le cinéma soviétique à l'heure de la perestroika." *Vingtième Siècle. Revue d'histoire* 29: 85–89.

Görlich, Christopher. 2002. *Die 68er in Berlin. Schauplätze und Ereignisse*. Berlin: Homilius.

Görtemaker, Manfred. 1994. *Unifying Germany, 1989–1990*. New York: St. Martin's.

Grabner, Wolf-Jürgen, Christiane Heinze, and Detlef Pollack, eds. 1990. *Leipzig im Oktober: Kirchen und alternative Gruppen im Umbruch der DDR: Analysen zur Wende*. Berlin: Wichern.

Grémion, Pierre. 1985. *Paris/Prague: La gauche face au renouveau et à la régression tchécoslovaques, 1968–1978*. Paris: Julliard.

———. 1995. *L'intelligence de l'anticommunisme*. Paris: Fayard.

Grierson, John, and Joris Ivens. 1997. "Der Dokumentarfilm wird zerstört." In Mauersberger 1997: 121–22.

Grunert, Horst. 1991. "Aspekte internationaler Entwicklungen." In Agde 1991: 15–19.

Grüning, Barbara. 2010. "The Art of Narrating and the Question of Cultural Acknowledgment: The Case of Die Kinder von Golzow and a Reunified Germany." *The Sociological Review* 58: 44–59.

Guigueno, Vincent, and Christian Delage. 2004. "Les contraintes d'une expérience collective. Nuit et brouillard." In *L'historien et le film*, ed. Christian Delage and Vincent Guigueno. Paris: Gallimard. 59–78 and 291–92.

Gumbert, Heather. 2006. "Split Screens: Television in East Germany, 1952–1989." In *Mass Media, Culture and Society in Twentieth-Century*, ed. Karl-Christian Fuehrer and Corey Ross. New York: Palgrave Macmillan. 146–64.
Guyot-Bender, Martine. 2014. "Tracking the Global through the Local: Slon/Iskra's Documentaries of Displacement." *SubStance* 43, no. 1: 138–51.|
Habel, Frank-Burkhard. 2001. *Das grosse Lexikon der DEFA-Spielfilme*. Berlin: Schwarzkopf & Schwarzkopf.
Hadeln, Moritz de. 1990. *Roumanie. Le film documentaire: Une rétrospective (1890–1990)*. Nyon: Festival international du film documentaire.
Hagen, Eva-Maria. 1998. *Eva und der Wolf*. Munich: Econ & List.
Hahn, Brigitte J. 1997. *Umerziehung durch Dokumentarfilm?: ein Instrument amerikanischer Kulturpolitik im Nachkriegsdeutschland (1945–1953)*. Münster: Lit.
Hähnel-Mesnard, Carola. 2007. *La littérature autoéditée en RDA dans les années 1980 — Un espace hétérotopique*. Paris: Harmattan.
Hake, Sabine. 2002. *German National Cinema*. New York: Routledge.
Hanák, Dušan. 1993. "Die Wahrheit der Outsider." In *Filmkultur im Umbruch: Beispiel Slowakei*, ed. Hans-Joachim Schlegel. Graz: Edition Blimp. 43.
Havel, Václav, Roger Errera, and Jan Vladislav. 1989. *Essais Politiques*. Paris: Calmann-Lévy.
Hecht, Heidemarie. 1996. "Der letzte Akt 1989–1992." In Jordan and Schenk 1996: 234–69.
Heimann, Thomas. 1991. "Spielfilme und Kulturpolitik in der SBZ/DDR 1946 bis 1957." *Deutsche Studien* 29, no. 114: 158–78.
———. 1994. *DEFA, Künstler und SED-Kulturpolitik*. Berlin: Vistas.
———. 1996. "Von Stahl und Menschen." In Jordan and Schenk 1996: 48–90.
———. 2000. "Zwischen Alltäglichkeit und Nonkonformismus. Jürgen Böttchers Jahrgang 45." In Zimmermann and Moldenhauer 2000: 351–60.
———. 2002. "Modernisierung in Provisorien: Zur Programmentwicklung des DDR-Fernsehens (1968–1974)." In *Die Überwindung der Langeweile?*, ed. Claudia Dittmar and Susanne Vollberg. Leipzig: Leipziger Universitätsverlag. 63–102.
———. 2003. "Übersicht zur institutionellen Entwicklung des Deutschen Fernsehfunks 1952–1972." In *Die Programmentwicklung des DDR-Fernsehens zwischen 1956 und 1991. Programmstrukturelle Betrachtungen, statistische Vergleiche und senderinterne Entwicklungen*, ed. Thomas Heimann, Markus Schubert, and Hans-Jörg Stiehler. Leipzig: 63–102.
Hellwig, Gisela, and Hildegard Maria Nickel, eds. 1993. *Frauen in Deutschland 1945–1992*. Berlin: Akademie Verlag.
Herbst, Andreas, Winfried Ranke, and Jürgen Winkler. 1994. *So funktionierte die DDR*. Reinbek: Rowohlt.
Heym, Stefan. 1996. *Der Winter unseres Missvergnügens: Aus den Aufzeichnungen des OV Diversant*. Munich: btb.
Heynowski, Walter. 2007. *Der Film meines Lebens: Zerschossene Jugend*. Berlin: Das Neue Berlin.
———. 2013. "Aufnahmen, die um die Welt gingen." [Interview by Niels Seibert]. *Neues Deutschland*, 11 January.
Heynowski, Walter, and Gerhard Scheumann. 1997. "Positionen." In Mauersberger 1997: 92–98.

Hillebrand, Ernst. 1987. *Das Afrika-Engagement der DDR*. Frankfurt am Main: Peter Lang.
Hintze, Götz. 1999a. "Jugendradio DT 64." In Hintze 1999b: 144.
———. 1999b. *Rocklexikon der DDR*. Berlin: Schwarzkopf & Schwarzkopf.
Hirschman, Albert O. 1993. "Exit, Voice and the Fate of the German Democratic Republic: An Essay in Conceptual History." *World Politics* 45: 172–202.
Hofmann, Michael, and Dieter Rink. 1990. "Der Leipziger Aufbruch 1989: Zur Genesis einer Heldenstadt." In Grabner et al. 1990: 114–22.
Hogenkamp, Bert. 2000. "Der Einsatz von DEFA Filmen durch Arbeiterorganisationen 'im kapitalistischen Ausland' in den 1950er Jahren." In Zimmermann and Moldenhauer 2000: 283–88.
Holloway, Dorothea, and Ronald Dorothea Holloway. 1979. *O. is for Oberhausen: Weg zum Nachbarn*. Oberhausen: Westdeutsche Kurzfilmtage.
Hörl, Patrick. 1996. *Film als Fenster zur Welt. Eine Untersuchung des filmtheoretischen Denkens von John Grierson*. Constance: UVK-Medien Ölschläge.
Horton, Andrew, and Michael Brashinsky. 1992. *The Zero Hour: Glasnost and Soviet Cinema in Transition*. Princeton: Princeton University Press.
Hübner, Christoph. 1996. "'Die Dinge des Lebens': Gespräch mit Volker Koepp; Entretien de Christoph Hübner avec Volker Koepp." In *Dokumentarisch arbeiten: Im Gespräch mit Christoph Hübner*, ed. Gabriele Voss. Berlin: Vorwerk 8.
Hübner, Peter. 1995. *Konsens, Konflikt und Kompromiss: Soziale Arbeiterinteressen und Sozialpolitik in der SBZ/DDR 1945–1970*. Berlin: Akademie Verlag.
Hülbusch, Nikolas. 1997. *Die "Schwarze Serie" des polnischen Dokumentarfilms, 1955–1959, im diakronen Kontext dokumentarfilmtheoretischer Diskurse*. Alfeld/Leine: Coppi-Verlag.
Hürtgen, Renate, and Thomas Reichel. 2001. *Der Schein der Stabilität: DDR-Betriebsalltag in der Ära Honecker*. Berlin: Metropol.
Iordanova, Dina, ed. 2013. *The Film Festival Reader*. St Andrews: St Andrews Film Studies.
———. 2016. "The Film Festival and Film Culture's Transnational Essence." In De Valck et al.: 1–6.
———. 2017. "Yingying, Zhenzhen, and Fenfen? China at the Festivals." In Berry and Robinson: 217–235.
Iriye, Akira. 1991. "Culture and International History." In *Explaining the History of American Foreign Relations*, ed. Michael J. Hogan and Thomas G. Paterson. Cambridge: Cambridge University Press. 214–25.
Jacobsen, Hans A., ed. 1980. *Drei Jahrzehnte Aussenpolitik Der DDR: Bestimmungsfaktoren, Instrumente, Aktionsfelder*. Munich: Oldenbourg.
Jacobsen, Wolfgang. 2000. *50 Jahre Berlinale: Internationale Filmfestspiele Berlin*. Berlin: Nicolai.
Jäger, Manfred. 1994. *Kultur und Politik in der DDR, 1945–1990*. Cologne: Edition Deutschland Archiv.
Jäger, Wolfgang, and Ingeborg Villinger. 1997. *Intellektuellen und die deutsche Einheit*. Freiburg im Breisgau: Rombach.
Jarausch, Konrad H. 1999. *Dictatorship as Experience: Toward a Socio-Cultural History of the GDR*. New York: Berghahn Books.

Jarausch, Konrad H., Christian F Ostermann, and Andreas Etges, eds. 2017. *The Cold War: Historiography, Memory, Representation*. Berlin: De Gruyter Oldenbourg.
Jarausch, Konrad H., and Hannes Siegrist, eds. 1997. *Amerikanisierung und Sowjetisierung in Deutschland 1945–1970*. Frankfurt/New York: Campus.
Jeancolas, Jean-Pierre. 2001. *L'oeil hongrois: quatre décennies de cinéma à Budapest, 1963–2000*. Budapest: Magyar Filmunió.
———. 2003. "À quelles fins, l'histoire?" Special issue, "Cinéma hongrois," ed. Kristian Feigelson and Jarmo Valkola. *Théorème* 7: 245–48.
Jelenkovic, Dunja, ed. 2013. *The Short Film Fest—60 Years: Monograph on the Belgrade Documentary and Short Film Festival*. Belgrade: FEST Head Office.
———. 2017a. "The Film Festival as an Arena for Political Debate: The Yugoslav Black Wave in Belgrade and Oberhausen." In Kötzing and Moine 2017: 47–61.
———. 2017b. "Une histoire culturelle et politique du Festival yougoslave du film documentaire et du court-métrage, 1954–2004. Du socialisme yougoslave au nationalisme serbe." Ph.D., University Versailles Saint-Quentin-en-Yvelines.
Jesse, Eckard, and Armin Mitter, eds. 1992. *Die Gestaltung der deutschen Einheit*. Bonn: Bundeszentrale für politische Bildung.
Jessen, Ralph. 2009. "Die Montagsdemonstrationen." In *Erinnerungsorte der DDR*, ed. Martin Sabrow. Munich: Beck. 466–80.
Jordan, Günter. 1994. "Wochenschau, Dokumentarfilm, Kulturfilm." In Mückenberger and Jordan 1994: 197–366.
———. 1996. "Die frühen Jahre 1946–1952." In Jordan and Schenk 1996: 14–47.
———. 1998a. "Das Nadelöhr. Filmauswahl und ihre Kriterien." In Gehler and Steinmetz 1998: 105–117.
———. 1998b. "Diskussion zum Beitrag von R. Ritterbusch." In Gehler and Steinmetz 1998: 125–32.
———. 2000. "Schatten vergangener Ahnen . . . " In Zimmermann and Moldenhauer 2000: 103–32.
———. 2003. "Die Stimme. Stephan Hermlin und der Film." In *Apropos: Film 2003*, ed. Ralf Schenk and Erika Richter. Berlin: Neue Berlin. 46–81.
———. 2007. "Verlust der Un-schuld." In Schenk 2007: 54–58.
———. 2009. *Film in der DDR. Daten, Fakten, Strukturen*. Potsdam: Filmmuseum.
———. 2018. *Unbekannter Ivens: Triumph, Verdammnis, Auferstehung, 1948–1989*. Berlin: Bertz+Fischer.
Jordan, Günter, ed. 1991. *Erprobung eines Genres. DEFA-Dokumentarfilme für Kinder, 1975–1990*. Remscheid: Kinder- und Jugendfilmzentrum in der Bundesrepublik Deutschland.
Jordan, Günter, and Ralf Schenk, eds. 1996. *Schwarzweiß und Farbe. DEFA-Dokumentarfilme, 1946–1992*. Berlin: Jovis.
Judt, Matthias. 1997. *DDR-Geschichte in Dokumenten: Beschlüsse, Berichte, interne Materialien und Alltagszeugnisse*. Berlin: Ch. Links Verlag.
Kaelble, Hartmut, Jürgen Kocka, and Hartmut Zwahr, eds. 1994. *Sozialgeschichte der DDR*. Stuttgart: Klett-Cotta.
Kaiser, Monika. 1997. *Machtwechsel von Ulbricht zu Honecker. Funktionsmechanismen der SED-Diktatur in Konfliktsituationen 1962 bis 1972*. Berlin: Akademie Verlag.

Karl, Lars. 2007. *Leinwand zwischen Tauwetter und Frost: Der osteuropäische Spiel- und Dokumentarfilm im Kalten Krieg.* Berlin: Metropol.

Kathe, Steffen R. 2005. *Kulturpolitik um jeden Preis: Die Geschichte des Goethe-Instituts von 1951 bis 1990.* Munich: Martin Meidenbauer.

Katsakioris, Constantin. 2008. "Transgresser les frontières de la guerre froide: Militants, intellectuels et étudiants africains en Union soviétique, 1956–1991." *Présence africaine* 175–176–177, no. 1–2: 85–92.

Kersten, Heinz. 1995. "Erinnerungen an eine Landschaft: Beobachtungen zum Dokumentarfilm der DEFA seit den 60er Jahren as westicher Sicht." In Zimmermann 1995: 119–32.

Kilian, Werner. 2001. *Die Hallstein-Doktrin.* Berlin: Duncker & Humblot.

Kleinert, Burkhard. 1998. "Mein Achtundsechzig." *Sklavenaufstand* 51. Quoted in Engler 1999: 311.

Klejman, Naum. 2000. "Une histoire personnelle." In Eisenschitz 2000: 139–50.

Klessmann, Christoph. 1997. *Zwei Staaten, eine Nation: deutsche Geschichte 1955–1970.* Bonn: Bundeszentrale für politische Bildung.

Klunker, Heinz. 1993. "Ein jegliches hat seine Zeit. Die Chronik der 'Kinder von Golzow,' Lebensläufe." *DHM-Magazin* 8: 20–25.

Knopfe, Gerhard. 1996. "Kalendarium einer deutschen Spezies." In Jordan and Schenk 1996: 294–341.

Kopaněvová, Galina. 1996. "Un quart de siècle de métamorphoses." In Zaoralová and Passek 1996: 95–101.

Korff, Gottfried. 2009. "Feierabend." In François and Schulze 2009: 3:169–86.

Kott, Sandrine. 1999. "Zur Geschichte des kulturellen Lebens in DDR-Betrieben. Konzepte und Praxis der betrieblichen Kulturarbeit." *Archiv für Sozialgeschichte* 39: 167–97.

———. 2000. *Le communisme au quotidien: Les entreprises d'État dans la société est-allemande.* Paris: Belin.

———. 2001. "Die Arbeiterjugend 1970–1989." In Hürtgen and Reichel 2001: 229–49.

———. 2002. "Pour une histoire sociale du pouvoir en Europe communiste. Introduction thématique." *Revue d'histoire moderne et contemporaine* 49, no. 2: 5–23.

———. 2011. *Histoire de la société allemande au XXe siècle. La RDA 1949–1989.* Paris: La Découverte.

Kötz, Michael, and Günter Minas. 2001. *Zeitgeist mit Eigensinn. Eine Filmfestivalgeschichte Internationales Filmfestival Mannheim-Heidelberg.* Mannheim: Internationales Filmfestival Mannheim-Heidelberg.

Kötzing, Andreas. 2004. "Die Internationale Leipziger Dokumentar- und Kurzfilmwoche in den 1970er Jahren." Master's thesis, Universität Leipzig.

———. 2012. "Keine einfachen Wahrheiten: Die Leipziger Dokumentarfilmwoche und der Fall IM 'Walter.'" *Politische Bildung* (June). Accessed 31 January 2018. http://www.bpb.de/geschichte/zeitgeschichte/deutschlandarchiv/138558/keine-einfachen-wahrheiten?p=all on.

———. 2013. *Kultur- und Filmpolitik im Kalten Krieg: Die Filmfestivals von Leipzig und Oberhausen in Gesamtdeutscher Perspektive 1954–1972.* Göttingen: Wallstein.

———. 2017. "Cultural and Film Policy in the Cold War. The Film Festivals of Oberhausen and Leipzig and German-German Relations." In Kötzing and Moine 2017: 31–45.

Kötzing, Andreas, ed. 2014. *"Die Sicherheit des Festivals ist zu gewährleisten!"* Kritische Jugend, die Leipziger Dokfilmwoche und das Ministerium für Staatssicherheit. Halle: Mitteldeutscher Verlag.
Kötzing, Andreas, and Caroline Moine, eds. 2017. *Cultural Transfer and Political Conflicts: Film Festivals in the Cold War.* Göttingen:Vandenhoeck & Ruprecht.
Kötzing, Andreas, and Ralf Schenk, eds. 2015. *Verbotene Utopie: Die SED, die DEFA und das 11. Plenum.* Schriftenreihe der DEFA-Stiftung. Berlin: DEFA-Stiftung.
Krause, Anthony. 2002. "Les écrivains hongrois face à la normalisation kadarienne. Le cas Tibor Déry." *Revue d'histoire moderne et contemporaine* 49, no. 2: 203–23.
Krenzlin, Leonore. 1991. "Vom Jugendkommuniqué zur Dichterschelte." In Agde 1991: 150–51.
Kubina, Michael, and Manfred Wilke. 1995. *"Hart und kompromisslos durchgreifen." Die SED contra Polen 1980/81. Geheimakten der SED-Führung über die Unterdrückung der polnischen Demokratiebewegung.* Berlin: Akademie Verlag.
Kuehn, Karl Georg. 1997. *Caught: The Art of Photography in the German Democratic Republic.* Berkeley: University of California Press.
"Künstler Agentur der DDR." 2010. In *Wer war wer in der DDR: Ein Lexikon Ostdeutscher,* ed. Helmut Müller-Enbergs. Berlin: Ch. Links Verlag. 538.
Labaki, Amir. 1998. "Santiago Álvarez: Zur Ästhetik seiner Filme." In Gehler and Steinmetz 1998: 51–58.
Labin, Suzanne. 1980. *Chili: Le crime de resister.* Paris: Nouvelles Editions Debresse.
Labrousse, Agnès. 2003. "Les mutations de l'économie est-allemande depuis la réunification. Un éclairage institutionnel et évolutionnaire." Ph.D., Paris, Ecole des Hautes Études en Sciences Sociales.
Lamm, Hans-Siegfried, and Siegfried Kupper. 1976. *DDR und Dritte Welt.* Munich: R. Oldenbourg Verlag.
Langermann, Martina. 2002. "Der Streit um die "blinde Metapher": Brecht, Kafka und die Folgen." In Barck and Münz-Koenen 2002: 29–35.
Laser, Kurt. 2001. "Fernsehen auf getrennten Kanälen." *Berlinische Monatsschrift* 3: 157–65.
Latil, Loredana. 2005. *Le festival de Cannes sur la scène international.* Paris: Nouveau Monde.
Laurent, Natacha. 2000. *L'oeil du Kremlin: cinéma et censure en URSS sous Staline, 1928–1953.* Toulouse: Privat.
Lawton, Anna. 1989. "Toward a New Openness." In *Post New Wave Cinema in the Soviet Union and Eastern Europe,* ed. Daniel J. Goulding. Bloomington: Indiana University Press. 1–50.
———. 1992. *Kinoglasnost: Soviet Cinema in Our Time.* Cambridge: Cambridge University Press.
Lehmann, Kirsten, and Lydia Wiehring von Wendrin. 1997. *Filmografie der in Leipzig gelaufenen HFF-Filme 1961–1996: 40 Jahre Internationales Leipziger Festival für Dokumentar- und Animationsfilm.* Potsdam-Babelsberg: Hochschule für Film und Fernsehen. 1997.
Lektorat Rundfunkgeschichte, ed. 1985. *Erinnerungen sozialistischer Rundfunkpioniere. Ausgewählte Erlebnisberichte.* Berlin: Staatliches Komitee für Rundfunk.
Lemke, Michael. 2000. "Nationalismus und Patriotismus in den frühen Jahren der DDR." Special issue, "Zeitgeschichte." *Aus Politik und Zeitgeschichte* 50. Accessed

6 September 2017. http://www.bpb.de/apuz/25291/nationalismus-und-patriotismus-in-den-fruehen-jahren-der-ddr.
Leyda, Jay. 1967. *Filme aus Filmen: Eine Studie über den Kompilationsfilm*. Berlin: Henschelverlag.
Liehm, Mira, and Antonín J. Liehm. 1989. *Les cinémas de l'Est, de 1945 à nos jours*. Paris: Editions du Cerf.
Lindenberger, Thomas. 1999a. "Die Diktatur der Grenzen. Zur Einleitung." In Lindenberger 1999b: 13–44.
———. 1999b. *Herrschaft und Eigen-Sinn in der Diktatur. Studien zur Gesellschaftsgeschichte in der DDR*. Cologne: Böhlau.
———. 2003. "Secret et public: société et polices dans l'historiographie de la RDA." *Genèses* 52: 33–57.
———. 2005. "'Hoam solz gahn, Ami!' Heimat-Exploitation und Antiamerikanismus in frühen DEFA-Filmen." In *Anti-Amerikanismus im Kalten Krieg. Deutschland im europäischen Vergleich*, ed. Jan C Behrends, Árpád von Klimó, and Patrice G Poutrus. Bonn: Dietz.
———. 2009. "Terriblement démodée: zum Scheitern blockübergreifender Filmproduktionen im Kalten Krieg (DDR-Frankreich, 1956–1960)." In Fleury and Jilek 2009: 283–96.
———. 2014. "Ist die DDR ausgeforscht? Phasen, Trends und ein optimistischer Ausblick." Special issue, "Aufbruch '89." *Aus Politik und Zeitgeschichte* 24–26. Accessed 6 September 2017. http://www.bpb.de/apuz/185600/ist-die-ddr-ausgeforscht-phasen-trends-und-ein-optimistischer-ausblick?.
Lindenberger, Thomas, ed. 2006. *Massenmedien im Kalten Krieg: Akteure, Bilder, Resonanzen*. Cologne: Böhlau.
Lindeperg, Sylvie. 2007. *Nuit et brouillard: un film dans l'histoire*. Paris: Jacob.
———. 2014. *Night and Fog: A Film in History*, trans. Tom Mes. Minneapolis: University of Minnesota Press.
Loridan-Ivens, Marceline. 1997. "Eine wirklich schöne Geschichte!" In Mauersberger 1997: 57–60.
Lorrain, Sophie. 1994. *Histoire de la RDA*. Paris: Presses universitaires de France.
Löser, Claus. 1996. "Im Dornröschenschloss: Dokumentarfilme an der Babelsberger Filmhochschule." In Jordan and Schenk 1996: 342–55.
———. 2001. "Jürgen Böttcher und sein Film Barfuss und ohne Hut." In Gehler et al. 2001: 7.
———. 2011. *Strategien der Verweigerung. Untersuchungen zum politisch-ästhetischen Gestus unangepasster filmischer Artikulationen in der Spätphase der DDR*. Schriftenreihe DEFA-Stiftung. Berlin: DEFA-Stiftung.
Loth, Wilfried. 1994. *Stalins ungeliebtes Kind*. Berlin: Rowohlt.
Lüdtke, Alf. 1998. "La République allemande comme histoire. Réflexions historiographiques." *Annales. Histoire, Sciences Sociales* 53, no. 1: 3–39.
Lukeš, Jan. 1996. "La chute, la montée et l'incertitude: Le film tchèque de 1970 à 1996." In Zaoralová and Passek 1996: 135–43.
Lutz, Annabelle. 1999. *Dissidenten und Bürgerbewegung: Ein Vergleich zwischen DDR und Tschechoslowakei*. Frankfurt am Main: Campus.
Madeline, Emmanuelle. 2004. "La tradition documentaire." Special issue "Cinéma hongrois," ed. Kristian Feigelson and Jarmo Valkola. *Théorème* 7: 177.

Mählert, Ulrich. 1998. *Kleine Geschichte der DDR*. Munich: Beck.
Major, Patrick, and Rana Mitter. 2006. "Culture." In *Palgrave Advances in Cold War History*, ed. Saki Dockrill and Geraint Hughes. Basingstoke: Palgrave Macmillan. 240–62.
Mallinckrodt, Anita M. 1972. *Wer macht die Aussenpolitik der DDR?: Apparat, Methoden, Ziele*. Düsseldorf: Droste.
Marsolais, Gilles. 1974. *L'Aventure du cinéma direct: histoire, esthétique, méthodes, tendances, textes, chronologie, dictionnaire biographique et filmographique*. Paris: Seghers.
Martin, Marcel. 1993. *Le cinéma soviétique de Khrouchtchev à Gorbatchev (1955–1992)*. Lausanne: L'Age d'homme.
Martini, Heidi. 2007. *Dokumentarfilm-Festival Leipzig: Filme und Politik im Blick und Gegenblick*. Berlin: DEFA-Stiftung.
Mattelart, Tristan. 1995. *Le cheval de Troie audiovisuel. Le rideau de fer à l'épreuve des radios et télévisions transfrontières*. Grenoble: Presses Universitaires de Grenoble.
Matthews, Mervyn. 1978. *Soviet Sociology, 1964–75. A Bibliography*. New York: Praeger.
Maurin Jost. 2003. "Die DDR als Asylland: Flüchtlinge aus Chile 1973–1989." *Zeitschrift für Geschichtswissenschaft* 51: 814–831.
Mauss, Marcel. 1999. "Essai sur le don: Forme et raison de l'échange dans les sociétés archaïques." In *Sociologie et anthropologie*, by Marcel Mauss. 8th ed. Paris: PUF. 145–279.
Mazany, Donatien. 2015. *Tours, capitale du court métrage — Les journées internationales du court métrage, 1955–1971*. Chinon: Anovi.
Merkel, Ina. 1996. "Konsumkultur in der DDR: Über das Scheitern der Gegenmoderne auf dem Schlachtfeld des Konsums." *Mitteilungen aus der kulturwissenschaftlichen Forschung* 37 (February): 314–30.
———. 1999. *Utopie und Bedürfnis: Die Geschichte der Konsumkultur in der DDR*. Cologne: Böhlau.
Meuschel, Sigrid. 1991. "Wandel durch Ablehnung." In Deppe et al. 1991: 26–43.
———. 1992. *Legitimation und Parteiherrschaft. Zum Paradox vom Stabilität und Revolution in der DDR 1945–1989*. Frankfurt am Main: Suhrkamp.
Miard-Delacroix, Hélène. 2010. "Les mouvements pour la paix en République fédérale et en RDA dans les années 1980 — entremêlés, distincts, différents." *Allemagne d'aujourd'hui* 194 (October–December): 101–9.
———. 2013. *Willy Brandt*. Paris: Fayard.
Michalek, Boleslaw, and Frank Turaj. 1992. *Le cinéma polonais*. Paris: Centre Georges Pompidou.
Mignot-Lefebvre, Yvonne. 1994. "Le documentaire sociologique à l'épreuve de la television." *Xoana* 2: 67–90.
Mittenzwei, Werner. 1991. "Zur Kafka-Konferenz 1963." In Agde 1991: 84–92.
Moine, Caroline. 2002. "Ouvriers et réalisme socialiste: les films documentaires est-allemands." In *Les images de l'industrie, de 1850 à nos jours*, ed. Denis Woronoff and Nicolas Pierrot. Paris: Comité pour l'Histoire Economique et Financière de la France. 68–79.
———. 2004. "Gone with the Eastern Wind. The Film Festival of Leipzig and the Glasnost." *Film International* 8: 6–13.

———. 2005a. "Le Cinéma en RDA, entre autarcie culturelle et dialogue international: une histoire du Festival international de films documentaires de Leipzig: 1949–1990." Ph.D. dissertation, University Paris 1 Panthéon-Sorbonne.
———. 2005b. "Le fascisme ordinaire au festival de Leipzig: documentaire et déstalinisation en RDA." Special issue, "Cinéma et stalinisme." *Théorème* 8: 228–39.
———. 2007. "Un passé resté hors champ. Mémoire et oubli dans les films documentaires de la DEFA (1961-1990)." *CINéMAS* Fall: 135-151.
———. 2010a. "Cinéma d'actualités et documentaire." In *Dictionnaire d'histoire culturelle de la France contemporaine,* ed. Christian Delporte, Jean-Yves Mollier, and Jean-François Sirinelli. Paris: Presses universitaires de France. 147–50.
———. 2010b. "La RDA à l'heure de la 'Solidarité internationale': le festival de la jeunesse de Berlin-Est, août 1973." In *La République démocratique allemande: La vitrine du socialisme et l'envers du miroir (1949–1989–2009),* ed. Chantal Metzger. Brussels: Peter Lang. 289–300.
———. 2011a. "La FIAPF, une fédération de producteurs au cœur des relations internationales après 1945." In *Les producteurs. Enjeux créatifs, enjeux financiers,* ed. Laurent Creton, Yannick Dehée, Sébastien Layerle, and Caroline Moine. Paris: Nouveau Monde. 249–66.
———. 2011b. "Filmer pour témoigner: Documentaires et 'Solidarité internationale' contre le régime de Pinochet." In *Lorsque Clio s'empare du documentaire,* ed. Jean-Pierre Bertin-Maghit. Paris: Harmattan. 2:195–207.
———. 2012. "Festivals de cinéma et politiques culturelles dans l'Europe de la guerre froide: diversité des enjeux et des acteurs." In *Festivals & sociétés en Europe—XIXe–XXe siècles,* ed. Philippe Poirrier. Territoires contemporains 3. Accessed 4 September 2017. http://tristan.u-bourgogne.fr/CGC/publications/Festivals_societes/C_Moine.html on.
———. 2013. "Les festivals artistiques de la guerre froide: quel rôle dans le renouveau de l'espace culturel européen (années 1940–1960)?" In Fléchet et al. 2013: 41–53.
———. 2014a. *Cinéma et guerre froide: Histoire du Festival de Films Documentaires de Leipzig, 1955–1990.* Paris: Publications de la Sorbonne.
———. 2014b. "From Karlovy Vary to West Berlin and Venice. International Film Festivals in the Turbulent Year of 1968." *Illuminace: The Journal of Film Theory, History and Aesthetics* 1: 39–48.
———. 2015. "'Votre combat est le nôtre': Les mouvements de solidarité internationale avec le Chili dans l'Europe de la guerre froide." *Monde(s)* no. 8 (November): 83–103.
Moldenhauer, Gebhard, and Volker Steinkopff, eds. 2001. *Einblicke in die Lebenswirklichkeit der DDR durch dokumentare Filme der DEFA.* Oldenbourg: Bibliotheks- und Informationssystem der Universität Oldenburg.
Mouralis, Guillaume. 2008. *Une épuration allemande. La RDA en procès 1949–2004.* Paris: Fayard.
Mückenberger, Christiane. 1996. "Fenster zur Welt: Zur Geschichte der Leipziger Dokumentar- und Kurzfilmwoche." In Jordan and Schenk 1996: 364–80.
———. 1997. "Es gab keine Tabus mehr." In Mauersberger 1997: 111–16.
———. 1998. "Wandlungen und Übergänge nach 1989." In Gehler and Steinmetz 1998: 133–48.

———. 2000. "Auseinandersetzung im DEFA-Dokumentarfilm mit dem deutschen Faschismus unter besonderer Berücksichtigung der 50er Jahre." In Zimmermann, and Moldenhauer 2000: 43–55.
Mückenberger, Christiane, and Günter Jordan. 1994. *Sie sehen selbst, Sie hören selbst—: eine Geschichte der DEFA von ihren Anfängen bis 1949*. Marburg: Hitzeroth. 1994.
Müller, Christian, and Patrice Poutrus, eds. 2005. *Ankunft-Alltag-Abreise: Migration und interkulturelle Begegnung in der DDR-Gesellschaft*. Cologne: Böhlau.
Müller, Eggo. 1992. "Dokumente der Distanz." In *Mauer-Show: das Ende der DDR, die deutsche Einheit und die Medien*, ed. Rainer Bohn, Knut Hickethier, and Eggo Müller. Berlin: Ed. Sigma. 139–55.
Müllerová, Alena. 1996. "Le film documentaire des années 60 et 80." In Zaoralová and Passek 1996: 179–84.
Müncheberg, Hans, ed. 1984. *Experiment Fernsehen: Vom Laborversuch zur sozialistischen Massenkunst. Die Entwicklung fernsehkünstlerischer Sendeformen zwischen 1952 und 1961 in Selbstzeugnissen von Fernsehmitarbeitern*. Podium und Werkstatt 15/16. Berlin: Verband der Film- und Fernsehschaffenden der DDR.
Munitić, Ranko. 1992. "Le cinéma yougoslave." In *Le cinéma yougoslave*, ed. Jean-Loup Passek and Zoran Tasic. Paris: Centre Georges Pompidou. 49–103.
Muschter, Gabriele, and Jürgen Rostock. 1992. "Kultur im deutschen Einigungsprozess." In Jesse and Mitter 1992: 312–35.
Neubert, Ehrhart. 1997. *Geschichte der Opposition in der DDR, 1949–1989*. Berlin: Bundeszentrale für Politische Bildung.
Niederhut, Jens. 2007. *Wissenschaftsaustausch im Kalten Krieg: die ostdeutschen Naturwissenschaftler und der Westen*. Cologne: Böhlau.
Niemeyer, Christin, and Ulrich Pfeil, eds. 2014. *Der deutsche Film im Kalten Krieg*. Brussels: Peter Lang.
Niethammer, Lutz. 1985. "Fragen-Antworten-Fragen. Methodische Erfahrungen und Erwägungen zur Oral History." In *"Wir kriegen jetzt andere Zeiten": Auf der Suche nach der Erfahrung des Volkes in nachfaschistischen Ländern*, ed. Lutz Niethammer and Alexander von Plato. Berlin/Bonn: Dietz. 392–447.
Niney, François. 1990a. "L'art du réel vu de Léningrad." *Cahiers du cinéma*, 75–77.
———. 1990b. "Lettonie." *Cahiers du cinéma*, 79–80.
Nowak, Andreas. 1995. "Neues in Wittstock. Neues vom Dokumentarfilm. Ein Gespräch mit dem Regisseur Volker Koepp." In Zimmermann 1995: 155–59.
Nye, Joseph S. 2004. *Soft Power: The Means to Success in World Politics*. New York: Public Affairs.
Odin, Roger. 1998a. *L'Age d'or du documentaire. Vol 1: France, Allemagne (RFA/RDA), Espagne, Italie. Europe: années cinquantes*. Paris: Harmattan.
———. 1998b. "Le cinéma documentaire et le Groupe des Trente." In Odin 1998a: 19–52.
Offenberg, Ulrike. 1998. *"Seid vorsichtig gegen die Machthaber": Die jüdischen Gemeinden in der SBZ und der DDR 1945 bis 1990*. Berlin: Aufbau-Verlag.
Opgenoorth, Ernst, 1984. *Volksdemokratie im Kino. Propagandistische Selbstdarstellung der SED im DEFA-Dokumentarfilm, 1946–1957*. Cologne: Wissenschaft und Politik.

Ory, Pascal. 2003. "De la diplomatie culturelle à l'acculturation." *Relations internationales* 116 (Winter): 479–81.
———. 2004. "Introduction." In *Pour une histoire cinématographique de la France*, ed. Christophe Gauthier, Pascal Ory, and Dimitri Vezyroglou. *Revue d'histoire moderne et contemporaine* 51, no. 4: 7–9. Paris: Belin.
———. 2010 "Introduction." In Dulphy et al. 2010: 15–23.
Paulmann, Johannes. 2005. *Auswärtige Repräsentationen: deutsche Kulturdiplomatie nach 1945*. Cologne: Böhlau.
Perks, Robert, and Alistair Thomson, eds. 1998. *The Oral History Reader*. London/New York: Routledge.
Petersen, Jesper Strandgaard, and Carmelo Mazza. 2011. "International Film Festivals: For the Benefit of Whom?" *Culture Unbound: Journal of Current Culture Research* 3: 139–65 and 145–47.
Pfaff, Steven. 2006. *Exit-Voice Dynamics and the Collapse of East Germany: The Crisis and the Revolution of 1989*. Durham: Duke University Press.
Pfeil, Ulrich. 2004. *Die "anderen" deutsch-französischen Beziehungen: Die DDR und Frankreich 1949–1990*. Cologne: Böhlau.
Pflaum, Hans Günter, and Hans Helmut Prinzler. 1993. *Cinema in the Federal Republic of Germany: The New German Film*. Bonn: Inter Nationes.
Pike, David. 1992. *The Politics of Culture in Soviet-Occupied Germany, 1945–1949*. Stanford: Stanford Press.
Pilard, Philippe. 2010. *Histoire du cinéma britannique*. Paris: Nouveau Monde.
Pinel, Vincent, Françoise Pinel, and Christophe Pinel. 2009. *Le siècle du cinéma*. Paris: Larousse.
Pisu, Stefano. 2013. *Stalin a Venezia. L'URSS alla Mostra del cinema fra diplomazia culturale e scontro ideologico (1932–1953)*. Soveria Mannelli: Rubbettino.
———. 2016. *Il XX secolo sul red carpet. Politica, economia e cultura nei festival internazionali del cinema (1932–1976)*. Milan: FrancoAngeli.
———. 2017. *Transnational Mobilization and Domestic Political Exploitation: The 1977 Venice Biennale of Dissent*. In Kötzing and Moine 2017: 123–39.
Port, Andrew I. 2013. "The Banalities of East German Historiography." In *Becoming East German: Socialist Structures and Sensibilities after Hitler*, ed. Mary Fulbrook and Andrew I. Port. New York/Oxford: Berghahn Books. 1–30.
Poumet, Jacques. 1990. *La satire en RDA. Cabarets et presse satirique*. Lyon: Lyon Presses Universitaires.
Priess, Lutz, and Václav Kural, and Manfred Wilke. 1996. *Die SED und der "Prager Frühling" 1968. Politik gegen einen "Sozialismus mit menschlichem Gesicht."* Berlin: Akademie Verlag.
Prinzler. 1993. *Cinema in the Federal Republic of Germany*. Bonn: Inter Nationes.
Pusch, Steffi. 2000. *Exemplarisch DDR-Geschichte Leben: Ostberliner Dokumentarfilme 1989/1990*. Frankfurt am Main: Peter Lang.
Radevagen, Thomas Til. 1992. "Die DEFA zwischen dem Verschwinden der DDR und einem möglichen neuen Anfang. Vom November 1989 bis zum Sommer 1991." In *Mauer-Show: das Ende der DDR, die deutsche Einheit und die Medien*, ed. Rainer Bohn, Knut Hickethier, and Eggo Müller. Berlin: Ed. Sigma: 189–200.
Rauhut, Michael. 1991. "DDR-Rockmusik zwischen Engagement und Repression." In Agde 1991: 52–63.

———. 1993. *Beat in der Grauzone: DDR-Rock 1964 bis 1972. Politik und Alltag*. Berlin: BasisDruck.
Reichardt, Ann-Kathrin. 2003. "Zwischen Prag und Ost-Berlin." *Deutschland Archiv* 1: 67–75.
Rexin, Manfred. 1973. "Westdeutsche Jugendverbände bei den X. Weltfestspielen." *Deutschland Archiv* no. 9: 932–43.
Richter, Erika. 1994. "Zwischen Mauerbau und Kahlschlag 1961–1965." In Schenk 1994: 158–211.
———. 2000. "Frauenbilder im ost- und westdeutschen Dokumentarfilm." In Zimmermann and Moldenhauer 2000: 133–42.
———. 2001. "Abschied von der alten Welt. Zu Jürgen Böttchers Film *Die Mauer*." In Gehler et al. 2001: 17–19.
Roberts, Graham. 1999. *Forward Soviet! History and Non-fiction Film in the USSR*. London: I. B. Tauris.
Rolland, Denis, ed. 2004. *Histoire culturelle des relations internationales*. Paris: Harmattan.
Romero, Federico. 2014. "Cold War Historiography at the Crossroads." *Cold War History* 4: 685–703.
Rostock, Jürgen. 1999. "Ost-Berlin als Hauptstadt der DDR." In *Berlin. Die Hauptstadt: Vergangenheit und Zukunft einer europäischen Metropole*, ed. Werner Süss and Ralf Rytlewski. Berlin: Nicolai. 259–94.
Roth, Wilhelm. 1995. "Abbilder und Gegenbilder: Der DEFA-Dokumentarfilm der 80er Jahre." In Zimmermann 1995: 177–92.
———. 1997. " . . . und ein waches Publikum." In Mauersberger 1997: 86–91.
———. 1998. "Leipziger Dokumentarfilm-Entwicklungen." In Gehler and Steinmetz 1998: 13–23.
———. 2000. "Porträtfilm und Langzeitbeobachtung als Geschichte des Alltagslebens in der BRD und der DDR." In Zimmermann and Moldenhauer 2000: 143–58.
———. 2001. "Jürgen Böttcher und sein Film *Rangierer*." In Gehler et al. 2001: 12.
Rother, Hans-Jörg. 1996. "Auftrag: Propaganda 1960 bis 1970." In Jordan and Schenk 1996: 92–127.
Roudé, Catherine. 2017. *Le cinéma militant à l'heure des collectifs: Slon et Iskra dans la France de l'après-1968*. Paris: Presses universitaires de Rennes.
Roudé, Catherine, and Victor Barbat, eds. 2013. *De l'Unité populaire à la transition démocratique : représentations, diffusions, mémoires cinématographiques du Chili, 1970–2013*. Paris: actes des journées d'étude. Accessed 31 January 2018. http://hicsa.univ-paris1.fr/page.php?r=133&id=699.
Saunders, Frances Stonor. 1999. *Who Paid the Piper? The CIA and the Cultural Cold War*. London: Granata Books.
Schäfer, Kirstin Anne. 2009. "Die Völkerschlacht." In François and Schulze 2009: 2:187–201.
Schenk, Ralf. 2006. *Eine kleine Geschichte der DEFA: Daten, Dokumente, Erinnerungen*. Berlin: DEFA-Stiftung.
Schenk, Ralf, ed. 1994. *Das zweite Leben der Filmstadt Babelsberg, 1946–1992*. Berlin: Henschel.
———. 2007. *Bilder einer gespaltenen Welt. 50 Jahre Leipziger Dokumentarfilmfestival*. Berlin: Bertz + Fischer Verlag.

Schieber, Elke. 1996. "Im Dämmerlicht der Perestroïka." In Jordan and Schenk 1996: 180–233.
Schieder, Martin. 2009. "Die documenta I (1955)." In François and Schulze 2009: 2:637–51.
Schnitzer, Luda, Jean Schnitzer, and Marcel Martin. 1966. *Le cinéma soviétique par ceux qui l'ont fait.* Paris: Editeurs Français Réunis.
Schreiber, Eduard. 1996. "Zeit der verpassten Möglichkeiten 1970 bis 1980." In Jordan and Schenk 1996: 128–79.
Schröder, Klaus. 1998. *Der SED-Staat. Geschichte und Strukturen der DDR.* Munich: Böhlau.
Seebacher-Brandt, Brigitte. 1992. "Die deutsch-deutschen Beziehungen: Eine Geschichte von Verlegenheiten." In Jesse and Mitter 1992: 15–41.
Segert, Dieter. 2003. "Kunst als Ersatzöffentlichkeit? Thesen zum Vergleich der antitotalitären Wirkungen von Kunst in der DDR und der CSSR nach 1970." In *Sphären von Öffentlichkeit in Gesellschaften sowjetischen Typs. Zwischen partei-staatlicher Selbstinszenierung und kirchlichen Gegenwelten,* ed. Gábor T. Rittersporn, Malte Rolf, and Jan C. Behrends. Frankfurt am Main: Lang. 195–216.
Shaw, Tony. 2000. *British Cinema and the Cold War: The State, Propaganda and Consensus.* London: I. B. Tauris.
Shaw, Tony, and Denise J. Youngblood. 2010. *Cinematic Cold War: The American and Soviet Struggle for Hearts and Minds.* Lawrence: University Press of Kansas.
Shlapentokh, Dimitry, and Vladimir Shlapentokh. 1993. *Soviet Cinematography, 1918–1991 : Ideological Conflict and Social Reality.* New York : Aldine de Gruyter.
Siebs, Benno-Eide. 1999. *Die Aussenpolitik der DDR 1976–1989: Strategien und Grenzen.* Paderborn: Schöningh.
Sirinelli, Jean-François, and Henri-Georges Soutou, eds. 2008. *Culture et guerre froide.* Paris: Presses de l'université Paris-Sorbonne.
Slobodian, Quinn, ed. 2015. *Comrades of Color: East Germany in the Cold War World.* New York: Berghahn Books.
Sorlin, Pierre. 1998. "The Cinema: American Weapon for the Cold War." *Film History* 10: 375–81.
Spindler, Sabine. 1998. "*Erinnerung an eine Landschaft. Für Manuela.* Ein Dokumentarfilm." In *Heimat in DDR-Medien,* ed. Rainer Waterkamp. Bonn: Bundeszentrale für Politische Bildung. 81–101.
Staritz, Dietrich. 1990. *Geschichte der DDR: 1949–1985.* 3rd ed. Frankfurt am Main: Suhrkamp.
Stark, Trevor. 2012. "'Cinema in the Hands of the People': Chris Marker, the Medvedkin Group, and the Potential of Militant Film." *October* 139 (1 December): 117–50.
Steiner, André. 2004. *Von Plan zu Plan: Eine Wirtschaftsgeschichte der DDR.* Munich: Deutsche Verlags-Anstalt.
Steinle, Matthias. 2003. *Vom Feindbild zum Fremdbild. Die gegenseitige Darstellung von Bundesrepublik und DDR im Dokumentarfilm.* Constance: UVK.
———. 2008. "Cinéma et propagande en RDA dans les années 1950 et 1960: une arme acérée et puissante?" In *Une histoire mondiale des cinémas de propagande,* ed. Jean-Pierre Bertin-Maghit. Paris: Nouveau Monde. 615–42.
Steinmetz, Rüdiger. 1998. "Von der anti-imperialistischen Solidarität zu den Stärken des Sozialismus." In Gehler and Steinmetz 1998: 35–42.

Steinmetz, Rüdiger, and Tilo Prase. 2002. *Dokumentarfilm zwischen Beweis und Pamphlet: Heynowski und Scheumann und Gruppe Katins.* Leipzig: Leipziger Universitätsverlag.
Soutou, Henri-Georges. 2001. *La guerre de Cinquante Ans: Les relations Est-Ouest, 1943–1990.* Paris: Fayard.
Szczepanska, Ania. 2011. "Le groupe de production X d'Andrzej Wajda: un cinéma d'opposition en République populaire de Pologne (1972–1983)." Ph.D., University Paris1 Panthéon-Sorbonne.
Taillibert, Christel. 1999. *L'Institut international du cinéma éducatif. Regards sur le rôle du cinéma éducatif dans la politique internationale du fascisme italien.* Paris: L'Harmattan.
——. 2009. *Tribulations festivalières — les festivals de cinéma et audiovisuel en France.* Paris: L'Harmattan.
Tantzsche, Monika. 1994. *"Massnahme Donau und Einsatz Genesung": die Niederschlagung des Prager Frühlings 1968/69 im Spiegel der MfS-Akten.* Berlin: Der Bundesbeauftragte für die Unterlagen des Staatssicherheitsdienstes der ehemaligen DDR.
Tatur, Melanie. 1991. "Zur Dialektik der 'civil society' in Polen." In Deppe et al. 1991: 234–55.
Tchernava, Irina. 2014. "Le cinéma de non-fiction en URSS: création, production et diffusion (1948–1968)." Ph.D., EHESS Paris.
Todorova, Maria. 2009 (1997). *Imagining the Balkans.* New York: Oxford University Press.
Tok, Hans-Dieter. 1997. "Geh ins Kino, Tok!" In Mauersberger 1997: 74–78.
Troche, Alexander. 1996. *Ulbricht und die Dritte Welt: Ost-Berlins "Kampf" gegen die Bonner "Alleinvertretungsanmassung."* Erlangen: Palm und Enke.
Turovskaya, Maya. 1997. "Schickt ihn nach Leipzig!" In Mauersberger 1997: 61–62.
——. 1998. "Mikhaïls Romms *Gewöhnliche Faschismus*, Genesis und Rezeption." In Gehler and Steinmetz 1998: 43–48.
Uhlmann, Petra. 1993. *"Die Regierung ruft die Künstler": Dokumente zur Gründung der Deutschen Akademie der Künste (DDR, 1945–1953).* Berlin: Henschel.
Vaissié, Cécile. 1999. *Pour votre liberté et pour la nôtre: Le combat des dissidents de Russie.* Paris: Laffont.
Val, Perrine. 2018. "Les relations cinématographiques entre la France et la RDA (1946–1992)." Ph.D., Université Paris 1 Panthéon-Sorbonne.
Vallejo, Aida. 2014. "Festivales cinematográficos. En el punto de mira de la historiografía fílmica." *Secuencias. Revista de Historia del cine* 39: 13–42.
Veit, Patrice. 2009. "Bach." In François and Schulze 2009: 3:239–57.
Véray, Laurent. 2003. "La photographie et le cinéma en 1914–1918. Études de quelques exemples emblématiques." *Histoire et sociétés. Revue européenne d'histoire sociale* 8 (October): 118–31.
——. 2004. *Loin Du Vietnam: Film Collectif Réalisé Par Jean-Luc Godard, Joris Ivens, William Klein, Claude Lelouch, Chris Marker, Alain Resnais, Agnès Varda.* Paris: Editions Paris expérimental.
Veyne, Paul. 1976. *Le pain et le cirque: Sociologie historique d'un pluralisme politique.* Paris: Seuil.
Vingt ans de cinéma à Venise. 1952. Rome: Editions de l'ateneo.

Voigt, Jutta, Heinz Kersten, Heinz Klunker, Wilhlelm Roth, Hans-Dieter Tok, and Ralk Schenk. 1998. "Leipzig in der Filmkritik." In Gehler and Steinmetz 1998: 67–82.
Volonterio, Guglielmo. 1977. *Per uno spazio autonomo, Festival internazionale del film di Locarno*. Locarno: Edizioni Festival.
Vorsteher, Dieter, ed. 1997. *Parteiauftrag: ein neues Deutschland, Bilder Rituale und Symbole der frühen DDR*. Munich: Koehler und Amelang.
Voss, Margit. 1993. "Drehort Golzow. Auf den Spuren einer Chronik." *DHM-Magazin* 8, 12–17.
Vowinckel, Annette, Marcus M. Payk, and Thomas Lindenberger, eds. 2012. *Cold War Cultures: Perspectives on Eastern and Western European Societies*. New York: Berghahn Books.
Wach, Margarete. 1998. *Zwischen Realismus und Poesie Dokumentarfilm in Polen*. Stuttgart: Haus des Dokumentarfilms.
Wallon, Emmanuel. 2010. "Le festival international, un système relationnel." In Dulphy et al. 2010: 363–83.
Walther, Joachim. 1999. *Sicherheitsbereich Literatur: Schriftsteller und Staatssicherheit in der Deutschen Demokratischen Republik*. Berlin: Ullstein.
Weber, Hermann. 1987. "Geschichte der SED." In *Die SED in Geschichte und Gegenwart*, ed. Ilse Spittmann. Cologne: Wissenschaft und Politik. 6–42.
——. 1992. "Immer noch Probleme mit dem Archiv." *Deutschland Archiv* 6 (June): 580–87.
Wedel, Michael, Barton Byg, Andy Räder, Skyler Arndt-Briggs, and Evan Torner, eds. 2013. *DEFA international: Grenzüberschreitende Filmbeziehungen vor und nach dem Mauerbau (Film, Fernsehen, Medienkultur)*. Berlin: Wissenschaft und Politik.
Wedel, Michael, and Thomas Elsaesser. 2011. "Einblicke von außen? Die DEFA, Konrad Wolf und die internationale Geschichte." In *Filmgeschichte als Krisengeschichte: Schnitte und Spuren durch den deutschen Film*, ed. Michael Wedel. Bielefeld: Transcript. 327–62.
Wendt, Hartmut. 1991. "Die deutsch-deutschen Wanderungen. Bilanz einer 40 jahrigen Geschichte von Flucht und Ausreise." *Deutschland Archiv* 24: 386–95.
Wenzke, Rüdiger. 1995. *Die NVA und der Prager Frühling 1968: Die Rolle Ulbrichts und der DDR-Streitkräfte bei der Niederschlagung der tschechoslowakischen Reformbewegung*. Berlin: Ch. Links Verlag.
Werner, Michael, and Bénédicte Zimmermann. 2004. *De la comparaison à l'histoire croisée*. Paris: Seuil.
Werth, Nicolas. 2010. *Histoire de L'union Soviétique de Lénine à Staline (1917–1953)*. Paris: Presses universitaires de France.
Westad, Odd Arne. 2006. *The Global Cold War: Third World Interventions and the Making of Our Times*. Cambridge: Cambridge University Press.
Wichnewski, Klaus. 1991. "Die zornigen jungen Männer von Babelsberg." In Agde 1991: 171–88.
Wicke, Peter, and Lothar Müller, eds. 1996. *Rockmusik und Politik: Analyse, Interviews und Dokumente*. Berlin: Ch. Links Verlag.
Wiedemann, Dieter. 1998. "Die HFF Potsdam-Babelsberg Konrad Wolf auf der Dokfilmwoche." In Gehler and Steinmetz 1998: 61–66.

Wierling, Dorothee. 1994. "Die Jugend als innere Feind. Konflikte in der Erziehungsdiktatur der sechsiger Jahre." In *Sozialgeschichte der DDR*, ed. Hartmut Kaelble, Jürgen Kocka, and Hartmut Zwahr. Stuttgart: Klett-Cotta.

———. 2000. "Über die Liebe zum Staat: Der Fall der DDR." *Historische Anthropologie* 2: 236–63.

———. 2002. *Geboren im Jahr Eins*. Berlin: Ch. Links Verlag.

Wippel, Steffen. 1996. *Die Aussenwirtschaftsbeziehungen der DDR zum Nahen Osten. Einfluss und Abhängigkeit der DDR und das Verhältnis von Aussenwirtschaft zur Aussenpolitik*. Berlin: Das Arabische Buch.

Wisotzki, Jochen. 1993. "Von Leipzig bis Hamburg — zwei Diplomarbeiten und die Zwischenzeit." *Kinemathek* 83 (December): 128–264.

Wolf, Christa. 2003. *Ein Tag im Jahr*. München: Luchterhand.

Wolfrum, Edgar. 2009. "Die Mauer." In François and Schulze 2009: 1:552–68.

Wolle, Stefan. 1992. "In the Labyrinth of the Documents: The Archival Legacy of the SED State." *German History* 10, no. 3: 325–65.

———. 1998. *Die heile Welt der Diktatur: Alltag und Herrschaft in der DDR 1971–1989*. Berlin: Ch. Links Verlag.

Wötzel, Roland. 1989. "Zu einigen Aspekten der territorialen Reproduktion im Bezirk Leipzig." *Wirtschaftswissenschaft* 37: 660–69.

Yurchak, Aleksei. 2006. *Everything was Forever, Until it was No More: The Last Soviet Generation*. Princeton: Princeton University Press.

Zaoralová, Eva, and Jean-Loup Passek, eds. 1996. *Le cinéma tchèque et slovaque*. Paris: Centre Georges Pompidou.

Zimmermann, Peter. 1998. "Frères et sœurs ennemis dans la guerre froide des médias." In Odin 1998a: 1:101–23.

———. 2000. "Zur Ikonographie der Arbeiterklasse in den Dokumentarfilmen der DEFA." In Zimmermann and Moldenhauer 2000: 303–20.

Zimmermann, Peter, ed. 1995. *Deutschlandbilder Ost. Dokumentarfilme der DEFA von der Nachkriegszeit bis zur Wiedervereinigung*. Constance: UVK-Medien/Ölschläger.

Zimmermann, Peter, and Gebhard Moldenhauer, eds. 2000. *Der geteilte Himmel: Arbeit, Alltag und Geschichte im ost- und westdeutschen Film*. Constance: UVK-Medien/Ölschläger.

Zwahr, Hartmut. 2009. "'Wir sind das Volk!'" In François and Schulze 2009: 2:253–65.

Index

A

Abusch, Alexander, 52
Abuladze, Tengiz, xv
Academy Awards (U.S.), 132
Ackermann, Anton, 20, 24, 31, 33, 134
Adameck, Heinz, 105–6, 214, 125n13
Adamovich, Ales, 285
Adenauer, Konrad, 31, 105, 158, 170
Agarwal, Goverdhandas, 73
Allende, Salvador, 172, 175–6
Álvarez Santiago, 1, 73, 144, 162–6, 177, 308
Anderson, Lindsay, 132
antifascism, 21, 22, 61, 72, 77, 114, 115–18, 123, 153, 198, 264, 294
Appeldorn, Hans, 44
Agarwal, Goverdhandas, 73
Attenborough, Richard, 133

B

Bach, Johann Sebastian, 38
Bachmann, Gideon, 135
Baldi, Gian Vittorio, 73
Baskakov, Vladimir, 117
Baumert, Heinz, 106, 121
Becher, Johannes R., 19, 44, 52, 224, 303
Becker, Jurek, 223, 239
Beethoven, Ludwig van, 27
Belafonte, Harry, 240
Bellon, Yannick, 129n94
Bentzien, Hans, 90
Berger-Fiedler, Róza, 265, 277n78, 290
Berlin Wall, 59–62, 71, 90, 101, 110, 112, 131

Beyer, Frank, 124n1, 136–7, 220, 223–4, 286
Biermann, Wolf, xii, 1, 131, 136, 219–26, 228, 239, 241, 303, 312
Bisky, Lothar, 285–6, 291
Bitterfeld Way, 52–53, 84, 131–32
Bittorf, Wilhelm, 192
Boekel, Christoph, 235
Bonacina, Diego, 173
Bossak, Jerzy, xiv, 48, 67n18, 74–75, 81, 128n76, 195
Böttcher, Jürgen, xv, 1, 84–86, 88–89, 91, 93–94, 97n26, 118–21, 137–40, 144, 147–48, 153, 181, 203, 222, 224–27, 238–39, 289, 301–3, 309–10
Brandt, Willy, 77, 162
Brasch, Thomas, 144, 239, 289
Brault, Michel, 86
Braun, Volker, 131
Brecht, Bertolt, 22, 28
Brinkmann, Heinz, 224, 226
Bruk, Franz, 39n2
Buñuel, Luis, 129n94, 145
Burkert, Erwin, 260
Burkhardt, Bernd, 298

C

Cantow, Barbara, 298
Capra, Franck, 115
Carvajal, Samuel, 173
Castillo, Patrice, 237
Castillo, René, 237
Castro, Fidel, 144, 147, 163–4, 167

Cavalcanti, Alberto, xiv, 65, 72–75, 80, 92, 129n94, 310
Cayrol, Jean, 77
censorship, xii, xv, 1, 9, 40n16–17, 50, 54, 57, 58, 68n41, 77, 83, 87, 97n26, 103, 115, 120–124, 130, 136, 137, 139, 144, 146, 169, 195, 213–14, 220–21, 225, 229, 238–41, 243n23, 248, 255–56, 258, 262–63, 267, 274n16, 274n19, 275n37, 284–85, 286, 288, 289, 298, 300, 308, 310, 313; Eleventh Plenum, 101, 118–24, 136
Chanderli, Djamel, 64, 70n65
Chanjutin, Yuri, 115
Chaskel, Pedro, 173
Cherkasov, Nikolai, 68n36
Chodakowski, Andrzej, xv, 229
Christensen, Theodor, 74–75, 113, 128n76, 164
cinema of: Algeria, xvi, 64, 70n65, 157–58, 162, 163, 191, 308, Commission for the Establishment of Film Production, 157–58, 166, 191; Brazil, 65, 72–73, 164, 310, 313, 322–23; Canada, 86, 97n29; Ceylon (Sri Lanka), 163; Chile, xiv, 162, 164, 175, 176, 313, 322–33; China, xvi, 64; Cuba, ix, xiv, 1, 9, 65, 111, 127n53, 137, 144, 146–47, 162, 163–67, 184n26–28, 241, 308, 313, 322–23, Institute of Cinematographic Art and Industry (ICAIC), 164–65, Noticiero Newsreels, 165; Czechoslovakia, ix, xiii, 34–35, 38, 47–48, 53, 56, 59, 61, 66, 69n53, 69n59, 93, 95, 95n1, 96n12, 96n16, 130–31, 132–34, 139, 147, 164, 167, 195, 253, 263, 293, 322–23, Central Administration for Film, 132; Egypt, 47, 163; France, 28, 32, 40n4, 41n25–26, 47, 64, 67n8, 74, 75, 76–79, 81, 86–89, 92, 93, 94, 95, 95n1, 122–24, 127n54, 129n94, 142–44, 161, 168–69, 175, 180, 190–92, 215n4, 216n7, 218n40, 274n10, 287–88, 310, 313, 322–23, French Filmmakers' Union, 288, Group of Thirty, 76–79, 96n9, Union of French [Film] Producers, 123; Ghana, 64, 163; Great Britain, 28, 64, 65, 72–74, 75, 81, 92, 95n1, 128n76, 132–33, 144, 175, 205, 300, 322–23, British Film Institute, 35, 90; Hungary, xi, xiv, 48, 53, 91, 93, 95, 95n1, 98n46, 113, 127n66, 135, 193–95, 199, 204, 216n13, 216n15, 253–54, 255, 274n15, 289, 311, 312, Hungarian Filmmakers' Union, 254; India, 163; Indonesia, 163; Japan, 27, 28, 231–32, 322–23; Korea, 47; Latin America, ix, 1, 47, 64–65, 72, 145, 158–67, 173–77, 191, 299, 309, 313, 322–23, Noticiero Newsreels, 165; Lebanon, 163, 184n23; Mali, 163; Morocco, 163; Nigeria, 163; Palestine, 163, 184n23, 244n47, 265, 309, 313; Poland, xi, xiii, xv, 24, 35, 47, 48, 51, 53, 59, 66, 67n18, 69n53, 74, 75, 83, 93, 95, 95n1, 107, 113, 122, 167, 195–97, 228–30, 252, 254, 322–23, Black Series, 48, 132, Filmpolski, 67n18, Irzykowski Documentary Film Studio, 252, Warsaw Documentary Film Studio, 67n18; Socialist Countries, 53 (conference), 109; Soviet Union (USSR), xvii, 35, 40n15, 54, 61, 64, 69n53, 74, 80–82, 87, 95, 95n1, 102–3, 113–18, 127n67, 132, 135, 166, 190–91, 248–52, 256, 261–62, 285, 295, 312, 314, Central State Film and Photo Archive, 114, 264, Goskino (State Committee for Cinematography), 117, Soviet Filmmakers' Union, 254, 256, 259, 273, 285, VOKS (All-Union Society for Cultural Relations with Foreign Countries), 110, 126n48; United States, 32, 36, 50, 64, 72, 81, 83, 86–87, 92, 95n1, 115, 132–33, 166, 167–69, 174–75, 179, 192, 240, 256, 259, 262, 310; Vietnam, xvi, 25, 47, 64–65, 159, 164, 167–69, 263
Cinéma vérité, 86–88, 92, 93–95, 97n28, 123–24
Cohn-Vossen, Richard, 224, 226
Cortázar, Octavio, xiv, 137, 147, 162, 164

Coutant, André, 94
Curtis, Tony, 133

D
Dalos, György, 254, 263
Danielsen, Claas, xii, 2, 315–16
Davis, Angela, 179–80, 222, 224
de Antonio, Emile, 262
de Sica, Vittorio, 43
Dessau, Paul, 167, 224
Dietrich, Marlene, 115
Direct Cinema, 86–90, 95, 97n28
Drew, Robert, 86
Dubček, Alexander, 133–34, 293
Duckworth, Martin, 235–36

E
Eastern European politics, 53, 130–37, 273n1; Czechoslovakia, xv, 130–35, 144, 155n28, 228, 281–82, 293–94; East Germany (GDR), 27, 32, 36, 40n5, 40n9, 50, 273n1; Hungary, 48, 50, 105, 228, 263, 273n1, 281; Poland, 48, 107, 140, 162, 195, 198, 215, 228–30, 238
Eisenstein, Sergei, 74, 80, 87, 166
Eisler, Hanns, 77
Elek, Judit, xi, 194–95, 199
Éluard, Paul, 76

F
Fabiani, Henri, 77, 79, 129n94
Fenič, Fero, 274n16
film festivals, xiii, 7–9, 13n22, 31, 34–39, 125n24; Belgrade, 35; Berlin (Berlinale), xiv, xvii, 36–37, 42n45, 43, 54, 68n35, 77, 124n9, 204–6, 213–14, 255–56, 271; Bombay, 43; Brussels, 122; Cannes, 7, 35–36, 43, 51, 54, 77, 81, 96n10; Carthage, xiii, 136; Edinburgh, 27, 35, 43, 107; Karlovy Vary, xiii, xvii, 27, 30, 34–35, 51, 54, 57, 103, 109, 132–33, 136; Krakow, xiii, 107–8, 125n27; Locarno, 27, 35–36, 43, 51, 132, 135; London, 35, 122; Mannheim, xiv, 30, 37–38, 43, 47–48, 52, 54, 56–59, 62, 64–65, 75–76, 95, 107, 135, 171, 192, 224; Montevideo, 30, 163; Moscow (MIFF), xiii, xvii, 35, 54, 109, 111, 132, 147, 162, 176, 274n19; Neubrandenburg, 214, 241, 285; Nyon, 176, 192; Oberhausen, xiv, 37–38, 42n49, 46, 48–49, 56, 59, 64–65, 73, 75–77, 81, 95, 107, 135, 162, 177, 192, 195–96, 204, 213; Pula, xvii, 35; Tours, xiii, 35, 107, 120, 162; Tashkent, xiii, xvii; Venice, xiii, 35–36, 43, 54, 107, 135
film schools: Babelsberg (HFF), 21, 22, 24–25, 26, 40n14, 46, 49, 65, 84, 90–91, 122, 143–4, 148, 150–53, 158–59, 198, 225, 240, 258, 284, 285–86, 288–90, 292, 298, 312, 313, 323, 324; Belgrade, 91; Budapest, 91; Łódź, xiv, 24, 48, 195; Moscow (VGIK), xiv, 24; Munich, 2, 24; Paris, 91; Prague (FAMU), ix, xiv, 136, 147, 277n72; Vienna, 91; West Berlin (dffb), 24, 235
film studios: Balázs Béla Studio, 91, 194; Barrandov Studio, 132, 134, 136; DEFA Studios, xi, 6, 18–19, 20, 24, 30, 34, 40n11, 56, 84, 104–5, 109, 134, 136, 157, 171, 240, 309; DEFA Documentary Studio, 17, 20, 40n9, 40n11, 44, 46, 52, 56, 57, 78, 106, 125n13, 136, 170, 196–203, 241, 258, 266, 284–85, 298–99, 306n23; DEFA Feature Film Studio, 53, 90, 97n38, 134, 136, 138; Pathé, 41n26, 94; UFA, 21, 30, 37, 39n1, 41n20
Fischer, Kurt Joachim, 37, 46, 52, 58
Flaherty, Frances, 72–73
Flaherty, Robert, xiv, 72, 86–87, 92, 310
Fonda, Henry, 133
Fonda, Jane, 167, 168
formalism, 26, 84, 97n26,
Forman, Miloš, 93, 132
Forman, Stanley, 74, 144, 175, 300
Foth, Jörg, 247
Frank, Herz, xi, 258
Frick, Thomas, 286

G
Gass, Karl, xvi, 22, 32–33, 37, 44, 49, 58, 60–61, 73, 75, 82, 89–90, 92–94,

110, 147, 151–153, 170, 197, 203, 222, 225, 232, 264, 288–89, 298, 300
GDR organizations: Academy of Arts, 22, 90, 131, 224, 271; Artists' Association, 106; Association of Film and Television Workers (VFF), 21, 284; Association of State Owned Film Enterprises (VVB-Film), 52, 54, 57, 62, 103; Central School of Art and Literature, 102; Film clubs (Ciné clubs), 1, 106, 139–40, 146, 216n9, 243n29, 265; Association of GDR Film Clubs, 139, 278n84; Association of German Film Clubs, 37, 76; Filmmakers' Club, 19, 22–25, 32, 33, 43, 44, 51, 52, 56, 57, 62–63, 67n22, 68n36, 91, 93, 102, 105, 106, 112, 159; Free German Youth (FDJ), 19, 40n9, 103, 173, 179–81, 185n53, 209, 233, 266, 292, 306n25; GDR Committee for Peace, 110–11, 126n52; GDR Solidarity Committee, 158–159, 289; GDR Journalists' Union, 106; Ministry for State Security, see Stasi; Ministry of Culture, 18, 19–20, 34, 43, 52, 57, 62, 64, 92, 94, 105, 108, 109, 114, 122, 123, 181, HVFilm, 18, 19–22, 31, 51–52, 102, 103, 106, 107, 109, 119, 120, 122, 123, 135, 138–40, 166, 196, 202, 205, 214–15, 237–38, 258, 294; Ministry of Foreign Affairs (MfAA), 106, 108, 109; National People's Army (NVA), 39, 49, 154n6, 228, 233, Army Film Studio, 12n14, 241, 244n60; Progress Filmverleih, 62, 102, 103, 105; Society for Cultural Relations with Foreign Countries, 110; State Film Archive, 66, 91–92, 97n37–38, 105, 112, 114, 122–24, 129n97, 139, 145, 146, 258, 318, Film Research Institute, 121, 123; Writer's Union, 136
Gehler, Fred, 139–140, 145–46, 226, 313, 315
Gensch, Werner, 235
Gessner, Peter, 167
Godard, Jean-Luc, 150

Goethe, Johann Wolfgang von, 28, 38
Goldstücker, Eduard, 144, 155n28
Gómez Yera, Sara, 73
Gomułka, Władysław, 195
Gorbachev, Mikhail, 247–48, 253, 255, 273, 281, 286, 293, 295
Grass, Günter, 237, 239
Gregor, Ulrich, xvi, 135, 145, 171–72, 204, 214, 270–71
Gregor, Erika, xvi, 204, 214, 271
Grélier, Robert, 216n8
Grierson, John, xiv, 37, 73–75, 80–84, 92, 97n22, 97n29, 113, 133, 149, 163, 177, 308
Grigoriev, Roman, 61
Guzmán, Patricio, xiv, 162, 175–76

H

Haanstra, Bert, 73
Hager, Kurt, 20–21, 122, 250, 252, 254, 259–61, 264
Hallstein Doctrine, 33, 46, 49
Hanák, Dušan, xi, 263, 277n72
Harkenthal, Wolfgang, 102–104, 109, 112, 117–18, 136, 140, 143, 145, 149, 161, 181–82, 298
Harkenthal, Gisela, 104
Havel, Václav, 264, 293
Havemann, Robert, 136
Hein, Christoph, 282
Hellmich, Peter, 59, 171, 176
Hemingway, Ernest, 50
Herlinghaus, Hermann, 80, 82, 84, 93–95, 128n73, 134
Hermlin, Stephan, 27, 131, 221, 223, 239
Herrman, Konrad, 303
Heym, Stefan, 220–21, 241, 300
Heynowski, Walter, 73, 140, 167, 169, 170–72, 175–77, 222, 271, 308
Hindemith, Harry, 60
Hitler, Adolf, 61, 115, 174, 255, 301
Hoffman, Jerzy, 48
Hoffmann, Ernst, 52, 103
Hoffmann, Hans-Joachim, 20
Hoffmann, Hilmar, 37, 49, 56, 162
Hoffmann, Stanley, 74
Hohmann, Lew, 290

Honecker, Erich, 121, 171, 177–80, 182, 204, 217n28, 219, 231–32, 239, 254, 264, 270, 273, 282, 286, 292, 294
Hornig, Harry, 142
Huisken, Joop, 28, 47

I
international organizations: International Association of Film Journalists and Critics, 251; International Documentary Association (IDA), 75–76; International Federation of Film Critics (FIPRESCI), 111, 117, 135, 193, 205, 256, 263, 271; International Federation of Film Producer Associations (FIAPF), 36, 54, 56, 107, 123, 125n24; International Federation of Film Societies (Ciné Clubs) (IFFS or FICC), 273, 278n84, 293, 306n26; International League for Friendship with the GDR, 110; NATO, 33, 38, 51, 61, 122, 230, 232; International Radio and Television Organization (OIRT), 111, 127n54; Warsaw Pact, 33, 134–35, 144, 164, 228, 230; World Congress of Partisans for Peace, 110, 127n53; World Federation of Democratic Youth, 111, 185n53; World Federation of Trade Unions, 28, 111, 190; Women's International Democratic Federation, 30, 111
international solidarity, 25, 47, 110–11, 153, 157–86, 295, 299–300, 309, 314
ISKRA, 155n24, 191, 216n6
Italian Neorealism, 28, 311, 313
Ivens, Joris, xiv, 28–30, 44, 49–50, 68n36, 72–73, 75, 79–83, 91–92, 113, 142, 159, 161, 163–64, 177, 191, 289, 308, 310, 313

J
Jaap, Max, 27
Janka, Walter, 285, 303
Jara, Víctor, 174–75
Jara, Joan, 174
Jordan, Günter, 6, 22, 240, 256, 258, 267

Junge, Winfried, 91, 153, 189, 197–207, 213–15, 289, 298, 310
Juráček, Pavel, 135

K
Kacerová, Eva, 293
Kadár, Ján, 132
Kádár, János, 263
Kafka, Franz (conference), 131–32, 144
Karabasz, Kazimierz, 48, 75, 91, 300
Karmen, Roman, xiv, 64, 74–75, 96n3, 113, 117, 168, 175, 177, 308
Kazan, Elia, 133
Kernicke, Wolfgang, xii, 19, 44, 62–63, 76, 91, 102–104, 125
Kersten, Heinz, 214, 237, 263
Kerzabi, Ahmed, 159, 162
Khrushchev, Nikita, 33, 35, 48, 61, 109, 113, 115, 122, 132–33, 158
Kieślowski, Krzysztof, xi, 195–96, 229
kinoglaz (ciné-eye), 80, 114
kinopoezd (ciné-train), 1, 191
Kino-Pravda, 79–84
Klaue, Wolfgang, 91, 97n37, 114, 122–23
Klein, Günter, 19–20, 32, 46, 57–59, 62–64, 67n22, 75, 78, 80, 102, 110
Klein, William, 169
Klimov, Elem, 248, 254, 256
Klos, Elmar, 132
Kohlert, Werner, 87
Kósa, Ferenc, 127n66
Knoop, Walter, 44
Koepp, Volker, 148–49, 151–53, 189, 197, 206–9, 211, 213–15, 222, 242, 269, 288–89, 310
Kogan, Pavel, 250
Kohlert, Werner, 87, 224
Köhlert, Lutz, 151
Kopalin, Ilya, 81
Koutecký, Pavel, 253
Kovács, András, xiv, 95, 98n46
Kroske, Gerd, 290–91
Kunert, Joachim, 27, 44
Kunert Günter, 242n9
Kunert, Julia, 298
Kurella, Alfred, 224

L

Labaki, Amir, 166
Languepin, Jean-Jacques, 75, 79
Leacock, Richard, 73, 75, 86–87, 95
Leckebusch, Walter, 60
Lehmann, Christian, 88, 94, 120, 139, 147, 179, 211, 213, 240
Lehmann-Peddersen, Christian, 234
Leipzig, City of: 38–39; Bach Archives, 38; District and City Councils, 105; Gewandhaus Orchestra, 38; Karl Marx University, 65, 137; St. Thomas Church, 38; Trade Fair, 33, 38; Völkerschlachtdenkmal, 38–39
Leipzig Festival, awards, 25, 44, 48, 49, 61, 77, 78, 86, 88, 101, 110–12, 117, 127n62, 144, 159–61, 164, 166, 167, 169, 170–73, 176, 184n28, 185n48, 190, 204, 217n33, 232, 236, 241, 243n29, 244n47, 263–64, 271, 272, 277n81, 285, 292, 295, 313; Budget, 92, 106–7, 125n22, 241, 299, 300; Free Forum, 60, 80–84, 105; Information Program, 47, 67n16, 151, 166, 184n35; International jury, 54, 74, 79, 112, 128n76, 165, 167, 182, 191, 195, 204, 244n47, 263, 292; Organizing Committee, 62, 66n3, 66n22,105–108, 124, 178, 257, 287–88, 295, 319; Presidium, 21, 49, 62, 63, 69n60, 72, 74, 79, 165, 181; retrospective, 49–50, 72, 74, 80, 82, 91–92, 97n38, 114–15, 122–24, 129n94, 129n97, 140, 162, 177, 184n21, 231, 288, 300, 310, 315–16, 322–24; Selection Committee, 49, 101, 103–4, 106, 109, 121, 136, 142, 242, 256, 257, 258, 261–62, 275n39, 275n42, 276n44, 280, 299
Leiser, Erwin, 91, 115
Leupold, Hans-Eberhard, 179, 199, 217n25
Leyda, Jay, 115
Lhomme, Jean, 87–88
Liehm, Antonin, 135
Lissakowitch, Viktor, 127n67
Loach, Ken, 133
Lods, Jean, 73, 79
Loest, Erich, 282
Łozinski, Marcel, xi, 252
Loridan, Marceline [Loridan-Ivens], 79, 142–44, 191, 300
Luntz, Edouard, 77, 192n94

M

Maaß, Wilfried, 20
Machals, Alfons, 30, 44
Mäde, Hans-Dieter, 20, 39n2
Maetzig, Kurt, 26
Makarczyński, Tadeusz, 75
Makk, Károly, 311
Malraux, André, 40n4
Marker, Chris, xi, xiv, 1, 73, 79, 87–89, 101, 104, 123, 129n94, 139, 142, 164, 168, 177, 190–92, 220, 308, 313
Marschalleck, Ralf, 298
Martay, Oscar, 36
Martin, Marcel, 128n76
Maysles Albert and David, xiv, 86–87
Medvedkin, Alexander, 190
Meerapfel, Jeanine, 275n28, 299
Menegoz, Robert, 28, 79, 129n94
Menzel, Jiří, 93, 132–33, 135
Mészáros, Marta, xi, 194–95, 255
Misselwitz, Helke, 266, 269–71, 273, 278n87
Montagu, Ivor, 73–74, 128n76
Moore, Mickaël, 295
Morin, Edgar
Mückenberger, Jochen, 90, 121
Mückenberger, Christiane, 121, 298–99, 313, 315
Müller, Heiner, 242n9
Muel, Bruno, 175
Mund, Karl-Heinz, 303

N

Nadim, Saad, 73
Nasser, Gamal Abdel, 47
Navotny, Antonín, 136
Navrátil, Antonín, 134
Nazism: concentration camps, 77, 305n19; former Nazis, 40n9; in West Germany, 22, 61, 78, 170, 184n43,

255; *Kulturfilm,* 25–27, 41n20; *Kristallnacht,* 261; past, 24, 57, 116–18, 142, 224, 265, 283, 301; period, 18; propaganda, 80, 117; resistance against, 61, 114–15, 217n37, 265
Nazis,
Nehru, Jewaharlal, 47
Němec, Jan, 135
newsreels, 18, 19, 20, 26, 27, 34, 36, 38, 41n20, 44, 61, 82, 115, 165, 168, 174
New Wave, 11, 71, 124, 131–34, 135, 139, 148, 308
Nickel, Gitta, 152–53, 168, 216n22, 231, 278n83, 287

O
Ort-Šnep, Joszef, 135

P
Panfilov, Gleb, 256
Parajanov, Sergei, 256
Pasanen, Leena, 316
Passer, Ivan, 132
Patalas, Enno, 88–89, 146
Paula, Romanian, xi
Pieck, Wilhelm, 22
Pinochet, Augusto, 173, 175
Pehnert, Horst, 20, 214, 237–38, 294
Picasso, Pablo, xiv, 2, 28, 76, 112, 178
Philipe, Anne, 79
Philipe, Gérard, 28, 40n25, 67n8, 68n36, 79
Piwowski, Marek, xi, 195
Plenert, Thomas, 225–26, 270, 301
Podnieks, Juris, xv, 251, 295
Pozner, Vladimir, 28, 30, 44, 74, 79, 91, 300
Pozner, Ida, 79, 91, 300
prejudice: anti-Semitism, 83, 115, 195, 277n78–79; racism, 93, 295
press, international, xii, xiv, 10, 18, 19, 22, 32, 33, 35, 36, 37, 38, 46, 47, 48, 49, 53, 57, 58, 59, 60, 62–63, 65, 67n18, 73, 74, 75, 76, 78, 79, 81, 82, 83, 88, 94, 96n21, 101, 103, 105, 107, 110, 111–12, 115, 117, 118, 120, 121, 122, 124, 125n27, 127n58, 132, 134, 135, 136, 139, 141, 143, 145, 146, 158, 166, 168, 170, 172, 181, 192, 196, 202, 203, 204, 205, 214, 215n4, 216n6–7, 222, 223, 229, 232, 233, 235, 236–40, 242n12, 243n36, 248, 251, 256, 259, 260, 261, 262, 270, 273, 282, 284, 286, 289, 292, 295, 298, 299, 300, 304, 305n5, 306n21, 308, 312, 313, 315, 316, 319; GDR Journalists' Union, 106; German Film Journalists' Association (VDJ), 61, 106; International Association of Film Journalists and Critics, 251; International Journalists' Union, 232
Prévert, Jacques, 81
Prévert, Paul, 76
propaganda, 7, 9–10, 20–22, 30, 36, 41n20, 62, 80, 82–86, 88, 117, 124, 127n67, 133–34, 168, 169–170, 175–77, 182, 205, 232, 278n83, 299, 306n38; Propaganda Department (of the SED's ZK), 105, 109
Püchner, Jana, 286

R
Ramirez, Alvaro, 173
Reed, Dean, 174–75
Resnais, Alain, 76–78, 87, 123, 129n94, 133, 169
Richardson, Tony, 132
Richter, Erika, 25, 46, 80, 93, 273, 293
Richter, Rolf, 95
Rios, Héctor, 173
Ritterbusch, Richard, 242, 258–59
Robichet, Theo, 175
Rodenberg, Hans, 33, 39n2, 49, 60, 163
Román, José,173
Romm, Mikhail, 115–18, 122, 221, 264, 308
Rose, Werner, 63
Rossellini, Roberto, 93
Roth, Wilhelm, 118, 139, 146–47, 166, 192, 203–4, 214, 222, 225, 260, 315
Rotha, Paul, 65, 73–75, 92
Rouch, Jean, 86–87, 162
Ruspoli, Mario, 97n28

S
Sadoul, Georges, xiv, 68n36, 79, 111

Sanz, Luis Alberto, 173
Saurer, Karl, 235
Schamoni, Ulrich, 136
Schauer, Hermann, 124n2, 166
Scheumann, Gerhard, 73, 128n76, 140, 167, 169–72, 176–177, 182, 222, 224, 271
Schiller, Friedrich von, 27, 37
Schmutzer, Klaus, 298
Schnabel, Rolf, 19
Schnitzler, Karl-Eduard von, 89, 97n33, 151, 168, 221–22, 235, 241
Schönemann, Sibylle, 303
Schreiber, Eduard, 225, 303
Schumann, Dieter, 259, 266–69, 271, 278n85
Sefranka, Bruno, 73
Seghers, Anna, 22, 136
Seidowsky, Hans-Joachim, 257–59
Sergiyenko, Rollan, 251, 256
Sergent, Jean-Pierre, 79
Shostakovich, Dmitri, 28
Simmons, Anthony, 75
Simon, Jean-Daniel, 288
Simon, Rainer, 67n8
Ślesicki, Władysław, 48
Socialist Democratic Party of Germany (SPD), 40n9, 52, 183n2, 231, 238
Socialist Realism, 5, 26–27, 32, 48, 77, 80, 86, 132, 298, 311
Sokurov, Alexander, 256
Soosaar, Mark, 251, 262
Soviet influence, 9, 17–18, 20, 24, 26, 32–33, 36, 47, 54, 79, 104, 109–10, 113, 117, 120, 122, 133–34, 137, 166, 180, 232, 260, 261, 273, 285, 293, 309, 314; protest against, 140, 141, 146–47, 149, 166–67, 258, 313; 228–30
Soviet Occupation Zone, 12n15, 18, 26, 39n1, 170, 181, 242n8
Soviet reforms, 248–52, 254, 258, 273, 295, 314; glasnost, xv, xvii, 9, 247–48, 251, 257, 259, 273, 273n1, 285, 295, 309, 311–14; perestroika, x, xv, xvii, 247, 253, 259, 271, 276n63, 295
Springfeld, Gert, 20
Stasi (GDR Ministry of State Security, secret police), xv, xvii, 64, 135, 155n31, 179, 185n55, 222, 228–29, 233–41, 255–57, 260–62, 282, 286, 289–90, 297, 313, 315
Stalin, Joseph, 31–32, 48, 104, 114–15, 133
Stalinism, 114–18, 133–34, 216n16, 285; de-Stalinization, 11, 48, 113–14, 130–31; Stalinization, 283, 305n5, 308
Starke, Johannes, 20
Staudte, Wolfgang, 40n23
Steiner, Roland, 287, 294–95, 303, 306n28
Stier, Reinhard, 44
Stoph, Willy, 204
Storck, Henri, 73, 75, 177
Stoumen, Louis Clyde, 115
Studio H&S / H&S Studio, xi, 169–72, 175–77, 182, 224, 308–9
Süske, Kerstin, 286
Svoboda, Ludvík, 136

T

Táborský, Vaclav, 73
Tarkovsky, Andrei, 255
technological advances, 86–90, 92–95, 97n29; 70mm film, 104, 108, 124n9; access to equipment, 94, 98n46; handheld cameras, 85, 88, 90, 94, 190; light cameras, 98n46; sound, 94, 128n79; Super-8, 12n14; video, 12n14, 306n23
television, 9, 24, 30, 94, 137, 150, 156n46, 176, 178, 230, 266, 285, 297, 301, 303, 307; at film festivals, 106, 108, 137; at the Leipzig Festival, 11, 12n4, 101, 104–7, 111, 151, 152, 181, 308, 316; Great Britain (BBC), 27, 90; Czechoslovakia (ČST), 137, 154n15, 253, 293; GDR—Deutsche Fernsehfunk (DFF), 19, 60, 61, 78, 94, 97n33, 101–2, 104–7, 122, 125n11, 151, 170, 176, 178, 202, 205, 214, 217n28, 217n31, 241, 257, 260, 275n32, 278n85, 278n87, 285, 298, 312; Eurovision, 111; International Radio and Television Organization (OIRT), 111, 127n54; Intervision, 111,

127n55; Poland, 196, 229–30; FRG (West Germany), 30, 61, 104, 111, 193, 205, 221, 230, 243n25, 260–62; France, 95, 161, 274n10; Scotland, 73, 83; US, 87; USSR, 250
Tetzlaff, Kurt, 277n81, 184n23, 265, 282, 287
Theuerkauf, Herbert, 44, 49
Third World, 69n64, 74, 165, 305n19; at Leipzig Festival, xvi, 47, 60, 64–66, 106, 111, 127n53, 144, 160, 162, 164, 308, 172–77, 313; Algeria, xvi, 60, 64, 79, 87, 93, 110, 147, 216n7; Brazil, 173; China, 28, 30, 47, 74, 140; Chile, ix, xiv, 171, 172–75; Cuba, 60, 74, 79, 87, 146–47, 175, 240; Egypt, 47; India, 74; Vietnam, xiv, 74, 118, 123, 141–42, 166–69, 171–72, 289
Thorndike, Andrew, 21–22, 26–27, 49, 60, 64, 72–74, 80, 103–4, 121, 133–34, 147, 151–52, 170, 224, 288
Thorndike, Annelie, xii, 49, 73, 79, 121, 133–34, 152, 168, 170, 180–81, 222, 287, 298
Thomé, Ludwig, 32–33, 44
Tito, Jozip Broz, 47
Toeplitz, Jerzy, xiv, 74–75, 82–83, 95n4, 111, 195
Tosheva, Nevena, xi
Trampe, Tamara, 238–39
travel restrictions, 35, 52, 95, 102, 107, 128n83, 130, 145, 146, 159, 163, 203, 220–21, 231, 233, 239, 258, 266, 278n97
Trisch, Ronald, 161, 168, 180–82, 192, 196, 222, 234–36, 238, 240–42, 258–59, 261–62, 284, 287, 295, 298, 315
Trnka, Jiří, xiii, 38, 56
Truffaut, François, 150
Tschirner, Joachim, 240, 290
Tschörtner, Petra, 275n40, 304
Turovskaya, Maya, 115

U
Ugowski, Eberhard, 258
Ulbrich, Peter, 216n22, 238, 259
Ulbricht, Walter, 32, 48, 50, 52, 57, 117
Uralov, Oleg, 250

V
Vachek, Karel, 135
Varda, Agnès, 79, 129n94, 184n42
Vautier, René, xi, 70n65, 191
Vertov, Dziga, 79–82, 87, 92, 114, 159, 166, 190, 310
Vieira, José Luandino, 161
Vigo, Jean, 80, 129n94, 195
Voigt, Andreas, 290–91
Volkmann, Herbert, 91, 97n38,124, 129n97, 139
Vosz, Manfred, 236
Dušan Vukotić, 73

W
Wajda, Andrzej, 196, 229–30
Wagner, Siegfried, 20
Wegner, Hans, 102
Wehling, Will, 38, 46, 49, 59–60
Wehrstedt, Norbert, 298
Weigel, Helene, 30
Weisenborn, Christian, 192
Weiss, Konrad, 152, 288–90, 294, 297
Wildenhahn, Klaus, 193, 300
Wilkening, Albert, 39n2
Winterlich, Joachim, 235
Winzer, Otto, 110
Wischnewski, Klaus, 53, 101, 264, 298
Wiseman, Frederick, 192
Wisotzki, Jochen, 257, 304
Witt, Günter, 20, 107, 117, 121
Wolf, Christa, 67n8, 230, 242n9, 297
Wolf, Konrad, 40n14, 90, 136, 146, 224, 271
Wright, Basil, 73–75
Wulfes, Michael, 192

Y
Youth: 118–21, 132; and music, 118–21, 135; Free German Youth (FDJ), *see* GDR organizations; Gathering of German Youth, 103, 118, 124n8; World Federation of Democratic Youth, 185n53; World Youth Festival, 36

Z
Zafranović, Lordan, xi
Zahlbaum, Willi, 125n13
Zajaczkowski, Andrzej, xv, 229

Zavattini, Cesare, 133
Zielinski, Henryk, 196
Zygadlo, Tomasz, xi, 195

Film Index

20,000 matins (20,000 Mornings), France, Jean Lods, 1964, 79

79 Primaveras (79 Springs), Cuba, Santiago Álvarez, 1969, 166

Abgeordnete in Rostock – Im Vorfeld (Deputy in Rostock), GDR, Cohn-Vossen, 1976, 224

À bientôt, j'espère (Until Soon, I Hope), France, Chris Marker and Mario Marret, 1968, 190

Agoniya (Rasputin), USSR, Elem Klimov, 1973–75, 254

Algérie, année zéro (Algeria, Year Zero), France, Jean-Pierre Sergent and Marceline Loridan, 1962, 79

A Happy Mother's Day, USA, Richard Leacock and Joyce Chopra, 1963, 86

Allons enfants . . . pour l'Algérie (Arise, You Children . . . for Algeria), GDR, Karl Gass, 1961, 60

Anmut sparet nicht noch Mühe (Spare No Charm and Spare No Effort; Kinder von Golzow series), GDR, Winfried Junge, 1978–79, 217n23

Asse, GDR, Karl Gass, 1965, 97n34

Assemblea General (General Assembly), Cuba, Tomás Gutiérrez Alea, 1960, 184n26

Aufbruch'89 Dresden (New Beginning Dresden'89), GDR, Thomas Eichberg et al, 1989, 292

Aufgeben oder neu beginnen - Walter Janka (Give Up or Start Anew), Germany, Karlheinz Mund, 1990, 303

Augstākā tiesa (The Supreme Judgment), USSR, Herz Frank, 1987, 275n37

Barfuß und ohne Hut (Barefoot and without a Hat), GDR, Jürgen Böttcher, 1965, 118–120, 137, 289, 310

Berlin-Prenzlauer Berg. Begegnungen zwischen dem 1. Mai und dem 1. Juli 1990 (Berlin, Prenzlauer Berg), GDR, Petra Tschörtner, 1990, 304

Berlin um die Ecke (Berlin around the Corner), GDR, Gerhard Klein, 1965, 121

Bez leģendām (Without Legends), USSR, Herz Frank, 1967/1970, 275n37

Black Fox: The True Story of Adolf Hitler, USA, Louis Clyde Stoumen, 1962, 115

Brigada Ramona Parra (Ramona Parra Brigade), Chile, Alvaro Ramirez and Samuel Carvajal, 1970, 173

Carnet de viaje (Travel Notebook), Cuba, Joris Ivens, 1961, 164

Cerny Petr (Black Peter), Czechoslovakia, Miloš Forman, 1963, 132

Čili: vremja bor'by, vremja trevog (Chile: Time to Fight, Time to Agitate), USSR, Roman Karmen, D. Barsceski and O. Trifimova, 1973, 175

Chronique d'un été (Chronicle of a Summer), France, Jean Rouch and Edgar Morin, 1960, 86

Chuck Berry, Hail! Hail! Rock'n'Roll, USA, Taylor Hackford, 1987, 259

Chuyen Tu Te (*The Story of Kindness or How to Behave*), Vietnam, Tran Van Thuy, 1985–87, 253
Classe de lutte (*Fighting Class*), France, Medvekin Group collective, 1969, 190
Compañero: Victor Jara of Chile, UK, Stanley Forman and Martin Smith, 1975, 175
¡Cuba, Sí!, France, Chris Marker, 1961, 87
Cwiszenia Warsztatowe (*Workshop Exercise*), Poland, Marcel Łozinski, 1984, 252
Czlowiek z marmuru (*Man of Marble*), Poland, Andrzej Wajda, 1977, 196
Człowiek z żelaza (*Man of Iron*), Poland, Andrzej Wajda, 1981, 243n34

Das Ganze halt! (*It Stops Here*), GDR, Dieter Mendelsohn, 1961, 60
Das Jahr 1945 (*The Year 1945*), GDR, Karl Gass, 1985, 264
Das Kaninchen bin ich (*The Rabbit Is Me*), GDR, Kurt Maetzig, 1965, 128n85
Das Russische Wunder (*The Russian Miracle*), GDR, Annelie and Andrew Thorndike, 1963, 89, 103, 133–34, 151, 224,
Das weite Feld (*The Vast Field*), GDR, Volker Koepp, 1976, 213
Das Zeugnis (*The Testimony*), Czechoslovakia, Pavel Haser, 1961, 61
Den blodiga Titen (*Mein Kampf: A Blueprint for the Age of Chaos*), Sweden, Erwin Leiser, 1959, 115
Denk bloss nicht, ich heule (*Just Don't Think I'll Cry*), GDR, Frank Vogel, 1965, 128n85
Der erste Reis danach – Vietnam 2 (*And Then the First Rice*), GDR, Walter Heynowski and Gerhard Scheumann, 1977, 185n49
Der König geht (*The King Goes*), Germany, Klaus Wildenhahn, 1990, 300
Der Krieg der Mumien (*The War of the Mummies*), GDR, Walter Heynowski and Gerhard Scheumann, 1974, 175

Der Lachende Mann (*The Laughing Man*), GDR, Walter Heynowski, Gerhard Scheumann, 1966, 171–72
Der Sekretär (*The Party Secretary*), GDR, Jürgen Böttcher, 1967, 1, 138–140
Der Tod des Empedokles (*The Death of Empedocles*), FRG, Jean-Marie Straub, 1987, 275n28
Der Untergang der Graf Bismarck (*The Sinking of the Count Bismarck*), FRG, Wilhelm Bittorf, 1967, 192
Deutsche Kirchweih (*Church Anniversary*), FRG, Manfred Vosz, 1968, 244n47
Deutschland ist so gross und so schön (*Germany Is So Big and So Beautiful*), GDR, Jana Püchner, 1989, 286
Die Angst und die Macht (*Fear and Power*), Germany, Konrad Herrmann, 1990, 303
Die Dresdner Philharmoniker (*The Dresden Philharmonic*), GDR, Joachim Kunert, 1955, 27
Die eiserne Festung – Vietnam 4 (*The Iron Fortress*), GDR, Walter Heynowski and Gerhard Scheumann, 1977, 172, 185n49
Die Kinder Palästinas (*The Children of Palestine*), GDR, Kurt Teztlaff, 1980, 184n23, 278n81
Die Mauer (*The Wall*), GDR, Jürgen Böttcher, 1990, 300–302
Die Rolle des Meisters im System der sozialistischen Betriebswirtschaft (*The Role of the Foreman in the Management System of the Socialist Enterprise*), GDR, Volker Koepp, 1970, 197
Diese Golzower – Umstandsbestimmungen eines Ortes (*These Golzowers; Kinder von Golzow* series), GDR, Winfried Junge, 1984, 217n23
Die Teufelsinsel (*Devil's Island*), GDR, Walter Heynowski and Gerhard Scheumann, 1976, 185n49
Die Verliebten (*Days to Remember*), FRG, Jeanine Meerapfel, 1987, 275n28
Drehbuch: die Zeiten. Drei Jahrzehnte mir den Kindern von Golzow und

der DEFA (Screenplay: The Times. Three Decades with the Children of Golzow and the DEFA Documentary Film Studio), Germany, Barbara and Winfried Junge, 1993, 206
Drei Tage im Mai (Three Days in May), GDR, Heinz Müller, 1964, 103
Drei von vielen (Three of Many), GDR, Jürgen Böttcher, 1961, 97n26
Drifters, UK, John Grierson, 1929, 37, 81
Du und mancher Kamerad (You and Some Comrade), GDR, Andrew and Annelie Thorndike, 1955, 22, 51, 57

Egyszerü történet (A Commonplace Story), Hungary, Judit Elek, 1975, 194
Einmal in der Woche schrei'n (Yell Once a Week), GDR, Günter Jordan, 1982/89, 267
Ein Strom fließt durch Deutschland (A River Flows through Germany), GDR, Joachim Kunert, 1954, 46
Ein Tagebuch für Anne Frank (A Diary for Anne Frank), GDR, Joachim Hellwig, 1959, 57
Elf Jahre alt (Eleven Years Old; Kinder von Golzow series), GDR, Winfried Junge, 1966, 200, 204, 216n23
El golpe blanco – der weiße Putsch (The White Coup), GDR, Walter Heynowski and Gerhard Scheumann, 1975, 175
El golpe de estado (The Coup d'État; Part II of The Battle of Chile), Cuba/Chile/France, Patricio Guzmán, 1976, 175
Erfolge sind Pflicht (Successes Are Duty), GDR, Peter Ulbrich (Effekt group), 1970, 216n22
Erinnern heißt leben (Remembering Means Living), GDR, Róza Berger-Fiedler, 1987–88, 265,
Erinnerung an eine Landschaft – für Manuela (Memory of a Landscape), GDR, Kurt Tetzlaff, 1983, 265, 282
Es lebe die R. . . (Long Live the R. . .), GDR, Jörn Zielke, 292

Fabryka (The Factory), Poland, Krzysztof Kieslowski, 1970, 195

Feierabend (Leisure), GDR, Karl Gass, 1964, 89
Flammendes Algerien (Algeria in Flames), GDR, Willy Müller and René Vautier, 1961, 216n7
flüstern & SCHREIEN. Ein Rockreport (whisper & SHOUT), GDR, Dieter Schumann, 1988, 266–69, 311
Frau am Klavichord (Woman at the Clavichord), GDR, Jürgen Böttcher, 1981, 306n36
Friedrich Schiller, GDR, Max Jaap, 1956, 27
Für Angela (Angela), GDR, Werner Kohlert, 1972, 224

Gdzie diabel mówi dobranoc (Where the Devil Says Good Night), Poland, Kasimierz Karabasz and Władisław Ślesicki, 1956, 48

Hôtel Terminus (Hotel Terminus: The Life and Times of Klaus Barbie), France, Marcel Ophüls, 1988, 306n30
Hütes-Film (Dumplings), GDR, Volker Koepp, 1977, 213

Ich bereue aufrichtig (I Sincerely Repent), GDR, Walter Heynowski and Gerhard Scheumann, 1977, 185n49
Ich war ein glücklicher Mensch (I Was a Happy Person), GDR, Eduard Schreiber, 1990, 303
Ich war, ich bin, ich werde sein (I Was, I Am, I Will Be), GDR, Walter Heynowski and Gerhard Scheumann, 1974, 175–76
Ich war neunzehn (I Was Nineteen), GDR, Konrad Wolf, 1967, 146
Imbiss spezial (Snack Bar Special), GDR, Thomas Heise, 1990, 306n38
Im Lohmgrund (In the Lohm Valley), GDR, Jürgen Böttcher, 1976–77, 225
In der Fremde (Far from Home), FRG, Klaus Wildenhahn, 1967, 193
Istenmezején 1972–73-ban (A Hungarian Village), Hungary, Judit Elek, 1973, 194

Jahrgang 45 (*Born in '45*), GDR, Jürgen Böttcher, 1966, 121, 137, 139

Kamerad Krüger (*Comrade Krüger*), GDR, Walter Heynowski and Gerhard Scheumann, 1988, 271

Katjuscha, USSR, Viktor Lissakowitch, 1964, 127n67

Kolokol Chernobylya (*The Bell of Chernobyl*), USSR, Rollan Sergiyenko, 1987, 251, 256, 258

Kommando 52, GDR, Walter Heynowski, 1965, 171

Komm in den Garten (*Come into the Garden*), Germany, Heinz Brinkmann and Jochen Wisotzki, 1990, 304

La insurrección de la burguesía (*The Insurrection of the Bourgeoisie*; Part I of *The Battle of Chile*), Venezuela/France/Cuba, Patricio Guzmán, 1975, 175

La Rotonda/Vicenza. In Erinnerung an Prof. Lothar Kühne (*La Rotonda/Vicenza*), GDR, Roland Steiner, 1990, 303

La Seine a rencontré Paris (*The Seine Meets Paris*), France, Joris Ivens, 1957, 81–82, 129n94

Lásky jedné plavoulásky (*The Loves of a Blonde*), Czechoslovakia, Miloš Forman, 1965, 153

LBJ, Cuba, Santiago Álvarez, 1968, 162, 166

Leben in Wittstock (*Life in Wittstock*), GDR, Volker Koepp, 1984, 206, 209, 211, 213–14

Lebensläufe – Die Geschichte der Kinder von Golzow in einzelnen Porträts (*Children of Golzow: Individual Portraits*), GDR, Winfried Junge, 1981, 202–206, 213–14, 217n23

Leben und Weben (*Living and Weaving*), GDR, Volker Koepp, 1981, 206, 213

Le Fond de l'air est rouge (*A Grin without a Cat*), France, Chris Marker, 1977, 192

Leipzig im Herbst (*Leipzig in the Fall*), GDR, Andreas Voigt and Gerd Kroske, 1989, 290–92, 300

Le Joli Mai (*The Lovely Month of May*), France, Chris Marker, 1963, 87–89, 93–94, 101, 104

Les Enfants des courants d'air (*Children Adrift*), France, Edouard Luntz, 1959, 77, 129n94

Les Enfants du paradis (*Children of Paradise*), France, Marcel Carné, 1945, 124n4

Les Statues meurent aussi (*Statues Also Die*), France, Alain Resnais, Chris Marker and Ghislain Cloquet, 1953, 87

Le Train en marche (*The Train Rolls On*), France, Chris Marker, 1971, 191

Lied der Ströme (*Song of the Rivers*), GDR, Joris Ivens, 1954, 28, 34, 51, 82

Loin du Vietnam (*Far from Vietnam*), France, Chris Marker, Joris Ivens, William Klein, Jean-Luc Godard, Alain Resnais and Agnès Varda, 1967, 168–69

Ludwig van Beethoven, GDR, Max Jaap, 1954, 27, 51

Mädchen in Wittstock (*Wittstock Girls*), GDR, Volker Koepp, 1975, 206–7, 242

Makulatur 7/10/89 (*Waste Paper 10/7/89*), GDR, Kerstin Süske, 1989, 286

Manchmal möchte man fliegen (*Sometimes You'd Like to Fly*), GDR, Gitta Nickel, 1981, 278n83

Martha, GDR, Jürgen Böttcher, 1978, 278n89

Maximaliste v mikrosvete (*Maximalists in a Microcosm*), Czechoslovakia, Pavel Koutcky, 1986, 253

Mein Kind (*My Child*), GDR, Joris Ivens, 1954, 30, 44, 51

Mit Netz und Spinne (*With Web and Spider*), GDR, Karl Gass (Effekt group), 1971, 216n22

Musiikki s ostrava Kihnu (*Man of Kihnu*), Estonia, Mark Soosaar, 1986, 251

Nanook of the North, USA, Robert Flaherty, 1922, 72

Napló gyermekeimnek (*Diary for My Children*), Hungary, Márta Mészáros, 1984, 255

Nehéz emberek (*Difficult People*), Hungary, András Kovács, 1964, 98n46

Neues in Wittstock (*Modern Times in Wittstock*), Germany, Volker Voepp, 1992, 206

No es hora de llorar (*No Time for Tears*), Chile, Pedro Chaskel and Luis Alberto Sanz, 1971, 173

Notre Algérie (*Our Algeria*), Algeria, Djamel Chanderli, 1959, 64

Now, Cuba, Santiago Álvarez, 1965, 166

Nuit et brouillard (*Night and Fog*), France, Alain Resnais, 1956, 77–78, 87, 129n94

Nyolc év után (*After Eight Years*), Hungary, István György, 1973, 204

Obchod na korze (*The Shop on Main Street*), Czechoslovakia, Jan Kadár and Elmar Klos, 1965, 132

Obrazy Stareho Sveta (*Images of the Old World*), Czechoslovakia, Dušan Hanák, 1972, 263

Obyknovennyy fashizm (*Ordinary Fascism*), USSR, Mikhail Romm, 1965, 115–18, 121–22, 221, 264

Ofenbauer (*Furnace Makers*), GDR, Jürgen Böttcher, 1962, 84–86, 88–89, 121, 203

Oktober kam... (*October Came...*), GDR, Karl Gass, 1969–70, 289

Oratorium pro Prahu (*Oratorio for Prague*), Czechoslovakia, Jan Němec, 1968, 135

Ostern 68 (*Easter '68*), GDR, Harry Hornig, 1968, 142

Paris la belle (*Paris the Beautiful*), France, Pierre Prévert, 1960, 76

Phoenix, GDR, Walter Heynowski and Gerhard Scheumann, 1979, 172

Pierwsze lata (*The First Years*), Poland/Czechsolovakia/Bulgaria, Ivens, 1947, 82–83

Piloten im Pyjama (*Pilots in Pyjamas*), GDR, Walter Heynowski and Gerhard Scheumann, 1968, 172

Por primera vez (*For the First Time*), Cuba, Octavio Cortázar, 1967, 184n28

Por qué nació el Ejército Rebelde? (*Why Was the Rebel Army Born?*), Cuba, José Massip, 1960, 164

Potters Stier (*Potter's Bull*), GDR, Jürgen Böttcher, 1981, 306n36

Primary, USA, Robert Drew, Richard Leacock et al., 1960, 95

Profis – Ein Jahr Fussball mit Paul Breitner und Uli Hoeness (*Professionals: A Year of Soccer with Paul Breitner and Uli Hoeness*), FRG, Christian Weisenborn and Michael Wulfes, 1979, 192–93

Proshchanie (*Farewell*), USSR, Elem Klimov, 1981, 256

Psalm 18, GDR, Walter Heynowski and Gerhard Scheumann, 1974, 177

Pueblo en armas (*People at Arms*), Cuba, Joris Ivens, 1961, 184n27

Rangierer (*Shunters*), GDR, Jürgen Böttcher, 1984, 226–27

Reportaje a Lota (*Report to Lota*), Chile, Diego Bonacina and José Román, 1970, 173

Robotnicy '80 (*Workers '80*), Poland, Andrzej Chodakowski and Andrzej Zajaczkowski, 1980, 229

Roger & Me, USA, Michael Moore, 1989, 295

Rosenthaler Str. 51, GDR, Heiner Sylvester, 1976, 225

Rozmarné léto (*Capricious Summer*), Czechoslovakia, Jiří Menzel, 1968, 133

Salut les Cubains (*Greetings, Cubans*), France, Agnès Varda with Chris Marker and Anne Philipe, 1963, 79

Schaste (*Happiness*), USSR, Alexander Medvekin, 1932, 1

Schaut auf diese Stadt (*Look at this City*), GDR, Karl Gass, 1962, 61, 90, 97n33, 156n47, 289
Septembre chilien (*Chilean September*), France, Bruno Muel and Theo Robichet, 1973, 175
Showman (aka, *Mr. Levine*), USA, Albert and David Maysles, 1963, 86–87
Sieben vom Rhein (*Seven from the Rhine*), Andrew and Annelie Thorndike, 1954, 22, 27, 34
Sign 'o' the Times, USA, Prince, 1987, 259
Skorbnoye beschuvstviye (*Mournful Unconcern*), USSR, Alexander Sokurov, 1984, 256
Skoro Leto (*Summer Will Soon Be There*), USSR, Pavel Kogan, 1987, 250
So viele Träume (*So Many Dreams*), GDR, Heiner Carow, 1986, 256
Sprízneni volbou (*Elective Affinities*), Czechoslovakia, Karel Vachek and Joszef Ort-Šnep, 1968, 135
Spur der Steine (*Trace of Stones*), GDR, Frank Beyer, 1966/1990, 136, 220, 286
Spzital (*Hospital*), Poland, Krzysztof Kieslowski, 1977, 195
Stars, GDR, Jürgen Böttcher, 1963, 88, 94, 118, 121, 278n89

Tema (*The Theme*), USSR, Gleb Panfilov, 1979/1987, 256
The Bridge on the River Kwai, UK/USA, David Lean, 1957, 124
Toute la mémoire du monde (*All the Memory of the World*), France, Alain Resnais and Chris Marker, 1957, 123, 129n94
Tu enfanteras sans douleur (*Birth without Fear*), France, Henri Fabiani, 1956, 77
Turbine 1, GDR, Joop Huisken and Karl Gass, 1953, 34
Turksib, USSR, Victor Tourine, 1929, 87

Um die Europameisterschaft (*The European Cup*), FRG, Walter Knoop, 1951, 44

Un dimanche à Pékin (*Sundays in Peking*), France, Chris Marker, 1956, 87
Unsere Kinder (*Our Children*), GDR, Roland Steiner, 1989, 294–96
Unternehmen Teutonenschwert (*Operation Teutonic Sword*), GDR, Annelie and Andrew Thorndike, 1958, 22
Urlaub auf Sylt (*Holiday on Sylt*), GDR, Annelie and Andrew Thorndike, 1957, 22
Uroki Pravdy (*Lessons in Truth*), USSR (Ukrainian entry), 1987, 250
Uruguay. Fernes Land nah gesehen (*Uruguay, Distant Country, Observed from Nearby*), GDR, Joop Huisken, 1956, 47
Uwaga, chuligani! (*Look Out, Hooligans!*), Poland, Jerzy Hoffman, 1955, 48

Vai viegli but jaunam? (*Is It Easy to Be Young?*), USSR, Juri Podnieks, 1986, 251, 258, 295
Velikaya otechestvennaya (*The Great Patriotic War*), USSR, Roman Karmen, 1965, 117
¡Venceremos!, Chile, Pedro Chaskel and Héctor Rios, 1970, 173
Venus nach Giorgione (*Venus by Giorgione*), GDR, Jürgen Böttcher, 1981, 306n36
Verbrennt nicht unsere Erde (*Do Not Burn Our Earth*), GDR, Gitta Nickel, 1980, 231
Verriegelte Zeit (*Locked Up Time*), Germany, Sybille Schönemann, 1990, 303
Vom Alex zum Eismeer (*From Alexanderplatz to the Arctic*), GDR, Karl Gass, 1954, 37

Weggefährten – Begegnungen im 25. Jahre der DDR (*Traveling Companions*), collective under the direction of Rolf Schnabel, 1974, 224
Wenn man vierzehn ist (*When You Are Fourteen*; *Kinder von Golzow* series), GDR, Winfried Junge, 1969, 201, 217n23

Wer die Erde liebt (Those Who Love the Earth), GDR, Joachim Hellwig, 1973, 179–80

What's Happening! The Beatles in the U.S.A., USA, Albert and David Maysles, 1964, 86

Wieder in Wittstock (Back in Wittstock), GDR, Volker Koepp, 1976, 206

Winter Adé, GDR, Helke Misselwitz, 1988, 266, 269–72, 311

Wittstock III, GDR, Volker Koepp, 1978, 206

Wittstock, Wittstock, Germany, Volker Koepp, 1997, 206

Zehn Tage im Oktober (Ten Days in October), GDR, Thomas Frick, 1989, 286, 292

Zhizn'bez . . . (A Life Without . . .), USSR, Mark Soosaar, 1987, 262

Zum Beispiel . . . Silbitzer im Wettbewerb (For Example . . . Silbitzers in Competition), GDR, Gitta Nickel, 1971, 216n22

Zwei Tage im August – Rekonstruktion eines Verbrechens (Two Days in August: Reconstruction of a Crime), GDR, Karl Gass, 1982, 232

www.ingramcontent.com/pod-product-compliance
Lightning Source LLC
Chambersburg PA
CBHW061400030325
22857CB00013B/514